DELL CROSSWORD

DICTIONARY

By KATHLEEN RAFFERTY

Published by
DELL PUBLISHING CO., INC.
1 Dag Hammarskjold Plaza
New York, N.Y. 10017

Copyright, © 1960, by
DELL PUBLISHING CO., INC., New York, N. Y.

First printing—July 1960
Fifth printing—July 1963
Tenth printing—September 1964
Fifteenth printing—April 1966
Twentieth printing—November 1967
Twenty-fifth printing—April 1969
Thirtieth printing—October 1970
Thirty-fifth printing—December 1971
Thirty-sixth printing—January 1972
Thirty-seventh printing—March 1972
Thirty-eighth printing—May 1972
Thirty-ninth printing—July 1972
Fortieth printing—October 1972
Forty-first printing—January 1973
Forty-second printing—April 1973
Forty-third printing—June 1973
Forty-fourth printing—September 1973
Forty-fifth printing—October 1973
Forty-sixth printing—December 1973

Printed in U.S.A.

ABOUT THIS BOOK . . .

Looking for an "Assam silkworm"? Can't find a "Brazilian coin"? Don't know a "candlenut tree"? You will—with the aid of this book.

The purpose of this dictionary is to give puzzlers the pleasure of COMPLETING, down to the last three-letter word, every crossword that they begin. It is meant to eliminate the frustration of filling in "all but a few" of those final puzzle squares. Here in handy, workmanlike form, is a complete 384-page reference book that can be used by puzzle solvers to find all of those little-known, but much-used, crossword words.

This DELL CROSSWORD DICTIONARY has not only been newly revised and greatly enlarged, but it also brings you, for the first time, the exclusive new cross-referenced Word-Finder. We believe this book is the most useful book ever published exclusively for crossword solvers.

It is the outgrowth of many years of exhaustive research and was prepared by the editor of the three famous DELL CROSSWORD magazines, OFFICIAL CROSSWORD PUZZLES, DELL CROSSWORD PUZZLES and POCKET CROSSWORD PUZZLES—all leaders in the puzzle world.

KATHLEEN RAFFERTY
Compiler and Editor

ABBREVIATIONS USED IN THIS BOOK

abbr. .... abbreviation
Abyssin. .... Abyssinia(n)
Afgh. .... Afghanistan
Afr. .... Africa(n)
Am. .... American
Arab. .... Arabia(n)
Arch. .... Architecture
A.-S. .... Anglo-Saxon
Austr. .... Austria(n)
Austral. .... Australia(n)
Babyl. .... Babylonian
Bibl. .... Biblical
biol. .... biology
bot. .... botany; botanical
Braz. .... Brazil(ian)
Cent. Am. ... Central America(n)
Chin. .... Chinese
comb. form .... combining form
Dan. .... Danish
Du. .... Dutch
Du. E. Ind. .... Dutch East Indies
E. .... East
Egyp. .... Egypt(ian)
E. Ind. .... East Indies
Eng. .... England; English
Eur., Europ. .... Europe(an)
fort. .... fortification
Fr. .... France; French
geol. ...... geology; geological
geom. .... geometry
Ger. .... German(y)
Goth. .... Gothic
govt. .... government
Gr. .... Greek
Hebr. .... Hebrew
Her. .... heraldry
Himal. .... Himalayan
Holl. .... Holland
Ind. .... India(n)
Indo-Chin. ...... Indo-Chinese
Ir. .... Ireland; Irish
Is. .... Island

Ital. .... Italian; Italy
Jap. .... Japan(ese)
Lat. .... Latin
math. .... mathematics
med. .... medical
Medit. .... Mediterranean
Mex. .... Mexican; Mexico
milit. .... military
Min. .... Minor
mus. .... music; musical
myth. .. mythological; mythology
N., No. .... North
naut. .... nautical
N. Hebr. .... New Hebrides
N. T. .... New Testament
N. Z. .... New Zealand
Nor. .... Norway; Norwegian
O. Eng. .... Old English
P. I. .... Philippine Islands
P. R. .... Puerto Rico
Pacif. .... Pacific
Pers. .... Persian
pert. .... pertaining
pharm. .... pharmacy
philos. .... philosophical
poet. .... poetry
Polyn. .... Polynesia(n)
Port. ..... Portugal; Portuguese
Pruss. .... Prussian
R. C. .... Roman Catholic
Rom. .... Roman
Russ. .... Russian
S. .... South
S. Afr. .... South Africa(n)
Scot. .... Scottish
Sp. .... Spanish
Teut. .... Teutonic
Turk. .... Turkey; Turkish
W. .... West
W. Ind. .... West Indian
WW .... World War
zool. .... zoology

TABLE OF CONTENTS

DEFINITIONS SECTION

CROSSWORD DEFINITIONS AND ANSWERS

HOW TO USE THIS SECTION:

Here are crossword DEFINITIONS, arranged alphabetically.

Look up the DEFINITION of a crossword word, and you will find, in bold-face type, the word you want.

There are two kinds of crossword definitions. One is the almost unvarying definition: "Bitter vetch" or "Vetch" is used to define ERS. If you look in this dictionary under "B" for "bitter vetch" or under "V" for "vetch" you will find it there.

The other kind of definition, far more common, is the more varied definition where the puzzle-maker can choose from among many descriptive words when he defines a puzzle word: "India nurse," "Oriental nurse," "Oriental maid," "Oriental nursemaid" are all used in crossword puzzles as definitions for AMAH. For efficiency's sake, crossword words with varying definitions are listed here under the ESSENTIAL definition word. In the case of AMAH, the listing is under "nurse," "maid," and "nursemaid".

So, if you don't find your wanted word under the first word of the definition given, look for it under the other words of the definition.

The length of a word is important to crossword solvers, and so, when a definition fits two or more words the words are arranged according to length. For example: adage .... SAW, MAXIM, PROVERB.

Remember to use also the efficiently-arranged reference word lists in the SPECIAL SECTION, beginning on page 187.

A

a
Aaron's brother .... MOSES
Aaron's sister .... MIRIAM
Aaron's miracle worker ... ROD
Aaron's son, oldest .... NADAB
abaca .... LINAGA
abaca, top-quality ..... LUPIS
Abadan's land .... IRAN
abalone shell money
　　　　　　 ULLO, UHLLO
abandon　 MAROON, DISCARD
abandoned .... DERELICT
abate .... EBB, LESSEN
abatement .... LETUP
abbess .... AMMA
abbey: Sp. .... ABADIA
abbot: Lat. .... ABBAS
abbreviations
　　　 PTA, SRO, NATO (1949
　　　　　　　 pact)
abdominal .... VENTRAL
Abel's brother .... CAIN
abhor　 HATE, DETEST, LOATHE
Abie's girl .... ROSE
Abijah's son .... ASA
ability ...... POWER, TALENT
abject .... BASE
b
abode, blissful .... EDEN
abode of dead .. HADES, SHEOL
abode of dead: Egypt.
　　　　　　 AALU, AARU
abound .... TEEM
abounding .... RIFE
about .. OF, RE, ANENT, CIRCA
about: Lat. .... CIRCITER
above ..... O'ER, OVER, UPON
abrade .... RUB, CHAFE
Abraham's birthplace ..... UR
Abraham's brother
　　　　　 HARAN, NAHOR
Abraham's father ...... TERAH
Abraham's nephew .... LOT
Abraham's son
　　　 ISAAC, ISHMAEL
Abraham's wife . SARAH, SARAI
abrasive .... EMERY
abrogate .... ANNUL
abrupt flexure .... GENU
Absalom's cousin ..... AMASA
Absalom's sister ..... TAMAR
abscond ..... ELOPE, LEVANT
absence, license for .... EXEAT
absent ..... OFF, OUT, AWAY,
　　　　　　　 GONE
absolute .... UTTER, PLENARY
absolve sins .... SHRIVE

c
absorbed .... RAPT
abstruse .... ESOTERIC
abundance, in .... GALORE
abundant ...... RIFE, AMPLE
abuse: India .... GALI, GALEE
abuse ... VIOLATE, MISTREAT
abusive, be .... REVILE
abusive charges .... MUD
abut .... ADJOIN, BORDER
abyss .... GULF, HOLE, CHASM
Abyssinian ..... KAFA, KAFFA
Abyssin. fly .... ZIMB
Abyssin. grain .... TEFF
Abyssin. Hamite . AFAR, AGAO,
　　　　　　 BEJA, AFARA
Abyssin. language ...... SAHO
Abyssin. mountain wolf
　　　　　　　 KABERU
Abyssin. ruler's title ... NEGUS
Abyssin. ox .. GALLA, SANGA,
　　　　　　　 SANGU
Abyssin. Semitic dialect
　　　　　 GEEZ, GHESE
Abyssin. tree .... KOSO
Abyssin. tribesman ..... SHOA
Abyssin. vizier .... RAS
accent .... TONE
accent, Irish .. BLAS, BROGUE
d
access .... ENTREE
accommodate .... LEND
"— accompli" .... FAIT
according to . ALA, AUX, ALLA
accost .... HAIL, GREET
account entry ...ITEM, DEBIT,
　　　　　　　 CREDIT
accumulate .... AMASS,
　　　　　 HOARD, ACCRUE
accumulation .... FUND
accustomed ..... USED, WONT,
　　　　　　　 ENURED
acetic acid ester .... ACETATE
acetone derivative .... ACETOL
acetylene .... ETHIN, ETHINE
Achilles' adviser ...... NESTOR
Achilles' father ...... PELEUS
Achilles' mother ..... THETIS
Achilles' slayer .... PARIS
acid, kind of .. AMINO, BORIC
acid radical .... ACYL, ACETYL
acidity .... ACOR
acknowledge .... OWN
acknowledge frankly ... AVOW
acorns, dried ...... CAMATA
acoustics apparatus ... SIRENE
acquainted .... VERSANT
acquiesce .... ASSENT

6

a acquiesce, fully ..... ACCEDE
acquire .... WIN, GAIN, REAP
acrobat of India .... NAT
Acropolis of Thebes .. CADMEA
across: comb. form
TRAN, TRANS
acrostic, Hebrew .... AGLA
act ...... DEED, FEAT, EMOTE
act: Lat. .... ACTU, ACTUS
action, put into ...... ACTUATE
action word .... VERB
active .... SPRY, AGILE, BRISK,
LIVELY, NIMBLE
actor .... HISTRIO, HISTRION
actor's group .... TROUPE
actor's hint .... CUE
actor's valet .... DRESSER
actual .... REAL, TRUE
actual being .... ESSE
actuality .... FACT
adage .... SAW, MAXIM,
PROVERB
Adam's ale .... WATER
Adam's 1st mate: legend
LILITH
Adam's grandson ...... ENOS
Adam's son . ABEL, CAIN, SETH
adapt .... FIT
adept .... ACE
b add on .... AFFIX, ANNEX,
ATTACH
adder, common .... ASP
additions .... ADDENDA
addition, bill's .... RIDER
adequate .... DUE, FULL,
AMPLE, EQUAL
adhere .... CLING, STICK,
CLEAVE
adherent .... IST
adhesive .. GUM, GLUE, PASTE
ADJECTIVE ENDING, see SUF-
FIX, ADJECTIVE
adjust ...... FIX, SET, ADAPT,
ATTUNE, ORIENT
adjutant .... AIDE
adjutant bird .... ARGALA,
HURGILA, MARABOU
admonish .... WARN, EXHORT,
REPROVE
admonisher .... MONITOR
adolescence .... TEENS,
YOUTH, NONAGE
adopted son of Mohammed . ALI
Adriana's servant ...... LUCE
adroit ...... READY, HABILE,
SKILLFUL
adulterate .. DEBASE, DEFILE,
DENATURE
advance guard .... VAN
advantage .... USE, GAIN,
PROFIT, BENEFIT

c adventitious lung sound .. RALE
adventure ...... GEST, GESTE
adviser, woman ...... EGERIA
Aeëtes' daughter ..... MEDEA
Aegir's wife .... RAN
Aeneas' wife .... CREUSA
Aeneid author VERGIL, VIRGIL
Aesir ... TIU, TYR, ULL, FREY,
LOKE, LOKI, ODIN, THOR,
VALE, VALI, DONAR,
FREYA, BRAGI, WODEN,
BALDER
affectionate ... FOND, WARM,
LOVING, TENDER
affirm .. AVER, POSIT, ASSERT
affirmative .... AY, AYE,
YEA, YES
affirmative vote ..... AY, AYE,
YEA, YES
afflict ...... TRY, VEX, PAIN,
DISTRESS
affluence ...... EASE, RICHES,
WEALTH
affray .... BRAWL, FIGHT,
MELEE
Afghan prince .. AMIR, AMEER
Afghan title .... KHAN
afresh .... ANEW
d afraid: obsolete .... REDDE
AFRICAN .... see also SOUTH
AFRICAN and AFRICAN in
SPECIAL SECTION
AFRICAN ANTELOPE
see ANTELOPE
Afr. bass .... IYO
Afr. bustard .... KORI
Afr. cotton garment .... TOBE
Afr. disease .... NENTA
Afr. worm .... LOA
Afr. grass, millet-like .. FUNDI
Afr. hornbill .... TOCK
Afr. plant .... ALOE
Afr. scrub .... BITO
Afr. soldier .... ASKARI
Afr. squirrel .... XERUS
Afr. stockade .... BOMA
Afr. tableland .... KAROO
Afrikaans ...... TAAL, BOERS
aft .... ABAFT, ASTERN
after awhile .... ANON
aftermath .... ROWEN
afterpart of ship's keel
SKAG, SKEG
afterpiece, comic ..... EXODE
aftersong .... EPODE
again .... ENCORE
against .... CON, ANTI,
CONTRA, VERSUS
agalloch wood .. AGAR, ALOE,
GAROO
Agamemnon's son .... ORESTES

7

Agate

a agate stone .... ACHATE
age .... EON, ERA, AERA,
　　　　　　　RIPEN, PERIOD
aged .... OLD, ANILE, SENILE
agave fiber .... ISTLE
agency, depression-era .. N R A
agency, govt. .... E C A, F H A
agency, wage, price ...... E S A
agency, ration-book .... O P A
agency, World-War II .. O P A
agent ...... DOER, FACTOR,
　　　　　　　FACIENT
agents acted through .. MEDIA
aggregate . SUM, MASS, TOTAL
agitate .... STIR
agitation ...... STIR, DITHER,
　　　　　　　TUMULT
agitation, be in state of SEETHE
agnomen .... NAME
agree ..... GIBE, JIBE, TALLY,
　　　　　　　ASSENT, CONCUR
agreeable: old Eng. ... AMENE
agreeableness of letters EUTONY
agreement ...... MISE, PACT,
　　　　　CONCORD, ENTENTE
agriculture goddess ..... CERES,
　　　　　VACUNA, DEMETER
Agrippina's son .... NERO
b Ahasuerus' minister .. HAMAN
ahead ...... ON, BEFORE, FORWARD
Ahiam's father .... SACAR
aid .., ABET, ASSIST, SUCCOR,
　　　　　　　FURTHER
aim ...... END, GOAL, ASPIRE
aims, with the same .... AKIN
air .. AER, ARIA, MIEN, TUNE
air apparatus ...... AERATOR
air current, ascending THERMAL
air, fill with .... AERATE
air, fresh .... OZONE
air passage ...... FLUE, VENT
air spirit .... SYLPH
air, upper .. ETHER, AETHER
aircraft, motorless .... GLIDER
airplane .... JET, AERO
airplane: Fr. .... AVION
airport marker .... PYLON
airport, Paris .... ORLY
airship . AERO, BLIMP, PLANE
airy ...... LIGHT, ETHEREAL
ait .... ISLE
Ajax, tale about ..... MYTH
Ajax's father ...... TELAMON
akin .... SIB
alang grass .... LALANG
alarm . SCARE, SIREN, AROUSE
alas! .. ACH, HEU, OCH, OIME
alas: Irish .. OHONE, OCHONE
alas: poetic .... AY
Alaska glacier .... MUIR

c ALBANIAN see COINS, TRIBES,
　　GAZETTEER in SPECIAL
　　　　　　　SECTION
Albanian dialect .. GEG, CHAM,
　　　　　　　GHEG, TOSK
albatross, sooty ...... NELLY
alchitran .... TAR, PITCH
alcohol radical .... AL
alcohol, solid . STERIN, STEROL
alcoholic drink .... GIN, RUM,
　　　　　　　RHUM
Alcott heroine ..... JO, AMY,
　　　　　　　MEG, BETH
alcove ...... BOWER, RECESS
alder tree: Scot .... ARN
ale mug .... TOBY
ale, sour .... ALEGAR
alewife fish .... POMPANO
ALEUTIAN see TRIBES, GAZET-
　　TEER in SPECIAL SECTION
Alexandrian theologian . ARIUS
Alexander victory
　　　　　　ISSUS, ARBELA
alfalfa .... LUCERN, LUCERNE
Alfonso's queen .... ENA
alga .... NORI
alga, one-cell .... DIATOM
algae genus, fan-shaped
　　　　　　　PADINA
algarroba tree ...... CALDEN
d Algerian governor ...... DEY
ALGERIA—see SPECIAL SEC-
　　　　　　　TION
ALGONQUIN .... see Page 192
Ali Baba's word ...... SESAME
Ali, caliph descendants ALIDS
Alien in Hebrew territory .. GER
alienate .... WEAN, ESTRANGE
align ... TRUE, ALINE, RANGE
alkali .... LYE, REH, USAR
alkaline solution .... LYE
alkaloid .. CAFFEIN, CAFFEINE
alkaloid, calabar bean
　　　　　　　ESERINE
all: Lat. .... TOTO
all religions, believer in
　　　　　　　OMNIST
all right .... OKAY, OKEH
allanite .... CERINE
allay .... CALM, ASSUAGE,
　　　　　　　RELIEVE
alleged force .... OD
allegory, religious ... PARABLE
Allepo native .... SYRIAN
alleviate ...... EASE, ALLAY,
　　　　　　　LESSEN
alley .... MIB, MIG
alliance .... UNION, LEAGUE
alliance, Western ...... NATO
alligator .... LAGARTO

8

a alligator pear ..... **AVOCADO**
alligator, S.A. ...... **CAIMAN, CAYMAN**
allot .... **METE, GRANT, ASSIGN, PORTION**
allotment .... **QUOTA, RATION**
allow .... **LET**
allowance **TARE, TRET, RATION**
alloy ...... **MOKUM, OROIDE**
alloy, aluminum ...... **DURAL**
alloy, copper .... **BRASS**
alloy, copper-tin ...... **BRONZE**
alloy, gold-silver: Egyp. . **ASEM**
alloy, lead-tin .. **CALIN, TERNE**
alloy, non-ferrous ...... **TULA**
alloy, yellow .... **AICH**
allspice .... **PIMENTO**
allure .... **TICE, TOLE, TEMPT, ENTICE**
allusion .... **HINT**
almond emulsion ..... **ORGEAT**
almost .... **ANEAR**
alms box or chest ..... **ARCA**
aloe .... **AGAVE**
aloe derivative .... **ALOIN**
aloes product .... **ALOIN**
alone, on stage .. **SOLA, SOLUS**
along .... **ON, BESIDE**
alp .... **PEAK**
b alpaca .... **PACO**
alphabet letter, old .... **RUNE**
Alps, Austro-It.
     TIROL, TYROL, TIROLO
Alps, one of .... **BLANC**
Alps pass .... **CENIS**
Alps, river rising in .. **RHONE**
Altar constellation ...... **ARA**
altar end of church ..... **APSE**
altar screen .... **REREDOS**
altar shelf **GRADIN, RETABLE**
altar side curtain .... **RIDDEL**
altar top .... **MENSA**
alternate .... **ROTATE**
alternative ...... **OR, EITHER**
alumni .... **GRADS**
always **AY, AYE, EER, EVER**
amadou .... **PUNK**
amass .. **HOARD, GATHER**
amateur **TIRO, TYRO, NOVICE**
Amazon cetacean ...... **INIA**
Amazon tributary .. **APA, ICA**
ambary .... **DA**
ambary hemp .... **NALITA**
ambassador **ENVOY, LEGATE**
amber fish
     RUNNER, MEDREGAL
Amen-Ra's wife .... **MUT**
amend **ALTER, EMEND, REVISE**
amendment, document .. **RIDER**
amends, make .... **ATONE**
ament .... **CHAT**

c Am. artist ..... **WEST, HICKS, HOMER, MARIN, PEALE, BEN-TON, COPLEY, INNESS, COR-BINO, ALBRIGHT**
AMERICAN INDIAN ...... see
     INDIANS, Page 192
Am. aloe fiber .... **PITA, PITO**
Am. author . **ADE, POE, AMES, BAUM, HARTE, WYLIE, YERBY, CORWIN, FERBER, HERSEY, KANTOR, MORLEY**
Am. author, illustrator ... **PYLE**
Am. capitalist .... **ASTOR**
Am. caricaturist ... **REA, NAST**
Am. dramatist . **AKINS, BARRY, ODETS, CROUSE**
Am. editor .... **BOK**
Am. educator .... **MANN**
Am. explorer . **BYRD, FREMONT**
Am. general
     LEE, OTIS, GREENE
Am. humorist ...... **ADE, NYE, COBB, NASH, ROGERS**
Am. jurist .... **TANEY**
Am. inventor ... **IVES, MORSE, TESLA, EDISON**
American: Mex. ...... **GRINGO**
Am. nature writer **BEEBE, SETON**
Am. nighthawk .... **PISK**
AM. PAINTER see **AM. ARTIST**
d Am. patriot ..... **HALE, OTIS, ALLEN, REVERE**
Am. philanthropist ...... **RIIS**
Am. philosopher ..... **EDMAN**
Am. pianist
     ARRAU, DUCHIN, LEVANT
Am. poet ... **POE, AUDEN, BENET, FROST, GUEST, RILEY, STEIN, MILLAY**
Am. poetess ... **STEIN, LOWELL**
Am. sculptor .... **CALDER**
AM. SINGER ... see **SOPRANO**
Am. statesman
     CLAY, BARUCH, DULLES
Am. suffragist .... **CATT**
Am. surgeon .... **PARRAN**
AM. WRITER see **AM. AUTHOR**
AMERIND (means any American Indian) See pages 192, 193
amide, pert. to .... **AMIC**
a mine: Corn. .... **BAL**
ammonia compound ... **AMIN, AMIDE, AMINE**
ammoniac plant ...... **OSHAC**
ammunition . **SHOT, SHRAPNEL**
ammunition, short for: . **AMMO, AMMU**
ammunition wagon ... **CAISSON**
among ...... **IN, MID, AMID**
amorously, stare .. **LEER, OGLE**
amount assessed ...... **RATAL**

9

a amount staked in gambling
MISE
amuse .... DIVERT
ampere .... WEBER
amphibian
FROG, TOAD, ANURAN
amphibian, order HYLA, ANURA
amphitheater .... ARENA
amphitheater, natural . CIRQUE
amplification factor .. MU
amulet .... CHARM, PERIAPT
analyze .... ASSAY, DISSECT
analyze grammatically . PARSE
ancestor of Irish .. IR, ITH,
MIL, MILED
ancestor of man, Hindu MANU
ancestral spirit, P. I ANITO
ancestral .... AVITAL
ancestral spirits LARES, MANES
anchor ..... FIX, TIE, MOOR,
KEDGE
anchor part .... FLUKE
anchor, small, light ... KEDGE
anchor tackle .... CAT
ancient Asiatic .... MEDE
ancient Briton .... CELT
ancient Chinese ...... SERES
anchovy sauce .... ALEC
ancient city, Asia Minor MYRA,
NICAEA
ancient country .. . GAUL
Ancient Egyp. kingdom SENNAR
ancient flute .. . TIBIA
ancient Greece division AETOLIA
ancient invader, India
SAKA, SACAE
b ancient people of Gaul .. REMI
ancient Persian .... MEDE
ancient Persian money . DARIC
ancient philosophy .... YOGA
ancient race .... MEDES
ancient Slav
VEND, WEND, VENED
ancient times .... ELD, YORE
ancient tribe of Britons . ICENI
ancient weight .... MINA
and .. TOO, ALSO, PLUS, WITH
and: Lat. .... ET
and not .... NOR
and so on: abbr. .... ETC.
Andes cold higher region . PUNA
Andes grass .... ICHU
Andes mountain .... SORATA
andiron .... DOG
"Andronicus,—" ...... TITUS
anecdotage or anecdotes
ANA, TALES
anent .... RE, ABOUT, BESIDE
anent, close — .... TO
anesthetic ...... GAS, ETHER
Angel of Death ...... AZRAEL
angel, Pers. .... MAH

c anger .... IRE, RAGE
RILE, CHOLER
anger, fit of .. PIQUE, TEMPER
angle, 57 degrees .... RADIAN
angle of leaf and axis ... AXIL
angle of leafstalk ...... AXIL
angle of stem, pert. to . AXILE
Anglo-Saxon "G" . YOK, YOGH
A.-S. god of peace ...... ING
A.-S. lord's man THANE, THEGN
A.-S. king .... INE
A.-S. money (coin) ...... ORA
A.-S. slave .... ESNE
A.-S. warrior . THANE, THEGN
Angora goat ...... CHAMAL
angry .... HOT, MAD,
SORE, IRATE
animal, Afr. .. CIVET, GENET,
POTTO, ZEBRA, GENETTE
animal, ant-eating . ECHIDNA
animal, aquatic . SEAL, OTTER,
WHALE, DUGONG,
WALRUS, MANATEE
animal, arboreal .... TARSIER
animal, Austral. .... ECHIDNA
animal, badgerlike, Java
TELEDU
animal body .... SOMA
animal, draft ......OX, OXEN
d animal, fabulous .... DRAGON
animal, giraffelike .... OKAPI
animal, India .... DHOLE
animal, Madagascar
FOSSA, FOUSSA
animals of area ..... FAUNA
animal-plant life ...... BIOTA
animal, Peru .... ALPACA
animal, sea .. SEAL, CORAL,
WHALE, WALRUS,
DUGONG, MANATEE
animal, S. Afr. ...... ZORIL
animal, S. Am. .. APARA, COATI
animal trail .... RUN, SLOT,
SPUR, SPOOR
animating principle .... SOUL
ankle . TALUS, TARSI, TARSUS
ankle, pert. to ...... TARSAL
Annamese measure .... TAO
ANNAMESE..see also ANNAM
in SPECIAL SECTION
Annapolis student PLEB, PLEBE
anneal ... TEMPER, TOUGHEN
annex .... ADD, ELL,
WING, ATTACH
annatto seeds: Sp. .. ACHIOTE
annihilate DESTROY, DISCREATE
ANNIVERSARY . see WEDDING
announce .... HERALD
annoy .. IRK, TRY, VEX, RILE,
PEEVE, TEASE, BOTHER,
MOLEST, PESTER, DIS-
TURB

a annual, as winds .... ETESIAN
annuity, form of .... TONTINE
annul .... UNDO, VOID,
CANCEL, REVOKE
annular die .... DOD
annulet: Her. .... VIRE
anoint ... OIL, ANELE, ENELE
another ... NEW, ADDITIONAL
ant .... EMMET, PISMIRE
antarctic bird ...... PENGUIN
antarctic icebreaker .... ATKA
antecedent . PRIOR, ANCESTOR
antelope, Afr. .... GNU, KOB,
BISA, GUIB, KOBA, KUDU,
ORYX, POKU, PUKU, TORA,
ADDAX, ELAND, ORIBI,
RHEBOK
antelope, Afr., large .. IMPALA
antelope, Afr., small .. DUIKER
antelope, Ind.
SASIN, NILGAI, NILGAU
antelope, Siberian ..... SAIGA
antelope, tawny .... ORIBI
antenna HORN, PALP, AERIAL
FEELER
antenna, with nodose
NODICORN
anthracite, inferior ..... CULM
anti-aircraft shells ..... FLAK
anti-tank gun .... PIAT
b antic ... DIDO, CAPER, PRANK
antique red color .. CHAUDRON
antiseptic .... EUPAD, EUSOL,
IODIN, SALOL, CRESOL,
IODINE
antiseptic, mercury
EGOL, METAPHEN
antitoxin ...... SERA, SERUM
antler point .... SNAG, TINE,
PRONG
antler, unbranched ...... DAG
antlers, stag's .... ATTIRE
"Anthony and Cleopatra" character .... IRAS
anvil .... INCUS, TEEST
anxiety .... CARE
any: dialect .... ONI
any one .... AN
aoudad .... ARUI
apathy ... ENNUI, DOLDRUMS
ape .... ORANG
ape, long-tailed, India .. KRA
appellation ..... NAME, TITLE
APERTURE . see also OPENING
aperture .... GAP, HOLE,
SLOT, VENT, ORIFICE
apex, at the .... APICAL
aphasia, motor .... ALALIA
aphorism . SAW, RULE, SUTRA
Aphrodite .... VENUS

c Aphrodite, got apple from
PARIS
Aphrodite, love of ... ADONIS
Aphrodite's mother .... DIONE
Aphrodite's son .... EROS
apocopate .... ELIDE
Apocrypha, book from . ESDRAS
Apollo's instrument ..... BOW,
LUTE, LYRE
Apollo's mother LETO, LATONA
Apollo's sister
DIANA, ARTEMIS
Apollo's son .... ION
Apollo's twin ...... ARTEMIS
Apollo's vale, sacred ... TEMPE
apoplexy, plant .... ESCA
Apostle (12) .... JOHN, JUDE
(THADDEUS), JAMES, JUDAS,
PETER (SIMON PETER), SI-
MON, ANDREW, PHILIP,
THOMAS (DIDYMUS), MAT-
THEW (LEVI), MATTHIAS,
BARTHOLOMEW
Apostle, Capernaum MATTHEW
Apostles, teaching of . DIDACHE
apparent ..... OVERT, PLAIN,
EVIDENT
apparition .. SPECTER, SPECTRE
appear .... LOOK, LOOM, SEEM
appearance . AIR, MIEN, GUISE
d appease ...... CALM, ALLAY
PLACATE
appellation ..... NAME, TITLE
append .... ADD, AFFIX,
ATTACH
appendage, caudal ... ...TAIL
appetizer . CANAPE, APERITIF
apple ... POME, TREE, FRUIT,
PIPPIN
apple acid .... MALIC
apple seed .... PIP
apple tree .... SORB
apple tree genus ...... MALUS
apple, winter .... ESOPUS
apples, crushed .... POMACE
apple-like fruit .... POME
appoint .. SET, NAME, CHOOSE
apportion DEAL, METE, ALLOT
appraise RATE, VALUE, ASSESS
apprise ...... ADVISE, NOTIFY
approach ...... NEAR, ANEAR,
ACCESS
appropriate, ... APT, FIT, MEET
appropriate, not INAPT, UNFIT
apricot, Jap. .... UME
apricot, Korean . ANSU, ANZU
apricots .... MEBOS
apropos .... PAT, FITTING
apteryx .... KIWI
aptitude ..... FLAIR, ABILITY

11

a aptitude, natural
            FLAIR, TALENT
aquamarine .... **BERYL**
AQUATIC . see SEA or MARINE
Arab ....**GAMIN, SEMITE**
Arab cloak, sleeveless .... **ABA**
Arab drink ...... **BOSA, BOZA,
                     BOZAH**
Arab name .... **ALI**
Arab's state of bliss ..... **KEF**
Arabia, people of ..... **OMANI**
ARABIAN . see ARAB, ARABIA,
            SPECIAL SECTION
Arabian chief . **SAYID, SAYYID**
Arabian chieftain . **AMIR, EMIR,
            AMEER, EMEER**
Arabian chieftain's domain
                 EMIRATE
Arabian cloth .... **ABA**
Arabian district .... **TEMA**
Arabian garment .... **ABA**
Arabian jasmine .... **BELA**
Arabian judge .... **CADI**
"Arabian Nights" dervish . **AGIB**
Arabian noble .. **AMIR, EMIR,
            AMEER, EMEER**
Arabian nomadic tribesman
                    SLEB
Arabian sailboat .. see VESSEL,
                  ARAB
Arabian sleeveless garment **ABA**
b Arabian tambourine
       TAAR, DAIRA, DAIRE
Arabic jinni, evil
     AFRIT, AFREET, AFRITE
Arabic letter . **GAF, KAF, MIM,
       WAW, ALIF, DHAL**
Arabic script ....**NESKI**
Arabic surname .... **SAAD**
arachnid . **MITE, TICK, SPIDER**
Arawakan language .... **TAINO**
arbitrator ... **UMPIRE, REFEREE**
arboreal .... **DENDRAL**
arc .... **LINE, CURVE**
arch of heaven .... **COPE**
arch, pointed .... **OGIVE**
archaeology, mound ..... **TERP**
archangel .... **URIEL**
archbishop .... **PRIMATE**
archbishop, Canterbury **BECKET**
archer in Eng. ballad
          CLIM, CLYM
archetype ... **MODEL, PATTERN**
archfiend .... **SATAN**
architect's drawing .... **EPURE**
architecture, school of
              BAUHAUS
architecture, type
        DORIC, IONIC
ARCTIC ..... see GAZETTEER
Arctic . **NORTH, POLAR, FRIGID**

c arctic air force base .... **THULE**
arctic dog .... **SAMOYED**
arctic gull .genus ...... **XEMA**
arctic plain .... **TUNDRA**
Arden .... **FOREST**
ardor ... **ELAN, ZEAL, FERVOR**
area measure .. **RADII, RADIUS**
area, small .... **AREOLA**
areca .... **BETEL**
arena .... **FIELD**
Ares' mother .... **ENYO**
Ares' sister .... **ERIS**
ares, 10 .... **DECARE**
Argonaut ... **JASON, ACASTUS**
Argonauts' leader ...... **JASON**
Argonauts' ship .... **ARGO**
argument .... **AGON,
         DEBATE, HASSLE**
arhat .... **LOHAN**
aria ...... **AIR, SOLO, SONG,
         TUNE, MELODY**
arias .... **SOLI**
aridity, having .... **XERIC**
arikara .... **REE**
arise .... **REBEL, ACCRUE,
           APPEAR**
arista .... **AWN**
Arizona aborigine ...... **HOPI**
ARIZONA INDIAN see page 192
d **ARIZONA** ... see also SPECIAL
                SECTION
Ark, porter of: Bible ..... **BEN**
Ark's landing place .. **ARARAT**
arm .... **LIMB, TENTACLE**
arm, movable with verniers
            ALIDADE
arm of sea . **BAY, FIRTH, FRITH**
armadillo ...... **APAR, APARA**
armadillo, Braz. . **TATU, TATOU**
armadillo, giant . **TATU, TATOU**
armadillo, large 12-banded
            TATOUAY
armadillo, 6-banded .. **PELUDO**
armadillo, small .. **PEBA, PEVA**
armadillo, 3-banded .... **APAR,
     APARA, MATACO, MATICO**
armed band .... **POSSE**
armed galley of old Northmen
                AESC
ARMOR .... see also SPECIAL
         SECTION, page 194
armor bearer .... **ARMIGER**
armor, body .... **CUIRASS**
armor, chain .... **MAIL**
armor, horse .. **BARD, BARDE**
armor, leg .... **JAMB, JAMBE**
armor, leg below knee **GREAVE**
armor, lower body ..... **CULET**

a armor part .... **LORICA**
armor part, throat ... **GORGET**
armor, skirt .... **TACE, TASSE, TASSET**
armor, thigh ... **CUISH, TUILE, CUISSE, TUILLE**
armpit .... **ALA**
army .... **HOST, TROOPS**
army group .... **CADRE**
army provisioner ...... **SUTLER**
aroid, an .... **ARAD, ARUM**
aromatic herb
  DILL, MINT, SAGE
aromatic herb, carrot genus
  CARUM
aromatic herb-plant .... **NARD**
aromatic seed
  CUMIN, CUMMIN
aromatic seed, plant ... **ANISE**
aromatic substance ... **BALSAM**
aromatic weed .... **TANSY**
around .... **CIRCA**
arouse .... **FIRE, STIR, PIQUE**
arpeggio .... **ROULADE**
arquebus support ...... **CROC**
arraign ..... **ACCUSE, INDICT**
arrange ...... **FIX, SET, FILE, DISPOSE**
arrangement: comb. form **TAX, TAXI, TAXO, TAXEO, TAXIS**
b arrangement, pert. to..**TACTIC**
array .. **DECK, ORDER, ATTIRE**
arrest .... **NAB, HALT**
arrest writ .... **CAPIAS**
arris .... **PIEN**
arrow .... **BOLT, DART**
arrow, body of ...... **STELE**
arrow, fit string to ..... **NOCK**
arrow, spinning .... **VIRE**
arrow wood .... **WAHOO**
arrowroot .... **PIA, ARARU**
arroyo .... **HONDO**
art: Lat. .... **ARS**
art style .... **DADA, GENRE**
Artemis . **UPIS, DELIA, PHOEBE**
Artemis' twin ...... **APOLLO**
Artemis' victim ...... **ORION**
artery, largest .... **AORTA**
artery of neck ...... **CAROTID**
artful .... **SLY, WILY**
arthritis aid **ACTH, CORTISONE**
Arthur's foster brother ... **KAY**
Arthurian lady
  ENID, ELAIN, ELAINE
article .... **AN, THE, ITEM**
article, Fr. ...... **LA, LE, DES, LES, UNE**
article, Ger. .... **DAS, DER**
article, Sp. .. **EL, LA, LAS, LOS**
articulated joint ...... **HINGE**
artifice ... **RUSE, WILE, TRICK**

c artificial language .... **RO, IDO**
ARTIST .... see also PAINTER and under Country of each artist
artist, primitive .... **MOSES**
artless .... **NAIVE**
arum family plant **TARO, CALLA**
arum plant ..... **ARAD, AROID**
Aryan .... **MEDE, SLAV**
as .. **QUA, LIKE, SINCE, WHILE**
as far as .... **TO**
as it stands: mus. .... **STA**
as written: mus. .... **STA**
asafetida .... **HING**
asbestos .... **ABISTON**
ascent .... **UPGO, CLIMB**
ascetic, ancient .... **ESSENE**
asceticism, Hindu ...... **YOGA**
ash, fruit, seed ...... **SAMARA**
ash key .... **SAMARA**
ashy pale .... **LIVID**
ASIA .. see also SPECIAL SECTION
Asia Minor district, old **IONIA**
Asia Minor region, pert. to
  EOLIC, AEOLIC
Asia native, S.E. .... **SHAN**
Asiatic ancient people .. **SERES**
d Asiatic country .. see page 210
Asiatic cow .... **ZO, ZOH**
Asiatic evergreen ...... **BAGO**
Asiatic fowl .... **SAT**
Asiatic gangster .... **DACOIT**
Asiatic sardine ...... **LOUR**
Asiatic shrub .... **TEA, TCHE**
Asiatic tree .... **ACLE, ASAK, ASOK, ASOKA**
"— asinorum" .... **PONS**
askew .... **WRY, AGr**
  ALOP, AWRY
aspect ... **SIDE, FACET, PHASE**
asperse .... **SLANDER**
aspire .... **HOPE**
ass, wild
  KULAN, ONAGER, QUAGGA
assail .... **BESET, ATTACK**
ASSAM ..... see also SPECIAL SECTION, Page 191
Assam hill tribe .... **AKA**
Assam mongol .... **NAGA**
Assam silkworm .... **ERI, ERIA**
Assam tribe, Naga Hills
  AO, NAGA
assault .... **ONSET, STORM**
assault, prolonged ...... **SIEGE**
assayer .... **TESTER**
assaying cup .... **CUPEL**
assemble ... **MEET, MUSTER, COLLECT**

13

a
assembly .... DIET, SYNOD
    SESSION, GATHERING
assembly, A.-S. GEMOT, GEMOTE
assembly, China, Hawaii .. HUI
assembly, Dutch .... RAAD
assent, solemn .... AMEN
assert .... AVER, POSIT, STATE
assert formally .... ALLEGATE
assess ..... TAX, LEVY, VALUE
assessment RATE, SCOT, RATAL
asseverate .... AVER
assignor of property ... CEDENT
assimilate .. ABSORB, DIGEST
assistance AID, HELP, SUPPORT
assistant .... AIDE
associate .. ALLY, COLLEAGUE
association, trade GILD, GUILD
assuage .... MITIGATE
ASSYRIAN .. see also SPECIAL
    SECTION, Page 198
Assyrian king .... PUL
Assyrian queen, myth.
    SEMIRAMIS
asterisk .... STAR
astern ..... AFT, BAFT, ABAFT
astringent .... ALUM, STYPTIC
astringent, black ...... KATH
astringent fruit .... SLOE
astrologer of India .... JOSHI

b
astronomical .... URANIC
astron. luminous "cloud"
    NEBULA
Aswan, ancient ...... SYENE
asylum ...... HAVEN, REFUGE
at all .... ANY
at any time .... EVER
at odds .... OUT
at the home of: Fr. ..... CHEZ
Atahualpa, king ... ... INCA
atap palm .... NIPA
atelier .... STUDIO
Athamas' wife .... INO
Athena .... PALLAS, MINERVA
Athena, appellation, title . ALEA
Athena, possession of ... EGIS
Athenian .... ATTIC
Athenian bronze coin CHALCUS
Athenian demagogue ... CLEON
Athens, last king of .. CODRUS
athlete, famous ...... THORPE
a-tiptoe .... ATIP
atmospheric pressure, of BARIC
at no time: poet. ...... NEER
atoll's pool .... LAGOON
atom part .... PROTON
atomic machine
    BETATRON, RHEOTRON
atomic physicist .. BOHR, RABI,
    UREY, FERMI, PAULI,
    COMPTON, MEITNER
    MILLIKAN

c
atomic submarine .... SKATE,
    SARGO, TRITON, NAUTILUS
atone for .... REDEEM
attach .... ADD, FIX, TIE,
    APPEND
attack .... BESET, ONSET
attack, mock .... FEINT
attar .... OTTO
attempt .... TRY, STAB, ESSAY
attendant, hunter's
    GILLY, GILLIE
attention ... EAR, CARE, HEED
attest ..... VOUCH, CERTIFY
attic ...... LOFT, GARRET
Attica resident .... METIC
Attila .... ATLI, ETZEL
attitudinize .... POSE
attribute .. IMPUTE, ASCRIBE
attune .... KEY, ACCORD
auction .... SALE
audience ...... EAR, HEARING
auditory .... OTIC, AURAL
auger .... BORE, BORER
augment .... EKE
augur ...... BODE, PORTEND
augury ...... OMEN, PORTENT
auk genus .. ALCA, ALLE, URIA
auk, little .. ROTCH, ROTCHE
aura, pert. to .... AURIC

d
aureola .... HALO
auric acid salt ...... AURATE
auricle .... EAR
auricular ...... OTIC, EARED
aurochs .. TUR, URUS, AURUS
aurora ...... EOS, DAWN
auspices .... EGIS, AEGIS
Australasian harrier-hawk
    KAHU
Australasian shrub genus
    HOYA
AUSTRALIA . see also SPECIAL
    SECTION
Australian boomerang .. KILEY
Austral. food .... KAI
Austral. gum tree
    KARI, TUART
Austral. hut .... MIAM, MIMI
Austral. marsupial
    TAIT, KOALA
Austral. scaly-finned fish
    MADO
Austral. tree, timber .. PENDA
Austrian folk dance .. DREHER
Austr. violinist .... MORINI
author .... PARENT
author, boys' .. ALGER, HENTY
author, nature stories .. SETON
authoritative .... MAGISTRAL
author unknown: abbr. ... ANON

a authority, name as **CITE, QUOTE**
auto, old .. **JALOPY, JALOPPY**
automaton .... **ROBOT**
automaton: Jew. legend **GOLEM**
automobile "shoe" . **TIRE, TYRE**
ave .... **HAIL**
avena .... **OAT**
avenger: Hebr. .... **GOEL**
average .... **PAR, MEAN,**
NORM, USUAL, MEDIAL
averse .... **LOTH, LOATH**
Avesta division
YASNA, GATHAS, YASHTS
avid .... **KEEN, EAGER**
avifauna .... **ORNIS**
avocado, Mex. .... **COYO**
avoid .... **SHUN, ESCHEW**

c avouch .... **AVER, ASSERT**
away .... **OFF, GONE, ABSENT**
aweather, opposed to .... **ALEE**
aweto .... **WERI**
awkward .... **INEPT**
awkward fellow .... **LOUT**
awn .... **ARISTA**
awned .... **ARISTATE**
awry .... **AGEE, AJEE, AGLEY**
axilla .... **ALA**
axilla, pert. to .... **ALAR**
axillary .... **ALAR**
axis deer .... **CHITAL**
Aztec god, sowing ...... **XIPE**
Aztec "Noah" (hero) ... **NATA**
Aztec "Noah's" wife .. **NANA**
Aztec spear .... **ATLATL**

B

babbler: Scot. ...... **HAVEREL**
Babism, founder .... **BAB**
babul tree pods .... **GARAD**
baby animal: Fr. .... **TOTO**
baby carriage .... **PRAM**
b **BABYLONIAN GODS, DEITY,**
see also GODS and also SPE-
CIAL SECTION on page 198
Babylonian abode of dead
ARALU
Babylonian city .... **IS**
Babylonian chief gods ... **EA,**
ANU, BEL, HEA, ENKI
Babylonian chief goddess
ISTAR, ISHTAR
Babylonian chief priest of
shrine .... **EN**
Babylonian division .... **SUMER**
Babylonian hero ...... **ETANA**
Babylonian lunar cycle
SAROS
Babylonian neighbor
ELAMITE
Babylonian numeral .... **SAROS**
Babylonian priestess .. **ENTUM**
Babylonian purgatory .. **ARALU**
Bacchanals' cry ...... **EVOE**
bacchante .... **MAENAD**
Bacchus' follower ..... **SATYR**
Bacchus' son .... **COMUS**
back .. **AID, AFT, FRO, ABET,**
HIND, REAR, SPONSOR
back, call .... **REVOKE**
back door .... **POSTERN**
back, flow ..... **EBB, RECEDE**
back, lying on ...... **SUPINE**
back of neck .... **NAPE**
back, pert. to ...... **DORSAL**

back, take .... **RETRACT**
back, thrust .... **REPEL**
back, toward .... **RETRAL**
back: Zool. **NOTA, NOTUM**
d backbone ...... **CHINE, SPINE**
bacteria-free .... **ASEPTIC**
bacteriologist's wire ..... **OESE**
bacteriostatic subst. . **CITRININ**
badge, Jap. .... **MON**
badger .... **DAS, BAIT**
badgerlike animal
PAHMI, RATEL
badgers, Old World .... **MELES**
baffle .... **FOIL, POSE, ELUDE**
bag .... **SAC**
bag net .... **FYKE**
bagatelle .... **TRIFLE**
bagpipe, hole in .... **LILL**
bagpipe sound .... **SKIRL**
bailiff, old Eng. .... **REEVE**
baize fabric .... **DOMETT**
baker bird .... **HORNERO**
baking chamber ... **OST, KILN,**
OAST, OVEN
baking pit .... **IMU**
balance .. **REST, POISE, SCALE**
balance, sentence ... **PARISON**
Balance, The .... **LIBRA**
balancing weight ... **BALLAST**
Balder's killer **LOK, LOKE, LOKI**
Balder's wife .... **NANNA**
baldness .... **ACOMIA**
Balkan .... **SERB**
ball, low .... **LINER**
ball, to hit
LOB, BUNT, SWAT

15

Ball

ball, yarn thread ...... **CLEW**
ballad .... **LAY, DERRY**
ballet jump .... **JETE**
ballet skirt .... **TUTU**
ballet turn .... **FOUETTE**
balloon basket **CAR, NACELLE**
ball-rope missile

BOLA, BOLAS
balm of Gilead ...... **BALSAM**
balsalike wood ...... **BONGO**
balsam .... **FIR, TOLU, RESIN**
Balt .... **ESTH**
BALTIC ... see also SPECIAL
SECTION
Baltic Finn .... **VOD**
Baltimore stove .... **LATROBE**
Balto-Slav .... **LETT**
Baluchistan tribe ...... **REKI**
Baluchistan tribesman .. **MARI**
"Bambi" author ...... **SALTEN**
bamboo .... **REED**
bamboo shoots, pickled **ACHAR**
Bana's daughter: Hindu **USHA**
banal .... **STALE, TRITE**
banana genus .... **MUSA**
banana, kind of .. **PLANTAIN**
banana, Polyn. .... **FEI**
band .... **BELT, TAPE,**
STRIP, FILLET
band: Arch. .. **FACIA, FASCIA**
band, muscle, nerve .. **TAENIA**
band, narrow .. **STRIA, STRIAE**
bandage ...... **STUPE, TAENIA**
bandicoot .... **RAT**
bandmaster, Am. .... **SOUSA**
banish ..... **EXILE, RELEGATE**
bank .... **RELY, DEPEND**
bank, of a river ... **RIPARIAN**
bank, river .... **RIPA**
banker, India .. **SARAF, SHROFF**
banner .... **FLAG,**
ENSIGN, BANDEROLE
banter ... **CHAFF, PERSIFLAGE**
BANTU see also TRIBES in
SPECIAL SECTION. Page 191
Bantu .... **KAFIR, KAFFIR**
Bantu, Congo ... **RUA, WARUA**
Bantu language .... **ILA**
Bantu nation .... **GOGO**
Bantu-speaking tribe
RAVI, RORI, PONDO
Bantu tribesman ..... **DUALA**
baobab, dried .... **LALO**
baobab leaves, powdered . **LALO**
baptism font .... **LAVER**
baptismal basin . **FONT**
bar .... **RAIL, INGOT,**
HINDER, STRIPE
bar legally .... **ESTOP**
bar, supporting .... **FID**
barb, feather .... **HARL, HERL**

Barbados native ...... **BIM**
barbarian .... **HUN, GOTH**
Barbary ape .... **MAGOT**
barber ...... **SHAVER, TONSOR**
bard, Goth. .... **RUNER**
bare .... **BALD, MERE, NUDE**
bargain .... **DEAL, PALTER**
bargain: Dutch .... **KOOP**
barge .... **HOY**
bark .... **BAY, YAP, YIP**
bark, bitter .. **NIEPA, NIOTA**
bark, inner .... **CORTEX**
bark, lime tree .. **BAST, BASTE**
bark, medicinal .... **COTO**
bark, paper mulberry .. **TAPA**
bark, pert. to ..... **CORTICAL**
bark remover .... **ROSSER**
bark, rough exterior .... **ROSS**
barking .... **LATRANT**
barn owl genus .... **TYTO**
barometric line ...... **ISOBAR**
barony, Jap. .... **HAN**
barracuda, small **SPET, SENNET**
barrelmaker .... **COOPER**
barrel slat .... **STAVE**
barren land .... **USAR**
Barrie character ...... **ALICE**
barrow, Russ. .... **KURGAN**
base .... **LOW, VILE**
base, architectural
SOCLE, PLINTH
base, attached by .... **SESSILE**
baseball position: abbr. .. **LF,**
RF, SS
Bashan, king of .... **OG**
bashful .... **COY, SHY, TIMID**
basilica, Rome ..... **LATERAN**
basin: Geol. .... **TALA**
basis of argument ... **PREMISE**
basket .... **KISH, CABAS,**
PANIER, PANNIER
basket, coarse .... **SKEP**
basket, Eng. ...... **PED, CAUL**
basket, fish ... **WEEL, CRAIL,**
CREEL, WICKER
basket grass, Mex. ..... **OTATE**
basket, large .... **HAMPER**
basket strip .... **RAND**
basketball player ..... **CAGER**
basketry rod .... **OSIER**
Basra native .... **IRAQI**
bass, Europ. .... **BRASSE**
basswood .... **LINDEN**
bast fiber .... **RAMIE**
bat .... **RACKET**
batfish .... **DIABLO**
bathe .... **LAVE**
bathing-suit .... **MAILLOT**
baths, Roman ..... **THERMAE**
Bathsheba's husband
URIA, URIAH

16

baton	ROD
batrachian	FROG, TOAD
batter	RAM
battering machine	RAM
battery plate	GRID
battle, Am. Rev.	CONCORD
battle area	SECTOR
battle, Arthur's last	CAMLAN
battle ax	TWIBIL, TWIBILL
battle, Civil War, Tenn.	SHILOH
battle cry, Irish	ABU, ABOO
battle, Eng.-Fr.	CRECY, CRESSY
battle formation	HERSE
battle, Franco-Pruss.	SEDAN
battle, 100 Years War	CRECY, CRESSY
"Battle Hymn of Republic" author	HOWE
battle, WWI	MARNE, SOMME, YPRES, VERDUN
battlefield	ARENA
bauble	BEAD
bay	COVE, BIGHT, INLET
bay, Orkney, Shetland	VOE
bay tree	LAUREL
bay window	ORIEL
bazaar	FAIR
be foolishly overfond	DOAT, DOTE
be silent: music	TACET
be still	SH, HUSH, QUIET
beach	SHORE, STRAND
beach cabin	CABANA
beads, prayer	ROSARY
beak	NEB, NIB, BILL
beam, supporting	TEMPLET, TEMPLATE
bean	SOY, URD, LIMA
bean, E. Ind.	URD
bean, field	PINTO
bean, green	HARICOT
bean, poisonous	CALABAR
bean, S. Am.	TONKA
bean tree	CAROB
bear	STAND, YIELD, ENDURE
Bear constellation	URSA
bear, nymph changed to	CALLISTO
bear, Austral.	KOALA
bear witness	VOUCH, ATTEST
beard of grain	AWN, ARISTA
bearded seal	MAKLUK
bearer, Ind.	SINDAR
bearing	MIEN, ORLE
bearing plate	GIB
bear's-ear	ARICULA
beast of burden	ASS, BURRO, LLAMA
beat	WIN, CANE, DRUB, FLAP, POMMEL, PULSE
beat about: naut.	BUSK

beater, mortar	RAB
beauty, goddess of: Hindu	SRI, SHRI, SHREE, LAKSHM¹
beauty, Greek	LAIS
beaver	CASTOR
beaver skin	PLEW
beche-de-mer	TREPANG
beckon	NOD
bed	KIP, PALLET
bed of dry stream	DONGA
bed of press, handle	ROUNCE
bed: slang	DOSS
Bedouin headband cord	AGAL
bee, honey, genus	APIS
bee house	APIARY, HIVE
bee, male	DRONE
bee tree	LINDEN
bees, pert. to	APIAN
bee's pollen brush	SCOPA
beech tree genus	FAGUS
beechnuts	MAST
beefwood: Polyn.	TOA, TOOA, BELAH
beehive, straw	SKEP
Beehive State	see page 209
beer	ALE, BOCK, LAGER
beer, Afr. millet	POMBE
beer ingredient	HOPS, MALT
beer mug	STEIN
beer, P. I. rice	PANGASI
beet variety	CHARD
Beethoven's birthplace	BONN
beetle	DOR, ELATER
beetle, burrowing	BORER
beetle, click	ELATER
beetle, fruit-loving	BORER
beetle genus, ground	AMARA
beetle, ground	CARAB
beetle, sacred Egyp.	SCARAB
beetle, wood	SAWYER
befall	HAP
before	ERE, PRE, ANTERIOR
before: obs.	ERER
before: naut.	AFORE
beget	EAN, SIRE
"Beggar's Opera" dramatist	GAY
beginner	TIRO, TYRO, NOVICE, NEOPHYTE
beginning	GERM, ONSET, ORIGIN, INITIAL
beginning	NASCENCY
behave toward	TREAT
behind	AFT, AREAR, ASTERN
behold	LO, ECCE, VOILA
behoove	DOW
beige	ECRU
being	ENS, ENTITY

17

Being

being, abstract **ENS, ESSE, ENTIA**
being, essential .... **ENS**
Bela, son of .... **IRI**
beleaguerment .... **SIEGE**
Belem .... **PARA**
belief .... **CREED,
FAITH, TENET**
believe .... **TROW,
CREDO, CREDIT**
believer in god of reason **DEIST**
bell, alarm .... **TOCSIN**
bell, sacring .... **SQUILLA**
bell tower .... **BELFRY,
CAMPANILE**
bell's tongue ...... **CLAPPER**
bellbird, N.Z. .... **MAKO**
bellowing .... **AROAR**
below: nautical ...... **ALOW**
belt .... **CEST, SASH**
belt, sword ...... **BALDRIC,
BAWDRIC, BALDRICK**
ben .... **BENE**
bench ...... **EXEDRA, SETTLE**
bench, judge's .. see **JUDGE'S
BENCH**
bench in a galley ..... **BANK**
bend .... **SNY, FLEX, GENU,
STOOP, FLEXURE**
benediction .... **BENISON**
benefactor .... **PATRON**
beneficiary: Law ...... **USES**
benefit .... **BOON, AVAIL**
Bengal native .... **KOL**
Bengal singer .... **BAUL**
Benjamin's first born .. **BELA**
bent .... **PRONATE**
bequeath .... **WILL**
bequest .... **DOWER**
Berber .... **RIFF**
Bermuda arrowroot
ARARU, ARARAO
Bermuda grass .. **DOOB, DOUB**
berserk ...... **AMOK, AMUCK**
beseech .... **PRAY,
OBTEST, ENTREAT**
beside .... **BY**
besides .. **TOO, YET, ALSO, ELSE**
bestow .... **AWARD,
CONFER, IMPART**
bets, fail to pay
WELCH, WELSH
betel leaf ...... **BUYO, PAUN**
betel nut .... **SERI, SIRI,
BONGA, SIRIH**
betel palm .. **ARECA, PINANG**
betel pepper ..... **IKMO, ITMO**
Bethuel's son .... **LABAN**
betoken .... **DENOTE**
betroth .... **AFFY**
between: prefix .... **INTER**
Bevan's nickname .... **NYE**

bevel .... **BEZEL, SLANT**
bevel out .... **REAM**
bevel ship timber .... **SNAPE**
bevel to join .. **MITER, MITRE**
BEVERAGE ... see also **DRINK**
beverage .... **ADE, ALE,
TEA, BEER**
beverage, curdled .... **POSSET**
beverage, hot wine .... **NEGUS**
beverage, Polyn.
KAVA, KAWA
beverage, S. Am. ...... **MATE**
bewitch .... **HEX, SPELL**
beyond: comb. form .. **ULTRA**
Bhutan pine .... **KAIL**
biased person .... **BIGOT**
BIBLICAL .. see also **SPECIAL
SECTION**
Biblical city .... **DAN,
BABEL, EKRON**
Biblical character .. **ARA, IRA,
ERI, ARAN, ATER, ONAN**
Biblical country , **EDOM, ENON
SEBA, SHEBA**
Biblical driver .... **JEHU**
Biblical judge .... **ELI,
ELON, GIDEON, SAMSON**
Biblical king **OG, ASA, AGAG,
AHAB, ELAH, OMRI, SAUL,
HEROD, NADAB**
Biblical kingdom ...... **ELAM,
MOAB, SAMARIA**
Biblical land .... **N.D**
Biblical lion .... **ARI**
BIBLICAL MEASURE ...... see
HEBREW MEASURE
BIBLICAL MOUNT see Page 197
Biblical name .... **ED, ER, IRI,
ONO, REI, TOI, ABIA, ADER,
ANER, ANIM, ASOM, DARA,
ENOS, IRAD, IVAH, REBA,
ABIAM, AHIRA, AMASA,
ASEAS**
Biblical name for part of Arabia
SHEBA
Biblical ornaments ..... **URIM**
Biblical priest, high ..... **ELI,
AARON, ANNAS**
Biblical region .. **ARAM, EDAR**
Biblical ruler .... **IRA**
Biblical sacred objects .. **URIM**
Biblical serpent .. **NEHUSHTAN**
Biblical son .... **HAM**
Biblical spy .... **CALEB**
Biblical tower .... **EDAR**
Biblical town in Samaria **ENON**
BIBLICAL TRIBE .... see
Page 197
Biblical weed .... **TARE**
Biblical well; spring . **AIN, ESEK**
Biblical wild ox .... **REEM**

18

Biblical

a
Biblical witch's home .. ENDOR
Biblical woman RAHAB, LEAH
Biblical word .. SELAH, MENE
Biblical word of reproach RACA
bicarbonate .... SODA
bice blue .... AZURITE
bicker .... CAVIL
bicycle for two ..... TANDEM
biddy .... HEN
"— bien" .... TRES
big casino .... TEN
bile .... GALL
bill ...... DUN, NEB, BEAK
bill of fare ... MENU, CARTE
bill, part of .... CERE
billiard shot .. CAROM, MASSE
billow .... SEA, WAVE
bind ...... TAPE, SWATH
biography .... LIFE, MEMOIR
biological .. BIOTIC, BIOTICAL
biological reproductive body
.... GAMETE
biotic community ..... BIOME

b
bird .... CLEE, COCK, CROW,
DOVE, FINK, GLED, HUIA,
IIWI, JACU, KALA, KIWI,
KOEL, KORA, KUKU, KYAH,
LARK, LOON, LORO, LORY,
LOUN, LOWA, LULU, LUPE,
MAKO, MAMO, MIRO,
MOHO, MORO, MYNA,
NENE, PAPE, PEHO, PISK,
RAIL, RAYA, ROOK, RUFF,
RURU, RYPE, SKUA, SMEE,
SMEW, SORA, STIB, SWAN,
TEAL, TERN, TOCK, TOCO,
TODY, UTUM, WAEG,
WREN, YENI, YUTU,
DRAKE, ROBIN, SERIN, EL-
ANET, SHRIKE, SISKIN,
bird, Am. .... TOWHEE
bird, Arctic .. BRANT, FULMAR
bird, Austral. .... EMU, KOEL,
COOEE, COOEY
bird, black ANI, ROOK, RAVEN
bird, blue .... JAY
bird, C. & S. Am. ..... COIN,
CONDOR, CONDORES
bird cry .... CAW, COO
bird, diving ..... AUK, LOON,
LOUN, SMEW
bird, ducklike .... COOT
bird, extinct .... MOA,
DODO, MAMO
bird, Europ. .... GLEDE, TEREK
bird genus ..... CRAX, RHEA
bird, gull-like .... TERN
BIRD, HAWAIIAN .... see
HAWAIIAN BIRD
bird house .... COTE
bird, hunting .... FALCON

c
bird, India .... SARUS
SHAMA, ARGALA
bird, laughing .... LOON
bird life .... ORNIS
bird, long-legged
AGAMI, STILT
bird, marsh .... RAIL,
SORA, BITTERN
bird, mythical .... ROC
bird, national .... EAGLE
bird nest collector .. OOLOGIST
bird of prey ...... ERN, ERNE,
HAWK, KITE, EAGLE,
CORMORANT
bird, orange .... ORIOLE
bird order ..... PICI, RASORES
bird, oscine .... CHAT, ORIOLE
BIRD, OSTRICHLIKE ...... see
OSTRICHLIKE BIRD
bird, Persian .... BULBUL
BIRD, SEA ..... see SEA BIRD
bird, shore. RAIL, SORA, SNIPE,
WADER, AVOCET, PLOVER
bird, small .... TIT, PIPIT
bird, small brown ...... WREN
BIRD, S. AM. .... see
S. AMER. BIRD
bird, swimming .. LOON, GREBE
bird, talking .. MYNA, MYNAH

d
bird, tropical ..... ANI, ANO,
TROGON, JACAMAR
bird, U. S.
COLIN, VEERY, TANAGER
BIRD, WADING .... see
..WADING BIRD
bird, wading, Afr.
UMBER, UMBRETTE
bird, water see WADING BIRD
BIRD, WEB-FOOTED .... see
WEB-FOOTED BIRD
bird, W. Ind. .... TODY
bird, white-plumed .... EGRET
bird, white-tailed .. ERN, ERNE
birds .... AVES
bird's beak .... NEB, NIB
bird's cry .... CAW, WEET
birds of region .... ORNIS
birds' route .... FLYWAY
biretta .... CAP
birth, by .... NEE
birth, of one's .... NATAL
birthmark
MOLE, NEVUS, NAEVUS
birthplace, Apollo, Diana DELOS
birthplace, Constantine's
NIS, NISH
birthplace, Mohammed's MECCA
birthplace, Muses, Orpheus
PIERIA

19

a birthstone .... Jan., **GARNET**; Feb., **AMETHYST**; March, **JASPER**, **AQUAMARINE**, **BLOODSTONE**; April, **DIAMOND**; May, **AGATE**, **EMERALD**; June, **PEARL**, **MOONSTONE**; July, **ONYX**, **RUBY**; Aug., **CARNELIAN**, **SARDONYX**, **PERIDOT**; Sept., **SAPPHIRE**; Oct., **OPAL**; Nov., **TOPAZ**; Dec., **TURQUOISE**, **ZIRCON**
birthwort, Europ. .. **CLEMATITE**
bishop .... **PRELATE**
bishop of Rome .... **POPE**
bishopric .... **SEE**
bishop's attendant ... **VERGER**
bishop's hat

    HURA, MITER, MITRE
bishop's office .... **LAWN**
bishop's seat ..... **SEE, APSE**
bishop's title, East ... **ABBA**
bite .... **CHAM, MORSEL**
bite upon .... **GNAW**
biting .... **ACERB, ACRID**
bitter .... **ACERB, ACRID**
bitter almonds compound

    AMARINE
bitter drug .... **ALOE**
bitter vetch .... **ERS**
b bittern .... **HERON**
bivalve .... **CLAM, MUSSEL**
bivalve genus .... **PINNA**
bizarre .... **OUTRE**
black ..... **JET, EBON, INKY, RAVEN, SABLE, TARRY, NIGRINE**
black and blue .... **LIVID**
black buck .... **SASIN**
black gum tree genus **NYSSA**
black haw .... **SLOE**
black kelpie .... **BARB**
black nightshade ... **DUSCLE**
Black Sea arm ... **AZOF, AZOV**
blackbird

    ANI, MERL, MERLE, RAVEN
blackbird, Europ.

    OSSEL, OUSEL, OUZEL
blackbird: variant ...... **ANO**
blacken .... **INK, SOOT**
black-fin snapper ...... **SESI**
blackfish .... **TAUTOG**
Blackmore heroine .... **LORNA**
blacksnake .... **RACER**
blacksmith's block .... **ANVIL**
blackthorn fruit .... **SLOE**
blackwood, India .... **BITI**
blade .... **OAR**
Blake's symbolic figure .. **ZOA**
Blake's symbolic figures **ZOAS**
blanch .... **ETIOLATE**

c blanket, cloak-like .. **PONCHO**
blanket, coarse wool .. **COTTA**
blanket, horse ...... **MANTA**
blanket, Sp.-Am. ..... **SERAPE**
blast furnace, stone in .. **TYMP**
blaubok, S. Afr. ...... **ETAAC**
blaze star .... **NOVA**
bleach .... **CHLORE**
bleaching vat .... **KEIR, KIER**
bleak .... **RAW**
blesbok .... **NUNNI**
bless .... **SAIN**
bless: Yiddish .... **BENSH**
blessing

    BOON, GRACE, BENEFICE
blight .... **NIP**
blight of drought, India **SOKA**
blind, as hawks .... **SEEL**
blind dolphin .... **SUSU**
blind god, Teut. **HOTH, HODER**
blind impulse to ruin ... **ATE**
blindness .... **CECITY**
blister .. **BLEB, BULLA, BULLAE**
block, small arch

    DENTEL, DENTIL
block, wood .... **NOG**
blockhead .... **ASS, DOLT**
blood factor .... **RH**
blood, lack of red

    ANEMIA, ANAEMIA
d blood of gods .... **ICHOR**
blood, part of .... **SERUM**
blood, pert. to .... **HEMAL**, **HEMIC, HAEMAL, HAEMIC**
blood vessel .... **VEIN**
blood vessel, main .. **AORTA**
blood, watery part of

    SERA, SERUM
blood sucker .... **LEECH**
blood-sucking parasite .. **TICK**
blouse, long .... **TUNIC**
blow..... **COUP, CRIG, ONER, SWAT, WAFT**
blubber, piece of ...... **LIPPER**
blubber, to strip ...... **FLENSE**
blue ..... **CADET, PERSE, SMALT, COBALT**
blue-dye yielding herb **WOAD**
blue dyestuff .... **WOAD**
"Blue Eagle" .... **NRA**
blue-footed petrel ...... **TITI**
blue grass (genus) .... **POA**
blue grape anthocyanin

    ENIN, OENIN
blue gray

    CHING, MERLE, SLATE
blue, greenish .... **BICE**

    SAXE, TEAL, EMAIL
blue mineral .... **IOLITE**
blue-pencil .... **EDIT**
blue pointer shark ..... **MAKO**

Blue

a blue pine .... **LIM**
Bluebeard's wife ..... **FATIMA**
bluebonnet .... **LUPINE**
bluff .... **CRUSTY**
bluish-white metal ...... **ZINC**
blunder .... **ERR**
blunt .... **DULL**
blushing .... **ROSY**
boa, ringed .... **ABOMA**
boast .... **BRAG, VAUNT**
boastful air .... **PARADO**
BOAT . see also SHIP, CANOE,
        GALLEY, VESSEL,
boat ...... **ARK, TUB, PUNT**
boat, assault .... **LST**
boat, Ceylon, India
        DONI, DHONI
boat, collapsible
        FALTBOAT, FOLDBOAT
boat, dispatch .... **AVISO**
boat, E. Ind. .... **DONI, DHONI**
boat, Egypt .... **BARIS**
boat, Eskimo .. **BIDAR, CAYAK,
KAYAK, UMIAK, OOMIAC,
OOMIAK, UMIACK**
boat, fishing
        TROW, DOGGER, CORACLE
boat, fishing, North Sea **COBLE**
boat, flat-bottomed
        SCOW, BARGE
b boat, freight ...... **LIGHTER**
boat front ...... **BOW, PROW**
boat, Ind. landing .. **MASOOLA**
boat, landing .... **LCI, LST**
boat, Levantine .... **BUM**
boat, light .... **WHERRY**
boat, mail .... **PACKET**
boat, Malay .... **PAHI, PRAH,
PRAO, PRAU, PROA,
PRAHU, PRAHO**
boat, Manila Harbor .. **BILALO**
boat, military ...... **PONTOON**
boat, Nile 2-masted .. **SANDAL**
boat, P. I. .. **BANCA, BANKA**
boat, racing .. **SCULL, SHELL**
boat, river
        BARGE, FERRY, PACKET
boat, river, Chin. ... **SAMPAN**
boat, small .... **DORY**
boat, 3-oar .... **RANDAN**
boat, used on Tigris
        GUFA, KUFA
boat, with decks cut
        RASEE, RAZEE
bob bait for fish .... **DIB**
bobbin .. **PIRN, REEL, SPOOL**
bobbins, frame for .... **CREEL**
bobwhite .... **COLIN**
Boche .... **HUN**
bodice, India .... **CHOLI**
bodily motion, pert. to **GESTIC**

c body .... **SOMA, LICHAM**
body, heavenly . **STAR, COMET**
body of laws .... **CODE**
body of men .... **FORCE**
body of persons ..... **CORPS**
body of retainers .... **RETINUE**
body of writing .... **TEXT**
body, part of
        THORAX, THORACES
body, pert. to **SOMAL, SOMATIC**
body, trunk of .. **TORSE, TORSO**
body: zool. .... **SOMA**
Boer general .... **BO H A**
bog.**FEN, MIRE, QUAG, MARSH**
boggy .... **FENNY**
boil .... **STEW, SEETHE**
boil down .... **DECOCT**
boiled rice without salt: P. I.
        CANIN
boiler, disk for hole in .. **SPUT**
"Bolero" composer .... **RAVEL**
boll weevil .... **PICUDO**
Bolshevik leader ...... **LENIN**
bolt .... **SCREEN**
bomb, defective .... **DUD**
bombardment, short, intense
        RAFALE
bombast .... **ELA**
bombastic **TURGID, OROTUND**
Bombyx .... **ERI**
d bond .... **NEXUS**
bond-stone .... **PERPEND**
bondman ..... **SERF, VASSAL**
bonds, chem. with 2 double
        DIENE
bone .... **OS**
bone, ankle **TALUS, ASTRAGAL**
bone, arm .... **ULNA**
bone, arm, pert. to ... **ULNAR**
bone, breast
        STERNA, STERNAL, STERNUM
bone, ear ..... **ANVIL, INCUS**
bone: Greek .... **OSTE**
bone, leg .... **FEMUR,
TIBIA, FIBULA, TIBIAE**
bone, pelvic, hip ...... **ILIUM**
bone, pert. to ...... **OSTEAL**
bone scraper .... **XYSTER**
bone, skull .... **VOMER**
bones .... **OSSA**
bones, dorsal .... **ILIA**
bones, end of spine .. **SACRA**
bones, hip .... **ILIA**
bonnet monkey **ZATI, MUNGA**
bonnyclabber .... **SKYR**
bony .... **OSTEAL**
book .... **MO, TOME, PRIMER**
book, case for **FOREL, FORREL**
book, largest .... **FOLIO**
book, manuscript
        CODEX, CODICES

21

book, map .... **ATLAS**
book, Bible .. see SPECIAL SEC-
TION, Page 196
book of devotions .... **MISSAL**
book of feasts, Catholic **ORDO**
book of hours .. **HORA, HORAE**
book palm, tree .... **TARA**
book, The .... **BIBLE**
books, Bible .... **GOSPEL**
bookbinding style ...... **YAPP**
bookkeeping entry
DEBIT, CREDIT
booklet .... **BROCHURE**
boor **OAF, CLOD, LOUT, CHURL**
boot, Eskimo .... **KAMIK**
booth .... **STALL**
booth, Oriental market
SUQ, SOOK, SOUK
bootlace .... **LACET**
booty .... **LOOT, PELF, SWAG**
booty, take .... **REAVE**
borax, crude .... **TINCAL**
border ...... **HEM, RIM, EDGE,**
RAND, SIDE, MARGE
border on .... **ABUT**
bore .... **TIRE, EAGRE,**
WEARY, CALIBER
borecole .... **KAIL, KALE**
boredom .... **ENNUI**
boric acid salts ...... **BORATE**
born .... **NEE**
born, being .... **NASCENT**
born: old Eng. .... **NATE**
Bornean squirrel shrew
PENTAIL
Borneo native .. **DYAK, DAYAK**
boron, pert. to .... **BORIC**
borough .... **BURG**
borrowed stock: Irish law **DAER**
bosh .... **ROT, POOH**
boss .... **STUD**
boss on shield .... **UMBO**
Bostonian .... **HUBBITE**
botanical suffix ..... **ACEAE**
botanist .... **MENDEL**
botch .... **FLUB, MESS**
both ears, involving use of
BINAURAL
bother ... **ADO, FUSS, TODO,**
TEASE, MOLEST, PESTER
bo-tree .... **PIPAL**
bottle, glass water .. **CARAFE**
bottle, oil, vinegar
CRUET, FLASK
bottomless pit .... **ABADDON**
boundary ...... **LINE, MERE,**
METE, LIMIT
boundaries, mark off
DEMARCATE
bounder .... **CAD**
bounding line .... **SIDE**

bounds .... **AMBIT**
bouquet .... **AROMA**
bovine .... **OX, COW**
bovine, male .... **STEER**
bow of ship .... **PROW**
bow, low Oriental
SALAM, SALAAM
bow-shaped .... **ARCATE**
bower .... **ARBOR**
bowfin .... **AMIA**
bowl: cricket .... **YARK**
bowling term .... **SPARE**
bowstring hemp **IFE, PANGANE**
box ...... **BIN, BINN, CASE,**
CIST, SPAR, CHEST
box, ecclesiastic ...... **ARCA**
box canyon: Sp. ...... **CAJON**
box, metal .... **CANISTER**
box opener .... **PANDORA**
box, papyrus rolls, Rom.
CAPSA
box, sacred, ancient Rom. **CIST**
box sleigh .... **PUNG**
boxing glove, Rom. .... **CESTUS**
boxing term .... **KO, TKO**
BOY'S NAME .. see MAN'S
NAME
boy ... **BUB, BUD, LAD, TAD**
boys in blue .... **ELI'S**
B.P.O.E. member .... **ELK**
brace .... **PAIR, TRUSS**
braced aback: nautical **ABOX**
bracing .... **TONIC**
brag .... **BOAST, VAUNT**
Brahman rule .. **SUTRA, SUTTA**
Brahmany bull .... **ZEBU**
braid ... **PLAT, PLAIT, QUEUE**
braid, kind of .... **LACET**
brain canal-passage .... **ITER**
brain, layer in .... **OBEX**
brain opening .... **LURA, PYLA**
brain part .... **PIA**
brain: P. I. .... **UTAC**
brain ridges .... **GYRI**
brain tissue .... **TELA**
brain ventricle opening **PYLA**
branch .... **ARM, LIMB, RAMI,**
RAME, RAMUS, SPRIG
branch-like **RAMOSE, RAMOUS**
branchia .... **GILL**
branch of learning ..... **ART**
brass, man of .. **TALOS, TALUS**
brassart .... **BRACER**
"Brave Bulls" author .... **LEA**
brawl .... **MELEE, FRACAS**
BRAZIL ..... see also SPECIAL
SECTION
Brazil drink .... **ASSAI**
Brazil red .... **ROSET**
Brazil dance .... **SAMBA**
Brazil heron .... **SOCO**

a Brazil Negro .... **MINA**
Brazil plant ..... **YAGE, YAJE**
Brazil rubber tree **ULE, HULE**
Brazil tree ...... **APA, ANDA**
Brazil capital .... **RIO**
breach .... **GAP**
bread, hard-baked ..... **RUSK**
bread crumbs, dish with
　　　　　　　PANADA
breadfruit: P. I. ...... **RIMA**
breadfruit: P. R. ... **CASTANA**
bread-tree seeds .... **DIKA**
break .... **SNAP**
break in .... **STAVE**
breakers .... **SURF**
breakwater ...... **MOLE, PIER**
breastbone, of ...... **STERNAL**
breastplate .... **URIM**
breastwork .... **PARAPET**
breastplate, Gr.
　　　THORAX, THORACES
breath of life .... **PRANA**
breathed .... **SPIRATE**
breathing, harsh
　　　　　RALE, STRIDOR
breech-cloth, Polyn. .. **MALO**
breeches: Scot. .... **TREWS**
breed ...... **REAR, RAISE**
Bremen's river ...... **WESER**
breviary ... **PORTAS, PORTASS**
b brewer's ferment .. **LOB, LOBB**
brewer's vat .... **TUN**
brewing .... **MALTING**
brewing, one
　　　GAAL, GAIL, GYLE
bribe .... **SOP**
brick carrier .... **HOD**
brick, sun-dried ...... **ADOBE**
bricklayer .... **MASON**
bricklayer's helper ..... **CAD**
bridal wreath .... **SPIREA**
bridge .... **SPAN**
bridge, floating ... **PONTOON**
bridge, maneuver .... **FINESSE**
bridge, Mississippi ..... **EADS**
bridge part **TRESSEL, TRESTLE**
brief .... **SHORT, TERSE**
brigand .... **LATRON**
Brigham Young U. site **PROVO**
bright .... **APT, NITID**
bright colored fish
　　BOCE, OPAH, WRASSE
bright: music .... **ANIME**
brilliance .... **ECLAT, ORIENCY**
brilliant group .... **PLEIAD**
bring forth .... **EAN**
bring on oneself ..... **INCUR**
bring together ...... **COMPILE**
bring up ...... **REAR, RAISE**
brisk: music .... **ALLEGRO**
bristle .... **SETA**

c bristles .... **SETAE**
bristle, pert. to .... **SETAL**
bristly .... **SETOSE**
Britain's ancient inhabitant
　　　　　　　PICT
BRITISH .. also see ENGLISH
British conservative ..... **TORY**
British king, legendary .. **LUD,
BELI, BRAN, BRUT, LUDD,
NUDD**
Britisher, early .... **PICT**
Brittany; city, ancient ...... **IS**
broach .... **RIMER**
broad band: Her. .... **FESS**
broadbill, E. Ind. ...... **RAYA**
broadbill duck .... **SCAUP**
broken glass to remelt .. **CALX**
broken seed coats ..... **BRAN**
broken spike of grain ... **CHOB**
broken stone, etc. ... **RUBBLE**
Bronte heroine .... **EYRE**
bronze, Rom. money ..... **AES**
brood ..... **SET, NIDE, COVEY**
brook, small ..... **RUN, RILL**
broom of twigs .... **BESOM**
broom-corn millet
　　　HIRSE, KADIKANE
brother .. **FRA, FRIAR, FRATER**
brought up .... **BRED**
brow of hill; Scot. ...... **SNAB**
d brown ..... **TAN, SEAR, SEPIA,
UMBER, BISTER, RUSSET,
SIENNA, SORREL**
brown kiwi .... **ROA**
brown, pale .... **ECRU**
brown, red-yellow ..... **PABLO**
brown, yellowish dull ... **DRAB**
brown-skinned race ... **MALAY**
brown sugar .... **PANELA**
browned .... **RISSOLE**
brownie ..... **NIS, NIX, NISSE**
Browning poem, girl in **PIPPA**
browse .... **GRAZE**
Brünnhilde's mother ... **ERDA**
brushwood .... **TINET, TINNET**
brusque .... **BLUNT, TERSE**
Brythonic .... **CORNISH**
Brythonic sea god ...... **LER**
bubble .... **BLEB**
buck, 4th year .... **SORE**
Buddha .... **FO**
Buddha, Jap. **AMIDA, AMITA**
Buddha's foe .... **MARA**
Buddha's mother ...... **MAYA**
Buddha's tree .... **PIPAL**
Buddhist angel .... **DEVA**
Buddhist language ..... **PALI**
Buddhist church in Jap. .. **TERA**
Buddhist monastery, Jap. **TERA**
Buddhist Mongol ...... **ELEUT**
Buddhist monk .... **BO, LAMA**

Buddhist

Buddhist pillar .... LAT
Buddhist monument .. STUPA
Buddhist novice ...... GOYIN
Buddhist priest .... LAMA
Buddhist relic .... STUPA
Buddhist sacred city .. LASSA
Buddhist sacred dialect PALI
Buddhist sacred mountain OMEI
Buddhist saint LOHAN, ARHAT
Buddhist scripture SUTRA, SUTTA
Buddhist sect, Jap. ZEN
Buddhist shrine TOPE, STUPA,
   DAGABA, DAGOBA, DAG-
   HOBA, DHAGOBA
Buddhist spirit of evil . MARA
buds, pickled .... CAPERS
buffalo, India
   ARNA, ARNI, ARNEE
buffalo pea .... VETCH
buffalo, water, P. I. CARABAO
buffet .... SLAP, SMITE, TOSS
buffoon .. FOOL, MIME, ZANY,
   CLOWN, MUMMER, JESTER
bug .... BEETLE
bugaboo: S. Afr. GOGA, GOGO
bugle call
   TATOO, TATTOO, TANTARA
bugle note .... TIRALEE
build .... REAR, ERECT
builder .... ERECTOR
builder, jetty-dam ...... EADS
building site .... LOT
building wing .... ELL, ANNEX
bulb, edible .... SEGO
bulb, Indian food
   CAMAS, CAMASS, CAMMAS
bulb-like stem .... CORM
BULGARIAN .. see also SPE-
   CIAL SECTION
Bulgarian czar .... BORIS
bulge, as eyes .... BUG
bulk .... MASS
bull, girl carried off on EUROPA
bull, sacred Egyp. ...... APIS
bullet, size of
   CALIBER, CALIBRE
bullet sound ..... ZIP, PHIT,
   PHUT, PIFF
bullfight .... CORRIDA
bullfight cry .... OLE
bullfighter on foot .. TORERO
bullfighter's queue .... COLETA
bullfinch, Eng. .... ALP
bully .... HECTOR
bulrush .... TULE
Bulwer-Lytton heroine .. IONE
bumblebee .... DOR
bumpkin .... LOUT
bunch .... TUFT, WISP
bunch grass .... STIPA
bundle .... BALE, PACK

bundle, small ......: PACKET
bundle, twig, stick .... FAGOT
bundling machine ...... BALER
bungle .... BOTCH
bunting .. ESTAMIN, ETAMINE,
   ORTOLAN, ESTAMENE
bunting bird .... CIRL
buoy, Eng. .... DAN
buoy, kind of. CAN, NUN, NUT,
   BELL, SPAR, WHISTLING
buoyancy .... FLOTAGE
burbot .... LING
burbot genus .... LOTA, LOTE
Burchell's zebra ...... DAUW
burden ... LADE, LOAD, ONUS
burden bearer .... ATLAS
burglar .... YEGG
burial place, Polyn. ..... AHU
BURMA .. see also SPECIAL
   SECTION
Burma Buddhist (native) MON
Burma chief ...... BO, BOH
Burmese capital, ancient AVA
Burmese demon (devil) .. NAT
Burmese gibbon .... LAR
Burmese governor WUN, WOON
Burmese hill-dweller ..... LAI
Burmese hills .... NAGA
Burmese knife .. DAH, DHAO
Burmese language .. WA, PEGU
Burmese mongoloid ...... LAI
Burmese native (s) WA,LAI,WAS
Burmese premier ...... UNU
Burmese 3-string viol .. TURR
Burmese wood sprite ... NAT
burn incense .... CENSE
burn ...... ASH, CHAR, SERE
Burnett, Frances, heroine SARA
burning bush .... WAHOO
burning, malicious .... ARSON
burnish .... RUB
burrowing animal MOLE, RATEL
burst asunder .... SPLIT
burst forth .... ERUPT
bury .... INTER, INHUME
bush or bushy clump .... TOD
bushel, fourth of ...... PECK
Bushmen .... SAN, SAAN
bushy .... DUMOSE
business .... TRADE
business cartel .... TRUST
"Bus Stop" author ..... INGE
bustard genus .... OTIS
bustle .... ADO, TODO
bustle about .... FISK
busy, to be .... HUM
but .... YET, ONLY, STILL
butcher's hook .... GAMBREL
butter, illipe .... MAHUA
butter, India ..... GHI, GHEE
butter, liquid ..... GHI, GHEE

24

butter tree .... SHEA
butter tub .... FIRKIN
butterbur .... OXWORT
butterfly .... IO, SATYR
butterfly, large ...... IDALIA
butterfly-lily .... SEGO
button .... STUD
button, part of ...... SHANK
buyer .... VENDEE
buyer: Law .... EMPTOR

buzzard .... BUTEO
buzzing sound .. WHIR, WHIZ
by .... AT, PER, PAST,
ALONG, BESIDE
by birth .... NEE
by hand, bred .... CADE
by means of .... PER
bygone .... AGO
Byron poem .... LARA
Byzantine capital .... NICAEA

C

C, mark under ...... CEDILLA
caama .... ASSE
cab, Near East .... ARABA
cabal .... PLOT
cabbage .... COLE, KAIL,
KALE, KEAL
cabbage type .... SAVOY
cabin, main .... SALOON
cabinet, open, bric-a-brac
ETAGERE
cactus fruit, edible ... COCHAL
cactus, genus .... CEREUS
cactus-like .... CACTOID
caddis fly worm ..... CADEW
Caddoan Indian .... REE
cadet .... LAD
Cadmus' daughter .... INO
Caen's river .... ORNE
Caesar's conspirator-slayer
CASCA, BRUTUS, CASSIUS
cafe .... CABARET
caffein in tea
THEIN, THEINA, THEINE
caffein-rich nut .. COLA, KOLA
cage .... MEW
Cain's brother .... ABEL
Cain's land .... NOD
Cain's son .... ENOCH
Cain's wife, Byron poem
ADAH
cake, rich ... TORTE, TORTEN
cake, small .... BUN, BUNN
calabar bean alkaloid
ESERIN, ESERINE
calamity .... WOE, DISASTER
calcium oxide .... LIME
calf of leg, pert. to ... SURAL
calf's cry .... BLAT
caliber .... BORE, DIAMETER
calico colors, mix .... TEER
calico horse .. PINTO, PIEBALD
calico-printing method .. LAPIS
California army base ...... ORD
Calif. fish ...... RENA, REINA
Calif. fort .... ORD

Calif. herb .... AMOLE
Calif. motto .... EUREKA
Calif. shrub, berry ..... SALAL
Calif. wine valley .... NAPA
Caliph .... ALI, IMAM
call .. CRY, DUB, DIAL, NAME,
ROUSE, WAKEN, MUSTER
call for hogs .... SOOK
call forth .. EVOKE, SUMMON,
ELICIT, EVOCATE
call, to attract attention
HEY, PST, HIST, PIST
calling .. METIER, VOCATION
Calliope's sister .... ERATO
calm .... LAY, COOL, LULL,
QUIET, STILL, PLACID, SE-
RENE, SMOOTH, SOOTHE
calorie ..... THERM, THERME
calumniate .... MALIGN
calumny .... SLANDER
Calvinists, Scotch .. BEREANS
calyx leaf .... SEPAL
cam .... TAPPET
cambric .... PERCALE
cambric grass .... RAMIE
CAME ....see COME
camel: Anglo-Ind. ..... OONT
camel hair cloth .... ABA
camel hair robe .... ABA
camel-like animal ..... LLAMA
Camelot lady .... ENID
cameo stone .... ONYX
camera platform ..... DOLLY
Cameroons tribe .... ABO
"Camille" author .... DUMAS
camlet .... PONCHO
camp, fortified ...... TABOR
camp, pert. to ...... CASTRAL
camphor, kind of ..... ALANT
campus, restrict. to Eng. GATED
Canaanite month ...... BUL
Canada goose ...... OUTARDE
canal bank ..... BERM, BERME
canal betw. N. and Balt. Seas
KIEL

canary yellow ...... **MELINE**
canasta play .... **MELD**
cancel .. **DELE, ANNUL, ERASE**
candid .... **OPEN, FRANK**
candidates list .. **LEET, SLATE**
candle ..... **DIP, TEST, TAPER**
candle holder
　　　　SCONCE, GIRANDOLE
candle wick .. **SNAST, SNASTE**
candlenut tree .... **AMA**
candlenut tree fiber ..... **AEA**
cane ... **RATTAN, MALACCA**
Canio's wife "I Pagliacci"
　　　　　　　　　NEDDA
canister, tea, alloy for .. **CALIN**
canna plant .... **ACHIRA**
cannabis .... **HEMP**
cannon .... **MORTAR**
cannon, old
　　　　MOYENNE, ROBINET
CANOE .. see also **BOAT**
canoe, Afr. .. **BONGO, BUNGO**
canoe, Hawaii ...... **WAAPA**
canoe, Malabar ...... **TONEE**
canoe, Malay (South Seas) out-
　rigger .... **PAHI, PRAH,
　PRAO, PRAU, PROA,
　PRAHO, PRAHU**
canoe, Maori .... **WAKA**
canoe, P. I. .. **BANCA, BANKA**
canon .... **LAW, RULE**
canonical hour .. **SEXT** (noon),
　**LAUDS, NONES, PRIME,
　MATINS, TIERCE**
canopy **COPE, SHADE, TESTER**
cant **TIP, TILT, SLANG, CAREEN**
cant-hook .... **PEAVY, PEEVY,
　　　　PEAVEY, PEEVEY**
cantankerous command.. **SCAT**
cantata, pastoral .. **SERENATA**
canticle, Scripture ...... **ODE**
"Cantique de Noel" composer
　　　　　　　　　ADAM
CANTON .. see the country in
　SPECIAL SECTION
canvas .. **DUCK, TUKE, SAILS**
canvas, piece of .... **TARP**
canvas shelter .... **TENT**
canyon mouth .... **ABRA**
canyon, small .... **CANADA**
CAP .. see **HEADGEAR**
capable .... **ABLE**
cape .... **NES, RAS,
　　　　NASE, NAZE, NESS**
cape, early .... **COPE**
cape, fur .... **PALATINE**
Cape Horn native .... **ONA**
cape, Pope's .. **FANON, ORALE**
Cape Verde native ..... **SERER**
Capek creature .... **ROBOT**

caper .... **DIDO, LEAP, ANTIC**
CAPITAL .. see SPECIAL SEC-
　　　　　　　　　TION
caprice **WHIM, FANCY, VAGARY**
captain, fiction ...... **AHAB**
captain, Nile ...... **RAIS, REIS**
capture **BAG, NAB, NET, SEIZE**
car .... **SEDAN**
car, last **CABOOSE, CAMBOOSE**
car, old make .... **REO**
caracal .... **LYNX**
Caradoc .... **BALA**
caravan .... **CAFILA**
caravansary
　　　　CHAN, KHAN, SERAI
caravel, Columbus **NINA, PINTA**
carbolic acid ...... **PHENOL**
carbon, powdery ...... **SOOT**
CARD .. see also GAME, CARD
card .. **ACE, PAM, SIX, TEN,
　TWO, FOUR, JACK, KING,
　NINE, TREY, KNAVE,
　POSTAL**
card game like bridge .. **VINT**
card game, 3-handed ... **SKAT**
card game, old ...... **TAROT**
card game, Sp. ...... **OMBER,
　　　　　　　　　OMBRE**
card holding .... **TENACE**
card in euchre .... **BOWER**
card, playing
　　　TAROC, TAROT, TAROCCO
card wool ... **TUM, TEASE**
cards, highest ...... **HONORS**
care for .... **RECK, TEND**
care, heavy .... **CARK**
careen ...... **TIP, LIST, TILT**
caress .... **PET**
cargo .... **LOAD, PORTAGE**
cargo, put on ... **LADE, LOAD**
"Carmen" composer .... **BIZET**
carnation .... **PINK**
carnelian .... **SARD**
carnivore, Afr. .... **RATEL**
carol .... **NOEL, SING**
carol singer .... **WAIT**
carom .... **RICOCHET**
carousal **ORGY, BINGE, SPREE**
carouse .... **REVEL**
carp .... **ID, CAVIL**
carp, Jap. .... **KOI**
carp, red-eyed .... **RUD, RUDD**
carpet, Afgh.. **HERAT, HERATI**
carpet, Caucasian **BAKU, KUBA**
carpet, India .... **AGRA**
carpet, Pers. ... **KALI, SENNA**
carriage .. **GIG, MIEN, POISE,
　CALASH, LANDAU, CARIOLE**
carriage: Fr. .... **FIACRE**
carriage, India ...... **EKKA**
carriage, Java, Oriental **SADO**

a carried away .... RAPT
carrier, of Orient .... HAMAL
Carroll heroine .... ALICE
carrot-family plant .... ANISE
carrot-like herb genus .. MEUM
carrot ridges .... JUGA
carry .... LUG, BEAR, TOTE
carry across water .... FERRY
carry on (a war) ...... WAGE
cart, heavy .... DRAY
carte .... MENU
Carthage, of .... PUNIC
Carthage queen .... DIDO
cartograph .... MAP
cartoonist
    ARNO, CAPP, NAST, KIRBY
carve in itaglio ...... INCISE
case, grammatical .... DATIVE
case of explosives .... PETARD
case, toilet, small
            ETUI, ETWEE
casing, bore-hole ...... LINER
cask .. KEG, TUB, TUN, BUTT,
    CADE, TIERCE, PUNCHEON
cassava .. AIPI, JUCA, YUCA
cassia leaves .... SENNA
cast, founded .. FUSIL, FUSILE
cast metal mass .. PIG, INGOT
cast off MOLT, SHED, MOULT
b caste AHIR, BICE, GOLA, JATI
caste, agricultural ...... MEO
caste, gardener .... MALI
caste, low KOLI, KULI, PARIAH
caste, Tamil merchant
            CHETTY
caster ...... CRUET, ROLLER
casting mold .... DIE
castor-oil bean poison RICIN
castor-oil plant .... KIKI
Castor's killer .... IDAS
Castor's mother .... LEDA
cat .... ANGORA
cat, Afr.
    CIVET, GENET, GENETTE
cat, Am.
    PUMA, COUGAR, OCELET
cat cry .... MEW, MIAU, MIAW,
    MIAOU, MIAOW, MIAUL
cat genus .... FELIS
cat-headed goddess, Egypt BAST
cat, spotted
    PARD, MARGAY, OCELET
cat, tailless .... MANX
catalogue ..... LIST, RECORD
catamaran ...... BOAT, RAFT
catapult .... ONAGER
cataract .... FALLS
catch .... NAB, HAUL, HOOK,
    SNAG, TRAP, DETENT
catchword ..... CUE, SLOGAN

c catechu-like resin ...... KINO
category .... GENRE, SPECIES
cater ...... PANDER, PURVEY
caterpillar .... LARVA
caterpillar hair .... SETA
caterpillar, N. Z. ...... WERI
catfish, Egypt ...... DOCMAC
catfish, S. Am. .... DORAD
cathedral .... MINSTER
cathedral city, Eng. ..... ELY
cathedral, famous .. CHARTRES
cathedral passage ..... SLYPE
cathedral, Russian .... SOBOR
Catholic, Greek UNIAT, UNIATA
Catholic tribunal .... ROTA
catkin ..... AMENT, AMENTA
catnip .... NEP
catspaw DUPE, TOOL, STOOGE
cattail ...... TULE, MATREED
cattail India, narrow .. REREE
cattail, N. Z. .... RAUPO
cattle, breed of .... DEVON
cattle dealer .... DROVER
cattle genus .... BOS
cattle stealing, crime of
            ABIGEAT
CAUCASIAN .... see
            CAUCASUS NATIVE
Caucasian bharal .... TUR
Caucasian goat .... TUR, TEHR
Caucasian ibex .... ZAC
d Caucasian language
            ANDI, AVAR
Caucasion Moslem
            LAZ, LAZZI
Caucasian race in China
            LOLO, NOSU
Caucasus native
    SVAN, SVANE, OSSET
caucho tree .... ULE
caudal appendage ..... TAIL
caulk lightly .... CHINSE
cause ...... CAUSA, REASON
caustic ... LYE, LIME, ACRID,
    ERODENT, MORDANT
caustic poison ...... PHENOL
cauterize .... SEAR
cautery plant .... MOXA
cautious WARE, WARY, CHARY
"Cavalleria Rusticana" heroine
            LOLA
cavalryman .... ULAN, UHLAN
cavalryman, Turk., Alg.
            SPAHI, SPAHEE
cave: archaic .... ANTRE
cave explorer .... SPELUNKER
cave: poet. .... GROT
cavern .. CAVE, GROT, GROTTO
caviar .... ROE, IKRA
caviar fish .... SHAD, STERLET
cavil .... CARP, OBJECT

27

Cavity

a cavity .... **ATRIA, ANTRA, SINUS, ANTRUM**
cavity, ear, nose .... **ANTRUM**
cavity, in a rock .. **VUG, VOOG, VUGG, VUGH, GEODE**
cavy .... **APEREA**
cease! .... **HALT, AVAST**
Cecrops' daughter .... **HERSE**
cedar, E. Ind. ...... **DEODAR**
Celebes ox .... **ANOA**
celebrated .... **EMINENT**
celery-like plant .... **UDO**
cella .... **NAOS**
cellulose acetate .... **ACETOSE**
cellulose: comb. form .. **CELLO**
Celt .... **ERSE, GAEL**
Celt, legendary **IR, ITH, MILED**
Celtic ... **ERSE, MANX, WELSH**
Celtic church early center **IONA**
Celtic dart .... **COLP**
Celtic god .... **TARANIS**
Celtic goddess
ANA, ANU, DANA, DANU
Celtic mother of gods
ANA, ANU, DANA, DANU
Celtic name meaning black
DHU
Celtic Neptune .... **LER**
b Celtic paradise ..... **AVALON**
Celtic sea god .... **LER**
Celtic sun god .... **LUG, LUGH**
cement ..**LUTE, PUTTY, SOLDER**
cement well lining .... **STEEN**
cenobite .... **MONK**
censure .**BLAME, CHIDE, SLATE**
center .... **HUB, CORE, FOCI, FOCUS, HEART**
center, away from .... **DISTAL**
center, toward ...... **ENTAD**
centerpiece .... **EPERGNE**
centesimal unit..**GRAD, GRADE**
centesimi, 100 .... **LIRA**
centipede: Tahiti .... **VERI**
central .... **MID, FOCAL**
Cent. Am. gum tree
TUNO, TUNU
Cent. Am. tree .... **EBO, EBOE**
central line .... **AXIS**
central points .... **FOCI**
century plant .... **AGAVE**
century plant fiber..**PITA, PITO**
cere .... **WAX**
cereal .... **FARINA**
cereal grain .... **OAT, RYE**
cereal grass ...... **OAT, RYE, WHEAT, MILLET**
cereal grass, E. Ind. ... **MAND, RAGI, RAGGI, RAGGEE**

c cereal grass genus ... **SECALE**
cereal plant: obs. ...... **RIE**
cereal spike .... **COB, EAR**
ceremonial chamber .... **KIVA**
Ceres' mother .... **OPS**
certificate, money ..... **SCRIP**
cerulean blue **COELIN, COELINE**
cervine animal .... **DEER**
cesspool .... **SUMP**
cetacean . **ORC, WHALE, NAR- WAL, NARWHAL, PORPOISE**
cetacean, dolphinlike, genus
INIA
Ceylon ape .... **MAHA**
Ceylon foot soldier ..... **PEON**
Ceylon governor .... **DISAWA**
Ceylon moss .... **AGAR**
Ceylon native
VEDDA, VEDDAH, WEDDAH
Ceylon sandstone ...... **PAAR**
Ceylon trading vessel .. **DONI**
chafe **RUB, FRET, FROT, GALL**
chaff .... **BANTER**
chaffinch ..... **CHINK, SPINK**
chain .... **CATENA**
chain, nautical .... **TYE**
chainlike .... **CATENATE**
chair .... **SEDAN**
chair part ...... **RUNG, SPLAT**
d chaise .... **GIG**
chalcedony ... **ONYX, AGATE**
chalcedony, red .... **SARD**
Chaldean astron. cycle .. **SAROS**
Chaldean city .... **UR**
chalice
AMA, AMULA, CALIX, GRAIL
chalice veil .... **AER**
chalky silicate .... **TALC**
challenge .. **DARE, DEFY, GAGE**
chamber .... **ROOM, CAMERA**
chamber, pert. to ... **CAMERAL**
champagne, Marne .... **AY**
chance .... **HAP, LOT, LUCK**
chances, excess of ..... **ODDS**
chanced upon .... **MET**
chancel part .... **BEMA**
chancel screen .... **JUBE**
chancel seat .. **SEDILE, SEDILIA**
change .... **FLUX, VARY, ALTER, AMEND**
change appearance .. **OBVERT**
change direction **CANT, KANT, TACK, TURN, VEER**
change: music .... **MUTA**
channel .... **GAT, MEDIA, STRIA, MEDIUM, STRIAL**
Channel Island .... **SARK**
channel marker .... **BUOY**
channels .... **MEDIA**

28

a chant .... **INTONE**
chanticleer .... **COCK**
chantry .... **CHAPEL**
chaos .... **NU, NUN**
chaos, Babyl. .... **APSU**
chaos, Egypt. ...... **NU, NUN**
chaos, Maori myth .... **KORE**
Chaos' son .... **EREBUS**
chap: S. Afr. .... **KEREL**
chapel, private .... **ORATORY**
chapel, sailor's ..... **BETHEL**
chaperon: Sp. **DUENA, DUENNA**
chaplain .... **PADRE**
chaplet .. **ANADEM, WREATH**
chapped .... **KIBY**
character .... **NATURE**
characteristic .... **TRAIT**
charcoal: Pharm. ...... **CARBO**
charge .... **FEE, COST,**
            DEBIT, INDICT
charge solemnly ...... **ADJURE**
charged particle .... **ION**
charger .... **STEED**
chariot, ancient Briton
    ESSED, ESSEDA, ESSEDE
chariot race site ..... **CIRCUS**
chariot, religious **RATH, RATHA**
charity .... **ALMS**
Charlemagne, race subdued by
                    AVARS
b Charlemagne's father ... **PEPIN**
Charlotte —, dessert .. **RUSSE**
charm .... **JUJU,**
    SPELL, AMULET, GRIGRI
Charon, payment for .. **OBOL**
Charon, river of .... **STYX**
chart .... **MAP**
Charybdis, rock opp. .. **SCYLLA**
chasm **GAP, ABYSS, CANYON**
chaste ...... **PURE, VESTAL**
chat, friendly ...... **COSE, COZE**
Chateaubriand heroine, novel
                    ATALA
chatelaine bag .... **ETUI**
chatter **GAB, GAS, YAP, PRATE**
chatterbox .... **PIET**
cheat .... **RENIG, RENEGE**
cheat .... **BAM,**
    CON, FOB, FUB, GIP, GYP,
    BILK, MUMP, COZEN, SHARP
cheaters: slang ...... **GLASSES**
check ...... **NIP, TAB, REIN,**
    STEM, BRAKE, STUNT
checking block .... **SPRAG**
cheek .... **GENA, JOLE, JOWL**
"cheek" .. **GALL, BRASS, NERVE**
cheek, pert. to ...... **MALAR**
cheek-bone .... **MALAR**
cheer .... **OLE, RAH,**
    BRAVO, ELATE, ENCORE
cheer pine .... **CHIR**

c cheer up .... **LIVEN**
cheerless .... **SAD, DRAB**
cheese ...... **EDAM, STILTON**
cheese, Dutch .... **EDAM**
cheese, hard brown .. **MYSOST**
cheese, soft .... **BRIE**
cheesy .... **CASEOUS**
cheetah, Ind. . **YOUSE, YOUZE**
chela .... **CLAW**
Chemical compound ... **IMID,**
    AMIDE, AMINE, IMIDE,
    IMINE, ESTER
CHEMICAL ELEMENT .... see
            SPECIAL SECTION
chemical ending **OL, INE, ENOL**
chemical prefix ... **ACI, OXA,**
            AMIDO, AMINO
chemical salt ..... **SAL, ESTER,**
            NITRE, BORATE
CHEMICAL SUFFIX .. see **SUF-**
    FIX, CHEMICAL
chemical unit .... **TITER**
chemist's pot .... **ALUDEL**
cherish ... **FOSTER, TREASURE**
cherry .... **GEAN**
cherry red .... **CERISE**
chess piece .... **MAN**
chess term,—passant .... **EN**
chessman ..... **KING, PAWN,**
d   **ROOK, QUEEN, BISHOP,**
    CASTLE, KNIGHT
chest, acacia wood ...... **ARK**
chest, antique .... **CIST, KIST**
chest, sacred **ARK, ARCA, CIST**
chest sound .... **RALE**
chestnut, Eur. .... **MARRON**
chestnut, Polyn. .... **RATA**
chevrotain .. **NAPU, MEMINNA**
chew ..... **BITE, CHAM, GNAW**
chew, leaf to .... **COCA**
chewink .... **TOWHEE**
Chibcha chief's title .... **ZIPA**
chick-pea .... **GRAM**
chicken snake .... **BOBA**
chide **SCOLD, BERATE, REPROVE**
chief ... **ARCH, HEAD, MAIN**
chief, Afr. tribe .... **KAID**
chief, Am. Ind. ...... **SACHEM**
chief: Chinook .... **TYEE**
chief deity, Panopolis .... **MIN**
chief in Italy .... **DUCE**
chief, India .... **SIRDAR**
Chief Justice 1921-30 ... **TAFT**
Chief Justice 1941-46 .. **STONE**
chief, Moslem ... **RAIS, REIS**
chief officer, India .. **DEWAN,**
            DIWAN
chief Norse god .... **ODIN,**
    WODAN, WODEN, WOTAN
chief, Pres. .... **MIR**
child .... **TIKE, TYKE**

29

child of streets . . **ARAB, GAMIN**
"Child of the Sun" . . . . . **INCA**
child, pert. to . . . . **FILIAL**
child: Scot. . . . . **BAIRN**
child: Tagalog, P. I. . . . . **BATA**
Chilean proletariat . . . . . **ROTO**
Chilean timber tree . . . . . **PELU**
Chilean volcano . . . . . **ANTUCO**
chill . . . . **ICE, AGUE**
chills and fever
. . . . **AGUE, MALARIA**
chimney: dialect . . . . **LUM**
chimney pipe . . . . **FLUE**
chin . . . . . . **MENTA, MENTUM**
China . . . . **CATHAY**
China blue . . . . **NIKKO**
China grass . . . . **BON**
Chinese . . **SERES, SERIC, SINIC**
Chinese aborigine . **YAO, MANS**
Chin. aboriginal population
division . . . . **MIAO**
Chin. are . . . . **MU**
Chin. boat . . . . **JUNK**
Chin. brick bed . . . . . . **K'ANG**
Chin. Causasian tribesman **LOLO**
Chin. characters in Jap. . **MANA**
Chin. club . . . . **TONG**
CHIN. COIN . . see also **COINS**
Page 190
Chin., coin, bronze . . . . . . **LI**
Chin., coin, early . . . . **PU**
Chin. Communist . . **MAO, CHOU**
Chin. cult . . . . **JOSS**
Chin. department . . . . **FU**
Chin. dialect . . . . **WU**
Chin. division . . . . **MIAO**
Chin. dynasty . **HAN, KIN, SUI,**
WEI, YIN, CH'IN, CHOU,
HSIA, T'ANG, MING, SUNG,
TS'IN, YUAN
Chin. factory . . . . **HONG**
Chin. feudal state . . . . **WEI**
Chin. flute . . . . **TCHE**
Chin. god . . . . **GHOS, JOSS**
Chin. govt. section
. . . . **HIEN, HSIEN**
Chin. guild . . . . **HUI**
Chin. idol . . . . . . **GHOS, JOSS**
Chin. instrument, stringed . **KIN**
Chin. kingdom, old
. . . . **WU, SHU, WEI**
CHIN. MEASURE . see also pages
188, 189
Chin. measure of length . **TSUN**
Chin. mile . . . . **LI**
Chin. monetary unit . . . . **YUAN**
CHIN, MONEY see also page 190
Chin. negative principle . . . **YIN**
Chin. noodles . . . . **MEIN**
Chin. official . . **KUAN, KWAN**
Chin. philos. principle . **LI, YANG**

Chin. plant . . . . **UDO**
Chin. pottery . . . . **CHUN,**
KUAN, MING, TING
Chin. ruler . . **YAO, YAU, YAOU**
Chin. secret society . . . . . **TONG**
Chin. shop: Du. E. Ind. . . **TOKO**
Chin. silk . . . . **PONGEE**
Chin. wax, wax insect . . **PELA**
Chin. wormwood . . . . . . **MOXA**
Chin. yellow . . . . **SIL**
chinin . . . . **COYO**
chink . . . . . **RIFT, RIMA, RIME**
chink-like . . **RIMAL, RIMATE**
chinky . . . . . . **RIMAL, RIMOSE,**
RIMOUS
chip . . . . **NICK**
chip of stone . . **SPALL, GALLET**
chipmunk . . . . **HACKEE**
chirp **CHEEP, TWEET, TWITTER**
chisel, primitive . . . . **CELT**
chisel, very broad . . . . . **TOOLER**
chocolate powder . . . . **PINOLE**
chocolate source . . . . . . **CACAO**
choice . . . . **CREAM, ELITE,**
PRIME, SELECT
choke up . . . . **DAM, CLOG**
choler . . . . . . **IRE, BILE, RAGE**
choose . . . . **OPT, ELECT**
chop . . . **AXE, CUT, HEW, LOP**
chop fine . . . . **MINCE**
chopped . . . . **HEWN**
choral music
. . . . **MOTET, CANTATA**
chord, 3 tones . . . . **TRINE**
chore . . . . **JOB, CHARE**
Chosen . . . . . . **COREA, KOREA**
Christ's thorn . . **NABK, NUBK**
Christmas . . . . **NOEL, YULE**
Christmas crib . . . . . . **CRECHE**
chromosome . . . . **IDANT**
chronicle . . . . **ANNAL, ANNALS**
chrysalis . . . . **PUPA**
chrysanthemum . . **MUM, KIKU**
chub, Europ. . . . . **CHEVIN**
chunk . . . . **GOBBET**
church . . . . **FANE**
church bench . . . . **PEW**
church, body of . . . . **NAVE**
church calendar . . . . **ORDO**
church contribution . . . . **TITHE**
church council . . . . **SYNOD**
church court . . . . **ROTA**
church dignitary . **POPE, BISHOP,**
PRELATE, CARDINAL
church dish . . . . **PATEN**
church, India . . . . **SAMAJ**
church living . . . . **BENEFICE**
church maintenance, canon's
. . . . **PREBEND**
church officer . . . . **ELDER**

a church official .... SEXTON, VERGER
church part ..... APSE, BEMA, NAVE, ALTAR
church, Pope's ..... LATERAN
church porch .... PARVIS
church property .... GLEBE
church reader .... LECTOR
church recess .... APSE
church, Scot. .... KIRK, KURK
church vessel .. AMA, PIX, PYX
churchman .... PRELATE
churl. CEORL, VILLAIN, VILLEIN
churl: var. .... CARLE
churn plunger .... DASHER
cibol .... ONION
cicatrix .... SCAR
cigar .... CLARO, SMOKE, CORONA, CHEROOT
cigar, cheap .. STOGY, STOGIE
cigarette, medicinal ... CUBEB
cigarfish .... SCAD
cincture .... BELT
cinnamon, kind of .... CASSIA
cion .... GRAFT
cipher .... ZERO, OUGHT
cipher system .... CODE
Circe's home .... AEAEA
circle .... CIRC, CIRQUE, RONDURE

b circle of light ... HALO, NIMB
circle, part of .... ARC
circle segment ...... SECTOR
circuit .... LAP, TOUR, AMBIT, ORBIT
circuit judge, court ..... EYRE
circular motion .... GYRE
circular plate ..... DISC, DISK
circular turn .... LOOP
circular saw .... EDGER
cirque, geol. .... CWM
cistern .... BAC, VAT
citation .... CITAL
cite .... QUOTE, ADDUCE
citron ...... ETROG, CEDRAT, ETHROG
citrus fruit ....LIME, LEMON, ORANGE, SHADOCK, SHADDOCK
CITY .. see also TOWN and GAZETTEER
city, ancient, Asia Min. . MYRA, TYRE, SARDES, SARDIS
city, ancient Thessalian LARISSA
city: Gr. .... POLIS
City of a Hundred Towers PAVIA
City of Bridges ...... BRUGES
City of God .... HEAVEN
City of Kings .... LIMA
City of Lights .... PARIS

c City of Luxury ...... SYBARIS
City of Masts .... LONDON
City of Rams .... CANTON
City of Refuge ...... MEDINA
City of Saints .... MONTREAL
City of the Prophet .. MEDINA
City of the Seven Hills .. ROME
City of the Violet Crown ATHENS
City of Victory .... CAIRO
city, pert. to .. CIVIC, URBAN
city, Philistines' ...... EKRON
city political division ... WARD
civet, Chinese .... RASSE
civet, Indian .... ZIBET
civet, Java .... DEDES
civet, Madagascar .... FOSSA, FOUSSA
civetlike cat . GENET, GENETTE
civic goddess, Gr. ..... ALEA
Civil War commander ..... LEE, POPE, GRANT, EWELL, MEADE, SCOTT, SYKES, HOOKER, CUSTER, FORREST, JACKSON
civil wrong or injury .... TORT
claim ...... ASSERT, DEMAND
clam genus .... MYA
clam, giant .... CHAMA
clam, razor .... SOLEN
clamor .... DIN, NOISE

d clamp .... VICE, VISE
clan .... GEN, SEPT, TRIBE
clan chieftain successor. TANIST
clan division: Gr. .... OBE
clan, Gr. .... GENOS
clan, head of .... ALDER
clarinet socket .... BIRN
clash .... JAR, COLLIDE
clasp . HASP, ENFOLD, INFOLD
clasp for a cope ..... MORSE
class .... ILK, CASTE, GENUS, GENERA, SPECIES
class leader, Eng. ...... DUX
class, lowest Jap. ... HEIMIN
class, scientific GENUS, GENERA
classic tongue .... LATIN
classification .... RATING
classification method . SYSTEM
classify .. RANK, RATE, SORT, TYPE, GRADE
claw .... NAIL, TALON, UNGUIS, UNGUES
claw, crustacean's CHELA, CHELAE
claw ornament .... GRIFF
claw: zool. .... UNCI, UNCUS
clay ..... BOLE, ARGIL, LOESS
clay, baked .... TILE

a clay bed .... **GAULT**
clay, building: Sp.
        ADOBE, TAPIA
clay-covered .... **LUTOSE**
clay, friable .... **BOLE**
clay layer .... **SLOAM, SLOOM**
clay, melting pot ..... **TASCO**
clay mineral .... **NACRITE**
clay molding plate ...... **DOD**
clay pigeon shooting ... **SKEET**
clay pipe .... **TD**
clay plug .... **BOTT**
clay, porcelain ...... **KAOLIN**
clay, potter's .... **ARGIL**
clayey .... **BOLAR**
clayey soil. **BOLE, MALM, MARL**
cleansing agent ...... **BORAX**
clear. **NET, RID, LUCID, LIMPID,**
    AUDIBLE, TRANSPARENT
clear, as anchor ..... **AWEIGH**
clear of charges ..... **ACQUIT**
clearing of land, Eng. ... **SART**
cleave ... **REND, RIVE, CLING**
cleaving tool .... **FROE**
cleft ...... **REFT, RIFT, RIMA**
Clemenceau's nickname . **TIGRE**
clement .... **MILD**
Cleopatra's attendant ... **IRAS**
Cleopatra's handmaid ... **IRAS**
b Cleopatra's needle ... **OBELISK**
Cleopatra's serpent .... **ASP**
clergyman .... **ABBE, CANON,**
    VICAR, CURATE, PRIEST,
    RECTOR
cleric, Fr. .... **ABBE**
clerical cap .... **BIRETTA**
clerical, not .... **LAIC, LAICAL**
clever .... **APT, HABILE**
click beetle ...... **DOR, DORR,**
    ELATER
climb .... **GRIMP, SCALE**
climbing plant ..... **IVY, VINE,**
    LIANA, LIANE
cling .... **STICK, ADHERE**
clingfish .... **TESTAR**
clinging, for .... **TENENT**
Clio, sister of .... **ERATO**
clip . **CUT, MOW, SNIP, SHEAR**
clique .... **SET**
CLOAK .... see also **GARMENT**
cloak ... **ABA, WRAP, CAPOT,**
    CAPOTE, MANTLE
cloak, Ind. .... **CHOGA**
cloak, Rom. . **SAGUM, ABOLLA,**
    ABOLLAE
cloak, woman's ..... **DOLMAN**
clock, ship-form .... **NEF**
clog-like shoe .... **PATTEN**
cloister .... **MONASTERY**
"Cloister-Hearth" author. **READE**

c close eyes of .... **SEEL**
close, keep .... **HUG**
close: musical .... **CODA**
close to . **AT, BY, NEAR, ANEAR**
close, to fit ..... **FAY, FADGE**
closed, as wings .... **PLIE**
closing measure, music .. **CODA**
CLOTH .... see also **SILK,**
    COTTON, FABRIC
cloth, bark .... **TAPA**
cloth, figured old ..... **TAPET**
cloth measure .... **ELL**
cloth, old wool ..... **CHEYNEY**
cloth, stout .... **BRIN**
cloth strip, India ..... **PATA**
cloth used in mourning . **CRAPE**
cloth, wrapping ...... **TILLOT**
clothe .... **GIRD, VEST, ENDUE**
clothes moth .... **TINEA**
clothespress, old Dutch ... **KAS**
clothing .. **DUDS, GARB, GEAR,**
    TOGS, RAIMENT
cloud .... **SMUR, CIRRI,**
    NUBIA, CIRRUS
cloud dragon, Vedic ...... **AHI**
cloud, luminous ..... **NIMBUS**
clouds, broken .... **RACK**
clouds, wind-driven. **RACK, SCUD**
cloudberry .... **MOLKA**
cloudy .... **DULL, LOWERY**
d clout .... **HIT, SWAT**
cloven-footed ...... **FISSIPED**
clover .... **HUBAM,**
    ALSIKE, MELILOT
clown .... **APER, GOFF, ZANY**
clown, Shakesperean . **LAVACHE**
cloy ... **PALL, SATE, ACCLOY**
club member, Gr. .... **ERANIST**
club, women's .... **ZONTA**
clubfoot ... **TALIPED, TALIPES**
clumsily, handle . **PAW, BOTCH**
clumsy ...... **INEPT, OAFISH**
cluster .... **NEP, TUFT**
cluster, grape .... **RACEME**
cluster pine ...... **PINASTER**
coach dog ...... **DALMATIAN**
coach, Eastern .... **ARABA**
coagulate ...... **GEL, CLOT**
coal dust ...... **COOM, SMUT**
coal, heat-treated ...... **COKE**
coal, live .... **EMBER**
coal, size of .. **EGG, NUT, PEA**
coal refuse .... **CULM**
coal scuttle .... **HOD**
coalfish .... **CUDDY**
coalition .... **UNION, MERGER**
coarse .... **GROSS**
coarse sugar, E. Ind. .... **RAAB**
coast bird ...... **GULL, TERN**
coast dweller ...... **ORARIAN**
coastal range, India .... **GHAT**

32

a COAT ..... see also GARMENT
coat .... LAYER
coat, animal .... PELAGE
coat, Arab .... ABA
coat, soldier's .... TUNIC
coat with alloy .... TERNE
cob .... SWAN
cobbler .... SUTOR
cobra ... HAJE, NAGA, MAMBA
cobra genus ..... NAIA, NAJA
cocaine source ... COCA, CUCA
cockatoo, Austral. .... GALAH
cockatoo, palm .. ARA, ARARA
cockboat .... COG
cockpit .... ARENA
coconut, dried .... COPRA
coconut fiber .... COIR, KOIR,
KYAR, COIRE
coconut, Ind. .... NARGIL
coconut palm, P. I. .... NIOG
cocoon insect .... PUPA
cocoon, silkworm ...... CLEW
cod genus .... GADUS
cod, pert. to .... GADOID
cod, young .... SCROD
code .... LAW, CIPHER
codfish, Eur. .... POOR
coffee ... RIO, JAVA, MOCHA
coffee-chocolate flavor .MOCHA
coffer-dam, Egypt ...... SADD
b coffin stand .... BIER
cognizant .... AWARE
cognomen ... NAME, EPITHET
cohere .... BIND
coil .... WIND, TWINE,
TWIST, WREATHE
COIN ..... see also SPECIAL
SECTION, Page 190
coin .... RIN, YEN, SPECIE
coin, cut edges of .... NIG
coin, edging .... REEDING
coin, gold .... LEV
coin, mill .... NURL
coin money .... MINT
coin, pewter .... TRA
coin, reverse side ...... VERSO
coin, silver .... SCEAT
coin tester, Orient
SARAF, SHROFF
coin, tin .... TRA
coincide .... JIBE, AGREE
colander .... SIEVE
cold .... ALGID, GELID
cold, producing ...... ALGIFIC
cold tableland, Andes .. PUNA
collar .. ETON, FICHU, GORGET
collar, clerical .... RABAT,
RABATO, REBATO
collar, deep .... BERTHA
collar, wheel-shaped .... RUFF
collect ...... AMASS, GARNER

c collection .... ANA, SET
collection .... SORTITE
collection, motley ...... RAFT
collection of facts ...... ANA
collection of sayings .... ANA
COLLEGE DEGREE . see DEGREE
college, Iowa .... COE
college, N.J., East Orange
UPSALA
college official .... DEAN
college quadrangle ..... QUAD
colloquialism .... IDIOM
colonists greeting to Ind. NETOP
colonize .... SETTLE
colonizer .... OECIST
colonnade .... STOA
colony, Eng. ...... CAROLINA
colony, Fr. .... ALGERIA
color .... DYE, HUE, TINT
color .. ASH, BAY, RED, TAN,
BLUE, FAON, FAWN, GRAY,
GREY, HOPI, JADE, LIME,
NAVY, NILE, PINK, PUCE,
ROSE, SAXE, AMBER, BEIGE,
CORAL, CREAM, EBONY,
HENNA, IVORY, MAUVE,
MOCHA, SEPIA, UMBER,
CERISE, CITRON, COBALT,
MAROON, RESEDA, SEVRES,
SIENNA, SORREL, CAR-
MINE, CELESTE, CITRINE,
MAGENTA
d color brown sugar ... CARAIBE
color changer, photo ... TONER
color, neutral .. GREGE, GREIGE
color, purplish-brown ... PUCE
color, slightly .... TINT, TINGE
color, stripe of .... PLAGA
color, terrapin .... FEUILLE
Colorado park .... ESTES
coloring agent .... RUDDLE
coloring matter in fustic. MORIN
colorless .... DRAB
colorless alkaloid ..... ESERIN
colorless oil .... CETANE
columbite, variety of. DIANITE
Columbus' birthplace .. GENOA
Columbus' city sailed from
PALOS
Columbus' ship .. NINA, PINTA
column, Buddhist-Hindu, building
LAT
column, Gr. .... DORIC, IONIC
column, memorial .... LAT
column, twisted . TORSE, TORSO
columns, arranged in TABULAR
coma .... TRANCE
comb horse .... CURRY
comb wool ..... CARD, TEASE
combat, field, place of . ARENA
combat, knight's ...... JOUST

33

Combat

a
combat, scene of ..... ARENA
combination .. UNION, CARTEL
combination, card .... TENACE
COMBINING FORMS:
above .... SUR
air ...... AER, AERI, AERO
all .... PAN, OMNI
ass .... ONO
bad .... MAL
bee .... API
beyond .... SUR
black .... MELA
blood .... HEMO
body ...... SOMA, SOMATO
bone .... OSTEO
both .... AMBI
boundary .... ORI
bread .... ARTO
bristle .... SETI
cetacean .... CETO
Chinese .... SINO
communications .... TEL
contemporary .... NEO
daybreak .... EO
dry .... XER
ear .... OTO, AURI
earth .... GEO
egg .... OO, OVI
eight .... OCT, OCTO
equal .... ISO, PARI

b
eye .... OCULO
far .... TEL, TELE
fat ... SEBI, STEAT, STEATO
fearful .... DINO
feast day .... MAS
female .... GYNE
firm .... STEREO
five .... PENTA
follower .... IST
food .... SITO
foot ...... PED, PEDI, PEDO
four-parted .... TETRA
fruit .... CARPO
gas .... AER, AERO
gate .... PYLE
glade .... NEMO
gland .... ADEN
gray .... POLIO
great .... MEGA
gums .... ULO
hair .... PIL, PILI
half ...... DEMI, SEMI
heat ..... THERM, THERMO
hundred ..... CENTI, HECTO
idea .... IDEO
ill .... MAL
individual .... IDIO
inner .... ENTO
in zoology .... EAE
late, latest .... NEO
line .... STICH

c
many .... POLY
medicine .... IATRO
middle .... MEDI
milk .... LACT, LACTO
monster .... TERAT
mountain .... ORO
mouth ...... STOM, STOMO
moving .... KINO
narrow .... STENO
neck types .... DERA
needle .... ACU
nerve .... NEURO
new .... NEO
nine .... ENNE, ENNEA
nose .... NASI
not .... UN, NON
numerical .... UNI
numerous .... MULTI
oil .... OLEO
one ...... UNI, MONO
on this side .... CIS
other .... HETER
outside .... ECTO
peculiar .... IDIO
power .... DYNA
powerful .... MEGA
quality .... ACY
recent .... NEO, CENE
reversal .... ALLO
ribbon .... TENE
round .... GYRO
sad .... TRAGI
seeds .... CARPO
seizure of illness .... AGRA
self .... AUT, AUTO
shoulder .... OMO
small .... STENO
solid .... STEREO
speak .... LALO
star .... ASTRO
stone .... LITH
strange .... XENO
sun .... HELIO
ten .... DECA
thin .... SERO
third .... TRIT
thread .... NEMA
threefold, thrice ...... TER
tooth .... ODONT
touch .... TAC
thought .... IDEO
thousand .... MILLE
up .... ANO
vapor .... ATMO
various ...... VARI, VARIO
watery .... SERO
white .... ALBO
whole .... TOTO
wind .... ANEMO
within .... ENT, ESO,
           ENDO, ENSO, ENTO

34

a
without .... ECT
wood .... XYLO
worker .... ERGATE
come . ENSUE, ACCRUE, ARRIVE
come back .... RECUR
come forth .... ISSUE,
EMERGE, EMERSE
come forth from .. JET, GUSH,
SPEW, EMANATE
comedian's foil ...... STOOGE
comedy .... FARCE
"Comedy of Errors" servant
LUCE
comfort .... EASE, SOLACE
comfortable .... COSH, SNUG
comforter .... SCARF
command .... BID, FIAT,
ORDER, DICTATE
command: archaic ..... HEST
command to horse
GEE, HAW, HUP
commander, Egypt .... SIRDAR
commander, Moslem
AGA, AGHA
commander, fortress CAID, QAID
commentary: Hebrew ... BIUR
commission, milit. .... BREVET
commodity .... WARE, STAPLE
common ... VULGAR, GENERAL
common brant .... QUINK
b
common: Hawaiian .... NOA
common man .... PLEB
commonplace . BANAL, TRITE
commotion . ADO, STIR, TO-DO
commune, Dutch, Holland EDE
COMMUNE see its country in
GAZETTEER
communion cup ...... AMA
communion dish ..... PATEN
communion service ..... MASS
communion table ..... ALTAR
compact ...... DENSE, SOLID
companion .... PAL, MATE
comparative conjunction . THAN
comparative suffix ending .. ER
compass point ... NE, SE, SW,
ENE, ESE, NNE, NNW, SSE,
SSW, WNW, WSW
compass point, mariner's RHUMB
compassion ...... PITY, RUTH
compel ...... MAKE, FORCE,
COERCE
compendium .... SYLLABUS
compensate .... PAY
compensation, N. Z. ...... UTU
competent .... ABLE
complain .... FRET, FUSS,
GRIPE, REPINE
complainant .... RELATOR
complete ...... TOTAL, UTTER,
ENTIRE, PLENARY

c
completely .... ALL, QUITE
completely occupy ... ENGROSS
complication ..... NODE, NODI
comply .... OBEY, YIELD
composer, Am. . NEVIN, SOUSA,
FOSTER, COPLAND
composer, Eng. .... ARNE,
ELGAR, COATES
composer, Fr. .. LALO, AUBER
BIZET, IBERT, RAVEL
composer, Ger. .... ABT, BACH,
WEBER
composer, Roum. ..... ENESCO
COMPOSITION . see also MUSIC
composition ... ESSAY, THEME
composition, mus. ...... OPUS,
ETUDE, MOTET, RONDO,
SUITE, SONATA, CON-
CERTO, FANTASIA
composition of selections . CENTO
composition, operatic ... SCENA
composition, sacred ... MOTET
compositor .... TYPO
compound, organic .... AMIDE
compound with oxygen . OXIDE
comrade-in-arms .... ALLY
concave .... DISHED
conceal: law .... ELOIN
concealed ..... INNER, PERDU
concealed obstacle ..... SNAG
concede .... ADMIT,
d
GRANT, YIELD
conceive .... IDEATE
concern .... CARE
concerning .... RE, INRE,
ABOUT, ANENT
conch .... SHELL
conciliate .... ATONE
conciliatory gift .... SOP
concise .. BRIEF, SHORT, TERSE
concluding passage music CODA
concoct .... BREW
concrete mixer .... PAVER
concur .. JIBE, AGREE, ASSENT
condescend .... DEIGN, STOOP
condiment .... SALT,
CURRY, SPICE
condition .. IF, STATE, STATUS
condition in agreement PROVISO
conduct ...... LEAD, GUIDE
conductor .... MAESTRO
conductor's stick ..... BATON
conduit . MAIN, DRAIN, SEWER
cone .... STROBIL, STROBILE
cone of silver .... PINA
confection .... COMFIT
confection, nut ...... PRALINE
confederate .... ALLY
Confederate soldier ...... REB
confederation .... LEAGUE
conference .... PALAVER

35

Confess

a
confess .... AVOW, ADMIT
confession of faith .... CREDO
confidence .... FAITH, TRUST
confidences .... SECRETS
confident .... RELIANT
confidential .... ESOTERIC
confine ..... BOX, HEM, PEN,
CAGE, CRAMP
confined .... PENT
confront .... MEET
confused, make .... ADDLE
confusion .... BABEL
congealed dew .... RIME
conger .... EEL
congregate .. MEET, GATHER
conical mass of thread ... COP
coniferous tree ..... FIR, YEW,
PINE, CEDAR, SPRUCE
conjunction .... OR, AND,
BUT, NOR
connect ... JOIN, LINK, UNITE
connecting strip of land
ISTHMUS
connection
NEXUS, CORRELATION
connective .... AND, NOR
connective tissue .... FASCIA
connubial .... MARITAL
conquer .... MASTER
conqueror, Mex.

b
CORTES, CORTEZ
Conrad's "Victory" heroine
LENA
conscript .... DRAFT
consecrate .... BLESS
consecrated .... OBLATE
consequence .... OUTCOME
conservative .... TORY
consider .... DEEM, RATE,
TREAT, REGARD
consonant, hard ...... FORTIS
consonant, unaspirated .. LENE
conspire .... PLOT
Constantine VIII's daughter . ZOE
constellation ...... ARA, LEO,
APUS, ARGO, LYNX, LYRA,
PAVO, URSA, VELA, ARIES,
CANIS, CETUS, DRACO,
LIBRA, MENSA, ORION,
VIRGO, AQUILA, GEMINI,
PISCES, TAURUS
constellation, Altar ...... ARA
constellation, Aquila ... EAGLE
constellation, Ara ... ALTAR
constellation, Aries .... RAM
constellation, Balance .. LIBRA
constellation, Bear ..... URSA
constellation, Bull ... TAURUS
constellation, Crab ... CANCER
constellation, Crane .... GRUS
constellation, Crow ... CORVUS

c
constellation, Dog .... CANIS
constellation, Dragon .. DRACO
constellation, Hunter ... ORION
constellation, Lion .... LEO
constellation near South Pole
APUS
constellation, northern .... LEO
constellation, Peacock .... PAVO
constellation, Ram ..... ARIES
constellation, Southern ... ARA,
APUS, ARGO, GRUS, PAVO,
VELA, INDUS
constellation's main star .. COR
constitution supporter .CARTIST
constrictor ..... BOA, ABOMA
constructor .... ERECTOR
consume: obs. .... ETE
container .... BOX, CAN, TIN,
TUB, VAT, URN, CASE
containing ore .... ORY
contempt, exclamation of .PISH
contempt, look of ..... SNEER
contend .... VIE, COPE,
DEAL, COMPETE
contest .... AGON, BOUT
continent: abbr. ..... NA, SA,
AFR, EUR
continue .... LAST,
ENDURE, RESUME
contort . WARP, GNARL, TWIST

d
contradict ..... DENY, REBUT,
NEGATE
contrition .... REMORSE
contrive .... MAKE, DEVISE
control .... STEER
controversial .... ERISTIC
controversy .... DEBATE
conundrum .. ENIGMA, RIDDLE
convert to Judaism ...... GER
conveyance of estate .. DEMISE
convoy .... ESCORT
cony .. DAS, DAMAN, GANAM
cook in cream .... SHIR, SHIRR
cooking odor .... NIDOR
cooking pot .... OLLA
cooky .... SNAP
cool .... ICE
coolie woman ...... CHANGAR
Cooper novel .... PILOT
copal .... ANIME
copper .... CENT
Copperfield, Mrs. .... DORA
copse .... HOLT, COPPICE
Coptic bishop .... ANBA
copy .... APE, MODEL, ECTYPE
copy, court record ... ESTREAT
coral .... POLYP
cord .... LINE, RAIP,
ROPE, WELT
cord, hat of Bedouin .... AGAL
cord, Hawaii .... AEA

36

a cordage fiber . **DA, COIR, ERUC, FERU, HEMP, IMBE, JUTE, RHEA, ABACA, SISAL**
cordage tree .... **SIDA**
Cordelia's father .... **LEAR**
"Cordiale, —" ..... **ENTENTE**
core ...... **AME, PITH, HEART**
core, casting mold ... **NOWEL**
core material of earth ... **NIFE**
core to fashion metal ... **AME**
core, wooden .... **AME**
cork .... **SPILE**
Cork County port .... **COBH**
cork, extract of .... **CERIN**
cork, flat .... **SHIVE**
cork helmet ..... **TOPI, TOPEE**
corkwood .... **BALSA**
corm .... **BULB**
corn crake bird .... **RAIL**
corn crake genus .... **CREX**
corn, hulled .... **HOMINY**
corn, India ... **RAGEE, RAGGEE**
corn lily .... **IXIA**
corn meal .... **MASA**
cornbread .... **PONE**
corner ... **NOOK, TREE, ANGLE**
cornerstone .... **COIN, COYN, COIGN, QUOIN, COIGNE**
cornice support .... **ANCON**

b Cornish prefix: town .... **TRE**
Cornish prefix in names . **LAN, ROS**
cornu .... **HORN**
Cornwall mine .... **BAL**
corolla part .... **PETAL**
corona ... **AUREOLA, AUREOLE**
coronach, Scot. .... **DIRGE**
coronation stone ...... **SCONE**
corpulent .... **OBESE**
corral: Sp. .... **ATAJO**
correct .. **OKEH, TRUE, AMEND, EMEND, REVISE**
correct behaviour, Chin. ... **LI**
correlative .... **OR, NOR**
correspond **JIBE, AGREE, TALLY**
corridor .... **HALL**
corrie .... **CWM**
corrode .... **EAT, RUST, ERODE**
corrupt ..... **TAINT, VENAL, VITIATE**
corrupt with money .... **BRIBE**
corsair .... **PIRATE**
corset bone .... **BUSK**
cortege .... **RETINUE**
corundum .... **EMERY**
cos lettuce .... **ROMAINE**
Cos, pert. to .... **COAN**
cosmic cycle .... **EON**
cosmic order: Vedic .... **RITA**
Cossack .... **TATAR**
Cossack chief ...... **ATAMAN**

c Cossack headman ... **HETMAN**
Cossack regiment . **POLK, PULK**
cosset .... **PET**
costa .... **RIB**
coterie .... **SET**
cottage, Ind. .... **BARI**
cotton batting .... **BATT**
cotton, Bengal .... **ADATI**
cotton, Egypt .... **SAK, PIMA, SAKEL**
cotton fabric ... **JEAN, LAWN, LENO, DENIM, SURAT, MADRAS**
cotton fabric, corded.**CANTOON**
cotton machine .... **GIN**
cotton, matted .... **BATT**
cotton tree .... **SIMAL**
cottonwood, Texas .... **ALAMO**
couch .... **LAIR**
cougar .... **PUMA, PANTHER**
council .... **SOVIET**
council, ecclesiastical . **SYNOD**
council, king's .... **WITAN**
"Council of —" ...... **TRENT**
counsel .... **REDE**
counselor .... **MENTOR**
count .... **ENUMERATE**
count, Ger. .... **GRAF**
counter .... **BAR**
counter, in cards ...... **MILLE**

d countercurrent .... **EDDY**
countermand .... **REVOKE**
counterpart .... **LIKE**
countersink .... **REAM**
counting frame ...... **ABACUS**
COUNTRY see also GAZETTEER, beginning on Page 210
country, ancient .... **ELAM**
country, ancient, Asia Min., Gr. **EOLIS, AEOLIA, AEOLIS**
country, ancient, Bib. .. **SHEBA**
country, ancient Greek ... **ELIS**
country bumpkin **RUBE, YOKEL, RUSTIC**
country: law .... **PAIS**
COUNTY.see also GAZETTEER, beginning on Page 210
county: Dan. .... **AMT**
county: Eng. .... **SHIRE**
county: Nor. .... **AMT, FYLKE**
county: Swed. .... **LAN**
couple .... **TWO, PAIR**
courage .... **METTLE**
courier .. **ESTAFET, ESTAFETTE**
course ...... **WAY, ROAD, TACK, ROUTE**
course, complete ...... **CYCLE**
course, meal . **SALAD, ENTREE**
course, part of ..... **LAP, LEG**
court .... **AREA**

37

a
court action .... SUIT
court, A.-S. .. GEMOT, GEMOTE
court, church .... ROTA
court cry .... OYES, OYEZ
court hearing .... OYER
court, inner .... PATIO
court, Jap. ..... DARI, DAIRO
court, old English .... LEET
court order .... ARRET
court panel .... JURY
court, pert. to church .. ROTAL
court proceeding ...... TRIAL
courtly .... AULIC
courtship strut, grouse's .. LAK
courtway .... AREA
courtyard .... PATIO
Covenant, — of the .... ARK
cover inner surface .... LINE
covering .. TEGMEN, TEGUMEN
covey .... BEVY, BROOD
cow .... BOSSY, BOVINE
cow house .... BYRE
cows .... KINE, BOSSIES
coward .... CRAVEN
cowboy garment ...... CHAPS
cowboy, S. Am. ..... GAUCHO
cowfish .... RAY, TORO
cowl .... HOOD
cowlike .... COUS
coxcomb .... FOP

b
coy .... ARCH
coyotillo .... MARGARITA
coypu .... NUTRIA
cozy .... HOMY, SNUG
cozy place .... DEN, NEST
crab-eating mongoose .. URVA
crab, front of ...... METOPE
crack . SNAP, CHINK, CREVICE
crackling .... CREPITANT
crackpot .... NUT
craft .... ART, TRADE
craftsman .... ARTISAN
crafty ...... SLY, FOXY, WILY
craggy hill .... TOR
cramp .... KINK
crane arm .... GIB, JIB
crane genus .... GRUS
crane, India .... SARUS
crane, pert. to ...... GRUINE
crane, ship's .... DAVIT
cranelike bird ...... CHUNGA
cranelike bird, S. Amer.
                    SERIEMA
cranial nerve ... VAGI, VAGUS
cravat .... TIE
crave . ASK, BEG, LONG, DESIRE
craw .... MAW, CROP
crayon .... CHALK, PASTEL
craze .... FAD, MANIA
crazy .... LOCO, LUNY, WILD

c
cream .... ELITE
credit transfer system .. GIRO
creed .... CREDO, NICENE
creek .... RIA, KILL
creek: N.Y. .... VLEI
creeper .... IVY
creeping .. REPENT, REPTANT
Cremona .... AMATI
crescent moon's point ... CUSP
crescent-shaped ...... LUNATE
crescent-shaped figure .. LUNE
crescent-shaped mark . LUNULA
crest . TOP, COMB, PEAK, TUFT
crest, sharp rugged mountain
                    ARETE
crested as birds ..... PILEATE
Cretan princess .... ARIADNE
Cretan spikenard .... PHU
CRETE . see SPECIAL SECTION
crevice ... CREVAS, CREVASSE
crew .... MEN, GANG,
                TEAM, EIGHT
cribbage pin or score ..... PEG
cribbage term .... NOB, NOBS
cricket .... GRIG
cricket, ball in .... EDGER
cricket, field parts ONS, OFFS
cricket, run in .... BYE
cricket term OVER, TICE, YORK

d
crime, Eccl. .... SIMONY
Crimean river .... ALMA
criminal .... FELON
crimp .... CURL, GOFFER
crimson ..... RED, CARMINE
crippled ...... HALT, LAME
criticize .... SLATE
criticize in a small way
                CARP, CAVIL
crocodile, India ...... GAVIAL
crocodile-head god, Egyp.
                SOBK, SEBEK
crocus .... IRID
crocus bulb .... CORM
Croesus' land .... LYDIA
crony .... PAL, CHUM, BUDDY
crony: old Eng. .... EME
crooked .... AGEE, AWRY
crooner, early .... VALLEE
crop .... MAW, CRAW
crop, spring, India ...... RABI
cross ..... IRATE, TRAVERSE
cross, church .... ROOD
cross-examine .... GRILL
cross of life, Egypt .... ANKH
cross oneself .... SAIN
cross out .... DELETE
cross-stroke .... SERIF
cross timber, ship ..... SPALE
crossbeam ..... TRAVE, TREVE
crossbill genus .... LOXIA
crossbow .... RODD

38

a crossing, fence .... STILE
crosspiece . BAR, RUNG, CLEAT
crosswise, vehicle ... EVENER
crossthreads ..... WEFT, WOOF
crosswise .... THWART
crossword champion, former
.... COOPER
crow .. ROOK, CRAKE, CORVUS
crow: Eng. .... BRAN
crow, Guam .... AGA
crow, kind of .... DAW
crowd, common ... MOB, RUCK
crowd together .. HERD, SERRY
crowded .... SERRIED
crown .... CAP, PATE,
.... TIARA, DIADEM
crown colony, Brit.
.... ADEN, BAHAMAS
crown of Osiris or Egypt .. ATEF
crown: poetic .... TIAR
crown, Pope's triple TIAR, TIARA
crucial point .... CRUX, PIVOT
crucible .... CRUSET
crucifix .... ROOD
crude . RAW, ROUGH, COARSE
crude metal .... ORE
crude sugar-molasses MELADA
cruel person .... SADIST
cruet .... AMA, CASTER
b cruising .... ASEA
crumbled easily ..... FRIABLE
Crusader's foe ...... SARACEN
Crusader's headquarters . ACRE
crush .... MASH, SUBDUE
crustacean .... CRAB, ISOPOD,
.... SHRIMP, LOBSTER
crustacean order, one of
.... DECAPOD
cry .... HO, HOA, SOB, HOWL,
.... WAIL, WEEP, LAMENT
cry, Austral. ... COOEE, COOEY
cry for silence, court
.... OYES, OYEZ
crystal-clear .... PELLUCID
ctenophores, no tentacle . NUDA
Cuban dance .... CONGA
Cuban rodent .... PILORI
Cuban secret police ... PORRA
Cuban timber tree ..... CUYA
cubic decimeter .... LITER
cubic measure .. CORD, STERE
cubic meter .... STERE
cubicle .... CELL
cubitus .... ULNA
Cuchulain's wife . EMER, EIMER
cuckoo, black, keel-billed . ANI
cuckoo, Oriental .. COEL, KOEL
cuckoopint .... ARUM
cucumber ...... CUKE, PEPO
cud .... QUID, RUMEN

c cudgel .... BAT, CLUB, DRUB,
.... BASTE, STAVE, STICK
cue .... HINT
cue, music .... PRESA
cuff fastener .... TAB
cuirass .... LORICA
cull .... SORT
culmination .... ACME, APEX
cultivate land .... HOE, PLOW,
.... TILL, HARROW
cultivation method, Bengal
.... JUM, JOOM
cultivation, soil .... TILTH
culture medium .... AGAR
cunning ... ART, CUTE, FOXY,
...... WILY, DEDAL, CALLID,
.... DAEDAL
cup .... CRUSE
cup, assaying .... CUPEL
cup, ceremonial .... AMA
cup, gem cutting .... DOP
cup stand of metal ..... ZARF
cup to hold gem .... DOP
cupbearer .... SAKI
cupbearer of gods ...... HEBE
cupboard .. AMBRY, CLOSET
Cupid .... AMOR, EROS
Cupid's title .... DAN
cupola .... DOME
cur .... MUT, MUTT
d curare ...... URALI, OORALI
curassow .... MITU
curassow genus .... CRAX
curdling powder ..... RENNET
cure-all ... ELIXIR, PANACEA
cure by salting .... CORN
cure with salt grass ..... DUN
curfew .... BELL
curios .... VIRTU
curl COIL, FRIZ, WIND, FRIZZ
curl of hair ...... FEAK, TRESS,
.... RINGLET
curling, mark aimed at ... TEE
currant genus .... RIBES
current .... AC, DC, EDDY,
.... RIFE, TIDE, STREAM
curt ...... BRUSK, BRUSQUE
curve .... ARC, BOW, ESS,
.... ARCH, BEND, SINUS
curve in a stream . HOEK, HOOK
curve, plane .... ELLIPSE,
.... PARABOLA
curve, sigmoid or double .. ESS
curved handle .... BOOL
curved in .. ADUNC, CONCAVE
curved out .... CONVEX
curved plank, vessel's .... SNY
Cush, son of .... SEBA
cushion ...... PAD, HASSOCK
custard .... FLAN
custard apple ...... ANNONA

39

Custard

custard cake .... **ECLAIR**
custard dish .... **FLAN**
custody .... **CHARGE**
custom .... **LAW, WONT,
HABIT, USAGE**
custom, India .... **DASTUR**
custom: Lat. .... **RITUS**
custom: obs. .... **URE**
customer .... **PATRON**
customs .... **MORES**
cut . **HEW, LOP, MOW, DOCK,
GASH, HACK, KERF, REAP,
SLIT, SNEE, SNIP, TRIM,
SEVER, SHEAR, SLIVE,
CLEAVE, TREPAN**
cut down .... **FELL**
cut edges of coins .... **NIG**
cut of meat .... **LOIN**
cut off ... **DOCK, SNIP, ELIDE**
cut off, as mane ..... **ROACH**
cut out .... **EXCISE**
cut: Shakespeare ...... **SLISH**
cut vertically
SCARP, ESCARP, ESCARPE
cutter .... **SLED**
cutting .... **SECANT, INCISAL**

cutting tool .. **AX, ADZ, AXE,
HOB, SAW, SAX, SYE, ADZE**
cuttlefish ...... **SEPIA, SQUID**
cuttlefish fluid .... **INK**
Cyclades, one of, see GAZET-
TEER
cycle, astronomical ..... **SAROS**
cyclorama .... **CYKE**
cylinder, moving ...... **PISTON**
cylindrical .... **TERETE**
cyma .... **GOLA**
cyma recta or reversa ... **OGEE**
cymbal, Orient .... **ZEL**
cymbals, India .... **TAL**
Cymbeline's daughter . **IMOGEN**
Cymric deity
GWYN, LLEU, LLEW
Cymry .... **WELSH**
cypher system .... **CODE**
cyprinoid fish .... **ID, IDE,
CARP, CHUB**
Cyrus' daughter ..... **ATOSSA**
cyst .... **WEN**
Czar .... **IVAN, FEDOR**
Czech .... **SLAV**
Czech, Eastern .... **ZIPS**

D

Dadaist .... **ERNST**
dado, pedestal ...... **SOLIDUM**
Daedalus' son .... **ICARUS**
dagger .. **DIRK, SNEE, BODKIN**
dagger, ancient . **SKEAN, SKENE**
dagger, Ir. **DHU, SKENE, SKEAN**
dagger, Malay .... **CRIS, KRIS,
CREES, KREES, CREESE,
KREESE**
dagger: obs. .... **SNEE**
dagger, thin .... **STILETTO**
Dahomey Negro .. **FON, FONG**
daily .... **DIURNAL**
dais .... **ESTRADE**
daisy . **MOON, OXEYE, SHASTA**
Dallas school .... **SMU**
dam .... **WAER, WEIR**
dam, Egypt ...... **SADD, SUDD**
dam site .... **ASWAN**
damage . **MAR, HARM, IMPAIR**
Damascus river ...... **ABANA**
damp .... **DANK**
damselfish .... **PINTANO**
dance .... **HOP, JIG, REEL,
GALOP, GAVOT, POLKA,
TANGO, RUMBA, REDOWA,
RHUMBA, GAVOTTA, GA-
VOTTE**
dance, country . **REEL, ALTHEA**
dance, Gr. .... **HORMOS**
dance, Israeli .... **HORA**

dance, lively ..... **JIG, REEL,
GALOP, POLKA, BOLERO**
dance, old Eng. ...... **MORRIS**
dance, Sp. ... **TANGO, BOLERO**
dance, stately, old
PAVAN, MINUET, PAVANE
dance step ..... **PAS, CHASSE,
GLISSADE**
dancer .... **KELLY, SHAWN,
BOLGER, ZORINA, ASTAIRE**
dancing girl, Egypt .... **ALMA,
ALME, ALMEH**
dancing girl, Jap. ..... **GEISHA**
dandy **FOP, DUDE, JAKE, TOFF**
DANISH ... see also DENMARK
in SPECIAL SECTION
Danish astronomer .... **BRAHE**
Dan. borough (in Eng.) .. **BORG**
Dan. chieftain .... **JARL, YARL**
Dan. division, territorial . **AMT**
Dan. fjord .... **ISE**
Dan. king ..... **CNUT, KNUT,
CANUTE**
Dan. measure .... **ALEN**
Dan. money ..... **ORA, ORAS**
Dan. physicist .... **BOHR**
Dan. speech sound ..... **STOD**
dank .... **WET**
Dante's patron .... **SCALA**
Danube city ...... **ULM, LINZ**
Danube, old name of ... **ISTER**

40

Danube tributary
.... INN, OLT, ISAR, PRUT
daring .... BOLD, NERVE
dark ...... MIRKY, MURKY
dark horse .... ZAIN
dark rock .... CHERT
dark wood ..... TEAK, EBONY
darkness ..... MIRK, MURK
darling: Ir. . ROON, ACUSHLA,
.... ASTHORE
darnel .... TARE
dart along .... FLIT
"Das Rheingold" role ... ERDA
dash .... ELAN
date, pert. to .... DATAL
date plum .... SAPOTE
date, Roman .... IDES, NONES
"David Copperfield" character
.... DORA, HEEP, DARTLE
David's captain .... JOAB
David's commander ... AMASA
David's daughter ..... TAMAR
David's father .... JESSE
David's nephew ..... AMASA
David's ruler, one of .... IRA
David's son .... SOLOMON
David's wife .... MICHAL
dawn .... DEW, EOS, AURORA
dawn, pert. to .... EOAN
day, Hebr. .... YOM
day, Rom. ...... IDES, NONES
day-breeze, It. .... ORA
days: Lat. .... DIES
day's march .... ETAPE
daybreak .... DAWN
dazing larks, device for DARE
deacon's stole ...... ORARION
dead ... FLAT, AMORT, INERT
dead, abode of . HADES, SHEOL
dead, region of: Egypt AMENTI
dead trees .... DRIKI
deadly ...... FATAL, LETHAL
deadly carrot .... DRIAS
deadly sins, 7 ENVY, LUST, AN-
...... GER, PRIDE, SLOTH, GLUT-
...... TONY, COVETOUSNESS
dealer .... MONGER
dealer, cloth
.... DRAPER, MERCER
dean ..... DOYEN, DOYENNE
dearth .... WANT
death .... MORT, DEMISE
death deity: Rom. ...... MORS
death note on hunter's horn
.... MORT
death notice .... OBIT
death rattle .... RALE
debate—debatable
.... AGON, MOOT
debauchee ...... RAKE, ROUE
debris, rocky .... SCREE

decade .... TEN
decamp ...... ELOPE, LEVANT
decay, dental ...... CARIES
decay tree ...... CONK, KONK
deceit .... SHAM, WILE,
.... FRAUD, GUILE
deceive .. BILK, DUPE, FOOL,
.... GULL, TRICK, ILLUDE
decelerate .... RETARD
deception HOAX, STRATAGEM
decide: Rom. law ...... CERN
decimal unit .... TEN
deck, ship's .... POOP
decks, cut away . RASEE, RAZEE
declaim .... RANT, RAVE,
.... ORATE, RECITE
declaration in whist . MISERE
declare ...... AVER, AVOW,
.... STATE, AVOUCH
declare, in cards .... MELD
decline .... EBB, SINK,
.... WANE, REFUSE
declivity ...... SCARP, SLOPE
declivity in menage . CALADE
decorate ...... DECK, ADORN
decorated letter .... FAC
decorated wall part .... DADO
decorous ..... STAID, DEMURE
decoy .... LURE, PLANT
decrease ...... EBB, WANE,
.... LESSEN, RECEDE
decree .... ACT, FIAT,
.... CANON, EDICT, ORDAIN
decree, Fr. law .... ARRET
decree, Moslem .... IRADE
decree, Rom. law .... DECRETE
decree, Russian ...... UKASE
deduce .... INFER
deed .... GEST, GESTE
deeds .... ACTA
deer, Asia ...... AHU, KAKAR,
.... SAMBAR, SAMBUR,
.... SAMBHAR, SAMBHUR
deer, barking .... KAKAR
deer, Chile, Andes ..... PUDU
deer, female . DOE, ROE, HIND
deer genus, E. Ind. ..... RUSA
deer, India .... AXIS
deer, Jap. .... SIKA
deer, Kashmir ...... HANGUL
deer, red .... ROE, HART
deer, S. Am. ...... GEMUL,
.... GUEMAL, GUEMUL
deer, spotted .... CHITAL
deer, Tibet .... SHOU
deer track .... SLOT
deerlet .... NAPUS
deerlike .... CERVINE
defamation .... LIBEL
defeat, chess .... MATE
defeat utterly ... BEST, ROUT

Defect

defect, weaving .... SCOB
defendant's plea .... NOLO
deference .... RESPECT
defraud .... GYP, BILK,
GULL, CHEAT
defy .... DARE
degrade ..... ABASE, LOWER,
DEBASE
degrading .... MENIAL
degree .... GRADE, STAGE
degree .. (dental) DDS, DDSC;
(engineer) CE, EE; (divinity) DD; (science) BSC;
(arts) BA, MA, MFA; (law)
LLB, LLD
degree, extreme .... NTH
degree taken, Cambridge
INCEPTOR
degrees, angle of 57.30. RADIAN
deified sky, Rom. ..... CAELUS
DEITY . see also GOD, GODDESS
and SPECIAL SECTION
deity .... GOD
deity, Buddhist ... DEV, DEVA
deity, Hindu ...... DEV, DEVA
deity, Jap. .. AMIDA, AMITA
deity, primeval .... TITAN
deity, Sumerian .... ABU
deity, Syrian .... EL
delay . WAIT, DETAIN, LINGER
delay, law .... MORA, MORAE
delicacy .... FINESSE
delight .... REVEL
delusion: Buddhism .... MOHA
demand . NEED, CLAIM, INSIST
demeanor .... AIR
Demeter's daughter CORA, KORE
demigod .... HERO
demolish .... RASE, RAZE
demon ... IMP, DEVIL, FIEND
demon, Arab, Moslem, Oriental
JIN, JINN, GENIE,
GENII, JINNI, JINNEE
demon, Hindu . ASURA, DAITYA
demon, sun-swallowing, Hindu
myth .... RAHU
demon, Zoroastrian
DEV, DIV, DEVA
demonstrative pronoun
THAT, THIS, WHOM
den ...... DIVE, LAIR, HAUNT
denary .... TEN
denial .... NO, NAY
DENMARK .. see also DANISH
and SPECIAL SECTION
denomination .... SECT
denote .... MEAN, SHOW,
INDICATE
denoting unfit ships in Lloyd's
registry .... AE

dense . CRASS, THICK, STUPID
density .... DORD
dental tool .... SCALER
deny .... NEGATE
depart ..... BEGONE, DECAMP
depart fast VAMOSE, VAMOOSE
depart: Lat. .... VADE
departed .. GONE, LEFT, WENT
department, Chin. .. FU, FOO
departure .... EXODUS
dependent .... MINION
depict .... DRAW, PAINT,
DESCRIBE
deplore .... LAMENT
deposit, alluvial DELTA, GEEST
deposit, clayey .... MARL
deposit, geyser ...... SINTER
deposit, mineral .... LODE
deposit, river
ALLUVIA, ALLUVIUM
deposit, wine cask ... TARTAR
depressed .... SAD
depression ...... DENT, FOVEA
deprivation .... LOSS
deprived .... REFT
depute .... SEND
deputy .... AGENT, VICAR
derby .... BOWLER
deride .... GIBE, JIBE
derrick ...... CRANE, STEEVE
dervish, "Arab. Nights" .. AGIB
dervish, Moslem ..... SADITE
descendant .... SON, CION
descendant, Fatima's
SAID, SEID, SAYID
descendants, male line .. GENS
descent, deep .... SCARP
descriptive term ..... EPITHET
desert dweller .... EREMITE
desert, Mongolia .... GOBI
desert plant .... AGAVE
deserter .... RAT
deserve .... EARN, MERIT
design .... AIM
desire .... YEN, URGE,
WANT, WISH
desire eagerly .... ASPIRE
desirous .... FAIN
desolate .... LORN, BLEAK
despoil .... RUIN
despot .. CZAR, TSAR, TZAR,
TYRANT, DICTATOR
dessert .... ICE, PIE, MOUSSE,
TRIFLE
destiny . DOOM, FATE, KARMA
destroy .... RASE, RAZE,
DECIMATE
destruction .... RUIN
detach .... WEAN
detachable button ...... STUD
detail .... ITEM

42

a
detain **CHECK, DELAY, ARREST**
detecting device ...... **SONAR**
detective .... **TEC, DICK**
detent .... **PAWL**
determination .... **WILL**
determine ...... **FIX, DECIDE, RESOLVE**
detest ...... **HATE, LOATHE**
dethrone .... **DEPOSE**
detonator .... **CAP**
"— deum" .... **TE**
devaluate .... **DEBASE**
developed compound animal **ZOON**
Devi .... **UMA**
deviate ... **ERR, YAW, DIVERGE**
deviation .... **LAPSE**
deviation from course .... **YAW**
devil . **DEMON, DEUCE, SATAN**
devil: Gypsy .... **BENG**
devil, Moslem **SHAITAN, SHEITAN**
devil, Russian folklore .. **CHORT**
devil worship ...... **SATANISM**
devilfish .... **MANTA**
Devon river .... **EXE**
devotee .... **FAN, IST**
devotion, nine-day .. **NOVENA**
devoutness .... **PIETY**
dewberry .... **MAYES**
b
dewy .... **RORAL, RORIC**
dexterity .... **ART**
dexterous .... **CLEVER**
diadem .... **TIARA**
diagonal .... **BIAS**
DIALECT . see also LANGUAGE
dialect . **IDIOM, LINGO, PATOIS**
dialect, Chin. ...... **CANTON**
dialect, Ethiopic ...... **TIGRE**
dialect, Gr. .... **DORIC, IONIC**
diamond corner .... **BASE**
diamond fragments ..... **BORT**
diamond holder .... **DOP**
diamond, impure industrial **BORT**
diamond, perfect .. **PARAGON**
diamonds, low quality .. **BORT**
Diana .... **ARTEMIS**
Diana's grove .... **NEMUS**
Diana's mother ...... **LATONA**
diaphanous ..... **THIN, SHEER**
diaphragm, pert. to .. **PHRENIC**
diatonic note .... **MI**
diatribe .. **SCREED, HARANGUE**
dibble .... **DAP, DIB**
Dickens character .. **PIP, TIM, DORA, GAMP, HEEP, FAGIN, DORRIT**
Dickens' pseudonym ...... **BOZ**
"Die Fledermaus" girl .. **ADELE**
die for making drain pipe . **DOD**
die, gambling .. **TAT, TESSERA**

c
"Dies —," "Day of Wrath" **IRAE**
diet .... **BANT, FARE**
differ ...... **VARY, DISAGREE**
difference between solar and
   lunar year .... **EPACT**
different ..... **OTHER, DIVERS**
difficulty .... **RUB, KNOT**
dig ..... **GRUB, PION, DELVE**
digest .... **PANDECT**
digit, foot .... **TOE**
digraph **AE, EA, OA, OE, SH, TH**
dike .... **LEVEE**
dilation .... **ECTASIA**
dilatory ...... **SLOW, TARDY, REMISS**
dilemma .... **FIX**
dill herb .... **ANET**
dilute .... **THIN, WATER**
dim, become .. **BLEAR, DARKLE**
diminish ... **EBB, BATE, SINK, WANE, ABATE, TAPER**
diminish front: military **PLOY**
dingle ...... **DALE, DELL, GLEN**
dining room, ancient ... **OECUS**
diocese center .... **SEE**
Dioscuri .... **ANAX**
dip .... **DAP, DIB, DOPP, DUNK, LADE**
dip out .... **BAIL**
diplomacy .... **TACT**
d
diplomat .... **ENVOY, CONSUL, ATTACHE**
diphthong ..... **AE, IA, OA, UO**
Dipper constellation ..... **URSA**
direct .... **AIM, LEAD**
direct attention .... **REFER**
direct steering of boat ... **CONN**
dirge .... **LINOS, LINUS**
dirigible .... **BLIMP**
dirk ....**SNY, SNEE**
dirty lock .... **FRIB**
disable .... **LAME, MAIM**
disagreeable .... **ILL**
disappear gradually . **EVANESCE**
disavow ...... **DENY, RECANT**
disbeliever .... **ATHEIST**
disburse ...... **SPEND, EXPEND**
discard . **DROP, SCRAP, REJECT**
discernment .... **TACT**
discharge .... **EMIT, FIRE, SACK, SHOOT**
discharged .... **SHOT**
disciple .... **APOSTLE**
disciple: India .... **CHELA**
disciplinarian ..... **MARTINET**
disclaim .... **DENY**
disclose ...... **BARE, REVEAL**
discolored ...... **DOTY, LIVID**
disconcert ..... **FAZE, ABASH**
discourse .. **HOMILY, DESCANT**
discourse, art of ... **RHETORIC**

a discover . SEE, SPY, ESPY, FIND
discriminate .... SECERN
discuss ...... TREAT, DEBATE
discussion group ...... FORUM
disease .... MAL, POX, HIVES
disease, Afr. .... NENTA
disease cause .... VIRUS
disease, diver's ...... BENDS
disease, fowl ..... PIP, ROUP,
PEROSIS
disease, fungus .... ERGOT
disease, grape-vine
ESCA, ERINOSE
disease, plant ... SMUT, SCALD
disease, skin .... ECZEMA
disease spreader
VECTOR, CARRIER
disease, tropical ...... SPRUE
disembark .... LAND
disembodied spirit: Chin.
KUEI, KWEI
disencumber .... RID
disengage .... FREE
disfigure ...... MAR, DEFACE
disgrace .... SCANDAL
disguise .... MASK
disgust, word of .... AW
DISH .... also see VESSEL
dish .... PLATE
dish, Hawaiian .... POI
b dish, highly seasoned
OLIO, OLLA
dish, hominy .... POSOLE
dish, Hungarian .... GOULASH
dish, It. .... RAVIOLI
dish, main .... ENTREE
dish, meat .... STEW, RAGOUT
dish, Mex. .. TAMAL, TAMALE,
TAMALI
dish, stemmed .... COMPOTE
dishearten .... DAUNT, DETER
dishonor .... SHAME, VIOLATE
dishonorable .... BASE
disinclined .... AVERSE
disinfectant , CRESOL, PHENOL,
CRESSOL, CRESSYL
disk, ice hockey .... PUCK
disk, like a .. DISCAL, DISCOID
disk, metal .... PATEN
dislocate .... LUXATE
dismal .... DREAR
dismantle .... STRIP
dismay ...... APPAL, DAUNT
dismiss .... DEMIT, FIRE
dismounted .... ALIT
disorder .... MESS, DERAY,
CLUTTER
disorderly flight .... ROUT
disparaging .... SNIDE
disparaging remark ..... SLUR
dispatch .... SEND, HASTE

c dispatch boat .... AVISO
dispelled .... GONE
display .... AIR, SHEW, SHOW,
ARRAY, EVINCE
display proudly
VAUNT, OSTENT
displease .... VEX, MIFF,
ANGER, ANNOY
disposed .... PRONE
disposition .... MOOD, TEMPER
dispossess .... OUST, EVICT
disprove .... REFUTE
disputable .... MOOT
dissertation ... THESES, THESIS
dissolute person .. RAKE, ROUE
dissonant .... ATONAL
distance, at-from a . OFF, AFAR
distant ... FAR, YON, REMOTE
distilling vessel .... MATRASS
distinctive air ... AURA, MIEN,
CACHET
distracted .... DISTRAIT
distraint: old Eng. law .. NAAM
distribute .. DEAL, DOLE, METE
DISTRICT .... see also REGION
district .... AREA, ZONE
district, old Eng. court
SOC, SOKE
disturb .... ROIL, MOLEST
disturbance ...... ROW, RIOT
d ditch .... FOSS, RINE,
FOSSE, TRENCH
ditch, castle .... MOAT
ditch, fort. .... RELAIS
ditch millet .... HUREEK
ditto .... SAME
divan .... SOFA
dive .... DEN, HEADER
dive bomber .... STUKA
diverge .... DEVIATE
divers .... SEVERAL
divest .... STRIP, DEPRIVE
divide .... PART, SHARE
divide for study ..... DISSECT
divided .... REFT, SPLIT
divider .... MERIST
dividing wall, membrance, parti-
tion ..... SEPTA, SEPTUM
divination by lots: Lat.
SORS, SORTES
"Divine Comedy" author DANTE
divine favor .... GRACE
divine law: Rom. .... FAS
divine revelation TORA, TORAH
divine utterance ..... ORACLE
divinity .... DEITY
divorce bill, Jewish law
GET, GETT
divorce, Moslem ...... TALAK
"— dixit" .... IPSE
dizziness, pert. to ..... DINIC

docile .... **TAME**
dockyard barge .... **LUMP**
doctor ..... **INTERN, INTERNE**
Dr. Brown's dog hero .... **RAB**
Dr. Jekyll's other self .. **HYDE**
doctrinaire .... **ISMY**
doctrine .. **ISM, DOGMA, TENET**
documents, box for .. **HANAPER**
dodder .... **AMIL**
dodo genus .... **DIDUS**
doe .... **HIND**
doe, young .... **TAG, TEG**
dog, ... **CANIS, CANINE**
dog .... **POM, CHOW, PEKE,
BASSET, POODLE, SPANIEL**
dog, chops of .... **FLEWS**
dog-faced ape .... **AANI**
dog-fisher .... **OTTER**
DOG, GUN see DOG, HUNTING
dog, Hungarian **PULI, KUVASZ**
dog, hunting (bird) ... **ALAN,
ALAND, ALANT, BASSET,
BEAGLE, SETTER, COURSER,
HARRIER, POINTER**
dog, John Brown's ...... **RAB**
dog, large .... **ALAN**
dog, "Odyssey" .... **ARGOS**
dog salmon .... **KETA**
dog, small-toy ..... **POM, PUG,
PEKE**
dog snapper, fish ..... **JOCU**
dog, Sputnik's .... **LAIKA**
dog star .... **SEPT, SOPT,
SEPTI, SIRIUS**
dog, tropical .... **ALCO**
dog, Welsh .... **CORGI**
dog, wild, Austral. ..... **DINGO**
dog, wild, India ...... **DHOLE**
doge, office of ...... **DOGATE**
dogfish .... **SHARK**
dogma .... **TENET**
dogwood .... **OSIER, CORNEL**
dole .... **METE**
dolphin fish .... **DORADO**
dolphin genus .... **INIA**
dolphin-like cetacean .... **INIA**
dolt ...... **ASS, OAF, CLOD,
LOUT, DUNCE**
domain .... **BOURN, REALM,
BOURNE, DEMENE, ESTATE,
DEMESNE**
dome .... **CUPOLA**
dome-shaped .... **DOMOID**
Domesday Book money ... **ORA**
domestic .... **MAID, LOCAL**
domestic animal ... **ASS, CAT,
COW, DOG, HOG, PIG,
RAM, SOW, MULE**
domestic slave .... **ESNE**
domesticated .... **TAME**
dominion .... **REALM, EMPERY**

domino .... **MASK**
Don Juan's mother ..... **INEZ**
donkey .... **ASS, MOKE,
BURRO, NEDDY**
doom .... **CONDEMN, DESTINE**
doom palm, Afr. .... **DUM**
door .... **PORTAL**
door: Lat. .... **JANUA**
door part ...... **JAMB, SASH,
SILL, LINTEL**
door section .... **PANEL**
doorkeeper, Masonic .... **TILER**
dorado, color .... **CUIR**
Doric frieze slab ..... **METOPE**
dormant ..... **ASLEEP, LATENT**
dormouse .... **LOIR**
dormouse, garden ..... **LEROT**
dormouse genus .... **GLIS**
dorsal .... **NOTAL**
dote .... **DRIVEL**
dots, paint with ..... **STIPPLE**
dotted with figures ..... **SEME**
double . **DUAL, TWIN, BINATE**
double cocoon .... **DUPION**
double dagger .... **DIESIS**
double, Egypt .... **KA**
double salt .... **ALUM**
double tooth .... **MOLAR**
doubletree .... **EVENER**
dovkie ...... **ROTCH, ROTGE,
ROTCHE**
Dovyalis .... **ABERIA**
dowel ...... **PIN, COAG, COAK**
dower, pert. to .... **DOTAL**
dower property .... **DOS**
down ..... **FUZZ, PILE, EIDER**
down, facing. **PRONE, PRONATE**
down quilt .... **DUVET**
"downunder" native clan ... **ATI**
downward, curve ...... **DEFLEX**
dowry .... **DOS, DOT**
drag ... **LUG, TUG, HAUL, SNIG**
dragnet .... **TRAWL**
dragon, like a ... **DRACONTINE**
dragon of darkness, Bibl. **RAHAB**
drain . **SAP, DEPLETE, VITIATE**
drain .... **SUMP, SEWER**
dram, small .... **NIP**
DRAMA ...... see also PLAY
Dravidian **KOTA, MALE, NAIR,
TODA, TULU, TAMIL**
draw ...... **TIE, TOW, LIMN,
PULL, DEPICT**
draw forth .... **EDUCE**
draw from .... **DERIVE**
draw out . **EDUCE, ATTENUATE**
draw tight: naut. .... **FRAP**
drawing curve .... **SPLINE**
drawing room .... **SALON**
dreadful .... **DIRE**
dream, day .... **REVERIE**

45

a "Dream Girl" playwright . **RICE**
dregs .... **FAEX, LEES,
DROSS, SEDIMENT**
drench .... **SOUSE, TOUSE**
drenched .... **WET, DEWED**
DRESS .... see also GARMENT
dress .... **GARB, CLOTHE,
ACCOUTER**
dress, as stone ...... **DAB, NIG**
dress feathers .... **PREEN**
dress leather ...... **DUB, TAN**
dress up .... **TOG, PREEN**
dressed .... **CLAD**
dressing wounds, material for
LINT, LINTS
dried berry: Sp. .... **PASA**
dried up .... **SERE**
drift .... **TREND**
drill .... **BORE, TRAIN**
drilling rod .... **BAR, BIT**
DRINK .... see also BEVERAGE
drink .... **GULP, SWIG,
QUAFF, IMBIBE**
drink, Christmas **NOG, WASSAIL**
drink, fermented ...... **MEAD**
drink, honey .... **MEAD**
drink, hot .... **TODDY**
drink, hot milk .... **POSSET**
drink of gods .... **NECTAR**
drink of liquor .. **NIP, BRACER**
b drink, old honey ...... **MORAT**
drink, palm .... **NIPA**
drink, rum-gin .... **BUMBO**
drink slowly .... **SIP, SUP**
drink, small ...... **NIP, PEG,
DRAM, SLUG**
drink to excess .. **TOPE, BOUSE**
drink, whiskey ...... **STINGER**
drinking bowl .... **MAZER**
drinking cup, Gr. .... **HOLMOS**
drinking vessel .... **CUP, MUG,
TIG, TYG, JORUM,
STEIN, TANKARD**
drive ..... **RIDE, URGE, IMPEL**
drive away .... **SHOO, DISPEL**
drive back
ROUT, REPEL, REPULSE
drive in .... **TAMP**
drivel .... **DROOL, SLAVER**
driver, fast reckless ...... **JEHU**
drizzle .. **MIST, SMUR, SMURR**
droll .... **ODD**
dromedary, female .... **DELUL**
dromedary, swift .... **MEHARI**
drone .... **BEE, DOR, HUM**
droop .... **LOP, SAG, WILT**
drooping .... **ALOP**
drop ..... **DRIB, FALL, SINK,
GUTTA, GLOBULE**
drop a fish line or bait .. **DAP**
drop, one .... **MINIM**

c drop: Prov. Eng. ..... **SIE, SYE**
dropsy .... **EDEMA**
dross .. **SLAG, SPRUE, SCORIA**
drought-tolerant plant .. **GUAR**
drove .... **HERD, RODE**
drove of horses .... **ATAJO**
drowse .... **NOD**
drudge ... **MOIL, TOIL, LABOR**
drug ..... **DOPE, SINA, ALOES,
OPIATE, DILANTIN**
drug, Hippocrates' .... **MECON**
drugged bliss .... **KEF**
drum-call to arms .... **RAPPEL**
drum roll, reveille ...... **DIAN**
drum, small . **TABOR, TABOUR,
TABRET**
drum, W. Ind. .... **GUMBY**
drumbeat .... **DUB, TATOO,
TATTOO**
drunkard .... **SOT, SOAK,
SOUSE, TOPER**
dry .... **SEC, ARID, SERE**
dry, as wine .... **SEC**
dry bed of river .... **WADI**
dry goods dealer ..... **DRAPER**
dub .... **NAME, KNIGHT**
duck .... **ANAS, SMEE,
TEAL, PEKIN**
duck, Arctic .... **EIDER**
d duck, breed of .... **ROUEN**
duck, diving .... **SMEW**
duck eggs, Chin. ...... **PIDAN**
duck, fresh water .... **TEAL**
duck genus .. **AEX, AIX, ANAS**
duck, like a .... **ANATINE**
duck lure .... **DECOY**
duck, male .... **DRAKE**
duck, Muscovy .... **PATO**
duck, pintail .... **SMEE**
duck, ring-necked ...... **DOGY**
duck, river ..... **TEAL, EIDER,
SHOVELER**
duck, sea ...... **COOT, SCAUP**
duck, sea, northern .... **SCOTER**
duck-shooting boat .... **SKAG**
duck to cook: Fr. ... **CANETON**
duct: anat. .... **VAS, VASA**
dude .... **FOP, DANDY**
due, India .... **HAK, HAKH**
duet .... **DUI, DUO**
dugout canoe **BANCA, PIROGUE**
dugout, India . **DONGA, DUNGA**
duke's dominion ...... **DUCHY**
dulcimer .... **CITOLE**
dulcimer, Oriental ..... **SANTIR**
dull . **DRY, DUN, DRAB, LOGY,
BLUNT, PROSY, BORING**
dull color .. **DUN, MAT, DRAB,
MATTE, TERNE**
dull in finish .... **MAT, MATTE**

a dull silk fabric .... **GROS**
dullard .... **BOOR**
Dumas hero
    ATHOS, ARAMIS, PORTHOS
dummy whist .... **MORT**
dung beetle .... **DOR**
dunlin bird .... **STIB**
dupe .... **USE, FOOL**
duration measure .... **TIME**
dusk .... **EVE**
dusky .... **DIM, DARK, SWART**
dusty: Scot. .... **MOTTY**
DUTCH see also NETHERLANDS,
      SPECIAL SECTION
Dutch: bit .... **DOIT**
     cupboard .... **KAS**
     donkey .... **EZEL**
     "mister" .... **HEER**
     out .... **UIT**
     woman .... **FROW**
Dutch cheese .... **EDAM**
Dutch commune .... **EDE**
Dutch early geographer .. **AA**
Dutch fishing boat .. **DOGGER**
Dutch measure, old ..... **AAM**
Dutch meter .... **EL**
Dutch minor coin .... **DOIT**
Dutch news agency, old **ANETA**
Dutch painter
    LIS, HALS, LELY, STEEN
Dutch two-masted vessel **KOFF**
duty .... **CHORE, TARIFF**
dwarf .. **RUNT, STUNT, TROLL**

c dwarf cattle, S. Am.
    NATA, NIATA
dwell ...... **BIDE, LIVE, ABIDE**
dwelling .... **ABODE**
dwindle .... **PETER**
Dyak knife .... **PARANG**
Dyak, sea .... **IBAN**
dye base .... **ANILINE**
dye, blue .... **WOAD**
dye, blue-red ...... **ORSELLE**
dye gum .... **KINO**
dye, indigo .... **ANIL**
dye, lichen
  ARCHIL, ORCHAL, ORCHIL
dye plant .... **ANIL**
dye, red   **AAL, ANATO, AURIN,**
  EOSIN, ANATTA, ANATTO,
  AURINE, EOSINE, ANNAT-
  TA, ANNATTO, ANNOTTO,
  ARNATTO
dye, red, poisonous
  AURIN, AURINE
dye stuff .. **EOSINE, MADDER**
dye, yellow .... **WELD,**
  WOLD, WOALD
dyeing apparatus ...... **AGER**
dyeing reagent .... **ALTERANT**
dyestuff from lichens .. **LITMUS**
dyewood tree .... **TUI**
dynamite inventor .... **NOBEL**
DYNASTY see CHIN. DYNASTY
dynasty, first Chin. ...... **HSIA**
dynasty, It. .... **SAVOY**

E

b eager .. **AGOG, AVID, ARDENT**
eagle .... **ERN, ERNE**
eagle, Bible .... **GIER**
eagle, tried to mount to heaven
  on .... **ETANA**
eagle, sea .... **ERN, ERNE**
eagle's nest
  AERY, EYRY, AERIE, EYRIE
eaglestone ... **ETITE, AETITES**
ear .... **LUG, HANDLE**
ear canal .... **SCALA**
ear cavity .... **UTRICLE**
ear doctor .... **AURIST**
ear inflamation ...... **OTITIS**
ear of wheat: archeol.
  SPICA, SPICAE
ear, pert. to .... **OTIC, AURAL**
ear, prominence **TRAGI, TRAGUS**
ear shell .. **ORMER, ABALONE**
ear stone .. **OTOLITE, OTOLITH**
earache ... **OTALGY, OTALGIA**
eared seal .... **OTARY**

d early Britisher .... **PICT**
early Christian priest ... **ARIUS**
earnest
  ARDENT, INTENT, SINCERE
earnest money: law .... **ARRA,**
  ARLES, ARRHA
earth .... **GEO**
earth deposit in rocks .. **GUHR**
earth: dial. .... **ERD**
earth god, Egypt. **GEB, KEB, SEB**
earth goddess ..... **GE, ERDA,**
  GAEA, GAIA
earth goddess, Khonds' .. **TARI**
earth goddess, Rom.
  CERES, TERRA
earth, kind of .... **LOAM**
earth, pert. to .... **GEAL**
earth's surface, made on
  EPIGENE
earthenware maker ... **POTTER**
earthly .... **TERRENE**
earthquake .. **SEISM, TEMBLOR**

Earthquake

a
earthquake, pert. to .. **SEISMIC**
earthquake, shock of.**TREMOR**
earthwork, Rom. ...... **AGGER**
East .. **ASIA, LEVANT, ORIENT**
E. African native ... **SOMALI**
E. Afr. spiritual power .. **NGAI**
E. Indian animal .... **TARSIER**
E. Ind. dye tree ...... **DHAK**
E. Ind. fruit **DURIAN, DURION**
E. Ind. grass .... **KASA**
E. Ind. herb .. **PIA, SESAME**
E. Ind. herb root **CHAY, CHOY**
E. Ind. palm ...... **NIPA**
E. Ind. plant .. **JUTE, SESAME**
E. Ind. shrubby herb .... **SOLA**
E. Ind. tanning tree .. **AMLA,
AMLI**
E. Ind. term of address **SAHIB**
E. Ind. timber tree..**ACH, SAJ,
SAL, SAIN, SAUL, TEAK**
E. Ind. tree, large ..... **SIRIS**
E. Ind. vine ..... **AMIL, GILO,
ODAL, ODEL, SOMA**
E. Ind. vine, milky ..... **SOMA**
E. Ind. weight .... **TOLA**
E. Ind. wood, strong, heavy **ENG**
E. Ind. woody vine **ODAL, GILO**
East Indies .... **INDONESIA**
east wind .... **EURUS**
east wind's opposite .... **AFER**
Easter ...... **PASCH, PASCHA**

b
Eastern .... **ORTIVE**
Eastern Catholic ...... **UNIAT**
Eastern Church doxology **DOXA**
Eastern European .... **SLAV**
Eastern garment .... **SARI**
Eastern name ..... **ALI, ABOU**
Eastern title ...... **AGA, RAS**
Eastern Turkey tribesman **KURD**
easy .... **SOFT**
easy gait .... **LOPE**
easy job **SNAP,CINCH,SINECURE**
eat away .... **ERODE**
eat voraciously
RAVEN, RAVIN, RAVINE
eaten away .... **EROSE**
eating away **CAUSTIC, ERODENT**
eccentric person .... **GINK**
eccentric piece, rotating .. **CAM**
ecclesiastic .... **PRELATE**
ECCLESIASTICAL see CHURCH
eclipse .... **DIM**
eclipse demon, Hindu
KETU, RAHU
ecru .... **BEIGE**
Ecuadorian extinct Indians **CARA**
edentate genus .... **MANIS**
edge .... **HEM, LIP, RIM,
ARRIS, BRINK, MARGE**
edged unevenly .... **EROSE**
edging .... **PICOT**

c
edging, make .... **TAT**
edible fungus .... **CEPE**
edible root ...... **OCA, YAM,
TARO, CASAVA, CASSAVA**
edible shoot, Jap. .... **UDO**
edict .... **LAW, FIAT, DECREE**
Edinburgh: poet ...... **EDINA**
edit .... **REVISE, REDACT**
editorial "I" .... **WE**
Edom district .... **TEMAN**
Edomite .... **OMAR**
Edomite city .... **PAU**
Edomite duke **UZ, ARAN, IRAM**
Edomite king, ruler ..... **BELA**
educated .... **BRED, LETTERED**
educator, Am. .... **MANN**
educe .... **EVOKE, ELICIT**
Edward Bradley's pseudo. **BEDE**
eel, marine .... **CONGER**
eel: old Eng. .... **ELE**
eel-shaped amphibian ... **OLM**
eel, S. Am. .... **CARAPO**
eel, young .... **ELVER**
eelworm .... **NEMA**
Eghbal's land .... **IRAN**
effervescent, to make .. **AERATE**
effigy .... **IDOL**
effluvium ... **MIASM, MIASMA**
effort .... **DINT, ASSAY,
NISUS, TRIAL**

d
effusive .... **GUSHING**
eft .... **EVET, NEWT**
egg .... **OVUM**
egg dish .. **OMELET, OMELETTE**
egg drink .... **NOG, NOGG**
egg, insect .... **NIT**
egg-shaped
OOID, OVAL, OVATE, OVOID
egg-shaped ornaments ... **OVA**
egg white, raw .... **GLAIR**
eggs .... **OVA, ROE**
ego .... **SELF**
Egypt, pert. to ...... **COPTIC**
Egyptian bird .... **IBIS**
Egyp. Christian .... **COPT**
Egyp. city, ancient **SAIS, THEBES**
Egyp. cobra .... **HAJE**
Egyp. crown .... **ATEF**
Egyp. dog-headed ape, deity
AANI
Egyp. gateway .... **PYLON**
Egyp. god of creation ... **PTAH**
**EGYPTIAN GODS — GODDESSES
—DEITY** see also GODS and
SPECIAL SECTION
Egyp. guard .... **GHAFIR**
Egyp. heaven
AALU, AARU, IALU, YARU
Egyp. immortal heart **AB, HATI**
Egyp. king .. **MENES, RAMESES**
Egyp. lute .... **NABLA**

48

a
Egyp. nationalist party . **WAFD**
Egyp. precious alloy .... **ASEM**
Egyp. primeval chaos ..... **NU**
Egyp. queen of gods ..... **SATI**
Egyp. sacred bird .. **BENU, IBIS**
Egyp. sacred bull .... **APIS**
Egyp. season .... **AHET**
Egyp. tambourine ...... **RIKK**
Egyp. thorn .... **KIKAR**
Egyp. writing surfaces **PAPYRI**
eh?: obs. .... **ANAN**
eight days after feast .. **UTAS**
eight, group of
     OCTAD, OCTET, OCTAVE
eight, set of ...... **OGDOAD**
eighth day of feast .... **UTAS**
eighth day, on ...... **OCTAN**
eighth note .... **UNCA**
Eire legislature .... **DAIL**
ejaculation, mystic ...... **OM**
eject ...... **EMIT, OUST, SPEW**
elaborate .... **ORNATE**
Elam, capital of .... **SUSA**
eland .... **IMPOFO**
elanet .... **KITE**
elasmobranch fish **RAY, SHARK**
Elbe, river to ..... **EGER, ISER**
Elbe tributary .... **EGER, ISER**
elbow .... **ANCON**
elder .... **SENIOR**

b
elder son of Zeus ...... **ARES**
elder statesmen, Jap. .. **GENRO**
eldest: law ...... **AINE, EIGNE**
electric catfish ...... **RAAD**
electric force .... **ELOD**
electric force unit ..... **VOLT**
electric reluctance unit .. **REL**
electric unit .. **ES, AMP, MHO,
     OHM, REL, PERM, FARAD,
     HENRY, AMPERE**
electrified particle ..... **ION**
electrode .. **ANODE, CATHODE**
electromagnet .... **RELAY**
electron tube
     TRIODE, KLYSTRON
elegance .... **GRACE**
elegant .... **FINE, POSH**
elegist .... **POET**
elegy .... **NENIA**
ELEMENT, non-metallic and me-
     tallic, gaseous on page 195
elemi .... **ANIME**
element, radioactive of **URANIC**
elephant goad .... **ANKUS**
elephant: India .... **HATHI**
elephant's cry .... **BARR**
elephant's ear .... **TARO**
elevated ground **MESA, RIDEAU**
elevation of mind .. **ANAGOGE**
elevator: Brit. .... **LIFT**

c
elf .... **SPRITE**
elf, Egypt. .... **OUPHE**
elfin .... **FEY**
Elia .... **LAMB**
elicit .... **EDUCE**
elide .... **DELE, OMIT**
Elija .... **ELIAS**
eliminate ... **DELETE, REMOVE**
Elizabeth I, name for **ORIANA**
elk, Am. .... **WAPITI**
elk, Europ. .... **MOOSE**
elk, Europ. genus .... **ALCES**
elliptical ...... **OVAL, OVOID**
elm .... **ULM, ULME**
elm fruit seed ...... **SAMARA**
elongated .... **PROLATE**
else .... **OTHER**
elude .... **DODGE, EVADE**
elver .... **EEL**
emaciation .... **TABES, MACIES**
emanation .... **AURA**
emanation, star .... **BLAS**
embankment ... **DAM, BUND,
     DIKE, DYKE, DIGUE, LEVEE**
embellish
     GILD, ADORN, DECORATE
embellished .... **ORNATE**
ember .... **ASH, COAL**
emblem ... **INSIGNE, INSIGNIA**

d
emblem of authority .... **MACE**
emblem of U.S. .... **EAGLE**
embrace
     HUG, CLASP, ENARM, INARM
embrocation ...... **LINIMENT**
embroidery frame
     TABORET, TABOURET
emend .... **EDIT**
emerald .... **BERYL, SMARAGD**
emerge **RISE, ISSUE, EMANATE**
emetic .... **IPECAC**
eminent .... **NOTED**
emit .... **REEK, EXUDE**
emmer .... **SPELT**
emmet .... **ANT**
Emperor of Russia
     CZAR, TSAR, TZAR
emphasis ... **ACCENT, STRESS**
empire .... **REALM**
employ .... **USE, HIRE, PLACE**
employed for wine, meas. **AAM**
employees .... **PERSONNEL**
employer .... **BOSS, USER**
employment .... **PLACE**
emporium ...... **MART, STORE**
Empress, Byzant. ...... **IRENE**
Empress, Russian .. **CZARINA,
     TSARINA, TZARINA**
empty .... **VOID, INANE,
     DEPLETE**
emulate .... **RIVAL**
enamel ware .... **LIMOGES**

49

enchantress .... **CIRCE, MEDEA**
encircle .... **ORB, GIRD, GIRT, RING, EMBAY**
encircled **GIRT, RINGED, SURROUNDED**
encircling band .... **ZONE**
enclose .... **MEW**
enclosure .... **MEW, PEN, REE, STY, CORRAL**
enclosure, cattle ..... **ATAJO**
enclosure: Sp. Am. ... **CANCHA**
encomium .... **ELOGE**
encompass .. **GIRD, GIRT, RING**
encompassed by .... **AMID**
encore .... **BIS**
encounter .... **MEET**
encourage .... **ABET**
end **TIP, FINIS, LIMIT, OMEGA**
end: music .... **FINE**
end result .... **PRODUCT**
end, tending to an .... **TELIC**
endeavor .. **TRY, ESSAY, NISUS**
ENDING ... see also SUFFIX or type of ending
ending, comparative . **IER, IOR**
ENDING, NOUN see SUFFIX, NOUN ENDING
ending, plural .... **EN, ES**
ending, superlative ..... **EST**
endow ...... **DOWER, INVEST**
endue .... **ENDOW**
endure .... **BEAR, LAST, WEAR**
endure: dial. .... **BIDE**
energy .... **PEP, VIM, ZIP, POWER, VIGOR, VIGOUR**
energy, potential ...... **ERGAL**
energy unit **ERG, RAD, ERGON**
enfeeble **WEAKEN, DEBILITATE**
engage **HIRE, ENTER, CHARTER**
engender .... **BEGET, BREED, PROMOTE, GENERATE**
engine, donkey ...... **YARDER**
engine of war .... **RAM**
engine part .... **STATOR**
engine, rotary ...... **TURBINE**
engineer, Am. .... **EADS**
engineer, military .... **SAPPER**
English actor .... **EVANS**
Eng. actress .... (Nell) **GWYN, TERRY, NEAGLE**
Eng. architect .... **WREN**
Eng. author .... **MORE, WEST, ARLEN, BACON, CAINE, DEFOE, DORAN, ELIOT, HARDY, READE, SHUTE, WAUGH, WELLS, AMBLER, AUSTEN, BARRIE, BELLOC, BRONTE, ORWELL, STERNE**
Eng. car .... **ROVER**
Eng. cathedral city **ELY, YORK**
Eng. city, historic **COVENTRY**

Eng. college ... **ETON, BALIOL**
ENG. COMPOSER see **COMPOSER, ENG.**
Eng. country festival .... **ALE**
Eng. dramatist **SHAW, PEELE, DRYDEN**
Eng. emblem .... **ROSE**
Eng. essayist .... **SALA, STEELE**
Eng. explorer ... **ROSS, CABOT**
Eng. historian .... **BEDE**
Eng. king **BRAN, CNUT, KNUT, CANUTE**
Eng. monk ..... **BEDE, BAEDA**
Eng. murderer .... **ARAM**
Eng. musician .... **ARNE**
ENG. NOVELIST .... see ENG. AUTHOR
Eng. painter .... **OPIE, ORPEN**
Eng. philosopher ... **HUME, JOAD, BACON, SPENCER**
Eng. playwright .... **SHAW**
Eng. poet ..... **GRAY, AUDEN, BLAKE, BYRON, CAREW, DONNE, ELIOT**
Eng. queen ..... **ANNE, MARY**
Eng. rebel leader, 1450 .. **CADE**
Eng. royal house **YORK, TUDOR**
Eng. scholar, schoolmaster **ARAM**
Eng. school, boys' ...... **ETON**
Eng. sculptor ...... **EPSTEIN**
Eng. spa .... **BATH, MARGATE**
Eng. spy .... **ANDRE**
Eng. statesman ... **EDEN, PITT**
Eng. theologian ..... **ALCUIN**
Eng. woman politician .. **ASTOR**
ENG. WRITER .... see ENG. AUTHOR and ENG. ESSAYIST
engraver ... **CHASER, ETCHER, GRAVER**
engraver, famous .. **PYE, DORE**
engraver's tool .... **BURIN**
engrossed .... **RAPT**
enigma .... **RIDDLE**
enlarge **DILATE, EXPAND, INCREASE**
enlarge a hole .... **REAM**
enlarging, as chimneys .. **EVASE**
enmity .... **ANIMUS**
Enoch's father .... **CAIN**
enough .... **ENOW**
enrol .... **ENTER, ENLIST**
ensign .... **FLAG**
ensnare .... **NET, WEB**
entangle .... **MAT, MESH**
enter .... **ENROL**
entertain **AMUSE, DIVERT, REGALE**
enthusiasm **ELAN, ARDOR, VERVE, SPIRIT**
enthusiastic .... **RABID**

a entice .... **BAIT, LURE, TOLE, TEMPT, ALLURE**
enticement .... **TICE**
entire man .... **EGO**
entity .... **ENS, ENTIA**
entomb .... **INURN**
entrance
ADIT, DOOR, GATE, PORTAL
entrance halls .... **ATRIA**
entreat .... **PRAY, PLEAD**
entreaty .... **PLEA**
entry, separate .... **ITEM**
entwine
WEAVE, ENLACE, WREATHE
enumerate .... **COUNT**
envelop **WRAP, ENFOLD, INFOLD**
environment .... **MILIEU**
envoy .... **LEGATE**
envy .... **COVET**
enzyme .... **ASE, LOTASE, RENNIN, MALTASE**
eon .... **OLAM**
ephah, 1/10 .... **OMER**
epic poetry .... **EPOS, EPOPEE**
epoch .... **ERA**
epochal .... **ERAL**
epode .... **POEM**
eponymous ancestor .... **EBER**
equal **IS, ARE, TIE, EVEN, PEER**
equality .... **PAR, PARITY**
b equally .... **AS**
equilibrium .... **POISE**
equine .... **HORSE**
equip .... **FIT, RIG**
equitable ... **JUST, IMPARTIAL**
equivalence .... **PAR**
equivocate .... **EVADE**
era .... **EPOCH**
eradicate .... **ERASE, UPROOT**
eral .... **EPOCHAL**
erase .... **DELE, DELETE**
erect .... **REAR, RAISE**
ergo .... **HENCE**
Eris' brother .... **ARES**
ermine, summer .... **STOAT**
Eros .... **CUPID**
errand boy .... **PAGE**
error, publication .... **TYPO, ERRATA, ERRATE, ERRATUM**
Esau .... **EDOM**
Esau's brother .... **JACOB**
Esau's father-in-law ... **ELON**
Esau's grandson ...... **OMAR**
Esau's home .... **SEIR**
Esau's wife .... **ADAH**
escape .. **LAM, ELUDE, EVADE**
eschew .... **SHUN**
escutcheon band .... **FESS**
Esdra's angel .... **URIEL**
eskers .... **OSAR**
Eskimo .... **ITA**

c Eskimo boat
KIAK, KYAK, KAYAK
Eskimo boot .... **MUKLUK**
Eskimo coat
PARKA, NETCHA, TEMIAK
Eskimo curlew .... **FUTE**
Eskimo house
IGLU, IGLOE, IGLOO, IGLOU
Eskimo settlement ..... **ETAH**
Eskimo summer hut .... **TOPEK**
Eskimos of Asia **YUIT, INNUIT**
esoteric .... **INNER**
espy .... **SEE, SPY**
esquire .... **ARMIGER**
essay ... **TRY, TEST, ATTEMPT**
essay, scholarly
THESIS, TREATISE
essence: Hindu religion .. **RASA**
essence, rose .... **ATTAR**
essential oils fluid ..... **NEROL**
essential part .... **CORE, PITH**
"— est" (that is) .... **ID**
establish .... **BASE, FOUND**
established value .... **PAR**
estate, landed, large .. **MANOR**
estate manager .... **STEWARD**
estate, not held by feudal tenure **ALOD, ALLOD, ALODIUM**
esteem .... **HONOR, PRIZE, ADMIRE, HONOR**
d ester, hydriodic acid ... **IODIDE**
ester, liquid .... **ACETIN**
ester, oleic acid ..... **OLEATE**
estimate .... **RATE, APPRAISE**
Estonian .... **ESTH**
estuary .... **RIA**
estuary, Brazil .... **PARA**
estuary, S. Am. .... **PLATA**
Eternal City .... **ROME**
eternity ..... **AGE, EON, OLAM**
ether compound .... **ESTER**
ethereal .... **AERY, AERIAL**
ETHIOPIA see also ABYSSINIA
Ethiopia .... **CUSH**
Ethiopian title .... **RAS**
Ethiopic .... **GEEZ**
ethos, opposed to .... **PATHOS**
Etruscan god .... **LAR**
Etruscan Juno .... **UNI**
Etruscan Minerva .... **MENFRA**
Etruscan title, peer **LAR, LARS**
eucalyptus secretion
LAAP, LARP, LERP
eucalyptus tree .... **YATE**
Eucharist case ...... **PIX, PYX**
Eucharist cloth
FANO, FANON, FANUM
Eucharist spoon .... **LABIS**
Eucharist wafer .... **HOST**
eulogy .... **ELOGE**
euphorbia .... **SPURGE**

a Eurasian dock plant .. **PARELLE**
eureka red .... **PUCE**
Euripides heroine ..... **MEDEA**
EUROPEAN see also specific word, as FISH, ANIMAL, etc.
European .... **POLE, SLAV**
Eur. colorful fish ...... **BOCE**
EUROP. FISH .. see FISH, EUR.
European, in Moslem East **FRANGI**
Europ. iris .... **ORRIS**
Europ. kite ..... **GLED, GLEDE**
Europ. porgy .... **PARGO**
Eurytus' daughter ...... **IOLE**
evade **SHUN, DODGE, ELUDE, SHIRK**
evaluate ..... **RATE, ASSESS**
Evangelist ...... **LUKE, MARK**
Evans, Mary Ann ...... **ELIOT**
Eve's grandson .... **ENOS**
even ..... **EEN, LEVEL, PLANE**
even if .... **THO**
evening party .... **SOIREE**
evening prayer .... **VESPER**
eventual lot .... **FATE**
ever .... **EER**
evergreen .... **FIR, YEW, PINE, CAROB, CEDAR, OLIVE, SAVIN, LAUREL, SABINE, SAVINE, SPRUCE**
b
evergreen, bean ...... **CAROB**
evergreen genus **OLAX, ABIES, CATHA**
evergreen, red-berry **YEW, WHORT**
evergreen, tropical .. **CALABA**
everlasting ... **ETERN, ETERNE**
evict .... **OUST**
evident **CLEAR, PLAIN, PATENT**
evil .... **MAL**
evil god, Egypt. ... **SET, SETH**
evil intent: law ...... **DOLUS**
evil spirit, Haiti **BAKA, BOKO**
evil spirit, Hindu ..... **ASURA**
evolve .... **EDUCE**
ewe, old .... **CRONE**
exact **BLEED, DEMAND, EXTORT**
exacerbate .... **IRE**
exact point .... **TEE**
examine ..... **PRY, SPY, SCAN**
excavate .. **DIG, PION, DREDGE**
excavation for extracting ore **STOPE**
excavation, mine .. **PIT, STOPE**
exceed .... **TOP**
exceedingly: music ..... **TRES**
excellence .... **VIRTU**
excellent .... **AONE**
except .... **BUT, SAVE**
excess ...... **LUXUS, NIMIETY**

c excess, fill to ... **GLUT, SATE**
excess of solar year ... **EPACT**
exchange medium, Chin. **SYCEE**
exchange premium, discount **AGIO**
exchequer .... **FISC, FISK**
excite .... **ELATE, ROUSE**
excited .... **AGOG, MANIC**
excitement, public **FUROR, FURORE**
exclamation .. **AH, EH, HA, HI, MY, OH, OW, UM, ACH, AHA, AUH, BAH, BAW, FIE, FOH, GRR, HAH, HAW, HAY, HEM, HEP, HEU, HEY, HIC, HIP, HOI, HOY, HUH, OHO, OUF, PAH, PEW, POH, PUE, SOH, TCH, TCK, TUT, UGH, WEE, WHY, WOW, YAH, YOI, YOW, ALAS, PHEW, ALACK**
exclamation, Fr. .... **HEIN**
exclamation, Ger. ...... **HOCH**
exclamation, Ir. ...... **ADAD, AHEY, ARAH, ARRA, ARRO, BOOH, EHEU, OCHONE**
exclude ... **BAR, OMIT, DEBAR**
exclusive .... **SOLE**
exclusive set .... **ELECT, ELITE**
exclusively .... **ONLY**
d excoriate .... **ABRADE**
excrete from skin ..... **EGEST**
excuse .. **PLEA, ALIBI, REMIT**
excuse, court **ESSOIN, ESSOINE**
execrated ..... **CURST, SWORE**
exemplar ... **MODEL, PATTERN**
exhaust **SAP, TIRE, SPEND, DEPLETE**
exhausted .... **EFFETE**
exhibits leaping ..... **SALTATE**
exigency .... **NEED**
exist .... **LIVE**
exist .. all forms of verb "BE"
exist, beginning to .. **NASCENT**
existence .... **ENS, ESSE**
existentialist leader ... **SARTRE**
existing **ALIVE, BEING, EXTANT**
exit .. **LEAVE, DEPART, EGRESS**
expand ..... **DILATE, DISTEND**
expanse .... **SEA**
expatriate .... **EXILE**
expectation .... **HOPE**
expedite .... **HURRY, HASTEN**
expedition .. **SAFARI, SUFFARI**
expert ... **ACE, ONER, ADEPT**
expiate .... **ATONE**
explain .... **DEFINE**
explode **POP, DETONATE, FULMINATE**
exploit **DEED, FEAT, GEST, GESTE**

a explosive
    CAP, TNT, GAINE, TONITE
explosive sound ... POP, CHUG
expose .... AIR, DISPLAY
expression, elegant . ATTICISM
expression, local ...... IDIOM
expressionless .... WOODEN
expunge DELE, ERASE, DELETE
extend
    JUT, LIE, REACH, BEETLE
extend the front ..... DEPLOY
extensive .... AMPLE
extent .... AREA
external .... EXOTERIC
external covering.HIDE, HUSK,
    PEEL, PELT, RIND, SKIN
extinct wild ox .... URUS
extirpate .. ROOT, ERADICATE
extort .... BLEED, EXACT
extra .... ODD, SPARE
extra leaf .... INSERT
extra, theatrical .... SUPE
extract DRAW, ELICIT, EVULSE
extraneous .... EXOTIC
extraordinary person, thing
    ONER

c extravagance .... ELA
extreme .... ULTRA
extreme unction, give
    ANELE, ENELE
exudate, plant
    GUM, LAC, RESIN
exude ..... EMIT, OOZE, REEK
exult .... ELATE
eye .... ORB, SEE, OGLE
eye cosmetic ... KOHL, KUHL
eye inflammation STY, IRITIS
eye, inner coat ...... RETINA
eye, layer .... UVEA
eye of bean .... HILA, HILUM
eye of insect .... STEMMA
eye, part of the ..... IRIS,
    UVEA, CORNEA, RETINA
eye, pert. to .... OPTIC
eye socket .... ORBIT
eye, symbolic .... UTA
eye-worm, Afr. .... LOA
eyelash ...... CILIA, CILIUM
eyes: old Eng. .... NIE
eyestalk .... STIPE
eyewink ...... LOOK, GLANCE
eyot .... ISLE, ISLET

F

b Fabian .... SHAW
fable .... APOLOG, APOLOGUE
fable writer ... ESOP, AESOP
fabled bird ...... ROC, RUKH
"Fables in Slang" author ADE
fabric ... REP, ACCA, BAFT,
    DRAB, DUCK, IKAT,
    LAWN, LENO, MOFF, REPP,
    SILK, SUSI, TAPA, TUKE,
    CRAPE, CREPE, MOIRE,
    NINON, ORLON, RAYON,
    CANVAS, COVERT, MAN-
    TUA, MOHAIR
farbic, Angora ..... CAMLET,
    MOHAIR
fabric, coarse cotton .. SURAT
fabric, coarse wool
    TAMIN, TAMINE
fabric, corded REP, REPP, PIQUE
fabric, cotton ... LENO, MULL,
    DENIM, MANTA, SCRIM,
    CALICO, CRETON, NAN-
    KIN, PENANG, NANKEEN,
    CRETONNE
fabric, curtain ... NET, SCRIM
fabric, felt-like ...... BAIZE
fabric, fig'd DAMASK, PAISLEY
fabric from remnants MUNGO
fabric, Ind. .. SHELA, SHELAH

d fabric, knitted .... TRICOT
fabric, light wool .... ALPACA
fabric, lustrous POPLIN, SATEEN
fabric, mourning ALMA, CRAPE
fabric, net .. TULLE, MALINE
fabric, plaid . MAUD, TARTAN
fabric, printed BATIK, BATTIK
FABRIC, RIBBED
    see RIBBED FABRIC
fabric, satin .. PEKIN, ETOILE
fabric, satiny
    SATINET, SATINETTE
fabric, sheer .... GAUZE,
    BEMBERG, ORGANZA
fabric, short nap ...... RAS
fabric, silk .... SURAH,
    PONGEE, SAMITE, TOB'NE
fabric, silk, gold, medieval ACCA
fabric, silk, thick ...... GROS
fabric, stiff .... WIGAN
fabric stretcher
    TENTER, STENTER
fabric, striped .. SUSI, DOREA,
    DORIA, DOOREA, MADRAS
fabric, thick .... DRAB
fabric, twilled .... REP
fabric, upholstery .. BROCATEL,
    BROCATALL, BROCATELL
    BROCATELLE

Fabric

a fabric, velvet-like .... **PANNE**
fabric, voile-like .... **ETAMINE**
fabric, wool .. **SERGE, TAMIN,
TAMIS, MERINO, TAMINE,
TAMINY, TAMISE, TAM-
MIN, ESTAMIN, ETAMINE,
STAMMEL, ESTAMINE**
fabric, worsted ...... **ETAMINE**
fabricate .... **MAKE**
fabulist ...... **ESOP, AESOP**
fabulous bird .... **ROC, RUKH**
face **MAP, MUG, PHIZ, FACADE**
face with stone .... **REVET**
facet of gem .. **BEZEL, BEZIL,
CULET, COLLET**
facile .... **EASY**
facing glacier .... **STOSS**
fact .... **DATUM**
fact, by the: law ..... **FACTO**
facts .... **DATA**
faction .... **SECT, SIDE, CABAL**
factor .... **GENE**
factory .... **PLANT**
faculty .... **SENSE**
fade ...... **DIE, DIM, WITHER**
"Faerie Queene" iron man
TALUS
"Faerie Queene" lady .... **UNA**
failure .... **DUD, FLOP**
fainting: med. ...... **SYNCOPE**
b fair . **BAZAR, FERIA, BAZAAR
KERMIS, KIRMES**
fair **JUST, CLEAR, IMPARTIAL**
fair-haired .. **BLOND, BLONDE**
fair-lead, naut. .... **WAPP**
fairy .. **ELF, FAY, PERI, SPRITE**
fairy fort .... **LIS, LISS**
fairy king .... **OBERON**
fairy queen .... **MAB, TITANIA**
fairy, Serbo-Croat **VILA, VILY**
fairylike creature ...... **PERI**
faith, article of ...... **TENET**
faith, pert. to .... **PISTIC**
faithful .... **LEAL,
TRUE, STANCH, STAUNCH**
falcon .... **SACER, SAKER,
LANNER, MERLIN, SAKERET**
falcon, Asia **LAGGAR, LUGGAR**
falcon genus .... **FALCO**
falcon-headed god
MENT, MENTU
falcon, Ind. **SHAHIN, SHAHEEN**
falcon of sea ...... **ERN, ERNE**
falconer's bait .... **LURE**
fall **DROP, PLAP, PLOP, SPILL**
fall back .... **RETREAT**
fallacy ...... **IDOLA, IDOLUM**
fallow-deer, female .... **TEG**
false excuse .... **SUBTERFUGE**
false friend .. **IAGO, TRAITOR**
false fruit of rose .... **HIP**

c false god .... **IDOL**
Falstaff's follower ...... **NYM**
fame .... **ECLAT, KUDOS,
RENOWN, REPUTE**
famed .... **NOTED**
familiar .... **VERSANT**
familiar saying .... **SAW, TAG**
family, Florentine .... **MEDICI**
family, Genoese ...... **DORIA**
family: Scot. .... **ILK**
famous .... **NOTED**
fan .... **ROOTER**
fan palm genus ...... **INODES**
fan's stick .... **BRIN**
fanatical .... **RABID**
fancy ... **IDEA, WHIM, IDEATE**
fanfare .... **TANTARA,
TANTARO, TANTARARA**
fanning device
PUNKA, PUNKAH
fare .... **DIET**
farewell ... **AVE, VALE, ADIEU**
farinaceous .... **MEALY**
farinaceous food **SAGO, SALEP**
farm group .... **GRANGE**
farm, small, Sp. Am. **CHACRA**
farm, Sw. small leased .. **TORP**
farm: Swedish .... **TORP**
farm, tenant .... **CROFT**
farmer .... **KULAK, GRANGER**
d farmyard, S. Afr. ...... **WERF**
Faroe Is. wind .... **OE**
Faroe judge .... **FOUD**
Farouk's father .... **FUAD**
fashion .... **FORM, MODE,
MOLD, MODEL, STYLE**
fasten .... **BOLT, LOCK, NAIL,
SEAL, SNIB, TACK, RIVET**
fasten: naut **BELAY, BATTEN**
fastener .... **NUT, PIN, BRAD,
CLIP, HASP, NAIL, SNAP,
STUD, CLASP, RIVET,
CLEVIS, COTTER**
fastener, wire .... **STAPLE**
fastener, naut. .... **BITT**
fastener, wood
FID, NOG, PEG, PIN
fastening .... **LATCH**
fastidious .... **NICE**
fasting month .... **RAMADAN**
fasting period .... **LENT**
fat **LARD, LIPA, SUET, OBESE**
fat, animal .. **ADEPS, TALLOW**
fat: comb. form **STEAT, STEATO**
fat, liquid part ...... **ELAIN,
OLEIN, ELAINE, OLEINE**
fat, natural .... **ESTER**
fat, of .... **SEBAIC**
fat, solid part
STEARIN, STEARINE
fatal ...... **FUNEST, LETHAL**

54

a fate .... **LOT, DOOM, KISMET**
Fates, Gr. & Rom. .... **MOIRA,
MORTA, PARCA, CLOTHO,
DECUMA, MOIRAI, PAR-
CAE, ATROPOS, LACHESIS**
fateful .... **DIRE**
father .... **SIRE, BEGET**
father: Arab. .... **ABU, ABOU**
father: Hebr. .... **ABBA**
father of modern engraving **PYE**
father's side, kinship on
AGNAT, AGNATE
fathom .... **PROBE, SOUND**
fatigue .. **FAG, TIRE, WEARY**
Fatima's huband .... **ALI**
fatty .... **ADIPOSE**
fatty gland secretion **SEBUM**
fatuous .... **INANE**
faucet ... **TAP, COCK, SPIGOT**
fault find ...... **CARP, CAVIL**
faultfinder .. **MOMUS, CAVILER**
faulty .... **BAD**
faux pas ...... **ERROR, GAFFE**
favor .... **BOON**
favorable vote .. **AY, AYE, YES**
favorite .... **PET, IDOL**
fawn color .... **FAON**
fawning favorite .... **MINION**
fear .... **PHOBIA**
fearful .... **TREPID**
b feast .... **REGALE**
feast day: comb. form .. **MAS**
feather **PENNA, PINNA, PLUME**
feather grass .... **STIPA**
feather palms .... **EJOO, IROK**
feather: zool. .... **PLUMA**
feathers, cast .... **MEW**
feathers of o-o .... **HULU**
feathered scarf .... **BOA**
feeble .. **PUNY, WEAK, DEBILE**
feel .... **SENSE**
feel one's way .... **GROPE**
feeler **PALP, PALPI, ANTENNA**
feet, having .... **PEDATE**
feet, pert. to **PEDAL, PEDARY**
feign .... **ACT, SHAM**
feline .... **CAT, PUMA**
felis leo .... **LION**
fellow ..... **GUY, LAD, BOZO,
CHAP, DICK, CHAPPY,
CHAPPIE**
felt ...... **GROPED, SENSATE**
female animal, parent
DAM, DOE
female camel .... **NAGA**
female disciple at Joppa
DORCAS
female insect .... **GYNE**
fence of shrubs .... **HEDGE**
fence of stakes .... **PALISADE**
fence step .... **STILE**

c fence, sunken, hidden
AHA, HAHA
fence to restrain cattle .. **OXER**
fencer's cry .. **HAI, HAY, SASA**
fencing dummy .... **PEL**
fencing position **CARTE, SIXTE,
QUARTE, QUINTE, TIERCE,
SECONDE, SEPTIME**
fencing sword ...... **EPEE, FOIL**
fencing term .... **TOUCHE**
fencing thrust ...... **LUNGE,
PUNTO, REMISE, RIPOST,
RIPOSTE, REPRISE**
fend .... **WARD**
fennel: P. I. .... **ANIS**
"Ferdinand the Bull" author
LEAF
feria, pert. to .... **FERIAL**
ferment .... **YEAST**
ferment: med. .... **ZYME**
fermented milk dessert **LACTO**
fern, climbing, P. I. .... **NITO**
fern, Polyn., edible .... **TARA**
fern root, N. Z. ...... **ROI**
fern "seed" .... **SPORE**
fern species .... **WEKI**
fern spore ..... **SORI, SORUS**
Ferrara ducal family .... **ESTE**
ferrum .... **IRON**
ferryboat .... **BAC**
d ferryboat, Afr. .... **PONT**
fertilizer ..... **MARL, GUANO**
fervent .... **ARDENT**
fervor ... **ZEAL, ZEST, ARDOR**
fester .... **RANKLE**
festival .. **ALE, FAIR, FETE,
GALA, FERIA, FIESTA, KER-
MIS, KIRMES**
festival, Creek Indian .. **BUSK**
festival, Gr.
AGON, DELIA, HALOA
fetid .... **OLID, RANK**
fetish .... **OBI, JUJU, OBIA,
ZEME, ZEMI, CHARM,
OBEAH, GRIGRI**
fetish, P. I. .... **ANITO**
fetter .... **GYVE, IRON**
feud, opposed to ...... **ALOD,
ALLOD, ALODIUM, ALLODIUM**
feudal benefice .... **FEU**
feudal estate **FEOD, FEUD, FIEF**
feudal land .... **BENEFICE**
feudal service, form of **AVERA**
feudal tax
TAILAGE, TALLAGE, TAILLAGE
feudal tenant .... **VASSAL**
fever, intermittent
AGUE, TERTIAN
feverish .... **FEBRILE**
fez .... **TARBUSH,
TARBOOSH, TARBOUCHE**

Fiber

a fiber .... JUTE, PITA,
          RAFFIA, STAPLE, THREAD
   fiber, bark
          TAPA, OLONA, TERAP
   fiber, coarse .... ADAD
   fiber, cordage .... DA, COIR,
          FERU, HEMP, IMBE, JUTE,
          RHEA, ABACA, SISAL
   fiber from palm .... ERUC
   fiber, hat or basket .... DATIL
   fiber knot .... NEP
   fiber plant
          ISTLE, IXTLE, IXLE, RAMIE
   fiber plant, Brazil .... CAROA
   fiber plant, E. Ind. SANA, SUNN
   fiber, textile .... SABA
   fiber, tropical
          IXLE, ISTLE, IXTLE
   fiber, woody .... BAST, BASTE
   fictional submarine character
          NEMO
   fiddle, medieval .... GIGA
   fiddler crab genus ...... UCA
   field LEA, ACRE, WONG, CROFT
   field deity .... PAN, FAUN
   field, enclosed: law ..... AGER
   field, stubble .... ROWEN
   fifth segment crustacean
          CARPOS
b fig marigold, Afr. ..... SAMH
   figs, Smyrna .. ELEME, ELEMI
   fight
          CLEM, FRAY, MELEE, AFFRAY
   figurative use of word .. TROPE
   figure .... SOLID
   figure, equal angles
          ISAGON, ISOGON
   figure, 4-sided .... TETRAGON
   figure, geom. .... SECTOR
   figure of speech
          TROPE, SIMILE, METAPHOR
   figure, oval .... ELLIPSE
   figure, 10-sided .... DECAGON
   figwort .... MULLEIN
   Fiji chestnut .... RATA
   Fiji tree .... BURI
   filament ..... FIBER, HAIR
   filament, flax ... HARL, HARLE
   filament, plant
          ELATER, THREAD
   filch .... STEAL
   file .... ROW
   file, coarse .... RASP
   file, three-square single-cut
          CARLET
   filled to capacity
          SATED, REPLETE
   fillet, architectural ORLE, ORLO
   fillet, narrow heraldic
          ORLE, ORLO, LISTEL
   fillet, shaft's ..... ORLE, ORLO

c fillip .... SNAP
   film, old green ..... PATINA
   filthy .... VILE
   filthy lucre .... PELF
   finale: music .... CODA
   finally: Fr. .... ENFIN
   finback whale .... GRASO
   finch .. MORO, LINNET, SISKIN
   finch, Europ.
          TARIN, TERIN, SERIN
   finch, S. Afr. .... FINK
   find fault ...... CARP, CAVIL
   fine, as a line .... LEGER
   fine, punish by ..... AMERCE
   fine, record of ...... ESTREAT
   finesse .... ART, SKILL
   Fingal's kingdom .... MORVEN
   finger .... DIGIT
   finger cymbals ... CASTANETS
   finger, 5th PINKIE, MINIMUS
   finger inflammation ... FELON
   finger nail half-moon
          LUNULA, LUNULE
   fingerless glove .... MIT, MITT
   fingerprint pattern .... WHORL
   finial ornament, slender .. EPI
   finisher .... EDGER, ENDER
   finishing tool .... REAMER
   FINLAND, FINNISH
          see also SPECIAL SECTION
d Finland .... SUOMI
   Finn in Ingria ..... VOT, VOTE
   Finns .... SUOMI
   Finnish god .... JUMALA
   Finnish poetry .... RUNES
   Finnish steam bath ... SAUNA
   fire basket .... CRESSET
   fire bullet .... TRACER
   fire god .... VULCAN
   fire god, Hindu .. AGNI, AKAL,
          CIVA, DEVA, KAMA, SIVA
   fire in heart: Buddhism RAGA
   fire opal: Fr. ...... GIRASOL
   fire, sacrificial, Hindu .. AGNI
   fire worshipper PARSI, PARSEE
   firearm . GUN, RIFLE, MAUSER,
          PISTOL, CARBINE, REVOLVER
   firecracker .... PETARD
   fired clay .... TILE
   firedog .... ANDIRON
   fireplace
          GRATE, INGLE, HEARTH
   fireplace side shelf .... HOB
   firewood bundle BARIN, FAGOT
   firewood, Tex. .... LENA
   firework .... GERB
   firm FAST, STANCH, STAUNCH
   firm: Hawaii .... HUI
   firmament .... SKY
   firn .... NEVE
   firs, true .... ABIES

56

a first **PRIME, INITIAL, ORIGINAL**
first American-born white
   child .... **DARE**
first appearance ...... **DEBUT**
first born: law .... **EIGNE**
first fruits of a benefice
                 ANNATES
first miracle site ..... **CANA**
first mortal, Hindu ..... **YAMA**
first part in duet ..... **PRIMO**
first principles .... **ABCS**
first-rate .... **ACE**
firth: Scot. .... **KYLE**
fish .. **ANGLE, TRAWL, TROLL**
fish .... **ID, EEL, IDE, CARP,
DACE, HAKE, HIKU, JOCU,
LIJA, LING, MADO, MASU,
OPAH, ORFE, PEGA, PETO,
PIKE, POGY, ROUD, RUDD,
SCAD, SCUP, SESI, SHAD,
SIER, SKIL, SOLE, SPET,
TOPE, TUNA, ULUA, PAR-
GO, POWAN, POWEN,
ROACH, SKATE, CONGER,
MULLET, SABALO, TOMCOD**
fish, ancient .. **ELOPS, ELLOPS**
fish, Atlant. **TAUTOG, ESCOLAR**
fish, boneless .. **FILET, FILLET**
fish, bony .... **CARP, TELEOST**
fish, butterfly .... **PARU**
b fish by trolling .... **DRAIL**
fish, Calif. surf .... **SPRAT**
fish, carplike
   RUD, DACE, ROUD, RUDD
fish cleaner .... **SCALER**
fish, climbing ...... **ANABAS**
fish, cod-like **CUSK, HAKE, LING**
fish, colorful
    BOCE, OPAH, WRASSE
fish, Congo .... **LULU**
fish, Cuban .... **DIABLO**
fish, cyprinoid
    ID, IDE, ORF, ORFE
fish, edible .... **SPRAT**
fish eggs .... **ROE**
fish, Egypt. .... **SAIDE**
fish, elongated **EEL, GAR, PIKE**
fish, Europ. .. **ID, BOCE, DACE,
BREAM, SPRAT, UMBER,
BARBEL, BRASSE, PLAICE,
SENNET, WRASSE**
fish, flat .. **DAB, RAY, SOLE,
BRILL, FLUKE, FLOUNDER**
fish, Florida .... **TARPON**
fish, food .. **COD, CERO, HAAK,
HAIK, HAKE, LING, SHAD,
TUNA, TUNNY, SARDINE**
fish, food: Ind. .... **HILSA**
fish, fresh water
    IDE, BASS, DACE, ESOX
fish from boat .... **TROLL**

c fish, game .... **BASS,
MARLIN, TARPON, TARPUN**
fish, gobeylike .... **DRAGONET**
fish, Gr. Lakes .. **CISCO, PERCH**
fish, Hawaiian .... **AKU**
fish, herringlike ...... **SHAD**
fish, hook for **GIG, GAFF, DRAIL**
fish, lancet .... **SERRA**
fish line ...... **SNELL, TRAWL**
fish line cork .... **BOB**
fish, linglike .... **COD**
fish, long-nosed .... **GAR**
fish, mackerellike
    CERO, TUNNY, TINKER
fish, many .... **SHOAL**
fish, marine **BONITO, TARPON**
fish measure .... **MEASE**
fish, Medit. .... **NONNAT**
fish, nest-building .... **ACARA**
fish net
    SEINE, TRAWL, SPILLER
fish, N. Z. .... **IHI**
fish, No. Pacif. .... **INCONNU**
fish, parasitic .... **REMORA**
fish, perch-like ...... **DARTER**
fish, Pers. myth .... **MAH**
fish pickle .... **ALEC**
fish, piece of ... **FILET, FILLET**
fish, pikelike .... **GAR**
d fish-pitching prong . **PEW, GAFF**
fish-poison tree .... **BITO**
fish, predatory .... **GAR**
fish, river .... **BLAY**
fish, Russian .... **STERLET**
fish sauce .... **ALEC, GARUM**
fish sign .... **PISCES**
fish, silvery .... **MULLET**
fish, small .. **ID, IDE, DARTER**
fish, snouted .... **SAURY**
fish, S. Am. ...... **ARAPAIMA**
fish, sparoid ..... **SAR, SARGO**
fish, spiny ..... **GOBY, PERCH**
fish, sucking .... **REMORA**
fish, trap .... **WEEL, WEIR**
fish, tropical
  SARGO, ROBALO, SALEMA
fish, warm sea
    GUASA, GROUPER
fish, W. Ind.
    BOGA, CERO, TESTAR
fish whisker .... **BARBEL**
fish with moving line .. **TROLL**
fish with net .. **SEINE, TRAWL**
fish, young .... **FRY**
fisherman's hut, Orkney
    SKEO, SKIO
fishhook line-leader ... **SNELL**
fishhook part .... **BARB**
fishing expedition: Scot. **DRAVE**
fishing grounds, Shetlands **HAAF**

fissure .... **RENT, RIFT, RIMA, RIME, CLEFT**
fissures, full of **RIMOSE, RIMOUS**
fist .... **NEAF**
fit .. **APT, RIPE, SUIT, ADAPT**
fit for cultivation .... **ARABLE**
fit for human consumption **POTABLE**
fit of sulks .... **HUFF**
five-dollar bill .... **VEE**
five-franc piece .... **ECU**
five, group of .... **PENTAD**
five in cards .... **PEDRO**
fix or fixed .... **SET**
fixed charge .... **FEE**
fixed income person .. **RENTIER**
fixed payment .... **KIST**
flaccid .... **LIMP**
flag **JACK, ENSIGN, BANDEROLE**
flag, flower, blue .... **IRIS**
flag, military .... **GUIDON**
flag, pirate .... **ROGER**
flag, small **BANNERET, BANNERETTE**
flagellants .... **ALBI**
flag's corner .... **CANTON**
flank .... **SIDE**
flank: dialect .... **LEER**
flannel .... **LANA**
flap .... **TAB, LOMA**
flap, as sails .... **SLAT**
flare .... **FUSEE, FUZEE**
flaring edge.. .. **LIP, FLANGE**
flashed lightning ... **LEVINED**
flask, drinking ..... **CANTEEN**
flat .... **EVEN, LEVEL, PLANE**
flat-bottomed boat **ARK, DORY, PUNT, SCOW**
flat, music ...... **MOL, MOLLE**
flatfish ..... **DAB, RAY, SOLE, BRILL, FLUKE, FLOUNDER**
flatten out .... **CLAP**
flattened .. **OBLATE, PLANATE**
flatter .... **PALP**
flattery .... **PALAVER**
flavor .... **LACE, TANG, AROMA, SAPOR, SEASON**
flavoring plant .. **HERB, LEEK, MINT, ANISE, BASIL**
flavoring root ...... **LICORICE**
flax fiber .... **TOW**
flax, like .... **TOWY**
flax, prepare .... **RET**
flee .... **LAM, BOLT**
fleece .... **FELL, WOOL**
fleece, poorest .... **ABB**
fleet .... **NAVY**
fleet, esp. Span. **ARMADA, ARMADO, ARMATA**
fleet, merchant ...... **ARGOSY**
fleur-de-lis .... **LIS, LYS, LISS**

fleur-de-lis, obs. ...... **LUCE**
flexible .... **LITHE**
flexible wood: dial. .... **EDDER**
flight ..... **HEGIRA, HEJIRA**
flight of ducks .... **SKEIN**
flight organ .... **WING**
flight, pert. to .... **AERO**
flightless bird **EMU, KIWI, WEKA, PENGUIN**
flip .... **SNAP**
flit .... **FLY, GAD**
float **BUOY, RAFT, SWIM, WAFT**
floating .... **NATANT**
floating vegetation on Nile **SADD, SUDD**
floating wreckage .. **FLOTSAM**
flock of quail .... **BEVY**
flock of swans .... **BANK**
flock, pert. to .... **GREGAL**
flock, small .... **COVEY**
flog **BEAT, LASH, WHIP, SWINGE**
flood .... **SEA, EAGRE, SPATE, FRESHET, TORRENT**
floodgate ..... **CLOW, SLUICE**
flora and fauna .... **BIOTA**
floral leaf ..... **BRACT, SEPAL**
Florentine family ..... **MEDICI**
Florida tree .... **MABI**
flounder **DAB, SOLE, FLUKE, PLAICE**
flour sieve .... **BOLTER**
flour, unsorted Ind. **ATA, ATTA**
flourish, music ..... **ROULADE**
flourishing: dialect ..... **FRIM**
flow .... **RUN, FLUX**
flow out .... **EMIT, SPILL**
flow, to stop **STANCH, STAUNCH**
flower cluster **CYME, ANADEM, RACEME**
flower extract **ATAR, OTTO, ATTAR, OTTAR**
flower, fall **ASTER, COSMOS, SALVIA**
flower, field .... **GOWAN**
flower, genus of .... **ROSA**
flower-goddess, Norse **NANNA**
flower-goddess, Rom. .. **FLORA**
flower leaf .. **BRACT, SEPAL**
flower, Oriental ...... **LOTUS**
flower part .... **PETAL, SEPAL, CARPEL, SPADIX**
flower, showy .... **CALLA**
flower spike .... **AMENT**
flowering plant .... **ARUM**
fluctuate .... **WAVER**
fluent .... **GLIB**
fluff, yarn .... **LINT**

58

a fluid, aeriform .... **GAS**
fluid, medical ... **SERA, SERUM**
fluid, serous .... **SERA, SERUM**
fluidity unit .... **RHE**
flume .... **SHUTE, SLUICE**
flushed .... **RED**
flute, ancient Gr. .. **HEMIOPE**
flute, India ... **BIN, MATALAN**
flute, small .... **FIFE**
flutter .. **FLAP, WAVE, HOVER**
fly **GNAT, SOAR, WING, AVIATE**
fly agaric .... **AMANITA**
fly aloft .... **SOAR**
fly, artificial
HARL, HERL, CAHILL, CLARET
fly, kind of .... **BOT**
fly, small ...... **GNAT, MIDGE**
fly, S. Afr. .... **TSETSE**
flycatcher
TODY, ALDER, PEWEE, PHOEBE
flying .... **VOLANT, VOLITANT**
"Flying Dutchman" saver **SENTA**
flying fox .... **KALONG**
flying lemur .... **COLUGO**
flying, of .... **AERO**
flying saucer .... **UFO**
foam .... **SUD, SUDS**
focus .... **CONCENTRATE**
fodder pit .... **SILO**
fodder storage place .... **SILO**
b fodder, to store ...... **ENSILE,
ENSILO, ENSILAGE, ENSILATE**
fog .... **MIST**
fog horn .... **SIRENE**
fog: old Eng. .... **RAG**
foist .... **FOB, PALM**
fold .... **LAP, PLY, PLIE,
RUGA, PLEAT, CREASE**
fold of skin .... **PLICA**
folds, arrange in ...... **DRAPE**
folded .... **PLICATE**
folio .... **PAGE**
folk dance, Slavic ...... **KOLO**
folklore being .... **TROLL**
folkway .... **MOS**
folkways .... **MORES**
follow .... **DOG, TAIL,
ENSUE, TRACE, SHADOW**
follow suit, not **RENIG, RENEGE**
follower .. **IST, ITE, ADHERENT**
foment .... **ABET**
fondle .... **PET, CARESS**
fondness: Ir. .... **GRA**
font .... **LAVER, STOUP**
food .... **FARE, MEAT,
MANNA, ALIMENT, PABULUM**
food bit .... **ORT**
food, farinaceous ..... **SAGO**
food for animals .... **FORAGE**
food forbidden Israelites **TEREFA**

c food, Hawaii .... **POI**
food: Maori, N. Z. ...... **KAI**
food of gods
AMRITA, AMREETA, AMBROSIA
food: Polyn. .... **KAI**
food, provide .... **CATER**
food, soft invalid's ...... **PAP**
foods, choice .... **CATES**
fool..**ASS, DOLT, GABY, RACA,
SIMP, IDIOT, NINNY**
fool's bauble .... **MAROTTE**
fool's gold .... **PYRITE**
foolish .. **DAFT, ZANY, INANE,
SILLY, HARISH, ASININE**
foot, animal's ..... **PAD, PAW**
foot, Chin. .... **CHEK**
foot, Gr. poet. .... **IONIC**
foot, having .... **PEDATE**
foot part, horse's .. **PASTERN**
foot, poet. ... **IAMB, IAMBIC,
IAMBUS, ANAPEST, ANAPAEST**
foot soldier .... **PEON**
foot soldier, Ir. **KERN, KERNE**
foot, two-syllable
SPONDEE, TROCHEE
foot, verse .... **IAMB,
DACTYL, ANAPEST, ANAPAEST**
football position: abbr. ... **FB,
HB, LE, LT, QB, RE, RT**
d footless .... **APOD, APODAL**
footless animal **APOD, APODE**
footless animal genus .. **APODA**
footlike .... **PEDATE**
footlike part .... **PES**
footpad .... **WHYO**
footstalk, leaf .... **STRIG**
footstool **HASSOCK, OTTOMAN**
for .... **PRO**
for example .... **EG**
for fear that .... **LEST**
for shame .... **FIE**
forage plant .. **GUAR, ALSIKE,
LUCERN, ALFALFA, LUCERNE**
foramen .... **PORE**
foray .... **RAID**
forbidden
TABU, TABOO, BANNED
Forbidden City .... **LASSA**
forbidding .... **STERN**
force ...... **VIS, DINT, DRIVE,
IMPEL, POWER, ENERGY,
VIOLENCE**
force, alleged
OD, BIOD, ELOD, ODYL
force, hypothetical .... **OD**
force, unit of .... **DYNE**
force, with .... **AMAIN**
foreboding .... **OMEN**
forefather .... **SIRE**
forefoot .... **PUD**
forefront .... **VAN**

forehead, of the .... METOPIC
forehead strap .... TUMP
foreign in origin ...... EXOTIC
foreign trade discount .. AGIO
foreigner: Hawaii ..... HAOLE
foreigners' quarter, Constanti-
nople .... PERA
foremost part
BOW, VAN, FRONT
foremost segment, insect's
ACRON
foreordain .... DESTINE
foreshadow .... BODE
forest: Brazil .... MATTA
forest clearing .... GLADE
forest: obsolete .... WOLD
forest ox .... ANOA
forest partly inundated GAPO
forest, pert. to
SILVAN, SYLVAN, NEMORAL
forest, P. I. .... GUBAT
forest warden .... RANGER
forestall .... AVERT, PREVENT
foretell .... AUGUR, INSEE
foreteller .... SEER
foretoken .... OMEN
forever .... AY, AYE
forever: Maori .... AKE
forever: poet. ETERN, ETERNE
forfeit .... LOSE, LAPSE
forfeits, Jap. .... KEN
forgetfulness fruit .... LOTUS
forgetfulness water ... LETHE
forgive .... REMIT
forgiving .... CLEMENT
forgo .... WAIVE
form a network .... PLEX
form: Buddhism ...... RUPA
form into line ALIGN, ALINE
form, pert. to .... MODAL
form, philos. .... EIDOS
formal choice .... VOTE
formation, military .. ECHELON
former .... ERST
former ruler CZAR, TSAR, TZAR
formerly .... NEE, ERST, ONCE
formerly: pref. .... EX
formic acid source ..... ANT
formicid .... ANT
formula .... LAW
forsaken .... LORN
fort ...... DIX, ORD, REDAN,
CITADEL, REDOUBT, RAVELIN
fort, N. Z. .... PA, PAH
forth .... OUT
forth, issuing ..... EMANANT
forthwith .... NOW
fortification
REDAN, RAVELIN, REDOUBT

fortification, ditchside
SCARP, ESCARP, ESCARPE
fortification, felled trees
ABATIS
fortification, slope .... TALUS
fortified place ..... LIS, LISS
fortify .... ARM, MAN
fortunate (India) .... SRI
fortune: Gypsy .... BAHI
forty days fast ...... CARENE
forty: Gr. .... MU
forward .... ON, AHEAD
fossil, mollusk .... DOLITE
fossil resin .... RETINITE
fossil worm track ... NEREITE
foul smelling
OLID, FETID, REEKY
found .... BASE
found, thing .... TROVE
foundation .. BED, BASE, BASIS
fountain .... FONS
four, group of ...... TETRAD
four-inch measure ..... HAND
fourth calif (caliph) ..... ALI
fourth estate .... PRESS
fowl .... HEN, CAPON, POULT
fowl's gizzard, etc. .... GIBLET
fox .... TOD
fox, Afr. .... FENNEC
fox hunter's coat ...... PINK
fox, S. Afr. ..... ASSE, CAAMA
"Fra Diavolo" composer AUBER
fraction ..... PART, DECIMAL
fragment, pottery
SHARD, SHERD, SHEARD
fragments .... ANA, ORTS
fragrant .... OLENT
frame, supporting
TRESSEL, TRESTLE
framework .... TRUSS
France .... GAUL
franchise .... CHARTER
Franciscan .... MINORITE
frank .... OPEN, HONEST
Franks, pert. to .... SALIC
frankincense ...... OLIBANUM
Frankish law .... SALIC
Frankish peasant .. LITI, LITUS
fraud .... SHAM
fraught .... LADEN
fray .... MELEE
free .... RID, GRATIS
free-for-all .... FRAY, MELEE
free from discount ..... NET
free from knots: obs. .. ENODE
freebooter .... PIRATE
freedman, Kentish law .. LAET
freehold land, Turkey ... MULK
freeman ...... CEORL, THANE
freight-boat .... ARK

a freight car .... **GONDOLA**
FRENCH WORDS: (accent marks
    omitted throughout)
    according to ..... **ALA, AUX**
    after .... **APRES**
    again .... **ENCORE**
    airplane .... **AVION**
    alas .... **HELAS**
    all .... **TOUT**
    among .... **ENTRE**
    and .... **ET**
    angel .... **ANGE**
    annuity .... **RENTE**
    arm .... **BRAS**
    article ...... **LA, LE, DE,**
    (plural) **DES, LAS, LES, UNE**
    at the home of ..... **CHEZ**
    aunt .... **TANTE**
    baby .... **BEBE**
    bacon .... **LARD**
    back .... **DOS**
    ball .... **BAL**
    bang! .... **PAN**
    bath .... **BAIN**
    beach .... **PLAGE**
    beast .... **BETE**
    before .... **AVANT**
    being .... **ETRE**
    bench .... **BANC**
    between .... **ENTRE**

b   beware .... **GARE**
    bitter .... **AMER**
    black .... **NOIR, NOIRE**
    blue .... **BLEU**
    bread crumbs ...... **PANURE**
    bridge .... **PONT**
    business house .... **CIE**
    but .... **MAIS**
    cabbage .... **CHOU**
    cake .... **GATEAU**
    carefully groomed .. **SOIGNE**
    carriage .... **FIACRE**
    charmed .... **RAVI**
    chicken .... **POULE**
    child .... **ENFANT**
    clear .... **NET**
    climax, theatre ..... **CLOY**
    cloth .... **DRAP**
    cloud .... **NUAGE**
    coarse cloth .... **BURE**
    connective .... **ET**
    cowardly .... **LACHE**
    cup .... **TASSE**
    dance, formal .... **BAL**
    dare .... **OSER**
    daughter .... **FILLE**
    deal .... **DONNE**
    dear .... **CHER, CHERI**
    deed .... **FAIT**
    defy .... **DEFI**

c department .... see SPECIAL
     SECTION, GAZETTEER
    depot .... **GARE**
    detective force .... **SURETE**
    devil .... **DIABLE**
    dirty .... **SALE**
    donkey .... **ANE**
    down with .... **ABAS**
    dream .... **REVE**
    duck to cook .... **CANETON**
    dugout .... **ABRI**
    duke .... **DUC**
    dungeon .... **CACHOT**
    ear of grain .... **EPI**
    east .... **EST**
    egg .... **OEUF**
    elegance .... **LUXE**
    enamel .... **EMAIL**
    equal .... **PAREIL**
    evening .... **SOIR**
    exaggerated .... **OUTRE**
    exclamation .... **HEIN**
    exist .... **ETRE**
    fabric .... **RAS, DRAP**
    father .... **PERE**
    fear .... **PEUR**
    finally .... **ENFIN**
    fingering .... **DOIGTE**
    fire .... **FEU**
    five .... **CINQ**

d for .... **CAR**
    friend .... **AMI, AMIE**
    froth .... **BAVE**
    full .... **PLEIN**
    game .... **JEU, JEUX**
    gift .... **CADEAU**
    god .... **DIEU**
    golden .... **DORE**
    good .... **BON**
    good-bye **ADIEU, AU REVOIR**
    grain ear .... **EPI**
    gray .... **GRIS**
    gravy .... **JUS**
    grimace .... **MOUE**
    ground .... **TERRE**
    half-mask .... **LOUP**
    hall .... **SALLE**
    handle .... **ANSE**
    head .... **TETE**
    health .... **SANTE**
    here .... **ICI**
    hill .... **PUY**
    his .... **SES**
    house .... **MAISON**
    hunting match .... **TIR**
    husband .... **MARI**
    idea .... **IDEE**

(French words continued on
pages 62 and 63)

61

French

FRENCH:

impetuosity	ELAN
in	DANS
income, annual	RENTE
is	EST
island	ILE
kind	SORTE
king	ROI
lamb	AGNEAU
land	TERRE
laugh	RIRE
laughter	RISEE
law	LOI, DROIT
leather	CUIR
lift	LEVE
lily	LIS
little	PEU
lively	VIF
lodging place	GITE
low	BAS
maid	BONNE
mail	POSTE
mask, half	LOUP
material	DRAP
May	MAI
meat dish	SALMI
milk	LAIT
mine	AMOI
mother	MERE
mountain	MONT
museum	MUSEE
nail	CLOU
name	NOM
near	PRES
network	RESEAU
night	NUIT
no	NON
nose	NEZ
nothing	RIEN
number, one	UNE
nursemaid	BONNE
of	DE
one	UNE
our	NOS, NOUS
out	HORS
outbreak	EMEUTE
over	SUR
oyster farm	PARC
petticoat	JUPE, COTTE
picnic spot	BOIS
pinion	AILE
poem	DIT
pork	SALE
pout	MOUE
preposition	DES
pretty	JOLI, JOLIE
pronoun	CES, ILS, MES, TOI, UNE, ELLE
queen	REINE
quickly	VITE
rabbit	LAPIN
railway station	GARE
read	LIRE
rear	ARRIERE
reception	ACCUEIL
rent	LOUER
river	RIVIERE
roast	ROTI
royal edict	ARRET
saint: abbr.	STE
salt	SEL
salted	SALE
school	ECOLE, LYCEE
scow	ACON
sea	MER
security	RENTE
senior	AINE
servant	BONNE
she	ELLE
sheath	ETUI
sheep	MOUTON
shelter	ABRI
shine	LUSTRE
shooting match	TIR
sickness	MAL
silk	SOIE
situated	SISE
small	PETIT
smitten	EPRISE
soldier	POILU
some	DES
son	FILS
soul	AME
spirit	AME
star	ETOILE
state	ETAT
stocking	BAS
storm	ORAGE
summer	ETE
superior quality	LUXE
superfluous	DETROP
surnamed	DIT
sweetmeat	DRAGEE
that	CE, CET, QUE, QUI, CELA
thee	TE
there!	VOILA
they	ILS
thirty	TRENTE
this	CE
thou	TOI
to be	ETRE
to go	ALLER
to love	AIMER
too much	TROP
under	SOUS
upon	SUR
us	NOUS
verb	ETRE
verse	RONDEL

62

a FRENCH:

very	TRES
vineyard	CRU
wall	MUR
water	EAU
wave	ONDE
weapon	ARME
well	BIEN
wine	VIN
wine, delicacy of	SEVE
wine-plant	CEP
wing	AILE
with	AVEC
with the	AU
without	SANS
wood	BOIS
yesterday	HIER
you	TOI
your	VOTRE

Fr., annuity	RENTE
Fr. art group	FAUVES
Fr. artist	DORE, DUFY, GROS, COROT, DEGAS, MANET, MONET, BRAQUE, DERAIN, RENOIR, CHAGALL, CHIRICO, MATISSE, UTRILLO
Fr. artist cult	DADA
Fr. author .. SUE, GIDE, HUGO, LOTI, ZOLA, CAMUS, DUMAS, RENAN, STAEL, VERNE, RACINE, SARTRE, COCTEAU

b

Fr. Calvinist	CALAS
Fr. chalk	TALC
Fr. coin, old	SOU
Fr. commercial company	CIE
FR. COMPOSER	see COMPOSER, FR.
Fr. dramatist	RACINE
Fr. ecclesiastic city	SENS
Fr. explorer	CARTIER
Fr. fort, battle of Verdun	VAUX
Fr. general .... FOCH, HOCHE, GAMELIN
Fr.-Ger. river basin	SAAR
Fr. guerillas	MAQUIS
Fr. Guiana tribesman	BONI
Fr. historical area	ANJOU
Fr. honeysuckle	SULLA
Fr. illustrator	DORE
Fr. island	ILE
Fr. lace-making town	CLUNY
Fr. marshal	NEY, MURAT
FR. NOVELIST see FR. AUTHOR	
FR. PAINTER see FR. ARTIST	
Fr. philosopher	COMTE
Fr. premier, former	LAVAL
Fr. priest	ABBE, PERE
Fr. protectorate	TUNIS
Fr. psychologist	BINET

c

Fr. Revolution month	NIVOSE, FLOREAL, PRAIRAL, VENTOSE, BRUMAIRE, FERVIDOR, FRIMAIRE, MESSIDOR, PLUVIOSE, THERMIDOR
Fr. revolutionist	MARAT
Fr. sculptor	RODIN
Fr. security	RENTE
Fr. singer	PIAF, SABLON
Fr. soprano	PONS, CALVE
Fr. statesman	COTY
FR. WRITER .. see FR. AUTHOR	
Frenchman	GAUL
frenzied	AMOK
frequently	OFT
fresh	NEW, SPICK
fresh supply	RELAY
freshet	FLOOD, SPATE
freshwater worm	NAID, NAIS
fretted	EROSE
Frey's wife	GERD
friar	FRA, MONK
friar, mendicant	SERVITE
friend: law	AMY
friends	KITH
Friendly Islands	TONGA
friendship	AMITY
frigate bird, Hawaiian	IWA
Frigg's brother-in-law	VE
Frigg's husband	ODIN
fright	FUNK, PANIC
frighten	FLEY, ALARM, SCARE
frill, neck	RUFF, JABOT
fringe of curls	FRISETTE
fringe: zool.	LOMA
frisk	PLAY, ROMP
frisky	PEART
FROCK see GARMENT	
frog	TOAD
frog genus	RANA
frogs, order of	ANURA
frogs, pert. to	RANINE
frolic ... LARK, PLAY, ROMP, CAPER, SPORT, SPREE	
from head to foot .	CAP-A-PIE
from: Lat.	DE
from: prefix	AB
front ... VAN, FORE, FACADE	
front page weather box ..	EAR
front, to extend	DEPLOY
frontier post	FORT
frontiersman	BOONE, CARSON
frost	ICE, HOAR, RIME
frosty	RIMY
froth	FOAM, SPUME
frothlike	SPUMY, YEASTY
frown	LOUR, GLOOM, LOWER, SCOWL, GLOWER
frugal	CHARY
fruit	BERRY, OLIVE
fruit, Afr.	PECEGO

d

63

Fruit

a fruit, aggregate ..... ETAERIO
fruit decay .... BLET
fruit dish
    COMPOTE, COMPOTIER
fruitdots, fern .... SORI, SORUS
fruit, dry .... ACHENE
fruit, fleshy ...... PEAR, PEPO
fruit, hard-shelled NUT, GOURD
fruit, India .... BEL
fruit-jelly .... RHOB
fruit, lemonlike ..... CITRON
fruit of maple ...... SAMARA
fruit pigeon, Polyn. ..... LUPE
fruit, plumlike .... SLOE
fruit, pulpy .... UVA, DRUPE
fruit shrub, E. Ind. .... CUBEB
fruit, small, 1-seeded
  AKENE, ACHENE, ACHENIUM
fruit, southern .... PAPAW
fruit squeezer ...... REAMER
fruit, tropical .. DATE, MANGO
fruit, vine .... MELON
fruit, yellow tropical
  PAPAW, PAPAYA, PAWPAW
fruiting spike .... EAR
frustrate ... SCOTCH, THWART
fry lightly .... SAUTE
Fuegan Indian .... ONA
fuel LOG, COAL, COKE, PEAT
fuel ship .... OILER, TANKER
fuel, turf .... PEAT, PEET
fugue theme .... DUX
fulcrum, oar .... THOLE
full .... PLENARY
full and clear ..... OROTUND
fullness .... PLENUM
fulmar .... NELLY, MALDUCK
fume .... REEK, SMOKE

c fun .... SPORT
function ..... GO, USE, WORK
function, trig. ... SINE, COSINE
fundamental
    BASIC, ELEMENTAL
funeral bell KNELL, MORTBELL
funeral music .... DIRGE
funeral notice .... OBIT
funeral oration ...... ELOGE
funeral pile .... PYRE
funeral song .... NENIA
fungi, tissue in .... TRAMA
fungus .... AGARIC
fungus, edible
  MOREL, MORIL, TRUFFLE
fungus, white-spored AMANITA
fur ...... SEAL, VAIR, GENET
  MARTEN, NUTRIA, MINIVER
fur cape .... PELERINE
fur: Her. PEAN, VAIR, VAIRE
furbelow ...... FRILL, RUFFLE
Furies, Gr. .... ERINYS
ERINNYS, ERINYES, ERINNYES
Furies, one of
ALECTO, MEGAERA, TISIPHONE
Furies, Rom. .... DIRAE
furlongs, eight .... MILE
furnish crew .... MAN
furnish with .... ENDOW
furnishings, mode of .. DECOR
furrows, with RIVOSE, RUTTED
further .... AID, YET
furtive .... SLY, SNEAKY
fury .... IRE
furze .... WHIN, WHUN,
  GORSE, GORST, GORSTE
fuse partly .... FRIT
fuss .... ADO, TO-DO

G

b gabl .... TARO
Gad, son of .... ARELI
gadget .... GISMO
Gael .... SCOT
Gaelic .. ERSE, CELTIC, KELTIC
Gaelic poem .... DUAN
Gaelic sea god .... LER
gaff .... SPAR
gain .... GET, WIN, EARN
goit .. LOPE, CANTER, GALLOP
gait, horse's ..... PACE, RACK
Galahad's mother ..... ELAINE
Galatea's beloved ..... ACIS
Galilee town .... CANA
galla ox ...... SANGA, SANGU
gallery, art .... SALON
gallery: hist. .... ALURE

d gallery, open .... LOGGIA
gallery protecting troops
    ECOUTE
galley, armed, old Northmen's
    AESC
galley, fast
    DROMON, DROMOND
galley, 1 oar bank UNIREME
galley, 2 oar banks .. BIREME
galley, 3 oar banks TRIREME
gallop, rapid .... TANTIVY
gallop slowly .... LOPE
Galsworthy heroine .... IRENE
Galway Bay, isles in .... ARAN
gamble .... GAME
gambling place ...... CASINO

a gambol .... **DIDO, CAPER**
game ... **LOTO, BINGO, LOTTO**
game, Basque .... **PELOTA**
game, board ... **CHESS, HALMA**
game, card .... **LU, LOO, NAP,
PAM, PUT, FARO, CINCH,
MACAO, MONTE, OMBER,
OMBRE, STUSS, TAROT,
WHIST, BASSET, CASINO,
ECARTE, ROUNCE, CA-
NASTA**
game, child's .... **TAG**
game, dice .... **LUDO**
game, follow .... **STALK**
game, gambling
FARO, PICO, STUSS
game, Hawaii .... **HEI**
game, Ind. guessing .. **CANUTE**
game, It. guessing .... **MORA**
game of skill ..... **POOL, CHESS**
game piece ... **MAN, DOMINO**
gamecock .... **STAG**
gamekeeper .... **RANGER**
gaming cube .... **DIE, DICE**
Ganges boat .... **PUTELI**
gangplank .... **RAMP**
gangster .. **MUG, THUG, WHYO**
gannet, common ...... **SOLAN**
gannet genus .... **SULA**
gap .... **HIATUS, LACUNA**
gap in hedge
b   **MUSE, MEUSE, MUSET**
gar fish .... **SNOOK**
garland .... **LEI, ANADEM**
GARMENT . see **COAT, BLOUSE**
garment .... **ROBE**
garment, Arab .... **ABA**
garment, bishop's
CHIMAR, CHIMER, CHIMERE
garment, church ..... **COTTA**
**GARMENT, CLERICAL OR EC-
CLESIASTIC,** see **GARMENT,
PRIESTLY**
garment, fitted .... **REEFER**
garment, India, Hindu .. **SARI,
SAREE, BANIAN, BANYAN**
GARMENT, LITURGICAL
see **GARMENT, PRIESTLY**
garment, loose .**CAMIS, CAMUS,
CYMAR, SIMAR, CAMISE**
garment, Malay .... **SARONG**
garment, Moslem ...... **IZAR**
garment, N. Afr. .... **HAIK**
garment, Old Ir. .... **INAR**
garment, outer
CAPOTE, PALETOT
garment, Polyn. ...... **PAREU**
garment, priestly .. **ALB, COPE,
AMICE, EPHOD, STOLE**
garment, rain .... **PONCHO**
garment, scarflike .... **TIPPET**

c garment, Turk. .... **DOLMAN**
garment, woman's
BODICE, MANTUA
garnishment .... **LIEN**
garret .... **ATTIC**
garter snake genus ... **ELAPS**
gas .... **FUEL, NEON**
gas apparatus ...... **AERATOR**
gas, charge with ..... **AERATE**
gas, colorless .... **OXAN**
gas, inert .... **ARGON, XENON**
gas, radioactive
RADON, NITON
GASEOUS ELEMENT
see **ELEMENTS, SPECIAL
SECTION, Page 195**
gaseous sky "cloud" ... **NEBULA**
GASTROPOD see also **MOLLUSK**
gastropod ...... **WELK, WILK,
WHELK, LIMPET**
gastropod, Haliotis .. **ABALONE**
gate .... **PORTAL**
gate, water .... **SLUICE**
gateway .... **PYLON**
gateway, Buddhist temple
TORAN, TORANA
gateway, Pers. .... **DAR**
gateway, Shinto temple . **TORII**
gather .... **AMASS, GLEAN,
GARNER, MUSTER**
gather, as grouse .... **LEK**
d gather in bundles .... **SHEAVE**
gathers, put in
SHER, SHIR, SHIRR
gaunt .... **SPARE**
Gawain's father .... **LOT**
gazelle .... **ARIEL**
gazelle, Afr. ... **ADMI, DAMA,
MOHR, KORIN, MHORR**
gazelle, Asia .... **AHU**
gazelle, black-tailed ..... **GOA**
gazelle, Pers. .... **CORA**
gazelle, Sudan .... **DAMA**
gazelle, Tibetan .... **GOA**
gear .... **CAM**
gear tooth .... **COG**
gear wheel, smallest .. **PINION**
Geb's consort .... **NUT**
Gelderland city .... **EDE**
gelid .... **ICY, COLD**
GEM .... see also **STONE**
gem ...... **JADE, ONYX, OPAL,
RUBY, SARD, AGATE, PEARL,
STONE, GARNET, SPINEL,
EMERALD, PERIDOT**
gem-bearing earth, Burma **BYON**
gem, carved .... **CAMEO**
gem facet ..... **BEZEL, BEZIL,
CULET, COLLET**
gem weight .... **CARAT**
Gemini's mortal half .. **CASTOR**

65

Gender

gender, a .... **NEUTER**
genealogy .... **TREE**
GENERAL, CIVIL WAR
 see CIVIL WAR COMMANDER
general, Morocco .... **KAID**
general Sitting Bull defeated
 CUSTER
generation .... **AGE**
Genesis matriarch ...... **SARAI**
genie, Egypt. .... **HAPI**
genip tree .... **LANA**
genipap wood .... **LANA**
gentle . **MILD, TAME, TENDER**
gentle breeze .... **AURA**
gentle heat .... **TEPOR**
genuflect .... **KNEEL**
GENUS . see PLANT or
 ANIMAL named
genus of plants .... **ARUM**
geode **VUG, VOOG, VUGG, VUGH**
geological division **LIAS, LYAS**
geol. epoch **BALA, ECCA, LIAS,
 MUAV, ERIAN, UINTA,
 PLIOCENE**
geol. formation ..... **TERRAIN,
 TERRANE, TERRENE**
geol. period .... **DYAS,
 EOCENE, MIOCENE**
geol. stage ..... **RISS, ACHEN**
geol. vein angle ...... **HADE**
geometric ratio .... **SINE**
geometric solid
 CONE, CUBE, PRISM
geometrical lines ..... **LOCI,
 LOCUS, SECANT**
geometry rule ...... **THEOREM**
geometry term .... **VERSOR**
geophagy .... **PICA**
George Sand novel ..... **LELIA**
Geraint's wife .... **ENID**
geranium lake color . **NACARAT**
germ .. **BUG, VIRUS, MICROBE**
germ-free **ASEPTIC, ANTISEPTIC**
germs, produced by .... **SEPTIC**
GERMAN . see also TEUTONIC
GERMAN WORDS: (umlauts
omitted throughout)
 "A" .... **EIN**
 above .... **UBER**
 again .... **UBER**
 alas .... **ACH**
 article ...... **DAS, DER, EIN**
 ass .... **ESEL**
 beer .... **BIER**
 blood .... **BLUT**
 conjunction .... **UND**
 count .... **GRAF**
 donkey .... **ESEL**
 dumpling .... **KNODEL**
 eat .... **ESSEN**

 eight .... **ACHT**
 evening .... **ABEND**
 everything .... **ALLES**
 exclamation .... **HOCH**
 four .... **VIER**
 gentleman .. **HERR, HERREN**
 hall .... **AULA, SAAL**
 heaven .... **HIMMEL**
 hunter .... **JAGER**
 "I" .... **ICH**
 ice .... **EIS**
 iron .... **EISEN**
 is .... **IST**
 it .... **ES**
 league (s) .... **BUND, BUNDE**
 love .... **LIEBE**
 mister .... **HERR**
 nation .... **VOLK**
 never .... **NIE**
 new .... **NEUE**
 no .... **NEIN**
 noble .... **EDEL**
 old .... **ALT**
 one .... **EIN, EINE**
 out of .... **AUS**
 pronoun .... **ICH**
 people .... **VOLK**
 school hall .... **AULA**
 softly .... **LEISE**
 song .... **LIED**
 spirit .... **GEIST**
 state .... **STAAT**
 steel .... **STAHL**
 temperament ...... **GEMUT**
 than .... **ALS**
 the .... **DAS, DER**
 three .... **DREI**
 thunder .... **DONNER**
 title .... **VON, PRINZ**
 town .... **STADT**
 us .... **UNS**
 very .... **SEHR**
 with .... **MIT**
 without .... **OHNE**
 yes .... **JA**
 you .... **SIE**
 your ...... **IHR, DEIN, EUER**

German .... **BOCHE**
Ger. admiral .... **SPEE**
Ger. bacteriologist ..... **KOCH**
Ger. camp, war ..... **STALAG**
GER. COMPOSER
 see COMPOSER, GER.
Ger.-Czech region ... **SUDETEN**
Ger. district, old ...... **GAU**
Ger. dive bomber ..... **STUKA**
Ger. emperor .... **OTTO**
Ger. highway ..... **AUTOBAHN**
Ger. John .... **HANS**

66

German

Ger. king .... OTTO
Ger. landscape painter .. ROOS
Ger. name prefix .... VON
Ger. philosopher . KANT, HEGEL
Ger. physicist .. OHM, ERMAN
Ger. president .... EBERT
Ger. princely family ..... WELF
Ger. theologian .... ARND
Ger. title .. VON, GRAF, PRINZ
Ger. tribal region
            GAU, GAUE, GAUS
Germanic deity .... DONAR
Germanic letter .... RUNE
gesture dance, Samoa; Fiji SIVA
get out! . SCAT, SHOO, SCRAM
ghastly .... LURID
ghost .... HANT, SPOOK,
            SPECTER, SPECTRE
ghost, India .... BHUT
ghost-town state: abbrev.: UT
giant .... TITAN
giant, frightful .... OGRE
giant, Hindu myth ..... BANA
giant, killed by Apollo .. OTUS
giant, Norse, Scand. myth YMER,
        YMIR, JOTUM, MIMIR
giant, Rom. .... CACA
giant, 1000-armed, Hindu BANA
giants, Bibl. .... ANAK, EMIM
gibbon, Malay .... LAR
gift, receiver of .... DONEE
gig .... NAPPER
gigantic person .... TITAN
"Gil —" LeSage novel .. BLAS
Gilead's descendant .... ULAM
Gilgit language, Kashmir SHINA
gills, four .... PINT
gilt .... DORE
gin .... TRAP
gingerbread tree .... DUM
ginkgo tree .... ICHO
GIPSY .... see GYPSY
giraffe-like animal .... OKAPI
girasol .... OPAL
girder .... TRUSS
girdle .... OBI, CEST, SASH
girl .... SIS, CHIT,
            DAME, SKIRT
GIRL'S NAME
        see WOMAN'S NAME
girth, saddle .... CINCH
gist .... NUB, PITH
give: law .... REMISE
give reluctantly ..... GRUDGE
give up .. CEDE, WAIVE, YIELD
give up wholly ...... DEVOTE
give way .... YIELD
glacial hill .... PAHA
glacial ice block, pinnacle SERAC
glacial ridge ... AS, OS, ASAR,
        KAME, OSAR, ESCAR,
        ESKAR, ESKER

glacial snow field FIRN, NEVE
glacial stage .... WURM
glacier chasm
            CREVAS, CREVASSE
glacier, facing a .... STOSS
gladiolus .... IRID
gladly .... FAIN
gland .... PINEAL, THYROID
gland, edible .... NOIX
glass .... LENS
glass, blue .... SMALT
glass bubble .... BLEB
glass defect .... TEAR
glass, flatten ...... PLATTEN
glass furnace mouth .. BOCCA
glass ingredient ..... SILICON
glass-like material .... PLASS
glass maker .... GLAZIER
glass, molten .... PARISON
glass, partly fused FRIT, FRITT
glass, transparent ..... UVIOL
glass vial .. AMPULE, AMPOULE
glassmaker's oven . LEER, LEHR
glasswort .... KALI
glassy .... HYALINE
glazier's tack .... BRAD
gleam .... GLINT
glide .... SKIM, SLIP,
            SKATE, SLIDE
glittering piece ..... SPANGLE
globe .... ORB, SPHERE
global .... ROUND, SPHERAL
gloom ...... MIRK, MURK
gloomy ...... DARK, DOUR,
            DREAR, DREARY
"Gloomy Dean" .... INGE
glossy-surfaced ...... GLACE
glottal stop: Dan. .... STOD
glove leather ..... KID, NAPA,
            MOCHA, SUEDE
glove shape, unstitched TRANK
glowing .... CANDENT
glucoside, root .... GEIN
glut ... SATE, GORGE, SATIATE
gnarl .... NUR, KNUR, NURR
gnat, small .... MIDGE
gnome .... NIS, GREMLIN
go .... WEND
go astray ..... ABERRATE
go astray slightly .... ERR
go back .... REVERT
go forth .... FARE
go hence: Lat. .... VADE
go on! .... GARN, SCAT
go shufflingly .. MOSY, MOSEY
goad .... PROD, SPUR, INCITE
goal .... AIM, END
goat, Alpine mountain .. IBEX
goat antelope .... GORAL
goat, Asian .... JAGLA

67

a
goat, genus .... **CAPRIA**
goat god .... **PAN**
goat, wild .. **TUR, IBEX, TAHR, TAIR, TEHR, THAR**
goatsucker .... **POTOO**
gob .... **TAR**
Gobi Desert .... **SHAMO**
goblet .... **HANAP**
goblin .... **POOK, PUCA, PUCK**
goblin, Egypt .... **OUPHE**
goblin, Norse **NIS,NISSE,KOBOLD**
goby, small .... **MAPO**
GOD . see also DEITY, and see also SPECIAL SECTION
god, Babyl. **EA, ABU, ANU, BEL**
GOD, CHIEF see CHIEF NORSE GOD, also BABYLONIAN CHIEF GOD
god: Chin. .... **SHEN**
god: Hebrew .... **EL**
god: Jap .... **KAMI**
god: Lat. .... **DEUS**
god of alcoholic drinks, **SIRIS**
god of Arcadia .... **PAN**
GOD OF CHAOS ... see CHAOS
god of darkness—evil, Egyp. **SET, SETH**
god of dead, Hindu .... **YAMA**
god of dead, Rom. .... **ORCUS**
b god of discord, Norse **LOK, LOKE, LOKI**
god of earth, Babyl. .. **DAGAN**
GOD OF EARTH, Egyptian see EARTH GOD
god of evil: Egyp. .. **SET, SETH**
god of evil, to ward off **BES,BESA**
god of fertility, Norse ... **FREY**
god of fields, flocks, forest **PAN, FAUN**
god of fire ... **AGNI, VULCAN**
god of Hades ..... **DIS, PLUTO**
god of harvests ...... **CRONUS**
god of light, Norse **BALDR, BALDER, BALDUR**
god of love, Gr. .... **EROS**
god of love, Rom. **AMOR, CUPID**
god of love, Vedic .... **BHAGA**
god of mirth .. **COMUS, KOMOS**
god (goddess) of mischief .. **ATE**
god of michief, Norse **LOK, LOKE, LOKI**
GOD OF MOON see MOON GOD
god of music .... **APOLLO**
god of north wind ... **BOREAS**
god of pleasure ..... **BES, BESA**
god of procreation, Egyp. **MIN**
god of prosperity, Teutonic **FREY**
god of revelry, Gr. ... **COMUS, KOMOS**
god of ridicule .... **MOMUS**
GOD OF SEA .... see SEA GOD
GOD OF SKY .... see SKY GOD

c God of Southeast Wind: Gr. **EURUS**
GOD OF STORMS see STORM GOD
GOD OF SUN .... see SUN GOD
god of thunder **THOR, DONAR**
god of Tuesday **TIU, TIW, TYR**
GOD OF UNDERWORLD see UNDERWORLD GOD
god of war, Assyrian **ASUR, ASSUR**
god of war, Babyl. . **IRA, IRRA**
god of war, Gr. .... **ARES**
god of war, Norse **TY, TYR, TYRR**
god of war, Rom. .... **MARS**
god of war, Teut. .... **ER**
god of wind, Norse .... **VAYU**
god of wind, storm, Babylonian **ZU, ADAD, ADDA, ADDU**
god of winds, Gr. .... **AEOLUS**
god of wisdom, Babyl. **NABU, NEBO**
god of wisdom, Norse .. **ODIN**
god of youth .... **APOLLO**
god skilled with bow, Norse **ULL**
god, Sumerian .... **ABU**
god, unknown, Hindu ..... **KA**
gods, Chief Teut., Norse **AESIR**
gods: Lat. .... **DI**
d gods, mother of .... **RHEA**
gods, mother of: Ir. **ANA, ANU**
GODS, QUEEN OF see QUEEN OF GODS
gods, the .... **DEI, DII**
GODDESS see also SPECIAL SECT.
GODDESS, CHIEF see BABYLONIAN CHIEF GODDESS
goddess, cow-headed ..... **ISIS**
goddess: Latin .... **DEA**
GODDESS, MOTHER see MOTHER GODDESS
goddess of agriculture **CERES, DEMETER**
goddess of art or science . **MUSE**
goddess of astronomy **URANIA**
goddess of beauty: Norse **FREYA**
goddess of betrothal, Norse **VOR**
goddess of chase . **DIAN, DIANA**
goddess of crops, Rom. **ANNONA**
goddess of dawn, Gr. ..... **EOS**
goddess of dawn, Rom. **AURORA**
goddess of dawn, Vedic .. **USAS**
goddess of dead ... **HEL, HELA**
goddess of deep, Babyl. . **NINA**
goddess of destiny, Norse **URD, URTH**
goddess of destruction ... **ARA**
goddess of discord .. **ATE, ERIS**
goddess of earth, Teut. . **ERDA**

68

goddess of earth ... GE, ERDA, GAEA, GAIA, TARI
goddess of earth: Rom. CERES, TERRA
goddess of faith, Rom. . FIDES
goddess of fate, Rom. NONA, PARCA
goddess of fate, Teutonic NORN
goddess of fertility ASTARTE
goddess of fertility, Anatolian MA
goddess of field, Rom. . FAUNA
goddess of flowers, Gr. CHLORIS
goddess of flowers, Norse NANNA
goddess of flowers, Rom. FLORA
goddess of grain CERES, DEMETER
goddess of harvest ...... OPS
goddess of harvest, Attica CARPO
goddess of healing ...... EIR
goddess of hearth ..... VESTA
goddess of heavens, Egyp. . NUT
goddess of hope .... SPES
goddess of hunt . DIAN, DIANA
goddess of infatuation .. ATE
goddess of justice . MA, MAAT
goddess of love ...... VENUS, ASTARTE, APHRODITE
goddess of love, Babylonian ISTAR, ISHTAR
goddess of love, Norse FREYA, FREYJA
goddess of magic .... HECATE
GODDESS OF MATERNITY see MATERNITY GODDESS
goddess of mischief .... ATE
GODDESS OF MOON see MOON GODDESS
goddess of nature CYBELE, ARTEMIS
GODDESS OF NIGHT, NORSE see NIGHT, NORSE
goddess of night: Rom.NOX,NYX
goddess of peace IRENE, EIRENE
goddess of plenty .... OPS
goddess of prosperity: Rom. SALUS
goddess of retribution .... ATE
goddess of retribution, Gr. ARA
goddess of revenge .. NEMESIS
GODDESS OF SEA see SEA GODDESS
goddess of seasons .... HORAE
goddess of splendor, Hindu UMA
goddess of truth, Egypt MA, MAAT
GODDESS OF UNDERWORLD see UNDERWORLD GODDESS

goddess of vegetation .. CORA, KORE, CERES
goddess of vengeance .... ARA
goddess of victory ...... NIKE
goddess of volcanoes, Hawaii PELE
goddess of war, Gr. .... ENYO
goddess of wisdom ATHENA, PALLAS
goddess of woods ...... DIAN, DIANA, ARTEMIS
goddess of youth ...... HEBE
goddess, Queen .. HERA, JUNO
goddesses of destiny ... FATES
goddesses of fate, Gr. MOERAE
goddesses of fate, Norse NORNS
Goethe drama .... FAUST
Goethe heroine ...... MIGNON
golconda .... MINE
gold .... AU, CYME, GILT
gold alloy, ancient ..... ASEM
Gold Coast Negro ...... GA
Gold Coast tong. CHI, TWI, TSHI
gold-colored metal . ORMOLU
gold, cover with .... GILD
gold deposit .... PLACER
gold district-field, Afr. .. RAND
gold: Her. .... OR
gold, mosaic .... ORMOLU
gold, pert. to .... AURIC
golden .... AUREATE
Golden Fleece keeper .. AEETES
Golden Fleece seeker .. JASON
golden in color .. DORE, DURRY
golden oriole .... PIROL
golden oriole, Eur. .... LORIOT
golden-touch king .... MIDAS
golf attendant .. CADY, CADDY
golf club ..... IRON, CLEEK, MASHIE, PUTTER
golf club, part .... TOE
golf club socket .... HOSEL
golf hole .... CUP
golf pro .... SNEAD
golf score .... PAR
golf stroke-shot .. PUT, BAFF, CHIP, LOFT, PUTT, DRIVE, SCLAFF
golf term ..... LIE, PAR, TEE
golfer .... TEER
gomuti .... ARENGA
gondolier's song BARCAROLE, BARCAROLLE
gone .... OUT, AWAY
gone by .... AGO, PAST, YORE
gonfalon .... BANNER
good-bye: Fr. ADIEU,AU REVOIR
good digestion .... EUPEPSIA
good health, in .... PEART
"Good King" .... HAL
good news EVANGEL, EVANGILE

Good

"Good Queen Bess," name for .... ORIANA
good: Tagalog .... MABUTI
goods .... WARES
goods in sea .... JETSAM
goods sunk at sea ..... LAGAN, LIGAN
goose barnacle genus .. LEPAS
goose cry ...... HONK, YANG
goose genus .... ANSER
goose, male .... GANDER
goose, sea .... SOLAN
goose, wild .... BRANT
gooseberry .... FABES
gopher tortoise ... MUNGOFA
gorge .... GLUT, CHASM, FLUME, RAVINE
Gorgons, one of ..... MEDUSA
gorse ... WHIN, WHUN, FURZE
goshawk genus . ASTUR, BUTEO
gospel ... EVANGEL, EVANGILE
gossamer .... WEB
gossip .... EME
gossip: India .... GUP
Gottfried's sister ...... ELSA
gourd fruit .... PEPO
gourd rattle .... MARACA
gourmet .... EPICURE
gout of knee ...... GONAGRA
government .... STATE
government control .... REGIE, STATISM
governor .... REGENT
governor, Mecca .... SHERIF, SHEREEF
governor, Persia ..... SATRAP
governor, Turkish ...... BEY GOWN ..... see GARMENT
grace .... ADORN
Graces' mother ...... AEGLE
Graces, The . AGLAIA, THALIA
graceful .... GAINLY
grackle .... DAW, MINA, MYNA, MYNAH
grade .... RANK, RATE, SORT, STEP
gradient .... SLOPE
Graf —, ship .... SPEE
graft .... CION, SCION
grafted: Her. .... ENTE
Grail, Holy, finder of .... BORS
grain .... OAT, RYE, SEED, WALE, SPELT, MILLET
grain beetle .... CADELLE
grain, chaff of .... BRAN
grain, coarse .... SAMP
grain given Romans . ANNONA
grain, sorghum, Ind., ... DARI, DORA, DURR, MILO, CHENA, DARRA, DARSO, DURRA, DHURRA, DOURAH, HEGARI

grain, sorghum, U. S. FETERITA
grain, stalks of ...... HAULM
grain to grind .... GRIST
gram molecule .... MOL
grammatically, describe . PARSE
grampus .... ORC
granary, India .... GOLA, GUNJ, GUNGE
grandparental .... AVAL
grandson, Adam's, Eve's. . ENOS
grant .... CEDE, MISE, REMISE
grant, India, Hindu .... ENAM
grant of rights .... PATENT, CHARTER
granular snow .... FIRN, NEVE
grape .... UVA, MUSCAT, CATAWBA, CONCORD
grape conserve .... UVATE
grape disease .... ESCA
grape genus .... VITIS
grape jelly .... SAPA
grape juice DIBS, MUST, STUM
grape juice sirup ...... SAPA
grape-like .. UVA, UVAL, UVIC
grape-like fruit .... UVA
grape refuse .... MARC
grape, white .... MALAGA
grapefruit .. POMELO, PUMELO
graphite .... KISH
grasp .... SEIZE
grass .... POA, REED, DARNEL
grass, Andes .... ICHU
grass, blue .... POA
grass, coarse .... REED, SEDGE
grass genus ...... AIRA, COIX, AVENA, STIPA
grass, kind of .... RIE
grass, marsh .... REED, SEDGE, FESCUE
grass, N. Afr. .... ALFA
grass, pasture .... GRAMA
grass rope: Sp. .... SOGA
grass, rope-making .... MUNG, MUNJ
grass, sour .... SORREL
grass stem .... CULM
grass tuff .... HASSOCK
grass, yard, wire .... POA
grasshopper .... GRIG
grassland .... SAVANNA, SAVANNAH
grassland, S. Afr. ..... VELDT
grasslands, Western ... RANGE
grate .... JAR, RASP, GRIDE
gratify . SATE, ARRIDE, PLEASE
grating . GRID, GRILL, GRILLE
gratuitous .... FREE
gratuity .... FEE, TIP
gratuity, customer ..... PILON
grave .... SOBER

70

a gravestone, Gr. & Rom. **STELA,**
    STELE, STELAE, STELAI
graving tool .... **STYLET**
Gray, botanist .... **ASA**
gray .... **OLD, HOAR,**
    ASHEN, SLATE
gray kingbird .... **PIPIRI**
gray, mole .... **TAUPE**
gray parrot .... **JAKO**
gray plaid, gray shawl .. **MAUD**
grayish-brown ... **DUN, TAUPE**
graze ...... **AGIST, BROWSE**
grease ... **OIL, LARD, AXUNGE**
great barracuda ...... **PICUDA**
Great Barrier Island, N. Z. **OTEA**
"Great Emancipator" .... **ABE**
great: Gypsy .... **BARO**
greater ...... **MORE, MAJOR**
Greece, ancient name . **HELLAS**
Greece, modern .... **ELLAS**
greedy .... **AVID**

   Greek Letters, Numbers:
Greek A, One .... **ALPHA**
Greek B, Two .... **BETA**
Greek D, Four .... **DELTA**
Greek E, Eight .... **ETA**
Greek I, Ten .... **IOTA**
Greek M, Forty .... **MU**
b Greek N, Fifty .... **NU**
Greek O, 800 .... **OMEGA**
Greek P, Eighty .... **PI**
Greek R, 100 .... **RHO**
Greek T, 300 .... **TAU**
Greek Z, Seven .... **ZETA**
Greek 90 .... **KOPPA**
Greek 900 .... **SAMPI**
Gr. ancient .... **ATTIC**
Gr. assembly .... **AGORA**
Gr. athletic contest .... **AGON**
Gr. authors .... **ZENO, AESOP,**
   HOMER, PLATO, TIMON,
   HESIOD, PINDAR, SAPPHO,
   STRABO, THALES, PLU-
   TARCH
Gr. city, ancient **ELIS, SPARTA**
Gr. city, word for ..... **POLIS**
Gr. colony, ancient .... **IONIA**
Gr. column ..... **DORIC, IONIC**
Gr. commonalty ...... **DEMOS**
Gr. community .... **DEME**
Gr. dialect ..... **EOLIC, AEOLIC**
Gr. district, ancient ... **ATTICA**
Gr. drama .... **MIME**
Gr. festival city ...... **NEMEA**
Gr. galley **TRIREME, UNIREME**
Gr. garment .... **CHITON**
Gr. ghost .... **KER**
GREEK GODS, GODDESSES . see
   SPECIAL SECTION and see
   GODS, GODDESSES
Gr. hero ...... **AJAX, JASON**

c Gr. historian .... **CTESIAS**
Gr. January .... **GAMELION**
Gr. legendary hero ...... **IDAS**
Gr. market place ..... **AGORA**
Gr. meeting place of voters
                  PNYX
Gr. musical term .. **MESE, NETE**
Gr. myth flier .... **ICARUS**
Gr. native .... **CRETAN**
Gr. patriarch .... **ARIUS**
Gr. philosopher **PLATO, THALES**
Gr. poet ..... **ARION, HOMER,**
              PINDAR
Gr. poetess .. **SAPHO, SAPPHO**
Gr. poetry, simple ..... **DORIC**
Gr. priest .... **MYST**
Gr. princess .... **IRENE**
Gr. province .... **NOME**
Gr. resistance group .... **EDES**
Gr. rose .... **CAMPION**
Gr. sculptor .... **PHIDIAS**
Gr. shield .... **PELTA**
Gr. slave .... **PENEST**
Gr. statesman .... **ARISTIDES**
Gr. temple .... **NAOS**
Gr. theologian .... **ARIUS**
Gr. township-commune .. **DEME**
Gr. underground .... **ELAS**
Gr. vase .... **PELIKE**
d Gr. weight, old ... **MNA, MINA**
green ..... **NILE, VERD, VERT,**
    OLIVE, RESEDA
green chalcedony ..... **JASPER**
green cheese .... **SAPSAGO**
green chrysolite ..... **PERIDOT**
green copper arsenate . **ERINITE**
green fly .... **APHID**
green: Her. .... **VERT**
Green Mountain hero ... **ALLEN**
green parrot: P. I. .... **CAGIT**
green stone ... **JADE, PERIDOT**
greenish yellow **OLIVE, RESEDA**
Greenland Eskimo .... **ITA**
Greenland geol. div. .... **KOME**
Greenland settlement, town,
   base .... **ETAH**
Greenland's colonizer ... **ERIC**
greeting .. **AVE, HAIL, SALUTE**
gridiron .... **GRILL**
grief .... **DOLOR, DOLOUR**
griffon genus .... **GYPS**
grimalkin .... **CAT**
grinding .... **MOLAR**
grindstone, Indian ..... **MANO**
grit .... **SAND**
grivet .... **WAAG**
grivet monkey .... **TOTA**
grommet, naut. ...... **BECKET**
groom, India . **SAIS, SICE, SYCE**
groove .... **RUT, SCARF**

71

Groove

a groove, pilaster **STRIA, STRIAE**
grooved ..... **LIRATE, STRIATE**
grope .... **FEEL**
gross .... **CRASS**
ground grain .... **MEAL**
ground wheat-husk .... **BRAN**
groundhog .... **MARMOT**
group .... **BAND, BODY,
CREW, TEAM**
group, animal .... **NID, NYE,
HERD, NIDE, COVEY,
DROVE, CLUTCH**
grouper .... **MERO**
grouse .... **PTARMIGAN**
grouse, red: Scot. . **MUIRFOWL**
grove, small-tree ... **COPSE**
grow .... **WAX, RAISE**
grow together ..... **ACCRETE**
growing out .... **ENATE**
growl .... **YAR, GNAR,
YARR, SNARL**
growth, skin .... **WEN**
grub .... **LARVA**
grudge .... **SPITE**
gruel, maize .... **ATOLE**
gruesome .. **GRISLY, MACABRE**
guarantees .... **SURETIES**
b guard .... **SENTRY**
guard, as door .... **TILE**
guardhouse .... **BRIG**
guardian, alert
ARGUS, CERBERUS
Guatemala fruit ...... **ANAY**
guava .... **ARACA**
Gudrun's husband
ATLI, SIGURD
Guenon monkey ...... **MONA**
guest house .... **INN**
Guiana tree .... **MORA**
guide .... **LEAD, PILOT, STEER**
guiding .... **POLAR**
guiding rule .... **MOTTO**
Guido's note ...... **UT, ELA**
guild, merchants' .... **HANSE**
guillemot ...... **COOT, MURR,
MURRE**
guilty .... **NOCENT**
guinea fowl's young .... **KEET**
guinea pig .... **CAVY**
gulch: Sp. .... **ARROYO**
GULF, ... also see GAZETTEER
gulf, Ionia sea .... **ARTA**
gulf, Medit. .... **TUNIS**

c gull ..... **MEW, SKUA, TERN,
WAEG, XEMA**
gull, fork-tailed .... **XEMA**
gull genus ...... **LARI, XEMA**
gulls, of, like .... **LARINE**
gullet .... **MAW, CRAW**
gullible person .. **DUPE, GULL**
"Gulliver's Travels," men
YAHOOS
gully: Afr. .... **DONGA**
gulp .... **SWIG**
gum .... **RESIN, BALATA**
gum arabic
ACACIA, ACACIN, ACACINE
gum, astringent .... **KINO**
gum resin .... **ELEMI, LOBAN,
MYRRH**
gum resin, aromatic ... **MYRRH**
gum, Somaliland ..... **MATTI**
gums .... **ULA**
gumbo ... **OCRA, OKRA, OKRO**
gumbo-limbo tree ... **GOMART**
gun .... **GAT**
gun, British .... **STEN**
gun fire, burst of ..... **SALVO**
gun, Ger. .... **BERTHA**
d gun, kind of .... **BREN**
gun lock catch .... **SEAR**
gun, P. I. .... **BARIL**
gun, slang ..... **ROD, HEATER
ROSCOE**
gun: S. Afr. ..... **ROER, ROHR**
gunny cloth .... **TAT**
gusto .... **ZEST**
gutta mixture .... **SOH**
gutta, Sumatra .... **SIAK**
guy-rope .. **STAT, STAY, VANG**
gym feat .... **KIP**
gymnast .... **TURNER**
gypsum, kind of . **YESO, GESSO,
YESSO, SELENITE**
gypsy .... **ROM, CALE, CALO,
ROAMER, ROMANY**
gypsy boy .... **ROM**
gypsy gentleman .... **RYE**
gypsy girl .... **CHAI**
gypsy husband .... **ROM**
gypsy lady .... **RANI**
gypsy married woman ... **ROMI**
gypsy: Sp. .... **GITANO**
gypsy tent, camp .... **TAN**
gypsy village .... **GAV**
gypsy word .... **LAV**
gypsy word for paper, book .**LIL**

H

H .... AITCH
habit .... RUT, WONT, USAGE
habitat plant form ..... ECAD
habitation .... ABODE
habituate ..... ENURE, INURE
habituated .... USED
hackney coach, Fr. .... FIACRE
hackneyed ..... STALE, TRITE
Hades ... DIS, ORCUS, PLUTO,
           SHEOL, TARTARUS
Hades: Old Eng. .... ADES
Hades, place before .. EREBUS
Hades river
        STYX, LETHE, ACHERON
hag .... CRONE
haggard .... DRAWN
Haggard, H. Rider, novel .. SHE
hail .... AVE, GREET
hail: naut. .... AVAST
hair, arrange .... COIF
hair, caterpillar .... SETA
hair coat .... MELOTE
hair-do, old .... TETE
hair dressing .... POMADE
hair, false . RAT, WIG, TOUPEE
hair, head of .... CRINE
hair, knot of .. BUN, CHIGNON
hair, lock of ... CURL, TRESS
hair net .... SNOOD
hair, remove .... EPILATE
hair, rigid .... SETA
hair, rough, matted .... SHAG
hair shirt .... CILICE
hair, standing .... ROACH
hair unguent .... POMADE
hairless: Sp. Am. ...... PELON
hairlike process
            CILIA, CILIUM
hairy . PILAR, COMOSE, PILOSE
Haiti bandit .... CACO
Halcyone's husband .... CEYX
half .... MOIETY
half-boot .... PAC
half-breed ... MESTEE, MUSTEE
half-caste .... METIS
half-moon figure .... LUNE
half-way .... MID
halfway house .... INN
halfpenny: Brit. .... MAG
hall: Ger. ..... AULA, SAAL
hallow .... BLESS
halo ...... NIMB, CORONA,
    NIMBUS, AUREOLA, AUREOLE
halt .... LAME, STOP
halting place, troops' .. ETAPE
Hamilton's party .... FEDERAL

Hamite .... SOMAL, BERBER,
                      SOMALI
Hamitic language AGAO, AGAU
hamlet ... BURG, DORP, TOWN
Hamlet's castle .... ELSINORE
hammer .... KEVEL
hammer head part ...... PEEN
hammer, heavy .... MAUL
hammer, large .... SLEDGE
hammer, lead .... MADGE
hammer, tilt .... OLIVER
hamper ..... CRAMP, FETTER,
                    TRAMMEL
Ham's son .... CUSH
hand .... PUD, NEAF, MANUS
hand, pert. to .... CHIRAL
hand, whist .... TENACE
handbill .... LEAF
handcuff .... MANACLE
handle ... EAR, LUG, PAW,
         ANSA, HILT, KNOB,
         HELVE, TREAT
handle, bench plane .... TOTE
handle, having ...... ANSATE
handle roughly ... PAW, MAUL
handle, scythe .... SNATH,
        SNEAD, SNEED, SNATHE
handstone for grinding . MANO
handwriting .... SCRIPT
handwriting on the wall . MENE,
    MENE, TEKEL, UPHARSIN
hang .... DRAPE, DROOP,
            HOVER, IMPEND
hank of twine .... RAN
Hannibal's defeat ...... ZAMA
Hannibal's victory .. CANNAE
happen ..... OCCUR, BEFALL,
            BETIDE, CHANCE
happening .... EVENT
happiness god, Jap.
            EBISU, HOTEI
harangue .... ORATE,
        TIRADE, DIATRIBE
Haran's son .... LOT
harass ..... NAG, BESET
harbinger .... HERALD
harbor .... BAY, COVE,
            PORT, HAVEN
hard cash .... SPECIE
harden .... GEL, SET
    ENURE, INURE, INDURATE
hardship .... TRIAL
hardtack .... PANTILE
hardwood .... ASH, OAK
Hardy novel heroine ..... TESS
hare: dialect .... WAT

73

a hare, genus .... **LEPUS**
hare, young, 1 year .. **LEVERET**
harem ... **ZENANA, SERAGLIO**
harem room .... **ODA**
harlot of Jericho, Bibl. . **RAHAB**
harm .**BANE, DAMAGE, INJURE**
harm: old Eng. .... **DERE**
harm: poetic .... **BALE**
harmful .... **NOCENT**
harmonize .... **ATTUNE**
harmony .. **UNISON, CONCORD**
harp, ancient .... **TRIGON**
Harp constellation ...... **LYRA**
harp guitar key .... **DITAL**
harp, kind of .... **EOLIC**
harp, Nubian .... **NANGA**
harpy, Gr. myth ...... **AELLO**
harquebus projection .... **CROC**
harrow .... **DRAG**
harsh to taste .... **ACERB**
hartebeeste .... **ASSE, TORA,
CAAMA, KAAMA**
harvest .... **REAP**
harvest festival, Rom. . **OPALIA**
harvest goddess .... **OPS**
harvest, India ... **RABI, RABBI**
has not: Old Eng. .... **NAS**
hashish .... **BHANG**
hasty pudding .... **SEPON**
HAT .... see HEADGEAR
b hat: Anglo-Ir. ...... **CAUBEEN**
hat plant .... **SOLA**
hat, straw .. **MILAN, PANAMA**
hatchet, archeol. ...... **HACHE**
hatchet, stone .... **MOGO**
hatred ... **ODIUM, AVERSION**
hatred: Buddhism ...... **DOSA**
hatter's mallet ...... **BEATER**
haul tight, naut. . **BOUSE, TRICE**
haunt, low .. **DEN, DIVE, NEST**
hautboy .... **OBOE**
haven .... **LEE**
having buttery account:
Oxford .... **BATTEL**
having holes, as cheese **EYEY**
having true luster when uncut
NAIF
haw!: P.I. .... **MANO**
haw, as cattle .... **HOI**
Hawaiian bird .. **IO, O-O, IIWI**
Hawaiian bird, extinct . **MAMO**
Hawaiian bird, red-tailed **KOAE**
Hawaiian blueberry ... **OHELO**
Hawaiian chant ...... **MELE**
Hawaiian cloth .. **TAPA, KAPA**
Hawaiian cudweed ... **ENAENA**
Hawaiian dance .... **HULA**
Hawaiian farewell, greeting
ALOHA
Hawaiian feather cloak . **MAMO**
Hawaiian fern .... **HEII**

c Hawaiian floral emblem **LEHUA**
Hawaiian food .... **POI**
Hawaiian food-game fish .**ULUA**
Hawaiian garland .... **LEI**
Hawaiian god .... **KANE**
Hawaiian goddess, fire .. **PELE**
Hawaiian goose .... **NENE**
Hawaiian gooseberry .... **POHA**
Hawaiian governor, 1st . **DOLE**
Hawaiian grass .... **HILO**
Hawaiian hawk .... **IO**
Hawaiian herb .... **HOLA**
Hawaiian loincloth .... **MALO**
Hawaiian musical instrument
PUA
Hawaiian porch ...... **LANAI**
Hawaiian president, 1st . **DOLE**
Hawaiian royal chief ... **ALII**
Hawaiian shrub .... **AKIA**
Hawaiian staple .... **POI**
Hawaiian starch .... **APII**
Hawaiian timber tree ... **OHIA**
Hawaiian tree
KOA, AULU, ALANI, ILIAHI
Hawaiian tree, dark .... **AALII**
Hawaiian tree fern ..... **PULU**
Hawaiian vine .... **IE**
Hawaiian volcano goddess.**PELE**
Hawaiian windstorm .... **KONA**
hawk .... **KITE**
d hawk, falconry .... **BATER**
hawk, fish .... **OSPREY**
hawk genus .... **BUTEO**
hawk-head god, Egypt . **HORUS**
hawk, India .... **SHIKRA**
hawk-like bird .... **KITE**
hawk, Scot. .... **ALLAN**
hawk, young .... **BRANCHER**
hawks .... **IOS**
hawk's cage .... **MEW**
hawk's leash .... **LUNE**
hawthorn .... **MAY**
hawthorn berry .... **HAW**
hay, spread to dry .... **TED**
haystack .... **RICK**
hazard ... **DARE, RISK, PERIL**
hazardous .... **CHANCY**
haze: Old Eng. .... **HASE**
hazelnut .... **FILBERT**
hazy, make ..... **DIM, BEDIM**
"he remains": Lat. ... **MANET**
head ..... **NOB, LEAD, PATE,
POLL, TETE, CAPUT, CHIEF,
CAPITA, LEADER, NODDLE,
NOODLE**
head covering .... **CAP, HAT,
TAM, HOOD, VEIL, BERET**
head covering, fleecy .. **NUBIA**
head, crown of .... **PATE**
head, having round ... **RETUSE**
head, membrane covering **CAUL**

a head, Moslem .... **RAIS, REIS**
head of Benjamin's clan .. **IRI**
head, shaved .... **TONSURE**
head: slang .... **NOGGIN**
head wrap .... **NUBIA, SHAWL**
headband, Gr. .... **TAENIA**
HEADDRESS
        see also HEADGEAR
headdress, bishop's
           MITER, MITRE
headgear, brimless ..... **TOQUE**
headgear, clerical
          BERETTA, BIRETTA
headgear, dervish .... **TAJ**
headgear, kind of ... **PANAMA**
headgear, military .... **SHAKO**
headgear, Moslem .. **TARBUSH,**
TARBOOCH, TARBOOSH,
TARBOUCHE
headgear, poetic .... **TIAR**
headgear, priest's
          BERETTA, BIRETTA
headgear, tropics
      TOPI, TERAI, TOPEE
headgear, Turk. .... **FEZ**
headland .. **RAS, CAPE, NASE,**
NESS, NOZE
headless: Her. .... **ETETE**
headstrong .... **RASH**
healing goddess .... **EIR**
health, in good .... **FIT**
b health-drinking word
         SALUD, PROSIT
health resort .... **SPA**
heap ...... **PILE, RAFF, RAFT**
hear ye! .... **OYES, OYEZ**
hearing: law .... **OYER**
hearken .. **HEAR, HEED, LIST,**
ATTEND, LISTEN
heart .... **COR, CORE**
heart auricle .. **ATRIA, ATRIUM**
heart contraction .... **SYSTOLE**
heart, immortal, Egyp. .... **AB**
heart trouble .... **ANGINA**
heartleaf .... **MEDIC**
heartless ... **CRUEL, SARDONIC**
heat .... **WARM, CALOR**
heated to whiteness .**CANDENT**
heath .... **MOOR**
heath genus .... **ERICA**
heathen .... **PAGAN**
heathen god .... **IDOL**
heather .... **LING, ERICA**
heating apparatus, vessel.**ETNA**
heave upward .... **SCEND**
heaven .. **SION, ZION, URANO**
heaven, eagle-borne flier to
           ETANA
heaven personified: Babyl.. **ANU**
heavens, pert. to .... **URANIC**
heavenly .... **EDENIC**

c heavenly being .... **ANGEL**
      SERAPH, SERAPHIM
heavenly Jerusalem **SION, ZION**
heavy blow .... **ONER**
HEBREW see also **JEWISH**
         and BIBLICAL
Hebr. Bible books .... **NEBIIM**
Hebr. Bible pronunciation aid
    GRI, KRI, KERE, KERI,
    QERE, QERI, QUERI
Hebr. drum .... **TOPH**
Hebr. dry measure .. **CAB, KAB**
Hebr. lyre .... **ASOR**
Hebr. measure .... **KOR, EPHA,**
      OMER, EPHAH
Hebr. precept .... **TORA**
HEBREW PROPHETS . see
  SPECIAL SECTION, Page 196
Hebr. proselyte .... **GER**
Hebr. reclaimer .... **GOEL**
Hebr. teacher ...... **RAB, REB**
Hebr. universe .... **OLAM**
Hebrews' ancestor, legend
            EBER
Hector's mother ..... **HECUBA**
hedge plant .... **PRIVET**
hedgerow: Eng. .... **REW**
heed .... **HEAR, MIND,**
       OBEY, RECK
heel .... **CAD, CALX**
d height .... **STATURE**
heir .... **SON, SCION,**
    HERITOR, LEGATEE
held, able to be .... **TENABLE**
Helen: It. .... **ELENA**
Helen of Troy's mother . **LEDA**
Helen's lover .... **PARIS**
helical .... **SPIRAL**
Helios .... **SUN**
hell .... **HADES, SHEOL**
Hellespont swimmer . **LEANDER**
helm position .... **ALEE**
helmet, light .... **SALLET**
helmet, medieval
    ARMET, HEAUME
helmet, Rom. .... **GALEA**
helmet-shaped ...... **GALEATE**
helmet-shaped part ... **GALEA**
helmsman .... **PILOT**
Heloise's husband ... **ABELARD**
help .. **AID, ABET, BACK, TIDE,**
  ASSIST, SUCCOR, SUCCOUR
helper .... **AIDE**
Helvetic .... **SWISS**
hem in .... **BESET**
hemp .... **TOW, RINE, RAMIE**
hemp, Afr. .... **IFE**
hemp, India ...... **KEF, BANG,**
  KEEF, KEIF, KIEF, BHANG,
  DAGGA, RAMIE
hemp, Manila .... **ABACA**

hemp narcotic ...... **CHARAS**
hemp shrub, India
     PUA, POOA, POOAH
hen .... **LAYER**
hen harrier, Europ. .... **FALLER**
hence .... **SO, OFF, AWAY**
Hengist's brother ..... **HORSA**
Henry IV birthplace ...... **PAU**
"Henry IV" character ... **PETO**
"Henry V" knave ...... **NYM**
"Henry VI" character ... **IDEN**
hep .... **ONTO**
her: obs. .... **HIR**
Hera's son .... **ARES**
herald .... **USHER**
HERALDIC TERMS . see also
    SPECIAL SECTION, Page 194
herald's coat .... **TABARD**
heraldic bearing **ORLE, FILLET**
heraldic cross .... **PATEE**
heraldic wreath .... **ORLE**
herb ..... **RUE, LEEK, MINT,
MOLY, WORT, ANISE, TANSY,
YARROW, OREGANO**
herb, aromatic **BASIL, DITTANY**
herb, bitter ...... **RUE, ALOE**
herb, carrot family .... **ANISE**
herb eve .... **IVA**
herb, fabulous **MOLY, PANACE**
herb, forage .... **SULLA**
herb genus .... **ABFA
GEUM, RUTA, ALETRIS**
herb, medicinal .. **ALOE, SENNA**
herb of grace .... **RUE**
herb, snake-charm .... **MUNGO**
herb with aromatic root .**NONDO**
herb, wooly .... **POLY**
Hercules' captive .... **IOLE**
Hercules, monster slain by
    HYDRA
Hercules' mother .. **ALCMENE**
herd .... **DROVE**
herd of horses .... **CAVIYA**
herd of whales .... **GAM, POD**
herdsman, Swiss ...... **SENN**
hereditary right .... **UDAL**
hereditary factor .. **GEN, GENE**
heretic, 4th cent.
    ARIAN, ARIUS
heretofore .... **ERENOW**
Hermes' mother .... **MAIA**
Hermes' son .... **PAN**
hermit . **EREMITE, ANCHORITE**
hero, legendary ...... **PALADIN**
Hero's love .... **LEANDER**
heroic .... **EPIC, EPICAL**
heroic poem **EPIC, EPOS, WORK**
heroic song .... **EDDA**
heron .... **EGRET**
heron brood, flock .... **SEDGE**
heron, kind of ...... **BITTERN**

herring .... **ALEC, BRIT, SILL**
herring, grayback ..... **CISCO**
herring keg .... **CADE**
herring small Eur. ...... **SPRAT**
hesitate
    DEMUR, FALTER, TEETER
hesitation syllable .... **ER, UM**
Hesperides, one of .... **AEGLE**
Heyward, Du Bose, heroine.**BESS**
Hezekiah's mother ...... **ABI**
hiatus .... **GAP, LACUNA**
hickory tree ...... **SHELLBARK**
hidden ..... **INNER, ARCANE,
COVERT, LATENT**
hide .... **VEIL, CACHE**
hide of beast ..... **FELL, SKIN**
hide, thongs of .... **RIEM**
hide, undressed .... **KIP**
hides, Russian leather ... **JUFTI**
hiding in .... **PERDU**
high in pitch: mus. ...... **ALT**
high on scale .... **ELA**
high priest ...... **ELI, AARON,
ANNAS**
highest note .... **ELA**
highest point .. **APEX, ZENITH**
highway .... **ITER, PIKE**
highway, Alaska-Canada **ALCAN**
highwayman .. **PAD, LADRONE**
hike .... **TRAMP**
hill .... **TOR**
hill, broad ... **LOMA, LOMITA**
hill dweller, Ceylon .... **TODA**
hill dweller, India ..... **DOGRA**
hill, flat-topped .... **MESA**
hill fort: Ir. .... **RATH**
hill, isolated .... **BUTTE**
hill, pointed .... **TOR**
hill, Rome
    CAELIAN, PALATINE
hill, S. Afr. ...... **KOP, BULT**
hill: Turk. .... **DAGH**
hillock .... **TUMP**
hillside: Scot. .... **BRAE**
hilltop .... **KNAP**
hilt, sword .... **HAFT, HANDLE**
Himalayan animal .... **PANDA**
Himal. broadmouth ..... **RAYA**
Himal. ibex .... **KYL**
Himal. monkshood ...... **ATIS**
Himal. mountain .... **API**
Himal. wild goat . **KRAS, TAHR,
TAIR, THAR**
hind ...... **ROE, BACK, REAR**
hinder by fear .... **DETER**
hindrance ...... **BAR, LET**
Hindu age, cycle ...... **YUGA**
Hindu ancestor ...... **MANU**
Hindu ascetic .... **JOGI,
YATI, YOGI, FAKIR,
SADHU, FAKEER**

Hindu bible .... **VEDA**
Hindu charitable gift ... **ENAM**
Hindu cymbal .... **TAL**
Hindu deity .... **DEVA, RAMA, SIVA, SHIVA**
HINDU DEITY . see also GOD and see SPECIAL SECTION
Hindu divorce law ..... **TALAK**
Hindu female slave ..... **DASI**
Hindu festival .... **HOLI**
Hindu festival, religious . **PUJA**
Hindu gentlemen **BABU, BABOO**
HINDU GODS .... see SPECIAL SECTION, Page 200, and also GOD
Hindu guitar .... **BINA, VINA, SITAR**
Hindu holy man .... **SADH**
Hindu laws, giver of ... **MANU**
Hindu legendary hero ... **NALA**
Hindu life energy ...... **JIVA**
Hindu, low caste .... **KORI**
Hindu magic .... **MAYA**
Hindu mantra .... **OM**
Hindu mendicant ...... **NAGA**
Hindu monastery ...... **MATH**
Hindu "Olympus" ...... **MERU**
Hindu philosophy ...... **YOGA**
Hindu poet .... **TAGORE**
Hindu prince **RAJA, RANA, RAJAH**
Hindu progenitor, myth **MANU**
Hindu queen .... **RANI, RANEE**
Hindu religious adherent **JAIN, JAINA**
Hindu rites .... **ACHARA**
Hindu sacred literature .. **VEDA**
Hindu sacred word .... **OM**
Hindu scripture ...... **AGAMA**
Hindu scriptures, pert. to **VEDIC**
Hindu sect, one of **SEIK, SIKH**
Hindu teacher .... **GURU**
Hindu temple .... **DEUL**
Hindu term of respect **SAHIB**
Hindu title ...... **AYA, SRI**
Hindu trader **BANIAN, BANYAN**
Hindu unknown god ..... **KA**
Hindu, unorthodox .... **JAINA**
Hindu widow, suicide .. **SUTTEE**
Hindu woman's garment **SARI, SAREE**
Hindu word .... **OM**
Hindu writings .... **VEDA**
Hinduism, elixir **AMRITA, AMREETA**
Hindustani .... **URDU**
hinge, kind of .... **BUTT**
hint .... **TIP, CLEW, POINTER**
hip .... **COXA, ILIA, ILIAC**
hipbone, of the .... **ILIAC**

Hippocrates' birthplace ... **KOS**
Hippodrome .... **ARENA**
hire **LET, RENT, ENGAGE, CHARTER**
hired carriage .... **HACK**
hired labor: S. Afr. ..... **TOGT**
history .... **LORE**
hitherto .... **YET**
Hittites ancestor .... **HETH**
hive for bees .... **SKEP**
hives .... **UREDO**
hoard .... **AMASS, STORE**
hoarder .... **MISER**
hoarfrost .... **RIME**
hoarfrost: Eng. .... **RAG**
hoary .... **OLD, GRAY**
hoax .... **RUSE, CANARD**
hobgoblin .... **PUCK, SPRITE**
hock, horse's ...... **GAMBREL**
hockey ball .... **ORR**
hodgepodge .... **MESS, OLIO**
hog cholera .... **ROUGET**
hog deer .... **AXIS**
hog, female .... **GILT**
hog plum, W. Ind. **AMRA, JOBO**
hog, wild .... **BOAR, PECCARY**
hog's heart, liver, etc. **HASLET**
Hogan, golfer .... **BEN**
hoist .... **HEAVE**
hold, as in war .... **INTERN**
hold back .... **DETER**
hold fast: naut. ...... **BELAY**
holding .... **TENURE**
holding device .. **VISE, TONGS**
hole for molten metal .. **SPRUE**
hole in embankment .... **GIME**
hole in mold .... **GEAT**
hole-in-one .... **ACE**
holidays, Roman .... **FERIA**
HOLLAND see NETHERLANDS SPECIAL SECTION
hollow .... **DENT, HOWE**
holly .... **HOLM, ILEX**
holly, U. S. .... **ASSI, YAPON, YUPON, YAUPON**
holm oak .... **ILEX**
"Holy Hill," Gr. .... **ATHOS**
Holy Land city .... **DAN**
holy orders, give .... **ORDAIN**
holy water font .... **STOUP**
homage .... **HONOR**
home .... **ABODE**
home of gods, Norse .. **ASGARD**
"Home Sweet Home" author **PAYNE**
homeopath school-founder **HERING**
Homer's epic .... **ODYSSEY**
hominy, Indian coarse .. **SAMP**
honey .... **MEL**
honey-badger .... **RATEL**

77

a honey buzzard .... **PERN**
honey drink .. **MEAD, MORAT**
honey eater bird
      IAO, MOHO, MANUAO
honeybee .... **DESERET**
honeycomb, like a ..... **FAVOSE**
honor .... **EXALT, REVERE**
honorarium .... **TIP**
honorary commission .. **BREVET**
Honshu bay .... **ISE**
Honshu port .... **KOBE**
hooded garment ...... **PARKA**
hoodoo .... **JINX, JYNX**
hoof ...... **UNGUES, UNGUIS**
hook, bent into ..... **HAMATE**
hook, double curve ...... **ESS**
hook, engine .... **GAB**
hook for pot .... **CLEEK**
hook money .... **LARI, LARIN**
hooks .... **HAMI**
hookah .... **NARGILE**
hooked .... **HAMUS,**
  HAMATE, HAMOSE, FALCATE
Hoover Dam lake ...... **MEAD**
hop-picker's basket ...... **BIN**
hope goddess, Rom. ..... **SPES**
hop plant .... **LUPULUS**
hopscotch stone ...... **PEEVER**
Horae, one of .... **DIKE,**
    EIRENE, EUNOMIA
Horeb .... **SINAI**
b horizontal stripe .... **BAR**
horizontal timber ..... **LINTEL**
horn .... **CORNU**
horn, crescent-moon ..... **CUSP**
horn, Hebr. **SHOFAR, SHOPHAR**
horn quicksilver .... **CALOMEL**
horn-shaped structure .. **CORNU**
horn sounded for kill .. **MORT**
horn tissue, bit of ..... **SCUR**
horneblende .... **EDENITE**
hornless, Eng. dial. ...... **NOT**
hornless stag .... **POLLARD**
hors d'oeuvre .... **CANAPE**
horse .. **BAY, COB, NAG, ARAB,**
   MARE, MERE, ROAN,
   MOUNT, STEED, EQUINE,
   JENNET
horse, Austral. .... **WALER**
horse, Barbary native ... **BARB**
horse blanket .... **MANTA**
horse breed .... **MORGAN**
horse, brown
     BAY, ROAN, SORREL
horse color **BAY, ROAN, SORREL**
horse dealer, Eng. ..... **COPER**
horse, disease of .... **SPAVIN**
horse, draft .... **SHIRE**
horse genus .... **EQUUS**
horse: gypsy .. **GRI, GRY, GRAS**
horse-mackerel .... **SCAD**

c horse-man, myth ... **CENTAUR**
horse, piebald .... **PINTO**
horse, race .... **PACER**
horse-radish, fruit of ... **BEN**
horse, saddle .... **MOUNT**
horse, small .... **GENET,**
  GENNET, JENNET, GENETTE
horse, Sp. Am. ..... **CABALLO**
horse, swift .. **ARAB, COURSER**
horse, talking, Gr. .... **ARION**
horse, war .... **CHARGER**
horse, white-flecked .... **ROAN**
horse, wild Asiatic ... **TARPAN**
horse, young .... **COLT, FOAL**
horses, goddess of ..... **EPONA**
horse's sideways tread ... **VOLT**
horsehair .... **SETON**
horsemanship, art of **MANEGE**
horseshoe gripper ...... **CALK**
horseshoeing stall
     TRAVE, TREVE
Horus' mother .... **ISIS**
Hosea's wife .... **GOMER**
host .... **ARMY, HORDE**
hostelry .... **INN**
hot air chamber ...... **OVEN**
hot iron to sear ..... **CAUTER**
hot spring, eruptive .. **GEYSER**
Hottentot .... **NAMA**
hourly .... **HORAL**
d house **ROOF, VILLA, COTTAGE**
house, like a .... **DOMAL**
house, mud, Afr. .... **TEMBE**
house urn: Rom. ... **CAPANNA**
housefly genus ...... **MUSCA**
housefly genus, lesser **FANNIA**
household **MENAGE, MAINPOST**
household god .... **LAR, LARES**
howl .... **ULULATE**
howling monkey **MONO, ARABA**
hub .. **NAVE, BOSTON, CENTER**
hubbub .. **ADO, STIR, TUMULT**
hue .... **COLOR, TINGE**
huge .... **VAST, ENORM**
Huguenot leader ..... **ADRETS**
hull .... **POD, HUSK**
humble .... **ABASE**
hummingbird
   AVA, TOPAZ, COLIBRI
humorist .... **WIT**
humpback salmon
     HADDO, HOLIA
Humphreys, Mrs. (pseudo.)
           RITA
hundred .... **CENTUM**
hundredweight ...... **CENTAL**
Hungarian dog .... **PULI**
Hungarian hero .... **NAGY**
Hungarian king .... **BELA**
Hungarian people ... **MAGYAR**
Hungarian pianist ... **SANDOR**

a Hungarian playwright **MOLNAR**
Hungarian violinist .... **AUER**
Huns, king of
      ATLI, ETZEL, ATTILA
hunt, Ind. .... **SHIKAR**
hunter ...... **ORION, NIMROD**
hunter, India .... **SHIKARI**
hunting cry .. **HO, YOI, TOHO, HALLOO, YOICKS, TALLY-HO**
hunting hat .... **TERAI**
hunting hound .... **ALAN**
huntress .... **ATALANTA**
huntsman .... **JAGER**
HUNTSMAN'S CRY see HUNT-ING CRY
hup: army .... **ONE**
hurdy-gurdy ..... **LIRA, ROTA**
hurry .... **HIE, HASTEN**
hurt .... **MAR, ACHE, LESION**

c hurt: old Eng. .... **DERE**
hurtful .... **MALEFIC**
husband's brother ..... **LEVIR**
hush .... **SH, HSH**
husk, cereal .... **BRAN**
hut, India .... **BARI**
hut, Mex. .... **JACAL**
hydrate, as lime ...... **SLAKE**
hydraulic pump .... **RAM**
hydrocarbon . **TOLAN, ETHANE, OCTANE, RETENE, TERPENE**
hydrogen compound ... **IMINE**
hydrogen isotope ... **PROTIUM**
hymn .... **ODE**
hymn of praise ..... **ANTHEM**
hypnotic state ...... **TRANCE**
hypothetical force
      OD, BIOD, ELOD, ODYL
hypothetical force of ... **ODIC**
hyson .... **TEA**

I

I .... **EGO**
"I have found it" .... **EUREKA**
"I love": Lat. .... **AMO**
Iago's wife .... **EMILIA**
b Iberians .... **IBERI, IBERES**
ibex .... **KYL, TUR, KAIL**
Ibsen character ... **ASE, NORA**
ice block, glacial ...... **SERAC**
ice mass .... **BERG, FLOE**
ice, slushy ..... **SISH, LOLLY**
iced .... **GLACE**
Iceland epic, literature, tales
      EDDA
Icelandic narrative ..... **SAGA**
icy .... **GELID**
"id —" (that is) .... **EST**
idea, Plato .... **EIDOS**
ideal .... **UTOPIAN**
ideal republic, imaginary
      OCEANA
ideal state .... **UTOPIA**
identical .... **ONE, SAME**
ideology .... **ISM**
idiocy .... **ANOESIA**
idiot .... **AMENT, CRETIN**
idle .... **OTIANT, OTIOSE**
idle, to be ..... **LAZE, LOAF**
idol: archaic .... **PAGOD**
idol: philos. .... **EIDOLON**
idolatrous .... **PAGAN**
ids, pert. to .... **IDIC**
Idumaea .... **EDOM**
if ever .... **ONCE**
if not .... **ELSE**
ignoble .... **BASE**

ignominy .... **SHAME**
ignorance, Hindu philos. **TAMAS**
ignorant .. **STUPID, UNAWARE**
ignore .... **ELIDE**
Igorot's neighbor tribesman **ATA**
d ill .... **EVIL**
ill-will .... **SPITE, RANCOR**
illumination unit .... **LUX**
illusion .... **CHIMERA**
illusory riches .... **MINE**
image .... **IDOL, IDOLON, IDOLUM, EIDOLON**
image, pert. to ...... **ICONIC**
image, religious .. **ICON, IKON**
imagine: arch. .... **WIS**
imbecile .... **AMENT, ANILE, CRETIN**
imbibe ... **SIP, GULP, DRINK**
imitate ... **APE, MIME, MIMIC**
imitation .... **MIMESIS**
imitation gems .... **PASTE**
immature seed .... **OVULE**
immature: zool. ..... **NEANIC**
immeasurable .... **BOUNDLESS**
immediately ..... **NOW, ANON**
immense .... **VAST**
immerse .. **DIP, DUNK, DOUSE**
immigrant, Greek ..... **METIC**
immunizing substance
      SERUM, HAPTEN, HAPTENE
imou pine .... **RIMU**
impair .. **MAR, DAMAGE, SPOIL**
impart .... **GIVE, LEND**
impartial .... **EVEN**
impede ..... **ESTOP, HAMPER**
impel .... **URGE**

79

Impertinent

a
impertinent ..... **PERT, SAUCY**
IMPLEMENT ... see also TOOL
implement, pounding .. **PESTLE**
implement to skid logs .. **TODE**
implied .... **TACIT**
import .... **SENSE**
important, critically ... **VITAL**
importune .... **URGE**
impose .... **LAY**
impost .... **TAX**
imposture .... **SHAM**
impoverish .... **IMPOOR**
impressionist painter .. **DEGAS**
        MANET, MONET, RENOIR
imprison .... **IMMURE**
improve .... **AMEND**
improvise music .... **VAMP**
impudence .... **LIP,**
        BRASS, CHEEK, NERVE
impure metal product .. **MATTE**
in addition .. **TOO, ALSO, YET**
in agreement .... **UNITED**
in disagreement .... **OUT**
in half, in — .... **TWO**
"in medias —" .... **RES**
in name only ...... **NOMINAL**
in same place .... **IBID**
in so far as .... **QUA**
in the know .... **AWARE**
in the matter of .... **INRE**
in the past .... **OVER**

b
in the very near future. . **ANON**
in unison .... **ONE**
in very truth .... **AMEN**
inability to hear ..... **ASONIA**
inactive .... **INERT**
inadequate .... **SCANT**
inborn .... **NATIVE**
incarnation, Hindu .... **RAMA,**
        AVATAR

incense ingredient
        GUM, SPICE, STACTE
incense receptacle, Rom.**ACERRA**
incense, Somali ...... **MATTI**
incentive .... **GOAD, MOTIVE**
incessantly .... **EVER**
inch, .001 of .... **MIL**
incidentally .... **OBITER**
incinerate .... **CREMATE**
incite ..... **EGG, PROD, URGE,**
IMPEL, SET ON, SUBORN
inciter .... **EGGER**
inclination .... **BENT**
incline .. **TEND, SLOPE, TREND**
inclined .... **APT, PRONE**
inclined way .... **RAMP**
income, annual, Fr. .... **RENTE**
incompletely .... **SEMI**
inconsiderable ..... **NOMINAL**
increase .... **WAX, RISE**
incrustation .... **SCAB**

c
incursion, predatory .... **RAID**
indeed: Ir. ...... **ARU, AROO**
indentation
        CRENA, CRENAE, CRENELET
index mark .... **FIST**
INDIA, INDIAN ... see also
        SPECIAL SECTION and see
        also HINDU
India farmer .... **MEO**
India minstrel .... **BHAT**
India native chief .... **SIRDAR**
India native servant ... **MATY**
India: poet. .... **IND**
India, swamp belt of .. **TERAI**
INDIAN .. see also page 192
Indian .... **SAC**
INDIAN, ALGONQUIN .... see
        page 192
Indian, Arawak ...... **ARAUA**
Indian, Arikara .... **REE**
Indian, Athapasca ..... **TAKU**
Indian buzzard .... **TESA**
Indian corn .... **MAIZE**
Indian corn: N. Z. ... **KANGA**
Indian elk .... **SAMBAR**
Indian farmer, Fla. ... **CALUSA**
Indian in Chaco .... **TOBA**
Indian mahogany tree .. **TOON**
Indian mulberry **AL, AAL, ACH**
Indian of Jalisco ...... **CORA**
Indian of Keresan .... **SIA**
Indian of Mex., scattered **CORA**

d
Indian ox .... **ZEBU**
Indian, Panamint ...... **KOSO**
INDIAN, PLAINS . see page 193
Indian race .... **JAT**
Indian shell currency
        ULO, UHLLO
INDIAN, SIOUAN see page 193
Indian, S. Peru .... **CHANCA**
INDIAN TREE.see TREE, INDIA
Indian, warlike ...... **APACHE**
Indian weight ..... **SER, TOLA**
Indian, whaler .... **HOH**
Indian yellow .... **PURI,**
        PIURI, PURREE
indicating succession **ORDINAL**
indict .... **ARRAIGN**
indifferent to pain
        STOIC, STOICAL
indigo plant .... **ANIL**
indistinct, make ...... **BEDIM**
indite .... **PEN, WRITE**
individual .... **ONE, SELF**
Indo-Chin. native **LAO,MRU,TAI**
Indo-Chin. tribe **TAI,LAOS,SHAN**
Indo-Chin. tribes .... **MOI**
Indo-European **ARYA, ARYAN**
Indo-Malayan animal .. **NAPU**
indolent ...... **OTIOSE, SUPINE**
Indonesian ..... **ATA, NESIOT**

a induce .... **LEAD**
Indus tribesman .... **GOR**
ineffectual .... **VAIN**
inelastic .... **LIMP**
inert .... **SUPINE**
infatuation .... **ATE**
infertile moor .... **LANDE**
infinity .... **OLAM**
infirm .... **ANILE, SENILE**
inflamed, be .... **RANKLE**
inflammable liquid .. **ACETONE**
inflammation: med. .. **ANGINA**
inflexible ...... **IRON, RIGID**
inflict .... **DEAL, IMPOSE**
inflorescence **RACEME, SPADIX**
inflorescence, racemose **AMENT**
influence .... **AFFECT**
informer: slang .... **NARK**
infusion .... **TEA**
ingenuous .... **NAIVE**
inhabitant .... **ITE**
inhabitant of a town ...... **CIT**
inheritance .... **ENTAIL**
inheritor .... **LEGATEE**
initiate .. **OPEN, BEGIN, START**
initiate, Gr. ... **EPOPT, EPOPTA**
injure ... **MAR, HARM, MAIM**
injury ...... **LESION, TRAUMA**
inlaid .... **MOSAIC**
inlaid decoration ...... **BUHL**
b inlet .. **ARM, BAY, RIA, FIORD**
inlet: Dutch .... **ZEE**
inlet, Orkneys .... **VOE**
inn .... **KHAN,
HOSTEL, POSADA, HOSPICE**
Inn, "Canterbury Tales" **TABARD**
inn, Oriental .... **SERAI**
inn, Turkish .... **IMARET**
inner .... **ENTAL**
inner meaning .. **CORE, HEART**
inner parlor: Scot. ...... **BEN**
innkeeper **PADRONE, BONIFACE**
insect ... **ANT, BEE, BUG, DOR,
FLY, FLEA, GNAT, MITE,
APHID, CADEW, EMESA,
BEETLE, CADDIS, CICADA,
CICALA, MANTIS**
Insect, adult .... **IMAGO**
insect body
THORAX, THORACES
Insect, immature ...... **PUPA,
LARVA, INSTAR**
Insect mature .... **IMAGO**
insect order .... **DIPTERA**
insect, plant sucking .. **APHID**
insect, ruinous **APHID, BORER**
insertion mark .... **CARET**
inset .... **PANEL**
insidious .... **SLY**
insincere talk .... **CANT**
insipid, become .... **PALL**

c insist .... **URGE, PRESS**
inspire .... **IMBUE**
install .... **INSTATE**
instance .... **CASE**
instant .... **MO. TRACE**
instar .. **PUPA, IMAGO. LARVA**
instigate .. **EGG. ABET INCITE**
instruct .... **BRIEF, EDUCATE**
INSTRUMENT .. see also MUS-
ICAL INSTRUMENT
Instrument, Afr. reed
GORA, GORAH, GOURA
instrument, Chin. ancient **KIN**
instrument, Hebr. ... **TIMBREL**
instrument, India ..... **RUANA**
instrument, Jap. ..... **SAMISEN**
instrument, lutelike **BANDORE**
instrument, lyrelike ... **KISSAR**
instrument, math. .... **SECTOR**
instrument, medieval .. **ROCTA**
instrument, naut.
PELORUS, SEXTANT
instrument, Sp. .... **CASTANET**
instrument, stringed ... **LYRE,
NABLA, REBAB, REBEC,
SAROD, SITAR, VIOLA,
CITHER, CITHARA, CITH-
ERN, CITTERN, GITTERN**
Instrument, surveying **TRANSIT**
instrumentality **MEDIA, MEDIUM**
d insulate .... **ISLE**
insult .... **CAG**
insurgent .... **REBEL**
intact .... **WHOLE**
intellect .... **MIND,
NOUS, MAHAT, REASON**
Inter .... **BURY, INHUME**
intercharged ..... **PERMUTED**
interdict .... **BAN**
interferometer ...... **ETALON**
interior, ancient temple **CELLA**
interjection for silence .... **TST**
interlace .... **WEAVE**
interlock .... **LINK**
international language **RO, IDO**
inter. money unit .... **BANCOR**
international pact ... **ENTENTE**
interpret .... **REDE**
intersect .... **MEET**
interstice, small
AREOLA, AREOLE
interstices, with .... **AREOLAR**
intervening: law ...... **MESNE**
interweave ... **TWINE, RADDLE**
intimidate **AWE, COW, DAUNT**
intone .... **CHANT**
intoxicant: India ...... **SOMA**
intoxicated .... **SOSH**
intricate .... **DEDAL, DAEDAL,
GORDIAN**

81

Intrigue

a intrigue .... **CABAL**
introduce
BROACH, INSERT, PRESENT
Introducer of jetties for deepening .... **EADS**
Inundation .... **SPATE**
inveigle ...... **LURE, ENTICE**
inventor, claim of rights **PATENT**
inventor, elevator ...... **OTIS**
inventor, sewing machine **HOWE**
inventor, steam engine **WATT**
invest ...... **ENDOW, ENDUE, INDUE, CLOTHE, ORDAIN**
invested .... **CLAD**
investigate .... **PROBE**
investigator .... **TRACER**
invite .... **ASK, BID**
involve **ENTAIL, ENTRAMMEL**
Io butterfly .... **KIHO**
iodine source .... **KELP**
ion, negative .... **ANION**
ion, positive .... **CATION**
Ionian city .... **TEOS**
iota .... **JOT, MITE**
Iowa college town ...... **AMES**
ipecac source .... **EVEA**
IRAN .. see also PERSIAN
Iran, former part of ... **ELAM**
Iranian .... **TAT, KURD**
b Iranian Turk .... **SART**
irascible .... **TESTY**
irate .... **MAD**
Ireland .... **EIRE, ERIN**
Ireland, old name ..... **IERNE**
Ireland personified .... **IRENA**
iridescent gem .... **OPAL**
iris .... **FLAG**
iris, Florentine, European **ORRIS**
iris, layer of .... **UVEA**
iris, of a layer .... **UVEAL**
iris root .... **ORRIS**
IRISH .. see also IRELAND
Irish .... **ERSE**
Ir. alphabet, early
OGAM, OGUM
Ir. ancestor **IR, MIL, ITH, MILED**
Ir. assembly .... **DAIL**
Ir. church .... **KIL**
Ir. city, ancient ..... **TARA**
Ir. clan, ancient ...... **SEPT**
Ir. competitive meet .... **FEIS**
Ir. crowning stone, — Fail **LIA**
Ir. dramatist .... **SYNGE**
Ir. exclamation .... **ARU, AROO, ARRA, WHIST, WURRA**
Ir. fairies .... **SHEE**
Ir. family .... **CINEL**
Ir. Free State .... **EIRE**
Irish-Gaelic .... **ERSE**
Ir. goddess, battle **BADB, BODB**

c **IR. GODS' MOTHER** see page 200
Ir. kings' home .... **TARA**
Ir. law, tribe .... **CINEL**
Ir. lower house parliament **DAIL**
Ir. nobleman .... **AIRE**
Ir. poet
AE, COLUM, MOORE, YEATS
Ir. rebel group .... **IRA**
Ir. tribe .... **SIOL**
Ir. writing .... **OGAM, OGHAM**
Irishman .. **AIRE, CELT, MICK**
iron disulfide .... **PYRITE**
iron, pert. to .... **FERRIC**
ironwood ...... **ACLE, COLIMA**
irony .... **SATIRE**
Iroquoian .... **ERIE**
Iroquois demon .... **OTKON**
irrational number ...... **SURD**
irregularity .... **JOG**
irrigation ditch **FLUME, SLUICE**
irritate ...... **VEX, GALL, RILE, NETTLE, RANKLE**
Isaac's son **EDOM, ESAU, JACOB**
Ishmael .... **PARIAH**
Ishmael, son of ...... **DUMAH**
Ishmael's mother ..... **HAGAR**
isinglass .... **MICA**
Isis, husband of .... **OSIRIS**
ISLAM .... see MOSLEM
d island ... **OE, AIT, CAY, KAY, KEY, EYOT, HOLM, ILOT, ISLE, ATOLL, ISLET, ISLOT**
ISLAND, AEGEAN .... see
GAZETTEER
island, Argyll .... **IONA**
island, coral .... **ATOLL**
island, Dodecanese . **COO, KOS, CASO, LERO, SIMI**
island, Great Barrier ... **OTEA**
island, Gr. (fine marble) **PAROS**
island, Gr., pert. to ... **CRETAN**
island, inhabiting an . **NESIOTE**
ISLAND, INNER HEBRIDES
see HEBRIDES GAZETTEER
island, Ionian .... **ZANTE**
island, Micronesia ... **PONAPE**
island near Ireland .... **ARAN**
island, near Italy ...... **CAPRI**
island off Scotland .... **IONA, ARRAN**
island, Riga Gulf ...... **OESEL**
island, river **AIT, EYOT, HOLM**
island, South Seas ... **ARU, TAITI, TAHITI, OTAHEITE**
island, west of Sumatra .. **NIAS**
islands, Gulf of Bothnia **ALAND**
islands, Irish .... **ARAN**
islands, off Timor ...... **LETI**
Isle of Man, pert. to ... **MANX**
islet .... **AIT, CAY, HOLM**
isolate .... **ENISLE**

82

a Israel .... JACOB
ISRAEL, KING OF ... see KING
OF ISRAEL
ISRAELITE .. see also HEBREW
and BIBLICAL
ISRAELITE JUDGE ...... see
BIBLICAL JUDGE
ISRAELITE KING .. see KING
OF ISRAEL
Israelite tribe .... DAN
Israelites .... SION, ZION
issue . EMIT, EMERGE, EMANATE
isthmus .... NECK
istle fiber .... PITA, PITO
it proceeds: music .... VA
ITALIAN WORDS: (accent marks
omitted throughout)
arts .... ARTES
article .... LA
canal (s) CANALE, CANALI
chest .... CASSO
custom house ..... DOGANA
day-breeze .... ORA
dear .... CARA, CARO
dough .... PASTA
drink .... BEVERE
enough .... BASTA
evening .... SERA
enthusiasm .... ESTRO
feast .... FESTINO
b field .... CAMPO
food .... PASTO
from beginning .... DACAPO
gentleman .... SER
goodby .... ADDIO
gondola cabin ...... FELZE
hamlet .... CASAL, CASALE
hair .... PELO
hand .... MANO
harbor .... PORTO
harp .... ARPA
hatred .... ODIO
Helen .... ELENA
holiday ...... FESTA, FESTE
host .... OSTE
Italy .... ITALIA
judge .... PODESTA
lady .... DONNA, SIGNORA
lake .... LAGO
little .... POCO
love .... AMORE
lover .... AMOROSO
mother .... MADRE
mountain peak ...... CIMA
nine .... NOVE
ninth .... NONO

c one .... UNO
paste .... PASTA
peak .... CIMA
pronoun .... MIA
right .... DESTRO
Rome .... ROMA
sign .... SEGNO
somebody .... UNO
street .... CALLE
three .... TRE
time .... TEMPO
tour .... GIRO
town ..... CASAL, CASALE
you .... TU
voice .... VOCE
well .... BENE
with .... CON

Italian actress .... DUSE
It., ancient
ITALI, OSCAN, SABINE
It. astronomer ...... GALILEO
It. author .... SILONE
It. car .... FIAT
It. cathedral city .... MILAN
It. commune .... ESTE
It. composer .... BOITO,
GUIDO, VERDI, ROSSINI
It. day breeze .... ORA
d It. family .... ESTE,
CENCI, DORIA, MEDICI
It. family royal name ... ESTE
It. gambling game ..... MORA
It. gentleman .... SER
It. guessing game ..... MORA
It. lady .... DONA, SIGNORA
It. millet ...... BUDA, MOHA
It. painter .... RENI,
LIPPI, VINCI, ANDREA,
CRESPI, GIOTTO
It. poet
DANTE, TASSO, ARIOSTO
It. resort .... LIDO
It. rice dish .... RISOTTO
It.: Rome .... ROMA
It. sculptor .... LEONI
It. singer .... AMATO
It. title, early .... SER
It. university city BARI, PADUA
It. violin maker ..... AMATI
It. wine .... ASTI
Italy .... ITALIA
itch .... PSORA
itemize .... LIST
ivory nut ...... ANTA, TAGUA
ivy crowned ..... HEDERATED
ivy thicket .... TOD

J

jack in cribbage .... NOB
jack-in-the-pulpit ARAD, AROID
jack tree .... JACA
jackal, Afr. .... THOS
jackal, India .... KOLA
jackal, N. Afr. .... DIEB
jackdaw .... DAW
jackdaw: Scot. .... KAE
JACKET .. see also GARMENT
jacket .. ETON, JUPE, BOLERO
jacket, armor .... ACTON
jacket, Malay .... BAJU
Jackson heroine .. RAMONA
Jacob's brother .. EDOM, ESAU
Jacob's son..DAN, GAD, ASER,
LEVI, ASHER
Jacob's twin brother .... ESAU
Jacob's wife .. LEAH, RACHEL
jaeger gull ..... SKUA, ALLAN
jagged line .... ZAG, ZIG
jai alai .... PELOTA
Jamashid .... YIMA
James II daughter ...... ANNE
Janizaries, Chief of ...... DEY
JAPANESE: . see also SPECIAL
SECTION
Jap. aborigine ... AINO, AINU
Jap. admiral .... ITO
Jap.-Am. .... ISSEI,
KIBEI, NISEI, SANSEI
Jap. army reserve ..... HOJU
Jap. army second line ... KOBI
Jap. art of self-defense JUDO
Jap. badge, family ...... MON
Jap. badge, imperial KIRIMON
Jap. beer, rice .... SAKE, SAKI
Jap. beverage .... SAKE
Jap. box, girdle .... INRO
Jap. bush clover ...... HAGI
Jap. cedar .... SUGI
Jap. celery-like vegetable UDO
Jap. cherry .... FUJI
Jap. clogs .... GETA
Jap. deer .... SIKA
Jap. drama ... NO, KABUKI
Jap. emperor's title ... TENNO
Jap. festival .... BON
Jap. fish .... TAI, FUGU
Jap. food, seaweed
KOBU, KOMBU
Jap. gods .... KAMI
Jap. happiness god
EBISU, HOTEI
Jap. harp .... KOTO
Jap. herb, stout .... UDO

Jap. immigrant .... ISSEI
Jap. mile measure .... RI
Jap. monastery .... TERA
Jap. national park ...... ASO
Jap. naval station .... KURE
Jap. news agency ... DOMEI
Jap. nobleman .... KUGE
Jap. outcast
ETA, YETA, RONIN
Jap. outer garment
MINO, HAORI, KIMONO
Jap. parliament .... DIET
Jap. perfecture .... FU
Jap. persimmon .... KAKI
Jap. plant .... UDO
Jap. plane .... ZERO
Jap. primitive ... AINO, AINU
Jap. province, old ... ISE, KAI
Jap. receptacle .... INRO
Jap. salad plant .... UDO
Jap. salmon .... MASU
Jap. sash, kimono .... OBI
Jap. school of painting KANO
Jap. ship name .... MARU
Jap. sock .... TABI
Jap. statesman .... ITO
Jap. straw cape .... MINO
Jap. sword .. CATAN, CATTAN
Jap. vegetable .. UDO, GOBO
Jap. verse .... UTA
Jap. village .... MURA
Jap. volcano .... FUJI
Jap. writing .... KANA
Japheth, son of ...... GOMER
jar ...... EWER, OLLA, CRUSE
jar ring .... LUTE
jar, wide-mouthed ..... OLLA
jargon ... CANT, ARGOT, PATOIS
Jason's father .... AESON
Jason's 2d wife ..... CREUSA
Jason's ship .... ARGO
Jason's wife .... MEDEA
jaunty .... PERK
Java plum: P. I. ..... DUHAT
Javanese carriage ..... SADO
Javanese language KAVI, KAWI
Javanese poison tree ... UPAS
javelin, Afr. ASSAGAI, ASSEGAI
javelin game .. JERID, JEREED
javelin, Rom. .... PILUM
jeer .... GIBE, SCOFF
jeer at ...... TAUNT, DERIDE
Jehoshaphat, father of ... ASA
Jehovah .... GOD
Jehovah: Hebr. .... JAH,
JAVE, JAVEH, YAHWEH

84

jejune .. DRY, ARID, BARREN
jelly base .... PECTIN
jelly fruit .... GUAVA
jelly, meat .... ASPIC
jeopardize .... ENDANGER
Jericho, land opposite .. MOAB
jersey, woollen .... SINGLET
Jerusalem, ancient name SALEM
Jerusalem: poet. ...... ARIEL
jest .... JAPE
jester ...... MIME, BUFFOON
jet, U.S. .. SABRE, SCORPION
Jether, son of .... ARA
jetty .... MOLE
Jew .... SEMITE
JEWEL ..... see GEM, STONE
jewelry setting .... PAVE
jewels, adorn with .... BEGEM
JEWISH .. see also HEBREW
Jewish ascetic ...... ESSENE
Jewish benediction ... SHEMA
Jewish bride .... KALLAH
Jewish ceremony SEDAR, SEDER
Jewish feast of tabernacles
                    SUCCOTH
Jewish festival PURIM, SEDER
Jewish law, body of .. TALMUD
Jewish marriage contract
                    KETUBA
Jewish offering .... CORBAN
Jewish prayer book .. MAHZOR
Jewish scholar .... RAB
Jewish sect, ancient .. ESSENES
Jewish teacher .... REB, RABBI
Jewish title of honor
                RAB, GAON
Jezebel's husband .... AHAB
Joan of Arc's victory ORLEANS
Job's-tears .... COIX
jog .... TROT, NUDGE
John: Gaelic, Scot. IAN, EOAN
John: Ir. .... EOIN, SEAN
John: Russ. .... IVAN
johnny-cake .... PONE
Johnson, Dr., hero .. RASSELAS
join ..... LINK, PAIR, SEAM,
    WELD, YOKE, MERGE,
    UNITE, ATTACH
join corners ... MITER, MITRE
join wood .... RABBET
joining bar .... YOKE
joint HIP, KNEE, NODE, HINGE
joint part TENON, MORTISE
joke with KID, RIB, JAPE, JOSH
joker .... WAG, WIT
Jordan city, ancient region
                    PETRA
Joseph's father ...... JACOB
Joseph's nephew ...... TOLA

Joshua tree .... YUCCA
Joshua's father ...... NUN
jostle .... JOG, ELBOW
jot .... IOTA, TITTLE
journey .... ITER, RIDE, TOUR,
        TREK, TRIP, TRAVEL
journey in circuit ...... EYRE
joy ..... DELIGHT, RAPT 'RE
joyous .... GLAD
Judah, city in ... ADAR, ENAM
Judah's son ...... ER, ONAN
Judaism scriptures
                TORA, TORAH
judge .. DEEM, RATE, ARBITER
JUDGE, BIB. ... see BIBLICAL
                    JUDGE
judge in Hades ...... MINOS
judge of dead, Egypt ... OSIRIS
judge's bench .... BANC
judge's chamber ... CAMERA
judges' rule, Israel KRITARCHY
judgment, Fr. law ..... ARRET
JUDICIAL see also LEGAL, LAW
judicial assembly ..... COURT
jug, large beer ..... RANTER
jug shaped like man ... TOBY
jug, wide-mouthed .... EWER
juice .... SAP
juice, thickened ...... RHOB
jujitsu .... JUDO
jujube .... BER, ELB
Jules Verne character ... NEMO
Juliet's betrothed ..... PARIS
Juliet's father, family CAPULET
jumble .... PI, PIE, MESS
jump: music .... SALTO
jumping disease, Malay LATA
jumping rodent ..... JERBOA
juncture, line of ...... SEAM
June bug .... DOR
Jungfrau's site .... ALPS
jungle clearing .... MILPA
juniper .... GORSE,
        SAVIN, SABINE, SAVINE
juniper, Europ. .... CADE
juniper tree, Bibl. EZEL, RETEM
Jupiter .... JOVE
Jupiter's moon, inner .... IO
Jupiter's wife .... HERA, JUNO
jurisdiction .... VENUE
jurisdiction, old Eng. SOC, SOKE
jurisprudence .... LAW
jury list .... PANEL
jury, writ summoning VENIRE
just .... MORAL
justice, goddess of . MA, MAAT
jute .... DESI
Jutlander .... DANE
jutting rock .... TOR
juxtaposition, place in APPOSE
jynx .... SPELL

K

a Kaffir language .... XOSA
   Kaffir tribe .... ZULU
   Kaffir war club .... KIRI
   Kaffir warrior .... IMPI
   Kalmuck ..... ELEUT, ELEUTH
   Kandh language .... KUI
   kangaroo, male ..... BOOMER
   kangaroo, young .... JOEY
   Katmandu's country ... NEPAL
   kava .... AVA
   kava bowl .... TANOA
   Kaw .... AKHA
   Keats poem-1820 .... LAMIA
   keel .... CAREEN
   keel, at right angle to ABEAM
   keel block wedge ... TEMPLET
   keel, having no ...... RATITE
   keel, kind of .... FIN
   keel, part of .... SKEG
   keel-shaped part
                   CARINA, CARINAE
   keen ACUTE, SHARP, ASTUTE
   keep account of .... TAB
   keepsake .... TOKEN
   keeve .... KIVER
b Kentucky coffee tree . CHICOT
   Kentucky college .... BEREA
   kerchief .... MADRAS
   kernel .... NUT
   ketch, Levant .... SAIC
   ketone, liquid ..... ACETONE
   ketone, oily .... CARONE
   kettledrum .. NAKER, ATABAL,
         ATTABAL, TIMPANI, TIM-
         PANO, TYMPANO
   key .... ISLE
   key fruit .... SAMARA
   key notch .... WARD
   key part .... BIT
   key-shaped ..... URDE, URDY
   keyed up .... AGOG
   Khedive's estate ..... DAIRA
   kid, undressed .... SUEDE
   kidney .... NEER
   kidney bean .... BON
   kidneys, pert. to .... RENAL
   killer whale .... ORCA
   kiln ...... OST, OAST, OVEN
   kiloliter .... STERE
   kind
      ILK, SORT, GENRE, SPECIES
   kind: Gr. .... GENOS
   kindle: dialect .... TIND
   kindly .... BENIGN
   kindness .... LENITY
   kindred .... SIB

c king .... REX, REY, REGES
   king —, cartoon character
                          AROO
   King Alfred's city: abbr. .. LON
   king, Amalekite .... AGAG
   King Arthur's abode
      AVALON, AVALLON, CAMELOT
   King Arthur's burial place
                   AVALON, AVALLON
   King Arthur's court .. CAMELOT
   King Arthur's father .. UTHER
   King Arthur's fool .. DAGONET
   King Arthur's lance ... RON
   King Arthur's mother IGERNA,
         IGERNE, YGERNE, IGRAINE
   King Arthur's queen
            GUINEVER, GUINEVERE
   KING, BIBLICAL .... see
                      BIBLICAL KING
   King Ethelred "The —"
                        UNREADY
   king, Gr. .... MINOS
   King Gradlon's capital .... IS
   king, Hebrew .... HEROD
   king, Midianite ...... REBA
   king, mythical ...... MIDAS
   king of beasts .... LION
d King of Colchis' daughter
                         MEDEA
   king of Crete .... MINOS
   king of elves ..... ERLKING
   king of gods, Egypt
            AMEN, AMON, AMUN
   king of Greece, ancient MINOS
   king of Israel ... AHAB, ELAH,
            OMRI, SAUL, NADAB
   king of Jews .... HEROD
   king of Judah ... ASA, AHAZ,
            AMON, UZZIAH
   king of Judea .... HEROD
   king of Naples ...... MURAT
   king of Persia .... CYRUS
   king of Sodom .... BERA
   king, pert. to ...... REGNAL
   king, Phrygian ...... MIDAS
   king, rich .... CROESUS
   king, Spartan AGIS, LEONIDAS
   king, Teut. Visigoth .. ALARIC
   king's bodyguard .... THANE
   king's yellow ..... ORPIMENT
   KINGDOM ..see also COUNTRY
   kingdom, ancient ..... MOAB
   KINGDOM, BIB. .. see page 197
   kingfish .... HAKU, OPAH
   kinkajou .... POTTO
   kinship, Moslem law ... NASAB
   Kipling hero .... KIM

a
kismet .... **FATE**
kiss .... **BUSS, SMᴧCK**
kitchen, ship's ...... **GALLEY**
kitchen tool
　　　　CORER, RICER, GRATER
kite, bird
　　　　GLED, GLEDE, ELANET
kittiwake gull, Shetlands **WAEG**
kitty, feed the .... **ANTE**
kiwi .... **ROA**
knave .... **ROGUE**
knave, in cribbage ..... **NOBS**
knave of clubs .... **PAM**
knead .... **ELT**
knead, in massage .... **PETRIE**
knee: Lat. .... **GENU**
kneecap ... **ROTULA, PATELLA**
KNIFE .. see also DAGGER
knife .... **CHIV, STAB,**
　　　　MACHETE, MACHETTE
knife, Burmese .... **DAH, DOW**
knife dealer .... **CUTLER**
knife, Eskimo .... **ULU**
knife, large ..... **SNY, SNEE**
knife, loop-cutting
　　TREVAT, TRIVAT, TRIVET
knife, P. I. .... **BOLO**
knife, single-edge .... **BOWIE**
knife, surgical ...... **SCALPEL**
knight **SIR, RITTER, TEMPLAR**
knight, heroic ..... **PALADIN**
knight, make .... **DUB**
knight, medieval ..... **BEVIS**
knight's mantel .... **TABARD**

c
knight's wife .... **DAME**
knitting stitch .... **PURL**
knob: anat. .... **CAPUT**
knobbed .... **TOROSE**
knoblike .... **NODAL**
knobkerrie .... **KIRI**
knockout .... **KO, KAYO**
knot .... **MILE, NODE, NODI,**
　　SNAG, GNARL, KNURL,
　　NODUS
knot, fiber .... **NOIL, NOYL**
knot in wood .... **BURL,**
　　KNAR, KNOR, KNUR, NURL
knot, insecure ..... **GRANNY**
knot lace .... **TAT, TATT**
knot, like a .... **NODAL**
knot of thread .... **BURL**
knots, fiber .... **NEP**
knots, having .... **NODED**
know .... **KEN, WIST**
knowledge ..... **KEN, LORE**
knowledge, pert. to .. **GNOSTIC**
knowledge, pure .... **NOESIS**
known as milo maize, grain
　　　　　　　　MILO
knucklebones, sheep ... **DOLOS**
kobold .... **NIS, NISSE**
Kol dialect .... **HO**
kopecks, 100 .... **RUBLE**
Koran chapter .... **SURA**
Koran interpreters .... **ULEMA**
Korea .... **CHOSEN**
Korean president ..... **RHEE**
Korean soldier .... **ROK**
Kronos' wife .... **RHEA**
kurrajong tree .... **CALOOL**

L

b
"La Boheme" heroine ... **MIMI**
Laban, daughter of .... **LEAH**
label .... **TAG, PASTER**
LABOR GROUP ... see **UNION**
laborer, China . **COOLY, COOLIE**
laborer, India .... **TOTY**
Labrador tea .... **LEDUM**
labyrinth .... **MAZE**
lac .... **RESIN**
lace .... **BEAT, LASH**
lace, barred **GRILLE, GRILLEE**
lace, Fr. ... **CLUNY, ALENCON**
lace, gold, silver .... **ORRIS**
lace, metal tip of
　　　　AGLET, AIGLET
lace, square hole ...... **FILET**
lacerate .... **RIP, TEAR**
laceration .... **RIP, TEAR**
lack .... **NEED, WANT**
lack of power .... **ATONY**

d
Laconian clan group ..... **OBE**
Laconian subdivision ..... **OBE**
ladder, scale fort wall with
　　SCALADE, SCALADO, ES-
　　CALADE, ESCALADO
ladderlike .... **SCALAR**
lady, India .... **BIBI**
"Lady of the Lake" outlaw **DHU**
ladylove, in poetry .... **DELIA**
lagoon .... **LIMAN**
lake .... **MERE**
lake, Afr. salt .. **SHAT, SHOTT**
lake, Blue Nile source .. **TANA**
Lake Erie battle officer **PERRY**
Lake, Great (5) **ERIE, HURON,**
　　ONTARIO, MICHIGAN, SU-
　　PERIOR
lake, mountain .... **TARN**
lake near Galilee sea .. **MEROM**
lake, resort .... **TAHOE**

a lake: Scot. .... **LOCH**
Lake Tahoe trout ...... **POGY**
lake whitefish .... **POLLAN**
lama, head .... **DALAI**
lamb .... **EAN, EWE, YEAN**
lamb, holy .... **AGNUS**
lamb: Lat. .... **AGNI, AGNUS**
lamb, young .... **COSSET**
Lamb's pen name ...... **ELIA**
Lamech, ancestor of ... **CAIN**
Lamech's son
NOAH, JABAL, JUBAL
lament .... **KEEN, WAIL,**
WEEP, GRIEVE, PLAINT
lamentation .... **LINOS**
lamp black .... **SOOT**
lamprey .... **EEL**
lance head .... **MORNE**
lance, mythical .... **RON**
lance rest, breastplate **FAUCRE**
lance, short .... **DART**
Lancelot's beloved ... **ELAINE**
lancer, Ger. ... **ULAN, UHLAN**
lancewood .... **CIGUA**
land, absolute property **ALOD,**
ALLOD, ALODIUM, ALLODIUM
land amid water .. **ISLE, ISLET**
land breeze .... **TERRAL**
land, church's .... **GLEBE**
b land held in fee simple
ODAL, UDAL
land: law .... **SOLUM**
LAND MEASURE .. see also
AREA in SPECIAL SECTION
land measure
AR, ARE, ROD, ACRE, ROOD
land ownership, pert. to **ODAL**
land snail genus ..... **CERION**
land spring .... **LAVANT**
land, tilled, plowed: Sp.
ARADA, ARADO
land under tenure: Scot. .. **FEU**
landing place ..... **KEY, PIER,**
QUAI, QUAY, LEVEE
landing place, India
GAUT, GHAT
landing ship .... **LST**
landmark .... **COPA**
landmark: Sp. .... **SENAL**
lands .... **ACRES**
language, Aramaic ... **SYRIAC**
language, Assam .... **AO, AKA**
language, dead ...... **LATIN**
language, early It. .... **OSCAN**
language, Egypt. .... **COPTIC**
language, Finnish ..... **UGRIC**
language form, peculiarity
IDIOM
language, Gilgit ...... **SHINA**
language, Hittite ...... **PALA**
language, Indic .... **HINDI**

c language, Indo-Chin. .... **AO,**
WA, AKA, ANU, LAI, LAO,
MRO, MRU, PWO, SAK,
AHOM, AKHA, AMOY,
BODO, GARO, KAMI, NAGA,
RONG, SGAU, SHAN
language, Ir. ... **CELTIC, KELTIC**
language, Kandh .... **KUI**
language, Kashmir .... **SHINA**
language, Mossi .... **MO, MOLE**
language, N. Afr. ..... **BERBER**
language of Bible days
ARAMAIC
language, P. I.
TAGAL, TAGALOG
language, Scot. **CELTIC, KELTIC**
language, Semitic .... **ARABIC**
language, Siberian
ENISEI, YENISEI
language, S. Afr. ...... **TAAL**
language, Sudanic **MO, MOLE**
language, synthetic .. **RO, IDO**
language, Welsh **CELTIC, KELTIC**
languages, E. Europ. ... **UGRIC**
languish .... **FLAG, PINE**
languor, drug-induced
KEF, KAIF, KIFF
langur .... **MAHA**
lantern feast .... **BON**
d Laomedon's father ...... **ILUS**
Laomedon's son
PRIAM, TITHONUS
Laos aborigine ... **KHA, YUN**
lapel .... **REVER**
lapidate .... **STONE**
Lapp's sledge ... **PULK, PULKA**
larboard .... **APORT**
larch **TAMARAC, TAMARACK**
large amount .... **SCAD**
lariat .... **LAZO, ROPE,**
LASSO, REATA, RIATA
lariat, metal eye of
HONDA, HONDO, HONDOO
larva .... **GRUB**
larva of fly ...... **BOT, BOTT**
lash .... **TIE, WHIP**
lasso
ROPE, REATA, RIATA, LARIAT
last .... **FINAL, OMEGA**
last but one .... **PENULT**
"Last Days of Pompeii" character .... **IONE**
last Imam .... **MAHDI**
last section .... **FINALE**
Last Supper picture ... **CENA**
Last Supper room .. **CENACLE**
latching: naut. ...... **LASKET**
late ... **NEW, TARDY, RECENT**
late, one at school ..... **SERO**
lateen-rigged boat ..... **DOW,**
DHOW, SETEE, MISTIC

latent .... **DORMANT**
lateral .... SIDE
lath .... SLAT
LATIN ...... see also ROMAN
LATIN:
  abbot .... ABBAS
  above ...... SUPER, SUPRA
  about .... CIRCITER
  across .... TRANS
  act .... ACTU, ACTUS
  after .... POST
  aged .... AET (abbr.)
  all .... TOTO
  alone .... SOLO, SOLUS
  and .... ET
  and others .... ETAL (abbr.)
  around .... CIRCUM
  art .... ARS
  backward .... RETRO
  before .... ANTE
  behold .... ECCE
  being .... ESSE
  believe, I .... CREDO
  beneath .... INERA
  bird .... AVIS
  book .... LIBER
  blessed .... BEATA
  bronze .... AES
  but .... SED
  cattle .... PECORA
  country .... RUS, RURIS
  cup .... CALIX
  custom .... RITUS
  day .... DIEM
  days .... DIES
  depart! .... VADE
  divination by lots .... SORS, SORTES
  door .... JANUA
  earth .... TERRA
  egg .... OVUM
  eight .... OCTO
  error .... LAPSUS
  event .... REI
  evil .... MALA, MALUM
  fate .... NONA
  field .... AGER
  fields .... AGRI
  fire .... IGNIS
  first .... PRIMUS
  fish .... PISCES
  force .... VIS
  from .... DE
  go! .... VADE
  god .... DEUS
  goddess .... DEA
  gods .... DI
  gold .... AURUM
  good .... BONUM, BONUS
  grandfather .... AVUS
  he .... ILLE

  he remains .... MANET
  he was .... ERAT
  head .... CAPUT
  high .... ALTA
  himself .... IPSE
  I love .... AMO
  in so far as .... QUA
  is .... EST
  itself .... IPSO
  ivory .... EBUR
  journey .... ITER
  knee .... GENU
  lamb .... AGNI, AGNUS
  land .... AGER
  learned .... DOCTUS
  life .... VITA, ANIMA
  lo .... ECCE
  man .... VIR
  mass .... MISSA
  mine .... MEUM
  more than .... SUPER
  mountain .... MONS
  name .... NOMEN
  nose, of the .... NAS
  not .... NON
  observe .... NOTA
  offense ..... MALA, MALUM
  once .... SEMEL
  or .... AUT
  other .... ALIA
  over .... SUPER
  pardon .... VENIA
  palm .... VOLA
  part .... PARS
  partly .... PARTIM
  peace .... PAX
  pin .... ACUS
  pledge .... VAS
  possessive .... SUA
  power .... VIS
  pronoun .... SUA
  property .... BONA
  quickly .... CITO
  rate .... RATA
  religious law .... FAS
  right .... DEXTER
  same .... IDEM
  scarcely VIX
  see .... VIDE
  side .... LATUS
  table .... MENSA
  tail .... CAUDA
  that is .... "ID EST"
  that one .... ILLE
  the same .... IDEM
  thing .... RES

Latin

LATIN(continued from page 89)

this one .... HIC, HAEC
thus .... SIC
throat .... GULA
to be .... ESSE
to use .... UTOR
tooth .... DENS
toward .... AD
twice .... BIS
under .... SUB
unless .... NISI
vein .... VENA
voice .... VOX
water .... AQUA
we .... NOS
well .... BENE
where .... UBI
within .... INTRA
without .... SINE
wool .... LANA
wrong ..... MALA, MALUM

Latvia, native of .... LETT
laugh .... FLEER
laugh, able to .... RISIBLE
laughing .... RIANT
laughing, pert. to .. GELASTIC
laurel .... BAY, DAPHNE
laurel bark, medicinal . COTO
lava .... AA, LATITE, SCORIA
lava, rough .... AA
lavender, Eur. .... ASPIC
lavish affection .... DOTE
law
JURE, RULE, CANON, EDICT
law, abstract .... JUS
law, D. E. Ind. .... ADAT
law excluding women from
reign .... SALIC
law of Moses .. TORA, TORAH
law, Rom. .... JUS, LEX
lawful .... LEGAL, LICIT
lawgiver, Gr.
DRACO, MINOS, SOLON
lawgiver, Hebr. .... MOSES
lawmaker .... SOLON
lawyer .... LEGIST
lawyers' patron saint ... IVES
lay .... PUT, DITTY
layer .... PLY,
LAMINA, STRATA, STRATUM
layer of a plant ..... PROVINE
layer, wood .... VENEER
layman .... LAIC
lazar .... LEPER
lazy .... OTIOSE
lead-colored .... LIVID
lead: music PRESA, PRECENT
lead, ore .... GALENA

lead, pellets of .... SHOT
lead, pencil ...... GRAPHITE
lead sulphide, native GALENA
lead telluride ...... ALTAITE
lead, white .... CERUSE
leaden color, having ... LIVID
leader, fishing .... SNELL
leader of movement .... VAN
leader, Rom. .... DUX
leaf appendage ...... STIPEL
leaf-cutting ant ...... ATTA
leaf division .... LOBE
leaf, fern .... FROND
leaf, flower .. BRACT, SEPAL
leaf-miner beetle ..... HISPA
leaf of book .... FOLIO
leaf vein .... RIB
league, Ger. .... BUND
league, trading .... HANSE
Leah's father .... LABAN
Leah's son .... LEVI
lean .. CANT, GAUNT, SPARE
lean-to .... SHED
Leander's love .... HERO
"Leaning Tower" city .. PISA
leap LUNGE, VAULT, CURVET
leap: music .... SALTO
leap: Scot. LOUP, LOWP, STEND
leaping .... SALTANT
learned .. ERUDITE, LETTERED
learning .... LORE
learning, man of
SAGE, PEDANT, SAVANT
Lear's daughter ...... REGAN
Lear's faithful follower KENT
least bit .... RAP
leather bottle .... MATARA
leather flask, Gr. ...... OLPE
leather, glove
KID, NAPA, MOCHA, SUEDE
leather, kind of ... ELK, BOCK
leather, prepare—make into
TAN, TAW
leather, soft
NAPA, ALUTA, SUEDE
leather thong, hawk's .. BRAIL
leatherfish .... LIJA
"leatherneck" .... MARINE
leave
GO, QUIT, EXEAT, DEPART
leave destitute ...... STRAND
leave of absence, school EXEAT
leave-taking .... CONGE
leaves, having: Her. .. POINTE
leaven .... YEAST
leaving .... ORT
leavings ..... DREGS, RESIDUE
Lebanese port, old .... TYRE
ledge, fort .... BERM, BERME
ledger entry
ITEM, DEBIT, CREDIT

lee, opposed to .... STOSS
leeangle .. LEAWILL, LEEWILL
leer .... OGLE
Leeward Island .... NEVIS
left: comb. form ...... LEVO
left-hand .... LEVO
left-hand page ... VO, VERSO
left, to turn .... HAW
leftover .... ORT
leg, covering, ancient PEDULE
leg, front of .... SHIN
leg joint, animal .... HOCK
leg-like part .... CRUS
leg of mutton, lamb .. GIGOT
leg, part of .... SHIN, SHANK
leg, pert. to calf of ... SURAL
legal action suit .. RES, CASE
legal claim .... LIEN
legal delays .... MORAE
legal injury .... TORT
legal job .... CASE
legal matter .... RES
legal offense .. DELIT, DELICT
legal order .... WRIT
legal paper .... DEED
legal profession ... BAR, LAW
legal prosecution ...... SUIT
legend ... MYTH, SAGA, TALE
legion division, Rom. COHORT
legislate .... ENACT
legislative assembly, Afr. RAAS
legislator ... SOLON, SENATOR
legislature ... DIET, SENATE
legislature: Sp. .... CORTES
legume ..... PEA, POD, BEAN
leisure .... REST, OTIUM
lemur .... MAKI, INDRI,
    LORIS, AYE-AYE, SEMIAPE
lemur, Afr. .... GALAGO
lemur, Asia, Ceylon LORI, LORIS
lemur, Ceylonese ...... LORI
lemur, flying ...... COLUGO
lemur, ruffed .... VARI
lemuroid .... POTTO
lengthily, address .. PERORATE
Leningrad's river .... NEVA
lens, hand .... READER
lentil .... ERVUM
leopard .... PARD
Leporidae, one of the .. HARE
leprosy .... LEPRA
Lepus genus, one of ..... HARE
lerp .... LAAP
Lesbos, poet of ...... ARION
"Les Etats —" .... UNIS
less .... MINUS
lessen BATE, ABATE, MITIGATE
let HIRE, RENT, LEASE, PERMIT
let bait drop .... DAP
let it stand! .... STA, STET

let up .... ABATE
lethal .... FATAL
lethargy
    COMA, STUPOR, TORPOR
letter .. AR (18), EF (6), EM
    (13), EN (14), EX (24),
    WY (25), BEE (2), CEE
    (3), DEE (4), ESS (19),
    GEE (7), JAY (10), PEE
    (16), TEE (20), VEE (22),
    WYE (25), ZED (26), ZEE
    (26), AITCH (8)
letter, according to .. LITERAL
letter, Ang.-Sax. ... EDH, ETH
letter, early Gr. .... SAN
LETTER, GR. and NUMBER . see
    also GREEK LETTER
letter, Gr. .... MU, NU, PI, XI,
    CHI, ETA, PHI, PSI, RHO,
    TAU, BETA, IOTA, ZETA,
    ALPHA, DELTA, GAMMA,
    KAPPA, OMEGA, SIGMA,
    THETA, LAMBDA, EPSILON,
    OMICRON, UPSILON
letter, Hebr. .. HE (5), PE (17),
    AIN (16), MEM (13),
    NUN (14), SIN (21), TAV
    (22), TAW (22), VAU
    (16), WAW (16), ALEF
    (11), AYIN (16), BETH
    (2), CAPH (11), ELEF (1),
    KAPH (11), KOPH (19),
    QOPH (19), RESH (20),
    SADE (18), SHIN (21),
    TETH (9), YODH, (10),
    ALEPH (13), GIMEL (3),
    LAMED (12), DALETH (4),
    LAMEDH (12)
letter of resignation .. DEMIT
letters, sloping ...... ITALICS
lettuce, kind of COS, ROMAINE
Levantine ketch .... SAIC
levee .... DIKE, DYKE
level EVEN, RASE, RAZE, PLANE
leveling slip .... SHIM
lever ..... PRY, PEVY, PEAVY,
    PEEVY, PEAVEY, PEEVEY,
    TAPPET
levy .... TAX, CESS, IMPOST
Lew Wallace hero .... HUR
Lhasa holy man .... LAMA
Lhasa's country .... TIBET
liability .... DEBT
liana .... CIPO
liang .... TAEL
liar .... ANANIAS
Liberian native .... VAI, VEI
Liberian tribes .. GI, KRA, KRU
license: slang .... READER
lichen .... MOSS
lichen genus USNEA, EVERNIA

lichen, kind **PARELLA, PARELLE**
lie in wait .... **LURK**
Liege, town near .... **ANS**
liegeman .... **VASSAL**
lieu .... **STEAD**
life .... **BIOS, BIOTA**
life: Lat. ...... **VITA, ANIMA**
life, of .... **VITAL**
life principle .... **PRANA**
life principle, Hindu .. **ATMAN**
life prolonger .... **ELIXIR**
life, relating to
        BIOTIC, BIOTICAL
life tenant .... **LIVIER**
lifeless **AMORT, AZOIC, INERT**
lifetime .... **AGE**
lifted with effort ...... **HOVE**
ligament .... **BOND**
light .... **LAMP, KLEIG,
        KLIEG, TAPER, ILLUME**
light and fine, as lines .. **LEGER**
light as a line .... **LEGER**
light bulb filler ...... **ARGON**
light, circle of
        HALO, NIMB, NIMBUS
light intensity unit ...... **PYR**
light, kind of .... **ARC**
light ring .... **CORONA**
light, science of ...... **OPTICS**
light, sun's **AUREOLA, AUREOLE**
light unit **PYR, LUMEN, HEFNER**
lighter, lamp .... **SPILL**
lighter, make .... **LEAVEN**
lighthouse .... **PHAROS**
lightning: poet. .... **LEVIN**
ligulate .... **LORATE**
like .... **AS, AKIN**
likely .... **APT**
likeness ...... **ICON, IMAGE**
likewise not .... **NOR**
lily .... **LIS, LYS, ALOE,
        ARUM, SEGO, CALLA**
lily family plant ..... **CAMAS
        CAMASS, CAMMAS**
lily genus .... **ALOE**
lily genus, plantain .... **HOSTA**
Lily Maid of Astolat
        ELAIN, ELAINE
lily, palm .... **TI**
limb ...... **ARM, LEG, MANUS**
limber .... **LITHE**
lime, to hydrate ..... **SLAKE**
lime tree ...... **TEIL, TEYL**
limestone, grainy ..... **OOLITE**
limestone, Irish .... **CALP**
limestone, soft **MALM, CHALK**
limicoline bird **SNIPE, PLOVER**
limit .... **TERM, BOURN,
        STENT, STINT, BOURNE**
limn............. **DRAW, PAINT**
Lindbergh's book .... **WE**

linden .... **LIN, TEIL, TEYL**
line .... **ROW, RANK**
line, cutting .... **SECANT**
line, fine, on type letter **CERIF,
        SERIF, CERIPH**
line, fishing .... **SNELL**
line, in a .... **AROW**
line, intersecting ..... **SECANT**
line inside of .... **CEIL**
line, math. .... **VECTOR**
line, naut. . **EARING, MARLINE**
line not forming angle **AGONE**
line on a letter .... **SERIF**
line, pert. to .... **LINEAR**
line, thin .... **STRIA, STRIAE**
line, waiting ..... **CUE, QUEUE**
line with stone **STEAN, STEENE**
lines, marked with
        RULED, STRIATE, STRIATED
lines, telescope-lens .. **RETICLE**
linen .... **CREA**
linen, fine ..... **LAWN, TOILE**
linen, household, table **NAPERY**
linen, one caring for royal
        NAPERER
linen tape, braid ...... **INKLE**
linger .... **WAIT, TARRY**
lingo .... **ARGOT**
lingua .... **GLOSSA**
liniment .... **ARNICA**
link .... **YOKE, CATENATE**
links connected ..... **CATENAE**
linnet .... **TWITE, LENARD**
lion .... **LEO, SIMBA**
lion group .... **PRIDE**
lion killed by Hercules **NEMEAN**
lion of God .... **ALI**
lionet .... **CUB**
lips, pert. to .... **LABIAL**
liqueur ...... **CREME, NOYAU**
liqueur, sweet .... **GENEPI**
liquid element
        BROMIN, BROMINE
liquid, made ... **FUSIL, FUSILE**
liquid, without ..... **ANEROID**
liquor .. **GIN, RUM, RYE, GROG**
liquor, malt .... **ALE, PORTER**
liquor, oriental ..... **ARRACK**
liquor, P. I. .... **VINO**
liquor, Russian **VODKA, VODKI**
liquor, sugar-cane
        TAFIA, TAFFIA
Lisbon's river .... **TAGUS**
lissome .... **SVELTE**
list .... **ROTA, SLATE,
ROSTER, CATALOG, CATALOGUE**
list of persons
        ROTA, PANEL, ROSTER
list, one of a .... **ITEM**
listen .... **HARK, HEAR**
listless, be .... **MOPE**

a listlessness .. ENNUI, APATHY
liter, Dutch .... AAM, KAN
literary collection .... ANA
literary extracts
ANALECTA, ANALECTS
literary master ...... STYLIST
literary scraps, bits ANA, NOTES
literate .. LEARNED, LETTERED
lithograph .... CHROMO
Lithuanian .... BALT, LETT
litter, E. Ind. .. DOOLI, DOOLY,
DOOLEE, DOOLEY, DOOLIE
"Little Boy Blue" poet .. FIELD
little casino .... TWO
little chief hare .... PIKA
little: music .... POCO
liturgy .... RITE
live .... all forms of verb "BE"
live oak, Calif. ...... ENCINA
lively .... PERT, BRISK, PEART
lively, make .... PERK
lively: music
VIVO, DESTO, ANIMATO
lively person .... GRIG
lively song .... LILT
liver .... HEPAR
liver, pert. to .... HEPATIC
liverwort genus .... RICCIA

b livid .... BLAE
living in currents ...... LOTIC
Livonian LIV
lixivium ...... LYE, LEACH
lizard .. GILA, GECKO, GUANA,
SKINK, VARAN, IGUANA
lizard, Am. .... ANOLE, ANOLI
lizard, beaded .... GILA
lizard, changeable CHAMELEON
lizard genus ... UTA, AGAMA
lizard, large .. GILA, MONITOR
lizard, old world ...... SEPS
lizard, small .... EFT, GECKO
lizard, starred .... AGAMA
lizard, tropical .... AGAMA
lizardlike .... SAURIAN
llamalike animal ..... ALPACA
load .... LADE, ONUS
loadstone .... MAGNET
loaf, small: dial. .... BAP
loam .... LOESS
loam, India .... REGUR
loath .... AVERSE
loathe .... ABHOR
lobster box .... CAR
local .... TOPICAL
locale .... SITE
locality .... AREA,
LOCUS, VENEW, VENUE
location ... SITE, SPOT, PLACE
lock .... CURL, TRESS

c locks, Panama Canal .. GATUN
lockjaw ... TETANUS, TRISMUS
locust .... ACACIA,
CICADA, CICALA
locust, N. Z. .... WETA
lodge, soldier's .... BILLET
lofty dwelling .... AERIE
log birling contest .... ROLEO
log drive, escape work on SNIB
log, spin floating ..... BIRL
log splitter .... WEDGE
logarithm unit .... BEL
loge .... STALL
logger's implement ... PEAVY,
PEAVEY
logic, omission of step in
proof .... SALTUS
logician .... DIALECTOR
Lohengrin's wife .... ELSA
Loire, city on .... BLOIS
loiter .... LAG
Loki's daughter .... HEL, HELA
Loki's son .... NARE
Loki's wife .... SIGYN
London district .... SOHO
long .... YEN, PINE,
CRAVE, YEARN, ASPIRE
long ago .... ELD, YORE
long journey .. TREK, ODYSSEY

d long line (fishing) with hooks
TROT
long live! .... VIVA, VIVE
long-suffering .... MEEK
look .... LO, SEE
look after ...... MIND, TEND
look askance .... LEER
look at .... EYE, SCAN, VIEW
look here! .... HIST
look narrowly PEEK, PEEP, PEER
look slyly .... LEER, OGLE
loom, heddles of ...... CAAM
loom, lever in .... LAM
loon genus .... GAVIA
loon, kind of .... DIVER
loop, edging .... PICOT
loophole .... MUSE, MEUSE
looplike structure, anat. ANSA
loose .... LAX
loose coat PALETOT, MANTEVIL
loose robe .... SIMAR
loosen .... UNDO, UNTIE
lop ... SNED, PRUNE, SNATHE
lopsided .... ALOP, ALIST
loquat tree .... BIWA
Lord High Executioner in
"Mikado" .... KOKO
Lord: Jacobite Church ... MAR
lord, Oriental .... KHAN
lord, Pers. .... KAAN,
KAUN, KAWN, KHAN
lord, privileged .... PALATINE

93

Lord

lord, Scot. .... LAIRD
lore, Norse .... RUNE
lorica .... CUIRASS
"Lorna Doone" character RIDD
lose .... AMIT
"Lost Chord" finale .... AMEN
lot .... FATE
Lotan's father .... SEIR
Lot's birthplace .... UR
Lot's father .... HARAN
Lot's son .... MOAB
lottery prize .... TERN
lotus enzyme .... LOTASE
Lotus: poet .... LOTE
lotus tree .... SADR
loud: music .... FORTE
loud-voiced one .... STENTOR
loudness, measurement unit
PHON
loudspeaker for high sound
TWEETER
loudspeaker for low sound
WOOFER
Louis XVI's nickname .. VETO
Louisiana county ..... PARISH
Louisiana native .... CREOLE
lounge .... LOAF, LOLL
love . JO, GRA, ADORE, AMOUR
love: Anglo-Irish ..... GRA
love apple .... TOMATO
love feast .... AGAPE
love god
LOVE GOD . see GOD OF LOVE
LOVE GODDESS . see GODDESS
OF LOVE
love, inflame with
ENAMOR, ENAMOUR
love knot .... AMORET
love to excess ... DOAT, DOTE
lover .... ROMEO
"Love's Labour's Lost" constable
DULL
loving
FOND, AMATIVE, AMATORY
low .... MOO, BASE
low caste Hindu .. PASI, TELI
low caste Indian .... DOM,
MAL, GADDI
Lowell, poetess .... AMY
lower ABASE, DEBASE, NETHER
lower: arch. .... VAIL
lower jaw, bird's ...... MALA
lower world gods, Rom. MANES
lowest deck .... ORLOP
lowest part of base ... PLINTH

lowest point .... NADIR
loyal .... LEAL,
TRUE, STANCH, STAUNCH
loyalist .... TORY
lozenge .... PASTIL, ROTULA
TROCHE, PASTILE, PASTILLE
loyalty fulfilling religious
obligations: Rom. . PIETAS
Lubeck, pert. to ...... LUBS
lucerne ... MEDIC, ALFALFA
luck: Ir. .... CESS
luck, pert. to ..... ALEATORY
lucky stroke .... FLUKE
lugubrious .... SAD
lukewarm .... TEPID
lumber along ... LOB, LOBB
Lumber State .... see page 208
lumberman .... SAWYER
lumberman's boot ...... PAC
lumberman's boots
PACS, OVERS
lumberman's hook .... PEVY,
PEAVY, PEEVY, PEAVEY,
PEEVEY
luminaire .... LAMP
luminary .... STAR
lump .... NUB, WAD,
CLOT, NODE, SWAD
lunar crater .... LINNE
lunar god, Phrygian .... MEN
luncheon .... TIFFIN
lurch .... CAREEN
lure .... BAIT, DECOY
luster .... GLOSS, SHEEN
lusterless .. DIM, MAT, MATTE
lustrous .... NITID
lute, Oriental .... TAR
luxuriant ..... LUSH, RANK
luxuriate .... BASK
Luzon native .... ATA, ITA,
AETA, ATTA, TAGAL,
TAGALA
Luzon negrito .... ATA,
AETA, ITA, ATTA
Luzon pagan .... ITALON
Lynette's knight .... GARETH
lynx, Afr. .... SYAGUSH
lynx, Pers. .... CARACAL
lyrebird genus ...... MENURA
lyric .... ODE, MELIC
lyric Muse .... ERATO
Lytton heroine .... IONE

94

M

a macaque Indian **BRUH, RHESUS**
macaw .... **ARA, ARARA**
macaw, Braz.
 ARA, ARARA, MARACAN
mace-bearer .... **BEADLE**
macerate ...... **RET, STEEP**
machine, finishing .... **EDGER**
machine, grain cleaner **AWNER**
machine gun .... **BREN, STEN**
machine, hummeling .. **AWNER**
machine, ore-dressing **VANNER**
machine part
 CAM, PAWL, TAPPET
machine, rubber .. **EXTRUDER**
mackerel net .... **SPILLER**
mackerel, young .... **SPIKE**
Madagascar mammal .. **LEMUR**
Madagascar native .... **HOVA**
madam .... **MUM, MAAM**
madder ..... **RUBIA, MUNJEET**
madder, common Eu. **GARANCE**
madder shrub genus ... **EVEA**
madness .... **MANIA**
mafura tree .... **ROKA**
maggot .... **LARVA**
Magi, one of .... **GASPAR**
magic .... **RUNE**
magic: Hindustan **JADU, JADOO**
magic, pert. to ...... **GOETIC**
b magic stone .... **AGATE**
magic: W. Ind. .... **OBEAH**
magician .... **MAGE,
 MAGI, MAGUS, MERLIN**
magistrate, Athens **ARCHON**
magistrate, It. .... **DOGE**
magistrate, Rom. ..... **EDILE,
 AEDILE, CONSUL, PRETOR**
magnate ... **MOGUL, TYCOON**
magnifying glass .... **LENS**
Magog, ruler of .... **GOG**
magpie .. **MAG, PIE, MAGG,
 PIET, PIOT, PYAT, PYET,
 NINUT, PIANET**
magpie genus .... **PICA**
mah-jongg piece .... **TILE**
mahatma
 ARAHT, ARHAT, ARAHAT
mahogany pine ...... **TOTARA**
mahogany, Sp. .... **CAOBA**
mahogany streak .... **ROE**
mahogany tree, Ind. ... **TOON**
MAHOMET .. see MOHAMMED
MAHOMETAN ... see MOSLEM
maid .... **LASS, BONNE**
maid, lady's .... **ABIGAIL**
maid-of-all-work ..... **SLAVEY**
maid, Oriental
 AMA, IYA, AMAH, EYAH
maiden .... **DAMSEL**

c maiden name, signifying .. **NEE**
maiden of myth .... **IO**
mail .... **POST, SEND**
mail, coat of . **BRINIE, BYRNIE**
mail, India **DAK, DAUK, DAWK**
main point ... **NUB, GIST, PITH**
maintain. **AVER, HOLD, ASSERT**
maize .... **CORN**
maize bread .... **PIKI**
maize genus .... **ZEA**
major: music .... **DUR**
major third: Gr. mus. .. **DITONE**
make .... **RENDER**
make as one: obs. ...... **UNE**
make evident ...... **EVINCE**
make fast: naut. ...... **BELAY**
make good by action . **REDEEM**
make happy .... **ELATE**
make public: Old Eng. **DELATE**
Makua .... **KUA**
malarial fever .... **AGUE**
malarial poison
 MIASM, MIASMA
Malay apple .... **KAWIKA**
Malay canoe
 PRAH, PRAO, PRAU, PROA
Malay chief or headman. **DATO,
 DATU, DATTO**
d Malay dagger .... **CRIS, KRIS,
 CREES, KREES, CREESE, KREESE**
Malay lanseh tree ..... **DUKU**
Malay law .... **ADAT**
Malay lugger .... **TOUP**
malay negrito ..... **ATA, ITA**
Malay nerve ailment ... **LATA**
MALAY OUTRIGGER see MALAY
 CANOE
Malay title of respect .. **TUAN**
Malay ungulate ...... **TAPIR**
Malay verse form ... **PANTUN**
Malay vessel
 PRAH, PRAO, PRAU, PROA
Malay, word meaning dark **AETA**
Malayan ape .... **LAR**
male cat .... **GIB, TOM**
male figure, used as support
 ATLAS, TELAMON
male swan .... **COB**
malefic .... **EVIL**
malic acid, fruit with
 ATTA, APPLE, GRAPE
malign .... **REVILE**
malignant .... **EVIL**
malignant spirit ... **KER, KERES**
malleable ..... **SOFT, DUCTILE**
mallet .... **MALL, GAVEL**
malt drink, pert. to ...... **ALY**
malt infusion .... **WORT**
maltreat .... **ABUSE**

Mammal

a
MAMMAL .. see also ANIMAL
mammal, sea aquatic .. SEAL,
    OTTER, WHALE, DUGONG,
    MANATEE
mammoth .... **GIANT**
man-eating monster ... **LAMIA**
man, handsome ...... **ADONIS**
man, rich .... **CROESUS**
man's name .. **ELI, GUY, IAN,**
    IRA, JOB, LEE, RAY, REX,
    ADAM, ALAN, AMOS,
    BRAM, CARL, DANA, DION,
    EBEN, EMIL, ENOS, ERIC,
    EVAN, EZRA, HANS, HUGH,
    HUGO, IVAN, JOEL, JOHN,
    JOSE, JUAN, JUDE, KARL,
    KNUT, LEON, LUKE, MARC,
    MARK, NEIL, NOEL, OTTO,
    OWEN, PAUL, SEAN, SETH,
    TEIG, BASIL, CALEB,
    CLARE, ENOCH, HIRAM,
    HOMER, SERGE, STEVE,
    TERRY, DEXTER, GASPAR,
    GEORGE, OLIVER, SAMSON,
    STEVEN, WARREN
man's nickname . **AL, ABE, ALF,**
    BEN, BOB, DON, GUS, JIM,
    JOE, KIT, LEW, LON, LOU,
    MAC, MAT, MAX, MOE,
    NED, PAT, ROB, SAM, SID,

b
    SIM, TED, TOM, ABIE,
    ALGY, ANDY, BART, BERT,
    BILL, BONY, DAVE, DAVY,
    DICK, DODE, FRED, GENE,
    JACK, JAKE, JOCK, JOEY,
    MART, MIKE, MOSE, NOLL,
    PETE, PHIL, RUBE, TOBY,
    TONY, WALT, ZACH, ZEKE
manageable .... **YARE**
manager .... **GERENT**
Manasseh, city of ...... **ANER**
Manasseh, son of ..... **AMON**
mandarin's home
    YAMEN, YAMUN
manducate .... **EAT**
maned .... **JUBATE**
manger ...... **CRIB, CRECHE**
mangle .... **MAUL**
mango, P. I. ...... **CARABAO**
mania .... **CRAZE**
manifest .... **SHOW,**
    OVERT, ATTEST, EVINCE
manifestation .... **AURA**
manifestation of god of lower
    world .... **SERAPIS**
maniple **FANO, FANON, FANUM**
manner
    AIR, WAY, MIEN, MODE
manner of walking ..... **GAIT**
manners .... **MORES**
manor .... **DEMENE, DEMESNE**

c
mantis crab .... **SQUILLA**
mantle .... **CAPE**
manual training, Swed. . **SLOID,**
    SLOYD
manuao .... **IAO**
Manxman .... **GAEL**
many .... **MAINT**
many-colored
    PIED, PINTO, MOTLEY
many-colored stone ... **AGATE**
Maori tattooing .... **MOKO**
Maori village ... **KAIK, KAIKA**
Maori wages .... **UTU**
Maori war club **MERE, MARREE**
Maori war-club wood ... **RATA**
map .... **PLAT**
map in a map .... **INSET**
maple fruit, seed .... **SAMARA**
maple genus .... **ACER**
maple tree tap .... **SPILE**
mar .... **DEFACE**
marabou .... **ARGALA**
marble **MIB, MIG, TAW, MIGG,**
    AGATE, AGGIE, MARMOR,
    MEALIE, SHOOTER
marble, Belgian **RANCE, RANSE**
marble, choice **ALAY, ALLEY**
marble, It. .... **CARRARA**
marble, Rom. .... **CIPOLIN**

d
marble, white .... **DOLOMITE**
marbles, game at ...... **TAW**
March King .... **SOUSA**
mare: Gypsy .... **GRASNI**
margin .... **RIM, EDGE, MARGE**
marginal reading, Hebrew
    Bible .... **KRI**
margosa tree .... **NIM, NEEM**
Marie Wilson, character played
    by .... **IRMA**
MARINE .. see also SEA
marine annelid .... **LURG**
marine fish, E. Ind. ... **DORAB**
marine measure, Jap. ..... **RI**
marine snail
    WELK, WILK, WHELK
marine snail genus .. **NERITA**
marine turtle genus . . **CARETTA**
marine worm .... **SYLLID**
marionette maker ..... **SARG**
mark .... **STIGMA, STIGMATA**
mark, diacritic **TILDE, MACRON**
mark of omission ..... **CARET**
mark, reference
    OBELI, OBELUS, OBELISK
mark, short vowel .... **BREVE**
marked with spots: bot. **NOTATE**
marker, Gr. & Rom. .. **STELA,**
    STELE, STELAE, STELAI

a market .... MART, SELL, VEND, RIALTO
market: India .... PASAR
market, Oriental
 SUQ, SOOK, SOUK
market place BAZAR, BAZAAR
market place, Gr. .... AGORA
marksman .... AIMER
marmalade tree
 MAMEY, SAPOTE
marmoset .... MICO
marmoset, S. Am. .. TAMARIN
"Marner, — " Eliot novel SILAS
marriage, absence of .. AGAMY
marriage notice BAN, BANNS
marriage portion, pert. to
 DOTAL
marriage portion: Scot.
 DOS, DOTE
marriage settlement
 DOS, DOT, DOWRY, DOWERY
marriage vows .... TROTH
marriageable .... NUBILE
marrow .... PITH
marry .... WED, WIVE
Mars .... ARES
Mars' outer satellite .. DEIMOS
Mars, pert. to .... AREAN
"Marseillaise" author .. LISLE
marsh .... BOG, FEN,
b SLUE, LIMAN, SWALE
marsh elder .... IVA
marsh fever .... HELODES
marsh gas .... METHANE
marsh hen .... RAIL
marsh mallow .... ALTEA
marsh marigold ...... CAPER
marsh plant
 REED, SEDGE, FESCUE
marshal, Waterloo ...... NEY
marshy .. PALUDAL, PALUDINE
marsupial, arboreal
 COALA, KOALA, POSSUM
marten .... SOBOL
martyr, 1st Christian . STEPHEN
marvel .... MIRACLE
Mascagni heroine ...... LOLA
MASCULINE
 see also MALE, MAN'S
mashy .... IRON
masjid ...... MOSK, MOSQUE
mask, half .... DOMINO
mask topknot, Gr. .... ONKOS
masons' pickax ..... GURLET
masquerade cloak ... DOMINO
mass ...... GOB, WAD, BULK
mass book .... MISSAL
mass meeting .... RALLY
mass, pert. to .... MISSATICAL
mass, rounded .... BOLUS
mast .... SPAR

c mast: obs. .... SPIR
mast, support .... BIBB
mast, wood for .... POON
master: archaic .... DAN
master, India
 MIAN, SAHEB, SAHIB
master, pert. to ...... HERILE
master, S. Afr. .... BAAS
master-stroke .... COUP
mastic tree .... ACOMA
masticate ...... CHAW, CHEW
mat, ornamental ...... DOILY
match, friction . FUSEE, FUZEE
match, wax .... VESTA
matchmaker .... EROS
MATERIAL ... see also FABRIC
maternity goddess, Egypt . APET
matgrass .... NARD
math quantity .SINE, OPERAND
math ratio, quantity .. PI, SINE
math term, hyperbolic function
 COSH, SECH, SINH, TANH
matter: law .... RES
matter-of-fact ..... LITERAL
matter: philos. .... HYLE
mattress case .... TICK
mature ..... AGE, RIPE, RIPEN
mature reproductive cell
 GAMETE
d maul .... MALLET
Mau Mau territory .... KENYA
Mauna — .... LOA
mausoleum, at Agra .... TAJ
maw: dialect .... MAA
maxilla ...... JAW, MALA
maxim . SAW, ADAGE, AXIOM,
 GNOME, MOTTO, SAYING
maxwell per ampere turn . PERM
May 1, Celtic ...... BELTANE
May fly .... DUN
MAYAN . see MAYAN INDIAN,
 page 192
Mayan year .... HAAB
Mayan year-end days .. UAYEB
mayor, Sp. . ALCADE, ALCALDE
meadow .... LEA, MEAD
meadow barley .... RIE
meadow grass genus ..... POA
meadow mouse .... VOLE
meadow saxifrage ..... SESELI
meadowsweet SPIREA, SPIRAEA
meager .... SCANT,
 LENTEN, SCANTY
meal .... REPAST
meal, boiled .... MUSH
meal, fine .... FARINA
meal, grain . PINOLA, PINOLE
meal, Indian, Hindu ATA, ATTA
meal, light .... BEVER

97

a meaning .... **SENSE, PURPORT**
meantime .... **INTERIM**
MEASURE ... Area, Liquid, Dry
    Length, Distance
    see SPECIAL SECTION
measure ...... **EM, EN, GAGE,
METE, PACE, GAUGE**
MEASURE, BIB. .. see HEBREW
                MEASURE
measure, Chin. length .... **LI**
"Measure for Measure"
    character .... **ANGELO**
MEASURE, DRY, BIB. .... see
    HEBREW DRY MEASURE
measure, Jap. distance .... **RI**
measure of distance, Ang.-Ind.
                  COSS
measure of spirits .... **PEG**
measure, old Arab ...... **SAA**
measure, old length ...... **ELL**
measure, poetry .... **SCAN**
measure, square ..... **AR, ARE**
meat, cut of ...... **HAM, RIB,
CHOP, LOIN, FILET,
STEAK, FILLET**
meat on skewer ...... **CABOB,
KABOB, KEBAB**
meat roll, fried ...... **RISSOLE**
Mecca pilgrim garb .... **IHRAM**
Mecca shrine .... **CAABA,**

b   **KAABA, KAABEH**
Mecca, trip to .... **HADJ**
mechanical man ...... **ROBOT**
mechanical part .... **CAM**
mechanics, branch of . **STATICS**
mechanics of motion
              DYNAMICS
meddle .... **PRY, TAMPER**
Medea's father .... **AEETES**
median line of valve ... **RAPHE**
medical .... **IATRIC**
medical fluid .... **SERUM**
medicinal capsule .... **CACHET**
medicinal fruit shrub .. **ALEM**
medicinal gum .... **KINO**
medicinal herb ...... **ALOE,
IPECAC, BONESET**
medicinal plant .... **ALOE**
medicinal plant, leaves **SENNA**
medicinal tablet ..... **TROCHE**
medicine man ...... **SHAMAN**
medicine man, S. Am.
           PEAI, PIAY
medieval lyric .... **ALBA**
medieval society **GILD, GUILD**
medieval tale, poem . **LAI, LAY**
Medina Arab .... **AUS**
MEDITERRANEAN ... see also
            GAZETTEER
Mediterranean, East of. **LEVANT**
Medit. grass .... **DISS**

c Medit. herb genus ...... **AMMI**
Medit. island: It. .... **RODI**
Medit. resort .... **NICE**
medlar .... **MESPIL**
medley .... **OLIO**
Medusa's slayer .... **PERSEUS**
meet .... **SIT**
meeting ..... **TRYST, SESSION**
meeting, political .... **CAUCUS**
megapode .... **MALEO**
melancholy . **SAD, BLUE, DREAR**
melancholy: poet. ..... **DOLOR**
mellow .... **AGE, RIPE**
melodic .... **ARIOSE**
melodious .... **ARIOSO**
melody .... **AIR, ARIA,
TUNE, MELOS**
melon ...... **PEPO, CASABA**
melt together ..... **FUSE, FUZE**
melted .... **MOLTEN**
membership .... **SEAT**
membrane ...... **WEB, TELA,
VELA, VELUM**
memento .... **RELIC**
memorabilia .... **ANA**
memorandum .... **CHIT, NOTE**
memorial post, Indian .. **TOTEM**
memory, pert. to
    MNESIC, MNEMONIC
Memphis chief god .... **PTAH**

d Memphis street, famous. **BEALE**
men .... **SONS**
mendacious person ..... **LIAR**
mender, chief ...... **TINKER**
mendicant, Mos.
    FAKIR, FAKEER
Menelaus' wife .... **HELEN**
menhaden fish .... **POGY**
menhaden, young ... **SARDINE**
Mennonite .... **AMISH**
Menotti heroine ...... **AMELIA**
men's party .... **STAG**
mental .... **PHRENIC**
mental deficiency ... **AMENTIA**
mental deficient **IDIOT, MORON**
mention .... **CITE**
Mercator .... **MAP, CHART**
mercenary . **VENAL, HIRELING**
merchandise .... **WARES**
merchant .... **TRADER**
merchant: India .... **SETH**
"Merchant of Venice" heiress
           PORTIA
merchant ship ...... **ARGOSY**
merchant vessel, Gr. . **HOLCAD**
Mercury, Gr. .... **HERMES**
Mercury's wand ... **CADUCEUS**
mercy, show .... **SPARE**
mere .... **SIMPLE**
merely .... **ONLY**

a merganser duck **SMEW, GARBILL**
merge .... **MELD**
merit .... **EARN**
merriment .... **GLEE**
merry-go-round ... **CAROUSAL, CAROUSEL, CARROUSAL**
"Merry Widow" composer **LEHAR**
"Merry Wives" character **PISTOL**
mesh .... **NET, WEB**
Mesopotamia ..... **IRAK, IRAQ**
Mesopotamian boat **GUFA, KUFA**
Mesopotamian city ..... **URFA**
mesquite bean flour ... **PINOLE**
mess, to make a ...... **BOTCH**
mestizo .... **METIS**
metal .... **TIN, MONEL**

metal alloy .... **BRASS, MONEL, BRONZE**
metal, bar of .... **INGOT**
metal bar on house door . **RISP**
metal casting .... **PIG, INGOT**
metal, coat with .**PLATE, TERNE**
metal-decorating art .. **NIELLO**
metal disk .... **MEDAL**
metal dross .... **SLAG**
metal filings .... **LEMEL**
metal fissure .... **LODE**
b metal leaf .... **FOIL**
metal mixture .... **ALLOY**
metal refuse .... **SCORIA**
metal spacer: print. ..... **SLUG**
metal suit .... **MAIL**
metal sulfide, impure . **MATTE**
metal, white .... **TIN**
metallic rock .... **ORE**
metalware, lacquered .... **TOLE**
metalwork, god of .. **VULCAN**
metarabic acid ..... **CERASIN**
meteor .... **LEONID**
meteor, exploding **BOLIS, BOLIDE**
meter, Dutch .... **EL**
meter, one-millionth .. **MICRON**
meters, 100 sq. ...... **AR, ARE**
metheglin .... **MEAD**
method .... **PLAN, ORDER**
Methuselah's grandson .. **NOAH**
methyl-phenol **CRESOL, CRESSOL**
metric measure ..... **AR, ARE, GRAM, KILO, LITER, METER, STERE, DECARE, HECTARE**
metric "quart" .... **LITER**
metrical beat .... **ICTUS**
metrical unit .... **MORA**
metropolitan .... **URBAN**
mew .... **GULL**
mew, cat's .... **MIAU, MIAW, MIAOU, MIAUL**

c Mexican dollar .... **PESO**
Mex. mush .... **ATOLE**
Mex. painter .... **RIVERA**
Mex. persimmon .... **CHAPOTE**
Mex. plant .... **JALAP**
Mex. president ...... **ALEMAN, CALLES, MADERO**
Mex. resin tree .... **DRAGO**
Mex. rodent .... **TUCAN**
Mex. slave .... **PEON**
Mex. spiny tree ...... **RETAMA**
Mex. timber tree ...... **ABETO**
Mex. wind instrument . **CLARIN**
mezzanine .... **ENTRESOL**
miasma .... **MALARIA**
mica, kind of .... **BIOTITE**
mica of muscovite ...... **TALC**
microbe .... **GERM**
microspores .... **POLLEN**
middle .... **MESAL, MESNE, MEDIAN**
middle, in the ...... **ATWEEN**
middle, toward .... **MESAD**
middling .... **SOSO**
Midgard Serpent slayer .. **THOR**
midge .... **GNAT**
midship, off .... **ABEAM**
d "Midsummer Night's Dream" character .. **PUCK, SNUG**
midwife: India .... **DHAI**
MID-EAST land .. **IRAK, IRAQ**
mien .... **AIR**
might .... **POWER**
mignonette ... **GREEN, RESEDA**
migrate .... **TREK**
migratory worker **OKIE, ARKIE**
Mikado's court . **DAIRI, DAIRO**
Milanion's wife .. **ATALANTA**
Milan's "Met" ..... **LA SCALA**
mild ...... **SHY, MEEK, SOFT, BLAND, GENTLE**
mildness .... **LENITY**
mile: naut. .... **KNOT**
mile, part of, Burma ... **DHA**
Miled, son of .... **IR, ITH, EBER**
milestone .... **STELE**
milfoil .... **YARROW**
military award .... **DSO**
military cap .... **KEPI**
military command ... **AT EASE**
military group . **CADRE, CORPS**
military maneuvers ... **TACTICS**
milk, coagulated ..... **CURD**
milk coagulator ..... **RENNIN**
milk, curdled ...... **CLABBER**
milk, part of **SERUM, LACTOSE**
milk, pert. to .... **LACTIC**
milk: pharm. .... **LAC**
milk protein .... **CASEINE**

99

a milk, watery part of .... **WHEY**
milkfish .... **AWA, SABALO**
Milky Way .... **GALAXY**
mill .... **QUERN**
MILLET
     see also GRAIN SORGHUM
millet, India **JOAR, JUAR, CHENA**
millimeter, 1000th part **MICRON**
millstone support ...... **RYND**
millwheel board .... **LADE**
millwheel bucket ...... **AWE**
Milton, masque by ..... **COMUS**
Milton rebel angel ..... **ARIEL**
mime .... **APER**
mimic ..... **APE, APER, MIME**
mimicking, practice of . **APISM**
mimosa .... **ACACIA**
minced oath .. **GAD, GED, GEE,**
    LUD, DRAT, EGAD, HECK,
    OONS, SWOW, MAFEY,
    MACKINS
mind .... **CARE, TEND**
mind, opposite of: Hindu
    ATTA, ATMAN
mind: philos. .... **NOUS**
Mindanao native, Indonesian
    ATA, AETA, MORO
mine ceiling .... **ASTEL**
mine entrance .... **ADIT**
mine narrow veins ..... **RESUE**

b mine passage .... **STULM**
mine roof support ...... **NOG**
mine shaft drain pit .... **SUMP**
mine step .... **LOB**
mineral, alkaline ..... **TRONA**
mineral, blue .... **IOLITE**
mineral group ...... **URANITE**
mineral group, pert. to **SALIC**
mineral, hard **SPINEL, SPINELLE**
mineral, lustrous .... **SPAR**
mineral, raw, native .... **ORE**
mineral salt .... **ALUM**
mineral, soft .... **TALC**
mineral spring .... **SPA**
mineral tar .... **BREA**
mineral, transparent .. **MICA**
mineral used gun-powder **NITER**
Minerva .... **ATHENA**
minim .... **DROP**
mining refuse .... **ATTLE**
mining road .... **BORD**
mining tool .... **GAD, BEELE**
minister, Moslem **VIZIR, VIZIER**
minister (to) .... **CATER**
mink, Amer. .... **VISON**
minority, legal ...... **NONAGE**
Minos' daughter .... **ARIADNE**
Minotaur's slayer ... **THESEUS**
minstrel .... **RIMER**
minstrel, medieval ... **GOLIARD**
minstrel, Norse . **SCALD, SKALD**

c mint .... **COIN**
mint, Europ. ... **CLARE, CLARY,**
    CLARRY, HYSSOP, DITTANY
mint genus .... **MENTHA**
mint herb .... **SAGE**
mints, the .... **NEPETA**
minus .... **LESS**
minute .... **WEE, TINY, SMALL**
mira .... **STAR**
miracle, scene of first .. **CANA**
mirage .... **SERAB**
miscellany .... **ANA**
mischief .... **HOB**
mischievous spirit ...... **PUCK**
misconceive .... **ERR**
Mishnah section .. **ABOT, ABOTH**
Mishnah section festivals .**MOED**
misinterpret .... **ERR**
mislay .... **LOSE**
misplay .... **ERROR**
misrepresent .... **BELIE**
Miss Dombey's suitor .. **TOOTS**
missile .... **DART, SNARK**
missile, guided ... **JUNO, NIKE,**
    THOR, ATLAS, TITAN,
    BOMARC, JUPITER, PERSH-
    ING, REGULUS, REDSTONE,
    BOLD ORION, MINUTEMAN
mist .... **HAZE, SMUR, MISLE**
mist: Eng. .... **RAG**

d mistake, stupid .... **BONER**
mistakes .... **ERRATA**
mistakes, make .... **ERR**
mite .... **ACARI, ATOMY,**
    ACARID, ACARUS
mite genus .. **ACARI, ACARUS**
mite, tick, order of
    ACARIDA, ACARINA
mitigate . **EASE, ABATE, ALLAY**
mix .... **STIR, ADDLE, KNEAD**
mixture .... **OLIO**
mixture, mineral .... **MAGMA**
Moab city, chief .... **UR**
Moab king .... **MESHA**
Moabites, Bibl. ...... **EMIM**
moat .... **FOSS, FOSSE**
"Moby Dick" pursuer .. **AHAB**
moccasin .... **PAC**
mock ..... **GIBE, JIBE, FLEER,**
    TAUNT, DERIDE
mock blow .... **FEINT**
mock orange .... **SYRINGA**
mockingbird genus ... **MIMUS**
model, perfect ..... **PARAGON**
moderate .... **BATE,**
    ABATE, LESSEN
modernist .... **NEO**
modest .... **SHY, DEMURE**
modify .... **VARY, ALTER,**
    EMEND, TEMPER
Mogul emperor ...... **AKBAR**

a MOHAMMEDAN .. see MOSLEM
Mohammedanism ...... ISLAM
Mohammed's adopted son . ALI
Mohammed's birthplace .MECCA
Mohammed's daughter .FATIMA
Mohammed's descendant
SAID, SEID, SAYID
Mohammed's son-in-law .. ALI
Mohammed's supporters .ANSAR
Mohammed's title .... ALI
Mohammed's tomb city MEDINA
Mohammed's uncle ..... ABBAS
Mohammed's wife ..... AISHA
Mohawk, city on ...... UTICA
Mohicans, last of the .. UNCAS
moiety .... HALF
moist .... WET, DAMP, DANK,
DEWY, UVID, HUMID
moist spot, rock-ledge .... SIPE
moisten ... DAMPEN, IMBRUE
moisture, having medium MESIC
mojarra fish .... PATAO
molasses .. TREACLE, TRIACLE
molasses, rum made from
TAFIA
mold .... MUST
mold, hole in casting .GIT, GEAT
molded clay .... PUG
molding .. CYMA, GULA, OGEE,
b TORUS, REGLET, REEDING
molding, concave
CONGE, SCOTIA
molding, convex
OVOLO, TORUS, ASTRAGAL
molding, curved . CYMA, OGEE
molding, edge of . ARIS, ARRIS
molding, flat .... FILLET
molding, rounded TORI, TORUS
molding, S-shaped ..... OGEE
molding, square ..... LISTEL
moldings, quarter-round .OVOLI
moldy .... MUSTY
mole .... NEVUS, NAEVUS
mole cricket, S. Am. . CHANGA
mole genus .... TALPA
molecule part .... ION
molelike mammal ... DESMAN
MOLLUSK.see also GASTROPOD
mollusk ...... CLAM, CHITON,
MUSSEL, ABALONE
mollusk, bivalve ...... SCALLOP
mollusk, chamber-shelled
NAUTILUS
mollusk, gastropod
SNAIL, ABALONE
mollusk genus ARCA, MUREX,
OLIVA, ANOMIA
mollusk, largest ...... CHAMA
mollusk's rasp organ .. RADULA
molt .... MEW, SHED

c molten rock ... LAVA, MAGMA
moment ..... MO, JIFF, TRICE
Monaco, pert. to
MONACAN, MONEGASQUE
monad .... ATOM, UNIT
monastery .... MANDRA
monastery church .. MINSTER
MONEY . see also SPECIAL
SECTION COINS
money .... CASH, CUSH, GELT
money, Amer. Ind. .. WAMPUM
money, bronze .... AES
money certificate .BOND, SCRIP
money, copper .... AES
money: dialect ..... SPENSE
money, early Eng. .... ORA
money drawer .... TILL
money exchange fee .... AGIO
money, fishhook . LARI, LARIN
money, medieval .... ORA
money of account .... ORA
money, piece of ...... COIN
money premium .... AGIO
money, put in .... INVEST
money reserve .... FUND
money, shell . SEWAN, SEAWAN
money, trade unit .... UNITAS
moneylender .... USURER
moneylender, Ind. .. MAHAJAN
Mongol ... HU, ELEUT, TATAR,
d ELEUTH, TARTAR
Mongol dynasty .... YUAN
Mongol warrior .... TATAR
Mongolian tent .... YURT
Mongoloid .... TURK, DURBAN
Mongoloid in Indo-China .SHAN
mongrel .... CUR, MUTT
monitor lizard .... URAN
monk .. FRA, FRIAR, CENOBITE
monk, Buddhist ...... ARAHT,
ARHAT, ARAHAT
monk, Eng. ...... BEDA, BEDE
monk, Gr. Church ... CALOYER
monk, head .... ABBOT
monk settlement .SCETE, SKETE
monk's hood .... COWL
monk's title ..... FRA, ABBOT
monkey .... APE, LAR, SAI,
SIME, SIMIAN, MARMOSET
monkey, Afr. .... MONA,
WAAG, GRIVET
monkey, Asia ..... LANGUR
monkey, capuchin .... SAI
monkey, Chin. .... DOUC
monkey genus .... CEBUS
monkey, guenon ...... NISNAS
monkey, howling ..... ARABA
monkey, P. I. .... MACHIN
monkey puzzle .... PINON
monkey, red, Afr. ..... PATAS
monkey, small .... LEMUR

101

a
monkey, S. Am. .. **SAKI, TITI,
ACARI, ARABA, SAJOU,
TETEE, PINCHE, SAGUIN,
SAMIRI, SAIMIRI, SAPAJOU**
monkey, spider, genus.**QUATA,
ATELES, COAITA**
monkshood .... **ATIS,
ATEES, ACONITE**
monolith .... **MENHIR**
monopoly ..... **TRUST, CARTEL**
monosaccharide .... **OSE**
Mons, language of ...... **PEGU**
monster .. **GOUL, GOWL, OGRE**
monster, Gr. myth .. **CHIMERA**
monster, half-man-bull
MINOTAUR
monster: med. ...... **TERAS**
monster, 100 eyes ..... **ARGUS**
monster slain by Hercules
HYDRA
month, Egypt. .... **AHET,
APAP, TYBI**
month, first day, Rom.
CALENDS, KALENDS
month, Hindu .... **ASIN, JETH,
KUAR, MAGH**
month, in last .... **ULTIMO**
month, Jewish ancient ..... **AB**
(11th), **BUL** (8th), **ZIF**
(8th), **ABIB** (7th), **ADAR**
(6th), **ELUL** (12th), **IYAR**,
(8th), **NISAN** (7th), **SEBAT**
(5th), **SIVAN** (9th), **TEBET**
(4th), **TIZRI** (1st), **TEBETH**
(4th), **TISHRI** (1st)
month, Moslem ...... **RABIA,
RAJAB, SAFAR, SHABAN,
RAMADAN**
month, Nisan .... **ABIB**
monument, stone.**LECH, CAIRN,
DOLMEN, CROMLECH**
moon . **LUNA, DIANA, PHOEBE**
moon, age at beginning of
calendar year ..... **EPACT**
moon angel .... **MAH**
moon flower .... **ACHETE**
moon god, Babyl. .. **SIN, ENZU**
moon goddess ...... **ASTARTE**
moon goddess, Gr. .... **SELENA,
SELENE, ARTEMIS**
moon goddess, Rom. ... **LUNA,
DIAN, DIANA**
moon nearest earth, point
PERIGEE
moon valley ..... **RILL, RILLE**
moor grass .... **NARD**
moorhen .... **GORHEN**
Moorish .... **MORISCAN**
moose genus .... **ALCES**
mop .... **SWAB, SWOB**

c
Moqul, one of .... **HOPI**
morals overseer ...... **CENSOR**
morass .... **QUAG, MARSH**
moray .... **EEL**
Mordecai, enemy of .. **HAMAN**
more .... **PLUS**
more! ...... **BIS, PIU, ENCORE**
more than enough ...... **TOO,
EXTRA, EXCESS**
More's island .... **UTOPIA**
morepork, N. Z. .. **PEHO, RURU**
morindin dye .... **AL**
moringa seed .... **BEN**
morning glory .... **IPOMEA**
morning music ...... **AUBADE**
morning: P. I. .... **UMAGA**
morning prayer ...... **MATINS**
morning song .... **MATIN**
Moro .... **SULU, LANAO**
Moro chief **DATO, DATU, DATTO**
Moro mantle .... **JABUL**
Moroccan Berber ...... **RIFF**
Moroccan land, public .. **GISH**
Moroccan native ...... **MOOR**
moron .... **AMENT, IDIOT**
morose ... **BLUE, GLUM, GRUM**
morsel .... **ORT**
mortar implement .... **PESTLE**

d
mortar ingredient ...... **LIME**
mortar mixer ... . **RAB**
mortar tray .... **HOD**
mortise insert .... **TENON**
Mosaic law .... **TORA, TORAH**
mosaic piece .... **TESSERA**
Moselle, river to .... **SAAR**
Moses, law given to here
SINA, SINAI
Moses' brother ...... **AARON**
Moses' death mountain .. **NEBO**
Moses' father-in-law .. **JETHRO**
Moses' spy in Canaan .. **CALEB**
MOSLEM ..... see also **MECCA**
Moslem .... **TURK**
Moslem ablution before prayer
WIDU, WUDU, WUZU
Moslem, Afr. .... **MOOR**
Moslem beggar .**FAKIR, FAKEER**
Moslem bible .... **KORAN**
Moslem call to prayer
ADAN, AZAN
Moslem chief .... **AGA,
IMAM, DATTO**
Moslem chief gold coin.**DINAR**
Moslem converts ...... **ANSAR**
Moslem deity ... **JANN, ALLAH**
Moslem demon .. **JANN, EBLIS**
Moslem Easter .... **EED**
Moslem fast ...... **RAMADAN**
Moslem festival ...... **BAIRAM**

Moslem fiat .... **IRADE**
Moslem fourth Caliph .... **ALI**
Moslem grant of property
     WAKF, WAQF, WUKF
Moslem guide .... **PIR**
Moslem holy city ..... **MECCA**
Moslem holy man
     IMAM, IMAUM
Moslem, hostile to Crusaders
     SARACEN
Moslem in Turkestan ... **SALAR**
Moslem judge .. **CADI, CAZI,**
   CAZY, KADI, KAZI, KAZY
Moslem leader . **IMAM, IMAUM**
Moslem marriage . **MOTA, MUTA**
Moslem marriage settlement
     MAHR
MOSLEM MORO ... see **MORO**
     CHIEF
Moslem mystic .... **SUFI**
Moslem name .... **ALI**
Moslem Negroids .... **MABA**
Moslem noble .... **AMIR, EMIR,**
     AMEER, EMEER
Moslem, N. W. India ... **SWAT**
Moslem official .... **AGA**
Moslem, orthodox .... **HANIF**
Moslem, P.I. .... **MORO**
Moslem potentate .... **AGA**
Moslem prayer .... **SALAT**
Moslem prayer place ... **IDGAH**
Moslem priest . **IMAM, IMAUM**
Moslem prince ... **AMIR, EMIR,**
     AMEER, EMEER
Moslem principle .... **IJMA**
Moslem pulpit ...... **MIMBAR**
Moslem reformer .... **WAHABI**
Moslem religion .... **ISLAM**
Moslem religious college
     ULEMA
Moslem ruler .... **HAKIM**
Moslem saber ...... **SCIMITAR**
Moslem saint .... **PIR**
Moslem school ...... **MADRASA**
Moslem spirit ... **JINN, JINNI**
Moslem spiritual guide ... **PIR**
Moslem teacher .. **ALIM, COJA**
Moslem temple . **MOSK, MOSQUE**
Moslem theologians ... **ULEMA**
Moslem title .... **AGA, RAIS,**
   REIS, SEID, SIDI, SYED,
   SYUD, CALIF, SAYID,
   SEYID, CALIPH
Moslem tunic .. **JAMA, JAMAH**
Moslem weight .... **ROTL**
Moslem woman's dress .. **IZAR**
Moslems, Sunnite .... **SART**
Moslemized Bulgarian . **POMAK**
mosque .... **MASJID**
mosque, central .... **JAMI**
mosque, Jerusalem .... **OMAR**
mosque student .... **SOFTA**

mosquito, genus, yellow-fever
     AEDES
mossbunker fish .... **POGY**
moss of Ceylon .... **AGAR**
moth .... **IO, LUNA,**
     EGGER, TINEA
moth, clearwing, genus . **SESIA**
moth, clothes .... **TINEA**
moth, green .... **LUNA**
mother goddess; Baby. . **ERUA**
mother goddesses, Hindu **MATRIS**
mother of Arthur .... **IGRAINE**
mother of gods .... **RHEA**
MOTHER OF IRISH GODS ... see
     page 200
mother-of-pearl ...... **NACRE**
mother-of-pearl shell . **ABALONE**
mother turned to stone . **NIOBE**
mother's side, related on
     ENATE, ENATIC
mother's side, relation on
     ENATE, ENATION
motherless calf .. **DOGY, DOGIE**
motion, producing .... **MOTILE**
motionless .... **INERT, STILL**
motive ...... **CAUSE, REASON**
motmot, S. Am. ..... **HOUTOU**
motor part .... **ROTOR**
mottled .... **PIED, PINTO**
mottled, as wood ...... **ROEY**
MOULDING .... see **MOLDING**
mound ...... **TUMP, BARROW**
mound, Polyn. .... **AHU**
Mount of Olives ...... **OLIVET**
mountain, Alps .... **BLANC**
mountain ash .. **SORB, ROWAN**
mountain, Asia Minor .... **IDA**
mountain, Bibl. .. **HOR, NEBO,**
   SEIR, SINA, HOREB,
   SINAI, ARARAT
   (see others on page 197)
mountain chain .... **SIERRA**
mountain climbing staff . **PITON**
mountain crest .... **ARETE**
mountain, Crete .... **IDA**
mountain, Edom .... **HOR**
mountain, fabled Hindu . **MERU**
mountain, famous .... **IDA**
mountain, Gr. ...... **HELICON**
mountain in Thessaly ... **OSSA**
mountain lion .... **PUMA**
mountain mint .... **BASIL**
mountain, Moab .... **NEBO**
mountain pass .... **COL**
mountain pass, Alps ... **CENIS**
mountain pass, India
     GAUT, GHAT
mountain peak .... **ALP**
mountain pool .... **TARN**
mountain recess .... **CWM**
mountain ridge .... **ARETE**

Mountain

a mountain ridge, Port. ... SERRA
mountain, 2nd highest N.A.
                      LOGAN
mountain sickness PUNA, VETA
mountain spinach ..... ORACH
mountain spur .... ARETE
mountains, Asia ...... ALTAI
mountains, myth ... KAF, QAF
mourn .... WEEP,
          GRIEVE, LAMENT
mournful .... SAD, DIRE
mourning band .... CRAPE
mouse .... VOLE
mouse, field .... VOLE
mouse genus .... MUS
mousebird ..... COLY, SHRIKE
mouth .... OS, ORA
mouth, away from .... ABORAL
mouth open .... AGAPE
mouth, river .... DELTA
mouth, tidal river ...... FRITH
mouth, toward .... ORAD
mouthful .... SIP, SUP
mouthlike orifice ..... STOMA
mouthpiece ..... REED, BOCAL
move .... STIR, AFFECT
move a camera .... PAN
move back ..... EBB, RECEDE
move to and fro
         WAG, FLAP, SWAY

b movement: biol. .... TAXIS
movement, capable of . MOTILE
movement: music .... MOTO
movement,with:music CONMOTO
movie: Sp. .... CINE
moving part .... ROTOR
mow, barn's .... LOFT
mow of hay .... GOAF
mowed strip .... SWATH
Mowgli's bear friend ... BALU,
                    BALOO
Mozambique native ...... YAO
muck .... MIRE
mud .... MIRE, MURGEON
mud deposit .... SILT
mud, slimy .... OOZE
mud, stick in .... MIRE
mud, viscous .... SLIME
mud, volcano .... SALSE
muddle .... MESS, ADDLE
muddy .... ROIL
muffin .... GEM
mug .... STEIN, NOGGIN
mug, small .... TOBY
mugger .... GOA
mulatto .... METIS
mulberry bark cloth .... TAPA
mulberry genus ...... MORUS
mulberry, India ...... AL, AAL
mulct .... FINE, AMERCE
mullet, red .... SUR

c multiform .... DIVERSE
multiplicand: math. . FACIEND
multiplier: math. .... FACIENT
multitude ...... HOST, HORDE
mum .... ALE
munch .... CHAMP
mundane .... TERRENE
Munich's river .... ISAR
municipal officer, Sp. . ALCADE,
          ALCAID, ALCAIDE,
               ALCAYDE
muntjac deer . KAKAR, RATWA
murder by suffocation . BURKE
murder fine, Scot. .... CRO
murderer, first .... CAIN
murmuring sound
        CURR, PURL, PURR
Musci, plant of .... MOSS
muscle .... THEW, SINEW
muscle coordination, lack of
               ATAXIA
muscle, deep, pert. to
             SCALENE
muscle, kind of
       ERECTOR, LEVATOR
muscle, like .... MYOID
muscle, round, rolling .. TERES
muscle, stretching .... TENSOR
muscles .... BRAWN

d muscular action, irregular
               ATAXIA
muscular spasm .... TIC
Muse, chief ...... CALLIOPE
muse in reverie .... REVE
Muse of astronomy ... URANIA
Muse of comedy ..... THALIA
Muse of dancing .TERPSICHORE
Muse of history ...... CLIO
Muse of lyric poetry
           CLIO, ERATO
Muse of music ...... EUTERPE
Muse of poetry ...... ERATO
Muse of sacred lyric
           POLYMNIA
Muse of tragedy . MELPOMENE
Muses, 9 .... PIERIDES
Muses' region .... AONIA
Muses, The .... NINE
musette .... OBOE
museum head ...... CURATOR
mush .... ATOLE, SEPON
mushroom .... MOREL, MORIL
mushroom cap .... PILEUS
music: as written .... STA
music character .... DOT,
          CLEF, REST
music drama .... OPERA
music for nine .... NONET
music for three .... TRIO
music for two .... DUET
music from the sign: abbr. . DS

104

a

music hall .... ODEA, ODEON, ODEUM
music interval ...... TRITONE
music: it proceeds ...... VA
music lines .... STAFF
music piece
     SERENATA, SERENATE
music, sacred
     CHORAL, CHORALE
music symbols, old ... NEUME
MUSICAL .... see also MUSIC
musical beat .... TAKT
musical composition, India
     RAGA
musical direction . STA, TACET
musical instrument .... ASOR, DRUM, FIFE, GIGA, HARP, HORN, LUTE, LYRE, OBOE, PIPE, REED, TCHE, TUBA, TURR, VINA, VIOL, CELLO, RAPPEL, SPINET, CLAVIER, HELICON, OCARINA
musical sign .. DOT, CLEF, REST
musical study .... ETUDE
musical work .... OPUS
musician, 11th century . GUIDO

c

musket ball, India ...... GOLI
Musketeer .... ATHOS, ARAMIS, PORTHOS
mussel, fresh-water ..... UNIO
must .... STUM
mustache monkey ... MOUSTOC
mustard family plant ... CRESS
musteline animal
     OTTER, RATEL
mustiness .... FUST
mutilate .... MAIM
muttonbird .... OII
muttonfish .... SAMA
"My Name is —" ..... ARAM
mysteries .... ARCANA
mysterious .... OCCULT
mystery .... RUNE
mystic word, Hindu ...... OM
mystic writing .... RUNE
mythical land ...... LEMURIA
mythical stream .... STYX
mythical submerged island
     ATLANTIS
mythical warrior ...... ARES
MYTHOLOGY .... see SPECIAL SECTION, Page 198

N

b

nab .... GRAB, ARREST
Nabal's wife: Bibl. ... ABIGAIL
NaCl .... SALT
nahoor sheep .... SNA
nail .... CLAW, TALON, UNGUES, UNGUIS
nail, hooked .... TENTER
nail, mining, surveying .. SPAD
nail, thin .... BRAD
nail with aperture ..... SPAD
nails, 100 lbs. .... KEG
namaycush .... TOGUE
NAME .... see also MAN'S NAME, WOMAN'S NAME
name .... DUB, TERM, CLEPE, NOMEN, TITLE, ENTITLE
name: Dan. .... NAAM
name plate, shop's .... FACIA
named ... Y-CLEPT, Y-CLEPED
namely .... VIZ
Naomi, name claimed by MARA
Naomi's daughter-in-law . RUTH
naos .... CELLA
nap, coarse, long ...... SHAG
nap-raising device ... TEASEL, TEASLE, TEAZEL, TEAZLE
nap-raising machine ..... GIG
nap, to raise .... TEASE
napoleon, game like ..... PAM

d

Napoleon's brother-in-law
     MURAT
Napoleon's isle .... ELBA
Napoleon's marshal general NEY
Napoleonic victory .JENA, LODI
Narcissus, nymph who loved
     ECHO
narcotic ...... DOPE, DRUG, HEROIN, OPIATE
narcotic, India . BANG, BHANG
narcotic plant .... DUTRA
narcotic shrub
     KAT, KAAT, KHAT
narcotic shrub, S. Am.
     COCA, CUCA
narrate .... TELL
narrow ...... LINEAL, STRAIT
nasal .... RHINAL
Nata's wife: myth ..... NANA
nation: Ger. .... VOLK
nation, pert. to ...... STATAL
NATIVE .... see TRIBES in SPECIAL SECTION, Page 191
native .... ITE, RAW, NATAL, ENDEMIC, INDIGENE
natural luster, having ... NAIF
natural talent . DOWER, FLAIR
nature ...... OUSIA, ESSENCE
nature goddess ...... CYBELE

Nature

a nature principal: Hindu . **GUNA**
nature spirit .... **NAT**
nature story writer ..... **SETON**
nautical .... **MARINE**
nautical cry
    AHOY, OHOY, AVAST
Navaho hut .... **HOGAN**
naval hero .... **PERRY**
navy jail .... **BRIG**
near . **AT, NIGH, ABOUT, CLOSE**
Near East native . **ARAB, TURK**
Near East river valley .. **WADI**
near the ear .... **PAROTIC**
near to .... **BY, ON**
nearest .... **NEXT**
nearsighted person .... **MYOPE**
nearsightedness ...... **MYOPIA**
neat ...... **TIDY, TOSH, TRIG,**
    TRIM, SPRUCE
neat cattle .... **NOWT**
neatly .... **FEATLY**
necessitate .... **ENTAIL**
neck, nape of .... **NUCHA**
necklace ..... **BEADS, RIVIERE**
neckline shape
    VEE, BOAT, CREW
neckpiece ...... **ASCOT, STOLE**
neckpiece, feather ...... **BOA**
neckpiece, woman's .... **FICHU**
NECKTIE .... see **TIE**

b need .... **WANT, REQUIRE**
needle .... **PROD, BODKIN**
needle bug .... **NEPA**
needle case .... **ETUI**
needle-shaped ...... **ACUATE,**
    ACERATE
needlefish .... **GAR**
needlelike bristle .... **ACICULA**
negative .... **NE, NO, NAY,**
    NON, NOT
negative pole ...... **CATHODE**
neglect .... **OMIT**
neglected school subject:
  abbr. .... **LAT.**
negligent .... **LAX**
negotiate .... **TREAT**
negrito . **ATA, ATI, ITA, AETA,**
    ATTA
NEGRO .... see also TRIBES in
  SPECIAL SECTION
Negro dance .... **JUBA**
Negro: India .... **HUBSHI**
NEGRO TRIBE .... see SPECIAL
  SECTION
Nelson's victory site ..... **NILE**
nematocyst .... **CNIDA**
nemesis .... **BANE**
Nepal Mongoloid .... **RAIS**
Nepal native .... **KHA**
Nepal people .... **RAIS**
nephew .... **NEPOTE**

c nephew, Fijian .... **VASU**
Neptune .... **LER**
Neptune's spear ..... **TRIDENT**
nerve cell .... **NEURON**
nerve-cell process ...... **AXON**
nerve layers, brain .... **ALVEI**
nervous .... **EDGY**
nervous disease .... **CHOREA**
nest .... **NID, NIDE,**
    NIDI, NIDUS
nest, eagle's .... **AERY, AERIE,**
    EYRY, EYRIE
nested boxes .... **INRO**
nestling .... **EYAS**
net .... **CLEAR**
net, fishing .... **STENT, SEINE,**
    STENT, TRAWL
net of hair-lines ..... **RETICLE**
NETHERLANDS
    see SPECIAL SECTION
netlike .... **RETIARY**
nettle family .. **RAMIE, RAMEE**
network .... **WEB, MESH,**
    RETE, RETIA
neuroglia .... **GLIA**
neve .... **FIRN**
— Nevis, Gt. Brit. peak .. **BEN**
new .... **NOVEL, RECENT**
New Caledonia bird .... **KAGU**
New England state: abbr. .. **RI**

d New Guinea area ...... **PAPUA**
New Guinea tribesman . **KARON**
New Guinea victory .... **GONA**
New Guinea wild hog .... **BENE**
New Jerusalem foundation
    JASPER
new, lover of .... **NEO**
new star .... **NOVA**
new wine .... **MUST**
New York harbor isle .... **ELLIS**
New Zealand aborigine ... **ATI**
N.Z. bird .... **HUIA, KAKI,**
    PEHO, RURU
N.Z. clan .... **ATI**
N.Z. evergreen .... **TAWA**
N.Z. fruit pigeon ...... **KUKU**
N.Z. laburnum .... **GOAI**
N.Z. mollusk .... **PIPI**
N.Z. native .... **MAORI**
N.Z. native fort ..... **PA, PAH**
N.Z. parson bird ...... **KOKO**
N.Z. plant .... **KARO**
N.Z. rail bird .... **WEKA**
N.Z. scabbard fish ..... **HIKU**
N.Z. shrub .... **KARO**
N.Z. shrub, poisonous .. **TUTU**
N.Z. subtribe .... **HAPU**
N.Z. timber tree . **GOAI, HINO,**
    MIRO, PELU, RATA, RIMU,
    HINAU, HINOU, KAURI,
    KAURY, TOTARA

N.Z. tree ... AKE, KOPI, NAIO, PUKA, TORO
N.Z. tree, lightwood ... WHAU
N.Z. tribe .... ATI
N.Z. wages .... UTU
N.Z. wood hen .... WEKA
news agency, Eng. ... REUTERS
news agency, Europ. ... ANETA
news agency, Jap. .... DOMEI
news agency, Rus. Soviet . TASS
news paragraph .... ITEM
newspaper service .... AP, UP, INS, UPI, REUTERS
newspapers .... PRESS
newt ..... EFT, EVET, TRITON
nibble ... GNAW, KNAB, KNAP
niche .... RECESS
Nichols' hero .... ABIE
Nick Charles' dog ...... ASTA
Nick Charles' wife ...... NORA
nickel steel alloy ...... INVAR
nicotine acid .... NIACIN
nictitate .... WINK
Niger delta native .... IJO
NIGERIA
see SPECIAL SECTION
Nigerian Negro ..... ARO, IBO
Nigerian tribe .... EDO
NIGERIAN TRIBE OR PEOPLE
see also SPECIAL SECTION
page 191
niggard .... MISER
nigh .... NEAR
night, Norse .... NATT, NOTT
nightingale, Pers. .... BULBUL
nightjar .... POTOO
nightmare demon, Teut. . MARA
nightmare, the ...... INCUBUS
nightshade, black
MOREL, MORIL
Nile, as god .... HAPI
Nile island .... RODA
Nile native .... NILOT
Nile sailboat .... CANGIA
Nile valley depression .. KORE
Nile, waste matter on
SADD, SUDD
Nilotic Negro ..... JUR, LUO, LWO, SUK
nimble .... SPRY, AGILE
nimbus .... HALO, NIMB
nimrod .... HUNTER
nine-angled polygon . NONAGON
nine, based on ..... NONARY
nine, group of ...... ENNEAD
nine inches .... SPAN
nine, music for ...... NONET
Nineveh's founder ..... NINUS
ninth day, every ...... NONAN
ninth: mus. .... NONA
niton .... RADON

nitrogen .... AZO, AZOTE
Noah, pert. to .... NOETIC
Noah's landing ..... ARARAT
Noah's 1st son .... SEM, SHEM
Noah's 2nd son .... HAM
Nobel prize, literature '04
MISTRAL
Nobel prize, science ..... UREY
noble, nobleman .. DUKE, EARL, LORD, PEER, BARON, COUNT
noble: Ger. .... GRAF, RITTER
NOBLEMAN ..... see NOBLE
nobleman, Jap .... KAMI
nocturnal mammal BAT, LEMUR
nod .... BOW, BECK
Nod, west of .... EDEN
nodding .... NUTANT
noddy tern: Hawaii .... NOIO
node .... KNOB, KNOT, KNUR, NODUS
"— noire" .... BETE
nomad ...... ARAB, SCENITE
Nome in Greece .... ELIS
nomenclature .... NAME
nominal value .... PAR
nominate .... NAME
non-gypsy: Romany ..... GAJO
non-Jew .... GOI, GOY
non-Moslem of Turkey or Ottoman Empire RAIA, RAYA
non-professional ... LAY, LAIC
non-union worker ...... SCAB
nonchalant .... COOL
none: dialect .... NIN
nonsense . PISH, POOH, HOOEY
nonsense creature ...... GOOP
noodles: Yiddish FARFEL, FERFEL
nook, sheltered ...... COVE
noose .... LOOP
Norn, one of URD,URTH,WYRD
Norse "Adam" .... ASKR
Norse bard ... SCALD, SKALD
Norse chieftain .. JARL, YARL
Norse epic .... EDDA
Norse explorer .... ERIC, LEIF
NORSE GOD or GODDESSES
see also GODS and GODDESSES and see also SPECIAL SECTION Page 200
Norse gods .... VANS, AESIR, VANIR
Norse letter .... RUNE
Norse myth. hero EGIL, EGILL
Norse myth. king .... ATLI
Norse myth. "Life" force LIF
Norse myth. woman .... IDUN
Norse neighbor .... FINN
Norse poetry .... RUNES
Norse prose .... EDDA
Norse sea goddess ...... RAN
Norseman ..... DANE, SWEDE

North

a North African .... **BERBER**
N. Afr. outer garment .. **HAIK**
North Carolina college .. **ELON**
North Carolinian .... **TARHEEL**
North Caucasian language
    UDI, AVAR, UDIC, UDISH
North, Mrs. of fiction .. **PAMELA**
North Sea fishing boat .. **COBLE**
North Sea, river into **ELBE, TEES**
North Star .... **POLARIS**
North Syrian deity .... **EL**
northern .... **BOREAL**
northern Scandinavian ... **LAPP**
northern tribe, China ..... **HU**
northernmost land ..... **THULE**
Northumberland river ... **TYNE**
Norway coin .... **ORE**
Norway territorial division **AMT**
Norwegian author .. **HAMSUN**
Norwegian composer .... **GRIEG**
Norwegian county **AMT, FYLKE**
Norwegian saint .... **OLAF**
nose .... **CONK, NASI,**
    NASUS, SNOOP
nose, having large ... **NASUTE**
nose, having snub .. **SIMOUS**
nose openings .. **NARES, NARIS**
nose, snub .... **PUG**
nostrils .... **NARES, NARIS**
b nostrils, of .... **NARIC,**
    NARIAL, NARINE
"— Nostrum," Mediterranean
    MARE
not at home .... **OUT**
not ever: poet. .... **NEER**
not genuine .... **TIN**
not in style ...... **OUT, PASSE**
not long ago .... **LATELY**
not moving ... **INERT, STATIC**
not one .... **NARY, NONE**
not so great .... **LESS, FEWER,**
    SMALLER
notch ... **KERF, NICK, NOCK,**
    CRENA, CRENAE
notched .. **SERRATE, SERRATED**
note .... **CHIT, MEMO**
note, double, whole .... **BREVE**
note, Guido's .... **UT, ELA**
note, Guido's low ..... **GAMUT**
note, half .... **MINIM**
note, high, highest .... **ELA**
note, marginal
    POSTIL, APOSTIL
note: music .. **DI, DO, FA, FI,**
    LA, LE, LI, ME, MI, RA, RE,
    RI, SE, SI, SO, TE, TI, SOL
note, old Gr. musical .... **NETE**
note, old musical .... **ELA**
NOTE, SCALE ..... see NOTE:
    MUSIC
notes, furnish with . **ANNOTATE**

c notes in Guido's scale .. **ELAMI**
nothing . **NIL, NIX, NUL, NULL,**
    ZERO, NIHIL
notion .... **BEE, IDEA**
notion, capricious .... **WHIM**
notional .... **IDEAL**
notorious .... **ARRANT**
Nott's son .... **DAG**
notwithstanding .... **YET**
nought .... **ZERO, NULL**
NOUN ENDING
    see SUFFIX, noun
noun form .... **CASE**
noun suffix of condition .. **ATE**
noun with only 2 cases. **DIPTOTE**
nourish .... **FEED, FOSTER**
nourishment .... **PABULUM**
Nova Scotia .... **ACADIA**
novel, advocate of .... **NEO**
novel by A. France ..... **THAIS**
novelty .... **FAD**
novice .... **TIRO, TYRO**
now: dial. .... **NOO**
noxious .... **MIASMIC**
Nubian .... **NUBA**
nucha .... **NAPE**
nuclear element ...... **PROTON**
nudge .... **POKE**
nuisance .... **PEST**
nullify .... **NEGATE**
d nullify, legally .... **VOID**
number, describable by .**SCALAR**
number under 10 ...... **DIGIT**
number, whole ...... **INTEGER**
numbered: Bib. .... **MENE**
numerous .. **MANY, MULTIPLE**
nun, Franciscan .... **CLARE**
nun, head .... **ABBESS**
nun's dress .... **HABIT**
nunbird .... **MONASE**
nuque .... **NAPE**
nurse, Oriental, India ... **AMA,**
    IYA, AMAH, AYAH, EYAH
nurse, Slavic .... **BABA**
nursemaid: Fr. .... **BONNE**
nut ..... **COLA, KOLA, LICHI,**
    ALMOND, CASHEW,
    LICHEE, LITCHI
nut, beverage .... **COLA, KOLA**
nut, hickory .... **PECAN**
nut, pert. to .... **NUCAL**
nut, P. I. .... **PILI**
nut, pine .... **PINON**
nut, stimulating .... **BE EL**
nut tree, Afr. .... **COLA, KOLA**
nuts for food .... **MAST**
nuthatch genus .... **SITTA**
nutlike drupe .... **TRYMA**
nutmeg husk .... **MACE**
nutria .... **COYPU**

108

nutriment ... **FOOD, ALIMENT**
nutritive .... **ALIBLE**
nymph .... **MAIA, LARVA**
nymph, fountain ..... **EGERIA**
nymph, laurel .... **DAPHNE**
nymph, Moslem .... **HOURI**

nymph, mountain ..... **OREAD**
nymph, ocean ...... **OCEANID**
nymph, water . **NAIAD, NEREID**
nymph, wood . **DRYAD, NAPEA,**
　　　　NAPAEA, HAMADRYAD
Nyx's daughter .... **ERIS**

O, plural .... **OES**
oaf .... **LOUT**
oak, Calif. .... **ENCINA**
oak, dried fruit of ... **CAMATA**
oak, evergreen .... **HOLM**
oak moss .... **EVERNIA**
oak, Turkey .... **CERRIS**
oakum, seal with ..... **CALK**
oar .... **ROW, BLADE, PROPEL**
oar at stern .... **SCULL**
oasis, N. Afr. ... **WADI, WADY**
oat genus .... **AVENA**
oats as rent ...... **AVENAGE**
oath, knight's .... **EGAD**
oath, old-fashioned . **ODS, EGAD**
oath, say under ..... **DEPOSE**
obeisance, Oriental
　　　　　BOW, SALAAM
obey .... **HEED, MIND**
object ... **AIM, CAVIL, DEMUR**
object of art .... **CURIO**
objection, petty ...... **CAVIL**
objective .... **AIM, GOAL**
obligation .... **TIE, DEBT**
　　　　　DUTY, ONUS
oblique ...... **CANT, BEVEL,**
　　　　　SLANT, SLOPE
obliterate .... **ERASE, EFFACE**
obliteration .... **RASURE**
oblivion ..... **LETHE, LIMBO**
oblivion stream .... **LETHE**
obscure ..... **DIM, FOG, DARK**
　　　　　BEDIM, CLOUD
obscure, render ..... **DARKLE**
observe .. **SEE, NOTE, BEHOLD,**
　　　REMARK, CELEBRATE
obstinate .... **SET, HARD**
obstruction, petty .... **CAVIL**
obtain .... **GET**
obvious .... **OPEN, PATENT**
obvious, not . **SUBTLE, SUBTILE**
occasional .... **ODD**
Occident .... **WEST**
occipital protuberances ... **INIA**
occultism .... **CABALA**
occupant .... **TENANT**
occupation .... **TRADE**
occupy .... **USE, FILL**
occurrence .... **EVENT**

ocean's rise, fall ...... **TIDE**
oceanic .... **PELAGIC**
oceanic tunicate .... **SALP**
ocher, black ..... **WAD, WADD**
octave, designating high .. **ALT**
octave of church feast ... **UTAS**
octopus .... **POULPE**
octoroon **METIS,MESTEE,MUSTEE**
odd-job man .... **JOEY**
Odin. **WODAN, WODEN, WOTAN**
Odin's brother ...... **VE, VILI**
Odin's granddaughter . **NANNA**
Odin's son ... **TY, TYR, THOR,**
　　　　TYRR, VALE, VALI
Odin's wife .... **RIND**
odor .... **AROMA, SCENT**
ODYSSEUS ... see also **ULYSSES**
Odysseus' companion . **ELPENOR**
Odysseus' friend ..... **MENTOR**
Odyssey beggar .... **IRUS**
Odyssey singer .... **SIREN**
Oedipus' father .... **LAIUS**
Oedipus' mother .... **JOCASTA**
of speed of sound ..... **SONIC**
of the age: abbr. .... **AET**
off .... **AWAY**
offend .... **CAG**
offense .... **CRIME**
offense: law .. **MALA, MALUM**
offer .... **BID, TENDER**
offered up .... **OBLATE**
offhand .... **CASUAL**
office, ecclesiastic .. **MATINS**
office, priest's ...... **MATINS**
office, R. C. curia
　　　DATARY, DATARIA
officer, church ...... **BEADLE**
officer, court: Scot. ... **MACER**
officer, municipal: Scot. **BAILIE**
officer, Rom. .... **LICTOR**
officer, synagogue .... **PARNAS**
officer, university
　　DEAN, BEADLE, BURSAR
official, Moslem .... **HAJIB**
official, Rom.
　　EDILE, AEDILE, TRIBUNE
official, subordinate .. **SATRAP**
official, weights ...... **SEALER**
offspring .... **SONS, HEIRS**

109

ogygian .... **AGED**
Ohio college town ...... **ADA**
oil .... **FAT, LARD, LUBE,**
.... **ATTAR, OLEUM**
oil beetle .... **MELOE**
oil bottle .... **CRUCE, CRUET,**
.... **CRUSE, CRUIZE**
oil, cruet .... **AMPULLA**
oil, edible .... **ACEITE**
oil, orange .... **NEROLI**
oil, pert. to .... **OLEIC**
oil, rub with .... **ANOINT**
oil-yielding Chinese tree . **TUNG**
oil-yielding tree ... **EBO, EBOE**
oilfish .... **ESCOLAR**
oilstone .... **HONE**
oily ketone .... **IRONE**
ointment ...... **BALM, NARD,**
.... **SALVE, CERATE, POMADE**
Ojibway secret order
.... **MEDA, MIDE**
O.K. .... **ROGER**
okra .... **GOMBO, GUMBO**
old ...... **AGED, ANILE, SENILE**
"Old Curiosity Shop" girl . **NELL**
old English army .... **FYRD**
old Eng. gold piece ..... **RYAL**
old Eng. rune .... **WEN, WYN**
old Greek coin .... **OBOL**
old Irish coin .... **RAP**
old Persian money .... **DARIC**
OLD TESTAMENT see BIBLICAL
.... and SPECIAL SECTION
Old Testament objects ... **URIM**
Old Test. people . **PHUD, PHUT**
old person .... **DOTARD**
old Sp. gold coin ..... **DOBLA**
old times .... **ELD, YORE**
old-womanish .... **ANILE**
oleaginous .... **OILY**
oleander genus ...... **NERIUM**
oleic acid salt ...... **OLEATE**
oleoresin .... **ANIME,**
.... **ELEMI, BALSAM**
olive fly genus .... **DACUS**
olive genus .... **OLEA**
olive, inferior .... **MORON**
olive, stuffed .... **PIMOLA**
Oliver's nickname ..... **NOLL**
Olympian deity-god-goddess
.... **ARES, HERA, APOLLO,**
.... **ATHENA, HERMES, AR-**
.... **TEMIS, DEMETER**
Olympus, mountain near . **OSSA**
Olympus queen .... **HERA**
Olympus, region by .... **PIERIA**
omen ...... **BODE, PRESAGE**
omission, vowel ..... **ELISION**
omit ...... **DELE, PASS, SKIP**
omit in pronunciation .. **ELIDE**

omitted, having part
.... **ELLIPTIC, ELLIPTICAL**
onager .... **ASS**
once: dial. .... **ANES**
one .... **AIN, UNIT**
one-base hit .... **SINGLE**
one behind other .... **TANDEM**
one-eighth Troy ounce .. **DRAM**
one-eyed giant ..... **CYCLOPS**
one-horse carriage ..... **SHAY**
one hundred sq. meters AR, **ARE**
one hundred thousand rupees
.... **LAKH**
one, music by .... **SOLI, SOLO**
one-spot .... **ACE**
one thousand .... **MIL**
one-year record ...... **ANNAL**
O'Neill heroine .... **ANNA**
onion .... **CEPA**
onion, Welsh .... **CIBOL**
onionlike plant .. **CIVE, LEEK,**
.... **CHIVE, SHALLOT, ESCHALOT**
only .... **MERE, SAVE, SOLE**
onward ...... **AHEAD, FORTH**
onyx, Mex. .... **TECALI**
oorial .... **SHA**
ooze ...... **LEAK, SEEP, SEIP,**
.... **SIPE, SYPE, EXUDE**
open .... **AJAR, OVERT,**
.... **BROACH, PATENT, UNWRAP**
open court .... **AREA**
open plain .... **VEGA**
opening .... **GAP, HOLE,**
.... **RIFT, SLOT, VENT, HIATUS**
opening, long .... **RIMA, SLOT**
opening, mouthlike
.... **STOMA, STOMATA**
opening, slit-like ...... **RIMA**
opening, small .... **PORE**
opera ... **AIDA, BORIS, ORFEO**
opera, Beethoven .... **FIDELIO**
opera, Bizet .... **CARMEN**
opera composer, modern
.... **BRITTEN, MENOTTI**
opera, Gounod .... **FAUST**
opera hat .... **GIBUS**
opera heroine ... **AIDA, ELSA,**
.... **MIMI, SENTA, ISOLDE**
opera house, Milan .... **SCALA**
opera, Massenet
.... **MANON, THAIS**
opera, Puccini .... **TOSCA**
opera scene .... **SCENA**
opera singer .... **MELBA**
opera soprano, star. **ALDA, PONS**
.... **BORI, RISE, RAISA, STEBER**
opera star .... **DIVA**
opera, Verdi ... **AIDA, ERNANI**
opera, Wagner .... **RIENZI**
operate ...... **RUN, MANAGE**
operetta composer ..... **FRIML**

110

a opium poppy seed ...... MAW
opossum, S. Am. ...... QUICA
opponent .. FOE, ANTI, RIVAL
opportune .... TIMELY
opportunity .... CHANCE
oppose .... IMPUGN
opposed, one .... ANTI
opposed to solo ...... TUTTI
opposite extremities ... POLES
opposite .... REVERSE
Ops' daughter .... CERES
Ops' husband .... SATURN
optical glass .... LENS
optical illusion ..... MIRAGE
optical instrument lines RETICLE
optimistic ... ROSY, ROSEATE
oracle, Apollo's ...... DELOS
oracle, Gr. .. DELPHI, DELPHOI
oral .... PAROL
orange-red stone ...... SARD
orange tincture, Her. .. TENNE
orangutan, Malay ...... MIAS
orarion .... STOLE
orator .... OTIS, RHETOR
orb of day .... SUN
orbit point .... APSIS, APOGEE
orchid genus .... DISA
orchid leaves for tea
            FAAM, FAHAM
orchid tuber .... SALEP

b ordain .... DECREE
order .... BID, FIAT,
     ARRAY, EDICT, DECREE
ordes, one of Catholic. MARIST
order, put in .... TIDY, SETTLE
orderliness .... SYSTEM
ordinance .... LAW
ordnance piece ...... MORTAR
ore deposit ...... LODE, MINE
ore of iron .... OCHER, OCHRE
ore receptacle ...... MORTAR
organ .... EAR, EYE
organ of algae .... PROCARP
organ part .... STOP
organ pipe .... REED
organ pipe, displayed MONTRE
organ prelude .... VERSET
organ, seed-bearing ... PISTIL
organ stop REED,SEXT,DOLCAN,
        CELESTE, MELODIA
organism, 1-cell
          AMEBA, AMOEBA
organism, simple
          MONAD, MONAS
organization .... SETUP
orgy .... REVEL
Orient .... EAST
Oriental ...... ASIAN, TATAR
Oriental dwelling .... DAR

c Oriental lute .... TAR
Oriental nursemaid .... AMA,
     IYA, AMAH, AYAH, EYAH
Oriental plane tree .. CHINAR
Oriental porgy .... TAI
Oriental potentate ..... AGA
Oriental sailing ship .. DHOW
Oriental servant ..... HAMAL
Oriental ship captain .... RAS
Oriental weight .... ROTL
orifice.PORE, STOMA, OSTIOLE
orifices, sponge ...... OSCULA
origin .... SEED
original .... NEW
original sin .... ADAM
originate ARISE, START, CREATE
Orinoco tributary .... ARO
oriole, golden .... LORIOT
ornament .... FRET
ornament, curly .... SCROLL
ornament in relief .. EMBOSS
ornament, spire .... EPI
ornamental border .... DADO
ornamental grass .... EULALIA
ornamental nailhead ... STUD
Orpheus' destination ... HADES
Orpheus' instrument .... LYRE
orris .... IRIS
orris-root ketone, oil ... IRONE
oscillate .... WAVE
osier .... WITHE

d Osiris' brother .... SET
Osiris' wife, sister ...... ISIS
ostentation .... POMP
ostracism ..... TABU, TABOO
ostrich, Am. .... RHEA
ostrich-like bird
          EMU, EMEU, RATITE
Otaheite apple .... HEVI
Othello was one .... MOOR
Othello's lieutenant, foe IAGO
otherwise .... ELSE
otic .... AURAL
otologist .... AURIST
otter brown, color ... LOUTRE
otter genus .... LUTRA
Ottoman .... TURK
Ottoman court .... PORTE
Ottoman official ..... PASHA
"Our Mutual Friend," ballad-
     seller in .... WEGG
oust .... EJECT, EVICT
out .... AWAY, FORTH
out-and-out .... ARRANT
out: Dutch .... UIT
out of style .... PASSE
out of the way .... ASIDE
outbreak, unruly ...... RIOT
outburst, sudden ...... SPATE
outcast
     LEPER, PARIAH, ISHMAEL

111

outcome, final .... **UPSHOT**
outcry .... **CLAMOR**
outer .... **ECTAL**
outer portion of earth ... **SIAL**
outfit .. **KIT, RIG, GEAR, SUIT**
outfit, queer .... **GETUP**
outlet .... **VENT**
outline .... **PERIMETER**
outlook .... **VISTA**
outmoded .... **PASSE**
OUTRIGGER see **MALAY CANOE**
outward .... **ECTAD**
ova .... **EGGS**
oval ... **ELLIPTIC, ELLIPTICAL**
oven .... **KILN, OAST**
oven, annealing .. **LEER, LEHR**
oven, Polyn. native ...... **UMU**
over .... **ATOP, ABOVE,**
AGAIN, ENDED, ACROSS
over-nice .... **FINICAL**
overnice person .... **PRIG**
over: poet. .... **OER**
over there ..... **YON, YONDER**
overact .... **EMOTE**
overcoat ... **ULSTER, PALETOT**
overdue payment ..... **ARREAR**
overflow .... **DEBORD**
overfond, be ..... **DOAT, DOTE**
overjoy .... **ELATE**
overlay .... **CEIL**
overripe grain .... **BRITE**
overseer, ranch: Sp. Am.
CAPORAL
overshadow .... **DOMINATE**
overshoe
GOLOE, GALOSH, GALOSHE
overskirt .. **PANIER, PANNIER**
overspreading mass ..... **PALL**

overt .... **OPEN, FRANK**
overwhelm .... **DELUGE**
overwhelming amount ... **SEA**
Ovid's "— Amatoria" .... **ARS**
ovule .... **SEED**
ovum .... **EGG**
owala tree .... **BOBO**
owl, barn, Samoa ...... **LULU**
owl, eagle .. **BUBO, KATOGLE**
owl, horned .... **BUBO**
owl, S. Asia .... **UTUM**
owl's cry .... **HOOT**
own up to .... **AVOW**
ownership, of land, old law
ODAL, UDAL
ox, extinct wild .... **URUS**
ox, forest .... **ANOA**
ox, long-haired .... **YAK**
ox of Caesar's time ... **URUS**
ox, wild .... **ANOA**
ox, wild: India .... **GAUR**
GOUR, ZEBU, GAYAL
oxalis, S. Amer. .... **OCA**
oxen .... **KINE**
oxhide strap .... **REIM, RIEM**
oxide .... **CALX**
oxidize .... **RUST**
oxygen compound **OXID, OXIDE**
oxygen, form of ..... **OZONE**
oxygen radical .... **OXYL**
oyster bed material
CULCH, CUTCH, CULTCH
oyster drill .... **BORER**
oyster farm: Fr. .... **PARC**
oyster, young .... **SPAT**
oysterfish .... **TAUTOG**
Ozarks, town west of in Okla.
ADA
Oz books author ...... **BAUM**

P

pace .... **RATE, STEP**
pachisi, kind of .... **LUDO**
pachyderm .... **ELEPHANT**
Pacific aroid food plant **TARO**
Pacific Island cloth ..... **TAPA**
Pacific pine .... **HALA**
Pacific shrub .... **SALAL**
pacify
CALM, SOOTHE, PLACATE
pack .... **WAD, STOW**
pack animal .... **ASS,**
BURRO, LLAMA, SUMPTER
pack horse ...... **SUMPTER**
pack down .... **RAM, TAMP**
package, India ...... **ROBBIN**
package of spun silk .. **MOCHE**
pad .... **TABLET**

padded jacket under armor
ACTON
padnag .... **TROT, AMBLE**
Padua, town near ...... **ESTE**
pagan god .... **IDOL**
page, "Love's Labor Lost" **MOTH**
page number .... **FOLIO**
pageantry .... **POMP**
"Pagliacci" character .. **CANIO**
"Pagliacci" heroine ... **NEDDA**
pagoda, Chinese ... **TA, TAA**
pagoda ornament ... **EPI, TEE**
paid notice .... **AD**
pail .... **SKEEL**
pain, dull .... **ACHE**
pain reliever **OPIATE, ANODYNE**
paint, face .... **FARD, ROUGE**

a pain-killer alkaloid source **COCA**
painted bunting: Creole .. **PAPE**
PAINTER .. see also ARTIST
and country of each artist
painter, modernist
KLEE, MIRO, ERNST
painting style .... **GENRE**
painting, wall .... **MURAL**
pair .... **DUO, DIAD,**
DUAD, DYAD, MATE
pair of horses ... **SPAN, TEAM**
pairing .... **MATING**
palanquin .... **JAUN**
palanquin bearer ... **HAMAL**
palanquin, Jap. .... **KAGO**
palatable, very ...... **SAPID**
pale .... **WAN, ASHY,**
ASHEN, PASTY
pale color .... **PASTEL**
pale-colored .... **MEALY**
Palestine in Jewish use **ERETS**
palisade: fort. .... **RIMER**
Pallas .... **ATHENA**
pallid .... **WAN, PALE**
palm .... **TI, COCO, TALA,**
TALIPAT, TALIPOT, TALI-
PUT
palm, Afr. .... **DUM**
palm, Asia .... **ARENG, BETEL**
palm, betel .... **ARECA**
palm, book .... **TARA**
b palm, Brazil .... **ASSAI**
palm, climbing ...... **RATTAN**
palm cockatoo .... **ARARA**
palm, dwarf genus .... **SABAL**
palm fiber **DOH, TAL, RAFFIA**
palm fiber, S. Amer. .... **DATIL**
palm genus .... **ARECA**
palm genus, Asia .... **ARENGA**
palm juice, fermented .. **SURA**
palm leaf
OLA, OLE, OLAY, OLLA
palm-leaf mat .... **YAPA**
palm lily .... **TI**
palm, liquor ..... **BENO, BINO**
palm, N. Z. .... **NIKAU**
palm, nipa ..... **ATAP, ATTAP**
palm off .... **FOB, FOIST**
palm, palmyra leaf .... **OLA,**
OLE, OLLA, OLAY
palm sago, Malay ... **GOMUTI**
palm sap .... **TODDY**
palm starch .... **SAGO**
palm, W. Ind. **GRIGRI, GRUGRU**
palmetto .... **SABAL**
palmyra leaf ...... **OLA, OLE,**
OLAY, OLLA
palmyra palm .... **BRAB**
palp .... **FEELER**
palpitation .... **PALMUS**

c pamper .... **COSHER, COSSET**
pamphlet .... **TRACT**
panacea .... **ELIXIR**
Panama gum tree **COPA, YAYA**
Panama, old name ... **DARIEN**
Panama tree, large .. **CATIVO**
Panay negrito .... **ATI**
panda .... **WAH, BEAR**
panel .... **PANE**
panel of jurors ...... **VENIRE**
pang .... **THROE**
pangolin .... **MANIS**
panic .... **FEAR, FUNK**
pannier .... **DOSSER**
Panopolis, chief god of .. **MIN,**
KHEM
pant .... **GASP**
pantry .... **AMBRY, LARDER,**
SPENCE, BUTTERY
— Paulo, Brazil .... **SAO**
papal cape ... **FANO, FANON,**
FANUM, ORALE, PHANO,
FANNEL
papal church .... **LATERAN**
papal collar .. **FANO, FANON,**
FANUM, ORALE, PHANO,
FANNEL
papal court ...... **SEE, CURIA**
papal fanon .... **ORALE**
papal letter .... **BULL, BULLA**
d papal scarf .... **ORALE**
papal veil .... **FANO, FANON,**
FANUM, ORALE, PHANO,
FANNEL
papal vestment .... **FANO,**
FANON, FANUM, ORALE,
PHANO, FANNEL
paper folded once ..... **FOLIO**
paper, imperfect, poor
CASSE, CASSIE, RETREE
paper, lighting .... **SPILL**
paper measure .. **REAM, QUIRE**
paper mulberry .... **KOZO**
paper mulberry bark .... **TAPA**
paper size
DEMY, POTT, OCTAVO
paper, thin crisp .... **PELURE**
par, 2 under .... **EAGLE**
Para, Brazil, capital .. **BELEM**
parade ...... **MARCH, STRUT**
paradise .... **EDEN**
paradise, Buddhist ..... **JODO**
paradise, like ...... **EDENIC**
"Paradise Lost" angel .. **ARIEL**
paragraph .... **ITEM**
parallelogram .... **RHOMB**
paralysis .... **PARESIS**
parapet, solid portion of **MERLON**
parasite .... **LEECH**

113

a parasite in blood .... TRYP
parasitic insect MITE, ACARID
parasitic plant MOSS, DODDER
paravane .... OTTER
Parcae .... FATES
Parcae, one of
    NONA, MORTA, DECUMA
parcel of land .... LOT, PLAT
parchment, book
    FOREL, FORREL
pardon .... REMIT, CONDONE
pardon, general .... AMNESTY
pare .... PEEL
Paris art exhibit ..... SALON
Paris, first bishop of
    DENIS, DENYS
Paris section .... PASSY
Paris subway .... METRO
Paris thug .... APACHE
Paris' father .... PRIAM
Paris' wife .... OENONE
parish head .... RECTOR
parley .... PALAVER
Parliament report .. HANSARD
parol .... ORAL
paroxysm ..... FIT, SPASM
parrot
    KEA, LORY, VASA, VAZA
parrot, Brazil ... ARA, ARARA
parrot-fish
b   LORO, LAUIA, SCARID
parrot, hawk .... HIA
parrot, monk .... LORO
parrot, N. Z. large KEA, KAKA
parrot, P. I., green .... CAGIT
parrot, sheep-killing ... KEA
parrot's bill, part of .... CERE
parrotlike .... ARINE
parry .... FEND, EVADE
Parsi priest .... MOBED
Parsi scripture .... AVESTA
parsley camphor .... APIOL
parsley, plant kin to
    ANISE, CELERY
parson bird
    POE, TUE, TUI, KOKO
parsonage .... MANSE
part .... ROLE, SOME, PIECE,
    BREAK, SEVER, SHARE,
    CLEAVE, ELEMENT
part, Greek play
    EXODE, EXODOS
part of church .... BEMA
    NAVE, AISLE, ALTAR
part of horse's foot ... PASTERN
part of speech .. NOUN, VERB
parted .... PARTITE
participle ending .... ING
parti-colored .... PIED, PINTO

c parti-colored horse
    ROAN, CALICO
particle ...... ACE, BIT, ION,
    JOT, ATOM, IOTA, DROP,
    MITE, MOTE, GRAIN,
    SHRED, TITTLE
particle, electrically charged
    ION
particle in cosmic rays MESON
particle of chaff ...... PALEA
particle, small
    JOT, ATOM, IOTA, MOTE
particular .... ITEM
Partlet .... HEN, BIDDY
partnership: Hawaii HUI, HOEY
partridge call ... JUCK, JUKE
partridge, sand ...... SEESEE
partridge, snow ...... LERWA
party .... SECT
parvenu .... UPSTART
pasha .... DEY
pass .... HAND, ELAPSE
pass a rope through ... REEVE
pass between peaks ... COL
pass by .... BYGO
pass on .... RELAY
pass over .. OMIT, SKIP, ELIDE
pass through .... REEVE
pass through mountains .. COL,
    DEFILE
passable .... SOSO
d passage .... GUT, ITER,
    CANAL, TRANSIT
passage, bastion .... POSTERN
passage, covered .... ARCADE
passage: hist. .... ALURE
passage: music TUTTI, STRETTA
passage out .... EXIT, EGRESS
passageway ADIT, HALL, AISLE
Passover ..... PASCH, PASCHA
Passover meal ... SEDAR, SEDER
passport endorsement VISA, VISE
past AGO, GONE, OVER, AGONE
paste .... STRASS
pasteboard .... CARD
pasted-up art work .. COLLAGE
pastel .... TINT
pastoral .... IDYLLIC
pastoral place ...... ARCADIA
pastoral poem .. IDYL, IDYLL
pastoral staff .. PEDA, PEDUM
pastry
    PIE, FLAN, TART, ECLAIR
pasture .... LEA
pasture: N. Eng. .... ING
pasture, to .... AGIST
pasty .... DOUGHY
pat .... DAB, TAP
pat, very .... APT
Patagonian cavy ...... MARA
patchwork, literary .... CENTO

patella .... ROTULA
paten .... ARCA, ARCAE
patent from monarch .. BERAT
path: Anglo-Ir. ..... CASAUN
path: math. .... LOCUS
path of planet .... ORBIT
pathos, false .... BATHOS
patriarch Jacob ...... ISRAEL
patriarch's title .... NASI
patron .... CLIENT
patron saint of France
         DENIS, DENYS
patronage ...... EGIS, AEGIS
pattern ...... NORM, TYPE,
    IDEAL, MODEL, PARAGON
pattern, large square   DAMIER
Paul, Apostle .... SAUL
Paul's birthplace ..... TARSUS
paulownia tree .... KIRI
pause .... REST
pause: poet. & music
   SELAH, CESURA, CAESURA
paver .... TUP
paver's mallet .... TUP
pavilion .... TENT
paving stone .... FLAG, SETT
paw .... PUD, FOOT
pawl .... DETENT
pawn .... HOCK
Pawnee Indian rite .... HAKO
Pawnee tribes .... CHAUI
pay ... ANTE, WAGE, REMIT
pay dirt .... ORE
pay, fixed .... STIPEND
pay for another ...... TREAT
pay homage: feudal law
             ATTORN
pay one's part .... ANTE
pay out .... SPEND
payable .... DUE
paymaster, India ..... BUXY
payment back ...... REBATE
payment for a bride, S. Afr.
            LOBOLA
payment for death, feudal CRO
payment for homicide ... ERIC
payment, press for ... DUN
payment to owner: Fr. law CENS
pea .... LEGUME
peace .... PAX
peace god, Anglo-Saxon .. ING
peace of mind .... REST
peaceful .. IRENE, IRENICAL
peach, clingstone ...... PAVY
peacock .... MAO, PAVO
peacock blue .... PAON
peacock butterfly .... IO
peacock fish .... WRASSE
peacock genus .... PAVO
peacock: Kipling .... MAO

peak ...... ALP, TOR, ACME,
    APEX, PITON, ZENITH
peak: Scot. .... BEN
peanut ..... MANI, GOOBER
pear, autumn .... BOSC
pear cider .... PERRY
pearl blue color ...... METAL
Pearl Buck heroine .... OLAN
pearl, imitation ...... OLIVET
pearl millet ... BAJRA, BA RI
pearlweeds .... SAGINA
peasant.CARL, CEORL, CHURL
peasant, India .... RYOT
peasant, Scot.
       COTTAR, COTTER
peat .... TURF
peat spade .... SLADE
pecan tree .... NOGAL
peccary, collared .... JAVALI
peck ...... DAB, NIP, KNIP
pedal .... TREADLE
peddle ... HAWK, SELL, VEND
peddle: Eng. .... TRANT
pedestal .... GAINE
pedestal part .. DADO, PLINTH
peduncle, plant ...... SCAPE
peel . BARK, PARE, RIND. SKIN
peep-show .... RAREE
PEER .... see also NOBLE
peer .... PEEK, PE??
Peer Gynt's mother .... ASE
peevish .... PETULANT
peg .... KNAG
peg, golf .... TEE
peg, wooden
   NOG, TRENAIL, TREENAIL
Pegu ironwood .... ACLE
Peleg's son .... REU
pellucid ...... CLEAR, LIMPID
pelma .... SOLE
pelota court ..... FRONTON
pelt . FELL, SKIN, STONE
pelvic bone, pert. to .... ILIAC
pelvic bones .... ILIA
pen name, Dickens ...... BOZ
pen name, G. Russell ..... AE
pen name, Lamb ...... ELIA
pen point .... NEB, NIB
pen-text .... RONDE
penman, Yutang .... LIN
penalty .... FINE
pendulum weight .... BOB
Penelope's father .. ICARIUS
penetrate
   GORE, ENTER, PERMEATE
penitential season .... LENT
penmanship .... HAND
pennies .... PENCE
Pennsylvania sect ..... AMISH
Pentateuch .... TORA, TORAH

115

People

PEOPLE .. see also TRIBES in SPECIAL SECTION
people .... MEN, FOLK, ONES, RACE, DEMOS
people, ancient Asian ... SERES
people: Ger. .... VOLK
people: Ir. .... DAOINE
people, Nigerian . BENI, BENIN
people: Sp. .... GENTE
people, spirit of ...... ETHOS
people, the .... DEMOS
pepper, climbing ..... BETEL
pepper, garden .... PIMIENTO
pepper plant, Borneo .... ARA
pepper shrub
          AVA, CAVA, KAVA, KAWA
pepper vine .... BETEL
Pequod's captain .... AHAB
"per —" .... DIEM, ANNUM
perceive .. SEE, SENSE, DESCRY
perception . EAR, TACT, SENSE
perch .... SIT, ROOST
perch genus .... PERCA
perchlike fish .... DARTER
percolate .. OOZE, SEEP, LEACH
peregrine .... ALIEN
perenially shifting sands region
          AREG
perfect .... IDEAL, MODEL
perforate ..... BORE, DRILL, PUNCH, RIDDLE
perform .... RENDER
performer
          DOER, ACTOR, ARTISTE
perfume
    ATAR, OTTO, AROMA, ATTAR
perfume base .... MUSK
perfume with incense .. CENSE
perfumed pad .... SACHET
Pericles' consort .... ASPASIA
periphery ... RIM, PERIMETER
period .... DOT
period, time
          AGE, EON, ERA, STAGE
periodic as Med. winds ETESIAN
permit .. LET, ALLOW, LICENSE
permission .... LEAVE
pernicious, something .... PEST
perplex
    BAFFLE, CONFUSE, BEWILDER
Persephone ..... CORA, KORE
Persephone's husband
          HADES, PLUTO
Persia .... IRAN
Persian .... IRANI
Persian coin, ancient .. DARIC
Pers. demigod .... YIMA
Pers. elf .... PERI
Pers. enameled tile ..... KASI
Pers. fairy .... PERI
Pers. governor, old ... SATRAP
Pers. headdress, ancient TIARA

Pers. lord ..... KAAN, KHAN
Pers. mystic .... SUFI
Pers. native .... LUR
Pers. poet .... OMAR
Pers. potentate .... SHAH
Pers. priestly caste .... MAGI
Pers. province, ancient .. ELAM
Pers. race, tribesman LUR,KURD
Pers. rug .. SENNA, HAMADAN
Pers. ruler .... SHAH
Pers. ruler of dead ..... YIMA
Pers. sect .... BABI
Pers. sprite .... PERI
PERS. TITLE .... see TITLE, PERSIAN
Pers. tribe member ..... LUR
Pers. weight .... SER
persimmon, E. Ind. GAB, GAUB
person of mixed blood
          METIS, MESTIZO
person, overnice .... PRIG
personage .... NIBS
personification of folly ... ATE
personification of light: Polyn.
          AO
personnel .... STAFF
perspiration .. SUDOR, SWEAT
perspire .... EGEST, SWEAT
pert girl .... CHIT, MINX
pertaining to the chin MENTAL
pertinent .... APT, PAT
perturb .... DERANGE, DISTURB, AGITATE, TROUBLE
PERU INDIAN .. see page 193
peruse ..... CON, READ, SCAN
peruser .... CONNER
Peruvian fertility goddess MAMA
Peruvian plant .... OCA
pervade .... PERMEATE
pester .... ANNOY, TEASE
pestle .... PILUM
pestle vessel .... MORTAR
pet .... CADE
pet lamb ...... CADE, COSSET
"Peter Pan" dog ...... NANA
"Peter Pan" pirate ...... SMEE
petiole .... STIPE
Petrarch's love .... LAURA
petrol .... GAS
peyote .... MESCAL
phantoms .... EIDOLA
Pharaoh .... RAMESES
Pharaoh after Rameses I .. SETI
phase .... FACET, STAGE
pheasant brood NID, NYE, NIDE
pheasant, Himal. . CHIR, CHEER
pheasant, India ...... MONAL
Phidias statue .... ATHENA
philippic .... TIRADE
PHILIPPINE ISLANDS
          see also SPECIAL SECTION

116

Philippine Islands attendant .... ALILA
P.I. bast fiber ...... CASTULI
P.I. cedar .... CALANTAS
P.I. chief DATO, DATU, DATTO
P.I. DWARF see P. I. NEGRITO
P.I. dyewood tree
.... TUI, IPIL, TUWI
P.I. food ...... POI, SABA
P.I. fort .... COTA, KOTA
P.I. grass ...... BOHO, BOJO
P.I. lighter .... CASCO
P.I. lizard .... IBID, IBIT
P.I. Moslem .... MORO
P.I. negrito, native, dwarf
.... ATA, ATI, ITA,
.... AETA, ATTA
P.I. palm wine ... BENO, BINO
P.I. peasant .... TAO
P.I. poisonous tree .... LIGAS
P.I. rice ...... PAGA, MACAN
P.I. sash .... TAPIS
P.I. servant .... ALILA
P.I. shrub, rope NABO, ANABO
P.I. skirt .... SAYA
P.I. tree .... DAO, IBA, TUA,
TUI, BOGO, DITA, IFIL,
IPIL, YPIL
P.I. warrior .... MORO
Philistine city .... GAZA,
GATH, EKRON
Philistine deity, principal DAGON
philosopher's stone .... ELIXIR
philosophical element .... RECT
philosophical theory MONISM
philosophy, pert. to Gr. ELEATIC
phloem .... BAST
phoebe .... PEWEE, PEWIT
Phoebus .... SOL, SUN
Phoenician city .... TYRE
Phoenician goddess .. ASTARTE
Phoenician port .... SIDON
Phoenician princess .. EUROPA
phonetic notation system
.... ROMIC
phonetical sound .... PALATAL
phosphate of lime ... APATITE
photo-developing powder METOL
photography solution ... HYPO
Phrygian god .... ATTIS
Phrygian lunar god ..... MEN
physical ... SOMAL, SOMATIC
physician ..... GALEN, MEDIC
physician's group .... AMA
physician's symbol CADUCEUS
physicist, Am. .... EINSTEIN
physicist, Eng. .... BOYLE
physicist, Fr. .... CURIE
physicist, Nobel prize-winner
1944 .... RABI
physiological individual .. BION

piano, upright ...... CLAVIAL
pick, miner's: Eng.
.... MANDREL, MANDRIL
pick out .... CULL, GLEAN
picket .... PALE
pickled bamboo shoots ACHAR
pickled meat .... SOUSE
pickling fluid .... BRINE
pickling herb .... DILL
pickpocket .... DIP
"Picnic" author .... INGE
picture ... DRAW, PORTRAIT
picture border .... MAT
picture, composite .. MONTAGE
picturesque .... SCENIC
pie, meat, small ...... PASTY
piebald .... PINTO
piebald pony ... PIED, PINTO
piece of eight .... REALS
piece out .... EKE
piece, thin .... SLAT
pier .... KEY, DOCK,
MOLE, QUAI, QUAY
pier, architectural ..... ANTA
pier support ... PILE, PILING
pierce ... GORE, STAB, SPEAR
pig. HOG, SOW, SHOAT, SHOTE
pig, wild .... BOAR
pig, young .... ELT, GRICE
pigs .... SUS
pigs' feet .... PETTITOES
pigs, litter of .... FARROW
pigs, red .... DUROC
pigeon ... NUN, BARB, DOVE,
POUTER, ROLLER
pigeon hawk .... MERLIN
pigeon pea. DAL, TUR, GANDUL
piglike animal .... PECCARY
pigment, blue-green .... BICE
pigment, brown ...... SEPIA
pigment, brown, from soot
.... BISTER, BISTRE
pigment, deep blue .... SMALT
pigment, red .... LAKE
pigment test crystalline DOPA
pigment, without .... ALBINO
pigmentation, lack of
.... ACHROMA
pigtail .... CUE, QUEUE
pike, full grown . LUCE, LUCET
pike, walleyed .... DORE
pilaster .... ANTA
pilchard .. FUMADO, SARDINE
pilchard-like fish ...... SPRAT
pile ...... NAP, HEAP, SPILE
pile driver .... OLIVER
pile driver ram .... TUP
pile of hay ..... RICK, STACK
pilfer .... STEAL
pilgrim .... PALMER

117

a pilgrimage city .... **MECCA**
pilgrimage to Mecca ..... **HADJ**
pill, large .... **BOLUS**
pillage .... **LOOT, SACK, STEAL**
pillage .... **RAPINE**
pillar, as of ore .... **JAMB**
pillar, Hindu .... **LAT**
pillar, resembling ...... **STELAR**
pillar, tapering ...... **OBELISK**
pillow .... **BOLSTER**
pilot .... **GUIDE, STEER**
pimento or —spice ..... **ALL**
pin .... **BROOCH**
pin, firing .... **TIGE**
pin, gunwale .... **THOLE**
pin, machine .... **COTTER**
pin, metal .... **RIVET**
pin, pivot .... **PINTLE**
pin, rifle firing .... **TIGE**
pin, Roman .... **ACUS**
pin, small, very .... **LILL**
pin, splicing .... **FID**
pin, wooden .. **FID, NOG, PEG,
COAG, COAK, DOWEL**
pin wrench .... **SPANNER**
pinafore .... **TIER**
pincer claw .... **CHELA**
pinch .... **NIP**
pinched with cold .... **URLED**
Pindar work .... **ODE**
b pine-cone, like a ...... **PINEAL**
pine, Mex. .... **OCOTE, PINON**
pine, Scot. .... **RIGA**
pine, textile screw
ARA, PANDAN
pineapple **NANA, PINA, ANANA**
pineapple genus .... **PUYA**
pinfeather .... **PEN**
pinion .... **WING**
pink .... **DAMASK**
pinnacle .... **TOP, APEX**
pinnacle, ice .... **SERAC**
pinniped .... **SEAL**
pinochle score, term
DIX, MELD
pint, half .... **CUP**
pintado fish .... **SIER**
pintail .... **SMEE**
pinworm .. **ASCARID, ASCARIS**
pious Biblical Jew ..... **TOBIT**
pipe .... **TUBE, RISER**
pipe, Irish .... **DUDEEN**
pipe joint, fitting .... **TEE**
pipe, pastoral .... **REED**
pipe, tobacco
BRIAR, BRIER, DUDEEN
pipe, water. **HOOKAH, NARGILE**
pipe with socket ends
HUB, HUBB
pipelike .... **TUBATE**
pique .... **PEEVE**

c pirate ...... **ROVER, CORSAIR**
pirate in War of 1812 **LAFITTE**
pismire .... **ANT, EMMET**
pistil part .... **CARPEL**
pistol .... **DAG, DAGG,
MAUSER, SIDEARM**
pistol: slang .... **HEATER**
pit ..... **HOLE, ABYSS, STONE**
pit for roots, Maori ..... **RUA**
pit: medical .... **FOSSA**
pit, small .. **FOVEA, LACUNA**
pitch ...... **KEY, TAR, TONE**
pitcher .... **JUG, EWER**
pitcher's false move ... **BALK**
pith .... **NUB, GIST**
pith helmet .... **TOPI, TOPEE**
pithy .... **TERSE**
pithy plant .... **SOLA**
pitiful quality ...... **PATHOS**
pittance .... **DOLE**
pitted .... **FOVEATE**
pity .... **RUTH**
placard .... **POSTER**
place .... **SET, LIEU, LOCI,
SPOT, LOCUS, STEAD, LO-
CALE**
place before .... **APPOSE**
place, camping .... **ETAPE**
place case is tried .... **VENUE**
place in office again .. **RESEAT**
d place, in relation ...... **POSIT**
place, market .... **FORUM**
place of shelter .. **GITE, HAVEN**
placid .... **CALM, SERENE**
plagiarize .... **STEAL**
plague .... **PEST, TEASE**
plain, arctic .... **TUNDRA**
plain, Argentine ...... **PAMPA**
plain, Asia .... **CHOL**
plain, Palestine .... **ONO**
plain, Russia .... **STEPPE**
plain, S. Am. .... **LLANO**
plain, treeless ...... **SAVANNA**
plain, treeless Arctic **TUNDRA**
plain, upland .. **WOLD, WEALD**
Plains Indian .... see page 193
plainly woven .... **UNI**
plait .... **PLY, BRAID**
plan .... **PLOT, INTEND**
plane, Fr. .... **SPAD**
plane, Ger. .... **STUKA**
plane, Jap. .... **ZERO**
plane part .... **FLAP,
NOSE, TAIL, WING**
plane, Russ. fighter ...... **MIG**
planets (in order of distance from
sun) **MERCURY (1), VE-
NUS (2), EARTH (3),
MARS (4), JUPITER (5),
SATURN (6), URANUS (7),
NEPTUNE (8), PLUTO (9)**

a planets in distance from Earth
(closest first)

1—VENUS	5—SATURN
2—MARS	6—URANUS
3—MERCURY	7—NEPTUNE
4—JUPITER	8—PLUTO

planets in size
(largest first)

1—JUPITER	6—VENUS
2—SATURN	7—PLUTO
3—NEPTUNE	8—MARS
4—URANUS	9—MERCURY
5—EARTH	

planetarium .... ORRERY
planetary aspect CUSP, TRINE
plank's curve on ship ..... SNY
plant .... SOW, SEED
plant, bayonet .... DATIL
plant broom .... SPART
plant, bulb
CAMAS, CAMASS, CAMMAS
plant cutter bird ..... RARA
plant cutting .. SLIP, PHYTON
plant disease ... RUST, SMUT
plant joined to another GRAFT
plant life .... FLORA
PLANT, LILY ...... see LILY
plant, lily-like
CAMAS, CAMASS, CAMMAS
plant louse .... APHID
plant, male .... MAS
b plant, medicinal, S. Am.
ALOE, SENNA, IPECAC
plant modified by environment
to abnormal development
ECAD
plant, mustard family
KALE, CRESS
plant organ .... LEAF
plant pod .... BOLL
plant, poisonous ...... LOCO
plant, sea-bottom ... ENALID
plant stem: bot. ..... CAULIS
plant stem tissue ...... PITH
plant used as soap ... AMOLE
plants of area .... FLORA
plantain lily genus ... HOSTA
plantation, osier ...... HOLT
planter .... SEEDER
plaster .... SMEAR
plaster, artist's painting. GESSO
plaster of Paris ...... GESSO
plastic .... LUCITE
plate, battery .... GRID
plate, Eucharist ...... PATEN
plate, reptile's ...... SCUTE
plate to hurl .... DISCUS
plateau .... MESA
plateau, Andes ...... PUNA
platform ...... DAIS, STAGE
platform, ancient ...... BEMA

c platform, mine shaft
SOLLAR, SOLLER
platinum, of .... OSMIC
platinum wire loop ..... OESE
Plato's "Idea" ... EIDE, EIDOS
play .... DRAMA
play on words .... PUN
play, part of ... ACT, SCENE
play unskillfully ...... STRUM
player .... ACTOR
playing card, old It. ... TAROT
playwright .... INGE
plea, to end: law .... ABATER
plead .... SUE, ENTREAT
pleading: law .... OYER
please .... SUIT
pleasing .... NICE
pleasure god, Egypt. . BES, BESA
pledge .... VOW,
GAGE, OATH, PAWN,
TROTH, ENGAGE
pledge, Rom. law ...... VAS
plexus .... RETE, RETIA
pliable .... WAXY
pliant .... LITHE
plinth .... ORLO, SOCLE
plot .... LOT,
PLAT, CABAL, CONSPIRE
plow, cutter COLTER, COULTER
plow part ... SHETH, SHEATH
plow, sole of .... SHARE
plowed field ... ERD, ARADA
plug .... BUNG,
CORK, SPILE, STOPPER
plum .... GAGE, SLOE
plume . EGRET, PREEN, AIGRET
plummet .... FATHOM
plump child .... FUB
plunder .... ROB, LOOT, PREY,
SACK, BOOTY, RAVEN,
RAVIN, REAVE, PILFER,
RAPINE, RAVAGE, RAVINE
plunder ruthlessly ... MARAUD
plunge ...... DIVE, DOUSE
plural ending .... EN, ES
plus .... AND
Pluto .... DIS, HADES, ORCUS
Pluto's mother-in-law DEMETER
pneumonia, kind of ... LOBAR
Po tributary .... ADDA
pochard .... SMEE
pocket billiards ...... POOL
pocket gopher, Mex. ... TUZA
pod, cotton .... BOLL
pods for tanning ...... PIPI
Poe poem .... RAVEN
poem .... ODE, ELEGY, EPODE
poem division, or part . CANTO
poem, 8 line .... TRIOLET

119

poem

poem, long heroic .. **EPIC, EPOS**
poem, love .... **SONNET**
poem, lyric ...... **ODE, EPODE**
poem, mournful .... **ELEGY**
poem, of a .... **ODIC**
poem, old Fr. .... **DIT**
poem, sacred .... **PSALM**
poet .... **BARD, ODIST**
poet, A.-S. .... **SCOP**
poet, Bengal .... **TAGORE**
poet, blind, epic ..... **HOMER**
poet, lyric .... **ODIST**
poet, Norse ... **SCALD, SKALD**
poet, poor .... **RIMER**
poetry .... **EPOS, POESY**
poetry, early .... **RUNE**
poetry, Finnish .... **RUNES**
poetry, mournful, pert. to
.... **ELEGIAC**
poetry, Norse god of
.... **BRAGE, BRAGI**
poi, source of .... **TARO**
point.**END, TIP, BARB, PUNTO**
point in moon's orbit nearest
earth .... **PERIGEE**
point of curve .... **NODE**
point of land .... **SPIT**
point of moon .... **CUSP**
point of view .... **ANGLE**
b point on mariner's compass
.... **RUMB**
point on tooth's crown ... **CUSP**
point, tennis or golf ... **ACE**
point won .... **GOAL**
pointed .... **SHARP, ACUATE**
pointed arch .... **OGEE**
pointed end .... **CUSP**
pointed missile **DART, SPEAR**
pointed remark .... **BARB**
pointed staff .... **PIKE**
pointer .... **WAND**
pointless .... **INANE**
poison .... **BANE, TAINT**
poison, arrow ... **INEE, UPAS,**
URALI, URARE, URARI,
CURARE, CURARI
poison, hemlock ..... **CONINE**
poison, India **BISH, BISK, BIKH**
poisonous protein **RICIN, RICINE**
poisonous weed .... **LOCO**
poke ..... **JAB, PROD, NUDGE**
poker stake ...... **POT, ANTE**
pokeweed ..... **POCAN, SCOKE**
Polar explorer .... **BYRD**
pole .... **MAST**
pole, Gaelic games
.... **CABER, CABIR**
Pole .... **SLAV**
pole, naut. .... **MAST, SPRIT**
pole to handle fish ... **PEW**
pole to pole, from **AXAL, AXIAL**

c polecat, Cape **ZORIL, ZORILLA**
police line .... **CORDON**
policeman ...... **COP, PEELER**
policeman, state .... **TROOPER**
policeman, S. Afr. ...... **ZARP**
polish .... **RUB, WAX,**
SHINE, LEVIGATE
POLISH ... see also POLAND
SPECIAL SECTION
Polish assembly ... **SEIM, SEJM**
Polish cake .... **BABA**
Polish general .. **BOR, ANDERS**
Polish title of address
.... **PAN, PANI**
polished ...... **SHINY, SLEEK,**
URBANE, ELEGANT
polisher .... **EMERY**
polishing material
.... **RABAT, ROUGE**
polite .... **CIVIL**
political booty .... **GRAFT**
pollack fish .... **SEY**
pollen brush .. **SCOPA, SCOPAE**
Pollux or Castor ...... **ANAX**
Pollux' mother .... **LEDA**
Pollux' twin .... **CASTOR**
polo stick ..... **MALLET**
Polynesian .... **MAORI**
Polyn. "Adam" .... **TIKI**
d Polyn. chestnut .... **RATA**
Polyn. cloth .... **TAPA**
Polyn. dance .... **SIVA**
Polyn. deity, demon
.... **AKUA, ATUA**
Polyn. drink .... **AVA**
Polyn. for nature's power **MANA**
Polyn. god .... **ATEO**
Polyn. god of forest .... **TANE**
Polyn. herb .... **PIA**
Polyn. hero .... **MAUI**
Polyn. island group ... **SAMOA**
Polyn. languages
.... **MAORI, MAHORI**
Polyn. lily .... **TI**
Polyn. stone heap .... **AHU**
pome .... **APPLE**
"Pomp and Circumstance" Com-
poser .... **ELGAR**
pompous .... **TURGID**
pond .. **MERE, POOL, LOCHAN**
ponder .... **MUSE, PORE**
pontiff .... **POPE**
pony .... **CAVY**
pony, student's .... **CRIB**
pool .... **MERE, TARN,**
LAGOON, PUDDLE
pool: Scot. ...... **DIB, CARR,**
LINN, LLYN
poon tree **DILO, DOMBA, KEENA**
poor .... **NEEDY**
poor joe .... **HERON**

120

a poor player .... DUB
poorly ILL
POPE .. see also PAPAL
Pope ... JOHN, PIUS, ADRIAN
Pope, English ...... ADRIAN
Pope John XXIII first name
ANGELO
Pope John XXIII last name
RONCALLI
Pope Pius XI .... RATTI
Pope Pius XII ...... PACELLI
POPE'S CAPE, COLLAR ... see
PAPAL CAPE, COLLAR
Pope's triple crown TIAR, TIARA
poplar ...... ALAMO, ASPEN
poplar, white ... ABELE, ASPEN
poppy red .... GRANATE
poppy seed .... MAW
populace, the .... DEMOS
popular girl .... BELLE
porcelain
CHINA, SEVRES, LIMOGES
porcelain, ancient .... MURRA
porcelain, Chin. ...... JU, KO
porcelain, Eng. ...... SPODE
porch .... ANTA, STOOP,
VERANDA, VERANDAH
porch, Gr. .... STOA
porch, Hawaiian ...... LANAI
b porch swing .... GLIDER
porcupine anteater ... ECHIDNA
porcupine, Canada .... URSON
pore .... PORUS, STOMA,
OSTIOLE, STOMATA
porgy .... SCUP
porgy, Europ. .... PARGO
porgy genus .... PAGRUS
porgy, Jap. (Oriental) .... TAI
porkfish .... SISI
porous rock ..... TUFA, TUFF
porpoise .... DOLPHIN
porridge ...... POB, BROSE
porridge, corn meal .... SAMP
porridge: Sp. Am. ..... ATOLE
Porsena of Clusium ...... LARS
PORT .. see also SPECIAL SEC-
TION — GAZETTEER
port .... HAVEN
port, banana, Hondurus .. TELA
port, Black Sea ...... ODESSA
Port Moresby land ... PAPUA
port of Rome .... OSTIA
port opp. Gibraltar .... CEUTA
port, South Seas .... APIA
port, Suez .... SAID
port wine city ...... OPORTO
portable chair .... SEDAN
portal .... DOOR, GATE
portend BODE, AUGUR, PRESAGE

c portent .... OMEN, SIGN
porter, Orient
HAMAL, HAMMAL
Portia's waiting woman NERISSA
portico .... STOA
portion.PART, SOME, SEGMENT
portion out DOLE, METE, ALLOT
portray .... DRAW,
LIMN, DEPICT, DELINEATE
Portuguese coin .... REI
Port. colony, India ...... GOA
Port. folk tune .... FADO
Port. lady .... DONA
Port. man .... DOM
Port. navigator .... GAMA
Port. title ..... DOM, DONNA
pose .... SIT
Poseidon .... NEPTUNE
Poseidon's son .... TRITON
posited .... SET
position ..... SITUS, STATUS
position without work SINECURE
positive .... THETIC
positive pole, terminal ANODE
possession, landed .... ESTATE
possum .... COON
possum, comic-strip ..... POGO
post .... MAIL, SEND
post-hole digger (slick) ...LOY
postpone .... DEFER
postulate .... POSIT
posture .... STANCE
pot .... OLLA
pot, chem. .... ALUDEL
pot, earthen .... CRUSE
pot herb .... WORT
pot, India LOTA, LOTO, LOTAH
pot liquor .... BREWIS
pot metal .... POTIN
potassium .... KALITE
potassium chloride .. MURIATE
potassium nitrate
NITER, GROUGH
potation, small .... DRAM
potato .... SPUD
potato, sweet .. YAM, BATATA
pother .... ADO
potpourri .... OLIO
potter's blade .... PALLET
pottery fragment ..... SHARD
pottery, pert. to .... CERAMIC
pouch .... SAC
pouch-shaped ...... SACCATE
poultry .... HENS, BIRDS
poultry disease .... PIP, ROUP
pounce .... SWOOP
pound .... TUND
pound down ...... RAM, TAMP
pour .... RAIN, TEEM
pour off gently ...... DECANT

121

a pour out .... **LIBATE**
poverty ...... **NEED, WANT**
powder, astringent .... **BORAL**
powder, mineral ingredient
.... **TALC**
powder of aloes .... **PICRA**
powdered pumice .... **TALC**
power .. **DINT, MANA, FORCE**
practical joke .... **HOAX**
practice .... **HABIT**
practice exercise, musical **ETUDE**
praise **LAUD, EXTOL, EXTOLL**
prance .... **CAPER**
prank .... **DIDO, CAPER**
prate .... **GAB, YAP**
prate: India ...... **BUKH, BUKK**
pray: Yiddish .... **DAVEN**
prayer **AVE, BEAD, BENE, PLEA,**
.... **CREDO, MATIN, ORISON**
prayer form .... **LITANY**
prayer, 9-day .... **NOVENA**
prayer-rug, Hindu ..... **ASANA**
prayer stick, Am. Ind.
.... **BAHO, PAHO, PAJO**
prayers, deacon's
.... **ECTENE, EKTENE**
prayerbook
.... **ORDO, PORTAS, PORTASS**
praying figure ...... **ORANT**
preacher, Gospel .... **EVANGEL**
b precepts .... **DICTA**
precipice, Hawaii .... **PALI**
precipitous .... **STEEP**
preclude ...... **AVERT, DEBAR**
preconceive .... **IDEATE**
predicament .... **SCRAPE**
predicate
.... **BASE, FOUND, AFFIRM**
predict
AUGUR, FORECAST, FORETELL
predisposed .... **PRONE**
preen .... **PLUME, PRINK**
preface .... **PROEM**
prefecture, Jap. .... **KEN**
PREFIX:
about .... **PERI**
above .... **HYPER**
across .... **DIA, TRANS**
again .... **RE**
against .... **ANTI**
ahead .... **PRE**
an .... **AE**
apart .... **DIS**
away .... **DE, DI, APO**
back .... **ANA**
backward .... **RETRO**
bad .... **MAL**
badly .... **MIS**
beauty .... **CALLI**
before .... **OB, PRE, ANTE**
blood .... **HAEM, HEMO**

c both .... **AMBI**
CHEMICALS .. see page 29
common .... **PRE**
distant .... **TEL, TELE**
double .... **DI**
down .... **DE, CATA**
eight ... **OCT, OCTA, OCTO**
equal .... **ISO**
far .... **TEL, TELE**
faulty .... **MIS**
fire .... **PYR**
former, formerly ...... **EX**
four .... **TETRA**
from .... **EC**
half ..... **DEMI, HEMI, SEMI**
ill .... **MIS**
mountain .... **ORO**
negative .... **IR, NON**
new .... **NEO**
not ... **IL, IM, IR, UN, NON**
not fully .... **SEMI**
numerical .... **UNI**
of atmospheric pressure **BARO**
of the stars .... **ASTRO**
on this side .... **CIS**
one .... **UNI**
out of .... **EC, EX**
d outer .... **ECT, EXO, ECTO**
outer skin .... **EPI**
outside .... **ECT, EXO**
over .... **EPI, SUPER,**
.... **SUPRA, SUPERB**
partly .... **SEMI**
people .... **DEMO**
pray .... **ORA**
recent .... **NEO**
same .... **ISO, EQUI, HOMO**
separation .... **DIS**
single .... **MONO**
ten .... **DEC, DECA**
thousand .... **KILO**
three .... **TER, TRI**
thrice .... **TER, TRIS**
threefold .... **TRI**
through .... **DIA, PER**
to .... **AP**
together .... **COM**
town .... **TRE**
turning .... **ROTO**
twice .... **BI**
two .... **DI, DUA**
twofold .... **DI**
under .... **SUB**
upon .... **EPI**
upward .... **ANA, ANO**
with .... **SYN**
within .... **ENDO**
wrong .... **MIS**

122

a
prehistoric implement ... **CELT**
prehistoric mound ...... **TERP**
prejudice .... **BIAS**
prelate, high .... **PRIMATE**
prelude .... **PROEM**
premium, exchange ..... **AGIO**
prepare .... **FIT, GIRD, MAKE, ADAPT, EQUIP**
prepare for publication .. **EDIT**
prepared opium **CHANDU, CHANDOO**
preposition ...... **AT, IN, ON, UP, INTO**
presage **OMEN, HERALD, PORTEND**
prescribed .... **THETIC**
prescribed quantity .... **DOSE**
present .. **GIFT, GIVE, DONATE**
present, be .... **ATTEND**
present in brief .... **SUM**
presently .**ANON, ENOW, SOON**
preserve .... **CAN, JAM, KEEP, SAVE, PROTECT, MAINTAIN**
preserve in brine .. **CORN, SALT**
Presidential nickname ... **ABE, CAL, IKE, TEDDY**
press together .... **SERRY**
pressure .... **DURESS**
pressure unit .. **BARAD, BARIE**
pretend .. **FAKE, SHAM, FEIGN**
b
pretense .... **SHAM**
pretensions .... **AIRS**
pretentious .... **SIDY**
prevail .... **WIN**
prevail on .... **INDUCE**
prevalent .... **RIFE**
prevent ... **DETER, PRECLUDE**
prevent by law .... **ESTOP**
prey .... **RAVIN**
prey upon **RAVEN, RAVIN, RAVINE**
Priam's son **PARIS, HECTOR, HEKTOR**
price .... **RATE**
price of transportation .. **FARE**
prickle .... **SETA**
prickles .... **SETAE**
prickly pear **TUNA, NOPAL, CACTUS**
prickly plant ... **BRIAR, BRIER, NETTLE**
prickly seed coat .. **BUR, BURR**
pride .... **PLUME**
PRIEST .. see also **CLERGYMAN**
priest **FRA, ABBE, CURE, PADRE**
priest, Celtic .... **DRUID**
priest, Gr. .... **MYST**

c
PRIEST, HIGH, see **HIGH PRIEST**
priest in "Iliad" .... **CALCHAS**
priest, Mongol ...... **SHAMAN**
priest, Moro **SARIP, PANDITA**
priestess, Gr. .... **AUGE**
priestess, Rom. ...... **VESTAL**
priesthood, Rom. ...... **SALII**
priestly caste ... **MAGI, MAGUS**
prima donna .... **DIVA**
PRIMA DONNA ...... see also OPERA SOPRANO
prime minister: Brit. ... **EDEN, PEEL**
primeval .... **OLD, EARLY, PRIMAL, PRISTINE**
prince, Abyssin. .... **RAS**
prince, Arabian .. **EMIR, SAYID, SAYYID, SHERIF, SHEREEF**
prince, India **RAJA, RANA, RAJAH**
prince of Argos ...... **DANAE**
Prince of Darkness .... **SATAN**
prince, Oriental .... **KHAN**
prince, Persian .. **AMIR, AMEER**
prince, petty .... **SATRAP**
prince, Slavic .... **KNEZ**
Prince Val's father ... **AGUAR**
princeling .... **SATRAP**
princely .... **ROYAL**
princess, Gr. myth ..... **IOLE**
princess, India .. **RANI, RANEE**
d
principal .... **TOP, ARCH, MAIN, CHIEF**
principal commodity .. **STAPLE**
principle, accepted **AXIOM, PRANA, TENET**
print .... **STAMP**
print measure .... **EM, EN**
printer, 1st colonial .... **DAYE**
printer's direction ...... **STET**
printer's mark .... **DELE**
printer's mistake **TYPO, ERRATUM**
printer's mistakes .... **ERRATA**
printing plate .... **STEREO**
printing roller .... **PLATEN**
prison.**JUG, GAOL, JAIL, QUOD**
prison sentence .... **RAP**
prison spy .... **MOUTON**
privation .... **LOSS**
privilege, commercial .. **OCTROI**
prize .... **PRY, AWARD**
pro .... **FOR**
"— pro nobis" .... **ORA**
probe, medical .... **STYLET**
problem .... **POSER**
proboscis .... **SNOUT**
proboscis monkey ...... **KAHA**
proceed ... **WEND, ADVANCE**
proceedings .... **ACTA**

123

a procession .... TRAIN, PARADE, MOTORCADE
proclaim .... CRY, VOICE, HERALD, DECLARE
prod .... URGE
produce .... BEGET, YIELD CREATE, INWORK, GENERATE
produce as an effect ... BEGET
produced, quantity ..... YIELD
producing cold ...... ALGIFIC
production, artistic .. FACTURE
profane .... VIOLATE
profane, Hawaiian ...... NOA
profession ART, CAREER, METIER
professional, not LAIC, LAICAL
profit ... GAIN, VAIL, AVAIL
profit, to yield .... NET
profits, taker of: law . PERNOR
profitable ...... FAT, USEFUL
profound .... DEEP
"— profundis" .... DE
progenitor ..... SIRE, PARENT
progeny .... ISSUE
prohibit .... BAN, BAR, VETO, DEBAR, ESTOP
prohibition BAN, VETO, EMBARGO
Prohibition, against ..... WET

b project ...... JUT, IDEA, PLAN
projectile .... MISSILE
projecting edge RIM, FLANGE
projecting piece ARM, RIM, TENON, FLANGE
projecting rim .... FLANGE
projecting tooth .... SNAG
projection . EAR, BARB, PRONG
projection, fireplace. HOB, HOBB
projection, jagged SNAG. TOOTH
projection, studlike .... KNOP
promenade .... MALL
promise .... WORD
promise to pay .... IOU, NOTE
"Promised Land" fountain AIN
promontory ..... CAPE, NASE, NAZE, NESS
promontory, Orkneys .... NOUP
promontory, rocky ...... TOR
promote .... FOSTER
prompt .... CUE, YARE
prone .... APT, FLAT
prong .... TINE, TOOTH
pronghorn .... CABREE, CABRET, CABRIE, CABRIT
pronoun .. IT, ME, US, WE, YE, HER, HIM, ONE, SHE, THAT, THIS, THEE, THEM, THEY, THOU, THESE, THOSE

c pronoun, possessive . MY, HER, HIS, ITS, OUR, HERS, MINE, OURS, YOUR
pronounce indistinctly ... SLUR
pronounce strongly ... STRESS
pronouncement DICTA, DICTUM
proof, corrected ...... REVISE
proof, printer's ...... GALLEY
proofreader's mark DELE, STET, CARET
prop .... HOLD, STAY, BRACE, BOLSTER, SUSTAIN
propeller .... OAR
proper .... DUE, FIT
properly .... FEATLY
property, hold on .... LIEN
property, India .... DHAN
property, item of ASSET, CHATTEL
property, landed ...... ESTATE
property owned absolutely ALOD, ALLOD, ALODIUM, ALLODIUM
property, receiver of .. ALIENEE
prophesy .... FORETELL
prophet ...... SEER, AUGUR, PREDICTOR, FORETELLER
PROPHETS, BIBLICAL ..... see SPECIAL SECTION
prophets .... VATES

d prophetic ... VATIC, VATICAL
proportion .... RATIO
proportionally assess PRORATE
proposition THESES, THESIS, PREMISE
proposition, logic .... LEMMA
proposition: math. .. THEOREM
prosecutor .... SUER
prosecutor: abbr. .... DA
proselyte to Judaism .... GER
"— prosequi," .... NOLLE
Proserpina ...... CORA, KORE
prospect .... VISTA
prosperity .... WEAL
prosperity god, Teut. .... FREY
Prospero's servant .... ARIEL
prostrate .... PRONE, REPENT
protagonist .... HERO
protected .... HOUSED
protection .... EGIS, AEGIS
protection right, Old Eng. MUND
protective building .... REDAN
protective influence EGIS, AEGIS
Protestant denomination: abbr. ME, PE, BAP, PRESB
prototype .... IDEAL
protozoan order .... LOBOSA
protuberance ..... JAG, NUB, HUMP, KNOB, KNOT, NODE, WART, KNURL, TORUS

124

protuberant .... **TOROSE**
prove: law .... **DERAIGN**
proverb ..... **SAW, ADAGE,**
AXIOM, MAXIM, SAYING
provide ..... **ENDOW, ENDUE**
provided .... **IF**
provided that .... **SO**
province, Rom. .... **DACIA**
provisional clause ... **PROVISO**
proviso .... **CLAUSE**
provoke............. **IRE, RILE,**
ANGER, ANNOY
prow .... **BOW, STEM**
prune: prov. Eng. ...... **SNED**
pruning knife .... **DHAW**
Prussian spa, town ..... **EMS**
pry .... **NOSE, LEVER, SNOOP**
Psalm, 51st .... **MISERERE**
Psalmist .... **DAVID**
Psalms, selection of .. **HALLEL**
Psalms, word in .... **SELAH**
pseudonym ...... **NOM, ALIAS**
pseudonym of Louise Del La
Ramee .... **OUIDA**
psyche .... **SOUL**
psychiatrist
JUNG, ADLER, FREUD
Ptah, embodiment of ... **APIS**
ptarmigan .... **RYPE**
pteropod genus ...... **CLIONE**
pua hemp .... **POOA**
public .... **OPEN, OVERT**
public: Chin. .... **KUNG**
public esteem .... **REPUTE**
public, make ... **AIR, DELATE**
public vehicle ... **BUS, TAXI**
publication, style of . **FORMAT**
publish .... **ISSUE, PRINT**
publish illegally ...... **PIRATE**
Puccini heroine .... **MIMI**
puck, hockey ...... **RUBBER**
pudding......... **DUFF, SAGO**
pueblo dweller .... **HOPI**
Pueblo Indian ... **HOPI, ZUNI,**
KERES, MOQUI, TANOA
Pueblo sacred chamber .. **KIVA**
Pueblo, Tanoan .... **HANO**
Puerto Rican plant ..... **APIO**
puff up .... **ELATE**
puffbird, Brazil .... **DREAMER**
puffbird genus .... **MONASA**
puffer fish .... **TAMBOR**
Pulitzer poet .... **FROST**
pull ... **TOW, TUG, DRAG, HALE**
pull with nautical tackle **BOUSE**
pulley .... **SHEAVE**
pulp, fruit .... **POMACE**
pulpit .... **AMBO, BEMA**
pulpy mass left in cider **POMACE**
pulverize .... **MICRONIZE**

pump handle .... **SWIPE**
pumpkin .... **PEPO**
punch .... **JAB**
"Punch and Judy" dog .. **TOBY**
punch, engraver's .. **MATTOIR**
punctuation mark **DASH, COLON**
pungent .. **TEZ, SPICY, TANGY**
punish by fine ...... **AMERCE**
punishment .... **FERULE**
punishment, of .... **PENAL**
punitive .... **PENAL**
Punjab native .... **JAT**
punk .... **AMADOU**
pupa .... **INSTAR**
pupil of eye .... **GLENE**
puppet .... **DOLL**
puppet, famous **JUDY, PUNCH**
puppeteer, famous ..... **SARG**
pure sirup .... **CLAIRCE**
pure thought .... **NOESIS**
purification, ancient Roman
LUSTRUM
purloin .... **STEAL**
purple
MAUVE, MODENA, TYRIAN
purple dye source .... **MUREX**
purple medic
LUCERN, ALFALFA, LUCERNE
purple ragwort ...... **JACOBY**
purple seaweed . **SION, LAVER**
purport, general ..... **TENOR**
purpose .... **AIM, END,**
GOAL, SAKE, INTENT
purposive .... **TELIC**
purse net .... **SEINE**
pursy .... **STOUT**
push up .... **BOOST**
put aside .... **DAFF**
put away .... **STORE**
put back .... **REPLACE**
put forth .... **EXERT**
put in bank .... **DEPOSIT**
put off .... **DEFER**
put out .... **OUST, EJECT**
put up .... **ANTE**
puzzle .... **POSER,**
REBUS, BAFFLE, ACROSTIC
puzzles .... **CRUCES**
Pygmalion's statue .. **GALATEA**
pygmy .... **ATOMY**
pygmy people, Congo
AKKA, ACHUAS
pygmy people, Equatorial Africa
BATWA, ABONGO, OBONGO
Pylos, kin of .... **NESTOR**
Pyramus, lover of .... **THISBE**
pyromaniac .... **FIREBUG**
Pythias' friend .... **DAMON**
python .... **BOA**

Q

a qua .... AS
"— qua non" .... SINE
quack IMPOSTOR, CHARLATAN
quack medicine .... NOSTRUM
quadrant .... ARC
quadrate .... SQUARE
"quae —" which see .... VIDE
quaff .... DRINK
quail .... COLIN, COWER
quake .... SHAKE,
    SHIVER, TREMOR, TREMBLE
Quaker .... FRIEND
Quaker Poet .... WHITTIER
quaking .... TREPID
qualify .... FIT, ADAPT,
    EQUIP, PREPARE
qualified .... FIT, ABLE
quality .... CALIBER, CALIBRE
quantity, indeterminate . SOME
quantity: math.
    SCALER, VECTOR

b quarrel .... ROW, FEUD,
    SPAT, TIFF
quarter of a year: Scot. RAITH
quartz .... JASPER
quartz, green .... PRASE
quartz, translucent ... PRASE
quash: law .... CASSARE
quaternion .... TETRAD
quay .... LEVEE
Quebec, district, town ... LEVIS
Quebec's patron saint .. ANNE
Queen .... CLEO
queen: Moslem BEGUM, BEEGUM
queen of gods, Egypt. ... SATI
queen of gods, Rom. ... HERA,
    JUNO
Queen of Italy .... ELENA
Queen of Ithaca ... PENELOPE
Queen of Roumania ... MARIE
Queen of Scots .... MARY
Queen of Spain, last ..... ENA
queen, "Romeo and Juliet"
    MAB

c queenly .... REGAL, REGINAL
Queensland hemp plant
    SIDA
Queensland tribe .... GOA
quell .... CALM, CRUSH
quench .... SLAKE
quench steel ..... AUSTEMPER
quern .... MILL
query .... ASK
queue .... LINE
question .... ASK, GRILL
question, hard .... POSER
quetzal .... TROGON
quibble ...... CAVIL, EVADE
quick .... FAST, AGILE,
    ALIVE, RAPID
quick: music .... TOSTO
quicken ... HASTEN, ENLIVEN
quickly .... CITO, APACE,
    PRESTO, PRONTO
quickly, move
    SCAT, SCUD, SKITE
quicksilver ...... HEAUTARIT
quid .... CUD

d "quid — quo," equivalent . PRO
quiescent LATENT, DORMANT
quiet .... CALM, LULL,
    STILL, SMOOTH
quiet! .... SH, PST, TST
quilkin .... FROG, TOAD
quill .... PEN, SPINE
quill feathers REMEX, REMIGES
quill for winding silk ..... COP
quilt .... EIDER, COVER
quince, Bengal .... BEL, BHEL
quinine .... KINA
quintessence ... PITH, ELIXIR
quirt, cowboy's ..... ROMAL
quit .... CEASE, LEAVE
quite .... ALL
quivering ... ASPEN, TREMOR
"quod — demonstrandum"
    ERAT
"Quo Vadis" tyrant character
    NERO
quoits, mark of .... MOT
quote .... CITE

126

R

Ra, consort of .... **MUT**
Ra, son of .... **SU, SHU**
rabbi, law-teaching ... **AMORA**
rabbit cage .... **HUTCH**
rabbit, Europ. . **CONY, CONEY**
rabbit, female .... **DOE**
rabbit fur .... **LAPIN**
rabbit home ...... **WARREN**
rabbit, small swamp .. **TAPETI**
rabbit, So. Am. ...... **TAPETI**
rabble .... **MOB**
rabies .... **LYSSA**
raccoon-like mammal .. **COATI**
RACE .. see also TRIBES in
    SPECIAL SECTION
race, boat .... **REGATTA**
race, kind of .... **RELAY**
race, short .... **SPRINT**
race-track .... **OVAL**
race-track circuit ...... **LAP**
race-track tipster ...... **TOUT**
races, pert. to ...... **ETHNIC**
Rachel's father ...... **LABAN**
racing boat .... **GIG**
racket, game .... **PELOTA**
radar screen .... **SCOPE**
radiate .... **EMANATE**
radical .... **RED**
radicle .... **STEMLET**
radio advertiser .... **SPONSOR**
radio bulletin .... **NEWSCAST**
radio-guided bomb ..... **AZON**
radio wave .... **MICROWAVE**
radio wire .... **LITZ**
radio-TV awards ..... **EMMIES**
radioactive counter .. **GEIGER**
radioactive element ... **NITON**
radioactive ray ...... **GAMMA**
radium discoverer ...... **CURIE**
radium emanation .... **NITON**
radius, pert. to ...... **RADIAL**
radon .... **NITON**
raft, kind of ... **CATAMARAN**
raft, Maori .... **MOKI**
rag doll .... **MOPPET**
rage .... **RAMP, RANT,**
        RESE, STORM
ragged person: Sp. ...... **ROTO**
raging monster, Bibl. .. **RAHAB**
ragout, game .... **SALMI**
ragweed genus .... **IVA**
raid .... **FORAY, INROAD**
raid, soldier's .... **COMMANDO**
rail at .... **REVILE**
rail bird **SORA, WEKA, CRAKE**
railing .... **PARAPET**

railroad bridge ...... **TRESSEL,**
        TRESTLE
railroad light .... **FLARE**
railroad signal
        TRIMMER, SEMAPHORE
railroad tie .... **SLEEPER**
railroad timber .... **TIE**
railway station: Fr. ..... **GARE**
rain after sunset ...... **SEREIN**
rain, fine .... **MISLE**
rain forest .... **SELVA**
rain gauge .... **UDOMETER**
rain serpent, Hindu .... **NAGA**
rain spout: Scot. ...... **RONE**
rain tree .... **SAMAN**
rainbow .... **ARC, IRIS**
rainbow goddess .... **IRIS**
rainbow, pert. to ... **IRIDAL**
raincoat .... **PONCHO**
rainy .... **WET**
raise . **REAR, BREED, ELEVATE**
raised .... **BRED**
raisin: Sp. .... **PASA**
raising device .... **JACK**
Rajah's lady ... **RANI, RANEE**
rake ..... **ROUE, LOTHARIO**
rake with gunfire .. **ENFILADE**
ram . **TUP, BUTT, TAMP, ARIES**
ram, male .... **TUP**
ram-headed god, Egypt
        AMEN, AMON, AMUN
Ramachandra, wife of .. **SITA**
ramble .... **GAD, ROVE**
Ramee, de la, penname . **OUIDA**
rammed earth building material
        PISE
rampart ..... **AGGER, VALLUM**
range .... **AREA, GAMUT,**
        SCOPE, SIERRA
Rangoon's state .... **PEGU**
rank .... **ROW, RATE, DEGREE**
ranks, press in .... **SERRY**
rankle .... **FESTER**
ransom .... **REDEEM**
rapeseed .... **COLSA, COLZA**
rapid, more: music .. **STRETTA,**
        STRETTE, STRETTI, STRETTO
rapids, river .... **SOO**
rapidly .... **APACE**
rapier .... **BILBO**
rare earth element ... **ERBIUM**
rascal .... **IMP, ROGUE**
rase .... **INCISE**
rasorial .... **GNAWING**
rasp .... **FILE, GRATE**

127

a raspberry, variety . **BLACKCAP**
rasse .... **CIVET**
rat .... **DESERTER**
rat, Ceylon, India . **BANDICOOT**
rat hare .... **PIKA**
rate .... **ESTIMATE**
rate, relative .... **AT**
ratify .... **SEAL**
ratio .... **RATE**
RATIO: MATH see MATH, RATIO
rational .... **SANE**
rational integer .... **NORM**
rational principle ..... **LOGOS**
rationalize .... **THOB**
ratite bird ...... **CASSOWARY**
rattan .... **CANE**
rattlesnake
          RATTLER, CROTALUS
rave .... **RANT**
"Raven" author .... **POE**
"Raven" character .. **LENORE**
ravine
     GAP, DALE, VALE, GORGE
ravine, Afr. .... **WADI, WADY**
ravine, Arabia .. **WADI, WADY**
rawboned .... **LEAN**
rawboned animal ..... **SCRAG**
ray fish .... **SKATE**
rays, like .... **RADIAL**
rayon ... **ACETATE, CELANESE**
b raze .... **DEVASTATE**
razor-billed auk
     ALCA, MURR, MURRE
reach across .... **SPAN**
react .... **RESPOND**
read, inability to .... **ALEXIA**
read metrically .... **SCAN**
read publically ..... **PRELECT**
reader, first .... **PRIMER**
reading desk .... **AMBO**
reading substituted: Bibl.
              KERE, KERI
ready: dialect .... **YARE**
ready-made tie ...... **TECK**
real being, pert. to .... **ONTAL**
real thing .... **MCCOY**
reality .... **FACT**
realm .... **DOMAIN**
reamer .... **BROACH**
rear ... **ERECT, RAISE, ARRIERE**
rear, to the
     AFT, ABAFT, ASTERN
rearhorse .... **MANTIS**
rearing of horse .... **PESADE**
reason .... **NOUS**
reason, deprive of ... **DEMENT**
reasoning .... **LOGIC**
reasoning, deductive .. **APRIORI**
reata
     LAZO, ROPE, LASSO, LARIAT

c rebec of India ...... **SAROD**
Rebecca's hairy son .... **ESAU**
rebound .. **CAROM, RICOCHET**
rebuff .... **SLAP, SNUB**
rebuke
     CHIDE, SCOLD, REPROVE
recalcitrant .... **RENITENT**
recant .... **RETRACT**
recede .... **EBB**
recent
     NEO, NEW, LATE, NEOTERIC
receptacle .... **BIN, BOX,
              TRAY, VESSEL**
reception, a.m. .... **LEVEE**
reception: Fr. .... **ACCUEIL**
reception, India ..... **DURBAR**
recess .... **APSE, ALCOVE**
recess, wall .... **NICHE**
recipient .... **DONEE**
recite metrically ...... **SCAN**
reckon .... **ARET, COUNT**
reckoning .... **TALLY**
reclaim .... **REDEEM**
recline .... **LOLL**
recluse .... **ASCETIC, EREMITE,
          ANCHORET, ANCHORITE**
recoil .... **SHY, RESILE**
recommit .... **REMAND**
recompense .. **PAY, FEES, MEED**
reconnaissance **RECCO, RECON**
reconnoiter .... **SCOUT**
reconstruct .... **REMODEL**
record ... **TAB, NOTE, ENROL,
     ENTER, ENTRY, REGISTER**
record of investigation REPORT
record, ship's .... **LOG**
record, year's .... **ANNAL**
records .... **ANNALS**
recorded proceedings ... **ACTA**
recording device .... **TAPE**
records, one who .... **NOTER**
recourse, have .... **REFER**
recover strength ...... **RALLY**
recovery, legal .... **TROVER**
recruit .... **BOOT**
rectifier, current ...... **DIODE**
rectify ...... **AMEND, EMEND**
recurring pattern .... **CYCLE**
d red .... **CARMINE,
          MAGENTA, NACARAT**
red, Brazil .... **ROSET**
red cedar .... **SAVIN, SAVINE**
red circle: Her. .... **GUZE**
red currant .... **RISSEL**
red deer .... **ELAPHINE**
red dye root ... **CHAY, CHOY**
red garden flower .... **CANNA**
red: Her. .... **GULES**
red horse .... **BAY, ROAN**
red ocher .... **KEEL, KIEL,
     TIVER, RADDLE, RUDDLE**

a red pigment .... **ROSET,
ASTACIN, ASTACENE**
red pine .... **RIMU**
red planet .... **MARS**
red powder, India ...... **ABIR**
red, painter's .... **ROSET**
Red River Rebellion leader
RIEL
red: Sp. .... **ROJO**
red squirrel ...... **CHICKAREE**
red swine .... **DUROC**
red, Venetian .... **SIENA**
red-yellow color ..... **ALOMA**
redact .... **EDIT**
redbreast .... **ROBIN**
redcap .... **PORTER**
reddish yellow .... **SUDAN**
redeem .... **RANSOM**
redshank .... **CLEE**
reduce .... **PARE, DEMOTE**
reduce sail .... **REEF**
reduce taxes .... **DERATE**
reebok .... **PEELE**
reedbuck .... **NAGOR**
reek .... **FUG, FUME**
reef .... **SHOAL**
reel, fishing-rod .... **PIRN**
refer .... **PERTAIN**
refer to repeatedly .... **HARP**
refined grace ...... **ELEGANCE**
b reflection .... **GLARE**
refracting device ...... **LENS**
refractor, light .... **PRISM**
refrain .... **FORBEAR**
refrain in songs .. **FALA, LALA,
DERRY, LUDDEN**
refrigerant .... **FREON**
refuge ...... **HAVEN, SHELTER**
refugee .... **EMIGREE**
refuse .... **DENY**
refuse .... **ORT, DROSS,
SCUM, OFFAL, TRASH**
refuse, bit of .... **SCRAP**
refuse, flax .... **POB**
refuse: law .... **RECUSE**
refuse, metal . **DROSS, SCORIA**
refuse, wool .... **COT**
refute .... **REBUT, DISPROVE**
regale .... **FETE**
regard ..... **ESTEEM, RESPECT**
regarding .... **RE, ANENT**
regenerate .... **RENEW**
regiment's framework .. **CADRE**
REGION .... see also DISTRICT
region ...... **CLIME, SECTOR**
region, Afr. .. **CONGO, NUBIA**
region, Boeotia ...... **AONIA**
region, Cent. Afr.
SUDAN, SOUDAN
region, Fr. .... **ALSACE**

c region, Gr. .... **DORIC**
region, Indo-China .... **LAOS**
region, pert. to .... **AREAL**
register .... **ENROL,
ENROLL, RECORD**
regret .... **RUE, DEPLORE**
reign: India .... **RAJ**
reign, pert. to .... **REGNAL**
reigning .... **REGNANT**
reigning beauty .... **BELLE**
reimbursed .... **PAID**
reindeer .... **CARIBOU**
reindeer, Santa's .... **DASHER,
DONDER, BLITZEN,
PRANCER**
reinstate .... **REVEST**
reiterate .... **REPEAT**
reject .... **SPURN, REPULSE**
relate .... **TELL,
RECITE, NARRATE**
related .... **AKIN, TOLD,
COGNATE, GERMANE**
related by blood .... **SIB**
related on mother's side **ENATE**
relation .... **SIB**
relative.**SIB, SIS, AUNT, NIECE**
relative amount ...... **RATION**
relative pronoun ...... **WHO,
THAT, WHAT**
relative speed .... **TEMPO**
d relatives .... **KIN**
relatives, favoring .. **NEPOTAL**
relax .... **EASE**
relaxing of state tensions
DETENTE
relay of horses ..... **REMUDA**
release .... **LOOSE**
release: law .... **REMISE**
release, phonetic .... **DETENTE**
relevant .... **GERMANE**
reliable .... **HONEST**
relief, — .... **BAS**
relief .... **DOLE**
relieve .... **EASE, ALLAY**
relieve: Scot. .... **LISS**
religieuse .... **NUN**
religion .... **FAITH**
religion, Jap. .... **SHINTO**
religious art, work of .. **PIETA**
religious brother .... **FRA,
MONK, FRIAR**
religious festival ...... **EASTER**
religious festival, India .. **MELA**
religious law, Rom. ...... **FAS**
religious laywoman .. **BEGUINE**
religious opinion .... **DOXY**
religious order, one in . **OBLATE**
religious sayings ...... **LOGIA**
relinquish .... **CEDE,
WAIVE, YIELD**

129

a reliquary .... APSE, ARCA, ARCAE, CHEST
relish .... GUSTO
reluctant ..... LOATH, AVERSE
rely .... TRUST
remain .... BIDE, STAY
remainder .... REST
remaining .... OVER
remark, witty .... MOT, SALLY
remiss .... LAX
remit .... SEND
remnant .... END, SHRED
remora fish . PEGA, LOOTSMAN
remove .. DELE, DOFF, DELETE
remove interior .... GUT
remove: law .... ELOIN, ELOIGN, ELOIGNE
remunerate .... PAY
rend ...... RIP, TEAR, WREST
render fat .... TRY
rendezvous .... TRYST
renegade .... APOSTATE
renounce .... ABNEGATE
renovated hat ..... MOLOKER
renown ...... FAME, NOTE, EMINENCE, PRESTIGE
rent .... LET, HIRE, TEAR, TORN, LEASE
rent, old Eng. law .... TAC
renter .... LESSEE

b repair .... DARN, MEND
repartee .... RIPOST, RIPOSTE
repast .... MEAL
repay .... REQUITE
repay in kind .... RETALIATE
repeat .... ECHO, ITERATE
repeat: music .... BIS
repeat performance .. ENCORE
repeat sign: music ... SEGNO
repeat tiresomely .. DIN, DING
repeated phrase ..... REPRISE
repeatedly hit ...... POMMEL
repetition .... ROTE
replete .... FULL
report, small .... POP
repose .... EASE, REST
representation .... IDOL
representative .... AGENT
reproach ..... BLAME, TAUNT
reproach, old term ...... RACA
reproductive body .. GAMETE
reproductive cell ...... SPORE
reptile, pert. to ..... SAURIAN
repulse .... REPEL
reputation .... NAME, REPUTE
repute .... CHARACTER
request .... PLEA
rescind .... REPEAL
resentment .... IRE
reserve supply .... STORE

c residence ..... HOME, ABODE
residence, ecclesiastical .MANSE
resident of .... ITE
resign .... QUIT, DEMIT
resin ..... GUM, LAC, ANIME, COPAL, ELEMI, JALAP, MYRRH, BALSAM, MASTIC
resin, fossil . AMBER, GLESSITE
resin, fragrant .... ELEMI
resist .... OPPOSE
resist authority .... REBEL
resisting pressure ... RENITENT
resistor, current ... RHEOSTAT
resort .... SPA
resort, Fr. .... PAU, NICE, CANNES
resources .... FUND, MEANS, ASSETS
respect .... ESTEEM
respond .... REACT
rest .... SIT, EASE, REPOSE
rest, lay at .... REPOSE
restaurant, small ..... BISTRO
resthouse ..... CHAN, KHAN
resting .... ABED
restive .... BALKY
restore .... RENEW
restrain .. CURB, REIN, DETER, STINT, TETHER

d restrict .... LIMIT
retaliate .... REPAY
retain .... HOLD, KEEP
retaliation .... TALION
retinue .... SUITE, TRAIN
retort, quick . RIPOST, RIPOSTE
retract .... RECANT
retreat .... RECEDE
retreat, cosy . DEN, NEST, NOOK
retribution .... NEMESIS
retribution, get .... VENGE
retrograde .... RECEDE
return ...... RECUR, RESTORE
return a profit .... PAY
return blow .... TIT
return on investment .. YIELD
returning .... REDIENT
reunion, hold a .... REUNE
reveille, call to .... DIAN
revelry, cry of .... EVOE
revelry, drunken .... ORGY
revenue, church: Scot. ANNAT
reverberate .... ECHO
reverberating ...... REBOANT
revere ...... HONOR, HONOUR
reverence .... AWE
reversed in order .. CONVERSE
reversion to type .... ATAVISM

a revert to state (land) ..... ESCHEAT
revise .... EDIT, AMEND
revive wine .... STUM
revoke legacy, grant .. ADEEM
Revolution hero . HALE, ALLEN
revolutions per minute .. REVS
revolve . SPIN, TURN, ROTATE
revolve: logging .... BIRL
revolver.GAT, GUN, ROD, COLT
reward .... MEED
rhebok .... PEELE
Rhine city .... MAINZ
Rhine tributary .... AAR
rhinoceros beetle ...... UANG
rhinoceros, black
BORELE, NASICORN
rhinoceros: obs.
ABADA, ABATH
Rhone tributary ...... SAONE
rhythm .... TIME, METER,
METRE, CADENCE
rhythmical accent ...... BEAT
rhythmical swing .... LILT
rib .... COSTA
rib, pert. to .... COSTAL
rib, woman from .... EVE
ribs, with .... COSTATE
ribbed fabric ..... REP, CORD,
REPP, PIQUE
b ribbon, badge ...... CORDON
ribbon: comb. form ..... TENE
ribbonfish .... GUAPENA
rice .... PADI, PADDY
rice dish ..... PILAU, PILAW
rice field, Java .... PADI
rice grass, P.I. .... BARIT
rice in husk .... PALAY
rice paste, Jap. .... AME
rice polishings .... DARAC
rich man .... MIDAS,
NABOB, NAWAB
rich silk cloth .... CAFFA
riches .... PELF
rid .... FREE
riddle .... ENIGMA
ridge .... ARETE,
SPINE, MOUNTAIN
ridge, camp's .... RIDEAU
ridge, glacial, sandy .... OS,
OSAR, ESKER, OESAR
ridge on cloth .... WALE
ridge on skin .... WELT
ridge, stony .... RAND
ridges, rounded .... GYRI
ridged area, Balkan .... BILO
ridicule .... GUY, MOCK,
RAZZ, DERIDE
ridicule personified, Gr.
MOMUS

c riding academy ..... MANEGE
riding dress .... HABIT
rifle .... KRAG, MINIE,
GARAND, CARBINE
rifle ball .... MINIE
rifleman, Ger. .... JAGER
right conduct, Buddhist .. TAO
right conduct: Taoism ..... TE
right hand: music .... DM
right-hand page .. RO, RECTO
right: law .... DROIT
right, pert. to ...... DEXTER
right to speak .... SAY
right, turn .... GEE
rights, of ..... JURAL, UDAL
Rigoletto's daughter ... GILDA
rigorous ...... HARSH, STERN,
STRICT, SEVERE, AUSTERE
rim ...... LIP, EDGE, FLANGE
rim of wheel .. FELLY, FELLOE
"Rime cold giant" . YMER, YMIR
ring ...... PEAL, TOLL, KNELL
ring, boxing .... ARENA
ring for reins . TERRET, TERRIT
ring, gun carriage ..... LUNET
ring, harness pad
TERRET, TERRIT
ring, lamp condensing ... CRIC
ring, little .... ANNULET
ring, naut. .... GROMMET
d ring of light .... HALO, NIMB,
NIMBUS, AUREOLA,
AUREOLE
"Ring of the Nibelung" goddess
ERDA
"Ring of the Nibelung" smith
MIME
ring out .... PEAL
ring, part of .... CHATON
ring, rubber jar .... LUTE
ring, seal .... SIGNET
ring-shaped ...... CIRCINATE
ring-shaped piece ..... QUOIT
ring, stone of .... CHATON
ringlet .... CURL, TRESS
ringworm ..... TINEA, TETTER
ripening agent .... AGER
ripple ...... LAP, RIFF, WAVE
rise above .... TOWER
rise aloft .... TOWER
rise: old Eng. .... RIS
risible .... GELASTIC
rites, religious .... SACRA
ritual .... RITE
RIVER . see also GAZETTEER in
SPECIAL SECTION
river .... RIO
river, Balmoral Castle's ... DEE
river bank .... RIPA
river bank, growing by
RIPARIAN

131

River

a river-bank stair, Ind.
    GAUT, GHAT
river bed, dry, Afr.
    WADI, WADY
river between Europe and Asia
    KARA
river, Bremen's .... **WESER**
river Caesar crossed . **RUBICON**
river, Dutch Meuse ..... **MAAS**
river in Baltic .... **ODER**
river in Essex .... **CAM**
river in Orleans .... **LOIRE**
river in Petrograd ...... **NEVA**
river into Moselle ...... **SAAR**
river into Rhone ...... **SAONE**
river islet .... **AIT**
river, "Kubla Khan" .... **ALPH**
river, Munich's .... **ISAR**
river mouth ..... **LADE, DELTA**
river nymph .... **NAIS**
river to the Humber
    OUSE, TRENT
River of Woe ..... **ACHERON**
river, Southwest .... **PECOS**
river: Sp. .... **RIO**
river: Tagalog .... **ILOG**
river to Medit. .... **EBRO**
river valley .... **STRATH**
rivulet .... **RILL**
road .... **VIA, PATH, ITER, AGGER**

b road: Roman .... **ITER**
road: Gypsy .... **DRUN**
roadhouse .... **INN**
roam .... **GAD, ROVE**
roast .... **CALCINE**
roasted meat strip .... **CABOB**
roasting rod .... **SPIT**
rob .... **REAVE, DESPOIL**
Rob Roy .... **CANOE**
robber .... **THIEF**
ROBE ..... see also GARMENT
robe .... **MANTLE**
robe to ankles .... **TALAR**
"Roberta" composer .... **KERN**
robot drama .... **RUR**
rock aggregate .... **AUGE**
rock, basic igneous .... **SIMA**
rock cavity ..... **VOOG, VUGG, VUGH, GEODE**
rock, dangerous ...... **SCYLLA**
rock, dark .... **BASALT**
rock, fine grained ..... **TRAP**
rock, flintlike .... **CHERT**
rock, granitoid **DUNITE, GNEISS**
rock, hard .... **WHIN**
rock, jutting .... **TOR**
rock, laminated .... **SHALE, SLATE, GNEISS**
rock, melted .... **LAVA**
rock, mica-bearing ... **DOMITE**

c rock, projecting ... **TOR, CRAG**
rock, rugged .... **CRAG**
rock snake .... **PYTHON**
rock whiting genus ..... **ODAX**
rock-wren .... **TURCO**
ROCKET .. see under MISSILE, GUIDED
rocket's goal .... **MOON**
rockfish ... **RASHER, TAMBOR**
rockfish, Calif. .. **RENA, REINA**
rockweed .... **FUCI, FUCUS**
Rocky Mt. peak .... **ESTES**
Rocky Mt. range
    TETON, UINTA
rocky peak, eminence, pinnacle .... **TOR**
rod ... **POLE, WAND, BATON, PERCH, STAFF**
rod, barbecue .... **SPIT**
rod, basketry .... **OSIER**
rod, billiard .... **CUE**
rod, chastening ...... **FERULE**
rodent .... **RAT, HARE**
rodent genus .... **MUS**
rodent, rabbit-like ..... **PIKA**
rodent, S. Am. .. **CAVY, DEGU, PACA, COYPU, AGOUTI**
rodent, W. Ind. ...... **HUTIA**
Rhoderick Dhu .... **SCOT**
rogue .... **PICARO**
roguish .... **SLY, ARCH**

d roister .... **REVEL**
Roland's destroyer ...... **GAN, GANO, GANELON**
roll and heave .... **TOSS**
roll of bread: dialect. .... **BAP**
roll of cloth .... **BOLT**
roll of paper .... **SCROLL**
roll up .... **FURL**
romaine .... **COS**
ROMAN GODS
    see SPECIAL SECTION
Rom. assembly ...... **COMITIA**
Rom. authors ... **CATO, LIVY, OVID, LUCAN, NEPOS, PLINY, CICERO, HORACE, SENECA, SILIUS, VERGIL, SALLUST**
Rom. barracks
    CANABA, CANNABA
Rom. box .... **CAPSA**
Rom. boxing glove ... **CESTUS**
Rom. bronze .... **AES**
Rom. brooch .... **FIBULA**
Rom. building .... **INSULA**
Rom. cap .... **PILEUS**
Rom. cavalry body
    TURM, TURMA
Rom. circus post ...... **META**
Rom. clan ..... **GENS, GENTES**
Rom. cloak ... **TOGA, ABOLLA**

132

Rom. coin, ancient
SEMIS, DINDER
Rom. coins .... AS, AES,
ASSES, SOLIDUS
Rom. Curia court ..... ROTA
Rom. date ...... IDES, NONES
Rom. dictator .... SULLA
Rom. dish .... LANX
Rom. emperor .... NERO,
OTHO, TITUS
Rom. farce .... EXODE
Rom. galley
TRIREME, UNIREME
Rom. gaming cube ..... TALUS
Rom. garment .. TOGA, STOLA,
TUNIC, PLANETA
Rom. goal post in racing . META
Rom. highway ..... VIA, ITER
Rom. historian ... LIVY, NEPOS
Rom. judge .... EDILE, AEDILE
Rom. law control ..... MANUS
Rom. legendary king ... NUMA
Rom. liquid measure .... URNA
Rom. list ...... ALBE, ALBUM
Rom. magistrate or official
EDILE, AEDILE, ARCHON,
CONSUL, PRETOR, TRIBUNE
Rom. market ... FORA, FORUM
Rom. meal .... CENA
Rom. money, copper .... AES
Rom. numerals 1-I, 5-V,
10-X, 50-L, 100-C,
500-D, 1000-M
ROMAN OFFICIAL
see ROMAN MAGISTRATE
Rom. patriot .... CATO
Rom. philosopher
CATO, SENECA
Rom. platter .... LANX
Rom. pledge .... VAS
Rom. poet .... OVID, LUCAN,
HORACE, VERGIL, VIRGIL
Rom. pound .... AS
Rom. province .... DACIA
Rom. public games ..... LUDI
Rom. public lands ..... AGER
Rom. religious festivals . VOTA
Rom. road .... VIA, ITER
Rom. robe .... TOGA
Rom. room, principal
ATRIA, ATRIUM
Rom. scroll .... STEMMA
Rom. statesman .... CATO
Rom. sword .... FALX
Rom. vessel .... PATERA
Rom. war garb ...... SAGUM
Rom. weight .... AS

Rom. well-curb ...... PUTEAL
Rom. writer .... MACER
romance, tale of . GEST, GESTE
ROMANIA .... see RUMANIA
Rome, a founder of ... REMUS
Rome's cathedral church
LATERAN
Rome's conqueror ..... ALARIC
Rome's river .... TIBER
Romulus' twin .... REMUS
rood .... CROSS
roof .... MANSARD
roof edge .... EAVE
roof of mouth .... PALATE
roof of mouth, pert. to
PALATAL
roof ornament .... EPI
roof, rounded . DOME, CUPOLA
roof, rounded like a ... DOMAL
roof, truncated .... HIP
roofing piece ...... RAG, TILE
roofing slate .... TILE
roofing timber .... PURLIN
rook's cry .... CAWK
room, Eng. college supply
BUTTERY
room, snug .... DEN
room, rooms .... SPACE, SUITE
room, architecture ..... OECUS
room for household goods,
linen, etc. .. EWRY, EWERY
room, main, Rom.
ATRIA, ATRIUM
room, mineshaft . PLAT, PLATT
room, Rom. .... ALA
roomy .... WIDE
roost .... PERCH
rooster .... COCK
root .... RADIX, RADICES
root, drug-yielding ..... JALAP
root, edible ..... OCA, TARO,
CASSAVA
root, tree used for sewing
WATAP
root, word .... ETYM
rootlet .... RADICEL, RADICLE
rootstock, edible ...... TARO
rootstock, fern (Maori) ... ROI
rootstock, fragrant ... ORRIS
rope ...... JEFF, LAZO, LASSO,
LONGE, REATA, RIATA,
LARIAT, MARLINE
rope, cringle
LEEFANG, LEEFANGE
rope fiber .. DA, COIR, FERU,
HEMP, IMBE, JUTE, RHEA,
ABACA, SISAL
rope for animals ..... TETHER
rope guide: naut. ...... WAPP
rope loop .... BIGHT

133

Rope

a rope, naut. ... **FOX, TYE, STAY,**
   VANG, HAWSER, RATLIN,
   LANIARD, LANYARD, RAT-
   LINE, SNOTTER
rope to tie boat ..... **PAINTER**
rope, weave .... **REEVE**
rope, yardarm ..... **SNOTTER**
ropes, unite .... **SPLICE**
rosary bead .... **AVE**
rose: Byron .... **GUL**
rose fruit .... **HIP**
rose genus .... **ROSA, ACAENA**
rose-like plant .... **AVENS**
rose of Sharon
   ALTHEA, ALTHAEA
rose oil derivative ..... **ATAR,**
   OTTO, ATTAR, OTTAR
rose ornament ...... **ROSETTE**
rose, Pers. .... **GUL**
rosewood .... **MOLOMPI**
rosolic acid ... **AURIN, AURINE**
rostellum .... **ROSTEL**
roster .... **LIST, ROTA**
rotate .... **ROLL, GYRATE**
rotating muscle ..... **EVERTOR**
rotating part .... **CAM, ROTOR**
rotation producer .... **TORQUE**
rotten .... **PUTRID**
rouge ...... **RADDLE, RUDDLE**
b rough ..... **RUDE, UNEVEN**
rough, as country ...... **HILLY**
rough copy .... **DRAFT**
rough in voice .... **GRUFF**
rough rock .... **KNAR**
roughness, sea .... **LIPPER**
roulette bet ...... **BAS, NOIR,**
   MILIEU
round, a ...... **ROTA, ROTULA**
round hand .... **RONDE**
round room .... **ROTUNDA**
Round Table Knight .... **KAY,**
   BORS, BORT, BALAN,
   BALIN, BOHORT, GAR-
   ETH, GAWAIN, GALA-
   HAD, PELLEAS
round-up .... **RODEO**
rounded projection ...... **LOBE**
rounder .... **RAKE, ROUE**
roundworm .... **NEMA,**
   ASCARID, ASCARIS
rouse . **WAKE, AWAKE, WAKEN**
Rousseau novel, hero .. **EMILE**
route .... **WAY, PATH**
route, plane's fixed ..... **LANE**
routine, fixed .... **ROTE**
row .... **LINE, SPAT, TIER**
rowan tree .... **ASH, SORB**
rowdy: slang .... **B'HOY**
rower .... **OAR**
rower's bench .... **ZYGA,**
   ZYGON, THWART

c royal authority ...... **SCEPTRE**
royal court, relating to . **AULIC**
royal edict: Fr. .... **ARRET**
royal family, Fr. ..... **VALOIS**
royal rights, having . **PALATINE**
royal rod .. **SCEPTER, SCEPTRE**
royal treasury ... **FISC, FISK**
royalty, Hawaii .... **ALII**
rub harshly .... **GRATE**
rub off .... **ABRADE**
rub out .... **ERASE**
rub roughly .... **SCRAPE**
rub to polish ... **BUFF, SHINE**
rub to soreness .... **CHAFE**
rubber .... **PARA,**
   LATEX, CAUCHO, ELASTIC
rubber, black .... **EBONITE**
rubber source ...... **KOKSAGYZ**
rubber, S. Am. . **PARA, CEARA**
rubber tree ...... **ULE, HULE,**
   SERINGA
rubber, wild .... **CEARA**
rubbery substance
   GUTTA, NOREPOL
rubbish .... **ROT, JUNK,**
   CULCH, RUBBLE
rubble masonry ..... **MOELLON**
rubella .... **MEASLES**
ruby .... **RED**
ruby red quartz ...... **RUBASSE**
d ruby spinel ... **BALAS, BALASS**
rudder bushing .... **PINTLE**
rudder fish .... **CHOPA**
ruddle .... **KEEL, KIEL**
rudiment .... **GERM**
rudiments .... **ABC**
rue .... **REGRET**
rue herb genus .... **RUTA**
ruff, female ..... **REE, REEVE**
ruffed lemur .... **VARI**
ruffer .... **NAPPER**
ruffle .... **CRIMP**
ruffle, neck ... **JABOT, RUCHE**
RUG .... see also CARPET
rug, long narrow
   KANARA, RUNNER
ruin .... **DOOM**
rule .... **LAW, DOMINEER**
"Rule Britannia" composer
   ARNE
rules, dueling .... **DUELLO**
ruler .... **REGENT**
ruler, Afghanistan ...... **EMIR,**
   AMEER, CALIF, EMEER,
   CALIPH, SULTAN
ruler, Arabian .. **EMIR, AMEER,**
   CALIF, EMEER, CALIPH,
   SULTAN
RULER, BIBLICAL .... see
   SPECIAL SECTION

134

a **RULER IN EAST**
    see RULER, ARABIAN
ruler, India .... **NAWAB**
ruler, Morocco
    SHERIF, SHEREEF
ruler, Moslem .. **EMIR, AMEER,
CALIF, EMEER, CALIPH,
SULTAN**
ruler of gods .... **ZEUS**
ruler, Oriental .... **CALIF**
ruler, Tunis .... **DEY**
RUMANIA
    see also SPECIAL SECTION
Rumanian composer ... **ENESCO**
Rumanian folk song ... **DOINA**
Rumanian king's title .. **DOMN**
rumen .... **CUD**
ruminant ...... **DEER, GOAT,
CAMEL, LLAMA, ANTELOPE**
ruminant genus .... **CAPRA**
ruminant, horned **DEER, GOAT**
ruminate ..... **MULL, PONDER**
Rumor personified ..... **FAMA**
rumor, to .... **BRUIT,
NORATE, REPORT**
b rumple .... **MUSS**
run at top speed ..... **SPRINT**
run before wind .... **SCUD**
run of the mill .... **PAR**
run out .... **PETER**
runner .... **SCARF,
STOLO, STOLON**
runner, distance ...... **MILER**
runner, plant .. **STOLO, STOLON**
rupees, 100,000 .... **LAC**
rural .... **RUSTIC, PASTORAL**
rural deity ..... **PAN, FAUNUS**
rural poem .... **GEORGIC**
rush .... **HASTE, SPEED**
rush, marsh .... **SPART**
Russell's viper
DABOIA, DABOYA
RUSSIA ...... see also SOVIET
    and SPECIAL SECTION
Russia, most northern town
KOLA
Russian .... **RED, RUSS, SLAV,
KULAK, TATAR**
Russ. basso........... **KIPNIS**
Russ. author .... **BUNIN**

c Russ. beer.**KVAS, QUAS, KVASS**
Russ. community .... **MIR**
Russ. convention ...... **RADA**
Russ. cooperative society.**ARTEL**
Russ. council .... **DUMA**
Russ. dress .... **SARAFAN**
Russ. edict .. **UKASE, DECREE**
Russ. emperor .... **CZAR,
TSAR, TZAR**
Russ. fiddle .... **GUDOK**
Russ. folk dance ...... **KOLO**
Russ. girl's name ...... **OLGA**
Russ. hemp .... **RINE**
Russ. labor union ..... **ARTEL**
Russ. lagoon .... **LIMAN**
Russ. Lapland capital ... **KOLA**
Russ. leather .... **YUFT**
Russ. liquid measure .... **STOF,
STOFF, STOOF**
Russ. log hut .... **ISBA**
Russ. marsh .... **LIMAN**
Russ. mile .... **VERST**
Russ. mountain range
ALAI, URAL
d Russian mts., pert. to..**ALTAIC**
Russ. name, given . **AKIM, IGOR**
Russ. news agency ... **TASS**
Russ. official .... **BERIYA**
Russ. opera .... **BORIS**
Russ. peninsula .... **KOLA**
Russ. sea, inland ...... **ARAL,
AZOF, AZOV**
Russ. secret police.**NKVD, OGPU**
Russ. tavern .... **CABACK**
Russ. tax, old .... **OBROK**
Russ. tea urn ...... **SAMOVAR**
Russ. trade guild ..... **ARTEL**
Russ. vehicle .. **ARBA, ARABA**
Russ. village .... **MIR**
Russ. whip .... **PLET**
Russ. writer ... **GORKI, GORKY**
Russ. "yes" .... **DA**
rust .... **EAT, ERODE**
Rustam's father .... **ZAL**
rustic .... **BOOR, RUBE, CARL,
CARLE, YOKEL, BUCOLIC,
PEASANT**
Ruth's husband .... **BOAZ**
Ruth's son .... **OBED**
rye, disease of .... **ERGOT**

S

a sable .... **SOBOL, MARTEN**
sac .... **BURSA**
saccharine source ...... **TAR**
sack fiber .... **JUTE**
sack, to .... **LOOT**
saclike cavity .... **BURSA**
sacred asp, symbol ... **URAEUS**
sacred bull, Egypt . **APIS, HAPI**
sacred chalice .... **GRAIL**
sacred city, India ... **BENARES**
sacred enclosure, Gr. .. **SEKOS**
sacred fig .... **PIPAL**
sacred Hindu word ...... **OM**
sacred image .... **ICON, IKON**
sacred lily .... **LOTUS**
sacred object: Oceania .. **ZOGO**
sacred picture .... **ICON, IKON**
sacred place .... **SHRINE**
sacred place, Gr.
         ABATON, HIERON
sacred tree, Hindu .. **BO, PIPAL**
sacrifice, place of ..... **ALTAR**
b sacrificial drink, Zoroaster's
         SOMA
sacrificial offerings ... **HIERA**
sad: comb. form ...... **TRAGI**
sad cry .... **ALAS, ALACK**
sad: music .... **MESTO**
saddle horses, fresh . **REMUDA**
saddle knob .... **POMMEL**
saddle, rear of .... **CANTLE**
safe .... **SECURE**
safe place ...... **PORT, HAVEN**
safe: thief's slang ...... **PETE**
safety lamp .... **DAVY**
safflower .... **KUSUM**
saga .... **EDDA**
sage .... **WISE**
sagacious .... **WISE,**
         ASTUTE, SAPIENT
sage genus .... **SALVIA**
sail fastener .... **CLEW**
sail-line .... **EARING**
sail nearer wind ...... **LUFF**
sail, square .... **LUG**
sail, square, edge of ... **LEECH**
sail, triangular .... **JIB**
sail yard: Scot. .... **RAE**
sail's corner .... **CLEW**
"Sails" of constellation Argo
         VELA
sailboat .... **YAWL, KETCH**
sailing race .... **REGATTA**
SAILING VESSEL .... see
        VESSEL, SAILING
sailmaker's awl ..... **STABBER**

c sailor.**GOB, TAR, SALT, SEADOG**
sailor, India .... **LASCAR**
St. Anthony's cross ..... **TAU**
saint, British .... **ALBAN**
saint, Buddhist
     ARAHT, ARHAT, ARAHAT
St. Catherine's home ... **SIENA**
saint, female: abbr. ...... **STE**
saint, 14th century .... **ROCH**
St. Francis' birthplace .. **ASSISI**
St. John's-bread ..... **CAROB**
"St. Louis Blues" composer
         HANDY
saint, Moslem .... **PIR**
St. Paul, deserter from . **DEMAS**
St. Vitus dance ...... **CHOREA**
sainte: abbr. .... **STE**
saint's relic box ...... **CHASSE**
salad green ...... **UDO, CRESS,**
     KERSE, CRESSE, ENDIVE
salamander .. **EFT, EVET, NEWT**
salient angle .... **CANT**
Salientia, the .... **ANURA**
sally .... **START, SORTIE**
"Sally in Our Alley" composer
         CAREY
d salmon, female .... **HEN**
salmon, male .... **COCK**
salmon net .... **MAUD**
salmon, silver .... **COHO**
salmon, third year .... **MORT**
salmon, 2 yr. .. **SMOLT, SPROD**
salmon, young .. **PARR, GRILSE**
salt ...... **SAL, HALITE, SALINE**
salt factory .... **SALTERN**
salt lake, Turkestan ..... **SHOR**
salt of tartaric acid .. **TARTAR**
salt pond or spring ... **SALINA**
salt, resembling ...... **HALOID**
salt, rock .... **HALITE**
salt, solution .. **BRINE, SALINE**
salt tax .... **GABELLE**
salt tree, Tamarisk ..... **ATLE**
salted .... **ALAT**
saltpeter ...... **NITER, NITRE**
saltwort .... **KALI**
saltworks ,.......... **SALINA**
salty water .... **BRINE**
salutation .... **AVE**
salutation: Ir. .... **ACHARA**
Salvation Army leader . **BOOTH**
salver .... **TRAY**
salvia .... **CHIA**
Sambal language .... **TINO**
sambar deer .... **MAHA, RUSA**
same .... **ILK, DITTO**

136

a

same place: abbr.	IBID
samlet	PARR
Samoan maiden	TAUPO
Samoan mollusk	ASI
Samoan political council.	FONO
Samuel, king killed by	AGAG
Samuel, teacher of	ELI
Samuel's son	ABIA
samurai, straying	RONIN
sanction	AMEN, FIAT
sanctuary	BEMA, FANE, NAOS, CELLA
sand	GRIT
sand bar	REEF, SHOAL
sand expanses	AREG
sand hill	DENE, DUNE
sand island	BAR
sand, sea bottom	PAAR
sand snake genus	ERYX
sandal, Egypt	TATBEB
sandal, Mex.	HUARACHE, HUARACHO
sandalwood tree	MAIRE
sandarac powder	POUNCE
sandarac tree	ARAR
sandbox tree genus	HURA
sandpiper	REE, RUFF, STIB, REEVE, STINT
sandpiper, Europ.	TEREK

b

sandpiper, red	KNOT
sandpiper, small	KNOT, PUME, STINT
sandstone	GRIT
sandstorm	HABOOB
sandwich	HERO
Sandwich Island discoverer	COOK
sandy	ARENOSE
Sankhya philos. term	GUNA
Sanskrit dialect	PALI
Sanskrit precept	SUTRA, SUTTA
Sanskrit school	TOL
Sao —, Brazil	PAULO
Sao Salvador	BAHIA
sap spout	SPILE
sapodilla	SAPOTA, SAPOTE
sapota tree	ACANA
Saracen	MOOR, MOSLEM
Sarah's slave	HAGAR
sarcasm	IRONY
Sardinia gold coin	CARLINE
sargeant fish	SNOOK
Sargon's capital	ACCAD
Sarmatia cave-dwellers	TAURI
sartor	TAILOR
sash, C. Amer.	TOBE
sash, Jap. kimono	OBI
sassafras tree	AGUE
Satan	DEVIL
Satan: Arab	EBLIS

c

satellite	MOON, PLANET
satellite	LUNIK, SPUTNIK, PIONEER, EXPLORER, VANGUARD, ATLAS-SCORE, DISCOVERER
satellite, navigation	TRANSIT
satellite, television	TIROS
satellite's path	ORBIT
satiate	CLOY, GLUT, SATE
satirical	DRY
satisfaction Maori	UTU
satisfy	SATE, SUIT, PLEASE
saturate	SOAK, IMBUE, STEEP
Saturn, satellite of	DIONE
Saturn's rings projection.	ANSA
Saturn's wife	OPS
Saturnalia	ORGY
satyr	FAUN
sauce	GRAVY
sauce, Chinese, Oriental	SOY
sauce, fish	ALEC
sauce, peppery	TABASCO
sauce, tomato	CATSUP, CATCHUP, KETCHUP
saucy	PERT
Saul's army leader	ABNER
Saul's chief herdsman	DOEG
Saul's father	KISH
Saul's grandfather	NER, ABIEL
Saul's successor	DAVID
Saul's uncle	NER
Sault Ste. Marie	SOO
saurel fish	SCAD

d

sausage, spiced	SALAME, SALAMI
savage	FERAL
Savage Island language	NIUE
save	HOARD, STINT, REDEEM, CONSERVE
saviour	REDEEMER
savory	SAPID, TASTY
saw	ADAGE, AXIOM, MAXIM, SAYING
saw-leaved centaury	BEHN, BEHEN
saw, notched like	SERRATE
saw notching	REDAN
saw, surgical	TREPAN, TREPHINE
sawbill duck	SMEW
sawlike organ, or part	SERRA
sawlike parts	SERRAS, SERRAE
sawtooth ridge	SIERRA
saxhorn	TUBA
Saxon god	ER, EAR
Saxon king	INE, ALFRED
Saxony natives	SORBS
say	UTTER
say again	ITERATE
saying	MOT, SAW, ADAGE, AXIOM, MAXIM
sayings	LOGIA

137

a
scabbard fish .... HIKU
scabbard, put into .. SHEATHE
scaffolding .... STAGING
scale .... GAMUT
scale, syllable of .. DO, FA, LA,
MI, RE, SO, TI, SOL
scale under blossom
PALEA, PALET
scales, having large . SCUTATE
scallop ..... CRENA, CRENAE
scallops, cut in small .... PINK
scalloped .... CRENATE
scalp disease .... FAVI, FAVUS
scamp ..... ROGUE, RASCAL
SCANDINAVIAN
see also NORSE
SCANDINAVIAN . see also
SWEDEN, NORWAY, in
SPECIAL SECTION
Scandinavian ... DANE, SWEDE
Scand., ancient ...... NORSE
Scand. countryman .... GEAT
Scand. explorer .... ERIC
Scand. fertility god .... NJORD
Scand. legend .... SAGA
Scand. measure .... ALEN
Scand. nation ...... GEATAS
Scandinavians in Russia
ROS, RUS

b
scanty .... SPARSE
scar, resembling a .... ULOID
scarce .... RARE
scarcely: Lat. VIX
scare away .... SHOO
scarf .... BOA, TIE,
ASCOT, ORALE
scarf, long .... STOLE
scarf, Sp. Am. ...... TAPALO
scarlet flower .... SALVIA
Scarlett O'Hara's home .. TARA
scatter ... SOW, TED, STREW
scatter: dial. .... SCOAD
scatter on .... LITTER
scattered: Her. .... SEME
scenario .... SCRIPT
scene ...... VIEW, TABLEAU
scene of action.ARENA, SPHERE
scenic view .... SCAPE
scent .... ODOR, AROMA
scented .... OLENT
schedule .... LIST
scheme .... PLAN, PLOT
schism .... RENT
scholar .... PEDANT
scholars, Moslem .... ULEMA
scholarship .... BURSE
school, boy's .... PREP
school, Fr. ...... ECOLE, LYCEE
school grounds ...... CAMPUS

c
SCHOONER ... see also BOAT,
SHIP, VESSEL
schooner, 3-masted ..... TERN
sciences .... ARTS
scientific farmer . AGRONOMIST
scientific study: abbr. . ANAT.
scientist, Am. . UREY, HOOTON,
PARRAN, COMPTON,
WAKSMAN, MILLIKAN
scientist, Austr. .... MEITNER
scientist, Czech .... CORI
scientist, Dan. .... BOHR
scientist, Eng. ...... HOGBEN,
FLEMING, HALDANE
scientist, Ger. .. BAADE, HABER
scientist, Ital. .... FERMI
scissors .... SHEARS
scoff ...... GIBE, JEER, JIBE,
RAIL, SNEER
scold ...... JAW, NAG, RATE
scold: dialect .... FRAB
scone: Scot. ..... FARL, FARLE
scoop .... DIP
scoot: Scot. ..... SKYT, SKITE
scope .. AREA, AMBIT, RANGE
scorch .... CHAR, SEAR,
SERE, SINGE
score .... TALLY
scoria .... SLAG, DROSS

d
scorpion fish .... LAPON
Scotch cake .... SCONE
scoter .... COOT
Scotland .... SCOTIA
Scott character .... ELLEN
Scott heroine .... ELLEN
Scott, poem by .... MARMION
SCOTTISH
see Pages of SCOTTISH WORDS
Scot. alderman .... BAILIE
Scot. author .... BARRIE
Scot. chemist ... URE, DEWAR
Scot. chief landholder
THANE, THEGN
Scot. cultural congress ... MOD
Scot. explorer .... RAE
Scot. highlander ...... GAEL
Scot. king .... BRUCE
Scot. lord .... THANE, THEGN
Scot. pillory .... JOUG
Scot. playwright ...... BARRIE
Scot. poet .... BURNS
Scot. pottage .... BROSE
Scot. proprietor ...... LAIRD
Scot. scholar .... NICOLL
Scot. singer .... LAUDER
SCOTTISH WORDS:
accept .... TAE
advise .... REDE
afraid .... RAD, RADE
age .... EILD

a

against .... **GIN**
alder tree ..... **ARN, ELLER**
an .... **AE**
animal, lean .... **RIBE**
any .... **ONY**
article .... **TA**
ashes .... **ASE**
ask .... **AX**
at all .... **AVA**
away .... **AWA**
awry .... **AJEE**
babbler .... **HAVEREL**
ball .... **BA**
bank .... **BRAE**
barter .... **TROKE**
beg .... **SORN**
bind .... **OOP**
biscuit .... **BAKE**
blockhead .... **CUIF, NOWT**
bloodhound .... **LYAM**
bone .... **BANE**
bound .... **STEND**
breeches .... **TREWS**
broth ...... **BREE, BROO**
brow of hill .... **SNAB**
built .... **BAG**
burden .... **BIRN**
bushel .... **FOU**
calves ...... **CAUR, CAURE**

b

came .... **CAM**
catch .... **KEP**
chalk .... **CAUK**
check .... **WERE**
chest .... **KIST**
child .... **BAIRN**
church ...... **KIRK, KURK**
comb .... **KAME**
contend .... **KEMP**
court, bring to ...... **SIST**
cut .... **KNAP, SNEG**
dairymaid .... **DEY**
damage .... **TEEN**
damaged .... **LESED**
dare .... **DAUR**
devil .... **DEIL**
did not know .... **KENNA**
die .... **DEE**
dig .... **HOWK**
dining room .... **SPENCE**
do .... **DAE, DIV**
do not know ...... **KENNA**
dread .... **DREE**
drip .... **SIE, SYE**
dusty .... **MOTTY**
earth .... **EARD**
elder .... **ELLER**
else .... **ENSE**
empty .... **TOOM**
endeavor .... **ETTLE**
endure .... **DREE**

c

extra .... **ORRA**
eye .... **EE**
eyes .... **EEN, EES**
family .... **ILK**
fidget .... **FIKE**
firth .... **KYLE**
fishing expedition ... **DRAVE**
fit of sulks .... **GEE**
flax refuse ..... **PAB, POB**
fog ..... **DAG, HAR, HAAR**
foretell .... **SPAE**
give .... **GIE**
glimpse .... **STIME**
grandchild .... **OY, OYE**
grant as property . **DISPONE**
great-grandchild .... **IEROE**
grief .... **TEEN**
have .... **HAE**
hawk .... **ALLAN**
heavy .... **THARF**
hill . **BEN, DOD, BRAE, DODD**
hillside .... **BRAE**
howl .... **YOWT**
hurt .... **LESED**
injure .... **TEEN**
injured .... **LESED**
intent .... **ETTLE**
keg .... **KNAG**

d

kinsman .... **SIB**
kiss .... **PREE**
knead .... **ELT**
knock .... **KNOIT**
lake .... **LOCH**
leap .. **LOUP, LOWP, STEND**
learning .... **LEAR**
list of candidates ..... **LEET**
loaf .... **SORN**
lop .... **SNATHE**
lout .... **CUIF**
love .... **LOE**
loyal .... **LEAL**
marriage portion ..... **DOTE**
millrace .... **LADE**
mire .... **GLAUR**
mist .... **URE**
mountain .... **BEN**
mouth, river .... **BEAL**
mouth .... **BEAL**
mud .... **GLAIR**
must .... **MAUN**
name .... **IAN**
near, nearest .... **NAR**
no .... **NAE**
none .... **NANE**
not matched .... **ORRA**
now .... **NOO**
nowhere .... **NAEGATE**
oak .... **AIK**

(Scottish words continued 140)

139

Scottish

oatmeal dish .... BROSE
odd .... ORRA
old age .... EILD
once .... ANES
one .... AIN, ANE, YIN
otherwise .... ELS
out .... OOT
own ...... AIN, ANE, AWN
pantry .... SPENCE
parlor .... BEN
payment .... MENSE
paw ground .... PAUT
peat cutter .... PINER
pig .... GRICE
pike .... GED, GEDD
pillory .... TRONE
pipe .... CUTTY
pluck wool .... ROO
pool .... DIB, CARR,
                LINN, LLYN
present .... GIE
pretty .... GEY
prop .... RANCE
propriety .... MENSE
prune .... SNED
puddle .... DUB
pull .... PU
quagmire .... HAG
quarter of a year ... RAITH
relieve .... LISS
revenue, church .... ANNAT
ridge of a hill ...... SHIN
river .... DOON
rowboat .... COBLE
sailyard .... RAE
same .... ILK
scone .... FARL, FARLE
scoot .... SKYT, SKITE
scratch .... RIT
seep .... SIPE
seize .... VANG
self .... SEL
serve .... KAE
severe blow .... DEVEL
sheepfold .... REE
sheepstick .... KED
sheep walk .... SLAIT
shelter ...... BIELD, SHEAL
sift .... SIE
since .... SIN, SYNE
slope .... BRAE
slouch .... LOUCH
sly .... SLEE
small .... SMA
snow .... SNA
so .... SAE
son of .... MAC
song .... STROUD
sore .... SAIR
sorrow .... TEEN
sow .... SOO

steward .... MORMAOR
stipend .... ANNAT
stone .STANE, STEAN, STEEN
stretch .... STENT
stupid one .... CUIF
suffer .... DREE
summit .... DOD, DODD
sweetheart .... JO
than .... NA
to .... TAE
toe .... TAE
tone .... TEAN
trench .... GAW
truant, play .... TRONE
try .... ETTLE
tune .... PORT
turnip .... NEEP
uncanny .... UNCO
uncle .... EME
urge .... ERT
very .... VERA
vex .... FASH
village .... REW
void, to render ...... CASS
waterfall ... LIN, LYN, LINN
wealthy .... BIEN
weep .... ORP
week .... OUK
well .... AWEEL
weighing machine ... TRON,
                       TRONE
wet .... WAT
whirlpool ..... WEEL, WIEL
whiskey drink ..... ATHOL,
                       ATHOLE
widow's third ...... TERCE
workhouse .... AVER
year, ¼ of .... RAITH
yell .... GOWL
scoundrel .... ROGUE, VARLET
scout unit . DEN, PACK, TROOP
scow ...... BARGE, LIGHTER
scow: Fr. .... ACON
scrap, table .... ORT
scraps of literature ...... ANA
scrape ... RAKE, RASP, GRAZE
scrape bottom ...... DREDGE
scratch .... MAR, RAKE
scrawny animal ...... SCRAG
screamer bird .... CHAJA
screed .... TIRADE
screen .... SIFT, SHADE
screen, altar .... REREDOS
screen, wind ..... PARAVENT
script, modern Syriac ... SERTA
script, upright .... RONDE
scripture, early .... ITALA
scripture passage ...... TEXT
scriptures, occult interpretation
                       CABALA
scrutinize .... EYE, SCAN

140

a scuffle .... **MELEE**
sculptor of "Thinker" . **RODIN**
scum, metal .... **DROSS**
scup .... **BREAM, PORGY**
scuppernong ..... **MUSCADINE**
scuttle .... **HOD**
scuttle, coal .... **HOD**
scythe .... **SY, SYE**
scythe handle . **SNATH, SNEAD,
SNEED, SNATHE**
sea anemone .. **POLYP, OPELET**
sea bird ... **ERN, ERNE, GULL,
SKUA, SCAUP, TERN, FUL-
MAR, GANNET, PETREL,
SCOTER**
sea bird, north .... **PUFFIN**
sea cow . **DUGONG, MANATEE**
sea cucumber ...... **TREPANG**
sea demon, Teut. ...... **WATE**
sea duck ...... **COOT, EIDER,
SCAUP, SCOTER**
sea eagle .... **ERN, ERNE**
sea-ear .... **ABALONE**
sea: Fr. .... **MER**
sea girdles .... **CUVY**
sea god .... **LER, TRITON,
NEPTUNE**
sea god, Gr. . **NEREUS, TRITON,
POSEIDON**
sea god, Rom. ...... **NEPTUNE**
sea god, Teut. .. **HLER, AEGIR**
sea goddess, Norse ...... **RAN**
b sea green .... **CELADON**
sea gull, Eur. .... **MEW**
sea, kept bow on . **ATRY, ATRIE**
sea lettuce ..... **ALGA, LAVER**
sea lettuce genus **ULVA, ULUA**
sea marker .... **DAN**
sea pheasant .... **SMEE**
sea robber .... **PIRATE**
sea mile, Austral. ...... **NAUT**
sea nymph .... **NEREID**
sea shell .... **TRITON**
(see also **SHELL**)
sea skeleton .... **CORAL**
sea slug genus . **DOTO, ELYSIA**
sea snail . **WELK, WILK, WHELK**
sea snake, Asia .... **KERRIL**
sea soldier .... **MARINE**
sea worm . **SAO, LURG, NEREIS**
seal .... **SIGIL**
seal, eared .... **OTARY**
seal, fur .... **URSAL**
seal, letter .... **CACHET**
seal, official .... **SIGNET**
seal, papal .... **BULLA**
seal, young .... **PUP**
seals, group of .... **POD**
seamark .... **BEACON**
seamen: Brit. .... **RATINGS**
seamlike ridge .... **RAPHE**

c seams of boat, fill ..... **CALK**
SEAPORT .... see PORT
search .... **GROPE**
search for ...... **HUNT, SEEK**
search for food ...... **FORAGE**
season ...... **AGE, FALL, SALT,
TIDE, SPRING**
season, church . **LENT, ADVENT**
season, Fr. .... **ETE**
seasons, goddesses of .. **HORAE**
seasonal phenomenon .. **EPACT**
seasoning .... **SAGE, SALT**
seasoning herb .... **SAGE,
BASIL, THYME**
seat, chancel .... **SEDILE**
seat, long ...... **PEW, SETTEE**
seat of oracle of Zeus. **DODONA**
seat, Rom. .... **SELLA**
seaweed ... **ORE, AGAR, ALGA,
KELP, ALGAE, LAVER,
VAREC**
seaweed ashes .... **KELP**
seaweed, brown .... **KELP**
seaweed, edible ...... **AGAR**
seaweed, edible Hawaiian .**LIMU**
seaweed, purple ...... **LAVER**
seaweed, purple, Jap. ... **NORI**
seaweed, red .... **DULSE**
Seb, consort of .... **NUT**
d secluded .... **REMOTE**
second . **ABET, TRICE, MOMENT**
second brightest star ... **BETA**
second-growth crop ... **ROWEN**
Second Punic War's end,
site of .... **ZAMA**
second team .... **SCRUB**
secondary .... **BYE, LESS**
secret ...... **RUNE, ARCANE,
COVERT, MYSTERY,
ESOTERIC**
secret agent .... **SPY**
secret society, Afr..**EGBO, PORO**
secret society in Sierra Leone
PORO
secrets .... **ARCANA**
secrets, one learning ... **EPOPT**
secretion, sweet
LAAP, LERP, LAARP
sect .... **CULT**
sect, Nepal . **ACHAR, ACHARA**
section of journey .... **LEG**
secular ... **LAY, LAIC, LAICAL**
secure . **FIX, GET, PIN, FAST,
NAIL, SAFE, FASTEN**
secure firmly . **MOOR, ANCHOR**
secure with rope .... **BELAY**
security .... **BOND**
Sec'y of State, 1933-44 .. **HULL**
sedate .... **STAID**
sedative .... **NEMBUTAL**

141

Sediment

a

sediment .... **LEES, SILT, DREGS, SILTAGE**
see .... **ESPY, LOOK**
see: Lat. .... **VIDE**
seed .... **PIP, PIT, GRAIN, SPORE, PYRENE**
seed coat or covering .. **ARIL, HULL, HUSK, TESTA, TEGMEN, TESTAE, TEGUMEN, TEGIMINA**
seed, edible ...... **PEA, BEAN, LENTIL, PINOLE**
seed, edible, Asia .... **SESAME**
seed, immature .... **OVULE**
seed, lens-shaped ..... **LENTIL**
seed, nutlike .... **PINON**
seed, opium poppy ..... **MAW**
seed plant .... **ENDOGEN**
seeds, remove .... **GIN**
seedless plant .... **FERN**
seek to attain .... **ASPIRE**
seem .... **LOOK**
seesaw .... **TEETER**
segment, last .... **TELSON**
segment of body .... **SOMITE**
segment of circle ...... **ARC**
segment, pert. to ...... **TORIC**
seine .... **NET**
seize .... **NAB, GRAB, GRASP, USURP, ARREST, COLLAR**

b

seize: archaic .... **REAVE**
selections, literary
.... **ANA, ANALECTA**
self .... **EGO**
self-assurance .... **APLOMB**
self-defense, art of ..... **JUDO**
self-denying .... **ASCETIC**
self-education doctrine
.... **BIOSOPHY**
self-locking nut ..... **PALNUT**
self-reproach .... **REMORSE**
sell .... **VEND**
seller .... **COSTER, VENDER, VENDOR**
semblance .... **GUISE**
semester .... **TERM**
semi-precious stone
.... **ONYX, SARD**
semicircular room ...... **APSE**
semidiameter .... **RADIUS**
semidiameters .... **RADII**
Seminole chief .... **OSCEOLA**
Semitic deity .... **BAAL**
sen, tenth of .... **RIN**
senate house .... **CURIA**
senate houses .... **CURIAE**
Senator, former .... **BORAH**
send back ... **REMIT, REMAND**
send money .... **REMIT**

c

send out .... **EMIT, ISSUE**
sending forth .... **EMISSIVE**
Senegambia gazelle .... **KORIN**
senility .... **DOTAGE**
senior .... **ELDER**
senior: Fr. .... **AINE**
senna, source of ...... **CASSIA**
sennet .... **SPET**
sense .... **FEEL**
senseless .... **INANE**
sensitive .... **SORE**
sentence, analyze ..... **PARSE**
sentence part .... **CLAUSE**
"Sentimental Journey" author
.... **STERNE**
sentinel, mounted ... **VEDETTE**
separate . **SIFT, APART, SECERN**
separated .... **APART**
separation .... **SCHISM**
sequence, 3-card ..... **TIERCE**
sequester .... **ISOLATE**
Sequoia national park ... **MUIR**
seraglio .... **HAREM, SERAI**
serene .... **SERENO**
serf .... **ESNE**
serf, Rom. .... **COLONA**
serf, Spartan, ancient .. **HELOT**
sergeant fish .... **COBIA**
series .... **SET, GAMUT**
series, in a .... **SERIATIM**

d

series of tones .... **SCALE**
serious ...... **GRAVE, EARNEST**
sermon .... **HOMILY**
serow .... **JAGLA**
SERPENT ..... see also **SNAKE**
serpent, Egypt. myth .... **APEPI**
serpent goddess, Egypt. . **BUTO**
serpent, Gr. .... **SEPS**
serpent, large .. **BOA, PYTHON**
serpent monster ...... **ELLOPS**
serpent, myth. ...... **BASILISK**
serpent worship ...... **OPHISM**
serpentine .... **OPHITE**
servant.......... **BOY, MAN, MAID, MENIAL**
servant, India ...... **HAMAL, FERASH, HAMMAL**
servant, man's .... **VALET**
servant, P. I. .... **BATA**
servants, for .... **MENIAL**
serve soup .... **LADLE**
server .... **TRAY**
service, religious ...... **MASS**
service tree .... **SORB**
servile .... **MENIAL**
serving boy .... **PAGE**
sesame .... **TIL, TEEL**
sesame oil ...... **BENI, BENNE**
sesame seed .... **GINGILI**
session, hold .... **SIT, MEET**

142

a set aside	**DEFER**
set in type	**PRINT**
set limits to	**STINT**
set price	**RATE**
set system	**ROTE**
set thickly	**STUD**
setback	**REVERSE**
Seth's brother	**CAIN**
Seth's mother	**EVE**
Seth's son	**ENOS**
setting	**SCENE, MILIEU**
setting sun, Egyp. god of	**TEM, TUM, ATMU, ATUM**
settled	**ALIT**
settler	**BOOMER**
seven	**SEPT**
Seven Dwarfs	**DOC, DOPEY, HAPPY, GRUMPY, SLEEPY, SNEEZY, BASHFUL**
seven, group of	**HEPTAD, PLEIAD, SEPTET, SEPTETTE**
"Seventh Heaven" heroine	**DIANE**
seventh order, of	**SEPTIC**
seventh, pert. to	**SEPTAN**
sever	**CUT, LOP, REND**
severe	**STERN**
severely criticize	**PAN, SLATE, ROAST**
b sew hawk's eyelids	**SEEL**
"Seward's —," Alaska	**FOLLY**
sexes, common to both	**EPICENE**
shabby	**WORN**
shabby woman	**DOWD**
shackle	**BOND, GYVE, IRON, FETTER**
shad	**ALLIS, ALOSA, ALOSE, ALLICE**
shaddock	**POMELO, PUMELO**
shade	**HUE, SCREEN**
shade of difference	**NUANCE**
shade of meaning	**NUANCE**
shaded walk	**MALL**
shadow	**TAIL**
shadow, eclipse	**UMBRA**
shaft	**POLE, SPINDLE**
shaft column, feather	**SCAPE**
shaft horse	**THILLER**
shaft of column	**FUST**
shaft, wooden	**ARROW**
shafter	**HORSE**
shake	**JAR, JOLT, NIDGE**
Shakespeare's elf	**PUCK**
Shakespeare's river	**AVON**
Shakespeare's theatre	**GLOBE**
Shakespeare's wife	**ANNE**
Shakesperian clown	**BOTTOM**
Shakesperian forest	**ARDEN**
Shakesperian king	**LEAR**

c Shakesperian shrew	**KATE**
Shakesperian villain	**IAGO**
shallow receptacle	**TRAY**
sham	**FAKE**
Shamash, wife of	**AI, AYA**
"Shane," star of	**LADD**
Shang dynasty	**YIN**
shank	**CRUS, SHIN**
shanks	**CRURA**
shanty	**HUT**
shape	**FORM, MOLD**
shaped like a club	**CLAVATE**
shaped like a needle	**ACUATE, ACERATE**
shaping tool	**LATHE, SWAGE**
share	**LOT, RATION**
share	**PARTAKE**
shark	**TOPE**
shark, Eur. small	**TOPE**
shark, long-nosed	**MAKO**
shark, nurse	**GATA**
shark parasite fish	**REMORA**
sharp	**ACERB, ACUTE, ACUATE**
sharp	**CHEAT**
sharp ridge	**ARETE**
sharpen	**EDGE, HONE, WHET**
sharpshooter	**JAGER, SNIPER**
shavetail: abbr.	**LT**
shawl	**MAUD, PAISLEY**
d shea tree	**KARITE**
sheaf of grain: Her.	**GERB**
shear	**CLIP**
sheath, petiole	**OCREA**
Sheba: Lat.	**SABA**
shed, as feathers	**MOLT, MOULT**
shed for sheep	**COTE**
sheen	**GLOSS**
sheep	**EWE, RAM, MERINO**
sheep, Afr. domestic	**ZENU**
sheep, Afr. wild	**ARUI, UDAD, AOUDAD**
sheep, Asia wild	**ARGALI**
sheep, Asia, wild, mountain	**SHA, SNA, RASSE, URIAL, BHARAL, NAHOOR, OORIAL**
sheep cry	**BAA, MAA**
sheep disease	**COE, GID, ROT**
sheep dog	**COLLIE**
sheep, Eng. black-faced	**LONK**
sheep, female	**EWE**
sheep genus	**OVIS**
sheep in 2nd year	**TEG, TEGG, BIDENT**
sheep, India, wild	**SHA, SNA, URIAL, NAHOOR, OORIAL**
sheep, large-horned	**AOUDAD, ARGALI**
sheep, Leicester	**DISHLEY**
sheep, male	**RAM, TUP**

Sheep

a

sheep, N. Afr. wild	**ARUI, UDAD, AOUDAD**
sheep, of	**OVINE**
sheep owner, Bibl.	**NABAL**
sheep pasture, old Eng.	**HEAF**
sheep, pert. to	**OVINE**
sheep, Tibet	**SHA, SNA, URIAL, BHARAL, NAHOOR, OORIAL**
sheep tick	**KED, KADE**
sheep, unshorn	**HOGG, HEDER**
sheep walk: Scot.	**SLAIT**
sheep, wild	**SHA, SNA, ARUI, UDAD, RASSE, BHARAL, NAHOOR, AOUDAD, AR-GALI, OORIAL**
sheep, young	**TAG, TEG**
sheepfold	**REE, COTE**
sheeplike	**OVINE**
sheepskin leather	**BOCK, ROAN, SKIVER**
sheerly	**SOLELY**
shekel, 1/4, Hebrew	**REBA**
shelf	**LEDGE**
shelf above altar	**RETABLE**
shell	**BOMB**
shell	**TEST, LORICA, TUNICA**
shell beads	**PEAG**
shell, large	**CONCH**
shell, marine	**TRITON**
shell money	**ULLO,**

b **COWRY, UHLLO, COWRIE**

shellfish, edible	**CRAB, ABALONE, SCALLOP**
shelter	**LEE, COTE, SHED, HAVEN, SCREEN**
shelter, hillside	**ABRI**
shelter: Scot.	**BIELD, SHEAL**
shelter, to	**ALEE**
sheltered	**ALEE**
Shem descendant	**SEMITE**
Shem's brother	**HAM**
Shem's son	**LUD, ARAM, ELAM, ASSHUR**
Sheol	**HADES**
shepherd prophet	**AMOS**
shepherd's crook	**PEDA, PEDUM**
shepherd's pipe	**OAT, REED**
shepherd's song	**MADRIGAL**
shepherdess, "Winter's Tale"	**MOPSA**
sheriff substitute	**ELISOR**
sheriff's men	**POSSE**
Sherwood	**FOREST**
Shetland court president	**FOUD**
Shetland hill pasture	**HOGA**
shield	**ECU, EGIS, AEGIS, PAVIS, DEFEND, PROTECT**
shield, Athena's	**AEGIS**
shield, Austral.	**MULGA**
shield-bearing or border.	**ORLE**

c

shield, medieval	**ECU**
shield, Rom.	**SCUTA, SCUTUM, CLIPEUS**
shield-shaped	**PELTATE, SCUTATE**
shield, small	**ECU**
shield strap	**ENARME**
shield's corner: Her.	**CANTON**
shift	**VEER**
shift position.	**GIBE, GYBE, JIBE**
shin	**CNEMIS**
shine	**GLOW, GLISTEN, ERADIATE**
shingle, wedge-shaped	**SHIM**
shingles	**ZONA**
shining	**NITID**
Shinto deity	**KAMI**
Shinto temple	**SHA**
Shinto temple gate	**TORII**
ship	**KEEL, SEND, LINER, TANKER, TENDER, VESSEL, CARAVEL**
ship, back part	**STERN**
ship boat	**GIG, DORY**
ship body or frame	**HULL**
ship bow, curve of	**LOOF**
ship canvas	**SAIL**
ship clock	**NEF**

d

ship drainage hole	**SCUPPER**
ship employee	**STEWARD**
ship, 1st Northwest Passage	**GJOA**
ship, forward part	**BOW, PROW**
ship, fur-hunting	**SEALER**
ship, ironclad	**MONITOR**
ship: Jap.	**MARO, MARU**
ship keel, rear part	**SKEG**
ship, large	**TONNER**
ship, lowest part	**BILGE**
ship, Medit.	**SETEE, SETTEE**
ship, middle part	**WAIST**
ship, mooring place	**DOCK, BERTH**
ship, oar-propelled	**GALLEY**
ship, part of	**RIB, DECK, HULL, KEEL**
ship plank	**STRAKE**
ship platform	**DECK**
ship pole	**MAST, SPAR**
ship shaped clock	**NEF**
ship side, opp. middle	**ABEAM**
ship timber, bevel	**SNAPE**
ship timber curve	**SNY**
ship timber, extra	**RIDER**
ship wheel	**HELM**
ship, wrecked	**HULK**
ship, 1-masted	**SLOOP**
ship, 2-masted	**BRIG, SNOW**
ship's kitchen	**GALLEY**
shipboard covering	**CAPOT**

a shipbuilding curve ..... SNY
shipbuilding piece
SPALE, THWART
shipworm .... BORER, TEREDO
shipwreck, causing
NAUFRAGEOUS
shirk .... GOLDBRICK
SHIRT .... see also GARMENT
shirt .... KAMIS, CAMISE
shirt, Oriental .... CAMISE
shoal .... REEF
shoal water deposit .... CULM
shock .... STUN,
APPAL, APPALL, TRAUMA
shock absorber ..... SNUBBER
shod, as monks ..... CALCED
shoe .... GAITER, SANDAL
shoe form .... LAST
shoe front .... VAMP
shoe gripper .... CLEAT
shoe, heavy.BROGAN, BROGUE
shoe latchet .... TAB
shoe, mule .... PLANCH
shoe part
LAST, RAND, WELT, INSOLE
b shoe strip ...... RAND, WELT
shoe, wooden ... GETA, SABOT
shoe, wooden-soled ..... CLOG
shoes .... SHOON
shoes, Mercury's winged
TALARIA
shoelace .... LACET
shoemakers' saint ... CRISPIN
shoemaker's tool .... AWL
shoot .... BAG, POT
shoot at from ambush SNIPE
shoot at, marble to ...... MIG
shoot, cotton ...... RATOON
shoot, plant .... BINE, CION,
GEMMA, SPRIT,
STOLO, STOLON
shoot, small .... SPRIG
shoot, sugar cane ... RATOON
shooter, hidden ...... SNIPER
shooter marble .... TAW,
AGATE, AGGIE
shooting match .... TIR
shooting match: Fr. ...... TIR
shooting star .... LEONID
shop .... STORE
shop, Rom. wine ... TABERNA
shops, Rom. wine .. TABERNAE
shop's name plate ...... FACIA
shore .... COAST, STRAND
SHORE BIRD . see BIRD, SHORE
short .... CURT,
BRIEF, TERSE, STUBBY

c short-breathed .... PURSY
short comedy sketch .... SKIT
short-spoken .. CURT, TERSE
short tail .... SCUT
shorten .... CUT, DELE, ELIDE
shortly
ANON, SOON, PRESENTLY
Shoshonean .... UTE
shoulder blade ..... SCAPULA
shoulder, of the
ALAR, SCAPULAR
shoulder ornament
EPAULET, EPAULETTE
shoulder, road .... BERM
shoulder wrap .... SHAWL
shout.CRY, CALL, ROAR, YELL
shove .... PUSH
shovel .... SPADE
show as false .... BELIE
show off .... FLAUNT
show place, Rom. .... CIRCUS
show, street .... RAREE
"Showboat" author .... FERBER
showy .... LOUD
shrew .... ERD, TARTAR
shrewd.SAGE, CANNY, ASTUTE
shrike genus .... LANIUS
d shrill .... PIPY
shrill, to .... STRIDULATE
shrimplike crustacean PRAWN
shrine .... ALTAR
shrink .... CONTRACT
shroud-stopper: naut. ... WAPP
SHRUB .... see also TREE
shrub and tree .... ALDER
shrub, Asia .... CHE
shrub, berry-bearing ... ELDER
shrub, berry, Pacific ... SALAL
shrub, Chin. .... TEA
shrub, Congo medical .. BOCCA
shrub, desert
RETEM, OCOTILLO
shrub, Eng. .... HEATH
shrub, evergreen .. BOX, YEW,
TITI, ERICA, HEATH, SAL-
AL, OLEANDER
shrub, flowering ITEA, AZALEA,
PRIVET, SPIREA, SPIRAEA,
SYRINGA
shrub genus BIXA, INGA, ITEA,
ROSA, ALDER, IXORA,
AZALEA
shrub, Hawaiian ..... OLONA
shrub, low spiny ...... GORSE
shrub, Medit. .... CAPER
shrub, poisonous
SUMAC, SUMACH
shrub, prickly .... CAPER

Shrub

a shrub, Rhus genus .... SUMAC, SUMACH
shrub, strong-scented .. BATIS
shrub with grapelike fruit .... SALAL
shrub, yellow flowers OLEASTER
shun .... AVOID, DODGE
shut up .... IMMURE
shy .... JIB, BALK
SIAM .. see also SPECIAL SECTION
Siamese .... THAI
Siam. coin .... ATT
Siam. garment ..... PANUNG
Siam. group ...... KUI, LAO
Siam. monetary unit .... BAHT
Siamese twin ... ENG, CHANG
SIBERIAN .. see also RUSSIAN
Siberian .... TATAR
Siberian wild cat ..... MANUL
Siberian squirrel ..... MINIVER
sibilant sound .... HISS
Sicilian resort .... ENNA
sickle, curved like ... FALCATE
sickle: variant .... SIVE
side, jewel's .... FACET
side arm .... GUN, SWORD, PISTOL, REVOLVER
b side: Lat. .... LATUS
side of head .. LORA, LORUM
side, pert. to .... COSTAL, LATERAL
side-post, door's ...... JAMB
sidetrack .... SHUNT
side street, Chin. ... HUTUNG
side timber: naut. .... BIBB
side, toward the .... LATERAD
sidereal .... ASTRAL
sidewalk .... PAVEMENT
sidewalk edge ... CURB, KERB
sidewinder .... CROTALUS
sidle .... EDGE
Siegfried's murderer ... HAGEN
siesta .... NAP
sieve .... SIFT, PUREE, BOLTER
sieve for clay .... LAUN
Sif, son of ...... ULL, ULLR
sift .... SCREEN
sift: dialect .... REE
sift: old Eng. .... LUE
sift: Scot. .... SIE
siffer .... SIEVE
sigh .... SOUF, SOUGH
sight, come into ...... LOOM
sight, dimness of .... CALIGO
sight on gun .... BEAD
sight, pert. to ...... OCULAR
sign ... MARK, OMEN, TOKEN

c sign, music .... PRESA, SEGNO
sign: old Eng. .... SEIN
sign, pert. to .... SEMIC
sign up ..... ENROL, ENROLL
signal for attention ..... PST
signal for parley ... CHAMADE
signal to act .... CUE
signal to begin .... CUE
signature, affix ...... SIGN, ENDORSE
signet .... SIGIL
signify ..... MEAN, DENOTE
"Silas Marner" author .. ELIOT
silence .... GAG, HUSH
silence: music .... TACET
silent ... MUM, MUTE, TACIT
silica .... SAND, SILEX
silica, rich in ...... ACIOLIC
silicate .... MICA
silk-cotton tree CEIBA, KAPOK
silk-cotton tree fiber ...... KAPOK, KUMBI
silk fabric ..... GROS, MOFF, PEKIN, SATIN, TULLE
silk filament .... BRIN
silk, fine ...... CRIN, TULLE
silk, heavy .... GROS
silk in cocoon .... BAVE
silk, India .... ROMAL, RUMAL
silk, old heavy .... CAMACA
d silk, raw .... GREGE
silk substitute ...... NYLON, RAYON, ORLON, DACRON
silk thread .... FLOSS
silk, twilled .... ALMA
silk, unravel .... SLEAVE
silken .... SERIC
silkworm, Assam ... ERI, ERIA
silkworm, China ..... TASAR
silkworm disease .... UJI
silly .... INANE
silver: Her. .... ARGENT
silver lactate .... ACTOL
silver ore .... PACO
silver, uncoined, in ingots SYCEE
silverfish .. TARPON, TARPUN
silverize .... PLATE
silvery .... ARGENT
silvery-white metal .. COBALT
simian .... APE
similar .... LIKE, SUCH
Simon .... PETER
simper .... SMIRK
simple .... EASY, MERE
simple sugar .... OSE
simpleton .... ASS, DAW, OAF, BOOB, COOT, FOOL, GABY, GAWK, GOWK, SIMP, GOOSE
simulate .... APE, SHAM, FEIGN, PRETEND

146

Sin

sin	ERR, EVIL
sin, grief for	ATTRITION
Sinai	HOREB
Sinbad's bird	ROC
since	AGO
since: Scot.	SIN, SYNE
Sinclair Lewis character	CASS
sine — non	QUA
sine qua —	NON
sinew	TENDON
sinewy	WIRY
sing	LILT, CAROL
sing, as a round	TROLL
sing softly	CROON
sing, Swiss style	JODEL, YODEL, YODLE
singer, synagogue	CANTOR
singing bird	OSCINE
singing girl, Egyptian	ALMA, ALME, ALMAH, ALMAI, ALMEH
singing, suitable for	MELIC
single	ONE, BILL, MONO, ONLY, UNAL
single out	CHOOSE
single: prefix	MONO
single thing	ONE, UNIT
singleton	ACE
sink, as putt	HOLE
sink: geol.	DOLINA
sinuous	WAVY, SERPENTINE
sinus cavities	ANTRA
Sioux, Siouan	OTO, OTOE
sir: India	MIAN
sir: Malay	TUAN
siren, Rhine	LORELEI
Sisera's killer	JAEL
sister	NUN, SIB
"Sistine Madonna" painter	RAPHAEL
sitatunga, Afr.	NAKONG
sitting	POSING, SEANCE, SESSION
sitting on	ASTRIDE
situation, difficult	STRAIT
siva snake	COBRA
Siva, wife of	DEVI, KALI, SATI
six, group of	SENARY, SESTET, SEXTET
six-line verse	SESTET, SESTINA
six on a die	CISE, SICE, SISE
six, series of	HEXAD
six: Sp.	SEIS
sixpence: slang	SICE
sixteen annas	RUPEE
sixth: music	SEXT
sixth sense: abbr.	ESP
size of shot	BB, FF, TT
sizing	SEALER
skate	RAY
skate genus	RAIA
skating area	RINK
skegger	PARR
skein of yarn	RAP, HANK
skeletal	BONY
skeleton, sea animal	CORAL, SPONGE
skeptic	AGNOSTIC
sketch	DRAW, OUTLINE
ski, heel spring	AMSTUTZ
ski race	SLALOM
ski run	SCHUSS, SLALOM
ski wax	KLISTER
skier, mark of	SITZMARK
skiing position	VORLAGE
skiing, zigzag	SLALOM
skilled person	ADEPT
skillful	ABLE, DEFT, ADEPT, HABILE
skillfully	ABLY
skim over	SKIP
skin	FLAY, DERMA
skin, deeper layer	CUTIS
skin, design on	TATOO, TATTOO
skin disease	ACNE, MANGE, PSORA, TETTER
skin disease, horse's	CALORIS
skin disease, Peru	UTA
skin infection	LEPRA
skin layer	DERM, CUTIS, DERMA, CORIUM, ENDERON
skin of a beast	FELL
skin, pert. to	DERIC, DERMIC
skinflint	MISER
skink, Egypt.	ADDA
skip	OMIT
skip a stone	DAP
skip happily	CAPER
skipjack	ELATER
skirmish	MELEE
skirt, ballet	TUTU
skirt section	PANEL
skittle	PIN
skulk	LURK
skull, pert. to	INIAL, INION
skull protuberance	INION
skullcap, Arab.	CHECHIA
skunk	CHINCHA, CHINCHE
sky	FIRMAMENT
sky god, Assyrian	ANAT
sky: Chin.	TIEN
sky god, Babyl.	ABU, ANU
sky god, Norse	TIU, TIW, TYR, ZIO, ZIU
sky, highest part	ZENITH
sky: Polyn.	LANGI
sky serpent, Vedic	AHI
slab, engraved	TABLET
slab, flooring, decorative	DALLE
slag	DROSS, SCORIA

147

Slam

a slam .... BANG
slam in cards .... VOLE
slander ...... LIBEL, ASPERSE
slang .... ARGOT
slant .... BEVEL, SLOPE
slanted edge .... BEVEL
slanted: naut. .... ARAKE
slanting .... SKEW, ASKEW
slanting type .... ITALIC
slantingly, drive .... TOE
slap .... CUFF, SPANK
slash .... JAG, SLISH
slater's tool, same as slate-
trimming tool
slate-trimming tool
SAX, ZAT, ZAX
Slav .... SERB
Slav, ancient
VEND, WEND, VENED
Slav, E. Ger. .... WEND
Slav in Saxony .... SORB
slave .... ESNE, SERF, THRALL
slave, fugitive ..... MAROON
slave, Spartan .... HELOT
sled, Swiss .... LUGE
sled to haul logs ...... TODE
sleep ...... NAP, NOD, DOZE
sleep, deep .... SOPOR
sleep lightly .... DOZE
b sleeping .... DORMANT
sleeping place BED, COT, BERTH
sleeping sickness fly .. TSETSE
sleeve, large .... DOLMAN
sleigh .... PUNG
sleight-of-hand ...... MAGIC
slender .... LANK, LEAN,
SLIM, THIN, REEDY
slender woman .... SYLPH
slice, bacon .... RASHER
slice of meat .... COLP
slice, thick .... SLAB
slick .... LOY
slide .... SKID, SLUE
sliding door, Jap. ... FUSUMA
sliding piece .... CAM
sliding valve .... PISTON
slight .... MERE, SLIM, FAINT
slight intentionally SLUR, SNUB
slimy .... OOZY
sling around .... SLUE
slip.ERR, BONER, GLIDE, LAPSE
slip by .... ELAPSE
slip out of course ...... SLUE
slip, plant .... CION, CUTTING
slipknot .... NOOSE
slipper .... MULE, MOYLE
slipper, P. I. .... CHINELA
slope ...... RAMP, GRADIENT
slope: fort. .... GLACIS

c slope of vein or lode ... HADE
slope: Scot .... BRAE
slope of land .... VERSANT
slope, steep .... SCARP, ESCARP
sloping edge
BASIL, BEZEL, BEZIL
sloth, three-toed .... AI
sloth, two-toed .... UNAU
slouch: Scot. .... LOUCH
slow .... POKY
slow loris .... KOKAM
slow: music .. TARDO, LARGO
LENTO, ADAGIO, ANDANTE
slower: music .... RIT
sluggish .... DOPEY
sluice .... CLOW
slump .... RECESSION
slur over .... ELIDE
slushy mass .... POSH
sly look ...... LEER, OGLE
sly: old Eng. .... SLEE, SLOAN
sly: Scot: .... SLEE
smack ...... BUSS, KISS, SLAP
small .... WEE, TINY,
PETIT, PETTY, PETITE
small amount .. DRAM, MINIM
small arachnid .... MITE
small bottle .... VIAL
small bunch .... WISP
d small case .... ETUI
small cluster .... SPRIG
small coin .... MITE
small creature MITE, MINIMUS
small dog .... POM, PUG,
PUP, PEKE, FEIST
small goby, Atlantic ... MAPO
small: law .... PETIT
small marine animal .... SALP
small monkey .... LEMUR
small pearl .... PEARLET
small poem .... ODELET
small: Scot. .... SMA
small stream RUN, RILL, RILLET
small: suffix .... ING
small weight ... GRAM, MITE
smallest .... LEAST
smallest integer .... ONE
smallpox .... VARIOLA
smaragd .... EMERALD
smart .... STING
smart CHIC, ASTUTE, CLEVER
smartly dressed ... CHIC, TRIG
smear on .... DAUB
smell, disagreeable
OLID, REEK, FETOR
smelting mixture ...... MATTE
smelting waste .. SLAG, DROSS
smirch .... SULLY
smith, aided Siegfried .. MIME

148

smock .... CAMISE
smoke .... FUME, REEK
smoke-colored .... FUMOUS
smoke, wisp of .... FLOC
smoked beef ...... PASTRAMI
smokeless powder ..... FILITE
smoking .... AREEK
smoking pipe ... BRIAR, BRIER
smoking pipe, Oriental
              HOOKAH, NARGILE
smoky .... FUMID
smooth
    EVEN, IRON, LEVEL, PREEN
smooth-breathing ...... LENE
smooth, make ..... LEVIGATE
smooth: phonetics ..... LENE
smooth-spoken .... GLIB
smoothing tool .... PLANE
snail, large.WHELK, ABALONE
snail, marine .... TRITON
snake ..... ASP, BOA, ADDER,
    VIPER, PYTHON, REPTILE
snake, Amer. .. ADDER, RACER
snake-bite antidote
              GUACO, CEDRON
snake, black .... RACER
snake charmer's clarinet BEEN
snake-haired woman GORGON,
    MEDUSA, STHENO, EURYALE
snake, India .... COBRA,
    KRAIT, DABOIA, DABOYA
snake-like .... SINUOUS
snake, S. Amer. ...... ABOMA
snake, tree .... LORA
snake, venomous, Ind..BONGAR
snakes, pert. to ..... OPHIOID
snakebird .... DARTER
snakeroot, white ..... STEVIA
snap up bargains ...... SNUP
snapper .... SESI, PARGO
snapper fish: Maori .. TAMURE
snapper: N. Z. ...... TAMURE
snare .. GIN, NET, WEB, TRAP
snarl .... GNAR, GNARR
snatch .... GRAB, SEIZE
sneer.GIBE, JIBE, FLEER, SCOFF
sniff .... NOSE
snipe, Europ. .... BLEATER
snipe's cry .... SCAPE
snoring .... STERTOR
snow field, Alpine.FIRN, NEVE
snow goose genus ...... CHEN
snow, ground down .... LOLLY
snow house
    IGLU, IGLOE, IGLOO, IGLOU
snow leopard .... OUNCE
snow lily .... VIOLET
snow, living in .... NIVAL
snow mouse .... VOLE

snow panther .... OUNCE
snow runner .... SKI, SKEE
snow: Scot. .... SNA
SNOW WHITE
            see SEVEN DWARFS
snuff .... RAPPEE
snuffbox bean
    CACOON, MACKAYBEAN
snug .... COSY, COZY
snuggery .... NEST
so .... THUS, TRUE, VERY
so be it! .... AMEN
so much: music ...... TANTO
so: Scot. .... SAE
soak .... RET, SOG, SOP, WET
soak flax .... RET
soap, fine .... CASTILE
soap-frame bar .... SESS
soap: pharm. .... SAPO
soap plant .... AMOLE
soap substitute ...... AMOLE
soap vine .... GOGO
soapstone .... TALC
soapy mineral .... TALC
sober .... GRAVE, STAID
social affair .... TEA
social division ...... CASTE
social unit or group .... SEPT
society, entrance into .. DEBUT
society swell .... NOB
sock, Jap. .... TABI
sock, Rom. .... UDO
sod .... TURF
sodium alum .... MENDOZITE
sodium carbonate .... TRONA
sodium chloride ...... SALT
sodium chloride: pharm. .. SAL
sodium compound ..... SODA
sodium nitrate .. NITER, NITRE
sofa .... DIVAN
soft
    LOW, EASY, WAXY, TENDER
soft area on bill .... CERE
soft drink
    ADE, POP, COLA, SODA
soft feathers ... DOWN, EIDER
soft ice from floes ..... LOLLY
soft job ..... SNAP, SINECURE
soft mass .... WAD
soft palate .... VELUM
soft palate lobe ...... UVULA
soft palate, pert. to
            VELAR, UVULAR
soft palates .... VELA
soft-spoken .... MEALY
soften in temper ..... RELENT
softly: music .... SOAVE
soil: comb. form .... AGRO
soil, organic part .... HUMUS

149

Soil

soil, rich .... **LOAM**
soil, sticky .. **GOMBO, GUMBO**
soil, type of .... **PEDOCAL**
solar disc ...... **ATEN, ATON**
solar over lunar year,
    excess of .... **EPACT**
soldier: Am. Rev. .. **BUCKSKIN**
soldier, Austral., N. Z. **ANZAC**
soldier, Brit. .... **ATKINS**
soldier, former .... **LANCER**
soldier, Gr. .... **HOPLITE**
soldier, Indo-Brit. ..... **SEPOY**
soldier, native India ... **SEPOY**
soldier's shelter ..... **FOXHOLE**
sole .... **PELMA**
sole of foot .... **VOLA**
sole of plow .... **SLADE**
solemn declaration.**VOW, OATH**
solicit .... **BEG, URGE,
                COURT, CANVASS**
solicitor's chamber ...... **INN**
solicitude .... **CARE**
solid .... **CONE, CUBE, PRISM**
solid, become **GEL, SET, HARDEN**
solid: comb. form .... **STEREO**
solidify .. **GEL, SET, HARDEN**
solitary .... **LONE, ONLY, SOLE**
solo .... **ARIA**
Solomon's aid giver ... **HIRAM**
Solomon's temple rebuilder
                        HIRAM
solution .... **KEY**
solution, strength of
                TITER, TITRE
solvent .... **ACETONE**
solvent, treat with .. **SOLUTIZE**
some .... **ANY**
somite .... **MEROSOME**
son: Fr. .... **FILS**
son-in-law .... **GENER**
son: Ir. .... **MAC**
son of .... **MAC**
son of Agrippina .... **NERO**
son of Joktan .... **OPHIR**
son of Reuben .... **PALLU**
son of: Scot. .... **MAC**
song ...... **LAY, ODE, DITE,
            DITTY, MELOS, TROLL**
song, Christmas
        NOEL, CAROL, WASSAIL
song for solo voices ..... **GLEE**
song: Ger. .... **LIED**
song, Hawaiian .... **MELE**
song, Jap. .... **UTA**
song, morning: poet. .. **MATIN**
song, of a .... **MELIC**
song of praise, joy
        PEAN, PAEAN, ANTHEM
"Song of the South" Uncle
                        REMUS

song, operatic .... **ARIA**
song, religious
        HYMN, CHANT, ANTHEM
song, sacred
        HYMN, CHANT, ANTHEM
song, sad .... **DIRGE**
song: Scot. .... **STROUD**
song, simple .... **DITTY**
song, Sp. .... **CANCION**
song thrush ... **MAVIE, MAVIS**
sonship .... **FILIETY**
soon .... **ANON**
sooner .... **ERE, ERER**
soot .... **COOM, SMUT**
soot: old Eng. .... **SOTE**
soothe .... **EASE, LULL**
soothing **ANODYNE, LENITIVE**
soothsayer .... **SEER**
Sophocles, play by ... **OEDIPUS**
soprano, prima donna .. **ALDA,
            BORI, PONS, RISE,
        RAISA, CALLAS, STEBER**
sora bird .... **RAIL**
sorceress .... **CIRCE**
sorceress, Hindu .... **USHA**
sorceress, myth. .... **LAMIA**
sorceress, "Odyssey," Greek
                        CIRCE
sorcery, W. Ind.
            OBE, OBI, OBEAH
sore, make .... **RANKLE**
sore: Scot. .... **SAIR**
sorghum variety .... **MILO**
sorrow ..... **DOLOR, REMORSE**
sorrow, feel
        RUE, LAMENT, REPENT
sorrowful . **SAD, BLUE, DOLENT**
sort .... **KIND,
            CLASS, GROUP, SPECIES**
sortie .... **SALLY**
sortilege .... **LOT**
sorting machine ..... **GRADER**
soul .... **ANIMA**
soul, Egyp. .... **BA, KA**
soul, Hindu .. **ATMA, ATMAN**
sound .. **TONE, NOISE, VALID**
sound, kind of ...... **PALATAL**
sound loudly .. **BLARE, LARUM**
sound, monotonous
                HUM, DRONE
sound perception .... **EAR**
sound, pert. to ...... **SONANT**
sound reasoning .... **LOGIC**
sound, resemblance of
                    ASSONANT
sound, solid .... **KLOP**
sound the ocean
                PLUMB, FATHOM

a sound waves, of ...... AUDIO
sound, without ..... ASONANT
sounding .... SONANT
soundless .... ASONANT
soup, heavy .. PUREE, POTAGE
soup spoon .... LADLE
soup, thick .... BISK,
    HOOSH, PUREE, BISQUE
soup vessel .... TUREEN
soupfin shark .... TOPE
sour .... ACID, ACERB,
    ACIDIC, ACETOSE
sour curdled milk: Nor. .. SKYR
sour-leaved plant ..... SORREL
sour milk drink. LEBAN, LEBEN
source, mineral .... ORE
source, obsidian's ...... LAVA
soursop .... ANNONA
south: Sp. .... SUR
South African .... BOER
SOUTH AFRICA ..... see also
    SPECIAL SECTION
S. Afr. assembly .... RAAD
S. Afr. dialect .... TAAL
S. Afr. Dutch .... BOER, TAAL
S. Afr. garter snake .... ELAPS
S. Afr. grass country .... VELD
S. Afr. greenhorn .... IKONA
S. Afr. gully .... DONGA
S. Afr. "out" .... UIT
b S. Afr. town .... STAD
S. Afr. village .... KRAAL
SOUTH AMERICA .... see also
    SPECIAL SECTION
South American animal . TAPIR
S. Amer. bird ... GUAN, JACU,
    SYLPH, TURCO, SERIEMA
S. Amer. game bird TINAMOU
S. Amer. Indian group .... GES
S. Amer. lizard .... TEJU
S. Amer. tree VERA, CEBIL, FOTUI
S. Amer. ungulate .... TAPIR
"South Pacific" hero .... EMILE
Southern Cross constellation
    CRUX
Southern France .... MIDI
Southern river .... PEEDEE
Southern state: abbr. .... ALA
Southwest river .... RED
sovereign (coin) ...... SKIV
sovereignty .... EMPERY
SOVIET .... see also RUSSIAN
Soviet news agency ..... TASS
Soviet newspaper .... PRAVDA
sow .... PIG, GILT
sow .... SEED, PLANT
sow: Prov. Eng. .... YELT
sow: Scot. .... SOO
sower .... SEEDER
sown: her. .... SEME
soybean .... SOJA, SOYA

c spa, Bohemian .... BILIN
spa, Eng. .... BATH
spa, Ger. .... EMS, BADEN
space between bird's eye
    and bill .... LORA, LORE,
    LORUM
space between triglyphs
    METOPE
space, small AREOLA, AREOLE
spaces on bird's face
    LORAE, LORES
spade .... LOY, SHOVEL
spade, narrow .... LOY, SPUD
spade-shaped .... PALACEOUS
spade, turf .... SLANE
Spain, ancient .... IBERIA
SPANISH see also SPAIN, SPE-
    CIAL SECTION
SP. ARTIST
        see SP. PAINTER
Sp. belle .... MAJA
Sp. cellist .... CASALS
Sp. coin, old .... PISTOLE
Sp. dance .... JOTA, BOLERO
Sp. epic .... CID
Sp. explorer
    CORTEZ, BALBOA, CORTES
d Sp. fabric .... CREA
Sp. fortress commander .. CAID
Sp. game of ball .... PELOTA
Sp. general, duke. ALBA, ALVA
Sp. hero .... CID
Sp. kettle .... OLLA
Sp. lady ..... DONA, SENORA
Sp. length unit .... VARA
Sp. man .... DON, SENOR
Sp. nun .... AVILA
Sp. painter
    GOYA, MIRO, SERT, PICASSO
Sp. poet .... ENCINA
Sp. pot .... OLLA
Sp. title. DON, SENOR, SENORA

SPANISH WORDS:
    (tilde omitted throughout)
    abbey .... ABADIA
    afternoon .... TARDE
    annatto seeds ... ACHIOTE
    another .... OTRO
    article .... EL, LA, LAS,
        LOS, UNO
    ass .... ASNO
    aunt .... TIA
    bay .... BAHIA
    bean .... HABA
    before .... ANTES
    being .... ENTE
    black .... NEGRA
    blue .... AZUL
    box canyon .... CAJON

151

Spanish

a

boy .... NINO
bravo! .... OLE
bull .... TORO
but .... PERO
canal .... CANO
chaperon . DUENA, DUENNA
chest .... CAJETA
chief .... JEFE, ADALID
child .... NINO
church .... IGLESIA
city .... CIUDAD
clay building . ADOBE, TAPIA
cloak .... CAPA
clothes .... ROPA
corral .... ATAJO
cut .... TAJO
day .... DIA
dining hall .... SALA
dove .... PALOMA
drawing room .... SALA
estuary .... RIA
evening .... TARDE
evil .... MALO
first .... PRIMUS
for .... POR
friend .... AMIGO
funds .... CAJA
girl .... NINA
God .... DIOS
gold .... ORO

b

good-bye .... ADIOS
grass fiber rope ...... SOGA
grille .... REJA
gulch .... ARROYO
gypsy .... GITANO
hall .... SALA
hamlet .... ALDA
harbor entrance ..... BOCA
health .... SANO
hello .... HOLLA
hill . ALTO, CERRO, MORRO
hillside .... FALDA
hotel .... POSADA
house .... CASA
Indian .... INDIO
inlet .... RIA, ESTERO
jail keeper .... CAID
judge .... JUEZ
king .... REY
lady .... DAMA
lake .... LAGO
landmark .... SENAL
latter .... ESTE
lawsuit .... ACTO
letter .... CARTA
lime .... LIMA
love .... AMOR
man .... HOMBRE
manservant .... MOZO
mayor .. ALCADE, ALCALDE

c

mouth .... BOCA
movie house .... CINE
meadow .... VEGA
my .... MIO
of .... DE
open space .... COSO
other .... OTRA
parish priest .... CURA
peak .... PICO
people .... GENTE
pine .... PINO
pole .... PALO
pole, wooden ...... PALO
porridge .... ATOLE
post office ...... CORREO
pot .... OLLA
priest .... CURA, PADRE
queen .... REINA
ragged person ...... ROTO
raisin .... PASA
red .... ROJO
river .... RIO
road .... CAMINO
room .... SALA
rum .... RON
saint, feminine .... SANTA
she .... ELLA
silver .... PLATA
six .... SEIS
snake .... CULEBRA
song .... CANCION
south .... SUR
street ...... CALLE, CALLI
sweet potato ..... CAMOTE
tall .... ALTA
this .... ESTA, ESTE
three .... TRES
to be .... SER, ESTE
tomorrow .... MANANA
trench .... TAJO
uncle .... TIO
very .... MUY
water .... AGUA
wax .... CERA
wit .... SAL
with .... DE
work .... OBRA
yes .... SI
you .... TE

spar ...... BOX, BOOM, GAFF,
         MAST, YARD, SPRIT
spar for colors .... GAFF
spar, heavy .... BARITE
spar, loading .... STEEVE
spar, small .... SPRIT
spare .... LEAN, EXTRA,
         GAUNT, LENTEN
sparkle .... GLITTER
sparkling, as wine . MOUSSEUX
sparrow, hedge ...... DONEY

d (markers in left margin beside respective sections)

152

a Sparta queen .... LEDA
Spartan army division .. MORA
Spartan magistrate ... EPHOR
spasm .... FIT, TIC, JERK
spawning place .... REDD
speak

UTTER, ORATE, DECLAIM

speak: comb. form ..... LALO
speak, inability to .. ALALIA
speak theatrically .... EMOTE
speaker ... ORATOR, LOCUTOR
speaking tube, pilot's.GOSPORT
spear .... DART, LANCE
spear, Afr. ASSAGAI, ASSEGAI
spear, fish .... GIG, GAFF
spear-like weapon PIKE, LANCE
spear-shaped ...... HASTATE
spear, 3-prong ...... TRIDENT
spear thrower, Austral.

WOMERA

special: Moslem law
KHAS, KHASS

species .... KIND, SORT
specific date .... DAY
specified time .... DATE
specimen .... SAMPLE
speck .... DOT, MOTE, FLECK
speckle .... DOT, STIPPLE
spectacle .... PAGEANT
b specter ...... BOGY, BOGEY,
GHOST, SHADE
speech ... LECTURE, ORATION
speech, art of ..... RHETORIC
speech defect

LISP, ALOGIA, STAMMER

speech goddess, Hindu
VAC, DEVI, VACH

speech, local .... PATOIS
speech, long .... SPIEL
speech, loss of ...... APHASIA
speech peculiarity ..... IDIOM
speech, violent ...... TIRADE
speechless ...... DUMB, MUTE
speed ..... HIE, RUN, PACE,
RACE, HASTE, HASTEN,
RAPIDITY

speed, at full .... AMAIN
spelt .... ADOR, EMMER
Spenser heroine .... UNA
Spenser's name for Ireland
IRENA

sphere .... ORB
sphere of action ..... ARENA
spice .... MACE
spice ball .... FAGOT, FAGGOT
spicknel .... MEU, MEW
spicy .... RACY
spider crab genus MAIA, MAJA
spider fluid: Pharm. ARANEIN

c spider monkey
QUATA, ATELES, COAITA
spider nest .... NIDUS
spigot .... TAP
spike .... EAR, GAD, BROB
spikenard .... NARD
spin

BIRL, REEL, TWIRL, ROTATE

spinal column ... AXIS, AXON
spinal cord .... MYELON
spinal membrane ...... DURA
spindle .... COP, AXLE
spindle, yarn .... HASP
spine .... AXIS, AXON
spine bones .... SACRA
spine, slender .... SETA
spineless cactus ...... CHAUTE
spiniform .... SPINATE
spinning jenny .... MULE
spiny shrub genus ..... ULEX
spiral formation ..... VOLUTE
spire ornament .... EPI
spirit .... ELAN, SOUL, METAL
spirit: Egyp. myth ..... BA, KA
spirit: Ger. .... GEIST
spirit, Ir. BANSHEE, BANSHIE
spirit lamp .... ETNA
spirit, Moslem ..... JIN, JINN,
GENIE, GENII, JINNI, JINNEE
spirit of air .... ARIEL
spirit of evil .. DEMON, DEVIL
d spirit of man: Egypt ..... AKH
spirit raiser .. ELATER, ELATOR
spirits and water ...... GROG
spirits of the dead .... MANES
spirited .... EAGER, CONMOTO
spirited horse .... STEED
spiritual body: Egypt. ... SAHU
spiritual struggle ..... PENIEL
spiritualist meeting ... SEANCE
splash .... LAP
spleen .... MILT
splendid .... GRAND
splendor .... ECLAT
splendor, goddess of: Hindu
UMA
split .... RIT, RENT, RIVE,
CLEFT, RIVEN, CLEAVE
split pulse .... DAL
spoil .... ROT, BOTCH
spoil, as eggs .... ADDLE
spoils of war .... LOOT
spoken .... ORAL
spoken word .... AGRAPH
spokes, having .... RADIAL
sponge, calcareous ... LEUCON
sponge gourd ... LOOF, LOOFA
sponge on ..... MUMP, LEACH
sponge spicule, bow-shaped
OXEA, TOXA, PINULUS
sponge, young .... ASCON

153

a

spongewood .... **SOLA**
sponsor .... **PATRON**
sponsorship ...... **EGIS, AEGIS**
spool .... **REEL**
spore .... **SEED**
spore cluster .... **SORUS**
spore fruit of rust fungi
**AECIA, TELIA, AECIUM,
TELIUM**
spore sac, fungus **ASCI, ASCUS**
sport .... **RUX, GAME,
GOLF, PLAY, POLO**
sports arena **STADIA, STADIUM**
sports center ... **RINK, ARENA**
sports hall .... **GYM**
spot in mineral ..... **MACLE**
spot on card .... **PIP**
spotted .... **PIED, PINTO,
DAPPLED, MACULOSE**
spotted cavy .... **PACA**
spotted deer **KAKAR, CHITAL**
spotted moth ...... **FORESTER**
spotted sting-ray ..... **OBISPO**
spotted, to make
DAPPLE, STIPPLE
spouse .... **MATE, WIFE**
spray .... **ATOMIZE**
spray, sea .... **LIPPER**

b

spread .... **TED**
spread by peening .... **RIVET**
spread by report
BRUIT, NORATE
spread out .... **FAN**
spread rumor .... **GOSSIP**
spread the word .... **TELL**
spread to dry, as hay ... **TED**
sprightly .... **PERT, PEART**
spring .... **SPA**
spring back .... **RESILE**
spring: Bible .... **AIN**
spring-like .... **VERNAL**
spring: old Eng. .... **KELD**
spring, mineral .... **SPA**
spring rice, India ...... **BORO**
spring, small .... **SEEP**
springs, warm ...... **THERMAE**
springboard .... **BATULE**
sprinkle **DEG, WATER, SPARGE**
sprinkling: her. ...... **SEME**
sprint .... **RUN, RACE**
sprite .. **ELF, FAY, PIXY, PIXIE**
sprite, tricksy .... **ARIEL**
sprout ... **CION, GROW, SCION**
spruce .... **TRIG, TRIM, NATTY**
spruce, Jap. .... **YEDDO**
spruce, white ...... **EPINETTE**
spume .... **FOAM**
spun wool .... **YARN**
spur .... **GAD, GOAD, CALCAR**
spur of mountain ..... **ARETE**

c

spur part .... **ROWEL**
spur wheel .... **ROWEL**
spurs, having .... **CALCARATE**
spurt .... **JET, GUSH**
spy, garment-trade slang **KEEK**
spy, British, Revolution **ANDRE**
squama .... **ALULA**
squander .... **SPEND**
square dance .... **REEL**
square-meshed net ..... **LACIS**
squash .... **PEPO,
CRUSH, GOURD, FLATTEN**
squash bug .... **ANASA**
squaw .... **MAHALA**
squawfish .... **CHUB**
squid genus .... **LOLIGO**
squirrel fur, Siberian
CALABAR, CALABER
squirrel, ground Europ. .. **SISEL**
squirrel-like animal **DORMOUSE**
squirrel skin .... **VAIR**
squirrel's nest ... **DRAY, DREY**
ST. .... see **SAINT**
stab .... **GORE**
stabilize .... **STEADY**
stable .... **FIRM, SOLID**
stable compartment .... **STALL**
stable-keeper, royal .. **AVENER**
stables, royal .... **MEWS**
stableman .... **OSTLER**

d

stack of hay .... **RICK**
staff .... **ROD, MACE**
staff-bearer .... **MACER**
staff, bishop's ...... **CROSIER**
staff of office .... **MACE**
staff, royal **SCEPTER, SCEPTRE**
stag ..... **DEER, HART, MALE**
stage direction
MANET, SENET, EXEUNT
stage equipment ...... **PROPS**
stage extra ..... **SUPE, SUPER**
stage horn signal .... **SENNET**
stage setting .... **SCENE**
stage whisper .... **ASIDE**
stagger .... **REEL**
stagger: Prov. Eng. ...... **STOT**
stagnation .... **STASIS**
stagnation, blood ..... **STASIS**
stain, **DYE, SOIL, SPOT, TASH**
stair part ..... **RISER, TREAD**
stair post .... **NEWEL**
staircase spindle .... **SPEEL**
stake .... **ANTE, WAGER**
stake, like a .... **PALAR**
stake, pointed ..... **PALISADE**
stake, poker .... **ANTE**
stakes .... **POT**
stakes, —, Epsom Downs Race
OAKS
stale .... **TRITE**
stalk .... **STEM**

a stalk, flower .. **SCAPE, PEDICEL**
stalk, frond .... **STIPE**
stalk, plant .... **CAULIS**
stalk, short .... **STIPE**
stalk, sugarcane ..... **RATOON**
stall in mud .... **STOG**
stammer .... **HAW, HEM**
stammering sound .... **ER**
stamp .... **MARK, SIGIL**
stamp battery block ..... **VOL**
stamp of approval .... **OK**
stamp-sheet part .... **PANE**
stamping device .... **DIE**
stamping machine .... **DATER**
stanch .... **STEM**
stand .... **RISE**
stand .. **BEAR, ABIDE, ENDURE**
stand, cuplike .... **ZARF**
stand in awe of .... **FEAR**
stand, small
     TABORET, TAROURET
stand, 3-legged **TRIPOD, TRIVET**
standard .. **PAR, FLAG, ENSIGN**
standard.**NORM, TYPE, NORMA**
standard of chemical strength
                            TITER
standard, Turk .... **ALEM**
standing .... **STATUS**
stannum .... **TIN**
stanza, last .... **ENVOY**
b stanza, Nor. .... **STEV**
stanza, part of .... **STAVE**
star .... **ASTRO**
star, blue .... **VEGA**
star, brightest .... **COR**
star cluster, distant
        NEBULA, NEBULAE
star, day .... **SUN**
star, evening .... **VENUS,**
     HESPER, VESPER, HESPERUS
star facet .... **PANE**
star, fixed .... **SUN, ALYA**
star: Fr. .... **ETOILE**
star in Aquarius .... **SKAT**
star in Aquilla .... **ALTAIR**
star in Argo .... **NAOS**
star in Big Dipper ..... **PHAD**
star in Bootes .... **IZAR**
star in Cetus .... **MIRA**
star in Cygenus **SADR, DENEB**
star in Draco .... **ADIB, JUZA**
star in Eridanus ... **AZHA, BEID**
star in Leo .. **DUHR, REGULUS**
star in Lyra ... **VEGA, WEGA**
star in Orion .... **RIGEL**
star in Pegasus **ENIF, MATAR**
star in Pleiades .... **MAIA**
   star in Perseus .... **ATIK**
   star in Scorpio ...... **ANTARES**

c star in Serpens .... **ALYA**
star in Taurus ..**NATH, PLEIAD**
star in Virgo .... **SPICA**
star near Mizar .... **ALCOR**
star, new .... **NOVA**
star-shaped .... **STELLATE**
star-shaped spicule
            ACTER, ACTINE
star, temporary .... **NOVA**
stars, dotted with ..... **SEME**
stars, pert. to ...... **ASTRAL**
starch .... **AMYL, ARUM,**
     SAGO, FARINA, CASSAVA
starchy rootstock ...... **TARO**
starfish .... **ASTEROID**
stark mad .... **RAVING**
starnose .... **MOLE**
— Starr, comic strip character
                       BRENDA
starred lizard **AGAMA, HARDIM**
start ... **BEGIN, SALLY, ROUSE**
starvation .... **INEDIA**
starwort .... **ASTER**
state .... **AVER**
STATE .. see also **GAZETTEER**
STATE FLOWERS . see page 208
state, New England: abbr. .. **RI**
state of affairs .... **PASS**
state, pert. to .... **CIVIL**
d state of: suffix .... **ERY**
state of being: suffix .... **URE**
state precisely .... **SPECIFY**
stately home .. **DOME, ESTATE**
statements, confused
                     RIGMAROLE
statesman, Brit. .... **PITT**
station .. **POST, DEPOT, PLACE**
stationary ..... **FIXED, STATIC**
stationary motor part **STATOR**
statistician .... **STATIST**
statute .... **ACT, LAW**
stave, barrel .... **LAG**
stay .... **WAIT, TARRY**
stay rope .... **GUY**
stays .... **CORSET**
stead .... **LIEU, PLACE**
steal **COP, ROB, GLOM, SNITCH**
steal cattle .... **RUSTLE**
steal: Eng. .... **GLOM**
steal, Eng. dialect ...... **NIM**
steel beam .... **GIRDER**
steel: Ger. .... **STAHL**
steel splint, armor skirt
            TACE, TASSE, TASSET
steep .... **RET, SOP**
steep .... **SHEER**
steep in lime .... **BOWK**
steer wildly .... **YAW**
steer, young: Prov. Eng. .. **STOT**

155

Steering

steering, direct ship's
COND, CONN
steersman .... COX
stellar ...... ASTRAL, STARRY
stem
CION, CORM, SCAPE, STALK
stem, fungus .... STIPE
stem, hollow .... CANE
stem, jointed .... CULM
stem of hop .... BINE
stem, rudimentary .. CAULICLE
stem, ship's .... PROW
stench .... ODOR, FETOR
stentorian .... LOUD
step .... GRADE, PHASE
step ... PACE, STAIR, TREAD
step, dance ..... PAS, CHASSE
step up to mark .... TOE
step, upright part of .. RISER
steps, outdoor .... PERRON
steps over fence ...... STILE
steppes, storm on ..... BURAN
stern GRIM, HARSH, AUSTERE
steward: Scot. ..... MORMAOR
stick .. BAR, BAT, ROD, CANE,
WAND, BATON, MUNDLE
stick .... GLUE,
PASTE, ADHERE, CLEAVE
stick, conductor's ..... BATON
stick together ...... COHERE
stick used in hurling .. CAMAN
sticks, bundle of ...... FAGOT
stickler for formality .. TAPIST
sticky substance ... GOO, GUM
stiffly nice .... PRIM
stigma .... BRAND
stigmatic point of mango NAK
still .... BUT, YET
stimulant, coffee
CAFFEIN, CAFFEINE
stimulant, tea THEIN, THEINE
stimulate .. FAN, WHET, ELATE
sting .... BITE, SMART
stinging ant .... KELEP
stinging herb .... NETTLE
stingy .... MEAN
stint .... TASK
stipend, church ..... PREBEND
stipend: Scot. .... ANNAT
stipulation .... CLAUSE
stir .. ADO, MIX, TODO, ROUSE
stir up .... RILE, ROIL
stitch .... PUNTO
stitchbird .... IHI
stitched fold .... TUCK
stithy .... ANVIL
stock .... BREED
stock .... STORE
stock exchange, membership in
SEAT
stock exchange, Paris BOURSE

stock market crash .... PANIC
stockade: Russ. .... ETAPE
stocking run .... LADDER
stockings .... HOSE
stocky .... STUB
stolen goods .... SWAG
stomach .... MAW, CRAW
stomach division, ruminant's
OMASUM
stomach, first ...... RUMEN
stomach, ruminant's ... TRIPE
stone .. AGATE, LAPIS, SLATE
Stone Age tool .... CELT,
EOLITH, NEOLITH
stone, aquamarine .... BERYL
stone, breastplate .... JASPER
stone chest .... CIST
stone chip .... SPALL
stone: comb. form ..... LITH
stone-cutter's chisel .... DROVE
stone fruit .... DRUPE
stone, green . BERYL, OLIVINE
stone hammer .... MASH
stone, hard ...... ADAMANT
stone heap ..... CARN, KARN,
CAIRN, CARNE, CAIRNE
stone, hollow .... GEODE
stone implement ...... CELT,
EOLITH, NEOLITH
stone, like a .... LITHOID
stone, monument ..... MENHIR
stone paving block ..... SETT
stone pillar .... STELE
stone, red ..... SARD, SPINEL
stone roller fish ...... TOTER
stone, rough .... RUBBLE
stone: Scot. .... STEAN, STEEN
stone set .... PAVER
stone, squared ...... ASHLAR
stone to death ..... LAPIDATE
stone, woman turned to NIOBE
stone worker .... MASON
stone, yellow TOPAZ, CITRINE
stonecrop
ORPIN, SEDUM, ORPINE
stonecutter MASON, LAPICIDE
stonecutter's chisel ... DROVE
stoneware: Fr. .... GRES
stool pigeon .... NARK
stop .... DAM, BALK, HALT,
STEM, WHOA, DESIST
stop, as engine .. CONK, STALL
stop by accident ..... STALL
stop: naut. ... AVAST, BELAY
stop short .... BALK
stoppage .... JAM
stopper .... BUNG, PLUG
storage battery plate ... GRID
storage place BIN, BARN SILO
store, army .... CANTEEN
store fodder .... ENSILE

156

a storehouse .... ETAPE
storehouse, army ..... DEPOT
storehouse, India .... GOLA
storehouse, public ..... ETAPE
stork .... MARABOU
storm FUME, FURY, RAGE, RAVE
storm, away from ...... ALEE
storm, dust .... SIMOON
storm: Fr. .... ORAGE
storm god, Babyl. ZU, ADAD, ADDA, ADDU
story, Norse .... SAGA
story, short .... CONTE
stoss, opposite of .... LEE
stout .... BURLY
stout, kind of .... PORTER
stove ...... ETNA, RANGE
"Stowe" character
EVA, TOM, TOPSY
straight .... DIRECT
straight-edge .... RULER
strain .... EXERT
strained .... TENSE
strainer .... SIEVE
strainer, wool cloth ... TAMIS
Straits Settlement region
PENANG
strange .... ODD
strap on falcon's leg .... JESS
strap-shaped .... LORATE
b strass .... PASTE
stratagem .... RUSE, WILE
stratagem, sudden ...... COUP
stratum .... LAYER
straw hat ...... BAKU, MILAN
stray .... ERR
stray .... WAIF
stray animal .... CAVY
streak .... ROE, LINE, VEIN, STRIA, STRAKE, STRIAE
streaky .... LINY, ROWY
stream
FLOW, RILL, BOURN, RIVER
streamlet ...... RILL, RUNNEL
street Arab .... GAMIN
street: It., Sp. .. CALLE, CALLI
street, narrow .... LANE
street roisterer .... MUN
street urchin .... ARAB
street, Venice water .. RIO, RII
strength .... POWER
strengthening .... ROBORANT
stress .... ICTUS
stressed beat, syllable .. ARSIS
stretch: Scot. .... STENT
stretched out ...... PROLATE
stretcher .... LITTER
stretching frame .... TENTER, STENTER
strewn with flowers: Her. SEME

c strife .... WAR
strife, civil .... STASIS
strike .. BAT, HIT, RAP, CONK, SLOG, SLUG, SOCK, SWAT, WHAM, SMITE
strikebreaker ..... FINK, SCAB
striking effect .... ECLAT
string of mules .... ATAJO
stringy .... ROPY
strip .. BARE, DIVEST, STRAKE
strip of land ... DOAB, DUAB
strip of wood .... LATH
strip off skin .... FLAY
strip, oxhide, S. Afr. ... RIEM
strip, wood, metal ... SPLINE
stripe .... BAR, BAND, WALE, WEAL, STREAK
stripe of color: zool. .. PLAGA
stripling .... BOY, LAD
strive .... AIM, VIE
strobile .... CONE
stroke .... FIT, ICTUS
stroke, brilliant .... COUP
stroll .... AMBLE
strong-arm man ...... GOON
strong, as cigars .... MADURO
strong desire .... HUNGER
strong man .... SAMSON
strong man, Gr. ...... ATLAS
strong point .... FORTE
d strong-scented ... OLID, RANK
strongbox .... SAFE
stronghold .. FORT, SION, ZION
struck with horror ... AGHAST
structure, tall .... TOWER
struggle .... COPE
struggle helplessly. FLOUNDER
struggled .... HOVE
stud .... BOSS
student in charge ... MONITOR
studio, art .... ATELIER
study ...... CON, PORE, READ
study group .... SEMINAR
stuff .... PAD, RAM, CRAM
stuffing .... KAPOK
stum .... MUST
stumble: prov. Eng. .... STOT
stump of branch ...... SKEG
stunted trees .... SCRUB
stupefied .... MAZED
stupefy .... DAZE, MAZE, STUN, BESOT
stupid ...... CRASS, DENSE
stupid person ...... ASS, OAF
CLOD, COOT, DOLT, LOON, LOUT, LOWN, MOKE
stupor .... COMA, SOPOR
sturgeon, small ..... STERLET
style .... MODE, NAME
style of art .... DADA, GENRE

157

Stylet

a
stylet, surgical	**TROCAR**
stymie	**IMPEDE**
Styx ferryman	**CHARON**
subbase	**PLINTH**
subdued shade	**PASTEL**
subject	**TOPIC, VASSAL**
subject in grammar	**NOUN**
subjoin	**ADD**
sublime	**NOBLE**
submarine	**PIGBOAT, SNORKEL**
submit	**BOW, YIELD**
subordinate	**MINOR, DEPENDENT**
subside	**EBB, SINK, ABATE, RELAPSE**
substance, lustrous	**METAL**
substances, class of	**LIPIN**
substantiate	**VERIFY**
substantive word	**NOUN**
substitute	**VICE, PROXY, ERSATZ**
substitute for: suffix	**ETTE**
subtle emanation	**AURA**
subtle variation	**NUANCE**
subtract	**DEDUCT**
subway, Eng.	**TUBE**
subway entrance	**KIOSK**
subway, Fr.	**METRO**
success	**HIT, WOW**

b
succession	**LINE**
successively	**AROW**
succinct	**TERSE**
succor	**AID**
succulent plant	**ALOE, HERB**
such	**SO**
sucking fish	**PEGA, REMORA**
Sudan lake	**CHAD**
Sudan native	**FUL**
Sudan Negroid	**SERE**
Sudan people	**HAUSA**
sudden attack: Med.	**ICTUS**
suet	**TALLOW**
suffer	**LET, BIDE**
suffer from hunger	**CLEM, STARVE**
suffer: Scot.	**DREE**
sufficient: poet.	**ENOW**

SUFFIXES:
act of	**TION**
action	**ANCE**
adjective	**ENT, IAL, INE, ISH, IST, ITE, OUS**
agent	**URE**
alcohol	**OL**
carbohydrate	**OSE**
chemical or chemistry	**ANE, ENE, IDE, INE, OLE, ONE, ENOL, ITOL, OLIC**

c
common ending	**ENT, INE, ING, ION**
common suffix	**ES, ESE, ESS, INE, IVE, ETTE, YNONE**
condition	**ATE, ILE, ISE, ANCE, SION, STER**
comparative	**IER, IOR**
compound	**ICAL, ILITY**
diminutive	**ET, IE, ULA, ULE, ETTE**
feminine	**INA, INE, ELLA**
feminine noun	**ESS**
follower	**IST, ITE**
forming nouns from verbs	**ER**
full of	**OSE**
inflammation	**ITIS**
inhabitant of	**ITE**
into	**EN**
like	**OID**
little	**ET**
made of	**EN**
make	**ISE**
medical	**IA, OMA**
mineral	**ITE, LITE**
native of	**ITE**
noun	**IA, OR, ATE, ENT, ERY, ESS, IER, ISE, IST, ITE, ANCY, ENCE, ENSE, STER**

d
noun ending	**STER**
noun forming diminutive	**CLE**
number	**TEEN**
or ordinal number	**ETH**
oil	**OL, OLE**
one who	**IST, STER**
one who does	**IST**
order of animals	**INI**
ordinal	**ETH**
origin, denoting	**OTE**
participle	**ING**
person	**ER**
plural	**(old EN), ES**
quality	**ANCE, ILITY**
rocks, of	**ITE, LITE**
science of	**ICS**
skin	**DERM**
small	**ING**
state of	**ERY, ANCE**
state of being	**URE**
substitute for	**ETTE**
superlative	**EST**
sympathizer	**ITE**
town	**TON**
tumor	**OMA**
verb	**ISE, ESCE**
with mineral names	**LITE**
zoological	**ATA**
Sufi disciple	**MURID**
sugar	**OSE, SUCROSE**
sugar cane disease	**ILIAU**

158

a sugar cane residue .. **BAGASSE**
  sugar, crude .... **GUR**
  sugar, fruit .... **KETOSE**
  sugar, raw .... **CASSONADE**
  sugar, simple .... **OSE**
  sugar source .... **CANE**
  suggestion .... **CUE, HINT**
  suit of mail .... **ARMOR**
  suitable.**APT, FIT, PAT, PROPER**
  suitcase ... **BAG, GRIP, VALISE**
  suitor .... **SWAIN**
  sullen .. **DOUR, GLUM, MOROSE**
  sullen, act .... **MOPE**
  sullen, be ...... **POUT, SULK**
  sully .... **SOIL, DIRTY**
  sultan, Turkish .... **SELIM**
  sultan's order .... **IRADE**
  sultan's residence ...... **SERAI**
  sultanate .... **OMAN**
  sultry .... **HUMID**
  Sulu Moslem .... **MORO**
  "sum," infinitive following **ESSE**
  sum paid as punishment .. **FINE**
  sumac genus .... **RHUS**
  sumac, P. I. .... **ANAM, ANAN**
  Sumatra squirrel shrew .. **TANA**
  Sumatra wildcat ...... **BALU**
  Sumatran silk .... **IKAT**
b "summa — laude" ...... **CUM**
  summary
        DIGEST, PRECIS, EPITOME
  summer: Fr. .... **ETE**
  summer-house
        ARBOR, PERGOLA
  summer, pert. to ..... **ESTIVAL**
  summit
        APEX, KNAP, PEAK, SPIRE
  summits .... **APICES**
  summon .... **CALL, CITE,**
        PAGE, CLEPE, EVOKE
  sun .... **SOL, HELIOS**
  sun apartments .... **SOLARIA**
  sun bittern .... **CAURALE**
  sun: comb. form ...... **HELIO**
  sun disk ...... **ATEN, ATON**
  sun-dried brick
        DOBE, DOBY, ADOBE, DOBIE
  sun god, Babyl. .. **UTU, UTUG,**
        BABBAR, SHAMASH
  sun god, Egypt. ..... **RA, TEM,**
        TUM, AMON, AMEN,
        AMUN, ATMU, ATUM
  sun god, Gr., Rom. ...... **SOL,**
        APOLLO, HELIOS
  sun god, Inca .... **INTI**
  sun, halo around .... **CORONA**
  sun, pert. to .... **SOLAR**
  sun porches .... **SOLARIA**
  sun tree, Jap. .... **HINOKI**

c sunbaked building
        DOBE, DOBY, ADOBE, DOBIE
  Sunday of Lent, 4th .. **LAETARE**
  sunder
        PART, REND, SPLIT, DIVIDE
  sundial, style of ..... **GNOMON**
  sunfish .... **BREAM**
  sunfish genus .... **MOLA**
  sunken fence ...... **AHA, HAHA**
  sunset, occurring at **ACRONICAL**
  sunspot center
        UMBRA, UMBRAE
  supercilious person ..... **SNOB**
  superfluous: Fr. .... **DE TROP**
  superintendent, office
        MANAGER
  superior, most .... **BEST, TOPS**
  superior quality: Fr. .... **LUXE**
  superiority, belief in .. **RACISM**
  superlative, absolute .. **ELATIVE**
  superlative ending ...... **EST**
  supernatural .... **OCCULT**
  supernatural being, Melanesia
        ADARO
  supernatural power, E. Afr. **NGAI**
  supernatural power, Polyn.
        MANA
  superscribe .... **DIRECT**
  superstition, object of
        FETICH, FETISH
d supper .... **TEA**
  supplication, make ..... **PRAY**
  supply ...... **STOCK, ENDUE**
  supply, fresh .... **RELAY**
  supply of horses ...... **REMUDA**
  support ...... **LEG, RIB, ABET,**
        BACK, PROP, BRACE
  support, one-legged .. **UNIPOD**
  suppose ... **ASSUME, IMAGINE**
  suppose: archaic .... **TROW**
  suppress ...... **ELIDE, QUASH**
  Supreme Being, Hebrew . **IHVH,**
        JHVH, JHWH, YHVH, YHWH
  surety agreement ...... **BOND**
  surf, roar of .... **ROTE**
  surface, attractive ... **VENEER**
  surface of gem .... **FACET**
  surface of a tool ...... **FACE**
  surfeit .... **CLOY, GLUT, SATE**
  surfeited .... **BLASE**
  surge .... **TIDE, BILLOW**
  surgeon's instrument .. **TREPAN,**
        TROCAR, ABLATOR, LE-
        VATOR, SCALPEL
  surgical thread .... **SETON**
  Surinam toad .... **PIPA**
  surly .... **GRUFF, SULLEN**
  surmise .. **INFER, GUESS, OPINE**
  surnamed: Fr. .... **DIT**

159

a surpass ...... **CAP, TOP, BEST**
surplice, chorister's .... **COTTA**
surplus ...... **EXTRA, EXCESS**
surrender
    CEDE, YIELD, DEDITION
surrender: law .... **REMISE**
surround **GIRD, BESET, INARM**
surrounding area ...... **ZONE**
surtout .... **COAT**
survey .... **MAP, POLL**
surveyor's assistant .. **RODMAN**
surveyor's instrument
    ROD, ALIDADE
surveyor's rod, sight on **TARGET**
Susa inhabitant ..... **ELAMITE**
suspend .... **HANG**
suspenders .... **BRACES**
suture .... **SEAM**
svelte .... **SLIM, TRIM**
swab .... **MOP**
swain .... **LOVER**
swallow **BOLT, GULP, MARTIN**
swallow, sea .... **TERN**
swamp .... **BOG, FEN, MARSH,**
    MORASS, SLEW, SLOO, SLUE
swamp gas .. **MIASM, MIASMA**
swamp, S. Afr. ... **VLEI, VLEY**
swampy belt, India ..... **TERAI**
swan, female .... **PEN**
swan genus .... **OLOR**

b swan, male .... **COB**
swan, whistling .... **OLOR**
swap .... **TRADE**
sward .... **SOD, TURF**
swarm .... **NEST, HORDE**
swarthy .... **DUN, DARK**
swastika .... **FYLFOT**
sway .... **ROCK, ROLL**
swear .... **AVER, CURSE**
sweat ...... **SUDOR, PERSPIRE**
SWEDISH .... see also SPECIAL
    SECTION—SWEDEN
Swedish:
    beer .... **OL**
    tea .... **TE**
    toe .... **TA**
    you .... **ER**
Swedish coin .... **ORE**
Swedish county, district .. **LAN**
Swedish explorer ...... **HEDIN**
Swedish order of merit .. **VASA**
Swedish royal guard **DRABANT**
Swedish sculptor ..... **MILLES**
sweep, scythe's ...... **SWATH**
sweet flag .. **SEDGE, CALAMUS**
sweet gale .... **GAGL**
sweet liquid .... **NECTAR**
sweet potato
    YAM, BATATA, OCARINA
sweet potato: Sp. .... **CAMOTE**

c sweet red wine .... **ALICANTE**
sweet-smelling
    OLENT, REDOLENT
sweet spire .... **ITEA**
sweetfish .... **AYU**
sweetheart: Ir. .... **GRA**
sweetheart: Scot. .... **JO**
sweetmeat: Fr. .... **DRAGEE**
sweetsop .... **ATA,**
    ATES, ATTA, ANNONA
swell .... **DILATE**
swell of water .... **WAVE**
swelling **LUMP, NODE, EDEMA**
swelling on plants .... **GALL**
swerve .... **SHY, SKEW**
swift .... **FAST, FLEET**
swift, common .... **CRAN**
swift horse .. **ARAB, PACOLET**
swiftly, run ...... **DART, SCUD**
swimming .... **NATANT**
swimming bell .. **NECTOPHORE**
swindle **GIP, GYP, DUPE, SWIZ**
swindler .... **COZENER**
swine .. **HOG, PIG, SOW, BOAR**
swine, feeding of ... **PANNAGE**
swine fever .... **ROUGET**
swine genus .... **SUS**
swing music .... **JIVE**
swing musician ...... **HEPCAT**

d swinish .... **PORCINE**
swipe .... **GLOM**
swirl .... **EDDY, GURGE**
SWISS .. see also SPECIAL SEC-
    TION—SWITZERLAND
Swiss capital ... **BERN, BERNE**
Swiss card game .... **JASS**
Swiss critic .... **AMIEL**
Swiss patriot .... **TELL**
Swiss state .... **CANTON**
switch .... **TOGGLE**
swollen .... **TURGID**
swoon .... **FAINT**
swoon: old Eng. ...... **SWEB**
sword .. **PATA, EPEE, BLADE,**
    SABER, SABRE, RAPIER
sword, Arthur's
    EXCALIBAR, EXCALIBUR
sword, curved .. **SABER, SABRE**
sword, fencing .... **EPEE**
sword, matador's ... **ESTOQUE**
sword, medieval ..... **ESTOC**
sword, Norse myth. .... **GRAM**
sword, put away .... **SHEATHE**
sword, St. George's
    ASCALON, ASKELON
sword-shaped ...... **ENSATE**
sword, Siegfried's .... **GRAM**
sword, slender ...... **RAPIER**
swordsman's dummy stake **PEL**
syllable, last .... **ULTIMA**

160

Syllable

a syllable, scale .... **DO, FA, LA, MI, RE, SO, TI, SOL**
syllable, short .. **MORA, MORAE**
sylvan deity **PAN, FAUN, SATYR**
SYMBOL, CHEMICAL .... see **SPECIAL SECTION**
symbol .... **TOKEN**
symbol of authority ... **MACE**
symbol of Crusaders ... **CROSS**
symbol of protection .... **EGIS**
sympathizer: suffix ...... **ITE**
synagogue .... **SHUL, TEMPLE**
syncopated music .... **RAG**
syncope ...... **FAINT, SWOON**
synod, Russian .... **SOBOR**
syntax, give the .... **PARSE**

c synthetic fabric or fiber **NYLON, ORLON, RAYON, DACRON**
synthetic rubber **BUNA, ELASTOMER**
Syria, ancient .... **ARAM**
Syrian, ancient port ... **SIDON**
Syrian bear .... **DUBB**
Syrian bishop's title .... **ABBA**
Syrian city, old ...... **ALEPPO**
system .... **ISM**
system of rule ...... **REGIME**
system of rules .... **CODE**
system of weights ..... **TROY**
system of worship ...... **CULT**
systematic regulation ... **CODE**

T

T-shaped .... **TAU**
tab .... **FLAP, LABEL**
tabard .... **CAPE**
table mountain, Abyssin. **AMBA**
tableland .... **MESA**
tablet .... **PAD, SLATE**
taboo, opposite of ...... **NOA**
b tabor, Moorish **ATABAL, ATTABAL**
Tacoma's Sound ...... **PUGET**
tack: naut. .... **BUSK**
tact .... **FINESSE**
tackle, anchor .... **CAT**
tael, part of .... **LI**
tag .... **LABEL**
tag, metal ... **AGLET, AIGLET**
Tagalog for river ...... **ILOG**
Tahitian national god ... **ORO**
Tai race branch .... **LAO**
tail, of ... **CAUDAL, CAUDATE**
tail of coin .... **VERSO**
tail, rabbit's .... **SCUT**
tail: zool. .... **CAUDA**
tailor .... **SARTOR**
Taino fetish ..... **ZEME, ZEMI**
Taj Mahal site .... **AGRA**
take away by force ... **REAVE**
take away: law ...... **ADEEM**
take back .... **RECANT**
take effect again ..... **REVEST**
take off .... **DOFF**
take one's ease .... **REST**
take on cargo ... **LADE, LOAD**
take out **DELE, ELIDE, EXPUNGE**
take part .... **SIDE**
take up again ...... **RESUME**
take up weapons ...... **ARM**
tale .... **SAGA, YARN, STORY**
tale, medieval Fr. .... **LAI**

tale, Norse .... **SAGA**
"Tale of Two Cities" girl **LUCIE**
"Tales of a Wayside —" .. **INN**
talent .... **FLAIR**
talented .... **SMART**
talisman .... **CHARM**
talisman, Afr. .... **GRIGRI**
talk ...... **GAB, GAS, CHAT, PRATE, PALAVER**
d talk: slang .... **YAK**
talk freely .... **DESCANT**
talk pompously **ORATE, HARANGUE**
talk, rambling ... **RIGMAROLE**
talk wildly ..... **RANT, RAVE**
Tallinn .... **REVAL**
tallow tree .... **CERA**
tally .... **SCORE**
Talmud commentary .. **GEMARA**
talon .... **CLAW, NAIL**
tamarack .... **LARCH**
tamarisk .... **ATLE**
tame, as hawks .... **MAN**
tan .... **BUFF, BEIGE**
tan skins .... **TAW**
tanager ..... **YENI, REDBIRD**
tanager, S. Am. **HABIA, LINDO**
tanbark .... **ROSS**
tangle ...... **SNARL, SLEAVE**
tangled mass .... **MAT, SHAG**
tanning gum .... **KINO**
tanning, plant for ... **ALDER**
tanning shrub **SUMAC, SUMACH**
tanning tree, India **AMLA, AMLI**
tantalize .... **TEASE**
Tantalus' daughter .... **NIOBE**
tantra .... **AGAMA**
tantrum .... **RAGE**
tap **PAT, COCK, SPIGOT, FAUCET**

161

Tapering

a tapering dagger ..... **ANLACE**
tapering piece .... **SHIM**
tapestry **ARRAS, TAPIS, DOSSER**
tapestry center .... **ARRAS**
tapeworm .... **TAENIA**
tapeworm larva ..... **MEASLE**
tapioca-like food ..... **SALEP**
tapioca source
      CASAVA, CASSAVA
tapir, S. Amer. ...... **DANTA**
Tapuyan .... **GE**
tarboosh .... **FEZ**
target .... **BUTT**
Tariff Act writer ..... **SMOOT**
Tarkington character .. **SAM**
tarnish .... **SPOT, SULLY**
taro ... **GABE, GABI, DASHEEN**
taro paste .... **POI**
taro root ... **EDO, EDDO, KALO**
tarpaulin .... **PAULIN**
tarpon .... **SABALO**
tarradiddle .... **FIB, LIE**
tarry .... **BIDE, WAIT,**
      STAY, LINGER
tarsus .... **ANKLE**
tarsus, insect .... **MANUS**
tart .... **ACID**
tartar, crude .. **ARGAL, ARGOL**
Tartini's B-flat .... **ZA**
b task .... **DUTY, CHORE,**
      STENT, STINT
task, punishing ...... **PENSUM**
taste ...... **SIP, SUP, SAPOR,**
      SNACK, PALATE
tasteful .... **ELEGANT**
tasty .... **SAPID**
Tatar .... **HU**
Tatar dynasty, China .... **WEI**
Tatar tribe, W. Siberia .. **SHOR**
tattle .... **BLAB**
tattler, idle .... **GOSSIP**
Tattler publisher ...... **STEELE**
tau cross .... **ANKH**
taunt ..... **JEER, MOCK, TWIT**
taut .... **TENSE**
taut, pull .... **STRETCH**
tavern .... **INN**
tax .. **CESS, GELD, LEVY, SCOT,**
    SESS, STENT, ASSESS, EX-
    CISE, IMPOST
tax, church .... **TITHE**
tea .... **CHA, CHAA**
tea, black
    PECO, BOHEA, PEKOE
tea bowl .... **CHAWAN**
tea box
    CADDY, CALIN, CANISTER
tea, China .... **BOHEA**
tea, Chin. green ...... **HYSON**

c tea genus .... **THEA**
tea-growing region ... **ASSAM**
tea, kind of
    OOPAK, OOLONG, OOPACK
tea, Labrador .... **LEDUM**
tea, marsh .... **LEDUM**
tea, medicinal **PTISAN, TISANE**
tea, oriental .... **CHA**
tea, Paraguay .. **MATE, YERBA**
tea, rolled .. **CHA, TCHA, TSIA**
tea tree .... **TI**
teacake ...... **SCON, SCONE**
teacher .... **DOCENT, MENTOR**
teacher, Hebrew ...... **RABBI**
teacher, Islam religious
    ALIM, MOLLA, MULLA
teacher, Jewish .... **RAB, REB**
teacher, Moslem
    ALIM, MOLLA, MULLA
teacher, Xenophon's .**ISOCRATES**
teacher's association: abbr. **NEA**
team of horses .... **SPAN**
team, 3-horse ...... **RANDEM**
teamster's command **GEE, HAW**
tear .... **RIP, REND, RENT**
tear apart
    REND, TATTER, DIVULSE
tease .... **TWIT, BOTHER**
technical name: biol. ... **ONYM**
technique .... **ART**
tedious writer .... **PROSER**
d teem .... **RAIN, POUR**
teeth, false ...... **DENTURES**
teeth, incrustation .. **TARTAR**
Telamon's son .... **AJAX**
telegraph inventor ... **MORSE**
telegraph key ...... **TAPPER**
telegraph signal ... **DOT, DASH**
telegraph, underwater .. **CABLE**
telegraphic speed unit .. **BAUD**
telephone exchange **CENTRAL**
telephone inventor .... **BELL**
telephone wire .... **LINE**
telescope part .... **LENS**
television .... **VIDEO**
television broadcast **TELECAST**
television cable .... **COAXIAL**
television recording **KINESCOPE**
television tube
    MONOSCOPE, ICONSCOPE
tell **IMPART, RELATE, NARRATE**
tell in detail .... **RECOUNT**
Tell, site of legend ...... **URI**
telling blow ...... **COUP, ONER**
temper .... **ANNEAL**
temper, fit of .... **PET**
temperament: Ger. .... **GEMUT**
"Tempest" sprite ..... **ARIEL**
"Tempest" slave .... **CALIBAN**
temple .. **FANE, RATH, RATHA**
temple, Asian .... **PAGODA**

162

a temple chamber, Gr. ... **NAOS**
temple, inner part .... **CELLA**
temple: Siam. .... **VAT, WAT**
temple tower, India .. **SHIKARA**
tempo: music .... **TAKT**
temporary decline ..... **SLUMP**
temporary fashion .... **FAD**
temporary relief ... **REPRIEVE**
tempt .... **LURE, TOLE**
temptation .... **ALLURE**
ten .... **DECAD**
ten ares .... **DECARE**
Ten Commandments
        DECALOG, DECALOGUE
"Ten Days that Shook the
    World" author ..... **REED**
ten million ergs .... **JOULE**
tenant .... **LESSEE**
tenant, early Ir. .... **SAER**
tend .... **SERVE**
tender .... **SOFT, OFFER**
tending toward .... **FOR**
tendril: bot. .... **CAPREOL**
tennis score .... **LOVE, DEUCE**
tennis shoe .... **SNEAKER**
tennis stroke **ACE, LOB, LOBB**
tennis term .... **LET**
Tennyson character .... **ENID,**
                    ARDEN
b Tennyson heroine
        ELAIN, ELAINE
Tennyson sailor ...... **ENOCH**
tenon .... **COG**
tenonlike piece .. **COAG, COAK**
tenor, famous ..... **MELCHIOR**
tense .... **TAUT**
tent dweller
        KEDAR, SCENITE
tent dwelling Arabs ... **KEDAR**
tent flap .... **FLY**
tentmaker, the .... **OMAR**
tents .... **CAMP**
tentacle .... **FEELER**
tenth part .... **DECI, TITHE**
tepid .... **WARM**
Tereus' son .... **ITYS**
term .... **NAME**
term .... **SESSION**
term: algebra .... **NOME**
TERM, GEOMETRY ...... see
        GEOMETRY, GEOMETRIC
term in office .... **TENURE**
term, math. .... **SINE, COSINE**
term of address .... **SIR, SIRE;**
                    MADAM
termagant .... **SHREW**
terminable .... **ENDABLE**
termite, P. I. .... **ANAI, ANAY**
tern .... **SKIRR**

c tern, black .... **DARR**
tern genus .... **STERNA**
tern, Hawaii .... **NOIO**
terpene alcohol ...... **NEROL**
terpene compound . **TEREBENE**
terrapin .... **EMYD,**
            POTTER, SLIDER
terrapin, red-bellied
            POTTER, SLIDER
terrestrial .... **GEAL**
terrible .... **DIRE**
terrier, kind of .. **SKYE, CAIRN**
terrier, Scottish breed of . **SKYE**
terrified .... **AFRAID**
territorial division .... **AMT**
territory .... **LAND, SOIL**
territory, additional
            LEBENSRAUM
territory, enclosed .. **ENCLAVE**
terror .... **PANIC**
terrorist .... **GOON**
tessellated .... **MOSAIC**
tessera .... **TILE**
test .... **ASSAY, TEMPT,**
        TRIAL, EXAMINE
test ground .... **BOSE**
testament .... **WILL**
testifier .... **DEPONENT**
testify ...... **DEPONE, DEPOSE**
d tetrachord, upper tone of .**NETE**
Teutonic, ancient ...... **GOTH**
Teutonic barbarian ..... **GOTH**
Teutonic deity .... **ER**
Teut. Fate ...... **NORN, URTH**
TEUTONIC GODS, GODDESSES,
    DEITY see NORSE SPECIAL
    SECTION
Teut. legendary hero ... **OFFA**
Teut. letter of alphabet . **RUNE**
Teut. people .... **GEPIDAE**
Teut. sea goddess ...... **RAN**
Teut. sky god .. **TY, TIU, TIW,**
        TYR, ZIO, ZIU, TYRR
Texas shrine .... **ALAMO**
textile screw pine
            ARA, PANDAN
texture .... **WALE,**
            WOOF, GRAIN
Thailand .... **SIAM**
Thames estuary .... **NORE**
than: Ger. .... **ALS**
than: Scot. .... **NA**
thankless person .... **INGRATE**
that is: abbr. ...... **E.G., I.E.**
that not .... **LEST**
that one: Lat. .... **ILLE**

That

a that which follows .... SEQUEL
thatch, grass to .... NETI
thatching palm .... NIPA
the: Ger. .... DAS, DER
"The Ballad of Reading —":
                           GAOL
"The Jairite" .... IRA
"The Lion of God" .... ALI
"The Red" .... ERIC
the same: Lat. .... IDEM
the squint .... SKEN
theatre .... ODEA, ODEON,
               ODEUM, STAGE
theatre box seat .... LOGE
theatre district ...... RIALTO
theatre floor .... PIT
theatre, Grecian ...... ODEA,
            ODEON, ODEUM
theatre group .... ANTA
theatre, part of Greek . SKENE,
       SCENA, SCENAE, SKENAI
theatre sign .... SRO
"Theban Bard" ...... PINDAR
Thebes deity .. AMEN, AMON,
   AMUN, MENT, AMENT, MENTU
Thebes, king of
           CREON, OEDIPUS
theme .... MOTIF
theme: music .... TEMA
then .... ANON

b then: music .... POI
theoretical .... PLATONIC
there: Fr. .... VOILA
therefore .... ERGO
theseli veil .... TEMPE
Theseus' father ..... AEGEUS
thesis, opp. of .... ARSIS
thespian .... ACTOR
Thessaly, king of .... AEOLUS
Thessaly mountain ...... OSSA
Thessaly valley .... TEMPE
they: Fr. .... ILS
thick-lipped .... LABROSE
thicket .. BOSK, SHAW, COPSE,
          COPPICE, SPINNEY
thicket: dialect .... RONE
thicket, game .... COVERT
thickness .... PLY
thief, gypsy .... CHOR
thief: Yiddish .... GANEF,
            GANOF, GONOF
thigh bone .... FEMUR
thigh, of the .... FEMORAL
thin ...... LANK, LEAN, RARE,
      SHEER, DILUTE, PAPERY,
       SPARSE, TENUOUS
thin cake .... WAFER
thin: comb. form ...... SERO
thin disk .... WAFER
thin layer .... FILM

c "Thin Man" dog ...... ASTA
"Thin Man" wife .... NORA
thin-toned .... REEDY
thin out .... ATTENUATE
thing: law (Latin) ...... RES
things added ..... ADDENDA
things done .... ACTA
things to be done
           AGENDA, AGENDUM
think ... DEEM, TROW, OPINE
think: archaic .... WIS
think (over) .... MULL, MUSE
third: comb. form ...... TRIT
third day, every .... TERTIAN
third king of Judah ...... ASA
third: music .... TIERCE
Third Reich special police: abbr.
                           SS
thirst-tortured king: Gr. myth
                      TANTALUS
thirsty .... DRY, ADRY
thirty: Fr. .... TRENTE
thirty, series of .... TRENTAL
this: Fr. .... CE
this: Sp. .... ESTA, ESTE
this one: Lat. ..... HIC, HAEC
thither .... THERE
Thomas Hardy heroine ... TESS
thong .... STRAP
thong, braided ...... ROMAL
thong-shaped ...... LORATE
thong, S. Afr. .... RIEM

d Thor's stepson ..... ULL, ULLR
Thor's wife .... SIF
thorax, crustacean's . PEREION
thorn ... BRIAR, BRIER, SPINE
thorn apple .... METEL
thorn, bearing a .... SPINATE
thornback ray .. DORN, ROKER
Thorne Smith character. TOPPER
thorny plant ... BRIAR, BRIER
thorny shrub ... NABK, NUBK
thoroughfare .... WAY, ROAD,
           AVENUE, STREET
thoroughgoing ...... ARRANT
those .... YON, YOND
those in power or office ... INS
thou: Fr. .... TU
thought .... IDEA
thought: comb. form .... IDEO
thoughts, form .... IDEATE
thousand .... MIL
thousand: comb. form . MILLE
Thrace, ancient people of EDONI
thrall .... ESNE, SLAVE
thrash .... LAM, BEAT
thread: comb. form .... NEMA
thread, cotton .... LISLE
thread, guiding ball of .. CLEW
thread-like .... NEMALINE
thread-like process ..... HAIR

164

a thread-like structure ... **FILUM**
thread, of a .... **FILAR**
threads, cross .... **RETICLE**
threads crossed by woof . **WARP**
threads crossing warp
    WEFT, WOOF
threads, lengthwise .... **WARP**
threaded fastener ...... **NUT**
threaten ... **IMPEND, MENACE**
three ...... **TER, TRIO, TRIAD**
three: Ger. .... **DREI**
three: Ital. .... **TRE**
three-legged stand
    TRIPOD, TRIVET
three-masted ship
    XEBEC, FRIGATE
3 parts, divided into: Her.
    TIERCE
3.1416 .... **PI**
three: Sp. .... **TRES**
three-spot .... **TREY**
threefold .... **TRINE, TREBLE,
    TERNARY, TERNATE**
threefold: comb. form .... **TER**
threshold .... **SILL**
threshold, psychology ... **LIMEN**
thrice: music .... **TER**
thrifty ..... **FRUGAL, SAVING**
thrive ..... **BATTEN, PROSPER**
b throat ...... **GORGE, GULLET**
throat: Lat. .... **GULA**
throat, pert. to .... **GULAR**
throb .. **BEAT, PULSE, PULSATE**
throe .... **PANG**
throng .. **MOB, HORDE, SWARM**
through .... **PER**
through: prefix .... **DIA**
throw .... **CAST, PITCH**
throw aside .... **FLING**
throw back .... **REPEL**
thrush ...... **VEERY, MISSEL**
thrush, Hawaiian ..... **OMAO**
thrush, India .... **SHAMA**
thrush, missel . **MAVIE, MAVIS**
thrust .... **LUNGE**
thrust back .... **REPEL**
thrust down .... **DETRUDE**
thunderfish .... **RAAD**
thurible .... **CENSER**
Thuringian city .... **JENA**
Thursday, source of name. **THOR**
thus .... **SO, SIC**
thus far .... **YET**
thwart .... **FOIL**
Tiber tributary .... **NERA**
Tibetan chief .... **POMBO**
Tibetan ox .... **YAK**
Tibetan priest .... **LAMA**
Tibetan tribe .... **CHAMPA**

c tibia .... **CNEMIS**
Tichborne Claimant ... **ORTON**
tick .... **ACARID**
tick genus .... **ARGAS**
tick, S. Amer. ..... **CARAPATO**
tickets, sell illegally ... **SCALP**
tickle .... **TITILLATE**
Ticonderoga's commander **GATES**
tidal flood ..... **BORE, EAGRE**
tidal wave, flow or bore. **EAGRE**
tidbit .... **CATE**
tide, lowest high ...... **NEAP**
tidings .... **NEWS, WORD**
tidings, glad .... **GOSPEL,
    EVANGEL, EVANGILE**
tidy ...... **NEAT, REDO, TRIM**
tie ...... **BIND, BOND, LASH,
    TRUSS, CRAVAT**
tie, kind of .... **ASCOT**
tie-breaking game ... **RUBBER**
tie off .... **LIGATE**
tie, railroad .... **SLEEPER**
tier .... **ROW**
tiger cat, S. Amer. .... **CHATI**
tiger, Persian ..... **SHER, SHIR**
tight .... **SNUG, TAUT, TENSE**
tight place .. **FIX, JAM, MESS**
tighten: naut. .... **FRAP**
tightly stretched ...... **TENSE**
til .... **SESAME**
d tile, hexagonal .... **FAVI**
tile, roofing .... **PANTILE**
tilelike .... **TEGULAR**
till the earth .... **FARM, PLOW**
tilled land ... **ARADA, ARADO**
tiller .... **HELM**
tilt .... **TIP, CANT, LIST**
tilt .... **JOUST**
tilting: naut. .... **ALIST**
timber bend .... **SNY**
timber, flooring ..... **BATTEN**
timber, nautical ..... **KEVEL**
timber, pine: Asia .... **MATSU**
timber rot ...... **DOAT, DOTE**
timber truck .... **WYNN**
timber wolf .... **LOBO**
timbrel .... **TABOR, TABOUR**
time ..... **ERA, TEMPI, TEMPO**
time before .... **EVE**
time being .... **NONCE**
time gone by .... **PAST**
time out .... **RECESS**
time, space of .... **WHILE**
time value, equalling in
    DIMORIC
times, old .... **ELD, YORE**
timetable .... **SCHEDULE**
timid .... **SHY, PAVID**
timorous .... **TREPID**
timothy .... **HAY**
Timothy's mother: Bib. ... **LOIS**

a
tin .... **CAN, STANNUM**
tin, containing .... **STANNOUS**
tin foil .... **TAIN**
tin plate .... **TAIN**
tin roofing .... **TERNE**
tinamou .... **YUTU**
tincture: Her. .... **OR, GULES,
VERT, AZURE, SABLE,
ARGENT, PURPURE**
tinder ...... **PUNK, AMADOU**
tine .... **PRONG**
tine of antler .... **SNAG**
tinge .... **TAINT**
tinge deeply .... **IMBUE**
tingle of feeling ..... **THRILL**
tinkle .... **TING**
tiny bird, W. Ind. ...... **TODY**
tip .... **END, FEE, APEX, KNAP**
tip .... **CANT, LEAN,
TILT, CAREEN**
tipping .... **ALIST, ATILT**
tiptoe, on .... **ATIP**
tire .... **FAG, JADE**
tire casing .... **SHOE**
tire, face of .... **TREAD**
tire support .... **RIM**
tissue .... **TELA**
tissue, of a .... **TELAR**
tissue, pert. to .... **TELAR**
TITAN . see SPECIAL SECTION,
GREEK MYTH page 200

b
Titania's husband .... **OBERON**
titanic iron-ore sand . **ISERENE**
titlark .... **PIPIT**
title ..... **EARL, NAME, TERM**
title, baronet's .... **SIR**
title, Benedictine .... **DOM**
title, church .... **PRIMATE**
title, East .... **COJA, HOJA**
title, Ethiopian .... **RAS**
title Hindu gives Moslem
MIAN
title, India .... **AYA, NAWAB,
SAHEB, SAHIB**
title, Jewish . **RAB, REB, RABBI**
title, knight's .... **SIR**
title, king's .... **SIRE**
title, lady's ... **DAME, MADAM**
title, Moslem ...... **AGA, ALI,
MOLLA, MULLA,
SHERIF, SHEREFF**
title of address .. **MME., MRS.,
SIR, MAAM, MADAM**
title of honor, Moslem . **SAYID,
SAIYID, SAYYID**
title of kings of Edessa . **ABGAR**
title of respect ..... **SIR, SIRE,
MADAME**
title of respect, Afr. ..... **SIDI**

c
title of respect, India .... **SRI,
SHRI, SAHIB, SHREE,
HUZOOR**
title of respect, Malay .. **TUAN**
title, Oriental .... **BABA**
title, Persian **MIR, AZAM, KHAN**
title, Spanish **DOM, DON, SENOR**
title to property or land . **DEED**
title, Turkish .. **PACHA, PASHA**
titleholder .... **TITLIST**
titmice, genus of ..... **PARUS**
titmouse .... **MAG, PARUS**
tittle .... **JOT, IOTA, WHIT**
Titus Andronicus' daughter
LAVINIA
Tiwaz .... **ER, TIU**
to .... **FOR, UNTO**
to: prefix .... **AP**
to: Scot. .... **TAE**
to be: Fr. .... **ETRE**
to be: Lat. .... **ESSE**
"to be," part of ..... **AM, IS,
ARE, WAS**
to go: Fr. .... **ALLER**
to love: Fr. .... **AIMER**
to the point that ...... **UNTIL**
to use: Lat. .... **UTOR**
toad genus .... **BUFO**
toad, huge .... **AGUA**
toad, order of .... **ANURA**
toad, tree genus .... **HYLA**
toadfish .... **SAPO**
toast, bit of .... **SIPPET**
toasting word .... **SALUD,
SKOAL, PROSIT**
tobacco ash .. **DOTTEL, DOTTLE**
tobacco, chewing ...... **QUID**
tobacco, coarse
SHAG, CAPORAL
tobacco, Cuban .... **CAPA**
tobacco, low grade ..... **SHAG**
tobacco, Peru .... **SANA**
tobacco, roll .... **CIGAR**
toddy palm juice ...... **SURA**
toe .... **DIGIT**
toe, fifth .... **MINIMUS**
toe: Scot. .... **TAE**
togs .... **DUDS**
toilet case .... **ETUI**
Tokyo Bay city .... **CHIBI**
Tokyo, old name ... **EDO, YEDO**
tolerable .... **SOSO**
toll .... **FEE, KNELL**
Tolstoi heroine .... **ANNA**
tomb, Moslem **TABUT, TABOOT**
tomboy .... **HOIDEN, HOYDEN**
tomcat .... **GIB**
tone down .... **SOFTEN**
tone, lack of .... **ATONY**
tone, of .... **TONAL**
tone quality .... **TIMBRE**

a
tone: Scot. .... **TEAN**
tones, series of ...... **OCTAVE**
tongue, gypsy .... **CHIB**
tongue of Agni .... **KALI**
tongue, pert. to ..... **GLOSSAL**
tongue, using the ..... **APICAL**
tongue, wagon .... **NEAP**
tonic .... **ROBORANT**
tonic, dried India
      CHIRATA, CHIRETTA
tonic herb ...... **ALOE, TANSY**
Tonkin native .... **THO**
too early .... **PREMATURE**
too much: Fr. .... **TROP**
tool, boring .... **AWL, BIT,
      AUGER, GIMLET**
tool, cutting .. **AX, ADZ, AXE,
   HOB, SAW, SAX, SYE, ADZE**
tool, engraver's
      BURIN, MATTOIR
tool, enlarging ...... **REAMER**
tool, grass-cutting .... **SITHE,
      SCYTHE, SICKLE**
tool, machine .... **LATHE**
tool, molding .... **DIE**
tool, pointed .... **BROACH**
tool, post hole digging .... **LOY**
tool shaper .... **SWAGER**
tool, splitting .... **FROE, FROW**
b
tool, stone, prehistoric
      CELT, EOLITH
tool, threading ...... **CHASER**
tool's biting edge .... **BIT**
tooth ...... **COG, TINE, MOLAR,
   CANINE, CUSPID, FANG**
tooth-billed pigeon ... **DODLET**
tooth, canine .... **CUSPID**
tooth: comb. form .... **ODONT**
tooth, gear .... **COG**
tooth: Lat. .... **DENS**
tooth-like ornament .. **DENTIL**
tooth, long **FANG, TUSH, TUSK**
tooth pulp .... **NERVE**
toothed formation ..... **SERRA**
toothed margin, having
      DENTATE
toothed wheel .... **GEAR**
toothless .... **EDENTATE**
toothless mammals . **EDENTATA**
top .... **APEX, CAP, LID**
top-notch .... **AONE**
top ornament ..... **EPI, FINIAL**
topaz humming bird .... **AVA**
topee material .... **SOLA**
toper .... **SOT, SOUSE**
topic .... **THEME**
topmast crossbar support .. **FID**
topsail .... **RAFFE**
torment ...... **BAIT, ANNOY,
   DEVIL, HARRY, TEASE**
torn: archaic .... **REFT**

c
torn place .... **RENT**
torrid region or zone .. **TROPIC**
tortoise .... **GALAPAGO**
tortoise, fresh water .... **EMYD**
tortoise, marsh genus ... **EMYS**
tortoise, order of ... **CHELONIA**
torturer .... **RACKER**
"Tosca" villain ...... **SCARPIA**
toss ...... **CAST, FLIP, HURL,
      FLING, PITCH**
tosspot ... . **SOT**
total ...... **ADD, SUM, UTTER**
total abstinence .. **NEPHALISM**
totalitarian ruler ... **DICTATOR**
totem pole .... **XAT**
toucan .... **TOCO**
toucan, S. Am. .... **ARACARI**
touch .... **ABUT**
touch lightly .... **PAT**
touch, organ of .... **PALP**
touch, pert. to **HAPTIC, TACTIC,
      TACTILE, TACTUAL**
touch sense, pert. to . **HAPTIC**
touchwood .... **PUNK**
tough .... **WIRY, HARDY,
      ROWDY, CHEWY**
tour: It. .... **GIRO**
tourmaline, colorless
      ACHROITE
d
tow .... **PULL, DRAW**
towai .... **KAMAHI**
toward: Lat. .... **AD**
toward stern ..... **AFT, ABAFF,
      ABAFT, ASTERN**
towel .... **WIPER**
towel fabric .... **HUCK, TERRY**
tower, Bibl. .... **BABEL**
tower, India ... . **MINAR**
tower, little .... **TURRET**
tower, mosque, slender
      MINARET
towering .... **STEEP**
towhead . **BLOND, BLONDE**
town, Arcadia ancient ... **ALEA**
town: Cornish prefix ..... **TRE**
town: Dutch .... **STAD**
town: Ger. .... **STADT**
town, India pilgrimage . **SORON**
town: It. .. **CASAL, CASALE**
town: Jap. .... **MACHI**
town: suffix .... **TON**
township, ancient Attica . **DEME**
townsman .... **CIT**
toxic protein .... **ABRIN**
toy with .... **TRIFLE**
trace .... **TINGE, VESTIGE**
track .... **TRACE**
track, animal ... **RUN, SLOT,
      SPUR, SPOOR**
track circuit .... **LAP**

a

track of ship .... **WAKE**
track, deer's .... **SLOT**
track, otter's .... **SPUR, SPOOR**
track, put off .... **DERAIL**
track, put on another
            SHUNT, SWITCH
tracker, India .... **PUGGI**
tract .... **LOT, AREA**
tract of farm land ...... **FIELD**
trade .... **SWAP, SWOP**
            BARTER, TRAFFIC
trade .... **METIER**
trade agreement .... **CARTEL**
trader ..... **DEALER, MONGER**
trader selling to soldiers
                    SUTLER
trading exchange .... **PIT**
trading vessel of Ceylon
            DONI, DHONI
traditional story .... **SAGA**
traduce .... **SLUR, DEFAME**
traffic .... **TRADE**
trail .... **SLOT, SPOOR, TRACK**
train of attendants
            SUITE, RETINUE
train, overhead .... **EL**
train, slow, many-stops . **LOCAL**
tramp .... **BO, HOBO**
trample .... **TREAD**
tranquil or tranquilize

b

            SERENE, SOOTHE
transaction ...... **DEAL, SALE**
transfer .... **CEDE**
transfer, property
            DEED, GRANT
transfer, sovereignty .. **DEMISE**
transferer, property .. **ALIENOR**
transform .... **CONVERT**
transgress .... **ERR, SIN**
transit coach .... **BUS**
"— transit gloria mundi" . **SIC**
translator of Freud, Amer.
                    BRILL
transmit .... **SEND**
transom .... **TRAVE**
transpire .... **OCCUR, HAPPEN,**
                    DEVELOP
transverse pin .... **TOGGLE**
trap .... **SNARE, ENSNARE**
trap door .... **DROP**
trap, mouse: dial. .... **TIPE**
trap, rabbit: dial. ...... **TIPE**
trappings .... **REGALIA**
travel .... **TREK**
traveler .... **PASSENGER**
tray .... **SALVER, SERVER**
tread softly ...... **PAD, SNEAK**
treasure .... **ROON, TROVE**
treasurer, college ..... **BURSAR**
treasury agents .... **TMEN**
treat .... **USE**

c

treat with acid ..... **ACIDIZE**
treat with malice .... **SPITE**
treatment .... **USE**
tree   (3 letters) **ASH, ELM,**
            FIR, LIN,   OAK,   YEW;
            (4 letters) **AKEE, AMLA,**
            AMLI,   ANAM,   ANDA,
            ARAR, ASAK, AULU, AUSU,
            AUZU, BARU, BIJA, BITO,
            BIWA, BOBO, BOGO, DALI,
            DILO, DOON, DOUM, DUKU,
            EBOE, EJOO, GOAI, GUAO,
            HINO, IFIL, IPIL, KINO,
            KIRI, KOPI, KOZO, LIME,
            LINN,   MAKO,   MYXA,
            NAIO, NEEM, NIOG, NIPA,
            ODUM, OHIA, PALM, PELU,
            PINE, PUKA, RATA, RIMU,
            ROKA, SAUL, SHEA, SUPA,
            TALA, TARA, TAWA, TEAK,
            TEIL, TEYL, TOON, TORO,
            TUNG, TUNO, TUWI, UPAS,
            WHAU, YATE, YAYA, YPIL;
            (5 letters) **ASPEN;** (6 let-
            ters) **LINDEN**

tree, African .... **AKEE, BAKU,**
            COLA, KOLA, ROKA,
            SHEA, AEGLE, ARTAR

d

tree, Afr. & Asia .... **SIRIS**
tree, Afr. gum .... **BUMBO**
tree, Afr. tallow .... **ROKA**
TREE, AMER. TROPICAL...see
            TREE, TROPICAL AMER.
tree, Argentine timber ... **TALA**
TREE, ASIATIC .. see ASIATIC
                        TREE
tree, arrow poison ...... **UPAS**
TREE, AUSTRAL. .... see
            AUSTRAL. TREE
tree, Bengal quince ...... **BEL**
tree, black gum ...... **TUPELO**
tree, body of .... **TRUNK**
tree, boxwood yielding . **SERON**
tree, buckwheat .... **TITI**
tree, butter .... **SHEA**
tree, caucho-yielding ..... **ULE**
tree, chicle .... **SAPOTA**
tree, Chin. ... **GINKO, GINKGO**
tree clump, prairie .... **MOTTE**
tree cobra .... **MAMBA**
tree, coniferous (cone) .. **FIR,**
            YEW, PINE, LARCH
TREE. E. IND. ... see E. IND.
            TREE and TREE, IND.
TREE, EVERGREEN .... see
                    EVERGREEN
tree, flowering ..... **CATALPA**
tree genus .... **MABA**
tree genus, Afr. ...... **OCHNA**

a tree genus, elms
ULMUS, CELTIS
tree genus, small ... **CATALPA**
tree, gum .... **ICICA**
tree, hardwood **ASH, OAK, IPIL**
tree, India .... **DAR, MEE, SAJ,
SAL, AMLA, AMLI, DHAK,
MYXA, NEEM, SHOQ, MA-
HUA, BANYAN**
tree knot .... **BURL**
tree, locust .... **ACACIA**
tree, maidenhair ..... **GINKGO**
tree, Malay .... **TERAP**
tree, Medit. .... **CAROB**
tree, mimosaceous ...... **SIRIS**
tree moss .... **USNEA**
tree, N. Am.
TAMARAC, TAMARACK
TREE, N. Z.
see **NEW ZEALAND TREE**
tree, oak .... **ENCINA**
tree of olive family .... **ASH**
tree, Pacific .... **KOU**
tree, palm .. **GRIGRI, GRUGRU**
tree, palm, Asiatic .... **ARENG**
TREE, P.I. ..... see **P. I. TREE**
tree, pod .... **CAROB**
tree, resinous ...... **FIR, PINE,
BALSAM**
b tree, showy Asia .... **ASAK**
tree-snake .... **LORA**
tree, sun, Jap. ...... **HINOKI**
tree, swamp .... **ALDER**
tree, tamarisk salt ...... **ATLE**
tree, tea .... **TI**
tree, thorny .... **ACACIA**
tree tiger .... **LEOPARD**
tree toad genus .... **HYLA**
tree, tropical .... **EBOE, PALM,
BALSA, MANGO, COLIMA,
SAPOTA, LEBBEK**
tree, tropical Amer. **CEBA, DALI,
GUAO, CEIBA, COLIMA,
GUAMA, CEDRON**
tree trunk .... **BOLE**
tree, W. Ind. .... **GENIP,
SAPOTE, LIBIDIBI**
trees of a region .... **SILVA**
treeless plain ...... **PAMPAS,
TUNDRA, STEPPES**
tremble ...... **QUAKE, DIDDER**
trembling ..... **ASPEN, TREPID**
trench .... **SAP**
trench extension .... **SAP**
trench, rear wall of .. **PARADOS**
trend .... **TENOR**
trespass .. **INFRINGE, INTRUDE**

c trespass for game .... **POACH**
trespass to recover goods
TROVER
triad .... **TRIO**
trial .... **TEST**
triangle .... **TRIGON, SCALENE**
triangle, side of .... **LEG**
triangular insert .... **GORE**
tribal symbol .... **TOTEM**
TRIBE
see also **SPECIAL SECTION**
tribe ..... **CLAN, FOLK, RACE**
TRIBE, BIBLICAL .... see
SPECIAL SECTION
tribe: Bib. tent-dwellers.**KEDAR**
tribe division, Rom.
CURIA, CURIAE
TRIBE, ISRAELITE .... see
ISRAELITE TRIBE
TRIBESMAN .. see **TRIBES** in
SPECIAL SECTION
tribulation .... **TRIAL**
tribunal .... **BAR, FORUM**
tribute .... **SCAT, SCATT**
tribute: Gaelic .... **CAIN**
trick **FLAM, GAWD, JEST, RUSE,
WILE, DODGE, FICELLE,
STRATAGEM**
tricks, game for no .... **NULLO**
tricks, win all .... **CAPOT**
d Trieste measure .. **ORNA, ORNE**
trifle ...... **TOY, DOIT, FICO,
STRAW, NIGGLE, PALTER**
trifling ...... **SMALL, SLIGHT**
trig .... **NEAT, TRIM**
trigonometry function
SINE, COSINE
trigonometry line ..... **SECANT**
trill, bird's .... **TIRALEE**
trim .... **NEAT, TRIG,
ADORN, DECORATE**
trimmed .... **SNOD**
trimming, dress . **GIMP, RUCHE**
trimmings, overlapping .. **FLOTS**
Trinidad tree .... **CYP**
trinket .... **GAUD**
triple .... **TRI, TREBLE**
triplet .... **TRIN**
tripletail, P. R. .... **SAMA**
tripod, 6-footed .... **CAT**
Tripoli: measure . see page 188
"Tristram Shandy" author
STERNE
Tristram's beloved ..... **ISOLT,
YSEUT, ISAUDE, ISAULT,
ISEULT, ISOLDE, ISOLTA,
ISOUDE, ISULTE**
trite .. **BANAL, CORNY, STALE**
triton ...... **EFT, EVET, NEWT**

troche ...... **PASTIL, ROTULA, PASTILE, PASTILLE**
TROJAN .... see also TROY
Trojan hero .. **PARIS, ENEAS, AENEAS, AGENOR, DARDAN, HECTOR, HEKTOR, ACHILLES**
trolley .... **TRAM**
troop-carrying group: abbr. **ATS**
troop, division, Gr. .... **TAXIS**
troops .... **MEN**
troops, spread .... **DEPLOY**
trophy .... **CUP**
tropic .... **SOLAR**
tropical Am. bird genus **CACICUS**
tropical disease . **BUBA, BUBAS**
tropical fever .... **DENGUE**
TROPICAL FRUIT ...... see FRUIT, TROPICAL
tropical plant .... **TARO**
tropical shrub genus **INGA, SIDA**
trot .... **JOG, AMBLE**
trouble ... **ADO, AIL, WORRY, EFFORT, MOLEST**
troubles .... **ILLS**
troublesome person **PEST, AGITATOR**
trough, inclined ...... **CHUTE**
trough, mining .... **SLUICE**
trout, British .. **SEWEN, SEWIN**
trout, brook .... **CHAR**
trowel, plasterers' ..... **DARBY**
Troy .... **ILION, ILIUM**
Troy, founder of .... **ILUS**
Troy, land of .... **TROAS**
Troy, last king of ..... **PARIS, PRIAM, PRIAMOS**
Troy, of ancient **ILIAC, ILIAN**
Troy: poetic .... **ILIUM**
truant, play: Scot. .... **TRONE**
truck ...... **LORRY, CAMION**
trudge .... **PACE, PLOD, SLOG**
true copy: law .... **ESTREAT**
true olives .... **OLEA**
trumpet ..... **HORN, CLARION**
trumpet call, reveille ... **DIAN**
trumpet, mouth of .... **CODON**
trumpet shell .... **TRITON**
trumpeter perch .... **MADO**
trumpeter, pigeon-like . **AGAMI**
trundle, as ore .... **RULL**
trunk of body .... **TORSO**
trunkfish .... **CHAPIN**
truss up .... **TIE**
trust .... **RELY, TROW, RELIANCE**
trustee of a wakf. **MUTAWALLI**
trusting .... **RELIANT**
truth: Chin. .... **TAO**

truth drug ...... **PENTOTHAL**
Truth personified ...... **UNA**
try .... **TEST, ESSAY, ATTEMPT**
try to equal ... **VIE, EMULATE**
tsetse fly .... **MAU, KIVU**
tsetse fly genus .... **GLOSSINA**
tub .... **VAT, KNAP, KNOP**
tub, brewer's .... **KEEVE**
tub, broad .... **KEELER**
tub, wooden: dialect ...... **SOE**
tube .... **DUCT**
tube, glass ... **PIPET, PIPETTE**
tube, plane's .... **PITOT**
tuber delicacy .... **TRUFFLE**
tuber, edible **OCA, OKA, YAM, TARO, POTATO**
tuber, orchid .... **SALEP**
tuber, S. Amer. .... **OCA, OKA**
Tuesday, god who gave name to **TIU, TYR**
tuft .... **CREST**
tuft: bot. .... **COMA**
tufted plant .... **MOSS**
tulip tree .... **POPLAR**
TUMERIC ..... see TURMERIC
tumor .... **OMA, WEN**
tumor, skin .... **WEN**
tumult .... **RIOT**
tune .... **AIR, ARIA, SONG, MELODY**
tune, bagpipe .... **PORT**
tune: Scot. .... **PORT**
tungstite ..... **OCHER, OCHRE**
tuning fork ...... **DIAPASON**
Tunis, ruler of ..... **BEY, DEY**
tunnel, train, Alps .... **CENIS**
tunny .... **AMIA, TUNA**
turban, Oriental .... **MANDIL**
turbid, make .... **ROIL**
turf .... **SOD**
turf, bit of: golf ..... **DIVOT**
Turkestan town dwellers . **SART**
turkey buzzard .... **AURA**
turkey red .... **MADDER**
turkeys, collection of .. **RAFTER**
Turkic person **TATAR, TARTAR**
Turkic person, 8th century **OGOR**
Turkish army corps ..... **ORDU**
Turkish army officer ..... **AGA**
Turkish caliph .... **ALI**
Turkish chamber .. **ODA, ODAH**
Turkish chieftain ...... **AMIR, ZAIM, AMEER**
Turkish commander . **AGA, ALI**
Turkish copper coin .... **PARA**
Turkish decree .... **IRADE**
Turkish flag .... **ALEM**
Turkish general .... **AGA**
Turkish gold coin ...... **LIRA, ALTUN, MAHBUB**

170

Turkish government .... **PORTE**
Turkish govt. summer residence
YALI
Turkish governor .. **VALI, WALI**
Turkish hostelry ..... **IMARET**
Turkish judge .... **CADI, KADI**
Turkish leader .... **AGA**
Turkish liquor .... **MASTIC**
Turkish magistrate.**CADI, KADI**
Turkish military district . **ORDO**
Turkish money of account
ASPER
Turkish officer .. **AGA, AGHA**
Turkish oxcart . **ARBA, ARABA**
Turkish palace .... **SERAI**
Turkish pavilion .... **KIOSK**
Turkish president, former
INONU
Turkish regiment .... **ALAI**
Turkish standard . **ALEM, TOUG**
Turkish sultan .... **SELIM**
Turkish title .... **AGA, AGHA,
BABA, EMIR, EMEER,
PASHA, BASHAW**
Turkish tribesman ..... **TATAR**
Turkish tribesman, Persia
GHUZ
Turkoman tribesman **SEID, SHIK**
turmeric .... **REA, ANGO**
turmoil .... **WELTER**
turn ..... **BEND, GYRE, VEER,
ROTATE, SWERVE**
turn aside.**SKEW, VEER, SHUNT**
turn back to .... **REVERT**
turn direction .... **VERT**
turn inside out .... **EVERT**
turn over: mus. .... **VERTE**
turning point ... **CRISES, CRISIS**
turning: prefix .... **ROTO**
turnover .... **PIE**
turnip ... **BAGA, NEEP, SWEDE**
turnip: Scot. .... **NEEP**
turpentine derivative
ROSIN, PINENE
turpentine distillate .... **ROSIN**
turpentine resin
ALK, GALLIPOT, GALIPOT
turtle, Amazon .... **ARRAU**
turtle, edible
TERAPIN, TERRAPIN
turtle, edible part of . **CALIPEE**
turtle enclosure ...... **CRAWL**
turtle genus .... **EMYS**
turtle, hawkbill .... **CARET**
turtle, order of .... **CHELONIA**
Tuscany art city .... **SIENA**
tusk, elephant .... **IVORY**
tutelary god ..... **LAR, LARES**
tutor .... **TUTE**

TV advertiser ...... **SPONSOR**
"Twelfth Night" clown .. **FESTE**
"Twelfth Night" heroine
VIOLA
twelve and one-half cents . **BIT**
twenty-fourth part
CARAT, KARAT
twenty quires .... **REAM**
twice .... **BIS**
twice: prefix .... **BI**
twig, willow .. **WITHE, WITHY**
twilight .... **EVE, DUSK,
GLOAM, EVENTIDE**
twilled coth .... **REP**
twilled wool fabric ..... **SERGE**
twin .... **GEMEL**
twin crystal .... **MACLE**
twin gods, Teut. .... **ALCIS**
twine .... **COIL, WIND, TWIST**
twining stem .... **BINE**
twist ..... **PLY, COIL, FEAK,
KINK, SKEW, GNARL,
WREATHE, CONTORT**
twist inwards .... **INTORT**
twist out of shape ..... **WARP**
twisted .... **AWRY, SKEW,
TORTILE**
twisted roll of fibers .... **SLUB**
twisted spirally .... **TORSE**
twitch .... **TIC**
twitching .... **TIC**
two .... **DUO, DUAD, PAIR**
two ears, affecting the **DIOTIC**
two elements, having . **BINARY**
two feet, verse of .... **DIPODY**
two-footed ... **BIPED, BIPEDAL**
two-horse chariot .... **BIGA**
two-hulled boat . **CATAMARAN**
two-masted ship . **YAWL, ZULU**
two-month period .. **BIMESTER**
two, music for .... **DUET**
two notes, group of .... **DUOLE**
two-pronged, as sponges
DICELLATE
two-pronged weapon .. **BIDENT**
two-spot .... **DEUCE**
two tenacles, having.**DICEROUS**
two-toed sloth .... **UNAU**
two-wheeled vehicle **GIG, CART**
two-year-old sheep
TEG, TEGG, BIDENT
"Two Years Before the Mast"
author .... **DANA**
twofold .. **DUAL, TWIN, BINAL**
twofold: prefix .... **DI**
tycoon .... **NABOB**
tymp arch of furnace ... **FAULD**
Tyndareus, wife of ..... **LEDA**
type collection .... **FONT**

171

Type

type, conforming to . **TYPICAL**
type face .... **RUNIC, CASLON**
type, 5½ point .... **AGATE**
type, jumbled .... **PI, PIE**
type, kind of .... **ELITE**
type measure .... **EM, EN**
type metal piece ...... **QUAD**
type, mixed .... **PI, PIE**
type of script .... **RONDE**
type part .... **KERN**
type set .... **FONT**

type size ..... **PICA, AGATE, BREVIER**
type, slanting .... **ITALIC**
type square .... **EM**
type tray .... **GALLEY**
typewriter roller ..... **PLATEN**
Tyr, Norse war god ...... **ER**
tyrant .... **DESPOT**
tyrant of Rome .... **NERO**
Tyre, king of .... **HIRAM**
Tyre, princess of ...... **DIDO**
tyro .... **NOVICE**

U

Uganda native .... **KOPI**
ukase .... **EDICT**
Ukraine legislature ..... **RADA**
"Ulalume" author .... **POE**
ulexite .... **TIZA**
ultra-conservative ...... **TORY**
ULYSSES ... see also ODYSSEUS
Ulysses' swineherd ... **EUMAEUS**
Ulysses' voyages .... **ODYSSEY**
umbrella .... **GAMP**
umbrella finial, Burma ... **TEE**
umbrella, India ...... **CHATTA**
umbrella part .... **RIB**
umpire .... **REFEREE**
unaccented vowel sound **SCHWA**
unadulterated .... **PURE**
unaffected .. **SIMPLE, ARTLESS**
Unalaskan .... **ALEUT**
unaspirate .... **LENE**
unassuming
    MODEST, NATURAL
unbeliever .... **HERETIC**
unbleached ..... **ECRU, BEIGE**
unburnt brick .. **DOBE, ADOBE**
Uncas' beloved .... **CORA**
uncanny ...... **EERY, EERIE, WEIRD**
unceasing **ETERNAL, PERPETUAL**
uncinate .... **HAMATE**
uncivil .... **RUDE**
uncle, dial. .... **EME**
uncle: Scot. .... **EME**
"Uncle Remus" author
    HARRIS
"Uncle Remus" rabbit ... **BRER**
unclean: Jewish law .... **TREF**
unclose .... **OPE, OPEN**
uncommon .... **RARE, SPECIAL**
unconcerned .... **CALM, OPEN, SERENE**
unconscious state ...... **COMA**
unconstrained .... **EASY**

uncouth person ... **CAD, BOOR, YAHOO, GALOOT**
unction .... **BALM**
unctuous .... **OILY, SUAVE**
under ...... **INFRA, NEATH, SOTTO, NETHER**
under: Fr. .... **SOUS**
under: naut. .... **ALOW**
under: prefix .... **SUB**
under side, pert. to .. **VENTRAL**
undergo: obs. .... **DREE**
underground bud .... **BULB**
underground reservoir, natural
    water .... **CENOTE**
underground stream, S. Afr.
    AAR
underhand, throw ...... **LOB**
undernsong .... **TIERCE**
undershirts .... **SKIVVIES**
undersized animal ...... **RUNT**
understand .... **GRASP**
understanding ... **KEN, SENSE, ENTENTE**
underwater box ..... **CAISSON**
underworld .... **HADES, SHEOL**
underworld, Egypt.
    DUAT, AMENTI
underworld god ... **DIS, PLUTO**
underworld god, Egypt. **OSIRIS, SERAPIS**
underworld goddess ...... **HEL**
underwrite ... **ENSURE, INSURE**
undeveloped .... **LATENT**
undraped .... **NUDE**
undulant fever .. **BRUCELLOSIS**
undulating .... **WAVY**
undulation .... **WAVE**
unequal .... **UNIQUE**
unequal angled ..... **SCALENE**
unequal conditions ...... **ODDS**
uneven .... **ODD, EROSE**
unevenly shaped .... **EROSE**

172

a unfadable .... FAST
unfair move .... FOUL
unfair shove in marbles . FULK
unfasten ..... UNTIE, LOOSEN
unfavorable .... BAD, ILL
unfeeling ... HARSH, CALLOUS
unfermented grape juice
                  STUM
unfit to eat, make . DENATURE
unfledged bird .... EYAS
unfold .... EVOLVE
unguent, Roman wrestlers'
              CEROMA
ungula .. CLAW, HOOF, NAIL
ungulate, S. Am. ...... TAPIR
unhappy .... SAD, BLUE,
       MOROSE, RUEFUL
unicorn fish ...... LIJA, UNIE
uniform .... EVEN
uniform in hue .. FLAT, FLOT
uninteresting .... DULL
union .... MERGER
union, labor ... AFL, CIO, ILA,
       ITA, ILGWU
union, political .... BLOC
union, Russ. workers' ... ARTEL
unique person .... ONER
unique thing: slang ..... ONER
unit .... ACE, ONE
b unit of capacity ...... FARAD
unit of conductance ..... MHO
unit of electrical intensity:
  abbr. .... AMP
unit of electrical resistance or
  reluctance .... REL
unit of electricity . OHM, WATT,
     FARAD, WEBER
unit of electromotive force
             VOLT
unit of energy .... ERG,
     RAD, ERGON
unit of fluidity .... RHE
unit of force .... DYNE
unit of heat .... CALORIE
unit of illumination ..... PHOT
unit of jet propulsion .... JATO
unit of light .... PYR, LUMEN,
      HEFNER
unit of power .... DYNE
unit of power, electric ... OHM,
    WATT, FARAD, WEBER
unit of pressure BARAD, BARIE
unit of reluctance .... REL
unit of resistance .... OHM
unit of weight .... WEY
unit of work ..... ERG, ERGON
unit, pert. to ...... MONADIC
unit, power ratio .... BEL

c unite .... WED, ALLY, JOIN,
     KNIT, WELD, YOKE,
     MERGE, INTEGRATE
unite edges .... RABBET
UNITED STATES
       see AMERICAN
unity .... ONE
univalent element .... MONAD
universal .. WORLD, GENERAL
universal language ... RO, IDO
universe .... WORLD, COSMOS
universe: Hindu ...... LOKA
universe, pert. to ..... COSMIC
university degree-holder
      LICENTIATE
University in Conn. ..... YALE
unkeeled .... RATITE
unkind ILL
unknown Hindu god .... KA
unless .... BUT, SAVE
unless: Lat. .... NISI
unlock .... OPE, OPEN
unmarried .... CELIBATE
unmatched .... ODD
unmixed .... PURE, SHEER
unmusical clang ...... TONK
unnecessary ...... NEEDLESS
unplowed strip .... HADE
unpredictable .... ERRATIC
d unprincipled person .... CAD,
    SCAMP, BOUNDER,
    REPROBATE
unprofitable, as rents .... SECK
unrefined .... EARTHY
unrelenting . IRON, ADAMANT
unruffled . CALM, SERENE
unruly outbreak .... RIOT
unruly person .... RANTIPOLE
unsophisticated ...... NAIVE
unsorted flour .... ATA, ATTA
unspoken .... TACIT
unstable ... ASTATIC, ERRATIC
unsuitable ..... INAPT, INEPT
untamed .... WILD, FERAL
untidy person .... SLOB
untidiness .... MESS, MUSS
until .... TILL
untrained .... RAW
unusual .... RARE, EXOTIC
unusual person or thing . ONER
unwavering .... SURE, STEADY
unwholesome ILL
unwieldly thing .... HULK
unwilling .... LOTH, LOATH,
     AVERSE
unwilling, be: archaic ... NILL
unyielding .. FIRM, ADAMANT
unyielding: naut. .... FAST

Up

up: comb. form .... ANO
Upanishad .... ISHA
upland plain .... WOLD
upbraid ...... CHIDE, SCOLD,
                    REPROACH
upon .... EPI, ATOP, ONTO
upon: law .... SUR
Upper Nile Negro ...... MADI
Upper Nile tribesman ... MADI
Upper Silurian .... ONTARIAN
uppermost part .... TOP
upright ...... ERECT, HONEST
upright column .... STELE
upright piece .... JAMB, STUD
uprising .... REVOLT
uproar .... DIN
upward, heave: naut. ... SCEND
uraeus .... ASP
Uranus' satellite ...... ARIEL
urban office-holder ... MAYOR
urchin ..... IMP, TAD, GAMIN
Urfa, modern .... EDESSA
urge .... EGG, PLY, YEN,
             IMPEL, PRESS
urge: Scot. .... ERT

urial .... SHA
urticaria .... HIVES
urus .... TUR
us: Ger. .... UNS
usage .... WONT
use a divining rod ..... DOWSE
use, be of .... AVAIL
use exertions .... STRIVE
use one's efforts ...... EXERT
used up ...... ATE, DEPLETED
useful ... UTILE, PRACTICAL
useless .... IDLE, FUTILE
               OTIOSE, INUTILE
usual .... NORMAL
Utah State flower ...... SEGO
utmost .... LAST, FINAL,
                    GREATEST
utmost hyperbole .... ELA
utter .... SAY, SHEER,
              SPEAK, STARK
utter, as greeting .... BID
utter loudly ..... VOCIFERATE
uttered ... ORAL, SAID, SPOKE
utterly .... STARK
Uz, brother of .... ARAN

V

V-shaped piece ...... WEDGE
vacant .... IDLE, EMPTY
vacuum .... VOID
vacuum, opposite of .. PLENUM
vacuum tube .... DIODE
vagabond . VAG, HOBO, TRAMP
vague .... HAZY, LOOSE
vainglory .... PRIDE
valance, short ...... PELMET
vale ..... DALE, DELL, VALLEY
Vali, mother of .... RIND
valiant ... BRAVE, STALWART
Valkyrie .... DIS, NORN
valley ..... DALE, DELL, VAIL,
             VALE, GLADE
valley, deep .... COULEE
valley, Jordan .... GHOR
value .... RATE, PRIZE,
          WORTH, APPRAISE
value, thing of little ... TRIFLE
valve .... COCK
vampire .... LAMIA
van .... FORE
vandal .... HUN
vanish .... EVANESCE
vanity .... PRIDE
vanity case .... ETUI
vantage, place of ... COIGN
vapid .... INANE, STALE

vapor .... STEAM
vapor: comb. form ..... ATMO
vapor: dialect......... ROKE
vapor in air ...... HAZE, MIST
Varangians .... ROS
variable .... PROTEAN
variable, most ..... PROTEAN
variable star .... MIRA, NOVA
variation, small
          SHADE, NUANCE
variegated .... SHOT
variegated in color
          PIED, CALICO
variety .... KIND
variety of bean
          SOY, LIMA, PINTO
various: comb. form
          VARI, VARIO
varnish ingredient
     LAC, COPAL, RESIN
varnish, kind of
     SHELLAC, SHELLAC
varnish material .... ELEM
vase .... URN
vat ...... BAC, TUB, CISTERN
vat, beer ... GAAL, GAIL, GYL
vat, brewer's ... KIVE, KEEV
vat, large .... KEIR, KIER
vault .... SAF

Vault

a
vault, church .... CRYPT
vaulted alcove .... APSE
vaunt .... BRAG, BOAST
vector, that which turns a
                        VERSOR
Vedic dialect .... PALI
VEDIC GODS
        see SPECIAL SECTION
veer ..... SHY, TURN, SHIFT
veer off .... SHEER
vegetable ... PEA, BEAN, BEET,
    KALE, OCRA, OKRA, OKRO,
    CHARD, ENDIVE, TOMATO,
    WOBBIE, CELTUCE
vegetable fuel .... PEAT
vegetables, pod .... PEASE
vehicle .... CAR, CART,
                CYCLE, HANSOM
vehicle, Am. Ind.
        TRAVOIS, TRAVOISE
vehicle 4-wheeled .... LANDAU
vehicle, light, India ... TONGA
vehicle, Near East ..... ARABA
vehicle, Russ. .... TROIKA
vehicle, war .... TANK
veil, chalice .... AER
vein: Lat. .... VENA
b
vein of body .... CAVA
vein, ore .... LODE, SCRIN
vein, ore: prov. Eng. .... ROKE
vein, ore beside .... RIDER
vein, throat .... JUGULAR
vellum .... PARCHMENT
velocity per second .... VELO
velum .... PALATE
velvet .... PANNE
velvet grass .... HOLCUS
vend .... SELL
vendetta .... FEUD
venerable .... OLD, HOARY
"Venerable" monk ...... BEDE
venerate ..... ESTEEM, REVERE
veneration .... AWE
Venetian nobleman ..... DOGE
Venetian painter ..... TITIAN
Venetian red .... SIENA
Venetian resort .... LIDO
Venetian rose .... SIENA
Venetian traveler ...... POLO
Venezuela copper center AROA
Venezuela Ind. language PUME
vengeance goddess ...... ARA
Venice marble bridge ..RIALTO
Venice canals .... RII
Venice district .... RIALTO
ventral .... HEMAD, HAEMAD
venture .... DARE

c
Venus, island of ..... MELOS
Venus' son .... CUPID
Venus, youth loved by ADONIS
veranda, Dutch, S. Afr. STOEP
veranda, Hawaii ...... LANAI
veranda, India .... PYAL
verb form .... IS, AM, ARE,
                    WAS, TENSE
verbal .... ORAL
verbal ending .. ED, ER, ES, ING
verbal noun .... GERUND
verbal rhythm .... METRE
verbally .... ALOUD
Verdi heroine .... AIDA
verily .... YEA, AMEN
verity .... TRUTH
versatile .... MOBILE
verse .... LINE, STICH
verse, Fr. .... RONDEL
verse, Ir. .... RANN
verse, pert. to kind of IAMBIC
version, Bible .... ITALA
vertebral bones SACRA, SACRUM
verticle line, in a .... APEAK
verticle timber: naut. ... BITT
vertigo .... DINUS
very .... SO
very abundant ... LUXURIANT
very: Fr. .... TRES
very: Scot. .... VERA
d
very: Span. .... MUY
Ve's brother .... ODIN
vesicle, skin .... BLISTER
VESSEL .. see also BOAT, SHIP,
        GALLEY
vessel .... ARK
vessel, anat. ..... VAS, VASA
vessel, Arab .... DOW, DHOW
vessel, chemical .... ETNA
vessel, coasting, E. Ind.
                    PATAMAR
vessel, cooking .... PAN, POT
vessel, drinking ...... GOURD
vessel for liquors .. DECANTER
vessel, glass .... BOCAL
vessel, Gr. CADUS, AMPHORA
vessel, heating .... ETNA
vessel, large .... TANK
vessel, liquor ...... FLAGON
vessel, Medit. .. SETEE, MISTIC
vessel, Rom. .... PATERA
vessel, sacred .... PIX, PYX
vessel, sailing .... SAIC,
                SETEE, XEBEC
vessel, shallow .... BASIN
vessel, supply .... COALER
vessel, 3-masted
            XEBEC, FRIGATE
vessel, 2-masted YAWL, ZULU

175

a vessel with two handles, Gr.
DIOTA
vessel's curved planking .. SNY
vestal .... CHASTE
vestige .. IOTA, RELIC, TRACE
vestment .. ALB, COPE, AMICE,
EPHOD, STOLE
vestment, white .. ALB, AMICE
vesuvianite, brown ... EGERAN
vetch .... TARE
vetch, bitter .... ERS
vetch, India .... AKRA
vetiver, grass .... BENA
vex GALL, RILE, ROIL, HARRY
vex persistently ...... NETTLE
vex: Scot. .... FASH
vexed .... RILY
via .... PER
viands .... DIET
viands, dainty .... CATES
Viaud's pseudonym ..... LOTI
vibrate .... THRILL
vibration: music .... TREMOLO
vice .... SIN
viceroy .... VALI
Vichy Premier .... LAVAL
vicious man .... YAHOO
victim .... PREY
victorfish .... AKU
victor's crown ...... LAUREL
victory, Eng. .. CRECY, CRESSY
victory trophy .... SCALP
b victuals .... FOOD
"— victus," woe to the con-
quered .... VAE
"—vide," "which see" .. QUAE
vie with .... EMULATE
Viennese park .... PRATER
view .... SCENE, VISTA
vigilant .... WARY, ALERT
vigor .... PEP, VIM,
VIS, ZIP, FORCE
Viking ... ERIC, OLAF, ROLLO
Viking explorer .... ERIC
vilify .... REVILE
village .. DORP, VILL, HAMLET
village, Afr. .... KRAAL
village, Java .... DESSA
village, Russ. .... MIR
village, Scot. .... REW
village, S. Afr. native .. STAD
villain .... KNAVE
villein .... CEORL
vindicate .... AVENGE
vindication .... REVENGE
vine .... IVY, BINE
vine: comb. form ...... VITI
vine, N. Z. .... AKA
vine, P. I. .... IYO

c vine, woody .. ABUTA, LIANA
"vin du —," wine of the
country .... CRU
vinegar of ale ...... ALEGAR
vinegar, pert. to ..... ACETIC
vinegar worm .... EEL, NEMA
vinous .... WINY
viol, ancient type ..... REBEC
viol, bass .... GAMBA
viol, Shetlands .... GUE
viola .... ALTO
violent .... HOT
violet-odored ketone .. IRONE
violin, bass .... CELLO
violin, early .. REBAB, REBEC
violin, famous .... STRAD
violin, It. .. AMATI, CREMONA
violin, small .... KIT
violin, tenor ... ALTO, VIOLA
violinist ...... ELMAN, YSAYE
viper .... ASP, ADDER
viper genus .... ECHIS
viper, horned ...... CERASTES
Virgil's hero .. ENEAS, AENEAS
Virgin Mary pictured mourning
PIETA
virus-fighting substance
ANTIVIRAL
visage .... FACE
viscous
d LIMY, ROPY, SIZY, SLIMY
viscous substance .. TAR, SLIME
Vishnu, incarnation, 7th RAMA
Vishnu, soul of universe VASU
Vishnu's bow .... SARAN
Vishnu's serpent ...... NAGA
visible juncture .... SEAM
Visigoth king ALARIC, ALARIK
vision, defective ..... ANOPIA
vision, pert. to .... OPTIC
visionary ...... AIRY, IDEAL,
DREAMY, UNREAL, IDEALIST
visit ...... SEE, CALL, HAUNT
visit at sea .... GAM
visit between whalers ... GAM
vison .... MINK
vital energy .... HORME
vital fluid .... SAP
vital principle .... SOUL
vitalize .... ANIMATE
vitamin ... CITRIN, ADERMIN,
ANEURIN, TORULIN
vitamin B NIACIN, THIAMINE
vitamin B2 .... FLAVIN
vitamin H .... BIOTIN
vitiate .... SPOIL, TAINT,
POLLUTE, INVALIDATE
vitriol-infused earth .... SORY
vituperate .... SCOLD

vivacious ..... AIRY, BRIGHT
vivacity .... ELAN, LIFE
vocal flourish ...... ROULADE
vocation .... CAREER
"— voce" .... SOTTO
voice .... SAY
voice
ALTO, BASS, VOCE, TENOR
voice: It. .... VOCE
voice: Lat. .... VOX
voice, loss of ...... APHONIA
voiced .... SONANT
voiced, not .... ASONANT
voiceless .... SPIRATE
voiceless consonant ..... SURD
void .... NUL, NULL,
ABYSS, SPACE, INVALID
void, to make. ANNUL, CANCEL
void, to render: Scot. ... CASS
voided escutcheon ...... ORLE
volcanic cinder .... SCORIA
volcanic islands, Atlantic
FAROE
volcanic rock
TUFA, TUFF, LATITE
volcanic scoria-matter
LAVA, SLAG
volcano .. ETNA, AETNA, PELEE
volcano crater .... MAAR
volcano hole .... CRATER

volcano, Martinique Is. .. PELEE
volcano mouth ...... CRATER
volcano, P. I. .... APO
volcano pit .... CRATER
volcano, Sicily ETNA, AETNA
volcano, W. Indies .... PELEE
volition .... WILL
volt-ampere .... WATT
Voltaire .... AROUET
Voltaire play: Fr. ..... ZAIRE
voluble .... GLIB
volume .... MO, TOME
vomiting .... EMESIS
voodoo charm .... MOJO
voodoo snake deity .... ZOMBI
vote .... BALLOT
vote into office .... ELECT
vote, right to .... FRANCHISE
vote, take a .... POLL
votes ...... AYES, NOES, YEAS
vouch for .... SPONSOR
voucher .... CHIT, NOTE
"vous —": Fr., you are .. ETES
vowel, line over ..... MACRON
vowel suppression .... ELISION
voyaging .... ASEA
vulcanite .... EBONITE
Vulcan's wife .... MAIA
vulgar .... COARSE
vulture AURA, URUBU, CONDOR

W

"W", old English .... WEN
wade across .... FORD
wading bird IBIS, RAIL, CRANE,
EGRET, HERON, STILT,
AVOCET, AVOSET, JAC-
ANA, FLAMINGO
wag .... WIT
wages .... PAY
Wagner heroine . ELSA, SENTA,
ISOLDE
Wagnerian role .... ERDA
wagon .. CART, DRAY, WAIN
wagon pin .... CLEVIS
wagon, Russ. .... TELEGA
wagon shaft .... THILL
wagon tongue .... NEAP, POLE
wagtail .... LARK
wahoo, fish .... PETO
wail .... KEEN, LAMENT
waist .... CAMISA, TAILLE
waistcoat VEST, GILET, JERKIN
wait .... BIDE
waken ...... ROUSE, AROUSE

wale .... WELT
Wales emblem .... LEEK
walk ..... PACE, STEP, TREAD
walk affectedly ...... MINCE
walk heavily .... PLOD, SLOG
walk, inability to .... ABASIA
walk lamely .... LIMP
walk stiffly .... STALK
walk, tree-lined .... ALAMEDA
walking stick ... CANE, STILT
wall, arena .... SPINA
wall around fortified place
RAMPART
wall, divided by .... SEPTATE
wall: Fr. .... MUR
wall material .... COB
wall, of a .... MURAL
wall paneling .... WAINSCOT
wall piece TEMPLET, TEMPLATE
wall section .... DADO, PANEL
wall, squeeze against .. MURE
walls .... SEPTA
wallaba tree, Brazil ..... APA
walled city, Nigeria ..... KANO

177

a wallflower .... KEIRI
wallop .... LAM
wallow .... WELTER
walrus .... MORSE
wampum PEAG,SEWAN,SEAWAN
wan .... ASHY, PALE, ASHEN
wand .... BATON
wander .. ERR, HAAK, ROAM,
    ROVE, RAMBLE, DIGRESS
wander idly .... GAD
wanderer .... VAG, NOMAD
"Wandering Jew" author .. SUE
wane .... EBB
want .... LACK, NEED, DESIRE
wapiti .... ELK
war-club, medieval ..... MACE
war correspondent
    PYLE, BALDWIN
war cry, ancient Gr. ... ALALA
war god .... ARES, MARS
war god, Babyl. ... IRA, IRRA
war god, Norse TY, TYR, TYRR
war god, Teut. .... ER
war goddess, Gr. ...... ENYO
war horse .... CHARGER
war, religious .... CRUSADE
war, Russ.-Eng. ...... CRIMEA
war vessel .... CRUISER
warble .. SING, TRILL, YODEL
b ward off .... FEND, AVERT,
    PARRY, REPEL, STAVE
ward politician ...... HEELER
warden, fire .... RANGER
warehouse .... DEPOT
warehouse room ...... LOFT
warm .... CALID, TEPID
warning of danger: biol.
    SEMATIC
warning signal .... SIREN
warning system, attack
    DEW, BMEWS
warp yarn .... ABB
warrant, from monarch BERAT
warrior, Samoa .... TOA
warship, sailing .... FRIGATE
wary .... CAGY
was not: dialect .... NAS
wash .... LAVE
wash leather .... LOSH
wash out .... ELUTE
washings: chem. ..... ELUATE
Washington Irving character RIP
wasp .... HORNET
wasps, the .... VESPA
waste .... LOSS
waste allowance .... TRET
waste away GNAW, ATROPHY
waste fiber .... NOIL
waste land .... MOOR
waste matter .... DROSS
waste silk ..... KNUB, FRISON

c waste time .... IDLE
wastes, growing in .. RUDERAL
watch .... SEE, GLOM
watch chain .... FOB
watchdog, Hel's .... GARM
watchful .... ALERT
watchful guardian .... ARGUS
watchful, name meaning . IRA
watchman, alert ...... ARGUS
watchman, night .... SERENO
watchtower .... MIRADOR
water ... SPRINKLE, IRRIGATE
water arum .... CALLA
water chestnut, Chin. .... LING
water cock .... KORA
water, covered by .... AWASH
water: Fr. ...... EAU, EAUX
water: Lat. .... AQUA
water lily .... LOTUS
water passage SLUICE, STRAIT
water pipe
    HOOKA, HOOKAH, NARGILE
water raising device
    TABUT, TABOOT
water reservoir, natural
    CENOTE
water scorpion genus ... NEPA
water, seek .... DOWSE
water, sound of .... PLASH
water: Sp. .... AGUA
d water spirit
    ARIEL, SPRITE, UNDINE
water sprite ...... NIX, NIXIE
water sprite: Gaelic .... KELPIE
water surface .... RYME
water vessel, India
    LOTA, LOTO, LOTAH
water wheel
    NORIA, DANAIDE, TURBINE
water wheel, Persian .. NORIA
water's surface: naut. .. RYME
watercourse ... LADE, BROOK,
    CANAL, RIVER, STREAM
watered appearance .... MOIRE
watered silk .... MOIRE
waterfall, Scot. LIN, LYN, LINN
watering place .. SPA, BADEN
waterproof canvas ..... TARP
waterskin .... MATARA
watertight, make CALK, CAULK
waterway ..... BAYOU, CANAL
waterway, narrow .... STRAIT
watery .... SEROUS
watery: comb. form ..... SERO
wattle tree .... BOREE
wattle honeyeater
    IAO, MANUAO
wave .... FLY, SEA
wave-crest comb. ...... COOM
wave: Fr. .... ONDE
wave, huge .... SEA

waver ...... FALTER, TEETER
wavy: Her.
UNDE, UNDY, NEBULE
wax .... CERE
wax ointment .... CERATE
wax, pert. to .... CERAL
wax: Sp. .... CERA
wax, yellow or white CERESIN
waxy chemical .... CERIN
waxy substance ...... CERIN
way ...... VIA, MODE, ROUTE
way of walking .... GAIT
way out .... EGRESS
wayside — .... INN
wayside stop, India .. PARAO
we: Lat. .... NOS
weak .... PUNY, FRAIL,
DEBILE, EFFETE, FEEBLE
weak cider .... PERKIN
weaken .... SAP, LABEFY,
VITIATE, ENERVATE, EN-
FEEBLE
weakfish, S. Am. .... ACOUPA
weakness .... ATONY
weal .... WALE
wealth, man of ...... NABOB
wealthy: Scot. .... BIEN
weapon .... LANCE,
SPEAR, SWORD, MUSKET
weapon, ancient .... CELT
weapon, dagger-like .. BALAS
weapon: Fr. .... ARME
weapon, gaucho's BOLA, BOLAS
weapon, Maori .... PATU
weapon, medieval ..... ONCIN
weapon, N. Z. .... PATU
weapon, P. I. .... BOLO
weapon, S. Am. .. BOLA, BOLAS
wear away EAT, ERODE, ABRADE
wear away slowly ... CORRODE
wear by friction .... RUB
wear off .... ABRADE
wearing down .... ATTRITION
weary .... BORE, TIRE
weasel VARE, ERMINE, FERRET
weasel: Eng.
STOT, STOAT, STOTE
weather indicator BAROMETER
weathercock .... VANE
weaverbird ..... BAYA, MAYA
weaverbird, S. Afr. .... TAHA
weaver's bobbin on shuttle PIRN
weaver's reed .... SLEY
weaving frame .... LOOM
weaving term .... LISSE
weaving tool .... EVENER

web .... TELA
web-footed bird . DUCK, LOON,
GOOSE
web-like membrane ..... TELA
web-spinning
RETIARY, TELARIAN
wed .... MARRY
wedding anniversaries 1st,
PAPER; 2nd, COTTON;
3rd, CANDY OR LEATHER;
4th, SILK, FRUIT, FLOW-
ERS, or LEATHER; 5th,
WOODEN; 6th, IRON OR
CANDY; 7th, WOOL, COP-
PER, OR FLORAL; 8th,
WOOL, BRONZE, OR POT-
TERY; 9th, WILLOW OR
POTTERY; 10th, TIN; 11th,
STEEL; 12th, SILK OR LIN-
EN; 13th, LACE; 14th,
IVORY; 15th, CRYSTAL;
20th, CHINA; 25th, SIL-
VER; 30th, PEARL; 35th,
CORAL; 40th, RUBY OR
EMERALD; 45th, RUBY OR
SAPPHIRE; 50th, GOLDEN;
55th, EMERALD; 75th,
DIAMOND
wedge, entering . COIN, COIGN,
QUOIN, COIGNE
wedge-like piece .... QUOIN
wedge-shaped ...... CUNEATE
wedge-shaped piece GIB, SHIM
wedge, steel .... FROE
Wednesday, source of name
WODEN
weed .... TARE, DARNEL
weed, coarse .... DOCK
week ..... SENNET, SENNIGHT
week day .... FERIA
weep
CRY, SOB, BOHO, LAMENT
weep, Scot. .... ORP
weeping statue .... NIOBE
weeping woman, Gr. myth NIOBE
weft .... WOOF
WEIGHT .. see also SPECIAL
SECTION
weight .... TON, HEFT
weight allowance TARE, TRET
weight, ancient
MINA, TALENT
weight, ancient: var. ... MNA
weight, Asiatic .... TAEL
weight, balance .... RIDER

179

Weight

weight, Danish .... **ORT**
weight, India ...... **SER, TOLA**
weight machine: Scot.
              TRON, TRONE
weight, metric unit of .. **GRAM**
weight of England ..... **STONE**
weight of silk before
    degumming .... **PARI**
weight, pert. to .... **BARIC**
weight system .... **TROY**
weir .... **DAM**
weird .... **EERY, EERIE**
welcome .... **GREET**
well, Bib. .... **AIN**
well-bred people ..... **GENTRY**
"well done" .. **EUGE, BRAVO**
well done: Eng. .... **EUGE**
well: Fr. .... **BIEN**
well: It. & Lat. .... **BENE**
well: Scot. .... **AWEEL**
Welsh dog .... **CORGI**
Welsh god of sea .... **DYLAN**
Welshman .... **CELT**
welt .... **WALE**
wen .... **TALPA**
Wend of Saxony ...... **SORB**
wergeld .... **CRO**
W. Australia capital ... **PERTH**
W. Afr. timber tree ... **ODUM**
W. Afr. tribe **IBO, BUBE, BUBI**
W. Ind. bayberry **AUSU, AUZU**
W. Ind. fish
    BOGA, CERO, TESTAR
W. Ind. idol. ..... **ZEME, ZEMI**
W. Ind. isle ... **CUBA, HAITI**
W. Ind. key .... **CAY**
W. Ind. scrapper .... **CAJI**
W. Ind. shrub plant ... **ANIL**
West Point mascot ..... **MULE**
West Pointer
    PLEB, CADET, PLEBE
West Saxon king .... **INE**
Western division of Osset **DIGOR**
Western European **CELT, KELT**
Western Indian .... **UTE**
Western shrub .... **SAGE**
"Western Star" author **BENET**
Western state .... **UTAH**
Westphalian city ..... **HERNE**
wet: Scot. .... **WAT**
wet .... **ASOP, MOIST**
whale .... **CET, ORC, ORK,**
    CETE, BELUGA, GRAMPUS
whale carcass **KRANG, KRENG**
whale hunter .... **AHAB**
whale oil cask .... **RIER**
whale-shark .... **MHOR**
whale tail part .... **FLUKE**
whale, white .... **BELUGA**

whale, white Caspian
             HUSE, HUSO
whales .... **CETE**
whales, herd of ... **GAM, POD**
whales, pert. to ...... **CETIC**
whales, school of .. **GAM, POD**
whalebone .... **BALEEN**
wharf..**KEY, PIER, QUAI, QUAY**
what is it? obs. .... **ANAN**
whatnot .... **ETAGERE**
wheal .... **WALE, WEAL**
wheat disease .... **BUNT**
wheat, German **EMMER, SPELT**
wheat, India ..... **SUJI, SUJEE**
wheat, kind of **EMMER, SPELT**
wheat middlings .. **SEMOLINA**
wheedle .... **COG, COAX**
wheedling .... **BUTTERY**
wheel .... **ROTA**
wheel band .... **STRAKE**
wheel center **HOB, HUB, NAVE**
wheel, furniture ..... **CASTER**
wheel, grooved ...... **SHEAVE**
wheel horse .... **POLER**
wheel part .... **HUB, RIM,**
          FELLY, SPOKE
wheel projection .... **CAM**
wheel shaft .... **AXLE**
wheel-shaped .... **ROTATE**
wheel spindle .. **AXLE, ARBOR**
wheel tread .... **TIRE**
wheels, pert. to .... **ROTAL**
where: Lat. .... **UBI**
whetstone, fine . **BUHR, HONE**
whey of milk .. **SERA, SERUM**
which see: abbr. .... **QV**
whiff .... **PUFF**
while .... **AS, WHEN**
whimper ..... **MEWL, PULE**
whin .... **GORSE**
whine .... **PULE**
whinny .... **NEIGH**
whip **CAT, BEAT, FLOG, LASH**
whip, cowboy .... **CHICOTE**
whip mark ..... **WALE, WEAL**
whip, Russ. ..... **KNOUT**
whipsocket .... **SNEAD**
whirl .... **REEL, SPIN**
whirlpool ..... **EDDY, GURGE,**
           VORTEX
whirlpool: Scot. .... **WEEL, WIEL**
whirlwind in Atlantic ..... **OE**
whirring sound .... **BIRR**
whiskers ..... **BEARD, GOATEE**
whiskey: Ir. .... **POTEEN**
whiskey drink: Scot.
       ATHOL, ATHOLE
whist win .... **SLAM**
whistle .... **PIPE, SIREN**
whit .... **BIT, JOT,**
    ATOM, DOIT, IOTA

a

white acid, pert. to .. TROPIC
white alkaline .... SODA
white ant, P. I. .. ANAI, ANAY
white, bitter compound LININ
white: comb. form ..... ALBO
"White Elephant" land .. SIAM
white ermine LASSET, MINIVER
white-flecked .... ROAN
White Friar .... CARMELITE
white: Ir. .... BAWN
white man: P. I. ... CACHILA
white matter, brain .... ALBA
white oak .... ROBLE
white poplar .... ABELE
white spruce ...... EPINETTE
white with age .... HOAR
whitefish .... CISCO
whiten .... ETIOLATE
whitish .... HOARY
whitlow grass .... DRABA
Whittier heroine ...... MAUD
whiz .... PIRR, WHIR, ZIZZ
whoa .... HOLLA
whole amount .... GROSS
whole: comb. form ...... TOTO
wholesome .... SALUTARY
wholly .... ALL
wicked .... EVIL
wicker basket .... CESTA,
                  KIPSY, PANNIER

b

wicker basket, Guiana PEGALL
wickerwork .... RATAN
wickerwork hut ...... JACAL
wicket, croquet .... HOOP
wide-mouthed vessel
                  EWER, OLLA
widgeon .... SMEE
widgeon genus ...... MARECA
widow .... RELICT
widow in cards .... SKAT
widow monkey .... TITI
widow's bit or coin .... MITE
widow's third: Scot. .... TERCE
wield .... PLY, USE
wife, Moroccan ruler's SHERIFA
wife ... FEME, FRAU, FEMME
wife's property .... DOS
wig .... PERUKE
wigwam .. TIPI, TEPEE, TEEPEE
wild .... FERAL, SAVAGE
wild animals, collection of
              ZOO, MENAGERIE
wild animal's trail
       SLOT, SPUR, SPOOR
wild apple .... CRAB, DOUCIN
wild ass, Afr. ...... QUAGGA
wild ass, Asia ...... ONAGER
wild boar genus .... SUS
wild buffalo, India
       ARNA, ARNI, ARNEE

c

wild buffalo, Malay ... GAUR,
       SLADANG, SALADANG,
              SELADANG
wild cat, Siberia, Tibet, steppes
                  MANUL
wild cattle, India GAUR, GOUR
wild ary .... EVOE
wild dog .... DHOLE
wild dog genus ...... THOS
wild dog, Japan .... TANATE
"Wild Duck" author .... IBSEN
wild garlic .... MOLY
wild ginger .... ASARUM
wild hog .... BOAR
wild honeybee, E. Ind. DINGAR
wild horse of Tartary TARPAN
wild lime .... COLIMA
wild olive tree ..... OLEASTER
wild ox .... ANOA
wild ox, Malay. .... BANTENG
wild plum .... SLOE
wild plum, Calif. ...... ISLAY
wild sheep, Asia
              RASSE, ARGALI
wild sheep, horned . MOUFLON
wild sheep, India ... SHA, SNA,
       URIAL, NAHOOR, OORIAL
wild sheep, N. Afr.
       ARUI, UDAD, AOUDAD
wild sheep, Tibet .... SHA

d

wild sheep, Tibet
       SNA, BHARAL, NAHOOR
wild turnip .... NAVEW
wild vanilla .... LIATRIS
wildcat .... BALU, LYNX
wildcat, Afr. & India .. CHAUS
wildcat, S. Am. ...... EYRA
wildcat, Sumatra ...... BALU
wildebeest .... GNU
wile .... ART
will addition ...... CODICIL
will, one inheriting from
                  DEVISEE
will, one making .... DEVISOR
will power, loss of .... ABULIA
William: Ir. .... LIAM
William I, half brother of ODO
William the Conqueror's
       daughter .... ADELA
willingly .... LIEF
willow .... ITEA, OSIER
willow, Europ. ...... SALLOW
willow genus, Virginia ... ITEA
Wilson's thrush ...... VEERY
wilt .... FADE, DROOP
wily .... FOXY
wimple .... GORGET
win .... GAIN
winch .... WHIN
wind .... GALE
wind, Adriatic .... BORA

181

wind, Andes ... **PUNA, PUNO**
wind, Austral. ...... **BUSTER**
wind, away from ...... **ALEE**
wind, cold Malta .... **GREGALE**
wind, cold Medit. .... **MISTRAL**
wind, cold Swiss Alps **BISE, BIZE**
wind: comb. form .... **ANEMO**
wind-deposited loam ... **LOESS**
wind, dry, from Sahara .. **LESTE**
wind, east .... **EURUS**
wind god, Babyl.
    ADAD, ADDA, ADDU
wind god, Hindu ...... **VAYU**
wind god, pert. to
    EOLIAN, AEOLIAN
wind, hot, dry ...... **KAMSIN,**
    SIMOOM, SIMOON, SIROCCO
wind, hot, Medit. .... **SOLANO**
wind indicator .. **SOCK, VANE**
wind instrument
    HORN, OBOE, PIPE, BUGLE
wind, Levant .... **ETESIAN**
wind, Madeira .... **LESTE**
wind, Medit. .... **ETESIAN**
wind, Medit., poet. ..... **SIROC**
wind, Mesop. .... **SHAMAL**
wind, north .... **BOREAS**
wind off Faroe Islands .... **OE**
wind, Peru Andes **PUNA, PUNO**
wind, sand-laden
    SAMIEL, SIMOOM, SIMOON
wind, Sahara .... **LESTE**
wind, South ... **NOTUS, AUSTER**
wind, southeast .... **EURUS**
wind, southwest .... **AFER**
wind, Trieste, cold ..... **BORA**
wind, warm dry **FOHN, FOEHN**
wind, west .... **AFER**
winds, south, Peru ..... **SURES**
windborne .... **AEOLIAN**
windflower .... **ANEMONE**
windlass .... **CAPSTAN**
windmill sail .... **AWE**
window lead .... **CAME**
window ledge .... **SILL**
window part .... **SASH**
window, semipolygonal .. **ORIEL**
window setter .... **GLAZIER**
windrow .... **SWATH**
windstorm
    OE, BURAN, TORNADO
windstorm, Asia **BURA, BURAN**
wine ...... **VIN, HOCK, PORT,**
    SACK, VINO, MEDOC, TO-
    KAY, CLARET, MALAGA,
    MUSCAT, SHERRY, MO-
    SELLE
wine, Am. .... **CATAWBA**
wine, ancient .... **MASSIC**
wine cask .... **TUN, BUTT**
wine city, It. .... **ASTI**

wine cup .... **AMA**
wine, delicacy of: Fr. ... **SEVE**
wine disorder .... **CASSE**
wine district, Calif. .... **NAPA**
wine drink .... **NEGUS**
wine, dry .... **SEC, BRUT**
wine, golden .... **BUAL**
wine, heavy .... **TOKAY**
wine, honey and ...... **MULSE**
wine, Madeira .... **BUAL**
wine measure, Trieste
    ORNA, ORNE
wine merchant .... **VINTNER**
wine, new .... **MUST**
wine pitcher, Gr. ...... **OLPE**
wine, red **PORT, TINTA, CLARET**
wine, sweet .... **MUSCAT**
wine, sweet: Fr. ..... **MASDEU**
wine, to make .... **VINT**
wine vessel ...... **AMA, OLPE,**
    AMULA, CHALICE
wine, white .... **HOCK,**
    SHERRY, SAUTERNE
wineberry, N. Z. ...... **MAKO**
wing .... **ALA, PENNA,**
    PINNA, PINION
wing, bastard .... **ALULA**
wing, beetle .... **TEGMAN,**
    TEGMINA, TEGUMEN
wing: Fr. .... **AILE**
wing-footed animal .. **ALIPED**
winglike .... **ALAR**
wing-like part .... **ALA, ALAE**
wing movement .... **FLAP**
wing tip, pert. to ... **ALULAR**
wings .... **ALAE**
wings, divested of
    DEALATA, DEALATED
wings, having .. **ALAR, ALATE**
wings: her. .... **VOL, AILE**
winged figure, Gr.
    IDOLON, IDOLUM, EIDOLON
winged fruit, indehiscent
    SAMARA
winged god ..... **EROS, CUPID**
winged seed .... **SAMARA**
winged victory .... **NIKE**
wingless .... **APTERAL**
wingless invertebrates **APTERA**
wink rapidly .... **BAT**
winning at bridge ...... **SLAM**
winnow .... **FAN**
winter, pert. to .... **BRUMAL,**
    HIEMAL, HYEMAL, HIBERNAL
winter squash ...... **CUSHAW**
wipe out .... **ERASE**
wire measure .... **MIL**
wire service .... **AP, UP,**
    INS, UPI, REUTERS

182

SPECIAL SECTION

READY REFERENCE WORD LISTS

In one compact section, here are lists of the most useful and widely-used word categories. Some of these words, having certain customary definitions, are also listed in the definitions' section of this book, but these complete word lists will be of greatest help when you are confronted with GENERALIZED definitions such as "Roman goddess," "South American Indian," "Heraldic term," or "African tribe."

All words in each separate listing are placed according to the number of their letters. This is a tremendous advantage to puzzle solvers, who are more concerned with the length of a word than with its alphabetical placement.

MEASURES

AREA MEASURES

AR, ARE, ACRE, DECARE (10 ARES), CENTIAR, CENTIARE
Annam .... MAU, QUO, SAO
Bengal .... BEGA
Czechoslovakia ... LAN, MIRA
Dutch E. Ind. ....'. BOUW
England, Old .... HYDE
Japan .... BU, SE, TAN
Norway .... MAL, MAAL
Paraguay .... LINO
Poland .... MORG
Rome, Ancient ..... CLIMA, CLIMATA
Serbia .... RIF, RALO
Shetlands, Orkney ...... URE
Siam .... RAI, NGAN
Sweden .... MORGEN

DRY MEASURES

PECK, PINT, STERE
Algeria .... TARRI
Austria .... MUTH
Borneo .... GANTANG
Brazil .... MOIO
Burma .... TENG
Calcutta .... KUNK, RAIK
Channel Is. .... CABOT
China .... HO, HU
Dutch .... KOP, ZAK
Egypt .... KADA, KILAH
Hebrew .... CAB, KAB, KOR, EPHA, OMER, SEAH, EPHAH
Italy .... SALM, SALMA
Japan .... SHO
Morocco .... SAHH
Netherlands ...... KOP, ZAK
Portugal .... MEIO, PIPA
Russia .... LOF
Tangier .... MUDD
Tunis ..... SAA, SAAH, UEBA

LENGTH, DISTANCE MEASURES

ELL, ROD, FOOT, HAND, INCH, MILE, YARD, METER, METRE, PERCH, MICRON, FURLONG
Annam .... LY, GON, NGU
Brazil .... PE
Calcutta .... DHAN, JAOB
China .... HU, LI, PU, TU, CH'IH, TCHI, TSUN
Czechoslovakia .. SAH, LATRO
Denmark FOD, MIL, MUL, ALEN
Domin. Repub. .... ONA
Dutch .... DUIM, VOET
D. E. Indies .... DEPA
Egypt .. PIC, PIK, KHET, THEB
Eritrea .... CUBI
Estonia .... LIIN, SULD
France .... AUNE
Greece .. PIC, PIK, BEMA, PIKI POUS, ACAENA
Hebrew .... EZBA
Iceland .... FET, ALIN, LINA
India .. GAZ, GEZ, GUZ, JOW, KOS, JAOB, KOSS
Italy .... CANNA
Japan .. BU, JO, RI (marine), CHO, DJO, KEN, RIN, HIRO

Java .... PAAL
Libya .... DRA, PIK, DRAH
Malabar .... ADY
Malacca .... ASTA
Netherlands .... DUIM, VOET
Norway .... FOT, ALEN
Persia ..... GAZ, GEZ, GUZ, ZAR, ZER
Poland .... MILA, PRET
Prussia .... RUTE
Rangoon . LAN, DAIN, TAUN
Rome, ancient ...... ACTUS, .. GRADUS, STADIA, STADIUM
Russia .... FUT, VERST
Siam .... WA, KUP, NIU, SEN, SOK, WAH, NIOU, SAWK
Spain .... BARA, CODO, DEDO, VARA
Sweden ...... FOT, REF, FAMN
Switzerland .... TOISE
Tripoli .... DRA, DRAA
Turkey .... PIC, PIK, KHAT, ZIRA

(liquid measures on page 189)

188

WEIGHTS

KIP, TON, GRAM, KILO, CARAT, GRAIN, OUNCE, CENTRAL
Abyssinia .... KASM, NATR, OKET, ALADA, NETER
Annam .... BINH
Arabia .... KELA
Austria .... UNZE
Bavaria .... GRAN
Brazil .... ONCA
Bulgaria .... OKA, OKE
Burma .... VIS, KYAT, VISS
Calcutta .. PANK, PAWA, RAIK
China .... LI, FEN, HAO, KIN, SSU, TAN, YIN, TAEL
Columbia .... SACO
Denmark ES, ORT, VOG, ESER, PUND
Dutch .... ONS, LOOD
Dutch E. Ind ...... TJI, HOEN, TALI, WANG
Egypt ... KAT, KET, OKA, OKE, HEML, KHAR, OHIA, OKIEH
England .... STONE
Estonia ...... NAEL, PUUD
Ethiopia .... See Abyssinia
France .... GROS
Germany .... LOT, LOTE, LOTH, STEIN
Greece .... MNA, MINA, OBOLE, OBOLUS
Guinea .... AKEY, PISO, UZAN, SERON

Hebrew .... BEKA, REBA
India .... SER, BHAR, PALA, RATI, TOLA, VISS, RATTI
Italian ...... SALM, SALMA
Japan ...... KIN, SHI, MORIN
Malay .... CHEE
Malta .... SALM, SALMA
Mexico .... LIBRA, ONZA
Mongolia .... LAN
Morocco .... ARTEL
Moslem .... ROTL
Netherlands ...... ONS, LOOD
Norway .... PUND
ORIENT ...... MANN, ROTL, TAEL, ARTAL
Palestine ...... ROTLA, ZUZA
Persia .... SER
Poland .... LUT
Portugal GRAO, ONCA, LIBRA
Rangoon .... RUAY
Rome, Ancient .... AS, BES, LIBRA, SOLIDUS
Russia .... LAN, PUD, DOLA, POOD, POUD
Siam .... PAI, KLAM, KLOM, TICAL
Shetland Island .. URE (ounce)
Spain .... ONZA
Sweden ASS, ORT, STEN, UNTZ
Turkey .... OCK, OKA, OKE, KILE, OCHA, KERAT

LIQUID MEASURES

TUN, DRAM, GILL, PINT, MINIM
Abyssinia ...... CUBA, KUBA
Annam .... TAO
Arabia .... SAA
Austria .... FASS
Brazil .... PIPA
Burma .... BYEE, SEIT
China ...... KO, QUEI, SHIH
Cyprus .... CASS
Dutch .. (old) AAM, AUM, KAN
Egypt .... HIN
England .... PIN, CRAN
Ethiopia .... see ABYSSINIA
Germany .... AAM, EIMER
Hebrew .... HIN

Hungary .... AKO
Japan .... KOKU, SHO
Malaya .... PAU
Netherlands . AAM, AUM, KAN
Portugal .... BOTA, PIPA
Rangoon .... BYEE, SEIT
Rome, Ancient ...... URNA
Russia ... STOF, STOFF, STOOF
Somaliland .... CABA
Spain .... COPA
Sweden .... AM, AMAR, KAPP
Switzerland ..... IMMI, SAUM
Tangier .... KULA
Trieste .... ORNA, ORNE
Yugoslavia .... AKOV

COINS, MONEY

Abyssinia ..... BESA, GIRSH, TALARI
Afghanistan .... AMANIA
Albania .... LEK
Anglo-Saxon .... ORA, SCEAT
Annam .... QUAN
Austria .... DUCAT
Biblical .. BEKA, MITE (small), SHEKEL, TALENT
Brazil .... REI
Bulgaria ... LEV, LEW, DINAR
Chile .... COLON
China .. LI, CASH, TAEL, TIAO, YUAN, PU (early)
Colombia .... REAL
Costa Rica .... COLON
Czechoslovakia ...... DUCAT, KRONE (plural, KRONEN)
Denmark ... ORA, ORE, ORAS, KRONE (plural, KRONER)
Dutch OORD, DALER, GULDEN, STIVER
D. E. Indies ..... BONK, DUIT
Egypt .... GIRSH
England ... ORA, RIAL (gold), RYAL, RYEL, GROAT, PENCE, FLORIN, GUINEA
Equador .... SUCRE
Ethiopia ...... see ABYSSINIA
Europe .... (old) GROS, DUCAT
France .. ECU (old), SOL, SOU, AGNEL (old), FRANC, LIARD (old), LOUIS, OBOLE, BESANT or BEZANT (old)
Genoa .... JANE (old)
Germany .... MARK, KRONE (former), TALER, THALER
Ger. E. Africa .... PESA
Greece .. OBOL or OBOLI (old), STATER (old)
Hungary ...... GARA, PENGO
Iceland .... AURAR, EYRIR, KRONA
India. LAC, PIE, ANNA, DAWM, FELS, HOON, LAKH, PICE (small bronze), TARA, MOHUR (old), RUPEE
Iran .... see PERSIA
Iraq .... DINAR
Ireland .... RAP (old)

Italy .... LIRA, LIRE, SOLDO, TESTER, TESTON, TESTONE, TESTOON
Japan .... BU, RIN, SEN, YEN, OBAN
Latvia .... LAT, LATU
Lithuania .. LIT, LITAI, LITAS
Macao .... AVO
Malaya TRA (tin, pewter), TRAH
Mexico ..... PESO, CENTAVO
Montenegro .... PARA
Morocco .... OKIA, RIAL
Nepal .... MOHUR
Netherlands .... DAALDER
Norway .... ORE, KRONE (KRONER)
Oman .... GAJ, GAZ, GOZ, GHAZI
Persia. PUL, KRAN, POUL, RIAL DARIC, DINAR, MOHUR (old), TOMAN, STATER
Peru .... SOL, DINERO
Poland .... DUCAT
Portugal ..... JOE, REI, PECA, DOBRA (former)
Rome, ancient . SEMIS, DINDER
Roman ...... AS, AES, ASSES, SOLIDUS
Rumania ..... LEU, LEY, BANI
Russia . COPEC, KOPEK, RUBLE
Siam .... AT, ATT, BAHT, TICAL or TIKAL
Sicily .... TARI
Somaliland .... BESA
South Africa ..... DAALDER
Spain ..... COB, DURO, PESO, REAL, DOBLA (old), PESETA, PISTOLE (old)
Sweden ORE, KRONA (KRONOR), KRONE (KRONER)
Switzerland .... BATZ
Thailand .... see SIAM
Timor .... AVO
Turkey .... LIRA (gold), PARA, ALTUN (gold), ASPER, MAHBUB (gold), PIASTER
United States .. CENT, DIME, EAGLE
Venice .... BETSO (old silver)
Yugoslavia .... DINAR

190

TRIBES (Including Peoples, Natives)

EUROPE:

Abyssinian .... SHOA
Albania .... GEG, CHAM,
GHEG, TOSK
Balto-Slav .... LETT
Celtic on Danube .... BOII
Finnish near Volga ..... VEPS,
VEPSA
Finnish, Ingria .... VOT, VOTE,
VOTH, WOTE
Lithuania .... BALT
Syryenian .... KOMI
Teuton, ancient .... UBII

MIDDLE EAST:

Arab .... AUS, IBAD
Bedouin .... ABSI, HARB
Turkey .... KURD
East Turkey .... KURD
Persia ...... see under ASIA

ASIA:

Afghanistan .... SAFI
Assam ..... AO, AKA; AHOM,
GARO, NAGA
Borneo .. DYAK, IBAN; DAYAK
Burma .... WA, LAI, KAW,
MON, WAS; AKHA, CHIN,
KADU, KUKI, TSIN; KAREN
Caucasus ... IMER, KURI, LASI,
LAZE, LAZI, SVAN; OSSET,
SVANE
Celebes, Malayan .... BUGI
China, Miao .... HEH
China, Nord .... USUN, UZUN;
USSUN
China, Tatar .... TOBA
India .... AWAN, BHIL,
BHEEL, TURI
Kolarian (India) .... BHAR
Japan, aborigine .. AINO, AINU
Madagascar .... HOVA
Manchu.............. DAUR
Mongol .... CHUD
Nepal .... AOUL, KHAS
Persia .... LUR, KURD,
FARSI, IRANIAN
Tibet .... CHAMPA

AFRICA:

Bantu .... KUA; BANE, BAYA,
BIHE, BULE, FANG, FUNG,
GOGO, GOLO, GOMA,
GUHA, HAKU, HEHE, JAGA,
LUBA, MAKA, NAMA,
SOGA, SUKU, VIRA, YAKA,
ZULU (largest); KAFIR;
KAFFIR
Bedouin .... ABSI
Berber DAZA, RIFF, TEDA, TIBU
Bushman ... SAN, SAAN, QUNG
Congo .... FIOT, SUSU
Central Africa ... ABO; BULO,
DOMA, KALI, KURI, LURI,
YAKO; LUREM
Dahomey .... FON, FONG
East Africa ... JUR, LUR, YAO;
AKKA, ALUR, ASHA, BARI,
BONI, GOLO, MADI, NUER,
VITI
Gold Coast .... AKAN, AKIM,
AKRA
Hamitic ... AFAR, BEJA, BENI,
BOGO, GALA, HIMA
Kaffir .... XOSA, ZULU
Kenya .... BONI
Lake Albert ..... ALUR, LURI
Liberia .... GI, KRA, KRU,
TOMA, VAI, VEI, KROO
Libya ..... FUL, FULA, MZAB
Mozambique .... YAO
Nigeria ... ARO, EDO, IBO, IJO;
BENI, BINI, EBOE, EKOI,
IDJO, IDYO, IDZO, NUPE;
BENIN
Nilotic .... SUK, BARI
Pygmy .... AKKA, DOKO
Slave Coast .... EGBA
Sudan ... FUL, FUR, VEI; FULA,
GOLO, MABA, MEGE,
NUBA, SUSU, TAMA
West Africa ... GA; AJA, EWE,
IBO, KRU, KWA; AGNI,
AKIM, APPA, BAGA, BINI,
EFIK, EGBA, EKOI, GENG,
GOLA, HABE, IKWE, JEBU,
JOAT, JOLA, KETU, NALU,
ONDO, REMO, SAPE, TCHI,
TSHI, VACA, WARI

ALASKA:

Aleutians .... ATKA

GREENLAND .... ITA

AUSTRALIA .... KOKO
NEW GUINEA .... KARON

SOUTH AMERICA:

Fr. Guiana .... BONI

191

INDIANS, INDIAN TRIBES

Alaska .... **ALEUT, SITKA**
Algonquin or Algonkian
  Indians ... **FOX, SAC, WEA;
    CREE, SAUK; MIAMI; LEN-
    APE, OTTAWA, PIEGAN;
    SHAWNEE**
Amazon .... **(lower) MURA,
    (upper) ANDOA**
Apache .... **LIPAN**
Araucanian .... **AUCA**
Arawak ..... **ARAUA, CAMPA,
    INERI**
Arikara .... **REE**
Arizona .. **HANO, HOPI, MOKI,
    PIMA, TEWA, YUMA;
    MOQUI; APACHE**
Athapascan Indians .... **DENE,
    HUPA, TAKU; LIPAN,
    TINNE; APACHE, NAV-
    AHO**
Aymara .... **COLLA**
Bolivia ...... **ITE, URO, URU;
    ITEN, LECA, MOJO, MOXO,
    URAN; CHOLO**
Brazil ...... **GE; YAO; CAME,
    DIAU, MAKU, MURA, PURI,
    PURU, TUPI; ACROA,
    ANDOA, ARAUA, CARIB,
    GUANA, SIUSI; ZAPARO**
Caddoan Indians .. **REE; ADAI;
    IONI, CADDO, BIDAI;
    PAWNEE**
California ...... **HUPA, KOSO,
    MONO, NOZI, POMO, SERI,
    TATU, YANA; MAIDU,
    YANAN; SALINA**
Canada .... **AHT, CREE, DENE,
    TAKU; NISKA, TINNE;
    SARCEE**
Carib .... **YAO, TRIO**
Carolina .... **CATAWBA**
Chaco .... **TOBA**
Chile .... **AUCA**
Colorado .... **UTE**
Colombia .... **BORO, DUIT,
    MUSO, MUZO, TAMA,
    TAPA; CHOCO; COLIMA**
Costa Rica ...... **BOTO VOTO**
Cowichan Indians .. **NANAIMO**

Dakotas .. **REE, SIOUX, TETON;
    MANDAN, SANTEE;
    ARIKARA**
Delaware .... **LENAPE**
Ecuador: ..... **CARA (extinct);
    ANDOA, ARDAN**
Eskimo .... **ATKA; ALEUT**
Florida: .... **CALUSA**
Fuegan .... **ONA**
Great Lakes .. **ERIE; HURON**
Guatemala ...... **MAM; CHOL,
    ITZA, IXIL, IXLI, MAYA,
    ULVA, VOTO; KICHE, PIPIL**
Honduras .... **PAYA**
Iowa .... **FOX, SAC; SAUK**
Indiana .... **WEA; MIAMI**
Iroquoian Indians,
  Iroquois: .... **ERIE, HURON,
    CAYUGA, MOHAWK,
    ONEIDA, SENECA**
Jalisco: .... **CORA**
Keresan Indians: . **SIA; ACOMA**
Kusan .... **COOS**
Lesser Antilles .... **INERI**
Mayan Indians: ... **MAM, CHOL**
Mexico ... **MAM, CHOL, CORA,
    MAYA, MIXE, PIMA, PIME,
    SERI, TECA, TECO, WABI;
    AZTEC, OTOMI, SERIA;
    TOLTEC**
Miami .... **WEA**
Mississippi ..... **TIOU, BILOXI**
Montana ...... **CROW, HOHE**
Muskohegan Indians: . **CREEK,
    YAMASI, CHOCTAW,
    SEMINOLE**
Nebraska .... **KIOWA**
Nevada .... **PAIUTE**
New Mexico . **SIA, PIRO, TANO,
    TAOS, TEWA, ZUNI;
    ACOMA, KERES, PECOS**
New York .... **SENECA**
Nicaragua . **MIXE, RAMA, ULVA**
Oklahoma .. **KAW, OTO; LOUP,
    OTOE; CADDO, CREEK,
    KANSA, KIOWA, OSAGE,
    PONCA; PAWNEE**
Oregon .... **COOS, KUSAN,
    MODOC, CHINOOK**

Panamint .... KOSO

Panama .... CUNA, CUEVA

Pawnee Indians .... LOUP

Payaguas .... AGAZ

Peru: .... ANDE, ANTI, BORO, CANA, INCA, INKA, LAMA, PEBA, PIBA, PIRO, YNCA; CAMPA, CHIMU, CHOLO, COLAN, YUNCA; CHANCA; QUICHU

Peru South .... CANA, COLLA, CHANCA

Piman Indians .. CORA, JOVA, MAYO, PIMA, XOVA, YAKI, YAQUI

Plains Indians ... CREE, CROW; KIOWA, OSAGE; PONCA, TETON, PAWNEE

Pueblo Indians .. HOPI, MOKI, TANO, TAOS, ZUNI; KERES, MOQUI

Rio Grande .... TANO

Sacramento Valley ..... YANA

Salishan Indians ..... ATNAH, LUMMI

Shoshonean Indians .... UTE; HOPI, KOSO, MOKI, MONO; MOQUI, PIUTE; UINTA, PAIUTE

Siouan Indians ... KAW, OTO; CROW, IOWA, OTOE; KANSA, OMAHA, OSAGE, PONCA; BILOXI, DAKOTA, MANDAN; CATAWBA

Sonora .... JOVA, PIMI, SERI

South America (widely distributed) .... GES, ONA, YAO; LULE, MOXO, PANO, PIRO, TOBA; CARIB, INERI; ARAWAK

South Carolina ..... CATAWBA

Tacanan Indians ..... CAVINA

Tanoan .... TEWA

Tapuyan Indians .... GE, GES, GHES, ACROA

Texas .... LIPAN

Tierra del Fuego: .... ONA

Tlingit: .... AUK, SITKA

Tupian .... ANTA

Utah: .... UTE

Washington .... HOH, LUMMI, MAKAH

Yucatan .... MAYA

Yukian .... TATU

Yukon .... TAKU

Yuncan .... CHIMU

ARMOR

Head	COIF, HELM; ARMET, VISOR; BEAVER, CAMAIL; BASINET, HAUBERK
Neck	GORGET
Shoulder	AILETTE, PAULDRON, EPAULIERE, PASSEGARDE
Body	TACE; CULET, TASSE; CORIUM, GORGET, LORICA, TASSET; CUIRASS, HAUBERK, SURCOAT; BRAGUETTE
Arm	BRASSARD, PALLETTE, VAMBRACE; CUBITIERE, REREBRACE
Hand	GAUNTLET
Thigh	CUISH, TASSE, TUILE; CUISSE, TASSET, TUILLE
Leg, foot	JAMB, JAMBE; GREAVE; CHAUSSE, PEDIEUX; SOLLERET
Complete suit	BARD, MAIL; BARDE

HERALDRY—HERALDIC TERMS

Heraldic bearings: BEND, ENTE, FESS, ORLE, FESSE, GIRON, GYRON, LAVER, PHEON; SALTIRE

Heraldic tinctures:
gold, OR; fur, PEAN, VAIR, VAIRE; green, VERT; blue, AZURE; red, GULES; black, SABLE; orange, TENNE; silver, ARGENT; blood-red, MURREY; purple, PURPURE

attitude of animal	SEJANT, GARDANT, PASSANT, RAMPANT
ball	ROUNDEL
band	FESS, ORLE, FESSE
barnacle	BREY
bend	COTISE
bird	MARTLET
circle	BEZANT, ANNULET
colter	LAVER
creature	LION, PARD; BISSE, WYVER; CANNET, WYVERN; GRIFFON, MARTLET
cross	CRUX, NOWY, PATY; FLORY, FORMY, PATEE, PATTE; CLECHE; SALTIRE
curved in middle	NOWY
curves, made of	NEBULE
division	PALE, PALY
dog, short-eared	ALANT
drops, seme of	GUTTE
duck	CANNET, CANETTE
fillet	ORLE
fish trap	WEEL
flower strewn	SEME
flying in air	FLOTANT
fountain	SYKE
grafted	ENTE
headless	ETETE
horizontal band	see band
leaves, having	POINTE
lines	UNDE, UNDY, URDY, NEBULY
lozenge	FUSIL, MASCLE
manacle	TIRRET
pointed	URDE
powdered	SEME
scattered	SEME
sheaf of grain	GERB, GERBE
shield	PAVIS
shield division	ENTE
shield's corner	CANTON
silver	ARGENT
sitting	ASSIS
snake	BISSE
sown	SEME
spangled	SEME
star-strewn	SEME
strewn	SEME
three parts, divided into	TIERCE
triangle	GIRON, GYRON
two-winged	VOL
voided escutcheon	ORLE
walking	PASSANT
wavy	ONDE, UNDE, UNDY, UNDEE, NEBULE
winged	VOL, AILE
wound	VULN
wreath	ORLE, TORSE

CHEMICAL ELEMENTS

METALLIC ELEMENTS	NON-METALLIC ELEMENTS	GASEOUS ELEMENTS
TIN	ARGON	ARGON
GOLD	BORON (inert)	CHLORINE
IRON	CARBON	FLUORINE
LEAD	HELIUM	HELIUM
ZINC	IODINE	HYDROGEN
CERIUM	NEON (inert)	KRYPTON
CESIUM	RADON-NITON	NEON (inert)
COBALT	SILICON	NITROGEN
COPPER	XENON	OXYGEN
ERBIUM		XENON
NICKEL		
RADIUM		
SILVER		
SODIUM		
YTTRIUM		

CHEMICAL SYMBOLS

Solver: Important Note—it is not necessary to list for you the chemical symbol of every element. The Chemical Symbol of any element not given below is found simply by writing down the first 2 letters of the name of the element. For example: Ruthenium's chemical symbol is simply RU.

Alabamine, **AB**
antimony, **SB;**
arsenic, **AS;**
boron, **B;**
cadmium, **CD;**
cesium, **CS;**
chlorine, **CL;**
chromium, **CR;**
columbium, **CB;**
copper, **CU;**
curium, **CM;**
gadolinium, **GD;**
gold, **AU;**

hafnium, **HF;**
iron, **FE**
lead, **PB;**
magnesium, **MG;**
manganese, **MN;**
mercury, **HG;**
neodymium, **ND;**
palladium, **PD;**
platinum, **PT;**
radon, **RN;**
rhenium, **RE;**
rubidium, **RB;**

samarium, **SM;**
silver, **AG;**
sodium, **NA;**
strontium, **SR;**
terbium, **TB;**
thallium, **TL;**
thulium, **TM;**
tin, **SN;**
ytterbium, **YB;**
zinc, **ZN;**
zirconium, **ZR;**

BIBLICAL REFERENCES

BOOKS OF THE BIBLE

Names and order of books of the:

OLD TESTAMENT

1 GENESIS	11 KINGS 1	21 ECCLESIASTES	30 AMOS
2 EXODUS	12 KINGS 2	22 SONG OF	31 OBADIAH
3 LEVITICUS	13 CHRONICLES 1	SOLOMON	32 JONAH
4 NUMBERS	14 CHRONICLES 2	23 ISAIAH	33 MICAH
5 DEUTERONOMY	15 EZRA	24 JEREMIAH	34 NAHUM
6 JOSHUA	16 NEHEMIAH	25 LAMENTATIONS	35 HABAKKUK
7 JUDGES	17 ESTHER	26 EZEKIEL	36 ZEPHANIAH
8 RUTH	18 JOB	27 DANIEL	37 HAGGAI
9 SAMUEL 1	19 PSALMS	28 HOSEA	38 ZECHARIAH
10 SAMUEL 2	20 PROVERBS	29 JOEL	39 MALACHI

Names and order of books of the:

NEW TESTAMENT

1 MATTHEW	9 GALATIANS	15 TIMOTHY 1	23 JOHN 1
2 MARK	10 EPHESIANS	16 TIMOTHY 2	24 JOHN 2
3 LUKE	11 PHILIPPIANS	17 TITUS	25 JOHN 3
4 JOHN	12 COLOSSIANS	18 PHILEMON	26 JUDE
5 THE ACTS	13 THESSALON-	19 HEBREWS	27 REVELATION
6 ROMANS	IANS 1	20 JAMES	
7 CORINTHIANS 1	14 THESSALON-	21 PETER 1	
8 CORINTHIANS 2	IANS 2	22 PETER 2	

BIBLICAL PROPHETS

AMOS (minor), ESAY, EZRA, JOEL (minor), HOSEA (minor), JONAH (minor), MICAH (minor), MOSES, DANIEL (major), NAHUM (minor), ELISHA, HAGGAI (minor), ISAIAH (major), EZEKIEL (major), JEREMIAH (major)

BIBLICAL PATRIARCHS

REU; ADAM, EBER, ENOS, NOAH, SETH, SHEM; ISAAC, JACOB, JARED, NAHOR, PELEG, SERUG, TERAH; LAMECH

BIBLICAL RULERS

OG; ASA (Judah), GOG, IRA; AGAG, AHAB, AHAZ, AMON, ELAH, JEHU, OMRI, SAUL; CYRUS, DAVID, DEBIR, HEROD, HIRAM, JORAM, NADAB, PEKAH, PIRAM, REZIN, SIHON, ZIMRI; ABIJAH, BAASHA, CAESAR, DARIUS, HEZION, HOSHEA, JAPHIA, JOSHUA, JOSIAH, JOTHAM, UZZIAH

BIBLICAL PEOPLES—TRIBES

DAN, GOG; ANAK, ARAD, CUSH, EMIM, MOAB, PHUD, PHUT (o.t.); ARKITE, HAMITE, HIVITE, KENITE, SEMITE, SHELAH, SINITE; EDOMITE, HITTITE, LEHABIM, MOABITE, REPHAIM

BIBLICAL PLACES

City . DAN, GATH, GAZA, ZOAR; BABEL, EKRON, SODOM; HEBRON

Country .... EDOM, ENON, SEBA; SHEBA

Hill, Jerusalem's .... ZION

Kingdom .... ELAM, MOAB; SAMARIA

Land .... NOD

Land of plenty .... GOSHEN

Mt. HOR, EBAL, NAIN, NEBO, PEOR; HOREB, SEIR, SINA, SINAI, TABOR; ARARAT, GILEAD, HERMON

Place .... ENON, AENON; JORDAN, SHILOH

Pool .... SILOAM

Region .. ARAM, EDAR; BASHAN

Town ...... CANA (1st miracle), NAIN (miracle site); BETHEL

River .... ARNON, JORDAN

BIBLICAL MEN

OG, UZ; ARA, DAN, ELI, GOG, HAM, IRA, LOT, NUN, URI; ABEL, AMOS, BOAZ, CAIN, CUSH, DOEG, EBAL, ENON, ENOS, ESAU, HETH, IRAD, JADA, JEHU, JOAB, KISH, LEVI, MASH, MOAB, OBAL, OBED, OMAR, OREB, OZEM, SETH, SODI, ULAM, UNNI, URIA; AARON (high priest), ABIAH, ABIEL, AHIRA, AMASA, ANNAS, CALEB, CHUZA, ENOCH, HAMAN, HARAN, HIRAM, HOHAM, IBZAN, ISAAC, JACOB, JAMES, JARED, MASSA, MOREH, NABAL, NAHBI, NAHOR, OPHIR, REZON, SACAR, TERAH, URIAH, ZAHAM; SAMSON; ANANIAS, ISHMAEL

BIBLICAL WOMEN

EVE; ADAH, JAEL, LEAH, MARY, RUTH; DINAH, EGLAH, HAGAR, JULIA, JUNIA, LYDIA, MERAB, NAOMI, PHEBE, RAHAB, SARAH, SARAI, SHUAH, TAMAR; ABITAL, BILHAH, DORCAS, ESTHER, HANNAH, HOGLAH, MAACAH, MAHLAH, MICHAL, MILCAH, MIRIAM, PERSIS, RACHEL, RIZPAH, SALOME, VASHTI, ZILLAH, ZILPAH; ABIGAIL, HAMUTAL

BIBLICAL NAMES

ED, ER; IRI, NER, ONO, REI, TOI; ABIA, ADER, ANER, ANIM, ASOM, DARA, ELON, ENOS, IRAD, IVAH, REBA; ABIAM, AHIRA, AMASA, ASEAS

GODS (DEITIES), GODDESSES
AND MYTHOLOGY

ASSYRIAN GODS
ANAT (sky), ASUR or ASSUR (war)

BABYLONIAN GODS
Chief gods: EA, ABU or ANU, BEL
EA (chief), ZU (wind), ABU or ANU (chief, sky, sun), BEL (chief), HEA (see EA), IRA (war), SIN (moon), UTU (sun), ADAD or ADDA or ADDU (wind, storm), APSU (chaos), ENKI (see EA), ENZU (see SIN), IRRA (war), NABU or NEBO (wisdom), UTUG (sun), DAGAN (earth), ETANA (eagle rider), SIRIS (alcoholic drinks), BABBAR (sun), SHAMASH (sun)

BABYLONIAN GODDESSES
AI or AYA (consort of Shamash), ERUA (mother), NINA (watery deep), NANAI (daughter of Anu), ISTAR or ISHTAR (chief, love)

BRYTHONIC GODDESS
DON (ancestress of gods)

CELTIC GODS—GODDESS
ANA, ANU, DANA, DANU (mother, queen), LER (sea), LUG, LUGH (light, sun), DAGDA (chief)

CYMRIC GODS
GWYN, LLEU, LLEW (solar)

EGYPTIAN GODS
RA (sun), SU (solar deity), BES (evil, pleasure), GEB (earth), KEB (earth), MIN (procreation), SEB (earth), SET (evil), SHU (see SU), TEM or TUM (sun), AANI (dog-headed ape, sacred to Thoth), AMEN (king), AMON (sun and king), AMUN (king), ATMU or ATUM (sun), BESA (see BES), HAPI (the Nile as a god), KHEM (see MIN), MENT (falcon-headed), PTAH (Memphis god), SOBK (crocodile-headed), AMMON (see AMEN), HORUS (hawk-headed), MENTU (see MENT), SEBEK (see SOBK), THOTH (wisdom, magic), OSIRIS (underworld), SERAPIS (see OSIRIS)

EGYPTIAN GODDESSES
MA (same as MAAT), MUT (Amen's wife), NUT (heavens), ANTA, APET (maternity), BAST (cat- or lion-headed), BUTO (serpent), ISIS (cow-headed, Horus' mother), MAAT (truth, justice), SATI (queen), ATHOR (see HATHOR), HATHOR (love, mirth, cow-headed)

198

EGYPTIAN MYTH

BA (soul of man), KA (body of man), NU (chaos), AKH (spirit of man), NUN (see NU), APIS (sacred bull), ATEN (solar disk), DUAT (see AMENTI), HAPI (Nile or Amenti's jinnee), AMENTI (underworld region)

GREEK GODS

DIS (underworld), PAN (field, flocks, forest), ZAN (old name for Zeus), ARES (war, Eris' brother), EROS (love), ZEUS (chief of Olympian gods), COMUS (mirth and revelry), EURUS (southeast wind), HADES (underworld), KOMOS (see COMUS), MOMUS (ridicule), PLUTO (underworld), AEOLUS (wind), APOLLO (sun, youth), AUSTER (south wind), BOREAS (north wind), CRONUS (a Titan, Rhea's spouse; harvest), HELIOS (sun), HERMES (herald), KRONOS (see CRONUS), NEREUS (sea), PLUTUS (wealth), TRITON (sea), BACCHUS (wine), POSEIDON (sea)

GREEK GODDESSES

GE (earth, mother of Titans), ARA (destruction, retribution, vengeance), ATE (discord, mischief, infatuation), EIR (healing), EOS (dawn), ALEA (ATHENA), CORA (see KORE), DICE or DIKE (one of Horae), ENYO (Ares' mother, war), ERIS (discord, sister of Ares), GAEA or GAIA (see GE), HEBE (youth), HERA (queen), HORA (one of Horae), KORE (vegetation), LEDA (Tyndareus' wife), NIKE (victory), RHEA (mother of gods, wife of Kronos), UPIS, ARTEMIS, HORAE (three goddesses of seasons), IRENE (peace), METIS (Zeus' first wife), MOIRA (fate or Fates), ATHENA (wisdom), CLOTHO (a Fate, thread spinner), CYBELE (nature), EIRENE (see IRENE), HECATE (moon, magic), MOERAE (see MOIRA), PALLAS (wisdom), SELENA and SELENE (moon), ARTEMIS (moon, woods, nature), ATROPOS (one of the Fates, thread cutter), DEMETER (grain, agriculture), CHLORIS (flowers), NEMESIS (revenge), LACHESIS (one of the Fates, thread length), APHRODITE (love)

GREEK MYTH

IO (Zeus' beloved changed to a heifer), INO (Cadmus' daughter), PAN (field, flocks, forest), ANAX (one of Dioscuri), AUGE (Arcadian princess), CEYX (Halcyone's husband turned into kingfisher), CLIO (Muse of History), FAUN (see PAN), IDAS (hero, killed Castor), IOLE (Hercules' captive), LETO (Apollo's mother), MAIA (Hermes' mother), OTUS (giant killed by Apollo), ALTIS (sacred grove, Olympic games), ATLAS (held up heavens), CREON (Oedipus' brother-in-law), DIONE (Aphrodite's mother), ENEAS (Troy's defender), ERATO (Clio's sister), HADES (underworld), HELLE (fell into Hellespont with golden fleece), HYDRA (9-headed monster), MINOS (king), NIOBE (weeping stone), SATYR (part-horse demigod), THEIA (Hyperion's sister, wife), ADONIS (beautiful youth), AENEAS (see ENEAS), AGENOR (Trojan warrior), ALECTO (a Fury), DAPHNE (Apollo's nymph turned into tree), EUROPA (carried off by Zeus in form of white bull), HECTOR (Trojan warrior), NEREID (sea nymph to Poseidon), NESTOR (wise king, fought Troy), THETIS (Achilles' mother), TITHON (see TITHONUS), TRITON (sea demigod,

Poseidon's son), URANIA (astronomy), ARIADNE (Theseus' love), ATHAMAS (Ino's husband), CENTAUR (half man, half horse), CYCLOPS (1-eyed giant), ERINYES, (avenging spirits), EUTERPE (Muse of Music), SILENUS (woodland deity, horse-goat-human), ATALANTA (picked up golden apples—lost the race), TARTARUS (infernal regions), TITHONUS (immortal king of Troy, Eos' favorite), TISIPHONE (one of Erinyes)
The Gorgons: MEDUSA, STHENO, EURYALE
The Graces: AGLAIA, THALIA
The Titans or Titanesses: primeval deities: GAEA or GE (mother of Titans). URANUS (father of Titans). Titans: RHEA, COEUS, CREUS, THEIA, CRONUS or KRONOS, PHOEBE, THEMIS

HINDU GODS

KA (unknown), AGNI (fire), AKAL (Immortal), CIVA (see SIVA), DEVA or DEWA (divine being), KAMA (love), RAMA (incarnation of Vishnu), SIVA (supreme), VAYU (wind), YAMA (judge of dead), BHAGA (love), DYAUS (heaven, sky), VISHNU (supreme), KRISHNA (avatar of Vishnu)

HINDU GODDESSES

SRI (beauty, wealth, luck, Vishnu's wife), UMA (splendor), VAC (speech), DEVI (any divinity, Siva's consort), KALI (evil), SHRI (see SRI), USAS (dawn), VACH (see VAC), SHREE (see SRI), MATRIS (mothers), LAKSHMI (see SRI)

HINDU MYTH

BANA (1,000-arm giant), KALI (tongue of Agni), KETU (Rahu's tail), NAGA (Vishnu's serpent), RAHU (dragon, swallows sun), USHA (Bana's daughter)

INCA GOD

INTI (sun)

IRISH—see CELTIC

NORSE GODS

ER (war), TY (see TIU), VE (Odin's brother, slayed Ymir), EAR (see ER), LOK (see LOKI), TIU (sky, war, Tiwaz), TIW (see TIU), TYR (sky, war), ULL (bow skill), VAN (sea), ZIO (sky), ZIU (see ZIO), FREY (fertility), HLER (sea), HOTH (blind god), LOKE or LOKI (discord, mischief), ODIN chief god, war, wisdom, slayed Ymir), THOR (thunder), TYRR (war), ULLR (see ULL), VALE (see VALI), VALI (Odin's son), VANS (see VANIR), VILI (Odin's brother), AEGIR (sea), AESIR (chief), ALCIS (twin gods), BALDR (see BALDER), BRAGE or BRAGI (poetry), DONAR (see THOR), HODER or HOTHR (see HOTH), VANIR (early race of gods), WODAN or WODEN or WOTAN (see ODIN), BALDER or BALDUR (light)
The Aesir or chief gods: TIU, TYR, ULL, FREY, LOKI, ODIN, THOR, VALI, BRAGI, DONAR, WODEN, BALDER

NORSE GODDESSES

EIR (healing), HEL (Loki's daughter, underworld, dead), RAN (sea, death, wife of Aegir), SIF (Thor's wife), URD (destiny), VOR (betrothal), ERDA (earth), FREA or FRIA (see FRIGG), GERD (Frey's wife), HELA (see HEL), NORN (fate), RIND (Odin's wife, Vali's mother), SAGA (golden beaker), URTH (see URD), FREYA (love, beauty), FRIGG (Odin's wife), NANNA (flowers), NORNA or NORNS (see NORN), FREYJA (see FREYA)

NORSE MYTH

ASK (see ASKR), DIS (female spirit), ASKR (first man), ATLI (king), EGIL (story hero), GARM (Hel's watchdog, slays Tyr), GERI (Odin's wolf), IDUN (Bragi's wife), MARA (nightmare demon), NATT or NOTT (night), WATE (giant), YMIR or YMER ("rime-cold giant"), EGILL (see EGIL), MIMIR (giant), ASGARD (abode of gods)

PHOENICIAN GODDESS

ASTARTE (fertility, love)

ROMAN GODS

DIS (underworld), SOL (sun), AMOR (love), FAUN (field, herds, half goat), JOVE (chief god), MARS (war), MORS (death), COMUS (mirth, joy), CUPID (love), EURUS (southeast wind), KOMOS (see COMUS), MANES (spirits of dead, gods of underworld), ORCUS (dead), APOLLO (sun, music), AUSTER (south wind), BOREAS (north wind), FAUNUS (rural deity), VULCAN (fire), NEPTUNE (sea)

ROMAN GODDESSES

NOX or NYX (night), OPS (harvest, plenty), DIAN (moon, chase, woods), IRIS (rainbow, Zeus' messenger), JUNO (queen), LUNA (moon), MAIA (Vulcan's consort), NONA (Fate), SPES (hope), CERES (earth, grain, agriculture, vegetation), DIANA (see DIAN), EPONA (horses), FIDES (faith), FAUNA (field), FLORA (flowers), MORTA (a Fate), PARCA (a Fate), SALUS (prosperity), TERRA (earth), VENUS (love), VESTA (hearth), ANNONA (crops), AURORA (dawn), DECUMA (a Fate), PARCAE (the Fates), VACUNA (Sabine huntress)
The Fates or Parcae: NONA, MORTA, DECUMA

TEUTONIC GODS—see NORSE GODS

TEUTONIC GODDESSES—see NORSE GODDESSES

VEDIC GODS—see HINDU GODS

VEDIC GODDESSES—see HINDU GODDESSES

WELSH GOD
DYLAN

FIRST AND LAST NAMES

(common to crossword puzzles)

You often find in crossword puzzles definitions like "Writer Aldous ——." or "—— Pavlova." The following list contains the most commonly used names, first names and last names. The part of the name which is usually given in the definition is here in light-face type, arranged alphabetically. The rest of the person's name follows in bold-face type.

Aaron .... BURR
Abbott .... BUD
Adams .... MAUDE
Addams ..... JANE
Adelina ..... PATTI
Adolph ..... OCHS
Adolphe .... ADAM
Adoree ..... RENEE
Aherne ..... BRIAN
Alan .. HALE, LADD,
    PATON, REED
Albani ...... EMMA
Alban .... BERG
Albert ..... ANKER,
    CAMUS
Aldo .... RAY
Aldous .... HUXLEY
Alexis ...... KIVI
Alexander
    FLEMING, POPE,
    SEROV
Alexandre .. DUMAS
Alfred ..... DRAKE,
    LUNT
Alfred B. ... NOBEL
Alighieri .... DANTE
Allegra ...... KENT
Allen ...... ETHAN,
    IDA, MEL
Allison ...... FRAN
Allyson .... JUNE
Alois .... LANG
Alonzo ..... CANO
Ambler ...... ERIC
Ambrose ... BIERCE,
    FLEMING
Amon ...... CARTER
Amundsen .. ROALD
Anatole ... FRANCE
Andersen .... HANS
Andre .... GIDE
Andrews .... DANA
Andy ..... DEVINE
Aneurin Bevan . NYE
Angelo ... GIOTTO,
    MOSSO, PATRI

Anita .... LOOS
Anna .. CASE, HELD,
    STEN, NEAGLE
Anthony ..... EDEN,
    SUSAN, TUDOR
Anton ...... DOLIN
Anya .... SETON
Arden ... EVE, TONI
Arnaz .... DESI
Arnold .... HAP
Arsene ..... LUPIN
Artemus ... WARD
Arthur Conan . DOYLE
Ataturk ... KEMAL
Attlee ... CLEMENT
Auguste .... RODIN
Autry ...... GENE
Axel .... GADE
Bagnold ..... ENID
Bailey ..... PEARL
Bainter ...... FAY
Bambi ...... LINN
Bampton .... ROSE
Barkley .... ALBEN
Bartok ...... BELA
Barton ..... CLARA
Basie ...... COUNT
Baxter ..... ANNE
Bayes ...... NORA
Beerbohm ... MAX
Beery ...... NOAH
Begley .... ED
Ben ...... HOGAN
Bennett ..... CERF
Benzell ..... MIMI
Berg ...... ALBAN
Berger ...... ERNA
Bernard .... SHAW
Bernhardt .. SARAH
Bernie ...... BEN
Bert ...... LAHR
Best .... EDNA
Bette ...... DAVIS
Betty ...... FIELD
Bevin .... ERNEST
Billings ..... JOSH

Billy . ROSE, SUNDAY
Blanche ..... RING,
    SWEET
Blandish ... SERENA
Blas .... GIL, RUY
Bloch .... RAY
Blum .... LEON
Blyth .... ANN
Bohr .... NIELS
Boleyn ..... ANNE
Bolger .... RAY
Bolivar .... SIMON
Bonar ...... LAW
Bonheur .... ROSA
Bowman ...... LEE
Boyd .... ORR
Bradley .... OMAR
Brendel .... EL
Bret ...... HARTE
Brigham ... YOUNG
Brodie ..... STEVE
Brown ... JOE EVAN
Broz .... TITO
Bruce ..... CABOT
Brynner ...... YUL
"Buffalo Bill" . CODY
Bull .... OLE
Burl .... IVES
Burns .... BOB
Burr ...... AARON
Burrows ..... ABE
Byington ... SPRING
Cabeza de .. VACA
Calloway .... CAB
Cameron ..... ROD
Camillo Benso
    CAVOUR
Canada ...... LEE
Cantor .... IDA
Capek ..... KAREL
Carl .... CORI
Carl Marie von
    WEBER
Carney ...... ART
Carnera ... PRIMO
Carrel .... ALEXIS

202

204

Karel ..... CAPEK
Karl .... MARX
Kay .... STARR
Kaye .... NORA
Kazan ...... ELIA
Keith .... IAN
Kelly . GENE, EMMET
Kenton ...... STAN
Khachaturian .ARAM
Khan .. AGA, ALI, ALY
Kibbee ...... GUY
Kiepura ...... JAN
Kim .... HUNTER
Kitchell ...... IVA
Knight ..... ERIC
Koussevitzky . SERGE
Kovacs ...... ERNIE
Kurt .... ADLER
Kyser .... KAY
Lafcadio .... HEARN
Lagerkvist .... PAR
Lagerlof .... SELMA
Lahr .... BERT
Laing ...... HUGH
Lanchester ... ELSA
Lange ...... HOPE
Lanny ...... ROSS
Lardner ..... RING
Lauck, Chester . LUM
Laura Hope . CREWS
Laurel ...... STAN
Laurence ... STERNE, OLIVIER
Laurie ..... PIPER
Law .... BONAR
Lazarus .... EMMA
Learned .... HAND
Lee .. OMA, CANADA
Le Gallienne ... EVA
Lehmann ... LOTTE
Lehr .... LEW
Lena ...... HORNE
Leslie ..... BANKS
Levant ..... OSCAR
Levene ...... SAM
Levenson .... SAM
Lew .. AYRES, CODY
Lewin, Liliane . LILO
Lewis . ADA, JOHN, LAWES, STONE, TED
"Light-horse Harry" LEE
Lillian . GISH, ROTH
Lillie ... BEA, PEEL
Lily .... PONS
Linkletter .... ART
Linn ...... BAMBI
Liszt ..... FRANZ
Lollobrigida .. GINA

Lombardo ..... GUY
Long .... HUEY
Loos .... ANITA
Loren ..... SOPHIA
Lorre ...... PETER
Louise ..... ANITA
Lowell ...... AMY
Lucas .. FOSS, SCOTT
Lucrezia ..... BORI
Ludwig ...... EMIL
Lugosi .... BELA
Luise ..... RAINER
Lupescu ... MAGDA
Lupino .... IDA
Lynn .... BARI
Lyons ...... GENE
Mack .... TED
MacMahon ... ALINE
Madame de .. STAEL
Madge .... EVANS
Magnani .... ANNA
Major ..... BOWES
Malbin .... ELAINE
Mann IRIS, HORACE
Marco ...... POLO
Maria ..... CALLAS
Marie ...... CURIE
Mario ..... LANZA
Mark ...... CLARK
Markey ...... ENID
Marner ..... SILAS
Marquette .... PERE
Marquis ..... DON
Marshall .... ALAN
Martha HYER, RAYE
Martini ..... NINO
Mary ...... ASTOR, GARDEN, URE
Mary Baker .. EDDY
Marx ...... CHICO, HARPO, KARL
Masaryk JAN, TOMAS
Mason ..... JAMES, PAMELA
Massey CURT, ILONA
Mata .... HARI
Maude .... ADAMS
Maurice .... RAVEL
Maxwell ..... ELSA
Maynard ..... KEN
McCarey .... LEO
McCoy .... TIM
Meg ...... MUNDY
Mel .. ALLEN, OTT, TORME
Menken. ADA, HELEN
Merimee . PROSPER
Meriwether .. LEWIS
Merkel ...... UNA
Merman .... ETHEL
Meyerson .... BESS

Milton ...... CROSS
Miranda ...... ISA
Mischa ..... AUER, ELMAN
Mitzi ...... GREEN
Mollet ...... GUY
Montagu .... LOVE
Montez ..... LOLA, MARIA
Moorhead .. AGNES
Morgana FATA, NINA
Morini ..... ERICA
Mostel ...... ZERO
Mowbray .... ALAN
Mundt ...... KARL
Munson ...... ONA
Murray .. DON, JAN, KEN, MAE
Musial ...... STAN
Myra .... HESS
Nahum ...... TATE
Nazimova .... ALLA
Ned ...... SPARKS
Neilson ...... ADA
Nelson ..... GENE, MILES
Nethersole .. OLGA
Nicholas .... AMATI
Nicholas Murray BUTLER
Nikolaidi ... ELENA
Niels .... BOHR
Noel ..... COWARD
Nora . BAYES, KAYE
Novello ..... IVOR
O. Henry . PORTER
O'Casey ..... SEAN
O'Connor .... UNA
Ogden . NASH, REID
Oley ...... SPEAKS
Oliver ..... HARDY
Olsen .... OLE
Oma .... LEE
Onegin ..... EUGEN
O'Neill ..... OONA
Opie ...... READ
Oren .... ROOT
Orlando .... LASSO
Oscar .... LEVANT, WILDE
Ott .... MEL
Page .... PATTI
Paine .... TOM
Palmer LILLI
Parker ...... FESS
Pastor ...... TONY
Pasternak .. BORIS
Paton ...... ALAN
Paul ..... DRAPER, MUNI, POTTER
Pauline ..... LORD

205

206

Verne ...... **JULES**
Vernon ..... **CASTLE**
Victor **BORGE, HUGO**
Vincent ..... **PRICE**
Vitus ...... **BERING**
Vivien ..... **LEIGH**
Vivienne ... **SEGAL**
Vladimir ... **LENIN**
W.C. .... **FIELDS**
W. Mackenzie **KING**
Wallace .. **HENRY,**
AGARD, LEW
Wallach .... **ELI**
Wally .... **PIP**
Walter ..... **ABEL,**
BRUNO, REED
Warburg .... **OTTO**
Washington
BOOKER
Waugh ...... **ALEC**
Webb .... **ALAN**

Weber and —
FIELDS
Weill ...... **KURT**
Wheeler ..... **BERT**
White .... **PEARL,**
WILLIAM ALLEN
Whitelaw .... **REID**
Whitfield .... **MAL**
Whitman ... **WALT**
Whitney ..... **ELI**
Wilbur ..... **CROSS**
Wilhelm von . **OPEL**
Willa .... **CATHER**
William .. **BOOTH,**
HANDY, HART,
HOLDEN, HULL,
INGE, PENN,
PITT
William Butler **YEATS**
William Cullen
BRYANT

William Randolph
HEARST
William Rose **BENET**
William Sidney
PORTER
Williams ... **ROGER,**
TED
Wills **CHILL, HELEN**
Winslow .... **HOMER**
Winterhalter . **HUGO**
Wolfert ...... **IRA**
Wynn .... **ED**
Xavier ..... **CUGAT**
Young ... **CY, GIG,**
ALAN
Youskevitch .. **IGOR**
ZaSu .... **PITTS**
Zebulon ..... **PIKE**
Zernial .... **GUS**
Zetterling .... **MAI**
Zola ...... **EMILE**
Zorina ...... **VERA**

PRESIDENTS OF THE UNITED STATES

(In order)

1. GEORGE WASHINGTON
2. JOHN ADAMS
3. THOMAS JEFFERSON
4. JAMES MADISON
5. JAMES MONROE
6. JOHN QUINCY ADAMS
7. ANDREW JACKSON
8. MARTIN VAN BUREN
9. WILLIAM HENRY HARRISON
10. JOHN TYLER
11. JAMES KNOX POLK
12. ZACHARY TAYLOR
13. MILLARD FILLMORE
14. FRANKLIN PIERCE
15. JAMES BUCHANAN
16. ABRAHAM LINCOLN
17. ANDREW JOHNSON
18. ULYSSES SIMPSON GRANT
19. RUTHERFORD BIRCHARD HAYES

20. JAMES ABRAM GARFIELD
21. CHESTER ALAN ARTHUR
22. GROVER CLEVELAND
23. BENJAMIN HARRISON
24. GROVER CLEVELAND
25. WILLIAM McKINLEY
26. THEODORE ROOSEVELT
27. WILLIAM HOWARD TAFT
28. WOODROW WILSON
29. WARREN GAMALIEL HARDING
30. CALVIN COOLIDGE
31. HERBERT CLARK HOOVER
32. FRANKLIN DELANO ROOSE-VELT
33. HARRY S. TRUMAN
34. DWIGHT DAVID EISENHOWER
35. JOHN FITZGERALD KENNEDY
36. LYNDON BAINES JOHNSON

37. RICHARD MILHOUS NIXON

U.S. STATE GENERAL INFORMATION TABLE

STATE	ABBREV.	RANK BY AREA	STATE CAPITAL	RANK BY POP.	STATE NICKNAME	STATE FLOWER
ALABAMA	Ala.	29	Montgomery	19	Yellow Hammer, Cotton, Heart of Dixie	Goldenrod
ALASKA	Alsk.	1	Juneau	50	The Last Frontier	Forget-Me-Not
ARIZONA	Ariz.	6	Phoenix	35	Grand Canyon, Sunset Land, Apache	Saguaro Cactus
ARKANSAS	Ark.	27	Little Rock	32	Wonder, Land of Opportunity, Bear	Apple Blossom
CALIFORNIA	Calif., Cal.	3	Sacramento	2	Golden, Grizzly Bear	Golden Poppy
COLORADO	Colo.	8	Denver	33	Centennial, Rover	Columbine
*CONNECTICUT	Conn.	48	Hartford	26	Constitution, Nutmeg	Mountain Laurel
*DELAWARE	Del., Dela.	49	Dover	46	First, Diamond, Blue Hen	Peach Blossom
†DISTRICT OF COLUMBIA	D.C.					American Beauty Rose
FLORIDA	Fla.	22	Tallahassee	12	Sunshine, Everglade, Live Oak, Peninsula	Orange Blossom
*GEORGIA	Ga.	21	Atlanta	16	Empire State of the South, Peach, Cracker	Cherokee Rose
HAWAII	Haw.	47	Honolulu	44	Paradise of the Pacific	Hibiscus
IDAHO	Id.	13	Boise	42	Gem, "Potato"	Lewis Mockorange
ILLINOIS	Ill.	24	Springfield	4	Prairie, Sucker	Violet
INDIANA	Ind.	38	Indianapolis	10	Hoosier	Peony
IOWA	Ia.	25	Des Moines	23	Hawkeye, "Corn"	Wild Rose
KANSAS	Kan., Kans.	14	Topeka	29	Sunflower, Corn Cracker, Garden, Jayhawk	Sunflower
KENTUCKY	Ky.	37	Frankfort	21	Blue Grass	Goldenrod
LOUISIANA	La.	31	Baton Rouge	20	Pelican, Creole, Sugar	Magnolia
MAINE	Me.	39	Augusta	36	Pine Tree, Lumber, Potato	Pine Cone and Tassel
*MARYLAND	Md.	42	Annapolis	22	Old Line, Free, Cockade	Black-Eyed Susan
*MASSACHUSETTS	Mass.	45	Boston	9	Bay, Old Colony	Arbutus
MICHIGAN	Mich.	23	Lansing	7	Wolverine	Apple Blossom

*One of The Thirteen Original States
†District

208

STATE	ABBREV.	RANK BY AREA	STATE CAPITAL	RANK BY POP.	STATE NICKNAME	STATE FLOWER
MINNESOTA	Minn.	12	St. Paul	18	North Star, Gopher, Land of 10,000 Lakes	Moccasin Flower
MISSISSIPPI	Miss.	32	Jackson	28	Magnolia, Bayou	Magnolia
MISSOURI	Mo.	19	Jefferson City	13	Show Me, Bullion	Hawthorn
MONTANA	Mont.	4	Helena	41	Treasure, Bonanza	Bitterroot
NEBRASKA	Nebr.	15	Lincoln	34	Beef, Cornhusker, Antelope	Goldenrod
NEVADA	Nev.	7	Carson City	49	Sagebrush, Silver, Battle-Born	Sagebrush
*NEW HAMPSHIRE	N.H.	44	Concord	45	Granite	Lilac
*NEW JERSEY	N.J.	46	Trenton	8	Garden	Violet
*NEW MEXICO	N.M.	5	Santa Fe	39	Sunshine	Yucca
*NEW YORK	N.Y.	30	Albany	1	Empire, Excelsior	Rose
*NORTH CAROLINA	N.C.	28	Raleigh	11	Tar Heel, Old North, Turpentine	Dogwood
NORTH DAKOTA	N.D.	17	Bismarck	43	Sioux, Flickertail	Wild Prairie Rose
OHIO		35	Columbus	6	Buckeye	Scarlet Carnation
OKLAHOMA	Okla.	18	Oklahoma City	27	Sooner	Mistletoe
OREGON	Ore.	10	Salem	31	Beaver, Webfooter	Oregon Grape
*PENNSYLVANIA	Penna., Pa., Penn.	33	Harrisburg	3	Keystone, Quaker	Mountain Laurel
*RHODE ISLAND	R.I.	50	Providence	37	Little Rhody, Gunflint	Violet
*SOUTH CAROLINA	S.C.	40	Columbia	25	Palmetto	Yellow Jessamine
SOUTH DAKOTA	S.D.	16	Pierre	40	Coyote, Sunshine	Pasque Flower
TENNESSEE	Tenn.	34	Nashville	17	Volunteer, Big Bend	Iris
TEXAS	Tex.	2	Austin	5	Lone Star	Bluebonnet
UTAH		11	Salt Lake City	38	Beehive, Mormon	Sego Lily
VERMONT	Vt.	43	Montpelier	47	Green Mountain, Granite	Red Clover
*VIRGINIA	Va.	36	Richmond	15	Old Dominion, Cavalier, "Mother of Presidents"	Dogwood
WASHINGTON	Wash.	20	Olympia	24	Evergreen, Chinook	Rhododendron
WEST VIRGINIA	W. Va.	41	Charleston	30	Mountain, Panhandle	Great Rhododendron
WISCONSIN	Wisc., Wis.	26	Madison	14	Badger, Cheese	Violet
WYOMING	Wyo.	9	Cheyenne	48	Equality	Indian Paintbrush

*One of The Thirteen Original States

†District

209

GAZETTEER

OR

GEOGRAPHICAL DICTIONARY

Cities, States, Countries, Counties, Provinces, Towns, Rivers, Communes, Ports and Harbors, Regions, Lakes, Mountains, Islands, Volcanoes, Settlements, Kingdoms, Districts, Divisions, Peninsulas, Mountain Ranges, Nomes, etc.; n = North; s = South

A

ABYSSINIA ..... city, **HARAR, GONDAR, HARRAR**; town, **ADOWA,** (s) **MEGA,** province, **TIGRE**; river, **OMO, ABBA**; lake, **TANA, TSANA**

ADRIATIC ... port and harbor, **FIUME**; peninsula, **ISTRIA**; resort, **LIDO**

AEGEAN .... river, **STRUMA**; island, **MELOS, SAMOS, TENOS**; gulf, **SAROS**

AFGHANISTAN .. city, **HERAT**

AFRICA .... (see also SOUTH AFRICA page 216)

AFRICA .. (n) country, **TUNIS, UGANDA, ALGERIA, TUNISIA, TUNISIE**; lake, **NYASA**; province, **LAGOS, NATAL**; river, **UMO, NILE, TANA, CONGO, NIGER**; city (n) **ORAN, DAKAR, TUNIS**; mountains, **ATLAS**; region, **CONGO, NUBIA, SUDAN, SOUDAN**; port (w) **DAKAR**

ALABAMA ...... city, **SELMA ANNISTON**

ALASKA .. city, **NOME, SITKA**; island, **ADAK, ATKA, ATTU**; peninsula, **UNGA**; mountain, **ADA**; inlet, **COOK**; river, **YUKON**; highest peak in North Amer., **McKINLEY**; glacier, **MUIR**

ALBANIA ... capital, **TIRANA**; river, **DRIN**

ALEUTIANS ... islands, **ADAK, ATKA, ATTU**

ALGERIA .... city, port, **ORAN**

ALPS ...... mountain, **BLANC, MATTERHORN**

ANNAM .. .... capital, **HUE**

ANTARCTIC .... sea, **ROSS**

ARABIA .. city, **ADEN, BEDA, BERA, SANA**; state, **ASIR, OMAN, YEMEN**; port, **ADEN**; district, **TEMA**; kingdom, **NEJD**; gulf, **ADEN, OMAN**

ARCTIC .. gulf, **OB**; sea, **KARA**

ARIZONA . city, **MESA, YUMA**; river, **GILA**

ARMENIA .... river, **ARAS**

ASIA . mountains, **ALTAI**; lake, **ARAL**; sea, **ARAL**; river, **OB, ILI, AMUR, LENA, ONON, TIGRIS**; kingdom, **NEPAL, SIAM**; country, **ANAM, IRAK, IRAN, BURMA, CHINA, KOREA, SYRIA, TIBET, SITSANG**; kingdom E. Asia, **KOREA**; desert, **GOBI**

ASIA MINOR .. district, **IONIA**; mountains, **IDA**

ASIATIC .... (see ASIA)

AUSTRIA .. city, **GRAZ, WEIN, VIENNA;** river, **MUR, ENNS, RAAB, RABA**

AUSTRALIA .. peninsula, **EYRE;** river, **SWAN;** city **PERTH**

AZORES ..... port and harbor, **HORTA;** island, **PICO, FAYAL, FLORES;** volcano, **PICO, (ALTO)**

B

BALEARIC ISLANDS .... port, **PALMA;** island, **MAJORCA**

BALTIC island, **OSEL** (opposite **RIGA);** gulf, **RIGA;** capital, **RIGA;** river, **ODER**

BAVARIA .. river, **NAB, ISAR, NAAB**

BELGIAN CONGO .. river, **UELE**

BELGIUM .. city, **HUY, MONS, GHENT, LIEGE, MALINES;** commune (town), **ANS, ATH, SPA, LEDE, MONS, NIEL, ROUX, NAMUR;** river, **LYS, YSER, MEUSE, SENNE;** port and harbor, **OSTEND;** province, **LIEGE**

BOHEMIA .. river, **ELBE, ISER;** mountains, **ORE**

BOMBAY .. city, **POONA;** district, **SURAT;** seaport and harbor, **SURAT**

BOTHNIA .... islands, **ALAND**

BRAZIL .... city, **RIO, BELEM;** port and harbor, **PARA, BELEM, NATAL, SANTOS, PELOTAS;** state, **PARA, BAHIA;** river, **APA, ICA, PARA;** capital, **RIO**

BRITISH WEST INDIES . island, **NEVIS**

BULGARIA ..... capital, **SOFIA**

BURMA (see also INDIA).capital (former) **AVA,** (present) **RANGOON;** district, **PROME**

C

CALIFORNIA .... city, **LODI,** NAPA, POMONA, ALAMEDA, SALINAS; town, **OJAI;** county, **NAPA, YOLO, MODOC, MADERA;** lake, **TAHOE;** mountain peak, **LASSEN, SHASTA;** valley, **NAPA**

CANADA .. mountains, **LOGAN, ROBSON;** peninsula, **GASPE;** province, **ALBERTA (ALTA.), BRITISH COLUMBIA (B.C.), MANITOBA (MAN.) NEW BRUNSWICK (N.B.), NEWFOUNDLAND (NEWF.), NOVA SCOTIA (N.S.), ONTARIO (ONT.), PRINCE EDWARD ISLAND (P.E.I.), QUEBEC (QUE.), SASKATCHEWAN (SASK.);** national park, **JASPER**

CANAL ZONE .. city, **ANCON, COLON;** lake, **GATUN**

CARIBBEAN .... island, **CUBA**

CAROLINES .. island, **PALAU (PELEW), PONAPE, TRUK, YAP**

CAPE VERDE.island, **SAL, FOGO**

CASPIAN .. seaport and harbor, **BAKU**

CENTRAL AFRICA .... region, **SUDAN, SOUDAN**

CENTRAL AMERICA .... river, **LEMPA**

CEYLON .... province, **UVA**

CHANNEL ISLANDS island, **SARK**

CHILE .... river, **LOA;** port, harbor, town, **ARICA**

CHINA .. city, **AMOY, IPIN, CANTON;** port and harbor, **AMOY;** kingdom old, **WU, SHU, WEI;** river, **SI, HAN, KAN, PEI, AMUR, HWAI, CANTON;** province, **AMOY, AMUR, HONAN;** mountains, **OMEI;** division, **MIAO**

COLORADO .... city, **LAMAR, PUEBLO, DURANGO;** park, **ESTES;** town, **OURAY;** range, **RATON;** mountain, **OSO, EOLUS;** peak, **OSO;** county, **OTERO;** resort, **ASPEN**

COLOMBIA . . . . river, MAGDALENA; city, CALI

CONGO . . . . river, UELE

CONNECTICUT town, DARIEN, ANSONIA, MERIDEN

CORSICA . . . port and harbor, BASTIA

CRETE . . . . port and harbor, CANDIA; capital, CANEA; mountain, IDA

CRIMEA . . . . port and harbor, KERCH; river, ALMA

CUBA . . . . town, GUINES

CYCLADES . . island, IOS, NIOO, MILO, SYRA, DELOS, MELOS, TENOS, THERA

CZECHOSLAVAKIA . . . . . city, BRNO; BRUNN; river, EGER, GRAN, HRON, IPEL, ISER, ODER, OHRE, MOLDAU; region, SUDETEN; capital, PRAGUE (PRAHA); mountains, ORE

D

DENMARK . . . . island off, ALS, AERO; islands, FAROE

DOMINICAN REPUBLIC . . city, MOCA

DUTCH . . . . . . see Netherlands

DUTCH EAST INDIES . . island, BALI, JAVA NIAS; island group, ARU, ALOR, LETI; gulf, BONI; capital, BATAVIA

E

EAST ASIA . . kingdom, KOREA

EAST EUROPEAN . river, DRAU, TISA, DRAVA, DRAVE, TISZA, THEISS

EAST INDIES . see also (Dutch) East Indies) island, BORNEO

ECUADOR . . . . . province, ORO

EGYPT . . city, SAIS, CAIRO; ancient city, THEBES; town, KISH; province, GIZA; river, NILE

ENGLAND . . city, ELY, BATH, YORK, LEEDS, COVENTRY; port and harbor, HULL, DOVER, POOLE; town, ETON; river, ALN, CAM, DEE, EXE, NEN, URE, AVON, NENE, OUSE, TEES, TYNE, TRENT; county, KENT, YORK, BERKS, BUCKS, DERBY, DEVON, ESSEX, HANTS, WILTS, DORSET, SURREY, SUSSEX

ESTONIA . . . . . island, SAARE; province, SAARE; capital, REVAL

ETHIOPIA . . . . . . see Abyssinia

EUROPE . . . . river, ISAR, OISE, URAL, DANUBE; lake, BALATON (largest); peninsula, IBERIA; resort, LIDO

F

FIJI . . . . capital, SUVA

FINLAND . . port and harbor, ABO, KEM, PORI; town, north-ern, ENARE; lake, ENARE; islands, ALAND

FLORIDA . . . . . . county, DADE; resort, DELAND; city, OCALA; cape, SABLE

FRANCE . . . . city, AIX, DAX, PAU, AGEN, ALBI, CAEN, LAON, LYON, METZ, NICE, OPPY, VAUX, ARLES, ARRAS, BLOIS, DINAN, LILLE, (n) NESLE, PARIS, SEDAN, TULLE, CANNES, NANTES, SEVRES; colony, ALGERIA; commune, EU, AUX, AUBY, BRON, ISSY, LOOS, MERU, ORLY, SENS, VIMY, VIRE, CENON; port and har-bor, CAEN, MEZE, (s) SETE, BREST; resort, PAU, NICE, CANNES; department, VAR, GARD, JURA, NORD, ORNE, MEUSE, VENDEE; river, AIN, LOT, LYS, AIRE, AUDE, CHER, EURE, LOIR, OISE, ORNE, RHIN, SAAR, YSER, AISNE, ISERE, LOIRE (largest), MARNE, MEUSE, SAONE, SARRE, SEINE, SELLE (small), (n) VESLE, MOSELLE; Mount, BLANC; mountains, JURA; region, ANJOU, ALSACE

212

FRENCH EQUATORIAL AFRICA
river, **SHARI**

FRENCH INDO-CHINA
see Indo China

FRENCH MOROCCO .. capital,
RABAT; city, **RABAT**

FRENCH WEST AFRICA
city, **DAKAR**

FRIENDLY ISLANDS .. **TONGA**

G

GEORGIA ..... city, **MACON,
SPARTA, AUGUSTA**

GERMANY ... city, **EMS, ULM,
BONN** (capital W. Germany),
**GERA, JENA, LAHR, LINZ,
EMDEN, ESSEN, NEUSS;** com-
mune town, **AUE, WALD;** spa,
AIX, BADEN; canal, **KIEL;**
river, **EMS, ALLE, EDER, EGER,
ELBE, ISAR, MAIN, ODER, PRUT,
REMS, RUHR, SAAR, LIPPE,
MOSEL, REGEN, RHINE, SAONE,
WESER;** mountain, **ORE, HARZ;**
state, **HESSE;** district, **ALSACE;**
region, **SUDETEN**

GOLD COAST . port and harbor,
KETA

GREAT BARRIER ISLAND **OTEA**

GREECE .... city, **ELIS,
SPARTA, SPARTE;** colony, an-
cient, **IONIA;** island, **COS, IOS,
KOS, NIO, MILO, SCIO, SERO,
CRETE, DELOS, MELOS, PAROS,
SAMOS, IONIAN;** mountain,
OETA, OSSA, HELICON; nome,
ELIS; river, **ARTA;** peninsula,
MOREA; region, **DORIS;** dis-
trict, ancient, **ATTICA**

GREENLAND .... town, settlement, base, **ETAH**

GUAM .. city, capital, **AGANA;**
port and harbor, **APRA**

GUATEMALA .. volcano, **AGUA**

H

HAWAII .. chief city, **HILO;**
island, **MAUI, OAHU;** district,

HANA; islet, **KURE**

HEBRIDES, INNER ..... island,
IONA, SKYE, UIST

HOLLAND .. see NETHELANDS

HONDURAS ...... port, **TELA**

HONSHU .... bay, **ISE;** port
and harbor, **KOBE**

HUNGARY ...... city, **BUDA,
PECS;** commune, town, **ERLAU;**
river, **RAAB**

HYOGO .... capital, **KOBE**

I

IDAHO ...... capital, **BOISE;**
town, **ARCO**

ILLINOIS . city, **PANA, ALEDO,
ELGIN, PEKIN, CANTON, MO-
LINE, PEORIA, SPARTA**

INDIA ... capital, **MADRAS;**
city, **AGRA, DELHI, POONA,
SIMLA, MADRAS, BENARES;**
commune, town, **ARCOT, SOR-
ON;** kingdom (n) **NEPAL;** state,
**DHAR, JATH, JIND, ASSAM,
MYSORE, GWALIOR;** province,
**SIND, SWAT, ASSAM, BERAR,
DELHI, MADRAS;** Portuguese
possession, **GOA;** river, **SIND,
SWAT, GANGA, INDUS, KABUL,
GANGES;** district, **SIMLA, SA-
TARA**

INDIA, NORTH
see NORTH INDIA

INDIANA .... city, **GARY,
PERU, MARION**

INDOCHINA . country, **ANAM,
ANNAM;** kingdom, **ANAM,
ANNAM;** city, **HUE, HANOI,
SAIGON;** region, **LAOS;** state,
ANAM, LAOS; port and harbor,
ANNAM

INDONESIA .... island, **AROE,
BALI, JAVA, TERNATE,
CELEBES;** island group, **KAI,
OBI**

IOWA .. city **AMES** (college);
county, **IDA**

213

IRAQ ..... capital, **BAGDAD, BAGHDAD**; port and harbor, **BASRA**

IRAN .... see PERSIA

IRELAND .. old capital, **TARA**; port and harbor, **COBH, TRALEE**; county, **MAYO, CLARE**; island, **ARAN**; river, **LEE, BANN, ERNE, NORE**; lake, **REE, ERNE**; town, **TARA**

ISLE OF WIGHT .... port and harbor, **COWES**

ISRAEL ..... port and harbor, **ACRE, HAIFA**; plain, **SHARON**; desert, **NEGEB**

ITALY .. capital, **ROMA, ROME**; city, **BARI, COMO, PISA, ROMA, ROME, MILAN, PARMA, SIENA, TRENT, NAPLES, SIENNA, VENICE,** (s) **CASERTA**; commune or town, **BRA, ARCO, ASTI, ATRI, DEGO, ESTE, LARI, NOLA, SAVA, TODI, ADRIA, ASOLA, PADUA, TURIN, EMPOLI**; resort, **LIDO**; port and harbor, **OSTIA, TRANI**; province, **ALBA, CONI, POLA, ROMA, ZARA, UDINE**; river, **PO, ADDA, ARNO, NERA, RENO, PIAVE, TIBER**; lake, **COMO, ISEO, NEMI**; strait, **OTRANTO**; gulf, **SALERNO**

J

JALAUN ...... capital, **ORAI**

JAPAN ...... capital, **TOKIO, TOKYO** (old name **EDO**); resort city, **HONSHU**; capital, **NARA**; city, **KOBE, KOFU, CHIBA, OSAKA, OTARU, TOKIO, TOKYO**; harbor or port or seaport, **OSAKA, OTARU**; island, **HONDO** (largest), **SADO**; volcano, **ASO, FUJI**; bay, **ISE**; province, old, **ISE, IYO, YAMATO**; mountain, **FUJI**

K

KANSAS .. city, **ARMA, IOLA, SALINA**; county, **OSAGE**; river, **OSAGE**

KOREA ... city, **KEIJO, SEOUL**

KASHMIR .... river, **INDUS**

KENTUCKY .. county, **ADAIR LA RUE**

KENYA .. (Africa) river, **TANA**

L

LATVIA .. capital, port, **RIGA**; river, **AA**

LEBANON ...... port, **SIDON**

LIBYA ..... port and harbor, **DERNA**; capital, **TRIPOLI**

LITHUANIA .. seaport, **VILNA**

LITTLE AMERICA .. sea, **ROSS**

LUZON ...... province, **ABRA** river, **ABRA, AGNO**

M

MAINE ... bay, **CASCO**; town, **BATH,** (University) **ORONO**; city, **SACO**

MALAYA ...... state, **PERAK, JOHORE**; region, **PENANG**; island, **BALI, JAVA, TIMOR**; port, **PEKAN**

MALAY ARCHIPELAGO island, **CELEBES**

MALTA .... island, **GOZO**

MARTINIQUE . volcano, **PELEE**

MASSACHUSETTS ...... city, **SALEM, NEWTON**; cape, **ANN, COD**; mountain, **TOM**

MEDITERRANEAN . island, **IOS, GOZO, RODI, CAPRI, CRETE, MALTA**; gulf, **TUNIS**; resort, **LIDO, NICE**

MESOPOTAMIA .. river, **TIGRIS**

MEXICO .... town, **TULA**; state, **COLIMA**; lake, **CHAPALA**

MICHIGAN ..... city, **ALMA, CLARE, FLINT, SPARTA**; county, **EATON**

214

MINDANAO ... volcano, **APO**; gulf, **DAVAO**

MISSISSIPPI .... city, **BILOXI**; river, **YAZOO**

MISSOURI .... city, **SEDALIA**; resort, **AVA**; river, **SAC**

MOLUCCA ...... island, **OBI**, **TERNATE**

MONGOLIA ..... desert, **GOBI**

MONTANA ..... city, **BUTTE**; river, **TETON**

MOROCCO .. region, **RIF, RIFF**; mountains, **ANTI ATLAS**; province, **SUS**; port and harbor, **RABAT**; town, **IFNI**

MOZAMBIQUE ... town, **IBA**; port and harbor, **BEIRA**

N

NEBRASKA .. city, **ORD**; river, **LOUP, PLATTE**; county, **OTOE**; capital, **LINCOLN**

NEPAL .... mountain, **API**

NETHERLANDS ... city, **EDAM, UTRECHT**; commune or town, **EDE, EPE, BEEK, ECHT, ELST, OLST, UDEN, GEMERT**; port and harbor, **EDAM**; river, **EEM, MAAS** (Dutch Meuse), **MAES, RIJN, WAAL**; island, **SUMATRA**

NEVADA ... city, **ELY, ELKO, RENO**; lake, **TAHOE**

NEW GUINEA .. city, port and harbor, **LAE**; island, **PAPUA**

NEW HAMPSHIRE ..... lake, **OSSIPEE**; city, **KEENE, NASHUA, LACONIA**; county, **COOS**

NEW HEBRIDES .... port and harbor, **VILA**; island, **EPI, TANA, EFATE, TANNA**

NEW JERSEY .. city, **TRENTON**; river, **RARITAN**

NEW MEXICO .. town, **TAOS**; river, **GILA**; resort, **TAOS**

NEW YORK ...... city, town, **ROME, TROY, OLEAN, UTICA, ELMIRA, MALONE, OSWEGO**; island, **STATEN**; county, **TIOGA**; village, **ILION**

NEWFOUNDLAND peninsula, **AVALON**

NEW ZEALAND .... lake, **TAUPO**; island, reef, **OTEA**

NIGERIA .. town, **ABA, IWO, LERE**; region, **BENIN**

NICARAGUA ..... city, **LEON**

NORMANDY ..... town, **ST. LO**

NORTH CAROLINA .... river, **HAW, TAR, PEE DEE** (Yadkin); cape, **FEAR**; county, **ASHE**

NORTH DAKOTA . city, **MINOT**

NORTHUMBERLAND river, **TYNE**

NORTH INDIA kingdom, **NEPAL**

NORTH VIETNAM capital, **HANOI**

NORWAY .... capital, **OSLO**; river, **TANA**; city, **HAMAR**

O

OHIO .... county, **ROSS**; city, **ADA** (college town Ohio Northern), **KENT, LIMA, BEREA, ELIDA, NILES, XENIA, CANTON, FOSTORIA**

OKINAWA .. port and harbor, **NAWA, NAHA**

OKLAHOMA ...... city, **ADA, ENID, SHAWNEE**

OREGON .... city, **SALEM, ASTORIA**; peak, **HOOD**

ORKNEYS .... island, **HOY**

P

PACIFIC ISLANDS ... Island, **LAU, YAP, FIJI, GUAM, SULU, TRUK, WAKE, LEYTE, SAMOA, TAHITI**; island group, **PELEW**

215

PAKISTAN .... city, **LAHORE;**
river, **INDUS**

PALESTINE .. (see also separate
Biblical lists on page 197);
mountain, **EBAL, SION, ZION,
TABOR, HERMON** (highest); valley, **GHOR;** plain, **ONO;** area,
BEISAN; port, **ACRE, GAZA;**
town, **GAZA**

PANAMA .... port, **COLON**

PARAGUAY ...... city, **ITA;**
river, **APA**

PENNSYLVANIA .. city, **ERIE,
EASTON, CHESTER, TYRONE;**
port, **ERIE**

PERSIA ... city, **NIRIZ, SUSA,
RESHT**

PERU ...... department, **ICA;**
capital, **LIMA;** city, **ICA;** cold
district, **PUNO;** port and harbor, (s) **ILO, CALLAO;** river, **ICA**

PHILIPPINE ISLANDS (see also
Luzon and Mindanao); city, **IBA,
CEBU, NAGA, ILOILO;** mountain
or peak, **IBA, APO;** volcano,
APO; port and harbor, **ILOILO,
BATANGAS;** province, **DAPA;**
island, **CEBU, SULU, BATAN
SAMAR, PANAY**

POLAND ... city, **LIDA, LODZ,
LWOW, POSEN, SRODA;** river,
**SAN, STYR, BIALA, VISLA,
STRYPA, VISTULA**

PÓRTUGAL ...... cape, **ROCA**

PUNJAB .... river, **INDUS**

Q

QUEBEC .... peninsula, **GASPE;**
district and town, **LEVIS**

R

RAJPUTANA ... district, **ABU**

ROUMANIA ..... city, **ARAD,
IASI;** department, **ALBA;** river,
OLT

RUSSIA .... city, **KIEF, OMSK,
OREL;** port and harbor, **OREL,**
ODESSA; commune, town, **KOLA;**
river, **OB, OM, DON, ILI, OKA,
ROS, UFA, DUNA, LENA, NEVA,
ONON, SEIM, URAL, TEREK;**
lake, **ONEGA;** sea, **ARAL, AZOF,
AZOV;** mountains, **ALAI, URAL,
ALTAI;** peninsula, **KOLA, KRIM,
CRIMEA;** lake in European Rus-
sia, **SEG;** state in Dagestan,
AVAR; region, **OMSK**

S

SAMOA
port, capital and harbor, **APIA**

SAVAGE ISLAND . island. **NIUE**

SAXONY . commune, town, **AUE**

SCOTLAND .. port and harbor,
OBAN; seaport, **AYR;** county,
AYR, BUTE; river, **DEE, TAY**
(largest), **DOON, SPEY, TYNE,
AFTON;** city, **AYR;** mountains,
IME; lake, **AWE, LOCH:** district,
ATHOLE, ATHOLL; island off,
ARRAN

SERBIA ...... department or
capital, **NIS, NISH**

SIBERIA .... (see also Russia)
river, **OB, ENISEI, YENISEI**

SICILY ...... volcano, **ETNA,
AETNA;** commune, town,
RAGUSA; city, **ENNA;** province,
ENNA; resort, **ENNA**

SOCIETY ISLANDS
island, **TAHITI**

SOUTH AFRICA district, **RAND;**
river, **VAAL**

SOUTHEAST AFRICA
district. **NIASSA, NYASSA**

SOUTHWEST AFRICA
port and harbor, **DAKAR**

SOUTH AMERICA . river, **BENI,
PLATA, YAPURA;** district,
CHACO; mountains, **ANDES**

SOUTH CAROLINA
river, **SANTEE**

SOUTH DAKOTA capital, **PIERRE**

SOUTH PACIFIC .... isle, **FIJI,
BALI, COOK, SAMOA**

SOUTHWEST .... river, **PECOS**

SPAIN .... city, **JACA, JAEN,
LEON, AVILA;** province, **ADRA,
JAEN, LEON, LUGO, AVILA,
MALAGA;** port and harbor,
**ADRA, NOYA. VIGO, PALOS,
MALAGA;** river, **EBRO, MINHO,
TAGUS;** kingdom, **LEON, CAS-
TILE;** commune, town, **ORIA**

SPANISH MOROCCO (see also
Morocco) port and harbor,
CEUTA; district, **IFNI**

SUMATRA .... district, **DELI**

SWEDEN .. river, **UME, LULE;**
island off **ALAND;** port and harbor, **MALMO, OREBRO;** strait,
ORESUND

SWITZERLAND .... city, **BEX,
BALE, BERN, GENF, SION,
BASLE, BERNE, LOCARNO;**
commune, town, **AY, BAAR,
BIEL, CHUR, RUTI, WALD,
AARAU, MORAT;** canton, **URI
ZUG, BERN, VAUD, ZOUG,
BASLE, BERNE;** river, **AAR,
AARE;** lake, **ZUG, JOUY,
LUCERNE;** mountain, **TODI,
VISO, MATTERHORN;** resort,
DAVOS; capital, **BERN, BERNE;**
town, see commune

SYRIA .... city, **ALEP, HOMS,
ALEPPO;** port and harbor,
SIDON

T

TAHITI .... capital, **PAPEETE**

TEXAS .... county, **CLAY,
CARSON;** city, **WACO, LAREDO,
ABILENE**

TIBET . capital, **LASSA, LHASA;**
river, **INDUS**

TRANS-JORDON .. mountain,
HOR; mountain range, **SEIR**

TUNISIA ..... capital, **TUNIS**

TURKEY .... city, **ADANA,
ANGORA;** river, **ARAS;** vilayet,
ORDU, URFA; island, **TENEDOS**
TUSCANY ...... river, **ARNO**

U

UTAH .... city,
HEBER, LOGAN;
mountains, **UINTA**

V

VENEZUELA .... state, **LARA;**
island, **ARUBA;** river, **PAO**

VERMONT ...... city, **BARRE**

VIRGINIA .... river, **DAN,
RAPIDAN**

VIRGIN ISLANDS
capital, **CHARLOTTE AMALIE**

W

WALES .... river, **DEE, USK;**
lake, **BALA**

WASHINGTON .. city, **TACOMA**

WEST AUSTRALIA capital,
PERTH

WEST INDIES .... isle, island,
CUBA, HAITI, NEVIS

WISCONSIN .... city, **RIPON,
RACINE**

WYOMING .... city, **CASPER,
LARAMIE;** highest mountain
peak, **GANNETT;** range, **TETON**

Y

YEMEN .... capital, **SANA**

YORKSHIRE .... river, **OUSE;**
city, **LEEDS**

YUGOSLAVIA ... island, **RAB,
ARBE, SOLTA;** city, **NIS;** river,
SAVA, DRINA, NARENTA; dis-
trict and province, **BANAT**

YUKON .... city,
DAWSON; river, **HESS, PEEL,
ROSS**

217

WORD-FINDER

with CROSS-REFERENCES

FOR THE SOLVER

You can complete any unfinished 2-, 3-, or 4-letter word in the crossword you are working by using this WORD-FINDER. Even though you are at first unable to locate it in the Definition section for some reason, if you have just two letters of your wanted word (just one if it's a 2-letter word) you can find it here.

The WORD-FINDER words are listed according to the following Letter-Combination system:

XX - -	(for cases when the first two letters are known)
- XX -	(when the second and third letters are known)
- - XX	(when the last two letters are known)
X - - X	(when the first and last letters are known)

Let us say that you need to complete a word that is four letters long.

STEP ONE: Find the Letter-Combination that is the same as the letters which you have written into the crossword puzzle. Have you, for example, found "ON" as the end of a 4-letter word? Then turn to the "- - ON" Letter-Combination. Of course, since the WORD-FINDER is thorough-going, a number of words, all containing the same letter combination, are listed under this Letter-Combination.

- - ON Acon, agon, Amon, anon,
　　　　Avon, axon, azon, bion,
　　　　boon, cion, coon, Dion,
　　　　doon, ebon, Enon, Eton,
　　　　faon, Gaon, hoon, icon,
　　　　iron, Leon, lion, loon,
　　　　moon, neon, etc.

STEP TWO: You may know, after looking through the words listed under your Letter-Combination, the word which is the only correct possibility. If not, you now begin to eliminate words in the list by working with the words in the crossword puzzle which CROSS your unfinished word. You do this by experimentally inserting words from the Letter-Combination list. When the experimental insert produces such impossible-looking combinations with the crossing word as "bv," "pv" etc. it can be discarded.

STEP THREE: After eliminating the words which make highly unlikely or "impossible" combinations with the crossing words, you still may not be sure how to complete your unfinished puzzle. Here you make use of the invaluable CROSS-REFERENCE listings following the words in the WORD-FINDER. Each number following a word is the number of the page of the Definitions Section on which the word and one of its definitions will be found. The alphabetical letters a, b, c, d indicate in exactly which section of the definition page you will be able to locate the word with its meaning.

Example: adat (90b, 95d)

On page 90 of this Dictionary, in section b of the page, you will find the word ADAT in bold face type. The definition is "law, D. E. Ind". On page 95, section d, you will find another cross-reference to ADAT. The definition reads "Malay law."

STEP FOUR: Now re-examine the definition in your puzzle. Eliminate words in the WORD-FINDER by comparing definitions until you arrive at the "logical candidate" word for which you have been looking. Definitions in this dictionary and those in your puzzle will not always agree in exact wording. In that case, let the general meaning of the definitions be your guide. Everyday words are not always cross-referenced in this WORD-FINDER, nor are some words of exceptional terminology. Only some of the words listed in the Special Section are cross-referenced. If your definition calls for a word likely to be found in the Special Section, it is recommended that you look there first.

TWO-LETTER WORDS

A -   Aa (47a), aa (90b), Ab (48d,75b,102a), ab (63d), AC (39d), ad (90a,112d,167d), ae (42b,43c,d,122b,139a), Ae (82c,115d), ah (52c), ai (143c,148c), al (8c,80c,102c,104b), am (166c,175c), an (11b, 13b), Ao (13d,88b,c,116c), AP (107a,182d), ap (122d,166c), ar (88b,91c,98a,99b,110c), as (51b,67b,92b,126a,133a,b,180d), at (25c,32c,106a,123a,128a), au (63a,69c), aw (44a), ax (40c,139a, 167a), ay (7c,8b,9b,28d,55a,60a)

- A   Aa (47a), aa (90b), BA (42a), Ba (150d,153c), ba (139a), da (9b,37a, 56a,133d,135d), DA (124d), ea (43c), EA (15b,68a), fa (108b,138a, 161a), Ga (69c), ha (52c), ia (43d,158c), ja (66d), ka (45c), Ka (68c, 77b,150d,153c,173c), la (13b,61a,83a,108b,138a,151d,161a), ma, MA (42a), Ma (69a,b,85d), na (140c,163d), NA (36c), oa (43c,d), pa (60b,106d), ra (108b), Ra (159b), SA (36c), ta (112d,139a,160b), VA (83a), va (105a), wa (188), Wa (24c,d,88c), ya, za (162a)

B -   BA (42a), ba (139a,150d,153c), bb (147b), be, bi (122d,171c), bo (23d,24c,136a,168a), bu (190), by (18b,32c,106a)

- B   ab (63d,) Ab (48d,75b,102a), bb (147b), FB (59c), HB (59c), ob (122b), QB (59c)

C -   ce (62d,164c), CE (42a)

- C   DC (39d), ec (122c)

D -   da (9b,37a,56a,133d,135d), DA (124d), DC (39d), DD (42a), de (63d,89b,122b,122c,124a,152c,d), di (68c,89b,108b,122b,122c, 122d,171d), dm (131c), do (108b,138a,161a)

- D   ad, (90a,112d,167d), DD (42a), ed (175c), Ed (18d), id (26d, 40c,51c,57a,b,d), od (8d,59d,79c), td (32a)

E -   ea (43c), EA (15b,68a), ec (122c), ed (175c), Ed (18d), ee (139c), EE (42a), ef (91c), eg (59d,163d), eh (52c), el (13b,42a,47a,99b, 151d,168a), El (68a,108a), em (91c,98a,123d,172a,c), en (15b, 29c,50a,91c,98a,119d,123d,158c,d,172a), eo (34a), er (35b,76c, 137d,155a,158c,d,160b,175c), Er (18d,68c,85c,163d,166c,172c, 178a), es (49b,50a,66c,119d,158c,d,175c), et (10b,61a,b,89a,158c), ex (60b,91c,122c)

- E   ae (42b,43c,d,122b,139a), Ae (82c,115d), be, CE (42a), Ce (62d), ce (164c), de (63d,89b,122b,c,124a,152c,d), ee (139c), EE (42a), Ge (47d,69a), he (91c), ie (74c,158c,163d), LE (59c), le (13b,61a, 108b), me (108b,124b), Me. (124d), ne (35b,106b), oe (43c,54d, 82d,180d,182a,b), pe (91c), Pe. (124d), re (6b,10b,35d,108b,122b, 129b,138a,161a), RE (59c), se (35b,108b), te (43a,62d,108b,131c, 152d,160b,185d), Ve (63c,109c), we (48c,124b), We (92b), ye (124b)

F -   fa (108b,138a,161a), FB (59c), ff (147b), Fi (108b), Fo (23d), fu (42c,84c), Fu (30b)

- F   ef (91c), ff (147b), if (35d,125a), LF (16d), of (6b), RF 16d)

220

G - Ga (69c), Ge (47d,69a), Gi (91d), go (64c,90d)

- G eg (59d,163d), Og (16d,18c)

H - ha (52c), HB (59c), he (91c), hi (52c), ho (39b,79a), Ho (87c), Hu (101c,108a,162b)

- H ah (52c), eh (52c), oh (52c), Rh (20c), sh (17b,43c,79c,126d), th (43c)

I - ia (43d,158c), id (26d,40c,51c,57a,b,d), ie (74c,158c,163d), if (35d, 125a), il (122c), im (122c), in (9d,123a), io (74b,74c,103c,115b), Io (25a,85d,95c,186b), ir (99d,122c), Ir (10a,28a,82b), is (51a,166c, 175c), Is (15b,23c,86c), it (124b)

- I ai (143c,148c), bi (122d,171c), di (68c,89b,108b,122b,c,d,171d), fi (108b), Gi (91d), hi (52c), Ii (30a,b,37b,98a,108b,161b), mi (43b, 108b,138a,161a), pi (71b,85d,91c,165a,172a), ri (84c,96d,98a, 108b), RI (106c), si (108b,152d,185d), ti (92b,108b,113a,b,120d, 138a,161a,162c,169b), xi (91c)

J - ja (66d), jo (140c,160c), Jo (8c,94b), ju (121a)

K - ka (45c), Ka (68c,77b,150d,153c,173c), ko (22c,87c,121a)

- K OK (155a)

L - la (13b,61a,83a,108b,138a,151d,161a), le (13b,61a,108b), LE (59c), Lf (16d), Ii (30a,b,37b,98a,108b,161b), Lt (143c), LT (59c), lu (65a), lo (17d,93d)

- L al (8c,80c,102c,104b), Al (96b), el (13b,42a,47a,99b,151d,168a), El (68a,108a), il (122c), ol (29c,158b,d,160b)

M - ma, Ma (69a,b,85d), MA (42a), me (108b,124b), Me. (124d), mi (43b,108b,138a,161a), mo (21d,81c,101c), Mo (88c,177c), mu (10a, 30a,60c,71a,91c), my (52c,124c)

- M am (166c,175c), em (91c,98a,123d,172a,c), dm (131c), im (122c), om (49a,77a,77b,105c,136a), um (52c,76c)

N - na (140c,163d), NA (36c), ne (35b,106b), no (42b,106b), No (84b), nu (71b,91c), Nu (29a,49a)

- N an (11b,13b), en (15b,29c,50a,91c,98a,119d,123d,158c,d,172a), in (9d,123a), on (8b,9a,60c106a,123a), un (34c,122c)

O - oa (43c,d), ob (122b), od (8d,59d,79c), oe (43c,54d,82d,180d, 182a,b), of (6b), Og (16d,18c), oh (52c), OK (155a), ol (29c, 158b, d,160b), om (49a,77a,b,105c,136a), on (8b,9a,60c,106a,123a), oo (34a,74b), or (9b,36a,37b,69c,158c,166a,184b), os (21d,67b,104a, 131b), ow (52c), ox (10c,22c), oy (139c)

- O Ao (13d,88b,c,116c), bo (23d,24c,136a,168a), do (108b,138a 161a), eo (34a), Fo (23d), go (64c,90d), ho (39b,79a), Ho (87c), io (74b,c,103c,115b), Io (25a,85d,95c,186b), jo (140c,160c), Jo (8c, 94b), ko (22c,87c,121a), lo (17d,93d), mo (21d,81c,101c), Mo (88c, 177c), no (42b,106b), No (84b), oo (34a,74b), Ro (13c,81d,88c,131c, 173c), so (76a,108b,125a,138a,158b,161a,165b,175c), to (10b, 13c), uo (43d), vo (91a), yo, zo (13d,186b)

P - pa (60b,106d), pe (91c), Pe. (124d), pi (71b,85d,91c,165a,172a), pu (30b,140a)

- P ap (122d,166c), AP (107a,182d), up (123a), UP (107a,182d)

Q - QB (59c), q.v. (180d)

R - ra (108b), **Ra** (159b), **re** (6b,10b,35d,108b,122b,129b,138a,161a), **RE** (59c), **RF** (16d), **Rh** (20c), **ri** (84c,96d,98a,108b), **Ri** (106c), **Ro** (13c,81d,88c,131c,173c), **RT** (59c)

- R ar (88b,91c,98a,99b,110c), **er** (35b,76c,137d,155a,158c,d,160b, 175c), **Er** (18d,68c,85c,163d,166c,172c,178a), **ir** (99d,122c), **Ir** (10a, 28a,82b), **or** (9b,36a,37b,69c158c,166a,184b), **Ur** (6b,28d,94a, 100d)

S - **SA** (36c), **se** (35b,108b), **Se, sh** (17b,43c,79c,126d), **si** (108b,152d, 185d), **so** (76a,108b,125a,138a,158b,161a,165b,175c), **SS** (16d, 164c), **Su** (127a), **Sw** (35b), **Sy** (141a)

- S as (51b,67b,92b,126a,133a,b,180d), **es** (49b,50a,66c,119d,158c, d,175c), **is** (51a,166c,175c), **Is** (15b,23c,86c), **os** (21d,67b,104a, 131b), **S.S.** (16d,164c), **us** (124b)

T - ta (112d,139a,160b), **td** (32a), **te** (43a,62d,108b,131c,152d,160b, 185d), **th** (43c), **ti** (92b,108b,113a,b,120d,138a,161a,162c,169b), **to** (10b,13c), **tt** (147b), **tu** (83c,164d,185d), **Ty** (68c,109c,163d, 178a)

- T at (25c,32c,106a,123a,128a), **et** (10b,61a,b,89a,158c), **It** (124b), **Lt** (143c), **LT** (59c), **RT** (59c), **tt** (147b), **ut** (72b,108b), **Ut** (67a)

U - um (52c,76c), **un** (34c,122c), **Uo** (43d), **up** (123a), **Ur** (6b,28d, 94a,100d), **UP** (107a,182d), **us** (124b), **ut** (72b,108b), **Ut** (67a), **Uz** (48c)

- U au (63a,69c), **bu** (190), **fu** (42c,84c), **Fu** (30b), **Hu** (101c,108a, 162b), **ju** .(121a), **lu** (65a), **mu** (10a,30a,60c,71a,91c), **nu** (71b, 91c), **Nu** (29a,49a), **pu** (30b,140a), **Su** (127a), **tu** (83c, 164d, 185d), **Wu** (30b), **Zu** (68c,157a)

V - va (105a), **Va** (83a), **Ve** (63c,109c), **vo** (91a)

- V q.v. (180d)

W - wa (188), **Wa** (24c,d,88c), **we** (48c,124b), **We** (92b), **Wu** (30b), **wy** (91c)

- W aw (44a), **ow** (52c), **sw** (35b)

X - xi (91c)

- X ax (40c,139a,167a), **ex** (60b,91c,122c), **ox** (10c,22c)

Y - ya, ye (124b), **yo**

- Y ay (7c,8b,9b,28d,55a,60a), **by** (18b,32c,106a), **my** (52c,124c), **sy** (141a), **oy** (139c), **Ty** (68c,109c,163d,178a), **wy** (91c)

Z - za (162a), **zo** (13d,186b), **Zu** (68c,157a)

- Z Uz (48c)

THREE-LETTER WORDS

AA - aal (47c,80c,104b), **aam** (47a,49d,93a), **aar** (172d), **Aar** (131a)

A - A aba (12a,25d,32b,33a,65b), **Ada** (110a,112c,183c), **aea** (26a,36d), **aga** (35a,39a,48b,102d,103a,b,111c,166b,170d,171a), **aha** (52c,55c, 159c), **aka** (88b,c,176b), **Aka** (13d), **ala** (6d,13a,15c,61a,133d,

222

182c,d), **Ala** (151b), **ama** (26a,28d,31a,35b,39c,95b,108d,111c, 117b,182c), **ana** (10b,33c,60d,93a,98c,122b,d,140d,142b), **Ana** (28a,68d,100c), **apa** (23a,177d), **ara** (33a,114a,116a,118b,163d), **Ara** (9b,18c,36b,c,68d,69b,c,85a,95a,175b), **Asa** (6a,18c,71a,84d, 86d,164c), **ata** (58d,97d,158d,160c,173d), **Ata** (79c,80d,94d, 95d,100a,106b,117a,), **ava** (78d,86a,116a,120d,139a,167b), **Ava** (24c), **awa** (100a,139a), **aya** (77b,166b)

- AA   **baa** (143d), **maa** (97d,143d), **saa** (98a), **taa** (112d)

AB -   **aba** (12a,25d,32b,33a,65b), **abb** (58b,178b,185b), **ABC** (134d), **Abe** (71a,96a,123a), **Abi** (76c), **Abo** (25d), **Abt** (34c), **abu** (17a), **Abu** (15b,42a,55a,68a,c,147d)

A - B   **abb** (58b,178b,185b), **alb** (65b,176a)

- AB   **Bab** (15a), **cab** (75c), **dab** (46a,57b,58b,d,114d,115c), **gab** (29b, 78a,116c,122a,161c,183a), **jab** (120b,125c), **kab** (75c), **lab**, **Mab** (54b,126b,183d), **nab** (13b,26c,27b,142a), **pab** (139c), **rab** (17c,75c, 85b,102d,162c,166b), **Rab** (45a), **tab** (29b,39c,58b,86a,128d,145a)

AC -   **ace** (7a,26c,52d,57a,77d,110c,114c,120b.147a,163a,173a), **ach** (8b, 48a,52c,66b,80c), **aci** (29c), **act** (41d,55b,119c,155d), **acu** (34c), **acy** (34c)

A - C   **ABC** (134d), **arc** (31b,39d,92a,126a,127c,142a)

- AC   **bac** (31b,55c,174d), **fac** (41c), **lac** (53c,99d,130c,135b,174d), **Mac** (96a,140b,150b), **pac** (73b,94c,100d), **sac** (15d,121d), **Sac** (80c), **tac** (34d,130a), **Vac** (153b), **zac** (27c)

AD -   **Ada** (110a,112c,183c), **add** (10d,11d,14c,158a,167c), **ade** (18c, 149d), **Ade** (9c,53b), **ado** (22b,24d,35b,64c,78d,121d,156b,170a), **ady** (188), **adz** (40c,167a)

A - D   **aid** (14a,15b,64c,75d,158b), **add** (10d,11d,14c,158a,167c), **and** (36a,119d)

- AD   **bad** (55a,173a,184d), **cad** (22b,23b,75c,172c,173d), **dad, fad** (38b, 108c,163a), **gad** (58c,100a,b,127d,132b,153c,154b,178a), **Gad** (84a, 186d), **had, lad** (22c,25b,55b,157c,186a), **mad** (10c,82b), **pad** (39d, 59c,76c,157d,161a,168b), **rad** (50b,138d,173b), **sad** (29c,42c,94c, 98c,104a,150d,173a), **tad** (22c,174a,186a), **wad** (94d,97b,109c, 112b,149d)

AE -   **aea** (26a,36d), **AEF** (184d), **aer** (8b,28d,34a,b,175a), **aes** (23c, 89a,101c,132d,133a,b), **aet** (89a,109d), **Aex** (46d)

A - E   **Abe** (71a,96a,123a), **ace** (7a,26c,52d,57a,77d,110c,114c,120b. 147a,163a,173a), **ade** (18c,149d), **Ade** (9c,53b), **age** (51d,66a,92a, 97c,98c,116b,141c), **ake** (60a,107a), **ale** (17c,18c,50c,55d,92d, 104c), **ame** (37a,62d,131b), **ane** (61c,140a,158b), **ape** (36d,79d, 100a,101d,146d), **are** (51a,88b,98a,99b,110c,166c,175c), **ase** (51a, 139a), **Ase** (79b,115d), **ate** (81a,108c,158c,174c), **Ate** (20c,68b,d, 69a,b,116c,186b), **ave** (54c,71d,73a,122a,134a,136d), **awe** (81d, 100a,130d,175b,182b), **axe** (30c,40c,167a), **aye** (7c,9b,55a,60a)

- AE   **dae** (139b), **eae** (34b), **hae** (139c), **kae** (84a,140b), **Mae** (183c), **nae** (139d), **rae** (136b,138d,140b), **Rae** (183c), **sae** (140b,149c), **tae** (138d,140c,166c,d), **vae** (176b)

AF -   **AFL** (173a), **Afr.** (36c), **aft** (14a,15b,17d,128b,167d)

A - F   **AEF** (184d), **Alf** (96a)

223

- AF   gaf (12b), kaf (12b), Kaf (104a), oaf (22a,45b,146d,157d,185d), Qaf (104a)

AG -   aga (35a,39a,48b,102d,103a,b,111c,166b,170d,171a), age (51d, 66a,92a,97c,98c,116b,141c), ago (25a,69d,114d,147a)

- AG   bag (26c,139a,145b,159a), cag (81d,109d), dag (11b,118c,139c), Dag (108c), fag (55a,166a), gag (146c,183a), hag (140a,183a), jag (124d,148a), lag (93c,155d), mag (73b,95b,166c), Mag (183d), nag (73d,78b,138c,184d), rag (59b,77c,100c,133c,161a), sag (46b), tag (45a,54c,65a,87b,144a), vag (174b,178a), wag (85b,104a,183a), zag (84a)

AH -   aha (52c,55c,159c), Ahi (32c,147d), ahu (24c,41d,65d,103d,120d)

A - H   ach (8b,48a,52c,66b,80c), akh (153d), ash (24d,33c,49c,73d,134b, 168c,169a), auh (52c)

- AH   bah (52c), dah (24c,87a), hah (52c), Jah (84d), Mah (10b,57c, 102b), pah (52c,60b,106d), rah (29c), sah (188), wah (113c), yah (52c)

AI -   aid (14a,15b,64c,75d,158b), aik (139d), ail (170a), aim (42d,43d, 67d,109b,125d,157c), ain (18d,91c,110c,124b,140a,154b,180a), air (11c,12c,42b,44c,53a,96b,98c,99d,125b,170c), ait (82d,132a), Aix (46d)

A - I   Abi (76c), aci (29c), Ahi (32c,147d), Ali (7b,12a,25c,48b,55a,60c, 92d,101a,103a,164a,166b,170d), ami (61d), ani (19b,d,20b,39b), api (34a,76d), Ari (18d), asi (137a), ati (106d,107a), Ati (45d,106b, 113c,117a)

- AI   hai (55c), kai (59c), Kai (14d,84d), lai (98b,161b), Lai (24c,d,88c), mai (62a), rai (188), sai (101d), tai (84b,111c,121b), Tai (80d), Vai (91d)

- AJ   gaj (190), raj (129c), saj (48a,169a), taj (75a,97d)

AK -   aka (176b), Aka (13d,88b,c), ake (60a,170a), akh (153d), ako (189), aku (57c,176a)

A - K   aik (139d), alk (171b), ark (21a,29d,38a,58b,60d,175d), ask (38b, 82a,126c), auk (19b)

- AK   dak (95c), hak (46d), lak (38a), nak (156b), oak (73d,168c,169a), sak (37c), Sak (88c), yak (112c,161d,165b), zak (188)

AL -   ala (6d,13a,15c,61a,133d,182c,d), Ala. (151b), alb (65b,176a), ale (17c,18c,50c,55d,92d,104c), Alf (96a), Ali (7b,12a,25c,48b,55a,60c, 92d,101a,103a,164a,166b,170d), alk (171b), all (35c,118a,126d, 181a), alp (24b,103d,115c), als (66d,163d), alt (66c,76c,109c), aly (95d)

A - L   aal (47c,80c,104b), AFL (173a), ail (170a), all (35c,118a,126d,181a), awl (145b,167a)

- AL   aal (47c,80c,104b), bal (9d,37b,61a,61b), cal (183c), Cal (123a), dal (117d,153d), gal, Hal (69d), ial (158b), mal (34a,b,44a,52b,62c, 122b), Mal (94b), pal (35b,38d), sal (29c,48a,136d,149d,152d, 169a,183a), Sal (183d), tal (40c,77a,113b), Zal (135d)

AM -   ama (26a,28d,31a,35b,39c,95b,108d,111c,117b,182c), ame (37a, 62d,131b), ami (61d), amo (79a,89c), amp (49b,173b), amt (37d, 40d,108a,163c), amy (63c), Amy (8c,94b,183c)

224

A - M   aam (47a,49d,93a), aim (42d,43d,67d,109b,125d,157c), arm (22d, 60c,81b,92b,124b,161b), aum (189)

- AM   aam (47a,49d,93a), bam (29b), cam (48b,65d,95a,98b,134a,139b, 148b,180c), dam (30c,49c,55b,156d,180a), gam (76b,176d,180c), ham (98a,144b), Ham (18d,107c), jam (123a,156d,165c), lam (51b, 58b,93d,164d,178a), Mam (192), pam (26c,65a,87a,105b), Ram (36b), ram (17a,45b,50b,79c,112b,121d,143d,157d), Sam (96a, 162a), tam (74d), yam (48c,121d,160b,170c)

AN -   ana (10b,33c,60d,93a,98c,122b,d,140d,142b), Ana (28a,68d,100c), and (36a,119d), ane (61c,140a,158b), ani (19b,d,20b,39b), Ann (183c), ano (19d,20b,34d,122d,174a), Ans (92a), ant (49d,60b,81b, 118c), Anu (15b,28a,68a,d,75b,88c,147d), any (14b,150b)

A - N   ain (18d,91c,110c,124b,140a,154b,180a), Ann (183c), arn (8c, 139a), awn (12c,17b,140a)

- AN   ban (81d,97a,124a), can (24c,36c,123a,166a), dan (24c,97c), Dan (18c,39c,77d,83a,84a,141b), ean (17d,23b,88a), fan (43a,154b), 156b,182d), Gan (132d), Han (16c,30b,185b), lan (85b,96a,139d), kan (93a), lan (37b,37d,160b), man (29c,60c,64c,65a,142d,161d), Nan (183c), pan (34a,61a,104a,175d), Pan (56a,68a,68b,76b,120c, 135b,161a,184a), ran (73d), Ran (7c,107d,141a,163d), san (91c, San (24d), tan (23d,33c,46a,72d,90d), van (7b,59d,60a,63d,90c), wan (113a), Zan (186b)

A - O   Abo (25d), ado (22b,24d,35b,64c,78d,121d,156b,170a), ago (25a, 69d,114d,147a), ako (189), amo (79a,89c), ano (19d,20b,34d, 122d,174a), Apo (122b,177c), Aro (107a,111c), Aso (84c), azo (107c)

- AO   dao (117a), hao (189), iao (78a,96c,178d), Lao (80d,88c,146a, 161b), mao (115b), Mao (30b), sao (141b), Sao (113c), tao (10d, 131c,170b), Tao (117a), Yao (30a,c,104b)

AP -   apa (23a,177d), ape (36d,79d,100a,101d,146d), api (34a,76d), apo (122b), Apo (177c), apt (11d,23b,32b,58a,80b,92b,114d,116d, 124b,159a)

A - P   alp (24b,103d,115c), amp (49b,173b), asp (7b,32b,149a,174a, 176c)

- AP   bap (93b,132d), Bap (124d), cap (19d,39a,43a,53a,74d,160a,167b, 185c), dap (43b,c,46b,91b,147d), gap (11b,23a,29b,76c,110d,128a), hap (17d,28d), Jap (31b,37d,59b,127a,131d,153d,167d), map (27a,29b,54a,98d,160a), nap (65a,117d,146b,148a), pap (59c), rap (90d,110a,147c,157c), sap (45d,52d,85c,169b,176d,179a), tap (55a,114d,153c), yap (16c,29b,122a)

AR -   ara (33a,114a,116a,118b,163d), Ara (8c,9b,36b,c,68d,69b,c, 85a,95a,175b), arc (31b,39d,92a,126a,127c,142a), are (51a,88b, 98a,99b,110c,166c,175c), Ari (18d), ark (21a,29d,38a,58b,60d, 175d), arm (22d,60c,81b,92b,124b,161b), arn (8c,139a), Aro (107a, 111c), ars (13b,89a), Ars (112c), art (22d,38b,39c,43b,56c,124a, 162c,181d), aru (80c,82b), Aru (82d)

A - R   aar (172d), Aar (131a), aer (8b,28d,34a,b,175a), Afr. (36c), air (11c,12c,42b,44c,53a,96b,98c,99d,125b,170c)

- AR   aar (172d), Aar (131a), bar (37c,39a,46a,52c,76d,78b,91a,124a,

137a,156a,157c,169c), **car** (16a,61d,93b,175a) **dar,** (65c,111b,
169a), **ear** (14c,d,28c,63d,64a,73c,111b,116a,124b,137d,150d,
153c), **far** (44c), **gar** (57b,c,d,106b), **har** (139c), **jar** (31d,70d,143b),
lar (24c,51d,67a,78d,95d,101d,171b), **mar** (40b,44a,79a,d,81a,
140d), **Mar** (93d), **nar** (139d), **oar** (20b,124c,134b), **par** (15a,51a,
51b,c,69d,107c,135b,155a) **sar** (57d), **tar** (8c,68a,94d,111c,118c,
136a,c,176d), **war** (157c), **yar** (72a), **zar** (188)

AS - **Asa** (6a,18c,71a,84d,86d,164c), **ase** (51a,139a), **Ase** (79b,115d),
ash (24d,33c,49c,73d,134b,168c,169a), **asi** (137a), **ask** (38b,82a,
126c) **Aso,** (84c), **asp** (7b,32b,149a,174a,176c), **ass** (17b,20c,45b,
c,59c,110c,112b,146d,157d)

A - S **aes** (23c,89a,101c,132d,133a,b), **als** (66d,163d), **Ans** (92a), **ars**
(13b,89a), **Ars** (112c), **ass** (17b,20c,45b,c,59c,110c,112b,146d,
157d), **aus** (66c), **Aus** (98b)

- AS **bas** (62a,d,129d,134b), **das** (13b,15d,36d,66b,d,164a), **fas** (44d,89d,
129d), **gas** (10b,29b,59a,116d,161c), **has, kas** (32c,47a), **las** (13b,
(151d), **mas** (34b,55b,119a) **nas** (74a,89c,178b), **pas** (40d,
156a), **ras** (6c,26b,48b,51d,53d,61c,75a,111c,123c,166b), **vas** (46d,
89d,119c,133b,175d), **was** (166c,175c), **Was** (24d)

AT - **ata** (58d,97d,158d,160c,173d), **Ata** (79c,80d,94d,95d,100a,
106b,117a), **ate** (81a,108c,158c,174c), **Ate** (20c,68b,d,69a,b,
116c,186b), **ati** (106d,107a), **Ati** (45d,106b,113c,117a), **att** (146a)

A - T **Abt** (35c), **act** (41d,55b,119c,155d), **aet** (89a,109d), **aft** (14a,15b,
17d,128b,167d), **ait** (82d,132a), **alt** (66c,76c,109c), **amt** (37d,40d,
108a,163c), **ant** (49d,60b,81b,118c), **apt** (11d,23b,32b,58a,80b,92b,
114d,116d,124b,159a), **art** (22d,38b,39c,43b,56c,124a,162c,181d),
att (146a), **aut** (34d,89d)

- AT **bat** (39c,107c,156a,157c,182d), **cat** (10a,45b,55b,71d,161b,169d,
180d,183d), **eat** (37b,96b,135d,179b), **fat** (110a,124a), **gat** (28d,
72c,131a), **hat** (74d), **Hat** (183d), **Jat** (80d,125c), **kat** (105d), **lat**
(24a,33d,106b,118a), **mat** (46d,50d,94d,117c,161d), **Mat** (96a),
nat (7a,24c,24d,106a), **oat** (15a,28b,70b,144b), **pat** (11d,116d,
159a,161d,167c), **Pat** (96a), **rat** 16a,42d,73b,132c), **sat** (13d), **tat**
(48c,72d,87c), **Tat** (82a), **vat** (31b,36c,163a,170c), **wat** (73d,140d,
163a,180b), **xat** (167c), **zat** (148a)

AU - **auh** (52c), **auk** (19b), **aum** (189), **aus** (66c), **Aus** (98b), **aut** (34d,
89d), **aux** (6d,61a)

A - U **abu** (17a), **Abu** (15b,42a,55a,68a,c,147d), **acu** (34c), **ahu** (24c,41d,
65d,103d,120d), **aku** (57c,176a), **Anu** (15b,28a,68a,d,75b,88c,
147d), **aru** (80c,82b), **Aru** (82d), **ayu** (160c)

- AU **eau** (63a,178c), **gau** (66d,67a), **mau** (170c,188), **pau** (130c), **Pau**
(48c,76a), **tau** (71b,91c,136c,161a), **vau** (91c), **Yau** (30c)

AV - **ava** (78d,86a,116a,120d,139a,167b), **Ava** (24c), **ave** (54c,71d,73a,
122a,134a,136d)

- AV **gav** (72d), **lav** (72d), **tav** (91c)

AW - **awa** (100a,139a), **awe** (81d,100a,130d,175b,182b), **awl** (145b,167a),
awn (12c,17b,140a)

- AW **baw** (52c), **caw** (19b,d), **daw** (39a,70b,84a,146d), **gaw** (140c), **haw**
(35a,52c,74d,91a,155a,162c), **jaw** (97d,138c), **law** (26b,33a,40a,

226

48c,60b,85d,91a,111b,134d,155d), **maw** (38b,d,72c,111a,121a,
142a,156c), **paw** (32d,59c,73c), **raw** (20c,39a,105d,173d), **saw** (7a,
11b,40c,54c,97d,125a,137d,167a), **taw** (90d,91c,96c,d,145b,161d),
waw (12b,91c), **yaw** (43a,155d)

AX -   **axe** (30c,40c,167a)
A - X   **Aex** (46d), **Aix** (46d), **aux** (6d,61a)
- AX   **lax** (93d,130a), **Max** (96a), **pax** (89d,115b), **sax** (40c,148a,167a),
         tax (13a,14a,80a,91d), **wax** (28b,72a,80b,120c), **zax** (148a)

AY -   **aya** (77b,143c,166b), **aye** (7c,9b,55a,60a), **ayu** (160c)
A - Y   **acy** (34c), **ady** (188), **aly** (95d), **amy** (63c), **Amy** (8c,94b,183c), **any**
         (14b,150b)
- AY   **bay** (12d,16c,33c,73d,78b,81b,90a,128d), **cay** (82d,180b), **day**
         (153a), **fay** (32c,54b,154b), **Fay** (183c), **gay**, **Gay** (17d), **hay** (52c,
         55c,165d), **jay** (19b,91c), **kay** (82d), **Kay** (13b,134b), **lay**
         (16a,25c,80a,98b,107d,141d,150b), **may** (74d), **May** (183c), **nay**
         (42b,106b), **pay** (35b,128c,130a,d,177b), **ray** (38a,49a,57b,
         58b,147b), **Ray** (96a), **say** (131c,174c,177a), **way** (37d,96b,134b,
         164d)

AZ -   **azo** (107c)
A - Z   **adz** (40c,167a)
- AZ   **gaz** (188,190), **Laz** (27d)

BA -   **baa** (143d), **Bab** (15a), **bac** (31b,55c,174d), **bad** (55a,173a,184d),
         bag (26c,139a,145b,159a), **bah** (52c), **bal** (9d,37b,61a,b), **bam**
         (29b), **ban** (81d,97a,124a), **bap** (93b,132d), **Bap.** (124d), **bar** (37c,
         39a,46a,52c,76d,78b,91a,124a,137a,156a,157c,169c), **bas** (62a,d,
         129d,134b), **bat** (39c,107c,156a,157c,182d), **baw** (52c), **bay** (12d,
         16c,33c,73d,78b,81b,90a,128d)
B - A   **baa** (143d) **boa** (36c,55b,106a,125d,138b,142a,149a)
- BA   **aba** (12a,25d,32b,33a,65b), **iba** (117a)
B - B   **Bab** (15a), **bib, bob** (57c,115d), **Bob** (96a), **bub** (22c)
- BB   **abb** (58b,178b,185b), **ebb** (6a,15b,41c,43c,104a,128c,158a,178a)
B - C   **bac** (31b,55c,174d), **BSC** (42a)
- BC   **ABC** (134d)
B - D   **bad** (55a,173a,184d), **bed** (60c,148b), **bid** (35a,82a,109d,111b,
         174c), **bud** (22c)
BE -   **bed** (60c, 148b), **bee** (46b,81b,91c,108c), **beg** (38b,150a), **bei** (64a,
         93c,168d,173b,183d), **Bel** (15b,68a,126b), **ben** (78c,81b,102c,115c),
         Ben (12d,77c,96a,106c,139d,140a), **ber** (85c), **Bes** (68b,119c), **bet,
         bey** (70b,170d)
B - E   **bee** (46b,81b,91c), **bye** (38c,141d)
- BE   **Abe** 71a,96a,123a), **obe** (31d,87d,150d), **ube** (185b)
B - G   **bag** (26c,139a,145b,159a), **beg** (38b,150a), **big, bog** (97a,160a),
         bug (24b,66b,81b)
B - H   **bah** (52c), **boh** (24c)
BI -   **bib, bid** (35a,82a,109d,111b,174c), **big, Bim** (16c), **bin** (22c,59a,
         78a,128c,156d), **bis** (50a,90a,102c,130b,171c), **bit** (46a,86b,114c,
         167a,b,171c,180d), **biz**

227

- BI	**Abi** (76c), **obi** (55d,67b,84c,137b,150d), **ubi** (90a,180d,185b)
B - K	**Bok** (9c)
B - L	**bal** (9d,37b,61a,61b), **bel** (64a,93c,168d,173b,183d), **Bel** (15b,68a, 126d), **Bul** (25d,102a)
B - M	**bam** (29b), **Bim** (16c), **bum** (21b)
B - N	**ban** (81d,97a,124a), **ben** (78c,81b,102c,115c,139d,140a), **Ben** (12d, 77c,96a,106c), **bin** (22a,59a,78a,128c,156b), **bon** (30a,61d,86b,88c), **Bon** (84b), **bun** (25b,73b)
BO -	**boa** (36c,55b,106a,125d,138b,142d,149a), **bob** (57c,115d), **Bob** (96a), **bog** (97a,160a), **boh** (24c), **Bok** (9c), **bon** (30a,61d,86b,88c), **Bon** (84b), **boo**, **Bor** (120c), **Bos** (27c), **bot** (59a,88d), **bow** (11c,21b, 39d,60a,107c,109a,125a,144d,158a), **box** (36a,128c,145d,152d), **boy** (142d,157c), **Boz** (43b,115d)
B - O	**boo**
- BO	**Abo** (25d), **ebo** (28b,110a), **Ibo** (107a,180a)
B - P	**Bap.** (124d), **bap** (93b,132d)
B - R	**bar** (37c,39a,46a,52c,76d,78b,91a,124a,137a,156a,157c,169c), **ber** (85c), **Bor** (120c), **bur** (123b)
BS -	**BSC** (42a)
B - S	**bas** (62a,d,129d,134b), **Bes** (68b,119c), **bis** (50a,90a,102c,130b, 171c), **Bos** (27c), **bus** (125b,168b)
B - T	**bat** (39c,107c,156a,157c,182d), **bet**, **bit** (46a,86b,114c,167a,b, 171c,180d), **bot** (59a,88d), **but** (36a,52b,156b,173c)
- BT	**Abt** (35c)
BU -	**bub** (22c), **bud** (22c), **bug** (24b,66b,81b), **Bul** (25d,102a), **bum** (21b), **bun** (25b,73b), **bur** (123b), **bus** (125b,168b), **but** (36a,52b, 156b,173c), **buy**
- BU	**abu** (17a), **Abu** (15b,42a,55a,68a,c,147d)
B - W	**baw** (52c), **bow** (11c,21b,39d,60a,107c,109a,125a,144d,158a)
B - X	**box** (36a,c,128c,145d,152d)
BY -	**bye** (38c,141d)
B - Y	**bay** (12d,16c,33c,73d,78b,81b,90a,128d), **bey** (70b,170d), **boy** (142d,157c), **buy**
B - Z	**biz**, **Boz** (43b,115d)
CA -	**cab** (75c), **cad** (22b,23b,75c,172c,173d), **cag** (81d,109d), **cal** (183c), **Cal** (123a), **cam** (48b,65d,95a,98b,134a,139b,148b,180c), **can** (24c, 36c,123a,166a), **cap** (19d,39a,43a,53a,74d,160a,167b,185c), **car** (16a,61d,93b,175a), **cat** (10a,45b,55b,71d,161b,169d,180d), **Cat** (183d), **caw** (19b,d) **cay** (82d, 180b)
C - A	**cha** (162b,c)
- CA	**ECA** (8a), **oca** (48c,112c,116d,133d,170c,184d), **Uca** (56a)
C - B	**cab** (75c), **cob** (28c,78b,95d,160b,177d), **cub** (92d,185d)
C - D	**cad** (22b,23b,75c,172c,173d), **Cid** (151c,d), **cod** (57b,c), **cud** (126c, 135a)
CE -	**cee** (91c), **cep** (63a), **ces** (62b), **cet** (62d,180b)
C - E	**cee** (91c), **che** (145d), **cie** (61b,63b), **cle** (158d), **coe** (143d),

228

Coe (33c), cue (7a,27b,92c,117d,124b,132c,146c,159a)

- CE ace (7a,26c,52d,57a,77d,110c,114c,120b,147a,163a,173a), ice (30a, 36d,42d,63d)

C - G cag (81d,109d), cig, cog (33a,65d,163b,167b,180c)

CH - cha (162b,c), che (145d), chi (91c), Chi (69c), cho (188)

- CH ach (8b,48a,52c,66b,80c), ich (66c), och (8b), tch (52c)

CI - Cid (151c,d), cie (61b,63b), cig, CIO (173a), cis (34c,122c), cit (81a,167d)

C - I chi (91c), Chi (69c)

- CI aci (29c), ici (61d), Ici (9b), LCI (21b)

- CK ock (189), tck (52c)

CL - cle (158d)

C - L cal (183c), Cal (123a), col (103d,114c)

C - M cam (48b,65d,95a,98b,134a,139d,148b,180c), com (122d), cum (159b), cwm (31b,37b,103d)

C - N can (24c,36c,123a,166a), con (7d,29b,83c,116b,157d)

CO - cob (28c,78b,95d,160b,177d), cod (57b,c), coe (143d), Coe (33c), cog (33a,65d,163b,167b,180c), col (103d,114c), com (122d), con (7d,29b,83c,116b,157d), coo (19b), Coo (82d), cop (36a,120c, 126d,153c,155d), cor (36c,75b,155b), cos (91d,132d), cot (129b, 148b), cow (22c,45b,81d), cox (156a), coy (16d), coz

C - O cho (188), CIO (173a), coo (19b), Coo (82d), cro (104c,115b,180a)

C - P cap (19d,39a,43a,53a,74d,160a,167b,185c), cep (63a), cop (36a, 120c,126d,153c,155d), cup (46b,69d,118b,170a), cyp (169d)

CR - cro (104c,115b,180a), cru (63a,176c), cry (25c,124a,145c,179d)

C - R car (16a,61d,93b,175a), cor (36c,75b,155b), cur (101d)

C - S ces (62b), cis (34c,122c), cos (91d,132d)

- CS ics (158d)

C - T cat (10a,45b,55b,71d,161b,169d,180d,183d), cet (62d,180b), cit (81a,167d), cot (148b), cut (30c,32b,145c)

- CT act (41d,55b,119c,155d), ect (35a,122d,183b), oct (34a,122c)

CU - cub (92d,185d), cud (126c,135a), cue (7a,27b,92c,117d,124b,132c, 146c,159a), cum (159b), cup (46b,69d,118b,170a), cur (101d), cut (30c,32b,145c)

C - U cru (63a,176c)

- CU acu (34c), ecu (58a,144b,c)

CW - cwm (31b,37b,103d)

C - W caw (19b,d), cow (22c,45b,81d)

C - X cox (156a)

CY - cyp (169d)

C - Y cay (82d,180b), coy (16d), cry (25c,124a,145c,179d)

- CY acy (34c), icy (65d)

C - Z coz

DA - dab (46a,57b,58b,d,114d,115c), dad, dae (139b), dag (11b,118c, 139c), Dag (108c), dah (24c,87a), dak (95c), dal (117d,153d), dam

(30c,49c,55b,156d,180a), **dan** (24c,97c), **Dan** (18c,39c,77d,83a,
84a,141b), **dao** (117a), **dap** (43b,c,46b,91b,147d), **dar** (65c,111b,
169a), **das** (13b,15d,36d,66b,d,164a), **daw** (39a,70b,84a,146d), **day**
(153a)

D - A **dea** (68d,89b), **dha** (99d), **dia** (122b,d,152a,165b), **dra** (188), **dua**
(122d)

- DA **Ada** (110a,112c,183c), **Ida** (103d,183c), **oda** (74a,170d)

D - B **dab** (46a,57b,58b,114d,115c), **deb**, **Deb** (183d), **dib** (21b,43b,c,
120d,140a), **dub** (25c,46a,c,87a,105b,121a,140a)

D - C **dec** (122d), **doc** (143a), **duc** (61c)

DD - **DDS** (42a)

D - D **dad, did, dod** (11a,32a,43b,140c), **dud** (21c,54a)

- DD **add** (10d,11d,14c,158a,167c), **odd** (46b,53a,109b,157a,172d,173c)

DE - **dea** (68d,89b), **deb, Deb** (183d), **dec** (122d), **dee** (91c), **Dee** (131d,
139b), **deg** (154b), **dei** (68d), **den** (38b,44d,74b,130d,133c,140d),
der (13b,66b,d,164a), **des** (13b,61a,62b,d), **dev** (42a,b), **dew** (41a),
dey (8d,84a,114c,135a,139b,170d)

D - E **dae** (139b), **dee** (91c), **Dee** (131d,139b), **die** (27b,54a,65a,155a,
167a), **doe** (41d,55b,127a), **due** (7b,115b,124c), **dye** (33c,154d)

- DE **ade** (18c,149d), **Ade** (9c,53b), **Ede** (35b,65d), **ide** (40c,57a,b,d,
158b), **ode** (26b,79c,94d,118a,119d,120a,150b)

D - G **dag** (11b,118c), **Dag** (108c,139c), **deg** (154b), **dig** (52b), **dog** (10b,
45b,59b), **dug**

DH - **dha** (99d), **dhu** (40b), **Dhu** (28a,87d)

D - H **dah** (24c,87a), **doh** (113b)

- DH **edh** (91c)

DI - **dia** (122b,d,152a,165b), **dib** (21b,43b,c,120d,140a), **did, die** (27b,
54a,65a,155a,167a), **dig** (52b), **dii** (68d), **dim** (47a,48b,54a,74d,
94d,109b), **din** (31c,130b,174a), **dip** (26a,79d,117c,138c), **dis**
(122b,d), **Dis** (68b,73a,119d,172d,174b), **dit** (62b,d,120a,159d), **div**
(42b,139b), **dix** (118b), **Dix** (60b)

D - I **dei** (68d) **dii** (68d), **dui** (46d)

- DI **Udi** (108a)

DJ - **djo** (188)

D - K **dak** (95c)

D - L **dal** (117d,153d)

D - M **dam** (30c,49c,55b,156d,180a), **dim** (47a,48b,54a,74d,94d,109b),
dom (121c,166b,c), **Dom** (94b), **dum** (45c,67b,113a)

D - N **dan** (24c,97c), **Dan** (18c,39c,77d,83a,84a,141b), **den** (38b,44d,74b,
130d,133c,140d), **din** (130b,174a), **don** (151d,166c), **Don** (96a), **dun**
(19a,39d,46d,71a,97d,115b,160b)

DO - **Doc** (143a), **dod** (11a,32a,43b,140c), **doe** (41d,55b,127a), **dog** (10b,
45b,59b), **doh** (113b), **dom** (121c,166b,c), **Dom** (94b), **don** (151d,
166c), **Don** (96a), **dop** (39c,43b), **dor** (17d,24b,32b,46b,47a,81b,
85d), **dos** (45d,61a,97a,181b), **dot** (45d,97a,104d,105a,116b,153a,
162d), **dow** (17d,87a,88d,175d)

D - O   dao (117a) djo (188), DSO (99d), duo (46d,113a,171d)

- DO   ado (22b,24d,35b,64c,121d,156b,170a), edo (162a), **Edo** (107a, 166d), **Ido** (13c,81d,88c,173c), **Odo** (181d), udo (28a,30c,48c,84b, c,d,136c,149d)

D - P   dap (43b,c,46b,91b,147d), dip (26a,79d,117c,138c), dop (39c,43b)

DR -   dra (188), dry (46d,85a,137c,164c)

D - R   dar (111b,169a), der (13b,66b,d,164a), dor (17d,24b,32b,46b,47a, 81b,85d), dur (95c)

DS -   DSO (99d)

D - S   das (13b,15d,36d,66b,d,164a), **DDS** (42a), des (13b,61a,62b,d), dis (122b,d), **Dis** (68b,73a,119d,172d,174b), dos (45d,61a,97a,181b)

- DS   DDS (42a), ods (109a)

D - T   dit (62b,d,120a,159d), dot (45d,97a,104d,105a,116b,153a,162d)

DU -   dua (122d), dub (25c,46a,c,87a,105b,121a,140a), duc (61c), dud (21c,54a), due (7b,115b,124c), dug (46d), dui (46d), dum (45c,67b,113a), dun (19a,39d,46d,71a,97d,115b,160b), duo (46d,113a,171d), dur (95c), dux (31d,64a,90c)

D - U   dhu (40b), Dhu (28a,87d)

D - V   dev (42a,b), div (42b,139b)

D - W   daw (39a,70b,84a), dew (41a), dow (17d,87a,88d,175d)

D - X   dix (118b), Dix (60b), dux (31d,64a,90c)

DY -   dye (33c,154d)

D - Y   day (153a), dey (8d,84a,114c,135a,139b,170d), dry (46d,85a,137c, 164c)

- DY   ady (188)

- DZ   adz (40c,167a)

EA -   eae (34b), ean (17d,23b,88a), ear (14c,d,28c,63d,64a,73c,111b, 116a,124b,137d,150d,153c), eat (37b,96b,135d,179b), eau (63a, 178c)

E - A   ECA (8a), ela (21c,53c,72b,76c,108b,174c), Ena (8c,126b), era (8a, 51a,116b,165d), ESA (8a), eta (71a,84c,91c), Eva (157a,183c)

- EA   aea (26a,36d), dea (68d,89b), Hea (15b), kea (114a,b), lea (56a, 97d,114c,185b), Lea (22d), N.E.A. (162c), pea (32d,91b,142a,175a), rea (9c,171a), sea (19a,52d,58c,112c,178d), tea (13d,18c,79c,81a, 145d,149c,159d), Wea (192), yea (7c,175c), zea (95c)

EB -   ebb (6a,15b,41c,43c,104a,128c,158a,178a), ebo (28b,110a)

E - B   ebb (6a,15b,41c,43c,104a,128c,158a,178a), elb (85c)

- EB   deb, Deb (183d), Geb (47d), Keb (47d), neb (17b,19a,d,115d), reb (35d,75c,85b,162c,166b), Seb (47d), web (50d,70a,98c,99a,106c, 149b)

EC -   ECA (8a), ect (35a,122d,183b), ecu (58a,144b,c)

E - C   etc (10b)

- EC   dec (122d), sec (46c,182c), tec (43a)

ED -   Ede (35b,65d), edh (91c), edo (162a), Edo (107a,166d)

E - D   Eed (102d), eld (10b,93c,110b,165d), end (8b,67d,120a,125d,130a, 166a), erd (47d,119d,145c)

- ED   bed (60c,148b), Eed (102d), fed, ged (100a,140a), ked (140b,144a), led, Ned (96a), ped (16d,34b), red (33c,38d,59a,127b,134c,135b), Red (151b), sed (89a), ted (74d,138b,154b), Ted (96b), wed (97a, 173c), zed (91c)

EE -   Eed (102d), eel (36a,49c,57a,b,88a,102c,176c), een (52a,139c, 185d), eer (9b,52a), ees (139c)

E - E   eae (34b), Ede (35b,65d), eke (14c,117c), ele (48c), eme (38d,70a, 140c,172b), ene (35b,158b,c), ere (17d,150c), ese (35b,158c), ete (36c,62d,141c,159b), eve (47a,131a,143a,165d,171c), Eve (183c), ewe (88a,143d), Exe (43a), eye (93d,111b,140d)

- EE   bee (46b,81b,91c,108c), cee (91c), dee (91c), Dee (131d,139b), fee (29a,58a,70d,166a,d), gee (35a,91c,100a,131c,139c,162c), lee (74b, 144b), Lee (9c,31c,96a), mee (169a), nee (19d,22b,25c,60b,95c), pee (91c), ree (12c,50a,80c,134d,137a,140b,144a,146b), Ree (25a), see (20a,43c,44a,51c,53c,93d,109b,113c,116a,176d,178c,183b), tee (39d,52b,69d,91c,112d,115d,118b,172a), vee (58a,91c,106a), wee (52c,100c,148c), zee (81b,91c)

EF -   eft (93b,107a,136c,169d)

E - F   elf (54b,154b)

- EF   AEF (184d), kef (12a,46c,75d,88c), nef (32b,144c,d), ref

EG -   egg (32d,80b,81c,112c,174a), ego (51a,79a,142b)

E - G   egg (32d,80b,81c,112c,174a), eng (48a,146a), erg (50b,173b, 184c)

- EG   beg (38b,150a), deg (154b), Geg (8c), keg (27a,105b), leg (37d, 92b,141d,159d,169c), Meg (8c,183d), peg (38c,46b,54d,98a,118a, 184c), teg (45a,54b,171d)

E - H   edh (91c), eth (91c,158d)

- EH   Heh (191), reh (8d)

EI -   ein (66b,c), Eir (69a,75a), eis (66c)

E - I   Eli (18c,d,76c,96a,137a,185a), epi (56c,61c,d,111c,112d,122d, 133c,153c,167b,174a), eri (13d,21c,146c), Eri (18c)

- EI   dei (68d), fei (16a,185b), hei (65a), lei (65b,74c), rei (89b,121c), Rei (18d), Vei (91d), Wei (30b,162b)

EK -   eke (14c,117c)

E - K   elk (22c,90d,178a)

- EK   lek (65c)

EL -   ela (21c,53c,72b,76c,108a,174c), elb (85c), eld (10b,93c,110b, 165d), ele (48c), elf (54b,154b), Eli (18c,d,76c,96a,137a,185a), elk (22c,90d,178a), ell (10d,24b,32c,98a), elm (168c), els (140a), elt (87a,117c,139d), Ely (27c,50b)

E - L   eel (36a,49c,57a,b,88a,102c,176c), ell (10d,24b,32c,98a)

- EL   bel (64a,93c,168d,173b,183d), Bel (15b,68a,126d), eel (36a,49c, 57a,b,88a,102c,176c), gel (32d,73d,150a), Hel (68d,93c,172d), mel (77d), pel (55c,160d), rel (49b,173b), sel (62c,140b), tel (34a, b,122c), zel (40c)

EM -   eme (38d,70a,140c,172b), Ems (125a,151c), emu (19b,58c,111d)

232

E - M   elm (168c)

- EM   gem (104b), hem (22a,36a,48b,52c,155a), mem (91c), Sem (107c), Tem (143a,159b)

EN -   Ena (8c,126b), end (8b,67d,120a,125d,130a,166a), ene (35b,158b, c), eng (48a,146a) ens (17d,18a,51a,52d), ent (34d,158b,c)

E - N   ean (17d,23b,88a), een (52a,139c,185d), ein (66b,c), eon (8a,37b, 51d,116b), ern (19c,d,47b,54b,141a)

- EN   ben (78c,81b,102c,115c), Ben (12d,77c,96a,106c,139d,140a), den (38b,44d,74b,130d,133c,140d), een (52a,139c,185d), fen (21c,97a, 160a), gen (31d,76b), hen (19a,60c,114c,136c), ken (60b,87c,122b, 172d), men (38c,116a,117b,170a), Men (94d), pen (36a,50a,80d, 118b,126d,160a,185c), sen (190), ten (19a,26c,41c,42b), wen (40c, 72a,110a,170c,177b), yen (33b,42d,93c,174a), Zen (24a)

EO -   eon (8a,37b,51d,116b), Eos (14d,41a,68d)

E - O   ebo (28b,110a), edo (162a), Edo (107a,166d), ego (51a,79a,142b), eso (34d,183b), ETO (184d), exo (122d)

- EO   geo (34a,47d), Leo (36b,c,92d,186d), Meo (27b,80c), neo (34a,b, c,100d,106d,108c,122c,d,128c), Reo (26c)

EP -   epi (56c,61c,d,111c,112d,122d,133c,153c,167b,174a)

E - P   e.s.p. (147b)

- EP   cep (63a), hep (52c), kep (139b), nep (27c,32d,56a,87c,184b), pep (50b,176b), rep (53b,d,131a,171c), yep, Zep

ER -   era (8a,51a,116b,165d), erd (47d,119d,145c), ere (17d,150c), erg (50b,173b,184c), eri (13d,21c,146d), Eri (18c), ern (19c,d,47b,54b, 141a), err (21a,43a,67d,100c,d,147a,148b,157b,168b,178a), ers (20a,176a), ert (140c,174a), ery (155d,158c,d)

E - R   ear (14c,d,28c,63d,64a,73c,111b,116a,124b,137d,150d,153c), eer (9b,52a), Eir (69a,75a), err (21a,43a,67d,100c,d,147a,148b,157b, 168b,178a), Eur. (36c)

- ER   aer (8b,28d,34a,b,175a), ber (85c), der (13b,66b,d,164a), eer (9b, 52a), ger (8d,36d,75c,124d), her (124b,c), ier (50a,158c), Ker (71b, 95d), Ler- (23d,28a,b,64b,106c,141a), mer (62c,141a), ner (137c), o'er (6b,112a), per (25c,122d,165b,176a), ser (80d,83b,d,116c, 152d,180a), ter (34d,122d,165a), xer (34a), zer (188)

ES -   ESA (8a), ese (35b,158c), eso (34d,183b), esp (147b), ess (39d,78a, 91c,158c,184d), est (50a,61c,62a,79b,89c,158d,159c)

E - S   ees (139c), eis (66c), els (140a), Ems (125a,151c), ens (17d,18a, 51a,52d), Eos (14d,41a,68d), ers (20a,176a), ess (39d,78a,91c,158c, 184d)

- ES   aes (23c,89a,101c,132d,133a,b), Bes (68b,119c), ces (62b), des (13b,61a,62b,d), ees (139c), Ges (151b), les (13b,61a), mes (62b), nes (26b), oes (109a), pes (59d), res (80a,89d,91a,97c,164c), ses (61d), yes (7c,55a)

ET -   eta (71a,84c,91c), etc (10b), ete (36c,62d,141c,159b), eth (91c, 158d), ETO (184d)

E - T   eat (37b,96b,135d,179b), ect (35a,122d,183b), eft (93b,107a,136c, 169d), elt (87a,117c,139d), ent (34d,158b,c), ert (140c,174a), est (50a,62a,79b,89c,158d,159c)

233

- ET aet (89a,109d), bet, cet (62d,180b), get (44d,64b,109b,141d), jet (20b,35a,154c), ket (189), let (9a,76d,77c,116b,130a,158b,163a), met (28d), net (26c,32a,50d,53b,60d,99a,124a,142a,149b), pet (26d,37c,55a,59b,162d), ret (58b,95a,149c,155d), set (7b,11d,13a, 23c,32b,33c,37c,58a,73d,109b,118c,121c,142c,150a,186a), Set (52b, 68a,b,111d), vet, wet (40d,46a,101a,124a,127c,149c), yet (18b, 24d,64c,77c,80a,108c,156b,165b)

EU - Eur. (136c)

E - U eau (63a,178c), ecu (58a,144b,c), emu (19b,58a,111d)

- EU feu (55d,61c,88b), heu (8b,30c,52c), jeu (61d), leu (190), meu (153b), peu (62a), Reu (115d)

EV - Eva (157a,183c), eve (47a,131a,143a,165a,171c), Eve (183c)

- EV dev (42a,b), lev (33b) rev

EW - ewe (88a,143d)

- EW dew (41a), few, hew (40a), Jew, lew (190), Lew (96a), mew (25b, 27b,50a,55b,72c,74d,101b,141b,153b), new (11a,63c,88d,111c, 128c), pew (30d,52c,57d,120b,141c), rew (75c,140c,176b), sew, yew (36a,52a,b,145d,168c,d)

EX - Exe (43a), exo (122d)

- EX Aex (46d), hex (18c), lex (90b), rex (86c,96a), sex, vex (7c,10d, 44c,82c)

EY - eye (93d,111b,140d)

E - Y Ely (27c,50b), ery (155d,158c,d)

- EY bey (70b,170d), dey (8d,84a,114c,135a,139b,170d), fey (49c), gey (140a), hey (25c,52c), key (14c,82d,88b,117c,118c,150b,180c), ley (190), Ney (63b,97b,105d), rey (86c,152b), sey (120c), wey (173b)

- EZ fez (75a,162a), gez (188), nez (62b), tez (125c), yez

FA - fac (41c), fad (38b,108c,163a), fag (55a,166a), fan (43a,154b, 156b,182d), far (44c), fas (44d,89d,129d), fat (110a,124a), fay (32c,54b,154b), Fay (183c)

F - A Fha (8a), fra (23c,63c,101d,123b,129d)

- FA MFA (42a)

F - B fib (162a), fob (29b,59b,113b,178c), fub (29b,119d)

F - C fac (41c)

F - D fad (38b,108c,163a), fed, fid (16b,54d,118a,167b), fod (188)

FE - fed, fee (29a,58a,70d,166a,d), fei (16a,185b), fen (21c,97a,160a), feu (55d,61c,88b), few, fey (49c), fez (75a,162a)

F - E fee (29a,58a,70d,166a,d), fie (52c,59d), foe (111a)

- FE ife (22c,75d)

- FF off (6b,15c,44c,76a)

F - G fag (55a,166a), fig, fog (109b), fug (129a)

FH - FHA (8a)

F - H foh (52c)

FI - fib (162a), fid (16b,54d,118a,167b), fie (52c,59d), fig, fin (86a), fir (16a,36a,52a,168c,d,169a), fit (7a,11d,51b,75a,114a,123a, 124c,126a,153a,157c,159a), fix (7b,10a,13a,14c,43a,c,141d,165c)

234

```
F - I      fei  (16a,185b)
FL -       flo, flu, fly  (58c,81b,163b,178d)
F - L      Ful  (158b)
  - FL     AFL  (173a)
F - N      fan  (43a,154b,156b,182d), fen  (21c,97a,160a), fin  (86a), Fon  (40b),
           fun
FO -       fob  (29b,59b,113c,178c), fod  (188), foe  (111a), fog  (109b), foh
           (52c), Fon  (40b), foo  (42c), fop  (38a,40d,46c), for  (123d,163a,
           166c), fot  (188), fou  (139a), fox  (134a)
F - O      Flo, foo  (42c), fro  (15b)
  - FO     Ufo  (59a)
F - P      fop  (38a,40d,46d)
FR -       fra  (23c,63c,101d,123b,129d), fro  (15b), fry  (57d)
F - R      far  (44c), fir  (16a,36a,52a,168c,d,169a), for  (123d,163a,166c), fur
  - FR     Afr.  (36c)
F - S      fas  (44d,89d,129d)
F - T      fat  (110a,124a), fit  (7a,11d,51b,75a,114a,123a,124c,126a,153a,
           157c,159a), fot  (188), fut  (188)
  - FT     aft  (14a,15b,17d,128b,167d), eft  (93b,107a,136c,169d), oft  (63c)
FU -       fub  (29b,119d), fug  (129a), Ful  (158b), fun, fur, fut  (188)
F - U      feu  (55d,61c,88b), flu, fou  (139a)
F - W      few
F - X      fix  (7b,10a,13a,14c,43a,c,141d,165c), fox  (134a)
F - Y      fay  (32c,54b,154b), Fay  (183c), fey  (49c), fly  (58c,81b,163b,178d),
           fry  (57d)
F - Z      fez  (75a,162a)
GA -       gab  (29b,78a,116c,122a,161c,183a), gad  (58c,100a,127d,132b,
           153c,154b,178a), Gad  (84a,186d), gaf  (12b), gag  (146c,183a), gaj
           (190), gal, gam  (76b,176d,180c), Gan  (132d), gap  (11b,23a,29b,
           76c,110d,128a), gar  (57b,c,d,106b), gas  (10b,29b,59a,116d,161c),
           gat  (28d,72c,131a), gau  (66d,67a), gav  (72d), gaw  (140c), gay,
           Gay  (17d), gaz  (188,190)
G - A      goa  (65d,104b,126c), Goa  (121c), gra  (59b,94b,160c)
  - GA     aga  (35a,39a,48b,102d,103a,b,111c,166b,170d,171a)
G - B      gab  (29b,78a,116c,122a,161c,183a), Geb  (47d), gib  (17b,38b,95d,
           166d,179d), gob  (97b,136c)
G - D      gad  (58c,100a,b,127d,132b,153c,154b,178a), Gad  (84a,186d), ged
           (140a), Ged  (100a), gid  (143d), god  (42a), God  (84d)
GE -       Geb  (47d), Ged  (100a,140a), gee  (35a,91c,100a,131c,139c,162c),
           Geg  (8c), gel  (32d,73d,150a), gem  (104b), gen  (31d,76b), geo  (34a,
           47d), ger  (8d,36d,75c,124d), Ges  (151b), get  (44d,64b,109b,141d),
           gey  (140a), gez  (188)
G - E      gee  (35a,91c,100a,131c,139c,162c), gie  (139c,140a), gue  (176c)
  - GE     age  (51d,66a,92a,97c,98c,116b,141c)
G - F      gaf  (12b)
```

                                235

G - G   gag (146c,183a), Geg (8c), gig (26d,28d,57c,105b,127a,144c,153a, 171d), gog (95b)

- GG   egg (32d,80b,81c,112c,174a)

GH -   ghi (24d)

- GH   ugh (52c)

GI -   gib (17b,38b,95d,166d,179d), gid (143d), gie (139c,140a), gig (26d,28d,57c,105b,127a,144c,153a,171d), gin (37c,92d,139a,142a, 149b), gip (29b,160c), git (101a)

G - I   ghi (24d), goi (107c), gri (75c,78b)

G - J   gaj (190)

G - L   gal, gel (32d,73d,150a), gul (134a)

G - M   gam (76b,176d,180c), gem (104b), gum (7b,53c,80b,130c,156b), gym (154a)

GN -   gnu (11a,181d)

G - N   gan (132d), gen (31d,76b), gin (37c,92d,139a,142a,149b), gon (188), gun (56d,131a,146a)

GO -   goa (65d,104b,126c), Goa (121c), gob (97b,136c), god (42a), God (84d), gog (95b), goi (107c), gon (188), goo (156b), Gor (81a), got, goy (107c), gox (190)

G - O   geo (34a,47d), goo (156b)

- GO   ago (25a,69d,114d,147a), ego (51a,79a,142b)

G - P   gap (11b,23a,29b,76c,110d,128a), gip (29b,160c), gup (70a), gyp (29b,42a,160c)

GR -   gra (59b,94b,160c), gri (75c,78b), grr (52c), gry (78b)

G - R   gar (57b,c,d,106b), ger (8d,36d,75c,124d), Gor (81a), grr (52c), gur (159a)

G - S   gas (10b,29b,59a,116d,161c), Ges (151b), Gus (96a)

G - T   gat (28d,72c,131a), get (44d,64b,109b,141d), git (101a), got, gut (114d,130a)

GU -   gue (176c), gul (134a), gum (7b,53c,80b,130c,156b), gun (56d, 131a,146a), gup (70a), gur (159a), Gus (96a), gut (114d,130a), guy (55b,131b,155d), Guy (96a), guz (188)

G - U   gau (66d,67a), gnu (11a,181d)

- GU   ngu (188

G - V   gav (72d)

G - W   gaw (140c)

GY -   gym (154a), gyp (29b,42a,160c)

G - Y   gay, Gay (17d), gey (140a), goy (107c), gry (78b), guy (55b,131b, 155d), Guy (96a)

G - Z   gaz (188,190), gez (188), gox (190), guz (188)

HA -   had, hae (139c), hag (140a,183a), hah (52c), hai (55c), hak (46d), Hal (69d), ham (98a,144b), Ham (18d,107c), Han (16c,30b,185b), hao (189) hap (17d,28d), har (139c), has, hat (74d), Hat (183d), haw (35a,52c,74d,91a,155a,162c), hay (52c,55c,165d)

H - A   Hea (15b), hia (114b), hoa (39b)

- HA aha (52c,55c,159c), cha (162b,c), dha (99c), FHA (8a), Kha (88d, 106b), shá (110c,143d,144a,c,174c,181c)

H - B hob (40c,56d,100c,124b,167a,180c), hub (28b,118b,180c)

H - C hic (52c,90a,164c)

H - D had, hid, hod (23b,32d,102d,141a)

HE - Hea (15b), Heh (191), hei (65a), Hel (68d,93c,172d), hem (22a,36a, 48b,52c,155a), hen (19a,60c,114c,136c), hep (52c), her (124b,c), heu (8b,30c,52c), hew (40a), hex (18c), hey (25c,52c)

H - E hae (139c), hie (79a,153b), hoe (39c), hue (33c,143b)

- HE che (145d), rhe (59a), she (124b), She (73a), the (13b)

H - G hag (140a,183a), hog (45b,117c,160c), hug (32c,49d)

H - H hah (52c), Heh (191), Hoh (80d), hsh (79c), huh (52c)

HI - hia (114b), hic (52c,90a,164c), hid, hie (79a,153b), him (124b), hin (189), hip (52c,54b,85b,133c,134a), hir (76a), his (124c), hit (32d,157c,158a)

H - I hai (55c), hei (65a), hoi (52c,74b,185b), hui (14a,30b,56d,114c)

- HI Ahi (32c,147d), chi (91c), Chi (69c), ghi (24d), ihi (57c,156b), phi (91c)

H - K hak (46d)

H - L Hal (69d), Hel (68d,93c,172d)

H - M ham (98a,144b), Ham (18d,107c), hem (22a,36a,48b,52c,155a), him (124b), hum (24d,46b,150d)

- HM ohm (49b,67a,173b)

H - N Han (16c,30b,185b), hen (19a,60c,114c,136c), hin (189), Hun (16c,21d,174b)

HO - hoa (39b), hob (40c,56d,100c,124b,167a,180c), hod (23b,32d,102d, 141a), hoe (39c), hog (45b,117c,160c), Hoh (80d), hoi (52c,74b, 185b), hop (40b), Hor (103d), hot (10c,176c), how, hoy (16c,52c)

H - O hao (189)

- HO cho (188), mho (49b,173b), oho (52c), Rho (71b,91c), sho (188), tho (52a), Tho (167a), who (129c)

H - P hap (17d,28d), hep (52c), hip (52c,54b,85b,133c,134a), hop (40b), hup (35a), hyp

H - R har (139c), her (124b,c), hir (76a), Hor (103d), Hur (91d)

- HR ihr (66d)

HS - hsh (79c)

H - S has, his (124c)

H - T hat (74d), Hat (183d), hit (32d,157c,158a), hot (10c,176c), hut (143c)

HU - hub (28b,118b,180c), hue (33c,143b,) hug (32c,49d), huh (52c), hui (14a,30b,56d,114c), hum (24d,46b,150d), Hun (16c,21d,174b), hup (35a), Hur (91d), hut (143c)

H - U heu (8b,30c,52c)

- HU ahu (24c,41d,65d,103d,120d), dhu (40b), Dhu (28a,87d), phu (38c), Shu (30b,127a)

237

H - W   haw (35a,52c,74d,91a,155a,162c), hew (40a), how

H - X   hex (18c)

HY -   hyp

H - Y   hay (52c,55c,165d), hey (25c,52c), hoy (16c,52c)

- HY   shy (16d,99d,128c,160c,165d,175a), thy, why (52c)

IA -   ial (158b), Ian (85b,96a,139d), iao (78a,96c,178d)

I - A   iba (117a), Ida (103d,183c), IIa (16b), ILA (173a), ina (158c),
Ina (183c), Ira (18c,d,41a,68c,82c,96a,164a,178a,c), Ita (51b,71d,
94d,95d,106b,117a), ITA (173a), iva (76a,97b,127b,185b) iwa
(63c), iya (95b,108d,111c)

- IA   dia (122b,d,152a,165b), hia (114b), Lia (82b), mia (83c), pia (13b,
22d,48a,120d), ria (38c,51d,81b,152a,b), Sia (80c), tia (151d), via
(132a,133a,b,179a)

IB -   iba (117a), Ibo (107a,180b)

- IB   bib, dib (21b,43b,c,120d,140a), fib (162a), glb (17b,38b,95d,166d,
179d), jib (38b,136b,146a), mib (8d,96c), nib (17b,19d,115d),
rib (37c,85b,90c,98a,144d,159d,172a), sib (86b,129c,139d,147b)

IC -   ice (30a,36d,42d,63d), ich (66c), ici (61d), Ici (9b), ics (158d),
icy (65d)

- IC   hic (52c,90a,164c), pic (188), sic (90a,165b,168b), tic (104d,153a,
171c,d)

ID -   Ida (103d,183c), ide (40c,57a,b,d,158b), Ido (13c,81d,88c,173d)

I - D   Ind (80c)

- ID   aid (14a,15b,64c,75d,158b), bid (35a,82a,109d,111b,174c), Cid
(151c,d), did, fid (16b,54d,118a,167b), gid (143d), hid, kid (67d,
85b,90d,186a), lid (167b), mid (9d,28b,73b), nid (72a,106b,c,116d),
oid (158c), rid (32a,44a,60d), Sid (96a)

IE -   ier (50a,158c)

I - E   ice (30a,36d,42d,63d), Ide (40c,57a,b,d,158b), ife (22c,75d), Ike
(123a), ile (62a,63b,158c), ine (29c,158b,c), Ine (10c,137d,180b),
ire (10c,30c,52b,64c,125a,130b,185a), ise (40d,158c,d), Ise (78a,
84c), ite (59b,81a,105d,130c,158b,c,d,161a), ive (158c)

- IE   cie (61b,63b), die (27b,54a,65a,155a,167a), fie (52c,59d), gie
(139c,140a), hie (79a,153b), lie (53a,69d,162a), nie (53c), pie
(42d,85d,95b,114d,171b,172a), rie (28c,70d,97d), sie (46c,66d,
139b,140b,146b), tie (10a,14c,38b,45d,51a,88d,109b,127c,138b,
170b), vie (36c,157c,170c)

IF -   ife (22c,75d)

- IF   Lif (107d), rif (188), Sif (164d), vif (62a), Zif (102a)

I - G   ing (114b,d,148d,158c,d,175c), Ing (10c,115b)

- IG   big, cig, dig (52b), fig, gig (26d,28d,57c,105b,127a,144c,
153a,171d), jig (40b,d), mig (8d,96c,145b), Mig (118d); nig (33b,
40a,46a), pig (27a,45b,99a,151b,160c), rig (51b,112a), tig (46b),
wig (73b), zig (84a)

IH -   ihi (57c,156b), ihr (66d)

I - H   ich (66c), ish (158b), Ith (10a,28a,82b,99d)

238

I - I ici (61d), Icl (9b), ihi (57c,156b), ini (158d), Iri (18a,d,75a)

- II dii (68d), oii (105c), rii (157b,175b)

IJ - Ijo (107a)

IK - Ike (123a)

I - K ilk (31d,54c,86b,136d,139c,140b), ink (20b,40c), Irk (10d)

- IK aik (139d), pik*(188)

IL - Ila (16b), ILA (173a), ile (62a,63b,158c), ilk (31d,54c,86b,136d, 139c,140b), ill (43d,121a,173a,c,d), ILO (184c), ils (62b,d,164b)

I - L ial (158b), ill (43d,121a,173a,c,d)

- IL ail (170a), kil (82b), lil (72d), mil (80b,110c,164d,182d), Mil (10a), nil (108c), oil (11a,71a), pil (34b), sil (30c,185c,d), til (142d)

IM - imp (42b,127d,174a), imu (15d)

I - M ism (45a,79b,161c)

- IM aim (42d,43d,67d,109b,125d,157c), Bim (16c), dim (47a,48b,54a, 74d,94d,109b), him (124b), Jim (96a), Kim (86d), lim (21a), mim (12b), nim (96d,155d), rim (22a,48b,96d,116b,124b,166a,180c), Sim (96b), Tim (43b), vim (50b,176b)

IN - ina (158c), Ina (183c), Ind (80c), ine (29c,158b,c), Ine (10c, 137d,180b), ing (114b,d,158c,d,175c) Ing (10c,115b), ini (158d), ink (20b,40c), inn (72b,73b,78c,132b,150a,161c,162b,179a), Inn (41a), Ino (14b,25b), ins (164d), INS (107a,182d)

I - N Ian (85b,96a,139d), inn (72b,73b,78c,132b,150a,161c,162b,179a), Inn (41a), ion (11c,29a,49b,101b,114c,158c)

- IN ain (18d,91c,110c,124b,140a,154b,180a), bin (22c,59a,78a,128c, 156d), din (31c,130b,174a), ein (66b,c), fin (86a), gin (37c,92d, 139a,142a,149b), hin (189), jin (42b,153c), kin (30b,81c,129d) Kin (30b), lin (140c,168c,178d), Lin (115d,186c), Min (29d,68b, 113c), nin (107d), pin (45d,54d,141d,147d), rin (33b,142b), sin (91c,140b,147a,168b,176a), Sin (102b), tin (36c,99a,b,108b,155a, 179c), vin (63a,182b), win (7a,17b,64b,123b), yin (140a), Yin (30b, 143c,185b)

IO - ion (11c,29a,101b,114c,158c), ior (50a,158c), ios (74d), IOU (124b)

I - O iao (78a,96c,178d), Ibo (107a,180b), Ido (13c,81d,88c,173c), Ijo (107a), ILO (184c), Ino (14b,25b), iso (34a,122c,d), Ito (84a,c, 186d), iyo (7d,176b)

- IO CIO (173a), mio (152c), rio (33a,131d,132a,152c,157b), Rio (23a), tio (152d), Zio (147d,163d)

I - P imp (42b,127d,174a)

- IP dip (26a,79d,117c,138c), gip (29b,160c), hip (52c,54b,85b,133c, 134a), kip (17c,72d,76c,189), lip (48b,58b,80a,131c), nip (20c, 29b,45d,46a,b,115c,118a), pip (11d,44a,121d,142a,154a), Pip (43b), rip (87b,130a,162c), Rip (178b), sip (46b,79d,104a,162b), tip (26b,d,50a,70d,77b,78a,120a,165d), yip (16c), zip (24b,50b, 176b)

IR - Ira (18c,d,41a,68c,82c,96a,164a,178a,c), ire (10c,30c,52b,64c,

239

125a,130b,185a), irl (18a,d,75a), irk (10d)

I - R ier (50a,158c), ihr (66d), ior (50a,158c)

- IR air (11c,12c,42b,44c,53a,96b,98c,99d,125b,170c), Eir (69a,75a), fir (16a,36a,52a,168c,d,169a), hir (76a), mir (29d,135c,d,166c,176b), pir (103a,b,136c), sir (163b,166b), tir (61d,62c,87a,145b), vir (89c)

IS - ise (40d,158c,d), Ise (78a,84c), -ish (158b), ism (45a,79b,161c), iso (34a,122c,d), ist (7b,34b,43a,59b,66c,158c,d)

I - S ics (158d), ils (62b,d,164b), ins (164d), INS (107a,182d), ios (74d), its (124c)

- IS bis (50a,90a,102c,130b,171c), cis (34c,122c), dis (122b,d), Dis (68b,73a,119d,172d,174b), eis (66c), his (124c), lis (54b, 58b,60c,62a,92b), Lis (47a), mis (122b,c,d,185c), nis (23d,67d, 68a,87c), Nis (19d), ris (131d), sis (67b,129c), tis (59d,89b,d, 90b,176b), wis (79d,164c)

IT - Ita (51b,71d,94d,95d,106b,117a), ITA (173a), ite (59b,81a,105d, 130c,158b,c,d,161a), Ite (130c), Ith (10a,28a,82b,99d), Ito (84a, c,186d), its (124c)

I - T ist (7b,34b,43a,59b,66c,158b,c,d)

- IT ait (82d,132a), bit (46a,86b,114c,167a,b,171c,180d), cit (81a, 167d), dit (62b,d,120a,159d), fit (7a,11d,51b,75a,114a,123a,124c, 126a,153a,157c,159a), git (101a), hit (32d,157c,158a), kit (112a, 176c), Kit (96a,183d), lit, mit (56c,66d,183b), nit (48d), pit (52b, 142a,164a,168a), rit (148c,140b,153d), sit (98c,116a,121c,130c, 142d), tit (19c,130d), uit (47a,111d,151a), wit (78d,85b,177b)

I - U imu (15d), I.O.U. (124b)

- IU piu (102c), Tiu (7c,68c,147d,163d,166c,170c), Ziu (147d,163d)

IV - iva (76a,97b,127b,185b), ive (158c), ivy (32b,38c,176b)

- IV div (42b,139b), Liv (93b)

IW - iwa (63c)
- IW Tiw (68c,147d,163d)

- IX Aix (46b), dix (118b), Dix (60b), fix (7b,10a,13a,14c,43a,c,141d, 165c), mix (156b), nix (23d,108c,178d), pix (31a,51d,175d), six (26c), vix (89c,138b)

IY - iya (95b,108d,111c), iyo (7d,176b)

I - Y icy (65d), ivy (32b,38c,176b)

- IZ biz, viz (105b)

JA - jab (120b,125c) jag (124d,148a) Jah (84d), jam (123a,156d,165c), Jap, jar (31d,70d,143b), Jat (80d,125c), jaw (97d,138c), jay (19b, 91c)

J - B jab (120b,125c), jib (38b,136b,146a), job (30d,184c), Job (96a)

JE - jet (20b,35a,154c), jeu (61d), Jew

J - E Joe (96a)

J - G jag (124d,148a), jig (40b,d), jog (82c,85c,170a), jug (118c,123d)

J - H Jah (84d)

JI - jib (38b,136b,146a), jig (40b,d), Jim (96a), jin (42b,153c)

- JI tji (189), uji (146d)

240

J - M jam (123a,156d,165c), Jim (96a), jum (39c)

J - N jin (42b,153c)

JO - job (30d,184c), Job (96a), Joe (96a), jog (82c,85c,170a), jot (82a, 114c,166c,180d), jow (188), joy

- JO djo (188), ljo (107a)

J - P Jap

J - R jar (31d,70d,143b), Jur (107b)

J - S jus (61d,90b)

J - T Jat (80d,125c), jet (20b,35a,154c), jot (82a,114c,166c,180d), jut 53a,124a)

JU - jug (118c,123d), jum (39c), Jur (107b), jus (61d,90b), jut (53a, 124a)

J - U jeu (61d)

J - W jaw (97d,138c), Jew, jow (188)

J - Y jay (19b,91c), joy

KA - kab (75c), kae (84a,140b), kaf (12b), Kaf (104a), kai (59c), Kai (14d,84c), kan (93a), kas (32c,47a), kat (105d), kay (82d), Kay (13b,134b)

K - A kea (114a,b), Kha (88d,106b), koa (74c), Kra (11b,91d), Kua (95c)

- KA aka (176b), Aka (13d,88b,c), oka (170c,184a,189)

K - B kab (75c), Keb (47d), kob (11a)

K - D ked (140b,144a), kid (67d,85b,90d,186a)

KE - kea (114a,b), Keb (47d), ked (140b,144a), kef (12a,46c,75d,88c), keg (27a,105b), ken (60b,87c,122b,172d), kep (139b), Ker (71b, 95d), ket (189) key (14c,82d,88b,117c,118c,150b,180c)

K - E kae (84a,140b)

- KE ake (60a,107a), eke (14c,117c), lke (123a), oke (189)

K - F kaf (12b), Kaf (104a), kef (12a,46c,75d,88c)

K - G keg (27a, 105b)

KH - Kha (88d,106b)

- KH akh (153d)

KI - kid (67d,85b,90d,186a), kil (82b), Kim (86d), kin (30b,81c, 129d), Kin (30b), kip (17c,72d,76c,189), kit (112a,176c), Kit (96a, 183d)

K - I kai (59c), Kai (14d,84c), koi (26d), kri (75c,96d), Kri (75c), Kui (86a,88c,146a)

- KI ski (149c)

K - L kil (82b), Kol (18b), kyl (76d,79b)

K - M Kim (86d)

K - N kan (93a), ken (60b,87c,122b), kin (30b,81c), Kin (30b)

KO - koa (74c), kob (11a), koi (26d), Kol (18b), kop (76d), kor (75c), Kos (77c,82d), kou (169a)

- KO ako (189), TKO (22c)

K - P kep (139b), kip (17c,72d,76c,189), kop (76d), kup (188)

241

KR -   **Kra** (11b,91d), **kri** (75c,96d), **Kru** (91d)

K - R   **Ker** (71b,95d), **kor** (75c)

K - S   **kas** (32c,47a), **Kos** (77c,82d)

K - T   **kat** (105d), **ket** (189), **kit** (112a,176c), **Kit** (96a,183d)

KU -   **Kua** (95c), **Kui** (86a,88c,146a), **kup** (188)

K - U   **kou** (169a), **Kru** (91d)

- KU   **aku** (57c,176a)

KY -   **kyl** (76d,79b)

K - Y   **kay** (82d), **Kay** (13b,134b), **key** (14c,82d,88b,117c,118c,150b, 180c)

- KY   **sky** (56d)

LA -   **lab, lac** (53c,99d,130c,135b,174d), **lad** (22c,25b,55b,157c,186a), **lag** (93c,155d), **Lai** (24c,d,88c), **lai** (98b,161b), **lak** (38a), **lam** (51b, 58b,93d,164d,178a), **lan** (37b,d,160b), **Lao** (80d,88c,146a,161b), **lap** (31b,37d,59b,127a,131d,153d,167d), **lar** (24c,51d,67a,78d,95d, 101d,171b), **las** (13b,151d) **lat** (24a,33d,106b,118a), **lav** (72d), **law** (26b,33a,40a,48c,60b,85d,91a,111b,134d,155d), **lax** (93d,130a), **lay** (16a,25c,80a,98b,107d,141d,150b), **Laz** (27d)

L - A   **lea** (56a,97d,114d,185b), **Lea** (22d), **Lia** (82b), **loa** (7d,53c,97d,184d)

- LA   **ala** (6d,13a,15c,61a,133d,182c,d), **Ala.** (151b), **ela** (21c,53c,72b, 76c,108b,174c), **Ila** (16b), **ILA** (173a), **ola** (113b), **ula** (72c,158c)

L - B   **lab, LLB** (42a), **lob** (15d,23b,94c,100b,163a,172b)

- LB   **alb** (65b,176a), **elb** (85c), **LLB** (42a)

LC -   **LCI** (21b)

L - C   **lac** (53c,99d,130c,135b,174d)

L - D   **lad** (22c,25b,55b,157c,186a), **led, lid** (167b), **LLD** (42a), **lud** (100a), **Lud** (23c,144b)

- LD   **eld** (10b,93c,110b,165d), **LLD** (42a), **old** (8a,71a,77c,123c,175b)

LE -   **lea** (56a,97d,114d,185b), **Lea** (22d), **led, lee** (74b,144b), **Lee** (9c, 31c,96a), **leg** (37d,92b,141d,159d,169c), **lei** (65b,74c), **lek** (65c), **Leo** (36b,c,92d,186d), **Ler** (23d,28a,b,64b,106c,141a), **les** (13b, 61a), **let** (9a,76d,77c,116b,130a,158b,163a), **leu** (190), **lev** (33b), **lew** (190), **Lew** (96a), **lex** (90b), **ley** (190)

L - E   **lee** (74b,144b), **Lee** (9c,31c,96a), **lie** (53a,69d,162a), **loe** (139d), **lue** (146b), **lye** (8d,27d,93b)

- LE   **ale** (17c,18c,50c,55d,92d,104c), **cle** (158d), **ele** (48c), **ile** (62a,63b, 158c), **ole** (24b,29b,113b,152a,158b,d), **ule** (23a,27d,134c,158c, 168d)

L - F   **Lif** (107d), **lof** (188)

- LF   **Alf** (96a), **elf** (54b,154b)

L - G   **lag** (93c,155d), **leg** (37d,92b,141d,159d,169c), **log** (64a,128d), **lug** (27a,45d,47b,73c,136b), **Lug** (28b)

LI -   **Lia** (82b), **lid** (167b), **lie** (53a,69d,162a), **Lif** (107d), **lil** (72d), **lim** (21a), **lin** (92c,140c,168c,178a), **Lin** (115d,186c), **lip** (48b,58b,80a, 131c), **lis** (54b,58b,60c,62a,92b), **Lis** (47a), **lit, Liv** (93b)

242

L - I   **lai** (98b,161b), **Lai** (24c,d,88c), **LCI** (21b), **lei** (65b,74c), **loi** (62a)

- LI   **Ali** (7b,12a,25c,48b,55a,60c,92d,101a,103a,164a,166b,170d), **Eli** (18c,d,76c,96a,137a,185a)

L - K   **lak** (38a), **lek** (65c), **Lok** (15d,68b)

- LK   **alk** (171b), **elk** (22c,90d,178a), **ilk** (31d,54c,86b,136d,139c,140b)

LL -   **LLB** (42a), **LLD** (42a)

L - L   **lil** (72d)

- LL   **all** (35c,118a,126d,181a), **ell** (10d,24b,32c,98a), **ill** (43d,121a,173a, c,d), **Ull** (7c,68c,146b,164d)

L - M   **lam** (51b,58b,93d,164d,178a), **lim** (21a), **lum** (30a)

- LM   **elm** (168c), **olm** (48c), **ulm** (49c), **Ulm** (40d)

L - N   **lan** (37b,d,160b), **lin** (140c,168c,178d), **Lin** (115d,186c), **Lon** (86c, 96a), **lyn** (140c,178d)

LO -   **loa** (7d,53c,97d,184d), **lob** (15d,23b,94c,100b,163a,172d), **loe** (139d), **lof** (188), **log** (64a,128d), **loi** (62a), **Lok** (15d,68b), **Lon** (86c, 96a), **loo** (65a), **lop** (30c,40a,46b,143a), **los** (13b,151d), **lot** (24b, 28d,55a,65d,114a,119c,143c,150d,168a), **Lot** (6b,73d), **Lou** (96a, 183d), **low** (16c,149d), **loy** (121c,148b,151c,167a)

L - O   **Lao** (80d,88c,146a,161b), **Leo** (36b,c,92d,186c), **loo** (65a), **Luo** (107b), **Lwo** (107b)

- LO   **Flo**, **ILO** (184c), **ulo** (34b,80d)

L - P   **lap** (31b,37d,59b,127a,131d,153d,167d), **lip** (48b,58b,80a,131c), **lop** (30c,40a,46b,143a)

- LP   **alp** (24b,103d,115c)

L - R   **lar** (24c,51d,67a,78d,95d,101d,171b), **Ler** (23d,28a,28b,64b,106c, 141a), **Lur** (116c)

LS -   **Lst** (21a,b,88b)

L - S   **las** (13b,151d), **les** (13b,61a), **lis** (54b,58b,60c,62a,92b), **Lis** (47a), **los** (13b,151d), **lys** (58b,92b)

- LS   **als** (66d,163d), **els** (140a), **ils** (62b,d,164d)

L - T   **lat** (24a,33d,106b,118a), **let** (9a,76d,77c,116b,130a,158b,163a), **lit**, **lot** (24b,28d,55a,65d,114a,119c,143c,150d,168a), **Lot** (6b,73d), **Lst** (21a,b,88b), **lut** (189)

- LT   **alt** (66c76c,109c), **elt** (87a,117c,139d), **Olt** (41a)

LU -   **lud** (100a), **Lud** (23c,144b), **lue** (146b), **lug** (27a,45d,47b,73c,136b), **Lug** (28b), **lum** (30a), **Luo** (107b), **Lur** (116c), **lut** (189), **lux** (79d)

L - U   **leu** (190), **Lou** (96a,183d)

- LU   **flu**, **ulu** (87a)

L - V   **lav** (72d), **lev** (33b), **Liv** (93b)

LW -   **Lwo** (107b)

L - W   **law** (26b,33a,40a,48c,60b,85d,91a,111b,134d,155d), **lew** (190), **Lew** (96a), **low** (16c,149d)

L - X   **lax** (93d, 130a), **lex** (90b), **lux** (79d)

LY -   **lye** (8d,27d,93b), **lyn** (140c,178d), **lys** (58b,92b)

L - Y   **lay** (98b,107d,141d,150b), **ley** (190), **loy** (121c,148b,151c,167a)

- LY aly (95d), Ely (27c,50b), fly (58c,81b,163b,178d), ply (59b,90b, 118d,164b,171c,174a,181b,184c), sly (13b,38b,64c,81b,132c)

L - Z Laz (27d)

MA - maa (97d,143d), Mab (54b,126b,183d), Mac (96a,140b,150b), mad (10c,82b), Mae (183c), mag (73b,95b,166c), Mag (183d), Mah (10b, 57c,102b), mai (62a), mal (34a,b,44a,52b,62c,122b), Mal (94b), Mam (192), man (29c,60c,64c,65a,142d,161d), mao (115b), Mao (30b), map (27a,29b,54a,98d,160a), mar (40b,44a,79a,d,81a,140d), Mar (93d), mas (34b,55b,119a), mat (46d,50d,94d,117c,161d), Mat (96a), mau (170c,188), maw (38b,d,72c,111a,121a,142a,156c), Max (96a), may (74d), May (183c)

M - A maa (97d,143d), MFA (42a), mia (83c), mna (71d,179d), moa (19b), Mya (31c)

- MA ama (26a,28d,31a,35b,39c,95b,108d,111c,117b,182c), oma (158c,d, 170c), sma (140b,148d), Uma (43a,69b,153d)

M - B Mab (54b,126b,183d), mib (8d,96c), mob (39a,127a,165b)

M - C Mac (96a,140b,150b)

M - D mad (10c,82b), mid (9d,28b,73b), Mod (138d), mud (6c)

ME - mee (169a), Meg (8c,183c), mel (77d), mem (91c), men (38c,116a, 117b,170a), Men (94d), Meo (27b,80c), mer (62c,141a), mes (62b), met (28d), meu (153b), mew (25b,27b,50a,55b,72c,74d,101b,141b, 153b)

M - E Mae (183c), mee (169a), Mme. (166b), Moe (96a)

- ME ame (37a,62d,131b), eme (38d,70a,140c,172b), Mme. (166b), ume (11d)

MF - MFA (42a)

M - G mag (73b,95b,166c), Mag (183d), Meg (8c,183c), mig (8d,96c, 145b), Mig (118d), mug (46b,54a,65a)

MH - mho (49b,173b)

M - H Mah (10b,57c,102b)

MI - mia (83c), mib (8d,96c), mid (9d,28b,73b), mig (8d,96c,145b), Mig (118d), mil (80b,110c,164d,182d), Mil (10a,82b), mim (12b), Min (29d,68b,113c), mio (152c), mir (29d,135c,d,166c,176b), mis (122b,c,d,185c), mit (56c,66d,183b), mix (156b)

M - I mai (62a), Moi (80d)

- MI ami (61d)

M - L mal (34a,b,44a,52b,62c,122b), Mal (94b), mel (77d), mil (80b,110c, 164d,182d), Mil (10a,82b), mol (58b,70c), mul (188)

MM - Mme. (166b)

M - M Mam (192), mem (91c), mim (12b), mom, mum (30d,95a,146c)

MN - mna (71d,179d)

M - N man (29c,60c,64c,65a,142d,161d), men (38c,116a,117b,170a), Men (94d), Min (29d,68b,113c), mon (15d,84b) Mon (24c), mun (157b)

MO - moa (19b), mob (39a,127a,165b), Mod (138d), Moe (96a), Moi (80d), mol (58b,70c), mom, mon (15d,84b), Mon (24c), moo (94b), mop (160a), mos (59b), mot (126d,130a,137d,183b), mow (32b,40a)

M - O	mao (115b), Mao (30b), Meo (27b,80c), mho (49b,173b), mio (152c), moo (94b), Mro (88c)
- MO	amo (79a,89c), omo (34d)
M - P	map (27a,29b,54a,98d,160a), mop (160a)
- MP	amp (49b,173b), imp (42b,127d,174a)
MR -	Mro (88c), Mrs. (166b), Mru (80d,88c)
M - R	mar (40b,44a,79a,d,81a,140d), Mar (93d), mer (62c,141a), mir (29d, 135c,d,166c,176b), mur (63a,177d)
M - S	mas (34b,55b,119a), mes (62b), mis (122b,c,d,185c), mos (59b), Mrs. (166b), Mus (104a,132c)
- MS	Ems (125a,151c)
M - T	mat (46d,50d,94d,117c,161d), Mat (96a), met (28d), mit (56c,66d, 183b), mot (126d,130a,137d,183b), mut (39c), Mut (9b,127a)
- MT	amt (37d,40d,108a,163c)
MU -	mud (6c), mug (46b,54a,65a), mul (188), mum (30d,95a,146c), mun (157b), mur (63a,177d), Mus (104a,132c), mut (39c), Mut (9b,127a), muy (152d,175d)
M - U	mau (170c,188), meu (153b), Mru (80d,88c)
- MU	emu (19b,58c,111d), imu (15d), SMU (40b), umu (112a)
M - W	maw (38b,d,72c,111a,121a,142a,156c), mew (25b,27b,50a,55b,72c, 74d,101b,141b,153b), mow (32b,40a)
M - X	Max (96a), mix (156b)
MY -	Mya (31c)
M - Y	may (74d), May (183c), muy (152d,175d)
- MY	amy (63c), Amy (8c,94b,183c)
NA -	nab (13b,26c,27b,142a), nae (139d), nag (73d,78b,138c,184d), nak (156b), Nan (183c), nap (65a,117d,146b,148a), nar (139d), nas (74a, 89c,178b), nat (7a,24c,d,106a), nay (42b,106b)
N - A	NEA (162c), noa (35b,124a,161a), NRA (8a,20d)
- NA	ana (10b,33c,60d,93a,98c,122b,d,140d,142b), Ana (28a,68d,100c), Ena (8c,126b), ina (158c), Ina (183c), mna (71d,179d), Ona (26b, 64a), sna (105b,140b,143d,144a,149c,181c,d), Una (54a,153b, 170c,183c)
N - B	nab (13b,26c,27b,142a), neb (17b,19a,d,115b), nib (17b,19d,115d), nob (38c,74d,84a,149d) nub (67b,94d,95c,118c,124d)
N - D	Ned (96a), nid (72a,106c,116d), nod (17c,46c), Nod (18d,25b)
- ND	and (36a), end (8b,67d,120a,125d,130a,166a), Ind (80c), und (66b)
NE -	N.E.A. (162c), neb (17b,19a,d,115b), Ned (96a), nee (19d,22b,25c, 60b,95c), nef (32b,144c,d), neo (34a,b,c,100d,106d,108c,122c,d, 128c), nep (27c,32d,56a,87c,184b), ner (137c), nes (26b), net (26c, 32a,50d,53b,60d,99a,124a,142a,149b), new (11a,63c,88d,111c, 128c, Ney (63b,97b,105d), nez (62b)
N - E	nae (139d), nee (19d,22b,25c,60b,95c), nie (53c,66c), NNE (35b), nye (72a,116c), Nye (9c,18b)
- NE	ane (61c,140a,158b), ene (35b,158b,c), ine (29c,158b,c), Ine (10c, 137d,180b), NNE (35b), one (79a,b,80b,d,124b,147a,148d,173a,c),

245

une (13b,61a,62b,95c)

N - F   **nef** (32b,144c,d)

NG -   **ngu** (188)

N- G   **nag** (73d,78b,138c,184d), **nig** (33b,40a,46a), **nog** (20c,46a,48d,54d, 100b,115d,118a)

- NG   **eng** (48a,146a), **ing** (114b,d,148d,158c,d,175c), **Ing** (10c,115b)

N - H   **nth** (42a)

NI -   **nib** (17b,19d,115d), **nid** (72a,106c,116d), **nie** (53c,66c), **nig** (33b, 40a,46a), **nil** (108c), **nim** (96d,155d), **nin** (107d), **nip** (20c,29b,45d,46a,b,115c,118a), **nis** (23d,67d,68a,87c), **Nis** (19d), **nit** (48d), **nix** (23d,108c,178d)

- NI   **ani** (19b,d,20b,39b), **ini** (158d), **oni** (11b), **uni** (34c,118d,122c), **Uni** (51d)

N - K   **nak** (156b)

- NK   **ink** (20b,40c)

N - L   **nil** (108c), **nul** (108c,177a)

N - M   **nim** (96d,155d), **nom** (62b,125a), **Nym** (54c,76a)

NN -   **NNE** (35b), **NNW** (35b)

N - N   **Nan** (183c), **nin** (107d), **non** (34c,62b,89c,106b,122c,147a), **nun** (24c,91c,117d,147b), **Nun** (29a,85c)

- NN   **Ann** (183c), **inn** (72b,73b,78c,150a,161c,162b,179a), **Inn** (41a)

NO -   **noa** (35b,124a,161a), **nob** (38c,74d,84a,149d), **nod** (17c,46c,148a), **Nod** (18d,25b), **nog** (20c,46a,48d,54d,100b,115d,118a), **nom** (62b, 125a), **non** (34c,62b,89c,106b,122c,147a), **noo** (108c,139d), **nor** (10b,36a,37b,92b), **nos** (62b,90a,179a), **not** (78b,106b), **now** (60b, 79d), **Nox** (69b)

N - O   **neo** (34a,b,c,100d,106d,108c,122c,d,128c), **noo** (108c,139d)

- NO   **ano** (19d,20b,34d,122d,174a), **Ino** (14b,25b), **ono** (34a), **Ono** (18d,118d), **uno** (83c,151d)

N - P   **nap** (65a,117d,146b,148a), **nep** (27c,32d,56a,87c,184b), **nip** (20c, 29b,45d,46a,b,115c,118a)

NR -   **NRA** (8a,20d)

N - R   **nar** (139d), **ner** (137c), **nor** (10b,36a,37b,92b), **nur** (67d)

N - S   **nas** (74a,89c,178b), **nes** (26b), **nis** (23d,67d,87c), **Nis** (19d), **nos** (62b,90a,179a)

- NS   **Ans** (92a), **ens** (17d,18a,51a,52d), **ins** (164d), **INS** (107a,182d), **ons** (38c), **uns** (66d,174c)

NT -   **nth** (42a)

N - T   **nat** (7a,24c,d,106a), **net** (26c,32a,50b,53d,60d,99a,124a,142a, 149b), **nit** (48d), **not** (78b,106b), **nut** (24c,32d,38b,54d,64a,65d, 86b,141c,165a), **Nut** (69a)

- NT   **ant** (49d,60b,81b,118c), **ent** (34d,158b,c), **TNT** (53a)

NU -   **nub** (67b,94d,95c,118c,124d), **nul** (108c,177a), **nun** (24c,91c,117d, 147b), **Nun** (29a,85c,129d), **nur** (67d), **nut** (24c,32d,38b,54d,64a, 65d,86b,141c,165a), **Nut** (69a)

N - U   **ngu** (188)

246

- NU   **Anu** (15b,28a,68a,d,75b,88c,147d), **gnu** (11a,181d), **Unu** (24d)

N - W   **new** (11a,63c,88d,111c,128c), **NNW** (35b), **now** (60b,79d)

- NW   **NNW** (35b), **WNW** (35b)

N - X   **nix** (23d,108c,178d), **Nox** (69b), **Nyx** (69b)

NY -   **nye** (72a,116d), **Nye** (9c,18b), **Nym** (54c,76a), **Nyx** (69b)

N - Y   **nay** (42b,106b), **Ney** (63b,97b,105d)

- NY   **any** (14b,150b), **ony** (139a), **sny** (18a,39d,43d,87a,119a,144d,145a, 165d,176a)

N - Z   **nez** (62b)

OA -   **oaf** (22a,45b,146d,157d,185d), **oak** (73d,168c,169a), **oar** (20b,124c, 134b), **oat** (15a,28b,70b,144b)

O - A   **oca** (48c,112c,116d,133d,170a,184a), **oda** (74a,170d), **oka** (170c, 184a,189), **ola** (113b) **oma** (158c,d,170c), **Ona** (26b,64a), **OPA** (8a), **ora** (10c,40d,41b,45b,83a,c,101c,104a,122d,123d), **ova** (48d), **oxa** (29c)

- OA   **boa** (36c,55b,106a,125d,138b,142d,149a), **goa** (65d,104b,126c), **Goa** (121c), **hoa** (39b), **koa** (74c), **loa** (7d,53c,184d), **Loa** (97d), **moa** (19b), **noa** (35b,124a,161a), **poa** (20d,70d,97d), **roa** (23d,87a), **toa** (17c,178b), **Zoa** (20b)

OB -   **obe** (31d,87d,150d), **obi** (55d,67b,84c,137b,150d)

O - B   **orb** (50a,53c,67d,153b)

- OB   **bob** (57c,115d), **Bob** (96a), **cob** (28c,78b,95d,160b,177d), **fob** (29b, 59b,113b,178c), **gob** (97b,136c), **hob** (40c,56d,100c,124b,167a, 180c), **job** (30d,184c), **Job** (96a), **kob** (11a), **lob** (15d,23b,94c,100b, 163a,172d), **mob** (39a,127a,165b), **nob** (38c,74d,84a,149d), **pob** (121b,129b,139c), **rob** (119d,155d), **Rob** (96a), **sob** (39b,179d)

OC -   **oca** (48c,112c,116d,133d,170a,184a), **och** (8b), **ock** (189), **oct** (34a, 122c)

O - C   **orc** (28c,70c,180b)

- OC   **Doc** (143a), **roc** (19c,53b,54a,147a), **soc** (44c,85d)

OD -   **oda** (74a,170d), **odd** (46b,53a,109b,157a,172d,173c), **ode** (26b,79c, 94d,118a,119d,120a,150b), **Odo** (181d), **ods** (109a)

O - D   **odd** (46b,53a,109b,157a,172d,173c), **oid** (158c), **old** (8a,71a,77c, 123c,175b), **Ord** (25b,60b)

- OD   **cod** (57b,c), **dod** (11a,32a,43b,140c), **fod** (188), **god** (42a), **God** (84d), **hod** (23b,32d,102d,141a), **Mod** (138d), **nod** (17c,46c), **Nod** (18d,25b), **pod** (76b,78d,91b,141b,180c), **rod** (6a,72d,88b,131a, 154d,156a,160a), **sod** (160b,170d), **tod** (24d,60c,83d), **Vod** (16a)

OE -   **o'er** (6b,112a), **oes** (109a)

O - E   **obe** (31d,87d,150d), **ode** (26b,79c,94d,118a,119d,120a,150b), **oke** (189), **ole** (24b,29b,113b,152a,158b,d), **one** (79a,b,80d,124b,147a, 148d,173a,c), **ope** (172b,173c), **ore** (39a,99b,108a,115b,141c,151a, 160b), **ose** (102a,146d,158b,c,d,159a), **owe**, **ote** (158d), **oye** (139c)

- OE   **coe** (143d), **Coe** (33c), **doe** (41d,55b,127a), **foe** (111a), **hoe** (39c), **Joe** (96a), **loe** (139d), **Moe** (96a), **poe** (114b), **Poe** (9c,d,128a, 172a), **roe** (27d,41d,48d,57b,76d,95b,157b), **soe** (170c,184a), **toe** (43c,69d,148a,156a), **voe** (17a,81b), **woe** (25b), **Zoe** (36b,183c)

OF -   off (6b,15c,44c,76a), oft (63c)

O - F   oaf (22a,45b,146d,157d,185d), off (6b,15c,44c,76a), orf (57b,185c), ouf (52c)

- OF   lof (188)

- OG   bog (97a,160a), cog (33a,65d,163b,167b,180c), dog (10b,45b,59b), fog (109b), gog (95b), hog (45b,117c,160c), jog (82c,85c,170a), log (64a,128d), nog (20c,46a,48d,54d,100b,115d,118a), sog (149c), tog (46a), vog (189)

OH -   ohm (49b,67a,173b), oho (52c)

O - H   och (8b)

- OH   boh (24c), doh (113b), foh (52c), Hoh (80d), poh (52c), soh (52c, 72d,) zoh (13d,186b)

OI -   oid (158c), oii (105c), oil (11a,71a)

O - I   obi (55d,67b,84c,137d,150d), oii (105c), oni (11b), ori (34a), ovi (34a)

- OI   goi (107c), hoi (52c,74b,185b), koi (26d), loi (62a), Moi (80d), poi (44a,59c,74c,117a,162a,164b), roi (55c,62a,133d), toi (62b,d,63a), Toi (18d), yoi (52c,79a)

OK -   oka (170c,184a,189), oke (189)

O - K   oak (73d,168c,169a), ock (189), ork (180b), ouk (140c)

- OK   Bok (9c), Lok (15d,68b), Rok (87c), sok (188), yok (10c,185a)

OL -   ola (113b), old (8a,71a,77c,123c,175b), ole (24b,29b,113b,152a, 158b,d), olm (48c), Olt (41a)

O - L   oil (11a,71a), owl

- OL   col (103d,114c), Kol (18b), mol (58b,70c), sol (108b), Sol (117b, 159b), tol (137b), vol (155a,182d)

OM -   oma (158c,d,170c), omo (34d)

O - M   ohm (49b,67a,173b), olm (48c)

- OM   com (122d), dom (121c,166b,c), Dom (94b), mom, nom (62b,125a), pom (45a,148d), rom (72d), tom (95d), Tom (96b,157a), yom (41a)

ON -   Ona (26b,64a), one (79a,b,80b,d,124b,147a,148d,173a,c), oni (11b), ono (34a), Ono (18d,118d), ons (38c) ony (139a)

O - N   own (6d)

- ON   bon (30a,61d,86b,88c), Bon (84b), con (7d,29b,83c,116d,157d), don (151d,166c), Don (96a), eon (8a,37b,51d,116b), Fon (40b), gon (188), ion (11c,29a,49b,101b,114c,158c), Lon (86c,96a), mon (15d,84b), Mon (24c), non (34c,62b,89c,106b,122c,147a), ron (152c), Ron (86c,88a), son (42d,75d), ton (158d,167d,179d), von (66d,67a), won, yon (44c,112a,164d)

OO -   oop (139a), oot (140a)

O - O   Odo (181d), oho (52c), omo (34d), ono (34a), Ono (18d,118d), oro (34c,122c,152a), Oro (161b), oto (34a) Oto (147b)

- OO   boo, coo (19b), Coo (82d), foo (42c), goo (156b), loo (65a), moo (94b), noo (108c,139d), roo (140a), soo (127d,140b,151b), Soo (137c), too (18b,102c), woo, zoo (181b)

OP -   OPA (8a), ope (172b,173c), Ops (28c,69a,b,74a,137c), opt (30c)

O - P   oop (139a), orp (140c,179d)

- OP   cop (36a,120c,126d,153c,155d), dop (39c,43b), fop (38a,40d,46d), hop (40b), kop (76d), lop (30c,40a,46b,143a), mop (160a), oop (139a), pop (52d,53a,130b,149d), sop (23b,35d,149c,155d), top (38c,52b,118b,123d,160a,174a,186b), wop

OR -   ora (10c,40d,41b,45b,83a,c,101c,104a,122d,123d), orb (50a,53c, 67d,153b), orc (28c,70c,180b), Ord (25b,60b), ore (39a,99b,108a, 115b,141c,151a,160b), orf (57b,185c), ori (34a), ork (180b), oro (34c,122c,152a), Oro (161b), orp (140c,179d), orr (77c), ort (59b, 90d,91a,102c,129b,140d,180a,184d), ory (36c)

O - R   oar (20b,124c,134b), oer (6b,112a), orr (77c), our (124c)

- OR   Bor (120c), cor (36c,75b,155b), dor (17d,24b,32b,46b,47a,81b,85d), for (123d,163a,166c), Gor (81a), Hor (103d), ior (50a,158c), kor (75c), nor (10b,36a,37b,92b), por (152a), tor (38b,76d,85d,115c, 124b,132b,c), Vor (69a)

OS -   ose (102a,146d,158b,c,d,159a), ost (15d,86b)

O - S   ods (109a), oes (109a), ons (38c), Ops (28c,69a,b,74a,137c), ous (158b)

- OS   Bos (27c), cos (91d,132d), dos (45d,61a,97a,181b), Eos (14d,41a, 68d), ios (74d), Kos (77c,82d), los (13b,151d), mos (59b), nos (62b, 90a,179a), ros (37b), Ros (138a,174d), SOS

OT -   ote (158d), oto (34a), Oto (147b)

O - T   oat (15a,28b,70b,144b), oct (34a,122c), oft (63c), Olt (41a), oot (140a), opt (30c), ort (59b,90d,91a,102c,129b,140d,180a,184d), ost (15d,86b), out (6b,14b,60b,69d,80a,108b,185c)

- OT   bot (59a,88d), cot (129b,148b), dot (45d,97a,104d,105a,116b,153a, 162d), fot (188), got, hot (10c,176c), jot (82a,114c,166c,180d), lot (24b,28d,55a,65d,114a,119c,143c,150d,168a), Lot (6b,73d), mot (126d,130a,137d,183b), not (78b,106b), oot (140a), pot (120b, 145b,154d,175d), rot (22b,134c,143d,153d), sot (46c,167b,c), tot (186a), Vot (56d)

OU -   ouf (52c), ouk (140c), our (124c), ous (158b), out (6b,14b,60b,69d, 80a,108b,185c)

- OU   fou (139a), IOU (124b), kou (169a), Lou (96a,183d), sou (63b), you

OV -   ova (48d), ovi (34a)

OW -   owe, owl, own (6d)

- OW   bow (11c,21b,39d,60a,107c,109a,125a,144d,158a), cow (22c,45b, 81d), dow (17d,87a,88d,175d), how, jow (188), low (16c,149d), mow (32b,40a), now (60b,79d), pow, row (44c,56b,92c,109a,126b, 127d,165c), sow (45b,117c,119a,138b,160c), tow (45d,58b,75d, 125b), vow (119c,150a), wow (52c,158a), yow (52c)

OX -   oxa (29c)

- OX   box (36a,c,128c,145d,152d), cox (156a), fox (134a), Nox (69b), pox (44a), vox (90a,177a)

OY -   oye (139c)

O - Y   ony (139a), ory (36c)

- OY   boy (142d,157c), coy (16d), goy (107c), hoy (16c,52c), joy, loy (121c,148b,151c,167a), Roy, soy (17b,137c,74d), toy (169d)

- OZ Boz (43b,115d), coz, goz (190)

PA - pab (139c), pac (73b,94c,100d), pad (39d,59c,76c,157d,161a,168b), pah (52c,60b,106d), pal (35b,38d), pam (26c,65a,87a,105b), pan (34a,61a,104a,175d), Pan (56a,68a,b,76b,120c,135b,161a,184a), pap (59c), par (15a,51a,b,c,69d,107c,135b,155a), pas (40d,156a), pat (11d,116d,159a,161d,167c), Pat (96a), Pau (48c,76a,130c), paw (32d,59c,73c), pax (89d,115b), pay (35b,128c,130a,d,177b)

P - A pea (32d,91b,142a,175a), pia (13b,22d,48a,120d), poa (20d, 70d,97c), pta (6a), pua (74c,76a)

- PA apa (23a,177d), OPA (8a), spa (75b,100b,130c,154b,178d)

P - B pab (139c), pob (121b,129b,139c)

P - C pac (73b,94c,100d), pic (188)

P - D pad (39d,59c,76c,157d,161a,168b), ped (16d,34b), pod (76b,78d, 91b,141b,180c), pud (59d,73c,115a)

PE - pea (32d,91b,142a,175a), ped (16d,34b), pee (91c), peg (38c,46b, 54d,98a,118a,184c), pel (55c,160d), pen (36a,50a,80d,118b,126d, 160a,185c), pep (50b,176b), per (25c,122d,165b,176a), pes (59d), pet (26d,37c,55a,59b,162d), peu (62a), pew (30d,52c,57d,120b, 141c)

P - E pee (91c), pie (42d,85d,95b,114d,171b,172a), poe (114b), Poe (9c, d,128a,172a), pre (17d,122b,c), pue (52c), Pye (50d,55a)

- PE ape (36d,79d,100a,101d,146d), ope (172b,173c)

P - G peg (38c,46b,54d,98a,118a,184c), pig (27a,45b,99a,151b,160c), pug (45a,101a,108a,148d)

PH - phi (91c), phu (38c)

P - H pah (52c,60b,106d), poh (52c)

PI - pia (13b,22d,48a,120d), pic (188), pie (42d,85d,95b,114d, 171b,172a), pig (27a,45b,99a,151b,160c), pik (188), pil (34b), pin (45d,54d,141d,147d), pip (11d,44a,121d,142a,154a), Pip (43b), pir (103a,b,136c), pit (52b,142a,164a,168a) piu (102c), pix (31a,51d, 175d)

P - I phi (91c), poi (44a,59c,74c,117a,162a,164b), psi (91c)

- PI api (34a,76d), epi (56c,61c,d,111c,112d,122d,133c,153c,167b, 174a), UPI (107a,182d)

P - K pik (188)

PL - ply (59b,90b,118d,164b,171c,174a,181b,184c)

P - L pal (35b,38d), pel (55c,160d), pil (34b), pul (190), Pul (14a)

P - M pam (26b,65a,87a,105b), pom (45a,148d)

P - N pan (34a,61a,104a,175d), Pan (56a,68a,b,76b,120c,135b,161a, 184a), pen (36a,50a,80d,118b,126d,160a,185c), pin (45d,54d,141d, 147d), pun (119c)

PO - poa (20d,70d,97c), pob (121b,129b,139c), pod (76b,78d,91b,141b, 180c), poe (114b), Poe (9c,d,128a,172a), poh (52c), poi (44a,59c, 74c,117a,162a,164b), pom (45a,148d), pop (52d,53a,130b,149d), por (152a), pot (120b,145b,154d,175d), pow, pox (44a)

P - O pro (59d,126d), Pwo (88c)

250

- PO   apo (122b), Apo (177c)

P - P   pap (59c), pep (50b,176b), pip (11d,44a,121d,154a), Pip (43b), pop (52d,53a,130b,149d), pup (141b,148d,185d)

PR -   pre (17d,122b,c), pro (59d,126d), pry (52b,91d,98b,123d)

P - R   par (15a,51a,b,c,69d,107c,135b,155a), per (25c,122d,165b,176a), pir (103a,b,136c), por (152a), pur, pyr (92a,b,122c,173b)

PS -   psi (91c), pst (25c,126d,146c)

P - S   pas (40d,156a), pes (59d), pus

- PS   Ops (28c,69a,b,74a,137c)

PT -   Pta (6a)

P - T   pat (11d,116d,159a,161d,167c), Pat (96a), pet (26d,37c,55a,59b, 162d), pit (52b,142a,164a,168a), pot (120b,145b,154a,175d), pst (25c,126d,146c), put (65a,69d,90b)

- PT   apt (11d,23b,32b,58a,80b,92b,114d,116d,124b,159a), opt (30c)

PU -   pua (74c,76a), pud (59d,73c,115a), pue (52c), pug (45a,101a,108a, 148d), pul (190), Pul (14a), pun (119c), pup (141b,148d,185d), pur, pus, put (65a,69d,90b), puy (61d)

P - U   Pau (48c,76a,130c), peu (62a), phu (38c), piu (102c)

PW -   Pwo (88c)

P - W   paw (32d,59c,73c), pew (30d,52c,57d,120b,141c), pow

P - X   pax (89d,115b), pix (31a,51d,175d), pox (44a), pyx (31a,51d,175d)

PY -   Pye (50d,55a), pyr (92a,b,122c,173b), pyx (31a,51d,175d)

P - Y   pay (35b,128c,130a,d,177b), ply (59b,90b,118d,164b,171c,174a, 181b,184c), pry (52b,91d,98b,123d), puy (61d)

- PY   spy (44a,51c,52b,141d)

QA -   Qaf (104a)

Q - A   qua (13c,80a,89c,147a)

Q - E   que (62d)

Q - F   Qaf (104a)

Q - I   qui (62d)

Q - O   quo (188)

QU -   qua (13c,80a,89c,147a), que (62d), qui (62d), quo (188)

RA -   rab (17c,75c,85b,102d,162c,166b), Rab (45a), rad (50b,138d,173b), rae (136b,138d,140b), Rae (183c), rag (59b,77c,100c,133c,161a), rah (29b), rai (188), raj (129c), ram (17a,45b,50b,79c,112b,121d, 143d,157d), Ram (36b), ran (73d), Ran (7c,107d,141a,163d), rap (90d,110a,147c,157c), ras (6c,26b,48b,51d,53d,61c,75a,111c,123c, 166b), rat (16a,42d,73b,132c), raw (20c,39a,105d,173d), ray (38a, 49a,57b,58b,147b), Ray (96a)

R - A   rea (9c,171a), ria (38c,51d,81b,152a,b), roa (23d,87a), rua (118c), Rua (16b)

- RA   ara (33a,114a,116a,118b,163d), Ara (9b,18c,36b,c,68d,69b,c,85a, 95a,175b), dra (188), era (8a,51a,116b,165d), fra (23c,63c,101d, 123b,129d), gra (59b,94b,160c), Ira (18c,d,41a,68c,82c,96a,164a, 178a,c), Kra (11b,91d), NRA (8a,20d), ora (10c,40d,41b,45b,83a,c,

251

101c,104a,122d,123d), **tra** (33b)

R - B   **rab** (17c,75c,85b,102d,162c,166b), **Rab** (45a), **reb** (35d,75c,85b, 162c,166b), **rib** (37c,85b,90c,98a,144d,159d,172a), **rob** (119d, 155d), **Rob** (96a), **rub** (6b,24d,28c,43c,120c,179b)

- RB   **orb** (50a,53c,67d,153b)

R - C   **roc** (19c,53b,54a,147a)

- RC   **arc** (31b,39d,92a,126a,127c,142a), **orc** (28c,70c,180b)

R - D   **rad** (50b,138d,173b), **red** (33c,38d,59a,127b,134c,135b), **Red** (151b), **rid** (32a,44a,60d), **rod** (6a,72d,88b,131a,154d,156a,160a), **rud** (26d,57b)

- RD   **erd** (47d,119d,145c), **Ord** (25b,60b), **urd** (17b,184b), **Urd** (68d,107d)

RE -   **rea** (9c,171a), **reb** (35d,75c,85b,162c,166b), **red** (33c,38d,59a,127b, 134c,135b), **Red** (151b), **ree** (12c,50a,80c,134d,137a,140b,144a, 146b), **Ree** (25a), **ref, reh** (8d), **rei** (89b,121c), **Rei** (18d), **rel** (49b, 173b), **Reo** (26c), **rep** (53b,d,131a,171c), **res** (80a,89d,91a,97c), **ret** (58b,95a,149c,155d), **Reu** (115d), **rev, rew** (75c,140c,176b), **rex** (86c,96a), **rey** (86c,152b)

R - E   **rae** (136b,138d,140b), **Rae** (183c), **ree** (12c,50a,80c,134d,137a, 140b,144a,146b), **Ree** (25a), **rhe** (59a,173b), **rie** (28c,70c,97d), **roe** (27d,41d,48d,57b,76d,95b,157b), **rue** (76a,b,129c,150d,183a), **rye** (28b,70b,72d,92d)

- RE   **are** (51a,88b,98a,99b,110c,166c,175c), **ere** (17d,150c), **ire** (10c, 52b,30c,64c,125a,130b,185a), **ore** (39a,99b,108a,115b,141c,151a, 160b), **pre** (17d,122b,c), **tre** (37b,83c,122d,165a,167d), **ure** (40a, 139d,155d,158b,d), **Ure** (138d,185d)

R - F   **ref, rif** (188)

- RF   **orf** (57b,185c)

R - G   **rag** (59b,77c,100c,133c,161a), **rig** (51b,112a), **rug**

- RG   **erg** (50b,173b,184c)

RH -   **rhe** (59a,173b), **rho** (71b,91b)

R - H   **rah** (29b), **reh** (8d)

RI -   **ria** (38c, 51d, 81b, 152a, b), **rib** (37c, 85b, 90c, 98a, 144d, 159d,172a), **rid** (28c,70d,97d), **rif** (188), **rig** (51b, 112a), **rii** (157b,175b), **rim** (22a,48b,96d),116b,124b,166a,180c), **rin** (33b,142b), **rio** (33a,131d,132a,152c,157b), **Rio** (23a), **rip** (87b, 130a,162c), **Rip** (178b), **ris** (131d), **rit** (140b,148c,153d)

R - I   **rai** (188), **rei** (89b,121c), **Rei** (18d), **rii** (157b,175b), **roi** (55c,62a, 133d)

- RI   **Ari** (18d), **eri** (13d,21c,146d), **Eri** (18c), **gri** (75c,78b), **Iri** (18a,d, 75a), **kri** (75c,96d), **ori** (34a), **sri** (60c,77b,166c), **Sri** (17c), **tri** (122d,169d), **Uri** (162d)

R - J   **raj** (129c)

R - K   **Rok** (87c)

- RK   **ark** (21a,29d,38a,58b,60d,175d), **irk** (10d), **ork** (180b)

R - L   **rel** (49b,173b)

R - M   **ram** (17a,45b,50b,79c,112b,121d,143d,157d), **Ram** (36b), **rim** (22a,

48b,96d,116b,124b,166a,180c), **rom** (72d), **rum** (8c,92d)

- RM   **arm** (22d,60c,81b,92b,124b,161b)

R - N   **ran** (73d), **Ran** (7c,107d,141a,163d), **rin** (33b),142b), **ron** (152c), **Ron** (86c,88a), **run** (10d,23c,58d,110d,148d,153b,154d,167d)

- RN   **arn** (8c,139a), **ern** (19c,d,47b,54b,141a), **urn** (36c,174d)

RO -   **roa** (23d,87a), **rob** (119d,155d), **Rob** (96a), **roc** (19c,53b,54a,147a), **rod** (6a,72d,88b,131a,154d,156a,160a), **roe** (27d,41d,48d,57b,76d, 95b,157b), **roi** (55c,62a,133d), **Rok** (87c), **rom** (72d), **ron** (152c), **Ron** (86c,88a), **roo** (140a), **ros** (37b), **Ros** (138a,174d), **rot** (22b, 134c,143d,153d), **row** (44c,56b,92c,109a,126b,127d,165c), **Roy**

R - O   **Reo** (26c), **rho** (71b,91c), **rio** (33a,131d,132a,152c,157b), **Rio** (23a), **roo** (140a)

- RO   **Aro** (107a,111c), **cro** (104c,115b,180a), **fro** (15b), **Mro** (88c), **oro** (34c,122c,152a), **Oro** (161b), **pro** (59d,126d), **S.R.O.** (6a,164a), **Uro** (192)

R - P   **rap** (90d,110a,147c,157c), **rep** (53b,d,131a,171c), **rip** (87b, 130a,162c), **Rip** (178b)

- RP   **orp** (140c,179d)

R - R   **rur** (132b)

- RR   **err** (21a,43a,67d,100c,d,147a,148b,157b,168b,178a), **grr** (52c), **orr** (77c)

R - S   **ras** (6c,26b,48b,51d,53d,61c,75a,111c,123c,166b), **res** (80a,89d, 91a,97c,164c), **ris** (131d), **ros** (37b), **Ros** (138a,174d), **rus** (89b), **Rus** (138a)

- RS   **ars** (13b,89a), **Ars** (112c), **ers** (20a,176a), **Mrs.** (166b)

R - T   **rat** (16a,42d,73b,132c), **ret** (58b,95a,149c,155d), **rit** (140b,148c, 153d), **rot** (22b,134c,143d,153d), **rut** (73a)

- RT   **art** (22d,38b,39c,43b,56c,124a,162c,181d), **ert** (140c,174a), **ort** (59b,90d,91a,102c,129b,140d,180a,184d)

RU -   **rua** (118c), **Rua** (116b), **rub** (6b,24d,28c,43c,120c,179b), **rud** (26d, 57b), **rue** (76a,b,129c,150d,183a), **rug, rum** (8c,92d), **run** (10d,23c, 58d,110d,148d,153b,154b,167d), **rur** (132b), **rus** (89b), **Rus** (138a), **rut** (73a), **rux** (154a,184d)

R - U   **Reu** (115d)

- RU   **aru** (80c,82b), **Aru** (82d), **cru** (63a,176c), **Kru** (91d), **Mru** (80d,88c), **Uru** (192)

R - V   **rev**

R - W   **raw** (20c,39a,105d,173d), **rew** (75c,140c,176c), **row** (44c,56b,92c, 109a,126b,127d,165c)

R - X   **rex** (86c,96a), **rux** (154a,184d)

RY -   **rye** (28b,70b,72d,92d)

R - Y   **ray** (38a,49a,57b,58b,147b), **Ray** (96a), **rey** (86c,152b), **Roy**

- RY   **cry** (25c,124a,145c,179d), **dry** (46d,85a,137c,164c), **ery** (155d,158c, d), **fry** (57d), **gry** (78b), **ory** (36c), **pry** (52b,91d,98b,123d), **try** (7c, 10d,14c,50a,51c,130a), **wry** (13d)

SA -   **saa** (98a), **sac** (15d,121d), **Sac** (80c), **sad** (29c,42c,94c,98c,104a,

253

150d,173a), **sae** (140b,149c), **sag** (46b), **sah** (188), **sai** (101d), **saj** (48a,169a), **sak** (37c), **Sak** (88c), **sal** (29c,48a,136d,149d,152d, 169a,183a), **Sal** (183d), **Sam** (96a,162a), **san** (91c), **San** (24d), **sao** (141b) , **Sao** (113c), **sap** (45d,52d,85c,169b,176d,179a), **sar** (57d), **sat** (13d), **saw** (7a,11b,40c,54c,97d,125a,137d,167a), **sax** (40c,148a,167a), **say** (131c,174c,177a)

S - A   **saa** (98a), **sea** (19a,52d,58c,112c,178d), **sha** (110c,143d,144a,c, 174c,181c), **sia** (80c), **sma** (140b,148d), **sna** (105b,140b,143d,144a, 149c,181c,d), **spa** (75b,100b,130c,154b,178d), **sta** (13c,91b,104d, 105a), **sua** (89d),

- SA   **Asa** (6a,18c,71a,84d,86d,164c), **ESA** (8a)

S - B   **Seb** (47d), **sib** (86b,129c,139d,147b), **sob** (39b,179d), **sub** (90a, 122d,172c)

S - C   **sac** (15d,121d), **Sac** (80c), **sec** (46c,182c), **sic** (90a,165b,168b), **soc** (44c,85d)

- SC   **BSC** (42a)

S - D   **sad** (29c,42c,94c,98c,104a,150d,173a), **sed** (89a), **Sid** (96a), **sod** (160b,170d), **sud** (59a)

SE -   **sea** (19a,52d,58c,112c,178d), **Seb** (47d), **see** (46c,182c), **sed** (89a), **see** (20a,43c,44a,51c,53c,93d,109b,113c,116a,176d,178c,183b), **sei** (62c,140b), **Sem** (107c), **sen** (190) **ser** (80d,83b,d,116c, 152d,180a), **ses** (61d), **set** (7b,11d,13a,23c,32b,33c,37c,58a,73d, 109b,118c,121c,142c,150a,186a), **Set** (52b,68a,b,111d), **sew, sex,** **sey** (120c)

S - E   **sae** (140b,149c), **see** (20a,43c,44a,51c,53c,109b,113c,116a,176d, 178c,183b), **she** (124b), **She** (73a), **sie** (46c,66d,139b,140b,146b), **soe** (170c,184a), **SSE** (35b), **ste** (62c,136c), **sue** (119c), **Sue** (63a, 178a,183d), **sye** (40c,46c,139b,141a,167a)

- SE   **ase** (51a,139a), **Ase** (79b,115d), **ese** (35b,158a), **ise** (40d,158c,d), **Ise** (78a,84c), **ose** (102a,146d,158b,c,d,159a), **SSE** (35b), **use** (7b, 47a,49d,64c,109b,168b,c,181b)

S - F   **Sif** (164d)

S - G   **sag** (46b), **sog** (149c)

SH -   **sha** (110c,143d,144a,c,174c,181c), **she** (124b), **She** (73a), **sho** (188), **Shu** (30b,127a), **shy** (16d,99d,128c,160c,165d,175a)

S - H   **soh** (52c,72d)

- SH   **ash** (24d,33c,49c,73d,134b,168c,169a), **hsh** (79c), **ish** (158b), **ush**

SI -   **Sia** (80c), **sib** (86b,129c,139d,147b), **sic** (90a,165b,168b), **Sid** (96a), **sie** (46c,66d,139b,140b,146b), **Sif** (164d), **sil** (30c,185c,d), **Sim** (96b), **sin** (91c,140b,147a,168b,176a), **Sin** (102b), **sip** (46b,79d, 104a,162b), **sir** (87a,163b,166b), **sis** (67b,129c), **sit** (98c,116a,121c, 130c,142d), **six** (26c)

S - I   **sai** (101d), **Sia** (80c), **ski** (149c), **sri** (60c,77b,166c), **Sri** (17c), **sui** (30b)

- SI   **asi** (137a), **psi** (91c)

S - J   **saj** (48a,169a)

SK -   **ski** (149c), **sky** (56d)

S - K   sak (37c), Sak (88c), sok (188), Suk (107b)

- SK   ask (38b,82a,126c)

SL -   sly (13b,38b,64c,81b,132c)

S - L   sal (29c,48a,136d,149d,152d,169a,183a), Sal (183d), sel (62c, 140b), sil (30c,185c,d), sol (108b), Sol (117b,159b)

SM -   sma (140b,148d), SMU (40b)

S - M   Sam (96a,162a), Sem (107c), Sim (96b), sum (8a,123a,167c)

- SM   ism (45a,79b,161c)

SN -   sna (105b,140b,143d,144a,149c,181c), sny (18a,39d,43d,87a,119a, 144d,145a,165d,176a)

S - N   san (91c), San (24d), sen (190), sin (91c,140b,147a,168b,176a), Sin (102b), son (42d,75d), sun (75d,111a,117b,155b), syn (122d,183b)

SO -   sob (39b,179d), soc (44c,85d), sod (160b,170d), soe (170c,184a), sog (149c), soh (52c,72d), sok (188), sol (108b) Sol (117b,159b), son (42d,75d), soo (127d,140b,151b), Soo (137c), sop (23b,35d, 149c,155d), SOS, sot (46c,167b,c), sou (63b), sow (45b,117c,119a, 138b,160c), soy (17b,137c,174d)

S - O   sao (141b), Sao (113c), sho (188), soo (127d,140b,151b), Soo (137c), S.R.O. (6a,164a)

- SO   Aso (84c), DSO (99d), eso (34d,183b), iso (34a,122c,d)

SP -   spa (75b,100b,130c,154b,178d), spy (44a,51c,52b,141d)

S - P   sap (45d,52d,85c,169b,176d,179a), sip (46b,79d,104a,162b), sop (23b,35d,149c,155d), sup (46b,104a,162b)

- SP   asp (7b,32b,149a,174a,176c), e.s.p. (147b)

S - Q   suq (22a,97a)

SR -   sri (60c,77b,166c), Sri (17c), S.R.O. (6a,164a)

S - R   sar (57d), ser (80d,83b,d,116c,152d,180a), sir (87a,163b,166b), sur (34a,62b,d,104b,151a,152d,174a)

SS -   SSE (35b), ssu (189), SSW (35b)

S - S   ses (61d), sis (67b,129c), SOS, sus (117c), Sus (160c,181b)

- SS   ass (17b,20c,45b,c,59c,110c,112b,146d,157d), ess (39d,78a,91c, 158c,184d)

ST -   sta (13c,91b,104d,105a), ste (62c,136c), sty (50a,53c)

S - T   sat (13d), set (7b,11d,13a,23c,32b,33c,37c,58a,73d,109b,118c, 121c,142c,150a,186a), Set (52b,68a,b,111d), sit (98c,116a,121c, 130c,142d), sot (46c,167b,c)

- ST   est (50a,61c,62a,79b,89c,158d,159c), ist (7b,34b,43a,59b,66c,158b, c,d), LST (21a,88b), ost (15d,86b), pst (25c,126d,146c), tst (81d, 126d)

SU -   sua (89d), sub (90a,122d,172c), sud (59a), sue (119c), Sue (63a, 178a,183d), Sui (30b), Suk (107b), sum (8a,123a,167c), sun (75d, 111a,117b,155b), sup (46b,104a,162b), suq (22a,97a), sur (34a,62b, d,104b,151a,152d,174a), sus (117c), Sus (160c,181b)

S - U   Shu (30b,127a), SMU (40b), sou (63b), ssu (189)

- SU   ssu (189)

S - W saw (7a,11b,40c,54c,97d,125a,137d,167a), **sew, sow** (45b,117c, 119a,138b,160c), **SSW** (35b)

- SW SSW (35b), **WSW** (35b)

S - X sax (40c,148a,167a), **sex, six** (26c)

SY - sye (40c,46c,139b,141a,167a), **syn** (122d,183b)

S - Y say (131c,174c,177a), **sey** (120c), **shy** (16d,99d,128c,160c,165d, 175a), **sky** (56d), **sly** (13b,38b,64c,81b,132c), **sny** (18a,39d,43d,87a, 119a,144d,145a,165d,176a), **soy** (17b,137c,174d), **spy** (44a,51c, 52b,141d), **sty** (50a,53c)

TA - taa (112d), **tab** (29b,39c,58b,86a,128d,145a), **tac** (34d,130a), **tad** (22c,174a,186a), **tae** (138d,140c,166c,d), **tag** (45a,54c,65a,87b, 144a), **tai** (84b,111c,121b), **Tai** (80d), **taj** (75a,97d), **tal** (40c,77a, 113b), **tam** (74d), **tan** (23d,33c,46a,72d,90d), **tao** (10d,131c, 170b), **Tao** (117a), **tap** (55a,114d,153c), **tar** (8c,68a,94d,111c,118c, 136a,c,176d), **tat** (43b,48c,72d,87c), **Tat** (82a), **tau** (71b,91c,136c, 161a), **tav** (91c), **taw** (90d,91c,96c,d,145b,161d), **tax** (13a,14a,80a, 91d)

T - A taa (112d), **tea** (13d,18c,79c,81a,145d,149c,159d), **tia** (151d), **toa** (17c,178b), **tra** (33b), **tua** (117a)

- TA ata (58d,97d,158d,160c,173d), **Ata** (79c,80d,94d,95d,100a,106b, 117a), **eta** (71a,84c,91c), **Ita** (51b,71d,94d,95d,106b,117a), **ITA** (173a), **Pta** (6a), **sta** (13c,91b,104d,105a), **uta** (53c,84d,93b,147c, 150b)

T - B tab (29b,39c,58b,86a,128d,145a), **tub** (21a,27a,36c,174d)

TC - tch (52c), **tck** (52c)

T - C tac (34d,130a), **tec** (43a), **tic** (104d,153a,171c,d)

- TC etc (10b)

T - D tad (174a,186a), **ted** (74d,138b,154b), **Ted** (96b), **tod** (24d,60c,83d)

TE - tea (13d,18c,79c,81a,145d,149c,159d), **tec** (43a), **ted** (74d,138b, 154b), **Ted** (96b), **tee** (39d,52b,69d,91c,112d,115d,118b,172a), **teg** (45a,54b,143d,144a,171d), **tel** (34a,b,122c), **Tem** (143a,159b), **ten** (19a,26c,41c,42b), **ter** (34d,122d,165a), **tez** (125c)

T - E tae (138d,140c,166c,d), **tee** (39d,52b,69d,91c,112d,115d,118b, 172a), **the** (13b), **tie** (10a,14c,38b,45d,51a,88d,109b,127c,138b, 170b), **toe** (43c,69d,148a,156a), **tre** (37b,83c,122d,165a,167d), **tue** (114b), **tye** (28c,134a)

- TE ate (81a,108c,158c,174c), **Ate** (20c,68b,d,69a,b,116c,186b), **ete** (36c,62d,141c,159b), **ite** (59b,81a,105d,130c,158b,c,d,161a), **ote** (158d), **ste** (62c,136c), **Ute** (145c,180b)

T - G tag (45a,54c,65a,87b,144a), **teg** (45a,54b,143d,144a,171d), **tig** (46b), **tog** (46a), **tug** (45d,125b), **tyg** (46b)

TH - the (13b), **tho** (52a), **Tho** (167a), **thy**

T - H tch (52c)

- TH eth (91c,158d), **Ith** (10a,28a,82b,99d), **nth** (42a)

TI - tia (151d), **tic** (104d,153a,171c,d), **tie** (10a,14c,38b,45d, 51a,88d,109b,127c,138b,170b), **tig** (46b), **til** (142d), **Tim** (43b), **tin** (36c,99a,b,108b,155a,179c), **tio** (152d), **tip** (26b,d,50a,70d,77b,78a,

256

120a,165d), **tir** (61d,62c,145b), **tis**, **tit** (19c,130d), **Tiu** (7c,68c, 147d,163d,166c,170c), **Tiw** (68c,147d,163d)

T - I   **tai** (84b,111c,121b), **Tai** (80d), **tji** (189), **toi** (62b,d,63a), **Toi** (18d), **tri** (122d,169d), **tui** (47c,114b,117a), **Twi** (69c)

- TI   **ati** (106d,107a), **Ati** (45d,106b,113c,117a)

TJ -   **tji** (189)

T - J   **taj** (75a,97d)

TK -   **TKO** (22c)

T - K   **tck** (52c)

T - L   **tal** (40c,77a,113b), **tel** (34a,b,122c), **til** (142d), **tol** (137b)

T - M   **tam** (74d), **Tem** (143a,159b), **Tim** (43b), **tom** (95d), **Tom** (96b, 157a), **tum** (26d), **Tum** (143a,159b)

TN -   **TNT** (53a)

T - N   **tan** (23d,33c,46a,72d,90d), **ten** (19a,26c,41c,42b), **tin** (36c,99a,b, 108b,155a,179c), **ton** (158d,167d,179d), **tun** (23b,27a,182b)

TO -   **toa** (17c,178b), **tod** (24d,60c,83d), **toe** (43c,69d,148a,156a), **tog** (46a), **toi** (62b,d,63a), **Toi** (18d), **tol** (137b), **tom** (95d), **Tom** (96b, 157a), **ton** (158d,167d,179d), **too** (18b,102c), **top** (38c,52b,118b, 123d,160a,174a,186b), **tor** (38b,76d,85d,115c,124b,132b,c), **tot** (186a), **tow** (45d,58b,75d,125b), **toy** (169d)

T - O   **tao** (10d,131c,170b), **Tao** (117a), **tho** (52a), **Tho** (167a), **tio** (152d), **TKO** (22c), **too** (18b,102c), **two** (26c,37d,80a,93a)

- TO   **ETO** (184d), **Ito** (84a,c,186d), **oto** (34a), **Oto** (147b)

T - P   **tap** (55a,114d,153c), **tip** (26b,d,50a,70d,77b,78a,120a,165d), **top** (38c,52b,118b,123d,160a,174a,186b), **tup** (115a,117d,127d,143d)

TR -   **tra** (33b), **tre** (37b,83c,122d,165a,167d), **tri** (122d,169d), **try** (7c, 10d,14c,50a,51c,130a)

T - R   **tar** (8c,68a,94d,111c,118c,136a,c,176d), **ter** (34d,122d,165a), **tir** (61d,62c,145b), **tor** (38b,76d,85d,115c,124b,132b,c), **tur** (14d,27c, 68a,79b,117d,174c), **tyr** (7c,68c,147d,163d,170c,178a)

TS -   **tst** (81d,126d)

T - S   **tis**

- TS   **its** (124c)

T - T   **tat** (43b,48c,72d,87c), **Tat** (82a), **tit** (19c,130d), **TNT** (53a), **tot** (186a), **tst** (81d,126d), **tut** (52c)

- TT   **att** (146a)

TU -   **tua** (117a), **tub** (21a,27a,36c,174d), **tue** (114b), **tug** (45d,125b), **tui** (47c,114b,117a), **tum** (26d), **Tum** (143a,159b), **tun** (23b,27a, 182b), **tup** (115a,117d,127d,143d), **tur** (14d,27c,68a,79b,117d, 174c), **tut** (52c)

T - U   **tau** (71b,91c,136c,161a), **Tiu** (7c,68c,147d,163d,166c,170c)

- TU   **utu** (35b,137c), **Utu** (96c,107a,159b)

T - V   **tav** (91c)

TW -   **Twi** (69c), **two** (26c,37d,80a,93a)

T - W   **taw** (90d,91c,96c,d,145b,161d), **Tiw** (68c,147d,163d), **tow** (45d, 58b,75d,125b)

257

T - X **tax** (13a,14a,80a,91d)

TY - **tye** (28c,134a), **tyg** (46b), **Tyr** (7c,68c,109c,147d,163d,170c,178a)

T - Y **thy, toy** (169d), **try** (7c,10d,14c,50a,51c,130a)

- TY **sty** (50a,53c)

T - Z **tez** (125c)

U - A **Uca** (56a), **ula** (72c,158c), **Uma** (43a,69b,153d), **Una** (54a,153b, 170c,183c), **uta** (53c,84d,93b,147c,150b), **uva** (64a,70c)

- UA **dua** (122d), **Kua** (95c), **pua** (74c,76a), **qua** (13c,80a,89c,147a), **rua** (118c), **Rua** (16b), **sua** (89d), **tua** (117a)

UB - **ube** (185b), **ubi** (90a,180d,185b)

- UB **bub** (22c), **cub** (92d,185d), **dub** (25c,46a,c,87a,105b,121a,140a), **fub** (29b,119d), **hub** (28b,118b,180c), **nub** (67b,94d,95c,118c 124d), **rub** (6b,24d,28c,43c,120c,179b), **sub** (90a,122d,172c), **tub** (21a,27a,36c,174d)

UC - **Uca** (56a)

- UC **duc** (61c)

UD - **Udi** (108a), **udo** (28a,30c,48c,84b,c,d,136c,149d)

U - D **und** (66b), **urd** (17b,184b), **Urd** (68d,107d)

- UD **bud** (22c), **cud** (126c,135a), **dud** (21c,54a), **lud** (100a), **Lud** (23c, 144b), **mud** (6c), **pud** (59d,73c,115a), **rud** (26d,57b), **sud** (59a)

U - E **ube** (185b), **ule** (23a,27d,134c,158c,168d), **ume** (11d), **une** (13b, 61a,62b,95c), **ure** (40a,139d,155d,158b,d), **Ure** (138d,185d), **use** (7b,47a,49d,64c,109b,168b,c,181b), **Ute** (145c,180b), **uve** (185b)

- UE **cue** (7a,27b,92c,117d,124b,132c,146c,159a), **due** (7b,115b,124c), **gue** (176c), **hue** (33c,143b), **lue** (146b), **pue** (52c), **que** (62d), **rue** (76a,b,129c,150d,183a), **sue** (119c), **Sue** (63a,178a,183d), **tue** (114b)

UF - **ufo** (59a)

- UF **ouf** (52c)

UG - **ugh** (52c)

- UG **bug** (24b,66b,81b), **dug** (129a), **fug** (129a), **hug** (32c,49d), **jug** (118c, 123d), **lug** (27a,45d,47b,73c,136b), **Lug** (28b), **mug** (46b,54a,65a), **pug** (45a,101a,108a,148d), **rug, tug** (45d,125b), **vug** (28a,66a)

U - H **ugh** (52c), **ush**

- UH **auh** (52c), **huh** (52c)

UI - **uit** (47a,111d,151a)

U - I **ubi** (90a,180d,185b), **Udi** (108a), **uji** (146d), **uni** (34c,118d,122c), **Uni** (51d), **UPI** (107a,182d), **Uri** (162d), **uvi** (185b)

- UI **dui** (46d), **hui** (14a,30b,56d,114c), **Kui** (86a,88c,146a), **qui** (62d), **Sui** (30b), **tui** (47c,114b,117a)

UJ - **uji** (146d)

- UK **auk** (19b), **ouk** (140c), **Suk** (107b)

UL - **ula** (72c,158c), **ule** (23a,27d,134c,158c,168d), **Ull** (7c,68c,146b, 164d), **ulm** (49c), **Ulm** (40d), **ulo** (34b,80d), **ulu** (87a)

U - L **Ull** (7c,68c,146b,164d)

258

- UL Bul (25d,102a), Ful (158b), gul (134a), mul (188), nul (108c,177a), pul (190), Pul (14a)

UM - Uma (43a,69b,153d), ume (11d), umu (112a)

U - M ulm (49c), Ulm (40d)

- UM aum (189), bum (21b), cum (159b), dum (45c,67b,113a), gum (7b, 53c,80b,130c,156b), hum (24d,46b,150d), Jum (39c), lum (30a), mum (30d,95a,146c), rum (8c,92d), sum (8a,123a,167c), tum (26d), Tum (143a,159b)

UN - Una (54a,153b,170c,183c), und (66b), une (13b,61a,62b,95c), uni (34c,118d,122c), Uni (51d), uno (83c,151d), uns (66d,174c), Unu (24d)

U - N urn (36c,174d)

- UN bun (25b,73b), dun (19a,39d,46d,71a,97d,115b,160b), fun, gun (56d,131a,146a), Hun (16c,21d,174b), mun (157b), nun (24c,91c, 117d,129d,147b), Nun (29a,85c), pun (119c), run (10d,23c,58d, 110d,148d,153b,154b,167d), sun (75d,111a,117b,155b), tun (23b, 27a,182b), wun (24c), Yun (88d)

U - O udo (28a,30c,48c,84b,c,d,136c,149d), ufo (59a), ulo (34b,80d), uno (83c,151d), Uro (192)

- UO duo (46d,113a,171d), Luo (107b), quo (188)

UP - UPI (107a,182d)

- UP cup (46b,69d,118b,170a), gup (70a), hup (35a), kup (188), pup (141b,148d,185d), sup (46b,104a,162b), tup (115a,117d,127d, 143d)

- UQ suq (22a,97a)

UR - urd (17b,184b), Urd (68d,107d), ure (40a,139d,155d,158b,d), Ure (138d,185d), Uri (162d), urn (36c,174d), Uro (192), Uru (192)

- UR bur (123b), cur (101d), dur (95c), Eur. (36c), fur, gur (159a), Hur (91d), Jur (107b), Lur (116c), mur (63a,177d), nur (67d), our (124c), pur, rur (132b), sur (34a,62b,d,104b,151a,152d,174a), tur (14d,27c,68a,79b,117d,174c)

US - use (7b,47a,49d,64c,109b,168b,c,181b), ush

U - S uns (66d,174c)

-US aus (66c), Aus (98b), bus (125b,168b), Gus (96a), jus (61d,90b), Mus (104a,132c), ous (158b), pus (89b,138a), rus (89b,138a), sus (117c), Sus (160c,181b)

UT - uta (53a,84d,93b,147c,150b), Ute (145c,180b), utu (35b, 137c), Utu (96c,107a,159b)

U - T uit (47a,111d,151a)

- UT aut (34d,89d), but (36a,52b,156b,173c), cut (30c,32b,145c), fut (188), gut (114d,130a), hut (143c), jut (53a,124a), lut (189), mut (39c), Mut (9b,127a), nut (24c,32d,38b,54d,64a,65d,86b,141c, 165a), Nut (69a), out (6b,14b,60b,69d,80a,108b,185c), put (65a, 69d,90b), rut (73a), tut (52c)

U - U ulu (87a), umu (112a), Unu (24d), Uru (192), utu (35b,137c), Utu (96c,107a,159b)

UV - uva (64a,70c), uve (185b), uvi (185b)

- UX	aux (6d,61a), **dux** (31d,64a,90c), **lux** (79d), **rux** (154a,184d)
- UY	buy, guy (55b,131b,155d), **Guy** (96a), **muy** (152d,175d), **puy** (61d)
- UZ	guz (188)
VA -	**Vac** (153b), **vae** (176b), **vag** (174b,178a), **Val** (91d), **van** (7b,59d, 60a,63d,90c), **vas** (46d,89d,119c,133d,175d), **vat** (31b,36c,163a, 170c), **vau** (91c)
V - A	via (132a,133a,b,179a)
- VA	ava (78d,86a,116a,120d,139a,167b), **Ava** (24c), **Eva** (157a,183c), iva (76a,97b,127b,185b), **ova** (48d), **uva** (64a,70c)
V - C	**Vac** (153b)
V - D	**Vod** (16a)
VE -	vee (58a,91c,106a), **Vei** (91d), **vet, vex** (7c,10d,44c,82c)
V - E	vae (176b), **vee** (58a,91c,106a), **vie** (36c,157c,170c), **voe** (17a,81b)
- VE	ave (54c,71d,73a,122a,134a,136d), **eve** (47a,131a,143a,165d,171c), **Eve** (183c), **ive** (158c), **uve** (185b)
V - F	vif (62a)
V - G	vag (174b,178a), **vog** (189), **vug** (28a,66a)
VI -	via (132a,133a,b,179a), **vie** (36c,157c,170c), **vif** (62a), **vim** (50b, 176b), **vin** (63a,182b), **vir** (89c), **vis** (59d,89b,d,90b,176b), **vix,** (89d,138b), **viz** (105b)
V - I	**Vai** (91d), **Vei** (91d)
- VI	ovi (34a), **uvi** (185b)
V - L	vol (155a,182d)
V - M	vim (50b,176b)
V - N	van (7b,59d,60a,63d,90c), **vin** (63a,182b), **von** (66d,67a)
VO -	**Vod** (16a), **voe** (17a,81b), **vog** (189), **vol** (155a,182d), **von** (66d, 67a), **Vor** (68d), **Vot** (56d), **vow** (119c,150a), **vox** (90a,177a)
V - R	vir (89c), **Vor** (68d)
V - S	vas (46d,89d,119c,133d,175d), **vis** (59d,89b,d,90b,176b)
V - T	vat (31b,36c,163a,170c), **vet, Vot** (56d)
VU -	vug (28a,66a)
V - U	**Vau** (91c)
V - W	vow (119c,150a)
V - X	vex (7c,10d,44c,82c), **vix** (89d,138b), **vox** (90a,**177a**)
V - Z	viz (105b)
- VY	ivy (32b,38c,176b)
WA -	wad (94d,97b,109c,112b,149d), **wag** (85b,104a,183a), **wah** (113c), **wan** (113a), **war** (157c), **was** (166c,175c), **Was** (24d), **wat** (73d, 140d,163a,180b), **waw** (12b,91c), **wax** (28b,72a,80b,120c), **way** (37d,96b,134b,164d)
W - A	**Wea** (192)
- WA	awa (100a,139a), **iwa** (63c)
W - B	web (50d,70a,98c,99a,106c,149b)
W - D	wad (94d,97b,109c,112b,149d), **wed** (97a,173c)

WE -   Wea (192), web (50d,70a,98c,99a,106c,149b), wed (97a,173c), wee (52c,100c,148c), Wei (30b,162b), wen (40c,72a,110a,170c,177b), wet (40d,46a,101a,124a,127c,149c), wey (173b)

W - E   wee (52c,100c,148c), woe (25b), wye (91c)

- WE   awe (81d,100a,130d,175b,182c), ewe (88a,143d), owe

W - G   wag (85b,104a,183a), wig (73b)

WH -   who (129c), why (52c)

W - H   wah (113c)

WI -   wig (73b), win (7a,17b,64b,123b), wis (79d,164c), wit (78d,85b, 177b)

W - I   Wei (30b,162b)

- WI   Twi (69c)

- WL   awl (145b,167a), owl

- WM   cwm (31b,37b,103d)

WN -   WNW (35b)

W - N   wan (113a), wen (40c,72a,110a,170c,177b), win (7a,17b,64b,123b), won, wun (24c) wyn (110a)

- WN   awn (12c,17b,140a), own (6d)

WO -   woe (25b), won, woo, wop, wow (52c,158a)

W - O   who (129c), woo

- WO   Lwo (107b), Pwo (88c), two (26c,37d,80a,93a)

W - P   wop

WR -   wry (13d)

W - R   war (157c)

WS -   WSW (35b)

W - S   was (166c,175c), Was (24d), wis (79d,164c)

W - T   wat (73d,140d,163a,180b), wet (40d,46a,101a,124a,127c), wit (78d,85b,177b)

WU -   wun (24c)

W - W   waw (12b,91c), WNW (35b), wow (52c,158a), WSW (35b)

W - X   wax (28b,72a,80d,120c)

WY -   wye (91c), wyn (110a)

W - Y   way (37d,96b,134b,164d), wey (173b), why (52c), wry (13d)

XA -   xat (167c)

- XA   oxa (29c)

XE -   xer (34a)

- XE   axe (30c,40c,167a), Exe (43a)

- XO   exo (122d)

X - R   xer (34a)

X - T   xat (167c)

YA -   yah (52c), yak (112c,161d,165b), yam (48c,121d,160b,170c), Yao (30a,c,104b), yap (16c,29b,122a), yar (72a), Yau (30c), yaw (43a, 155d)

Y - A   yea (7c,175c)

- YA   aya (77b,166b), Aya (143c), iya (95b,108d,111c), Mya (31c)

YE -   yea (7c,175c), yen (33b,42d,93c,174a), yep, yes (7c,55a), yet (18b, 24d,64c,77c,80a,108c,156b,165b), yew (36a,52a,b,145d,168c,d) yez

- YE   aye (7c,9b,55a,60a), bye (38c,141d), dye (33c,154d), eye (93d, 111b,140d), lye (8d,27d,93b), nye (72a,116d), Nye (9c,18b), oye (139c), Pye (50d,55a), rye (28b,70b,72d), sye (40c,46c,139b,141a, 167a), tye (28c,134a), wye (91c)

- YG   tyg (46b)

Y - H   yah (52c)

YI -   yin (140a), Yin (30b,143c,185b), yip (16c)

Y - I   yoi (52c,79a)

Y - K   yak (112c,161d,165b), yok (10c,185a)

- YL   kyl (76d,79b)

Y - M   yam (48c,121d,160d,170c), yom (41a)

- YM   gym (154a), Nym (54c,76a)

Y - N   yen (33b,42d,93c,174a), yin (140a), Yin (30b,143c,185b), yon (44c,112a,164d), Yun (88d)

- YN   lyn (140c,178d), syn (122d,183b), wyn (110a)

YO -   yoi (52c,79a), yok (10c,185a), yom (41a), yon (44c,112a,164d), you, yow (52c)

Y - O   Yao (30a,c,104b)

- YO   iyo (7d,176b)

Y - P   yap (16c,29b,122a), yep, yip (16c)

- YP   cyp (169d), gyp (29b,42a,160c), hyp

Y - R   yar (72a)

- YR   pyr (92a,b,122c,173b), Tyr (7c,68c,109c,147d,163d,170c,178a)

Y - S   yes (7c,55a)

- YS   lys (58b,92b)

Y - T   yet (18b,24d,64c,77c,80a,108c,156b,165b)

YU -   Yun (88d)

Y - U   Yau (30c), you

- YU   ayu (160c)

Y - W   yaw (43a,155d), yew (36a,52a,b,145d,168c,d), yow (52c)

- YX   Nyx (69b), pyx (31a,51d,75d)

Y - Z   yez

ZA -   zac (27c), zag (84a), zak (188), Zal (135d), Zan (186b), zar (188), zat (148a), zax (148a)

Z - A   zea (95c), Zoa (20b)

Z - C   zac (27c)

Z - D   zed (91c)

ZE -   zea (95c), zed (91c), zee (81b,91c), zel (40c), Zen (24a), Zep, zer (188)

Z - E   zee (81b,91c), Zoe (36b,183c)

262

Z - F   Zif (102a)

Z - G   zag (84a), zig (84a)

Z - H   zoh (13d,186b)

ZI -   Zif (102a), zig (84a), Zio (147d,163d), zip (24b,50b,176b), Ziu (147d,163d)

Z - K   zak (188)

Z - L   Zal (135d), zel (40c)

Z - N   Zan (186b), Zen (24a)

ZO -   zoa (20b), Zoe (36b,183c), zoh (13d,186b), zoo (181b)

Z - O   Zio (147d,163d), zoo (181b)

- ZO   azo (107c)

Z - P   Zep, zip (24b,50b,176b)

Z - R   zar (188), zer (188)

Z - T   zat (148a)

Z - U   Ziu (147d,163d)

Z - X   zax (148a)

FOUR-LETTER WORDS

AA - -   Aalu (6b,48d), Aani (45a,48d), Aare, Aaru (6b,48d)

- AA -   baal (142b), baas (97c), caam (93d), Faam (111a), gaal (23b,174d), Haab, (97d), haaf (57d), haak (57b,178a), haar (139c), kaan (93d, 116c), kaat (105d), laap (51d,91b,141d), maal (188), ma'am (95a, 166b), maar (177a), Maas (132a), Maat (69a,b,85d), Naab, naam (44c), Naam (105d), paal (188), paar (28c,137a), raab (32d), raad (14a,49b,151a,165b), Raad (151a), raas (91b), Saad (12b), saah (188), saal (66c,73b), Saan (24d), Saar (63b,102d,132a), Taal (7d, 88c,151a), taar (12b), Waac, waag (71d,101d)

- - AA   blaa, chaa (162b), draa (188)

A - - A   Abba (20a,55a,161c), Abfa (76b), Abia (18d,137a), abra (26b), Abra, acca (53b,d), acta (41d,123d,128d,164c), adda (147d), Adda (68c,119d,157a,182a), aera (8a), Aeta (94d,100a,106b,117a), Afra (183c), agha (35a,171a), agla (7a), agra (26d,34d), Agra (161b), agua (152d,166c,178c), Aida (110d,175c), Aira (70d), Akha (86a,c), akia (74c), Akka (125d), akra (176a), Akra (191), akua (120d), alba (98b,181a), Alba (151d), Alca (14c,128b), alda (152b), Alda (110d,150c), Alea (14b,31c,167d), alfa (70d), alga (141b,c), alia (89d), alla (6d), alma (40d,53d,146d,147a), Alma 38d, 183c), alta (89c,152d), Alva (151d), Alya (155b,c), amba (161a), amia (22c,170d), amla (48a,161d,168c,169a), amma (6a), amra (77c), anba (36d), anda (23a,168c), anna (190), Anna (110c,166d, 183c), anoa (28a,60a,112c,181c), ansa (73c,93d,137c), anta (83d, 117c,d,121a), Anta (164a), apia (121b), aqua (90a,178c), arba (135d,171a), arca (9a,22c,29d,115a,130a), Arca (101b), area (37d, 38a,44c,53a,93b,110d,127d,138c,168a,186d), aria (8b,98c,150a,c, 170c), arna (24a,181b), Aroa (175b), arpa (83b), arra (47d,52c,82b),

263

Arta (72b), **Arya** (80d), **asea** (39b,177c), **Asha** (191), **Asia** (48a), **asta** (188), **Asta** (107a,164c), **Atka** (11a), **atma** (150d), **atta** (58d, 90c,97d,160c,173d), **Atta** (94d,95d,100a,106b,117a), **atua** (120d), **Auca** (192), **aula** (66c,73b), **aura** (44c,49c,66a,96b,158a,170d, 177c), **Ausa, Azha** (155b)

AB - -   **abas** (61c), **Abba** (20a,55a,161c), **abbe** (32b,63b,123b), **Abby** (183d), **ABC's** (57a), **abed** (130c), **Abel** (7a,25b), **abet** (8b,15b,50a, 59b,75d,81c,141d,159d), **Abfa** (76b), **Abia** (18d,137a), **Abib** (102 a,b), **Abie** (96b,107a), **abir** (129a), **able** (26b,35b,126a,147c), **ably** (147c), **aboo** (17a), **Abot** (100c), **Abou** (48b,55a), **abox** (22d), **abra** (26b), **Abra, abri** (61c,62c,144b), **Absi** (191), **abut** (22a, 167c)

- AB -   **baba** (108d,120c,166c,171a), **babe, Babi** (116c), **babu** (77a), **baby, caba** (184c), **Faba, gabe** (162a), **gabi** (162a), **gaby** (59c,146d), **haba** (151d), **habe** (191), **Maba** (103a,168d), **mabi** (58d), **nabk** (30d, 164d), **nabo** (117a), **Nabu** (68c,183d), **Raba, rabi** (38d,74a), **Rabi** (14b,117b), **saba** (56a,117a), **Saba** (143d), **sabe, tabi** (84c, 149d), **tabu** (59d,111d), **Wabi** (192)

- - AB   **Ahab** (18c,26c,85b,86d,100d,116a,180b), **Arab** (30a,78b,c,106a, 107c,157b,160c,185d), **blab** (162b), **brab** (113b), **chab** (184a), **crab** (39b,144b,181b), **doab** (157c), **drab** (23d,29c,33d,46d,53b,d), **duab** (157c), **frab** (138c), **grab** (105b,142a,149b), **Haab** (97d), **Joab** (41a), **knab** (107a), **Moab** (18d,85a,86d,94a), **Naab, raab** (32d), **scab** (80b, 107d,157c), **slab** (148b), **snab** (23c,139a), **stab** (14c,87a,117c), **swab** (102b)

A - - B   **Abib** (102a,b), **Adib** (155b), **Agib** (12a,42d), **Ahab** (18c,26c,85b, 86d,100d,116a,180b), **Arab** (30a,78b,c,106a,107c,157b,160c,185d)

AC - -   **acca** (53b,d), **Acer** (96c), **ache** (79a,112d,185b), **acht** (66c), **achy, acid** (151a,162a), **Acis** (64b), **acle** (13d,82c,115d), **acme** (39c,115c, 186b), **acne** (147c), **acon** (62c,140d), **acor** (6d), **acre** (39b,56a,88b), **Acre, acta** (41d,123d,128d,164c), **acth** (13b), **acto** (152b), **Acts, actu** (7a,89a), **acus** (89d,118a), **acyl** (6d)

- A C -   **Bach** (35c), **back** (75d,76d,159d), **Caca** (67a), **caco** (73b), **dace** (57a,b), **each, face** (159a,176c), **fact** (7a,128b), **hack** (40a,77c, 184d), **jaca** (84a), **jack** (26c,58a,127c), **Jack** (96b), **jacu** (19a,151b), **lace** (58b,179c), **lack** (178a), **lact** (34c), **lacy, mace** (49d,108d,153b, 154d,161a,178a), **mack, nach, paca** (132c,154a), **pace** (64b,98a, 153b,156a,170b,177d), **pack** (24b,140d), **paco** (9b,146d), **pacs** (94c), **pact** (8a), **raca** (19a,59c,130b,184d), **race** (116a,153b,154b, 169c), **rack** (32c,64b), **racy** (153b), **sack** (43d,118a,119d,182b), **saco** (189), **tace** (13a,155d), **tack** (28d,37d,54d), **tact** (43c,d,116a), **Vach** (153b), **Waco, Zach** (96b)

- - AC   **utac** (22d), **Waac**

A - - C   **aesc** (12d,64d), **alec** (10a,57c,d,76c,137c), **amic** (9d), **avec** (63a, 183a)

AD - -   **adad** (52c,56a), **Adad** (68c,157a,182a), **Adah** (25b,51b), **Adam** (26b,96a,111c) **adan** (102d), **Adar** (85c,102a), **adat** (90b,95d), **adde** (147d), **Adda** (68c,119d,157a,182a), **Addu** (68c,157a,182a), **Addy** (183d), **aden** (34b), **Aden, Ader** (18d), **Ades** (73a), **Adib** (155b), **adit** (51a,100a,114d), **admi** (65d), **ador** (153b), **adry** (164c), **adze** (40c,167a)

264

- AD - Badb (82b), bade, cade (25c,27a,76c,85d,116d), Cade (30c', cad⁵
(12a,103a,171a), cady (69d), Dada (13b,63a,157d), dado (41c,111c,
115c,177d), Eads (23b,24b,50b,82a), fade (181d,183b), fado (121c),
fady, gade, hade (66a,148c,173c), hadj (98b,118a), jade
(33c,65d,71d,166a), jadu (95a), jady, kada (188), kade (144a), kadi
(103a,171a), Kadu (191), lade (24c,26d,43c,93b,100a,132a,139d,
161b,178d), Ladd (143c), lady, made, Madi (174a), mado (14d,57a,
170b), padi (131b), rada (135c,172a), rade (138d), sadd (33a,40b,
58c,107b), sade (91d), sadh (77a), sado (26d,84d), sadr (94a), Sadr
(155b), vade (42c,67d,89b), wadd (109c), wade, wadi (46c,106a,
109a,128a,132a), wady (109a,128a,132a)

- - AD adad (52c,56a), Adad (68c,157a,182a), arad (13a,c,84a), bead (17a,
122a,146b), brad (54d,67c,105b), Chad (158b), clad (46a,82a),
dead, diad (113a), duad (113a,171d), dyad (113a), ecad (73a,
119b), egad (100a,109a), Fuad (54d), glad (85c), goad (80b,154b),
grad (28b), head (29d), Ibad (191), Irad (18d), Joad (50c), lead
(35d,43d,72b,74d,81a), load (24c,26d,161b), mead (46a,78a,97d,
99b), Mead (78a), orad (104a), Phad (155b), quad (33c,172a), raad
(14a,49b,151a,165b), read (116d,157d), road (37d,164d), Saad
(12b), scad (31a,57a,78b,88d,137c), shad (27d,57a,b,c), . spad
(105b), Spad (118d), stad (151b,167d,176b), swad (94d), toad (10a,
17a,63d,126d), udad (143d,144a,181c), woad (20d,47c)

A - - D abed (130c), acid (151a,162a), adad (52c,56a), Adad (68c,157a,
182a), aged (110a), alod (51c,55d,88a,124c), amid (9d,50a), apod
(59d), arad (13a,c,84a), arid (46c,85a), Arnd (67a), Arod (86c), avid
(47b,71a,186b)

AE - - aera (8a), aeri (34a), aero (8b,34a,b,58c,59a), aery (47b,51d,106c),
aesc (12d,64d), Aeta (94d,95d,100a,106b,117a)

- AE - Caen, daer (22b), daez, faex (46a), Gaea (47d,69a), Gael (28a,96c,
138d), haec (90a,164c), haem (122b), Jael (147b), laet (60d), nael
(189), saer (163a), tael (91d,179d), waeg (19b,72c,87a), waer (40b)

- - AE alae (182d), blae (93b), brae (76d,139a,c,140b,148c), Irae (43c),
koae (74b), quae (176b), spae (139c)

A - - E Aare, abbe (32b,63b,123b), Abie (96b,107a), able (26b,35b,126a,
147c), ache (79a,112d,185b), acle (13d,82c,115d), acme (39c,115c,
186b), acne (147c), acre (39b,56a,88b), Acre, adze (40c,167a),
agee (13d,15c,38d), ague (30a,55d,95c,137b), aide (7b,14a,75d),
aile (62b,63a,182c,d), aine (49b,62c,142c), aire (82c), Aire, ajee
(15c,139a), akee (168c), alae (182d), albe (133a)
alee (15c,75d,144b,157a,182a), Alle (14c), alme (40d,147a), aloe
(7d,20a,76a,b,92b,98b,119b,158b,167a,183d), amie (61d), ance
(158b,c,d), Ande (193), ange (61a), Anne (50c,84a,143b,183c), ante
(87a,89a,115b,120b,122b,125d,154d), a-one (52b,167b), apse (9b,
20a,31a,128c,130a,142b,175a), arme (63a,179b), Arne (35c,50c,
134d), asse (25a,60d,74a), atle (136d,161d,169b), Aude, auge
(123c,132b), aune (188), axle (153c,180c)

AF - - afar (44c), Afar (6c), afer (48a,182b), affy (18b), Afra (183c)

- AF - baff (69d), baft (14a,53b), cafe, daff (125d), daft (59c), gaff (57c,
d,152d,153a), haft (76d), Kafa (6c), raff (75b), raft (27b,33c,58c,
75b), safe (141d,157d,174d), Safi (191), Taft (29d), Wafd (49a),
waft (20d,58c)

- - AF deaf, goaf (104b), Graf (37c,66b,67a,107c,186b), haaf (57d), heaf (144a), leaf (55c,73c,119b), loaf (79b,94b), neaf (58a,73c), Olaf (108a,176b), Piaf (63c), Wraf

A - - F alef (91c), alif (12b), arif (127d), atef (39a,48d), Azof (20b,135d)

AG - - Agag (18c,86c,137a), agal (17c,36d), Agao (6c,73c), agar (7d,28c, 39c,103c,141c), Agau (73c), Agaz (193), aged (110a), agee (13d, 15c,38d), ager (47c,56a,89b,c,131d,133b), agha (35a,171a), Agib (12a,42d), agio (52c,60a,101c,123a), Agis (86d), agla (7a), agni (88a,89c), Agni (56d,68b), agog (47b,52c,86b), agon (12c,36c,41b, 55d,71b), agra (26d,34d), Agra (161b), agri (89b), agro (149d), agua (152d,166c,178c), ague (30a,55d,95c,137b)

- AG - baga (171b), bago (13d), cage (36a), cagy (178b), dagg (118c), dagh (76d), Dago, gage (28d,98a,119c,d), gagl (160b), hagg, hagi (84b), Iago (54b,111d,143c), Jaga (191), jagg, kago (113a), kagu (106c), Iago (83b,152b), magg (95b), magg (95b), Magh (102a), magi (123c), Magi (95b.116c.183a), naga (13d,33a,55b,127c), Naga (24c,77a,88c,176c), Nagy (78d), Paga (117a), page (51b,59b, 142d,159b), raga (56d,105a), rage (10c,30c,157a,161d), ragi (28b), saga (79b,91a,138a,157a,161b,c,168a), Saga, sage (13a,90d,100c, 141c,145c,180b,183a), sago (54c,59b,113b,125b,155c), sagy, vagi (38b), wage (27a,115b), yage (23a)

- - AG Agag (18c,86c,137a), brag (21a,175a), coag (45d,118a,163b), crag (132c), drag (74a,125b), flag (16b,50d,82b,88c,115a,155a), knag (115d,139c), krag (131c), peag (144a,178a), quag (21c,102c), shag (73b,105b,161d,166d), skag (7d,46d), slag (46c,99a,138c,148d, 177a), snag (11b,27b,35c,87c,124b,166a), stag (65a,98d), swag (22a,156c), waag (71d,101d)

A - - G Agag (18c,86c,137a), agog (47b,52c,86b), ajog, areg (116a,137a)

AH - - Ahab (18c,26c,85b,86d,100d,116a,180b), Ahaz (86d), ahem, Ahet (49a,102a), ahey (52c), Ahir (27b), Ahom (88c), ahoy (106a), ahum

- AH - bahi (60c), baho (122a), baht (146a), haha (55c,159c), kaha (123d), kahu (14d), maha (28c,88c,136d), mahr (103a), Oahu, paha (67b), pahi (21b,26a), paho (122a), Rahu (42b,48b), saha (188), sahh (188), Saho (6c), sahu (153d), taha (179b), tahr (68a,76d)

- - AH Adah (25b,51b), Amah (95b,108d,111c), arah (52c), ayah (108d), blah, drah (188), Elah (18c,86d), Etah (51c,71d), eyah (95b,108d, 111c), Ivah (18d), kyah (19a), Leah (19a,84a,87b,183c), Noah (88a, 99b), odah (170d), opah (23b,57a,b,86d), prah (21b,26a,95c,d), Ptah (48d,98c), saah (188), seah (188), shah (116c), Utah (180b), yeah

A - - H acth (13b), Adah (25b,51b), aich (9a), Alph (132a), amah (95b, 108d,111c), ankh (38d,162b), arah (52c), arch (29d,38b,39d,123d, 132c), ayah (108d)

AI - - aich (9a), Aida (110d, 175c), aide (7b,14a,75d), aile (62b,63a,182c, d), aine (49b,62c,142c), Aino (84a,c), aint, Ainu (84a,c), aipi (27a), Aira (70d), aire (82c), Aire, airs (123b), airy (177a,176d)

- AI - bail (43c), bain (61a), bait (15d,51a,94d,167b), caid (35a,151c, 152b), cain (169c), Cain (6a,7a,50d,88a,104c,143a), Dail (49a, 82b, c), dain (188), dais (119b), fail, fain (42d,67c,183b), fair (17a,55d),

266

fait (6d,61b), Gaia (47d,69a), gail (23b,174d), Gail (183d), gain (7a, b,124a,181d), gait (96b,179a), haik (57b,65b,108a), hail (6d,15a, 71d), hair (56b,164d), jail (123d), Jain (77b), kaid (29d,66a), kaif (88c), kaik (96c), kail (18c,22a.25a,79b), Kain, kair, laic (32b,90b, 107d,124a,141d), laid, lain, lair (37c.42b), Lais (17c), lait (62a), Maia (76b,109a,153b,155b,177c), maid (45b.142d), mail (12d,99b, 121c), maim (43d,81a,105c), main (29d,35d,123d), mais (61b), Naia (33a), naid (63c), naif (74b,105d). naik, nail (31d,54d,141d,161d, 173a), naio (107a,168c), Nair (45d), nais (63c,132a), paid (129c), pail, pain (7c), pair (22d,37d,85b,171d), pais (37d), qaid (35a), raia (107d), Raia (147b), raid (59d,80c), raik (188,189), rail (16b,19b,c, 37a,97b,138c,150c,177b), rain (121d,162d), raip (36d), rais (26c, 29d,75a,103b), Rais (106b), saic (86b,91d,175d), said (174c), Said (42d,101a,121b), sail (144c,185a), sain (20c,38d,48a), sair (140b, 150d), sais (48d,71d), tail (11d,27d,59b,143b), tain (166a), tair (68a,76d), tait (14d), vail (94b,124a,174b), vain (81a), vair (64c, 154c), waif (157b), wail (39b,88a), wain (177b), Wain, wait (26d, 42b,92c,155d,162a), zaim (170d), zain (41a)

- - AI   alai (171a), Alai (135c), anai (163b,181a), chai (72d), goai (106d, 168c), ngai (48a,159c), peai (98b), quai (88b,117c,180c), Thai (146a)

A - - I   Aani (45a,48d), abri (61c,62c,144b), Absi (191), admi (65d), aeri (34a), agni (88a,89c), Agni (56d,68b), agri (89b), aipi (27a), alai (171a), Alai (135c), Albi (58a), alii (74c,134c), ambi (34a,122c), amli (48a,161d,168c,169a), ammi (98c), amoi (62a), anai (163b, 181a), Andi (27d), anti (7d,111a,122b), Anti (193), apii (74c), arni (24a,181b), arui (11b,143d,144a,181c), asci (154a), assi (77d), Asti 83d,182b), Atli (14c,72b,79a,107d), Atri, auri (34a)

AJ - -   ajar (110c), Ajax (71b,162d), ajee (15c,139a), ajog

- AJ -   baju (84a), caja (152a), caji (180b), gajo (107c), haje (33a,48d), maja (151c), Maja (153b), majo, Naja (33a), pajo (122a), raja (77a, 123c), Raja, tajo (152a,d), yaje (23a)

AK - -   Akal (56d), Akan (191), akee (168c), akey (189), Akha (86a,c), akia (74c), Akim (135d,191), akin (8b,92b,129c), Akka (125d), akov (189), akra (176a), Akra (191), akua (120d)

- AK -   baka (52b), bake (139a), baku (26d,157b,168c), cake, caky, fake (123a,143c), faky, hake (57a,b), hakh (46d), hako (115b), haku (86d), jake (40d), Jake (96b), jako (71a), kaka (114b), kaki (84c, 106d), lake (117d), lakh (110c), laky, make (35b,36d,54a,123a) maki (91b), mako (18a,19a,20d,143c,168c,182c), Maku (192), oaks (154d), oaky, rake (41b,44c,134b,140d), Saka (10a), sake (84b,125d), saki (39c,84b,102a), take, takt (105a,163a), Taku (80c), taky, waka (26a), wake (134b,168a), wakf (103a), waky, Yaka (191), Yaki (193)

- - AK   Anak (67a), asak (13d,168c,169a), beak (19a), coak (45d,118a, 163b), dhak (48a,169a), Dyak (22b), feak (39d,171c), flak (11a), haak (57b,178a), Irak (99a,d), kiak (51c), kyak (51c), leak (110c), peak (9a,38c,159b,186b), siak (72d), soak (46c,137d), teak (41a, 48a,168c), weak (55b)

A - - K   amok (18b,63c), Anak (67a), asak (13d,168c,169a), asok (13d), Atik (155b)

267

AL - - alae (182d), alai (171a), Alai (135c), alan (45a,79a,183), Alan, alar (15c,145c,182d), alas (52c,136b,183b), alat (136d), alay (96c), alba (98b,181a), Alba (151d), albe (133a), Albi (58a), albo (34d,181a), Alca (14c,128b), alco (45b), alda (152b), Alda (110d, 150c), Alea (14b,31c,167d), alec (10a,57c,d,76c,137c), alee (15c, 75d,144b,157a,182a), alef (91c), alem (98b,155a,170d,171a), alen (40d,138a), alfa (70d), alga (141b,c), Algy (96b), alia (89d), alif (12b), alii (74c,134c), alim (103b,162c), alin (188), alit (44b,143a), Alix (183c), alky, alla (6d), Alle (14c), allo (34c), ally (14a,35c,d, 173c), alma (40d,53d,146d,147a), Alma (38d,183c), alme (40d, 147a), alms (29a), alod (51c,55d,88a,124c), aloe (7d,20a,76a,b,92b, 98b,119b,158b,167a,183d) alop (13d,46b,93d), alow (18a,172c), Alph (132a), Alps (85d), also (10b,18b,80a), alta (89c,152d), alto (152b,176c,177a), alum (14a,45c), Alur (191), Alva (151d), Alya (155b,c), Alys (183c)

- AL - Aalu (6b,48d), Bala (26c,66a), bald (16c), bale (24b,74a), bali, Bali, balk (118c,146a,156d), ball, balm (110a,172c), Balt (93a), balu (104b,159a,181d), cale (72d), calf, calk (78c,109a,141c,178d), call (145c,159b,176d), calm (8d,11d,112b,118d,126c,d,172b,173d), calo (72d), calp (92b), calx (23c,75c,112c), dale (43c,128a,174b), dali (168c,169b), fala (129b), fall (46b,141c), falx (133b), gala (55d), Gala (191), gale (181d), gali (6c), gall (19a,28c,29b,82c,160c, 176a), galt, hala (112b), hale (125b), Hale (9d,131a), half (101a), hall (37b,114d), halm, halo (14d,31b,92a,107b,131d), Hals (47a), halt (13b,28a,38d,156d), lalu (48d), kala (19a), kale (22a,25a, 119b,175a), kali (26d,67c,136d,167a), Kali (147b), kalo (162a), lala (129b), lalo (16b,34d,153a), Lalo (35c), mala (89b,c,90a,94b, 97d,109d,185c), male (154d), Male (45d), mali (27b), mall (95d,124b,143b), malm (32a,92b), malo (23a,74c,152a), malt (17c), Nala (77a), pala (189), Pala (88b), pale (113a,117c,178a), pali (122b), Pali (23d,24a,137b,175a), pall (32d,81b,112a), palm (59b, 168c,169b), palo (152c), palp (11a,55b,58b,167c), paly (194), rale (7c,23a,29d,41b), ralo (188), sala (152a,b,c), Sala (50c), sale (14c,61c,62b,c,168b), salp (109c,148d), salt (35d,105b,123a,136c, 141c,149d), tala (16d,113a,168c,d), talc (28d,63b,99c,100b,122a, 149c), tale (91a,185b), tali (189), talk, tall (118d), vale (54c,128a, 174b), Vale (7c,109c), vali (171a,176a), Vali (7c,109c), wale (70b, 131b,157c,163d,179a,180a,c,d), wali (171a), walk, wall, Walt (96b), Yale (173c), yali (171a)

- - AL agal (17c,36d), Akal (56d), Aral (135d), aval (70c), axal (120b), Baal (142b), beal (139d), bual (182c), coal (49c,64a), cral, deal (11d,16c,36c,44c,81a,168b), dhal (12b), dial (25c), dual (45c,171d), eral (51a), etal (89a), foal (78c), gaal (23b,174d), geal (47d,163c), goal (8b,109b,120b,125d), heal (158c), ical (158c), keal (25a), kral, leal (54b,94c,139d), maal (188), meal (72a,130b), Neal, odal (48a,88b, 112c), opal (20a,65d,67b,82b) oral (114a,153d,174c,175c), oval (48c,49c,127a), paal (188), peal (131c,d), pyal (175c), real (7a), rial (190), ryal (110a,190), saal (66c,73b), seal (10c,d,54d,64c,96a, 118b,128a), sial (112a), Taal (7d,88c,151a), teal (19b,20d,46c,d), udal (76b,88b,131c), unal (147a), ural, Ural (135c), uval (70c), veal, vial (148c), weal (124d,157c,180c,d), zeal (12c,55d)

A - - L Abel (7a,25b), acyl (6d), agal (17c,36d), Akal (56d), amil (45a,4t

268

185c), **amyl** (155c), **anil** (47c,80d,180b), **Aoul** (191), **Aral** (135d), **aril** (142a), **aval** (70c), **axal** (120b), **axil** (10c), **azul** (151d)

AM - -   **amah** (95b,108d,111c), **amar** (189), **amba** (161a), **ambi** (34a,122c), **ambo** (125b,128b), **amen** (14a,80b,94a,137a,149c,175c,184b), **Amen** (86d,127d,159b,164a), **amer** (61b), **Ames** (9c,82a), **Amex** (184d), **amia** (22c,170d), **amic** (9d), **amid** (9d,50a), **amie** (61d), **amil** (45a,48a,185c), **amin** (9d), **amir** (7c,12a,103a,b,123c,170d), **amit** (94a), **amla** (48a,161d,168c,169a), **amli** (48a,161d,168c,169a), **amma** (6a), **ammi** (98c), **ammo** (9d), **ammu** (9d), **amoi** (62a), **amok** (18b,63c), **Amon** (86d,96d,127d,159b,164a), **amor** (152b), **Amor** (39c,68b), **Amos** (96a,144b), **Amoy** (88c), **amra** (77c), **Amun** (86d,127d,159b,164a), **amyl** (155c)

- AM -   **came** (182b), **Came** (192), **camp** (163b), **dama** (65d,152b), **dame** (67b,87c,166b), **damn**, **damp** (101a), **Fama** (135a), **fame** (130a), **famn** (188), **Gama** (121c), **game** (64d,154a), **gamp** (172a), **hami** (78a), **iamb** (59c), **jama** (103b), **jamb** (12d,45c,118a,146b,174a), **jami** (103b), **Kama** (56d), **kame** (67b,139b), **kami** (68a,84b), **Kami** (88c,107c,144c), **lama** (23d,24a,91d,165b), **Lamb** (49c), **lame** (38d, 43d,73b), **lamp** (92a,94c), **mama**, **Mama** (116d), **mamo** (19a,d,74b), **Nama** (78c), **name** (8a,11b,d,25c,46c,107c,130b,157d,163b,166b), **Rama** (77a,80b,176d), **rame** (22d), **rami** (22d), **ramp** (65a,80b, 127b,148b), **sama** (105c,169d), **same** (44d,79b), **samh** (56b), **samp** (70b,77d,121b), **Tama** (192), **tame** (45a,b,66a), **Tame**, **tamp** (46b, 112b,121d,127d), **vamp** (80a,145a), **Yama** (57a,68a), **Zama** (73d, 141d)

- - AM   **Adam** (26b,96a,111c), **anam** (159a,168c), **Anam**, **Aram** (18d,50c, 105c,144b,161c), **Azam** (166c), **beam**, **Bram** (96a), **caam** (93d), **cham** (20a,29d), **Cham** (8c), **clam** (20b,101b), **cram** (157d), **dram** (46b,110c,121d,148c), **edam** (29c), **Elam** (18d,37d,82a,116c,144b), **enam** (70c,77a), **Enam** (85c), **exam**, **Faam** (111a), **flam** (169c), **foam** (63d,154b), **gram** (29d,99b,148d,160d,180a), **Gram**, **Guam**, **imam** (25c,102d,103a), **klam** (189), **Liam** (181d), **loam** (47d,150a), **lyam** (139a), **ma'am** (95a,166b), **miam** (14d), **naam** (44c,105b), **ogam** (82b,c), **olam** (51a,d,75c,81a), **pram** (15a), **ream** (18c,37d, 50d,113d,171c), **roam** (178a), **seam** (85b,d,160a,176d,185a), **sham** (41c,55b,60d,80a,123a,b,146d), **Siam** (163d,181a), **slam** (180d, 182d), **swam**, **team** (38c,72a,113a), **Tiam**, **tram** (170a), **Ulam** (67b), **wham** (157c)

A - - M   **Adam** (26b,96a,111c), **ahem**, **Ahom** (88c), **ahum**, **Akim** (135d,191), **alem** (98b,155a,170d,171a), **alim** (103b,162c), **alum** (14a,45c), **anam** (159a,168c), **Anam**, **Anim** (18d), **Aram** (18d,50c,105c,144b, 161c), **arum** (13a,39b,58d,92b,155c), **Arum** (66a), **asem** (9a,49a, 69c), **Asom** (18d), **atom** (101c,114c,180d), **Atum** (143a,159b), **Azam** (166c)

AN - -   **anai** (163b,181a), **Anak** (67a), **anam** (159a,168c), **anan** (49a,159a, 180c), **Anas** (46c,d), **Anat** (138c,147d), **Anax** (43c,120c), **anay** (72b,163b,181a), **anba** (36d), **ance** (158b,c,d), **ancy** (158c), **anda** (23a,168c), **Ande** (193), **Andi** (27d), **Andy** (96b), **Aner** (18d,96b), **anes** (110c,140a), **anet** (43c), **anew** (7c), **ange** (61a), **ango** (171a), **anil** (47c,80d,180b), **Anim** (18d), **anis** (55c), **ankh** (38d,162b), **anna** (190), **Anna** (110c,166d,183c), **Anne** (50c,84a,143b,183c),

269

anoa (28a,60a,112c,181c), **anon** (7d,14d,79d,80b,123a,145c,150c, 164a), **ansa** (73c,93d,137c), **anse** (61d), **ansu** (11d), **anta** (83d, 117c,d,121a), **Anta** (164a), **ante** (87a,89a,115b,120b,122b,125d, 154d), **anti** (7d,111a,122b), **Anti** (193), **anzu** (11d)

- AN - **Aani** (45a,48d), **Bana** (67a), **banc** (61a,85c), **band** (72a,157c), **bane** (74a,106b,120b,139a), **bang** (75d,105d,148a), **bani** (190), **bank** (18a,58c), **bans, bant** (43c), **Cana** (57a,64b,100c), **cane** (17b, 128a,156a,159a,177d), **Cane, cang** (184a), **cano** (152a), **cant** (28d, 81b,84d,90c,109b,136c,165d,166a), **Dana** (28a,96a,171d), **Dane** (85d,107d,138a), **dang, dank** (40b,101a), **dans** (62a), **Danu** (28a), **fana, fane** (30d,137a,162d), **fang** (167b), **Fano** (51d,96b,113c,d), **gane** (185b), **gang** (38c), **Gano** (132d), **hand** (60c,114c,115d,184c), **hang** (160a), **hank** (147c), **Hano** (125b), **Hans** (66d,96a), **hant** (67a), **jane** (190), **Jane** (183c), **Jann** (102d), **kana** (84d), **Kane** (74c), **k'ang** (30a), **Kano** (84c,177d), **kant** (28d), **Kant** (67a), **lana** (58a,66a,90a,184b), **land** (44a,163c), **lane** (134b,157b), **lank** (148b,164b), **lanx** (133a,b), **mana** (30a,120d,122a,159c), **mand** (28b), **mane, mani** (115c), **mann** (189), **Mann** (9c,48c,185c), **mano** (71d,73d,74b,83b), **Mans** (30a), **Manu** (10a,76d,77a,b), **Manx** (27b, 28a,82d), **many** (108d), **nana** (118b), **Nana** (15c,105d,116d,186d), **nane** (139d), **Pana, pane** (113c,155a,b), **pang** (165b), **Pani** (120c), **pank** (189), **pant, rana** (77a,123c), **Rana** (63d), **rand** (16d,22a, 131b,145a,b), **Rand** (69c), **rang, rani** (72d,77b,123c,127c), **rank** (31d,55d,70b,92c,94d,157d), **rann** (175c), **rant** (41c,127b,128a, 161d), **sana** (56a,166d), **Sana** (185d), **sand** (71d,146c), **sane** (128a), **sang, sank, sano** (152b), **sans** (63a,183b), **tana** (159a), **Tana** (87d), **Tane** (120d), **tang** (30b,58b,186b), **tanh** (97c), **tank** (175a,d), **Tano** (192), **uang** (131a), **vane** (179b,182a), **vang** (72d,134a,140b), **Vans** (107d), **wand** (120b,132c,156a), **wane** (41c,43c), **wang** (189), **want** (41b,42d,87b,106b,122a), **wany, Yana** (192,193), **yang** (30b,70a), **yank, Yank, zany** (24a,32d,59c)

- - AN - **adan** (102d), **Akan** (191), **alan** (45a,79a,183c), **Alan** (96a), **anan** (49a,159a,180c), **Aran** (18c,48c,64d,82d,174c), **Awan** (191), **azan** (102d), **bean** (91b,142a,175a), **bran** (23c,39a,72a,79c,70b), **Bran** (23c,50c), **chan** (26c,130c), **clan** (169c), **Coan** (37b), **cran** (160c), **cyan, dean** (33c,109d), **dhan** (124c), **dian** (46c,130d,170b), **Dian** (68d,69a,c,102b), **duan** (64b), **elan** (12c,41a,50d,62a,153c,177a, 186b), **Eoan** (41a,85b), **Evan** (96a), **Ewan, flan** (39d,40a,114d), **gean** (29c), **Goan, gran, guan** (151b), **Iban** (47c), **Iran** (6a,48c, 116b), **Ivan** (40c,85b,96a), **jean** (37c), **Jean** (183c), **Joan** (183c), **juan** (113a), **Juan** (96a), **kaan** (93d,116c), **khan** (7c,26c,81b,93d, 116c,123c,130c,166c), **kran** (190), **kuan** (30b,c), **Kuan, kwan** (30b), **lean** (128a,148b,152d,164b,166a), **loan, mean** (15a,42b, 146c,156b), **mian** (97c,147b,166b), **moan, ngan, oban** (190), **Olan** (115c), **Oman** (159a), **Onan** (18c,85c), **Oran, oxan, pean** (65c), **plan** (99b,124a,138b), **quan** (190), **roan** (78b,c,114c,128d,144a, 181a), **Saan** (24d), **Sean** (85b,96a), **Shan** (13c,80d,88c,101d), **scan** (52b,93d,98a,116d,128b,c,140d), **span** (23b,107b,113a,128b,162c), **Svan** (27d), **swan** (19b,33a) **tean** (140c167a), **than** (35b), **tran** (7a), **tuan** (95d,147b,166c), **ulan** (27d,88a), **uran** (101d), **Uran, uzan** (189), **wean** (8d,42d), **yean** (88a), **yuan** (190), **Yuan** (30b,101d)

A - - N   acon (62c,140d), adan (102d), aden (34b), Aden, agon (12c,36c, 41b,55d,71b), Akan (191), akin (8b,92b,129c), alan (45a,79a, 183c), Alan (96a), alen (40d,138a), alin (188), amen (14a, 80b,94a,137a,149c,175c,184b),   Amen   (86d,127d,159b,164a), amin (9d), Amon (86d,96b,127d,159b,164a), Amun (86d,127d, 159b,164a), anan (49a,159a,180c), anon (7d,14d,79d,80b,123a, 145c,150c,164a), Aran (18c,48c,64d,82d,174c), Asin (102a), aten (150a,159b), aton (150a,159b), Avon (143b), Awan (191) axon (106c,153c), ayin (91c), azan (102d), azon (127b)

AO - -   aone (52b,167b), Aoul (191)

- AO -   faon (33c,55a), gaol (123d), Gaol (164a), Gaon (85b), Jaob, Laos (80d,129c), naos (28a,71c,137a,163a), Naos (155b), paon (115b), Taos (192), Yaou (30c)

- - AO   Agao (6c,73c), dhao (24c), grao (189), guao (168c,169b), Miao (30a,b), omao (165b), prao (21b,26a,95c,d), tiao

A - - O   aboo (17c), acto (152b), aero (8b,34a,b,58c,59a), Agao (6c,73c), agio (52c,60a,101c,123a), agro (149d), Aino (84a,c), albo (34d, 181a), alco (45b), allo (34c), also (10b,18b,80a), alto (152b,176c, 177a), ambo (125b,128b), ammo (9d), ango (171a), apio (125b), areo (34c), Argo (12c,36b,c), Arno (27a), aroo (80c,82b), arro (52c), arto (34a), asno (151d), Ateo (120d), atmo (34d,174d), auto (34d)

AP - -   Apap (102a), apar (12d), aper (32d), Apet (97c), apex (39c,76c, 115c,118b,159b,166a,167b), apia (121b), apii (74c), apio (125b), Apis (17c,24b,49a,125a,136a), apod (59d), apse (9b,20a,31a,128c, 130a,142b,175a), Apsu (29a), Apus (36b,c)

- AP -   capa (152a,166b), cape (75a,96c,124b,161a), caph (91c), capp (27a), gape (185b), gapo (60a), gapy, Hapi (66a,107b,136a), hapu (106d), jape (85a,b), kapa (74b), kaph (91d), kapp, Lapp (108a), mapo (68a,148d), napa (25c,67d,90d), Napa (182c), nape (15b, 108c,d), napu (29d,80d), papa, pape (19b,113a), rapt (6c,27a,50d), sapa (70c), sapo (149c,166d), tapa (16c,32c,53b,56a,74b,104b,112b, 113d,120d), tape (16a,19a,128d), tapu, wapp (54b,133d,145d), yapa (113b), Yapp (22a)

- - AP   Apap (102a), atap (113b), chap (55b), clap (58b), drap (61b,c, 62a), flap (17b,59a,104a,118d,161a,182d), frap (45d,165c), heap (117d), knap (76d,107a,139b,159b,166a,170c,185b), laap (51d,91b, 141d), leap (26c), neap (165c,167a,177b), plap (54b), reap (7a,40a, 74a), shap, slap (24a,128c,148c), snap (23a,36d,38b,48b,54d,56c, 58c,149d), soap, swap (168a), trap (27b,67b,132b,149b), wrap (32b,51a)

A - - P   alop (13d,46b,93d), Apap (102a), asop (180b), atap (113b), atip (14b,166a), atop (112a,174a)

AQ - -   aqua (90a,178c)

- AQ -   waqf (103a)

- - AQ   Iraq (99a,d)

AR - -   Arab (30a,78b,c,106a,107c,157b,160c,185d), arad (13a,c,84a), arah (52c), Aral (135d), Aram (18d,50c,105c,144b,161c), Aran (18c, 48c,64d,82d,174c), arar (137a,168c), Aras, arba (135d,171a), arca

271

(9a,22c,29d,115a,130a), **Arca** (101b), **arch** (29d,38b,39d,123d, 132c), **area** (37d,38a,44c,53a,93b,110d,127d,138c,168a,186d), **areg** (116a,137a), **areo** (34c), **Ares** (49b,51b,68c,76a,97a,105c,110b, 178a,186d), **aret** (128c), **Argo** (12c,36b,c), **aria** (8b,98c,150a,c, 170c), **arid** (46c,85a), **arif** (127d), **aril** (142a), **aris** (101b), **arme** (63a,179b), **arms, army** (78c), **arna** (24a,181b), **Arnd** (67a), **Arne** (35c,50c,134d) **arni** (24a,181b), **Arno** (27a), **arn't, Aroa** (175b), **Arod** (86c), **aroo** (80c,82b), **arow** (92c,158b), **arpa** (83b), **arra** (47d,52c,82b), **arro** (52c), **Arta** (72b), **arto** (34a), **arts** (138c), **arty, arui** (11b,143d,144a,181c), **arum** (13a,39b,58d,92b,155c), **Arum** (66a), **Arya** (80d)

- AR -   **Aare, Aaru** (6b,48d), **bara** (188), **barb** (20b,57d,78b,117d,120a,b, 124b), **bard** (12a,120a), **bare** (43d,157c), **bari** (79c), **Bari** (37c,83d), **bark** (115c), **barm** (185b), **barn** (156d), **baro** (71a,122c), **barr** (49b), **Bart** (96b), **baru** (168c), **cara** (83a), **Cara** (48b,183c), **card** (33d, 114d), **care** (11b,14c,35d,150a,184d), **cark** (26d,184d), **carl** (115c, 135d), **Carl** (96a), **carn** (156c), **caro** (83a,183d), **carp** (27d,38d, 40c,55a,56c,57a), **carr** (120d,140a), **cart** (171d,175a,177b), **Dara** (18d), **Dard**, **dare** (28d,41b,42a,74d,175b), **Dare** (57a), **dari** (38a, 70b), **dark** (47a,67d,109b,160b), **darn** (130b), **darr** (163c), **dart** (13b,88a,100c,120b,153a,160c), **Dart** (100c), **earl** (107c), **earn** (42d,64b,99a), **fard** (112d), **fare** (43c,59b,67d,123b), **farl** (138c, 140b), **farm** (165d), **faro** (65a), **gara** (190), **garb** (32c,46a), **gare** (61b,c,62c,127c,184b), **Garm** (178c), **garn** (67d,185b), **Garo** (88c), **Harb** (191), **hard** (109b), **hare** (91b,132c), **hark** (92d), **harl** (16b,56b, 59a), **harm** (40b,81a), **harp** (105a,129a), **hart** (41d,154d), **jarl** (40d, 107d), **kara** (132a), **Kari** (14d), **Karl** (96a), **karn** (156c), **karo** (106d), **Lara** (25c), **lard** (54d,61a,71a,110a), **lari** (78a,101c), **Larl** (72c), **lark** (19a,63d,177b), **larp** (51d), **Lars** (51d,121b), **mara** (114d), **Mara** (24a,d,105b,107b), **marc** (70c), **Marc** (96a), **mare** (78b,108b), **mari** (16a,61d), **mark, Mark** (52a,96a,146b,155a), **marl** (32a,42c, 55d), **maro** (144d), **Mars** (68c,118d,119a,178a), **mart** (49d,97a), **Mart** (96b,183d), **maru** (84c,144d), **Mary** (50c,126b,183c), **nard** (13a, 97c,102b,110a,153c), **Nare** (93c), **nark** (81a,156d), **nary** (108b), **oary, para** (134c,170d), **Para** (18a,51d), **parc** (62b,112c), **pard** (27b, 91b), **pare** (115c,129a), **pari** (34a,180a), **park, parr** (136d,147c), **pars** (89d), **part** (44d,60d,121c,159c), **paru** (57a), **rara** (119a), **rare** (138b,164b,172b,173d), **Sara** (24d,183c), **sard** (26d,28d,65d,111a, 142b,156d), **Sarg** (96d,125c), **sari** (48b,65b,77b), **Sark** (28d), **Sart** (82b, 103b, 170d), **tara** (22a, 55c, 113a, 168c), **Tara** (82b,c,138b), **tare** (9a,18d,41a,176a,179d), **tari** (47d,69a), **tarn** (87d,103d,120d), **taro** (13c,48c,49b,64b,112b,120a,133d,155c,170a, c), **tarp** (26b,178d), **tart** (114d), **vara** (151d), **vare** (179b), **vari** (34d,91b,134d,174d), **vary** (28d,43c), **ward** (31c,55c,86b), **ware** (27d,35a), **warf, warm** (7c,75b,163b), **warn** (7b), **warp** (36c,165a, 171c), **wart** (124d), **wary** (27d,176b), **yard** (152c), **yare** (96b,124b, 128b), **yark** (22c), **yarl** (40d,107d), **yarn** (154b,161b,184b), **yarr** (72a), **Yaru** (48d), **zarf** (39c,155a), **zarp** (120c)

- - AR   **Adar** (85c,102a), **afar** (44c), **Afar** (6c), **agar** (7d,28c,39c,103c,141c), **ajar** (110c), **alar** (15c,145c,182c), **amar** (189), **apar** (12d), **arar** (137a,168c), **asar** (67b), **atar** (58d,116c,134a), **Avar** (27d,108a), **bear** (27a,50b,113c,155c), **Bhar** (191), **boar** (77c,117c,160c,181c),

272

char (24d,138c,170b), czar (42d,49d,60b,135c), dear, Dhar, duar, Edar (18d), fear (113c,155a), gear (32c,112a,167b), gnar (72a), guar (46c,59d), haar (139c), hear (75b,c,92d), hoar (63d,71a, 181a), inar (65b), Isar (41a,104c,132a), Iyar (102b), izar (65b, 103b,155b), joar (100a), juar (100a), khar (189), knar (87c,134b), kuar (102a), kyar (33a), lear (139d), Lear (37a,143b, liar (98d), maar (177a), near (11d,32c,107b), omar (103b), Omar (48c,51b, 163b), osar (51b,67b,131b), paar (28c), pear (64a), rear (15b,23a, b,24a,51b,76d,127c), roar (145c) Saar (63b,102d,132a), scar (31a, 184d), sear (23d,27d,72d,138c), soar (59a), spar (22c,24c,64b, 97b,100b,144d), star (14a,21c,94c,100c), taar (12b), tear (67c, 87b,130a), thar (68a,76d), tiar (39a,75a,121a), tsar (42d,49d, 60b,135c), tzar (42d,49d,60b,135c), usar (8d,16c), wear (50b), year, Zoar

A - - R Abir (129a), Acer (96c), acor (6d), Adar (85c,102a), Ader (18d), ador (153b), afar (44c), Afar (6c), afer (48a,182b), agar (7d,28c, 39c,103c,141c), ager (47c,56a,89b,c,131d,133b), Ahir (27b), ajar (110c), alar (15c,145c,182d), Alur (191), amar (189), amer (61b), amir (7c,12a,103a,b,123c,170d), amor (152b), Amor (39c,68b), Aner (18d,96b), apar (12d), aper (32d), arar (137a,168c), asar (67b), Aser (84a), Askr (107d), asor (75c,105a), Asur (68c), atar (58d,116b,134a), Ater (18c), Auer (79a), Avar (27d,108a), aver (7c,14a,15c,41c,95c,140d,155c,160b,184c)

AS - - asak (13d,168c,169a), asar (67b), asci (154a), asea (39b,177c), asem (9a,49a,69c), Aser (84a), Asha (191), ashy (113a,178a), Asia (48a), Asın (102a), Askr (107d), asno (151d), asok (13d), Asom (18d), asop (180b), asor (75c,105a), asse (25a,60d,74a), assi (77d), asta (188), Asta (107a,164c), Asti (83d,182b), Asur (68c)

- AS - base (6a,43b,44b,51c,60c,79b,94b,122b), bash, bask (94d), bass (57b,c,177a), bast (16c,56a,117b,184a), Bast (27b), casa (152b), case (22c,36c,81c,91a,108c), cash (101c), cask, Caso (82d), cass (140c,177a), Cass (147a), cast (165b,167c), dash (125c,162d), dasi (77a), ease (7c,8d,35a,100d,129d,130b,c,150c), East (111b), easy (54a,146d,149d,172b), fash (140c,176a), fass (189), fast (56d, 126c,141d,160c,173a,d), gash (40a), gasp (113c), hase (74d), hash, hasp (31d,54d,153c), hast (160d), jass (160d), kasa (48a), kasi (116b), kasm (189), lash (58c,87b,165c,180d), Lasi (191), lass (95b, last (36c,50b,145a,174c), masa (37a), mash (39b,156c), mask (44a,45c), mass (8a,24b,35b,142d), mast (17c,108d,120b,144d,152d), masu (57a,84c), nase (26b,75a,124b), Nash (9c), nasi (34c,108a,115a), Nast (9c,27a), oast (15d,86b,112a), pasa (46a,127c,152c), pasi (94b), pass (110b,155c), past (25c,69d,165d), rasa (51c), rase (42b, d,91d), rash (75a), rasp (56b,70d,140d), sasa (55c), sash (18a,45c, 67b,182b), sass, tash (154d), task (156b), Tass (107a,135d,151b), vasa (46d,114a,160b,175d), Vasa, vase, vast (78d,79d), vasu (106c), Vasu (176d), wash, wasp, wast

- - AS abas (61c), alas (52c,136b,183b), Anas (46c,d), Aras, baas (97c), bias (43b,123a), blas (6c,49c), Blas (67b), bras (61a), Dyas (66a), ELAS (71c), eyas (106c,173a), gras (78b), Idas (27b,71c), Iras (11b,32a), khas (153a), kras (76d), kvas (135c), Lias (66a), Lyas (66a), Maas (132a), mias (111a), Nias (82d), oras (40d), quas

(135c), **upas** (84d,120b,168c,d), **Usas** (68d), **utas** (49a,109c), **Xmas,
yeas** (177c), **Zoas** (20b)

A - - S **abas** (61c), **ABC's** (57a), **Acis** (64b), **Acts, acus** (89d, 118a), **Ades**
(73a), **Agis** (86d), **Aias, Airs** (123b), **alas** (52c,136b,183b), **alms**
(29a), **Alps** (85d), **Alys** (183c), **Ames** (9c,82a), **Amos** (96a,144b),
Anas (46c,d), **Anes** (110c,140a), **anis** (55c), **Apis** (17c,24b,49a,
125a,136a), **Apus** (36b,c), **Aras, Ares** (49b,51b,68c,76a,97a,105c,
110b,178a,186d), **aris** (101b), **arms, arts** (138c), **ates** (160c), **atis**
(76d,102a), **Aves** (19d), **Avis** (89a,183c), **avus** (89b), **axis** (28b,
41d,77c,153c), **ayes** (177c)

AT - - **atap** (113b), **atar** (58d,116b,134a), **atef** (39a,48d), **aten** (150a,
159b), **Ateo** (120d), **Ater** (18c), **ates** (160c), **Atik** (155b), **atip**
(14b,166a), **atis** (76d,102a), **Atka** (11a), **atle** (136d,161d,169b),
Atli (14c,72b,79a,107d), **atma** (150d), **atmo** (34d,174d), **Atmu**
(143a,159b), **atom** (101c,114c,180d), **aton** (150a,159b), **atop** (112a,
174a), **Atri, atry** (141b), **atta** (58d,90c,97d,160c,173d), **Atta** (94d,
95d,100a,106b,117a), **Attu, atua** (120d), **Atum** (143a,159b)

- AT - **bata** (30a,142d), **bate** (43c,91b,100d), **bath, Bath** (50d,151c), **batt**
(37c), **batz** (190), **cata** (122c), **cate** (165c), **Cato** (132d,133b),
data (54a), **date** (64a,153a), **dato** (95c,102a,117a), **datu** (95c,102c,
117a), **eats, fate** (42d,52a,87a,94a), **gata** (143c), **gate** (51a,121b),
Gath (117a), **hate** (6a,43a), **hath, Hati** (48d), **jati** (27b), **jato** (173b),
Kate (143c,183d), **kath** (14a), **Katy** (183d), **lata** (85d,95d), **late**
(128c), **lath** (157c), **latu** (190), **mate** (18c,35b,41d,113a,154a,162c),
math (77a), **Matt, maty** (80c), **Nata** (15c,47c), **Nate** (22b), **Nath**
(155c), **Nato** (6a,8d), **natr** (189), **Natt** (107b), **oath** (119c,150a),
pata (32c,160d), **pate** (39a,74d), **path** (132a,134b), **pato** (46d), **patu**
(179b), **rata** (29d,56b,89d,96c,106d,120c,168c), **rate** (11d,14a,31d,
36b,51d,52a,70b,85c,112b,123b,127d,128a,138c,143a,174b), **rath**
(29a,76d,162d), **rati** (189), **rats, sate** (32d,52c,67d,70d,137c,159d),
sati, Sati (49a,126b,147b), **tate** (183a), **tatt** (87c), **tatu** (12d), **Tatu,
Wate** (141a), **watt, Watt** (82a,173b,177c), **yate** (51d,168c), **yati**
(76d), **zati** (21d)

- - AT **adat** (90b,95d), **alat** (136d), **Anat** (138c,147d), **beat** (58c,87b,131a,
164d,165b,180d), **bhat** (80c), **blat** (25b), **boat** (27b,106a), **brat,
chat** (9b,19c,161c), **coat** (160a), **doat** (17a,94b,112a,165d), **drat**
(100a), **Duat** (172d), **erat** (89c), **etat** (62d), **feat** (7a,52d), **fiat** (35a,
41d,48c,111b,137a), **Fiat** (81d), **flat** (41b,124b,173a), **frat, geat**
(77d,101a), **Geat** (138a), **ghat** (32d,88b,103d,132a), **gnat** (59a,
81b,99c), **goat** (135a), **heat, ikat** (53b,159a), **kaat** (105d), **khat**
(105d), **kyat** (189), **Maat** (69a,b,85d), **meat** (59b), **moat** (44d), **neat**
(165c,169d), **peat** (64a,175a), **piat** (11a), **plat** (22d,96c,114a,119c,
133d), **pyat** (95b), **scat** (26b,67a,d,126c,169c), **seat** (98c,156b),
shat (87d), **skat** (181b), **Skat** (155b), **slat** (58b,89a,117c,184a),
spat (112c,126b,134b), **stat** (72d), **swat** (15d,20d,32d,157c), **Swat**
(103a), **that** (42b,124b,129c), **what** (129c)

A - - T **abet** (8b,15b,50a,59b,75d,81c,141d,159d), **Abot** (100c), **abut** (22a,
167c), **acht** (66c), **adat** (90b,95d), **adit** (51a,100a,114d), **Ahet**
(49a,102a), **aint, alat** (136d), **alit** (44b,143a), **amit** (94a), **Anat**
(138c,147d), **anet** (43c), **Apet** (97c), **aret** (128c), **arn't, aunt** (129c)

AU - - **Auca** (192), **Aude, Auer** (79a), **auge** (123c,132b), **aula** (66c,73b),

274

aulu (74c,168c), aune (188), aunt (129c), aura (44c,49c,66a,96b, 158a,170d,177c), auri (34a), Ausa, ausu (168c,180b), auto (34d), auza (168c,180b)

- AU - baud (162d), baul (18b), Baum (9c,112c), cauk (139b), caul (16d, 74d), caur (139a), daub (95c), Daur (139b), dauw (24c), eaux (178c), faun (56a,68b,137c,161a,184a), gaub (116c), gaud (169d), gaue (67a), Gaul (10a,60d,63c), gaup, gaur (112c, 181c), gaus (67d), gaut (88b,103d,132a), haul (27b,45d), jaun (113a), kaun (93d), laud (122a), laun (146b), maud (53d,136d, 143c), Maud (181a,183c), Maui (120d), maul (73c), maun (139d), naut (141b), Paul (96a), paun (18b), paut (140a), Sauk (192), saul (48a,168c), Saul (18c,86d,115a), saum (189), taun (188), taut (163b,165c), Vaux (63b), yaup

- - AU Agau (73c), beau, Diau (192), Drau, Esau (82c,84a,128c), frau (181b), miau (27b,99b), prau (21b,26a,95c,d), sgau (88c), unau (148c,171d), whau (107a,168c)

A - - U Aalu (6b,48d), Aaru (6b,48d), Abou (48b,55a), actu (7a,89a), Addu (68c,157a,182a), Agau (73c), Ainu (84a,84c), ammu (9d), ansu (11d), anzu (11d), Apsu (29a), Atmu (143a,159b), Attu, aulu (74c,168c), ausu (168c,180b), auzu (168c,180b)

AV - - aval (70c), Avar (27d,108a), avec (63a,183a), aver (7c,14a,15c,41c, 95c,140d,155c,160b,184c), Aves (19d), avid (47b,71a,186b), avis (89a), Avis (183c), Avon (143b), avow (6d,36a,41c,112c), avus (89b)

- AV - bave (61d,146c), cava (116a,175b), cave (27d), cavy (72b,120d, 132c,157b), Dave (96b), Davy (96b,136b), eave (133c), favi (138a, 165d), gave, have, Java (33a), Jave (84d), kava (18c,116a), Kavi (84d), lava (101c,132b,151a,177a), lave (16d,178b), nave (30d,31a, 78d,114b,180c), navy (33c,58b), pave (85a), pavo (115b), Pavo (36b,c), pavy (115b), rave (41c,157a,161d), ravi, Ravi (16b), save (52b,110c,123a,173c), Tave (183d), Tavy (183d), wave (19a, 59a,111c,131d,160c,172d), wavy (147b,172d), yava

- - AV Muav (66a), Slav (13c,40c,48b,52a,120b,135b)

A - - V akov (189), Azov (20b,135d)

AW - - Awan (191), away (6b,69d,76a,109d,111d), awry (13d,38d,171c)

- AW - bawl, bawn (181a), cawk (133c), dawk (95c), dawm (190), dawn (14d,41b), fawn (33c), gawd (169c), gawk (146d), gawp, hawk (19c, 115c), jawy, kawa (18c,116a), Kawi (84d), kawn (93d), lawn (20a, 37c,53b,92c), pawa (189), pawl (43a,95a), pawn (29c,119c), sawk (188), sawn, tawa (106d,168c), yawl (136b,171d,175d), yawn, yawp

- - AW chaw (97c), claw (29c,105b,161d,173a), craw (38d,72c,156c), dhaw (125a), draw (42c,53a,92b,117c,121c,167d), flaw, gnaw (20a,107a, 178b), miaw (27b,99b), shaw (164b), Shaw (50c,53b), slaw, thaw

A - - W alow (18a,172c), anew (7c), arow (92c,158b), avow (6d,36a,41c, 112c)

AX - - axal (120b), axil (10c), axis (28b,41d,77c,153c), axle (153c,180c), axon (106c,153c)

- AX - saxe (20d,33c), taxi (13a,125b), taxo (13a), waxy (119c,149d)

275

- - AX   **Ajax** (71b,162d), **Anax** (43c,120c), **coax** (180c), **Crax** (19b,39d), **flax**, **hoax** (41c,122a), **Odax** (132c), **Olax** (52b)

A - - X   **abox** (22d), **Ajax** (71b,162d), **Alix** (183c), **Amex** (184d), **Anax** (43d,120c), **apex** (39c,76c,115c,118b,159b,166a,167b),

AY - -   **ayah** (108d), **ayes** (177c), **ayin** (91c)

- AY -   **baya** (179b), **Baya** (191), **cayo**, **Daye** (123d), **days**, **hayz**, **kayo** (87c), **maya** (179b), **Maya** (23d,186c), **Mayo** (193), **raya** (19b,23c,76d, 107d), **saya** (117a), **Vayu** (68c,182a), **ways**, **yaya** (113c,168c)

- - AY   **alay** (96c), **anay** (72b), **away** (6b,69d,76a,109d,111d), **blay** (57d), **bray**, **chay** (48a,128d), **Clay** (9d), **dray** (27a,154c,177b), **esay**, **flay** (147c,157c), **fray** (56b,60d), **gray** (33c,77c), **Gray** (50c), **okay** (8d), **olay** (113b), **piay** (98b), **play** (63d,154a), **pray** (18b,51a,159d), **quay** (88b,117c,180c), **ruay** (189), **shay** (110c), **slay**, **stay** (72d, 124c,130a,134a,162a), **sway** (104a)

A - - Y   **Abby** (183d), **ably** (147c), **achy**, **Addy** (183d), **adry**, (164c), **aery** (47b,51d,106c), **affy** (18b), **ahey** (52c), **ahoy** (106a), **airy** (176d, 177a), **akey** (189), **alay** (96c), **Algy** (96b), **alky** (52c), **ally** (14a,35c,d, 173c), **Amoy** (88c), **anay** (72b,163b,181a), **ancy** (158c), **Andy** (96b), **army**, **arty**, **ashy** (113a,178a), **atry** (141b), **away** (6b,69d,76a,109d, 111d), **awry** (13d,38d,171c)

AZ - -   **Azam** (166c), **azan** (102d), **Azha** (155b), **Azof** (20b,135d), **axon** (127b), **Azov** (20b,135d), **axul** (151d)

- AZ -   **caza**, **cazi** (103a), **cazy** (103a), **Daza** (191), **daze** (157d), **dazy**, **faze** (43d), **Gaza** (117a), **gaze**, **gazi**, **gazy**, **haze** (100c,174d), **hazy** (174b), **jazz**, **Kazi** (103a), **kazy** (103a), **laze** (79b), **Laze** (191), **Lazi** (191), **lazo** (88d,128b,133d), **lazy**, **maze** (87b,157d), **naze** (26b, 124b), **Nazi**, **raze** (42b,d,91d), **razz** (131b), **vaza** (114a)

- - AZ   **Agaz** (193), **Ahaz** (86d), **Boaz** (135d)

A - - Z   **Agaz** (193), **Ahaz** (86d)

BA - -   **Baal** (142b), **baas** (97c), **baba** (108d,120c,166c,171a), **babe**, **Babi** (116c), **babu** (77a), **baby**, **Bach** (35c), **back** (75d,76d,159d), **Badb** (82b), **bade**, **baff** (69d), **baft** (14a,53b), **baga** (171b), **bago** (13d), **bahi** (60c), **baho** (122a), **baht** (146a), **bail** (43c), **bain** (61a), **bait** (15d,51a,94d,167b), **baju** (84a), **baka** (52b), **bake** (139a), **baku** (26d,157b,168c), **Bala** (26c,66a), **bald** (16c), **bale** (24b,74a), **balk** (118c,146a,156d), **ball**, **balm** (110a,172c), **Balt** (93a), **balu** (104b, 159a,181d), **Bana** (67a), **banc** (61a,85c), **band** (72a,157c), **bane** (74a,106b,120b,139a), **bang** (75d,105d,148a), **bani** (190), **bank** (18a,58c), **bans**, **bant** (43c), **bara** (188), **barb** (20b,57d,78b,117d, 120a,b,124b), **bard** (12d,120a), **bare** (43d,157c), **bari** (37c,79c), **Bari** (83d), **bark** (115c), **barm** (185b), **barn** (156d), **baro** (71a,122c), **barr** (49b), **Bart** (96b), **baru** (168c), **base** (6a,43b,44b,51c,60c,79b,94b, 122b), **bash**, **bask** (94d), **bass** (57b,c,177a), **bast** (16c,56a,117b, 184a), **Bast** (27b), **bata** (30a,142d), **bate** (43c,91b,100d), **bath**, **Bath** (50d,151c), **batt** (37c), **batz** (190), **baud** (162d), **baul** (18b), **Baum** (9c,112c), **bave** (61d,146c), **bawl**, **bawn** (181a), **baya** (179b), **Baya** (191)

- BA -   **abas** (61c), **Ibad** (191), **Iban** (47c), **oban** (190)

- - BA   **Abba** (20a,55a,161c), **alba** (98a,181a), **Alba** (151d), **amba** (161a), anba (36d), arba (135d,171a), baba (108d,120c,166c,171a), boba (29d), buba (170a), caba (184c), ceba (169b), cuba (189), Cuba (180b), Egba (191), Elba (105d), ezba (188), Faba, haba (151d), isba (135c), juba (106b), koba (11a), kuba (26d,189), Luba (191), Maba (103a,168d), Nuba (108c), peba (12d), Peba (193), Raba, reba (144a), Reba (18d,86c), saba (56a,117a), Saba (143d), Seba (18c,39d), Toba (80c), tuba (105a,137d), ueba (188)

B - - A baba (108d,120c,166c,171a), baga (171b), baka (52b), Bala (26c, 66a), Bana (67a), bara (188), bata (30a,142d), baya (179b), Baya (191), Beda (101d), bega (188), Beja (6c,191), beka (189), bela (12a), Bela (18b,48c), bema (28d,31a,114b,119b,125b,137a), bena, (176a), Bera (86d), Besa (68b,119c), beta (71a,91c,141d), biga (171d), bija (168c), bina (77a), bisa (11a), biwa (93d,168c), Bixa (145d), blaa, boba (29d), boca (152b,c), boga (57d,180b), bola (16a, 179b), boma (7d), bona (89d,183c), Bona, bora (181d,182b), bosa (12a), bota (189), boza (12a), brea (100b), buba (170a), buda (83d), buna (161c), bura (182b)

- BB - Abba (20a,55a,161c), abbe (32b,63b,123b), Abby (183d)

- - BB bibb (97c,146b), Cobb (9c), dubb (161c), hobb (124b), hubb (118b), jibb, lobb (23b,94c,163a)

B - - B Badb (82b), barb (20b,57d,78b,117d,120a,b,124b), bibb (97c, 146b), blab (162b), bleb (20c,23d,67c), blob, blub, Bodb (82b), bomb (144a), boob (146d), brab (113b), brob (153c), bulb (37a, 172c)

- BC - ABC's (57a)

B - - C banc (61a,85c), bloc (173a), Bosc (115c)

B - - D bald (16c), band (72a,157c), bard (12d,120a), baud (162d), bead (17a,122a,146b), Beid (155b), bend (39d,171b), bind (33b,165c), biod (59d,79c), bird, bled, bold (41a), bond (92a,101c,141d,143b, 159d,165c), bord (100b), brad (54d,67c,105b), bred (23c,48c,127c), bund (49c,66c,90c), Byrd (9c,120b)

BE - - bead (17a,122a,146b), beak (19a), beal (139d), beam, bean (91b, 142a,175a), bear (27a,50b,113c,155a), beat (58c,87b,131a,164d, 165b,180d), beau, beck (107c), Beda (101d), Bede (48c,50c,101d, 175b), beef, been (149a), beer (18c), bees (185b), beet (175a), bega (188), behn (137d), Beid (155b), Beja (6c,191), beka (189), bela (12a), Bela (18b,48c,78d), Beli (23c), bell (24c,39d), Bell (162d), belt (16a,31a), bema (28d,31a,114b,119b,125b,137a), bena (176a), bend (39d,171b), bene (18a,83c,90a,106d,122a,180a), beng (43a), beni (116a,142d), Beni (191), beno (113b,117a), bent (80b), benu (49a), Bera (86d), berg (79b), berm (25d,90d,145c), Bern (160d), Bert (96b), Besa (68b,119c), Bess (76c,183d), best (41d, 159c,160a), beta (71a,91c,141d), bete (61a,107c), beth (91c), Beth (8c,183d), bevy (38a,58c)

- BE - abed (130c), Abel (7a,25b), abet (8b,15b,50a,59b,75d,81c,141d, 159d), Eben (96a), Eber (51a,75c,99d), ibex (67d,68a), obex (22d), obey (35c,75c), Obed (135d), uber (66b)

- - BE abbe (32b,63b,123b), albe (133a), babe, Bube (180b), cube (66b, 150a), dobe (159b,c,172b), Elbe (108a), gabe (162a), gibe (8a,42c, 84d,100d,138c,144c,149b), gybe (144c), Habe (191), Hebe (39c,

277

69c,186b), **imbe** (37a,56a,133d), **jibe** (8a,33b,35d,37b,42c,100d, 138c,144c,149b), **jube** (28d), **kibe, Kobe** (78a), **lobe** (90c,134b), **lube** (110a), **ribe** (139a), **robe** (65b), **rube** (37d,135d,185d), **Rube** (96b), **sabe, tobe** (7d,137b), **tube** (118b,158a)

B - - E **babe, bade, bake** (139a), **bale** (24b,74a), **bane** (74a,106b,120b, 139a), **bare** (43d,157c), **base** (6a,43b,44b,51c,60c,79b,94b,122b), **bate** (43c,91b,100d), **bave** (61d,146c), **Bede** (48c,50c,101d,117b), **bene** (18a,83c,90a,106d,122a,180a), **bete** (61a,107c), **bice** (20d, 117d), **Bice** (27b), **bide** (47c,50b,130a,158b), **bike, bile** (30c), **bine** (145b,156a,171c,176b), **bise** (182a), **bite** (29d,156b), **bize** (182a), **blae** (93b), **blue** (33c,98c,102c,150d,173a), **boce** (23b,52a,57b), **bode** (14c,60a,110b,121b), **bole** (31d,32a,169b), **bone, bore** (14c, 25b,46a,116a,165c,179b), **bose** (163c), **brae** (76d,139a,c,140b, 148c), **bree** (139a), **Brie** (29c), **Bube** (180b), **bure** (61b), **byee** (189), **byre** (38a)

- BF - **Abfa** (76b)

B - - F **baff** (69d), **beef, biff, buff** (134c,161d)

B - - G **bang** (75d,105d,148a), **beng** (43a), **berg** (79b), **bing, bong, borg** (40d), **brag** (21a,175a), **brig** (72b,106a,144d), **bung** (119d,156d), **burg** (22b,73c)

BH - - **Bhar** (191), **bhat** (80c), **bhel** (126d), **Bhil** (191), **b'hoy** (134b), **bhut** (67a)

- - BH **Cobh** (37a)

B - - H **Bach** (35c), **bash, bath, Bath** (50d,151c), **beth** (91c), **Beth** (8c, 183d), **bikh** (120b), **binh** (189), **bish** (120b), **blah, booh** (52c), **bosh, both, bruh** (95a), **bukh** (122a), **bush**

BI - - **bias** (43b,123a), **bibb** (97c,146b), **bibi** (87d), **bice** (20d,117d), **Bice** (27b), **bide** (47c,50b,130a,158b,162a,177b), **bien** (63a,140c,179a, 180a), **bier** (33b,66b), **biff, biga** (171d), **bija** (168c), **bike, bikh** (120b), **bile** (30c), **bilk** (29b,41c,42a), **bill** (17b,147a), **Bill** (96b), **bilo** (131b), **bina** (77a), **bind** (33b,165c), **bine** (145b,156a,171c, 176b), **bing, binh** (189), **Bini** (191), **binn** (22c), **bino** (113b,117a), **biod** (59d,79c), **bion** (117b), **bios** (92a), **bird, birl** (93c,131a,153c), **birn** (31d,139a), **birr** (180d), **bisa** (11a), **bise** (182a), **bish** (120b), **bisk** (120b,151a), **bite** (29d,156b), **biti** (20b), **bito** (7d,57d,168c), **bitt** (54d,175c), **biur** (35a), **biwa** (93d,168c), **Bixa** (145d), **bize** (182a), **bizz**

- BI - **Abia** (18d,137a), **Abib** (102a,b), **Abie** (96b,107a), **abir** (129a), **ibid** (80a,117a,137a), **ibis** (48d,49a,177b), **ibit** (117a), **obia** (55d), **obit** (41b,64c), **Ubli** (191)

- - BI **Albi** (58a), **ambi** (34a,122c), **Babi** (116c), **bibi** (87d), **Bubi** (180b), **cubi** (188), **gabi** (162a), **gobi, Gobi** (42d), **kobi** (84b), **mabi** (58d), **rabi** (38d,74a), **Rabi** (14b,117b), **sebi** (34b), **tabi** (84c,149d), **Tybi** (102a), **Wabi** (192), **Yobi**

B - - I **Babi** (116c), **bahi** (60c), **Bali, bani** (190), **bari** (79c), **Bari** (37c, 83d), **Beli** (23c), **beni** (116a,142d), **Beni** (191), **bibi** (87d), **Bini** (191), **biti** (20b), **Boii** (191), **Boni** (63b), **Bori** (110d,150c), **Bubi** (180b), **Bugi** (191), **buri** (56b)

- - BK **nabk** (30d,164d), **nubk** (30d,164d), **Sobk** (38d)

278

B - - K   **back** (75d,76d,159d), **balk** (118c,146a,156d), **bank** (18a,58c), **bark** (115c), **bask** (94d), **beak** (19a), **beck** (107c), **bilk** (29b,41c,42a), **bisk** (120b,151a), **bock** (17c,90d,144a), **bonk** (190), **book**, **bosk** (164b), **bowk** (155d), **buck**, **bukk** (122a), **bulk** (97b), **bunk**, **busk** (17b,37b,55d,161b)

BL - -   **blaa**, **blab** (162b), **blae** (93b), **blah**, **blas** (6c,49c), **Blas** (67b), **blat** (25b), **blay** (57d), **bleb** (20c,23d,67c), **bled**, **blet** (64a), **bleu** (61b), **blew**, **blob**, **bloc** (173a), **blot**, **blow**, **blub**, **blue** (33c,98c,102c,150d, 173a), **blup**, **blur**, **blut** (66b)

- BL -   **able** (26b,35b,126a,147c), **ably** (147c)

B - - L   **baal** (142b), **bail** (43c), **ball**, **baul** (18b), **bawl**, **beal** (139d), **bell** (24c,39d), **Bell** (162d), **bhel** (126d), **Bhil** (191), **bill** (17b,147a), **Bill** (96b), **birl** (93c,131a,153c), **boil**, **boll** (119b,d), **bool** (39d), **bowl**, **bual** (182c), **buhl** (81a), **bull** (113c), **burl** (87c,169a)

B - - M   **balm** (110a,172c), **barm** (185b), **Baum** (9c,112c), **beam**, **berm** (25d, 90d,145c), **boom** (152d), **Bram** (96a), **brim**

B - - N   **bain** (61a), **barn** (156d), **bawn** (181a), **bean** (91b,142a,175a), **been** (149a), **behn** (137d), **Bern** (160d), **bien** (63a,140c,179a,180a), **binn** (22c), **bion** (117b), **birn** (31d,139a), **Bonn** (17d), **boon** (18b,20c, 55a), **born**, **bran** (23c,39a,70b,72a,79c), **Bran** (23c,50c), **bren** (72d, 95a), **brin** (32c,54c,146c), **bunn** (25b), **burn**

BO - -   **boar** (77c,117c,160c,181c), **boat** (27b,106a), **Boaz** (135d), **boba** (29d), **bobo** (112c,168c), **boca** (152b,c), **boce** (23b,52a,57b), **bock** (17c,90d,144a), **Bodb** (82b), **bode** (14c,60a,110b,121b), **Bodo** (88c), **body** (72a), **Boer** (151a), **boga** (57d,180b), **bogo** (117a,168c), **Bogo** (191), **bogy** (153a), **boho** (117a,179d), **Bohr** (14b,40d,138c), **Boii** (191), **boil**, **bois** (62b,63a,183d), **bojo** (117a), **boko** (52b), **bola** (16a, 179b), **bold** (41a), **bole** (31d,32a,169b), **boll** (119b,d), **bolo** (87a, 179b), **bolt** (13b,54d,58b,132d,160a), **boma** (7d), **bomb** (144a), **bona** (89d), **Bona** (183c), **bond** (92a,101c,141d,143b,159d,165c), **bone**, **bong**, **Boni** (63b), **bonk** (190), **Bonn** (17d), **bony** (147c), **Bony** (96b), **boob** (146d), **booh** (52c), **book**, **bool** (39d), **boom** (152d), **boon** (18b,20c,55a), **boor** (47a,135d,172c), **boot** (128d), **bora** (181d, 182b), **bord** (100b), **bore** (14c,25b,46a,116a,165c,179b), **borg** (40d), **Bori** (110d,150c), **born**, **boro** (154b), **Boro** (193), **Bors** (70b,134b), **bort** (43b), **Bort** (134b), **bosa** (12a), **Bosc** (115c), **bose** (163c), **bosh**, **bosk** (164b), **boss** (49d,157d), **bota** (189), **both**, **Boto** (192), **bott** (32a,88d), **bout** (36c), **bouw** (188), **bowk** (155d), **bowl**, **boxy**, **boxa** (12a), **bozo** (55b)

- BO -   **aboo** (17a), **Abot** (100c), **Abou** (48b,55a), **abox** (22d), **eboe** (28b, 110a,168c,169b), **Eboe**, **ebon** (20b), **oboe** (74b,104d,105a,182a, 184a), **obol** (29b,110a)

- - BO   **albo** (34d,181a), **ambo** (125b,128b), **bobo** (112c,168c), **bubo** (112c), **Egbo** (141d), **Gobo** (84d), **hobo** (168a,174b), **jobo** (77c), **lobo** (165d,183c), **nabo** (117a), **Nebo** (68c,102d,103d,183a), **umbo** (22b), **zobo** (186d)

B - - O   **bago** (13d), **baho** (122a), **baro** (71a,122c), **beno** (113b,117a), **bilo** (131b), **bino** (113b,117a), **bito** (7d,52d,168c), **bobo** (112c,168c), **Bodo** (88c), **bogo** (117a,168c), **Bogo** (191), **boho** (117a,179d), **bojo** (117a), **boko** (52b), **bolo** (87a,179b), **boro** (154b), **Boro** (193), **Boto**

279

(192), **bozo** (55b), **broo** (139a), **bubo** (112c), **Bufo** (166c), **Buts** (142d), **buyo** (18b), **bygo** (114c)

B - - P   **blup, bump**

BR - -   **brab** (113b), **brad** (54d,67c,105b), **brae** (76d,139a,c,140b,148c), **brag** (21a,175a), **Bram** (96a), **bran** (23c,39a,70b,72a,79c), **Bran** (23c,50c), **bras** (61a), **brat, bray, brea** (100b), **bred** (23c,48c,127c), **bree** (139a), **bren** (72d,95a), **Brer** (172b), **Bres, brew** (35d), **brey** (194), **Brie** (29c), **brig** (72b,106a,144d), **brim, brin** (32c,54c,146c), **brit** (76c), **brob** (153c), **broo** (139a), **brow, bruh** (95a), **brut** (182c), **Brut** (23c)

- BR -   **abra** (26b), **Abra, abri** (61c,62c,144b), **Ebro** (132a), **obra** (152d, 184c)

B - - R   **barr** (49b), **bear** (27a,50b,113c,155a), **beer** (18c), **Bhar** (191), **bier** (33b,66b), **birr** (180d), **biur** (35a), **blur, boar** (77c,117c,160c,181c), **Boer** (151a), **Bohr** (14b,40d,138c), **boor** (47a,135d,172c), **Brer** (172b), **buhr** (180d), **burr** (123b)

- BS -   **Absi** (191)

- - BS   **dibs** (70c), **Lubs** (94c), **nibs** (116c), **nobs** (38c,87a)

B - - S   **baas** (97c), **bans, bass** (57b,c,177a), **bees** (185b), **Bess** (76c,183d), **bias** (43b,123a), **bios** (92a), **blas** (6c,49c), **Blas** (67b), **bois** (62b, 63a,183d), **Bors** (70b,134b), **boss** (49d,157d), **bras** (61a), **Bres, buss** (87a,148c)

- - BT   **debt** (91d,109b)

B - - T   **baft** (14a,53b), **baht** (146a), **bait** (15d,51a,94d,167b), **Balt** (93a), **bant** (43c), **Bart** (96b), **bast** (16c,56a,117b,184a), **Bast** (27b), **batt** (37c), **beat** (58c,87b,131a,164d,165b,180d), **beet** (175a), **belt** (16a, 31a), **bent** (80b), **Bert** (96b), **best** (41d,159c,160a), **bhat** (80c), **bhut** (67a), **bitt** (54d,175c), **blat** (25b), **blet** (64a), **blot, blut** (66b), **boat** (27b,106a), **bolt** (13b,54d,58b,132d,160a), **boot** (128d), **bort** (43b), **Bort** (134b), **bott** (32a,88d), **bout** (36c), **brat, brit** (76c), **brut** (182c), **Brut** (23c), **bult** (76d), **bunt** (15d,180c), **bust, butt** (27a,77b,127d,162a,182b)

BU - -   **bual** (182c), **buba** (170a), **Bube** (180b), **Bubi** (180b), **bubo** (112c), **buck, buda** (83d), **buff** (134c,161d), **Bufo** (166c), **Bugi** (191), **buhl** (81a), **buhr** (180d), **bukh** (122a), **bukk** (122a), **bulb** (37a,172c), **bulk** (97b), **bull** (113c), **bult** (76d), **bump, buna** (161c), **bund** (49c,66c,90c), **bung** (119d,156b), **bunk, bunn** (25b), **bunt** (15d, 180c), **buoy** (28d,58c), **bura** (182b), **bure** (61b), **burg** (22b,73c), **buri** (56b), **burl** (87c,169a), **burn, burr** (123b), **bury** (81d), **bush, busk** (17b,37b,55d,161b), **buss** (87a,148c), **bust, busy, Buto** (142d), **butt** (27a,77b,127d,162a,182b), **buxy** (115b), **buyo** (18b) **buzz**

- BU -   **abut** (22a,167c), **ebur** (89c)

- - BU   **babu** (77a), **kobu** (84b), **Nabu** (68c,183a), **tabu** (59d,111d), **Tibu** (191), **zebu** (22d,80d,112c)

B - - U   **babu** (77a), **baju** (84a), **baku** (26d,157b,168c), **balu** (104b,159a, 181d), **baru** (168c), **beau, benu** (49a), **bleu** (61b)

B - - W   **blew, blow, bouw** (188), **brew** (35d), **brow**

BY - - byee, (189), bygo (114c), Byrd (9c,120b), byre (38a)

- - BY Abby (183d), baby, doby (159b,c), gaby (59c,146d), goby (57d), kiby (29a), ruby (20a,65d,179c), toby (8c,85c,104b), Toby (96b, 125c)

B - - Y baby, bevy (38a,58c), b'hoy (134b), blay (57d), body (72a), bogy (153a), bony (147c), Bony (96b), boxy, bray, brey (194), buoy (28d,58c), bury (81d), busy, buxy (115b)

B - - Z batz (190), bizz, Boaz (135d), buzz

CA - - caam (93d), caba (184c), Caca (67a), caco (73b), cade (25c,27a,76c, 85d,116d), Cade (50c), cadi (12a,103a,171a), cady (69d), Caen, cafe, cage (36a), cagy (178b), caid (35a,151d,152b), cain (169c), Cain (6a,7a,50d,88a,104c,143a), caja (152a), caji (180b), cake, caky (178b), cale (72d), calf, calk (78c,109a,141c,178d), call (145c,159b, 176d), calm (8d,11d,112b,118d,126c,d,172b,173d), calo (72d), calp (92b), calx (23c,75c,112c), came (182b), Came (192), camp (163b), Cana (57a,64b,100c), cane (17b,128a,156a,159a,177d), Cane, cang (184a), cano (152a), cant (28d,81b,84d,90c,109b,136c,165d,166a), capa (152a,166d), cape (75a,96c,124b,161a), caph (91c), Capp (27a), cara (83a), Cara (48b,183c), card (33d,114d), care (11b, 14c,35d,150a,184d), cark (26d,184d), carl (115c,135d), Carl (96a), carn (156c), caro (83a), Caro (183d), carp (27d,38d,40c,55a,56c, 57a), carr (120d,140a), cart (171d,175a,177b), casa (152b), case (22c,36c,81c,91a,108c), cash (101c), cask, Caso (82d) cass (140c, 177a), Cass (147a), cast (165b,167c), cata (122c), cate (165c), Cato (132d,133b), Catt (9d), cauk (139d), caul (16d,74d), caup, caur (139a), cava (116a,175b), cave (27d), cavy (72b,120d,132c, 157b), cawk (133c), cayo, caza, cazi (103a), cazy (103a)

- CA - ecad (73a,119b), ical (158c), scab (80b,107d,157c), scad (31a,57a, 78b,88d,137c), scan (52b,93d,98a,116d,128b,c,140d), scar (31a, 184d), scat (26b,67a,d,126c,169c)

- - CA acca (53b,d), Alca (14c,128b), arca (9a,22c,29d,115a,130a), Arca (101b), Auca (192), boca (152b,c), Caca (67a), coca (29d,33a,105d, 113a), cuca (33a,105d), deca (34d,122d), Ecca (66a), esca (11c, 44a,70c), Inca (14b,30a), jaca (84a), juca (27a), mica (82c,100b, 146c), onca (189), orca (86b), paca (132c,154a), peca (190), pica (66b,95b,172c), puca (68a), raca (19a,59c,130b,184d), Teca (192), unca (49a), Ynca (193), yuca (27a)

C - - A caba (184c), Caca (67a), caja (152a), Cana (57a,64b,100c), capa (152a,166d), cara (83a), Cara (48b,183c), casa (152b), cata (122c), cava (116a,175b), caza, ceba (169b), cela (62d), cena (88d,133a), cepa (110c), cera (152d,161d,179a), chaa (162b), chia (136d), cima (83b,c), Civa (56d), coca (29d,33a,105d,113a), coda (32c,35d,55d, 56c), coja (103b,166b), cola (25b,108d,149d,168c), coma (91c, 157d,170c,172b), copa (88b,113c), cora (65d), Cora (42b,69c,80c, 116b,124d,172b,183c), cota (117a), coxa (77b), crea (92c,151d), cuba (189), Cuba (180b), cuca (33a,105d), Cuna (193), cura (152c), cuya (39b), cyma (101a,b)

C - - B chab (184a), chib (167a), chob (23c), chub (40c,154c), club (39c), Cobb (9c), comb (38c), crab (39b,144b,181b), crib (96b,120d), curb (130c,146b)

281

- CC -   acca (53b,d), Ecca (66a), ecce (17d,89a,c)

C - - C   chic (148d), circ (31a), cric (131c), croc (13a,74a)

C - - D   caid (35a,151d,152b), card (33d,114d), Chad (158b), chid, Chud (191), clad (46a,82a), clod (22a,45b,157d), coed, cold (65d), cond (156a), cord (39b,131c), curd (99d)

CE - -   ceba (169b), cede (67b,70c,129d,160a,168b,185d), ceil (92c,112a), cela (62d), cell (39b), celt (30c,123a,156c,167b,179b), Celt (10a, 180a,b), cena (88d,133a), cene (34c), cens (115b), cent (36d), cepa (110c), cepe (48c), cera (152d,161d,179a), cere (19a,114b,149d, 179a), cern (41c), cero (57b,c,d,180b), cess (91d,94c,162b), cest (18a,67b), cete (180b,c), ceto (34a), Ceyx (73b)

- CE -   Acer (96c), icer

- - CE   ance (158b,c,d), bice (20d,117d), Bice (27b), boce (23b,52a,57b), dace (57a,b), dice (65a), duce (29c), ecce (17d,89a,c), ence (158c), esce (158d), face (159d,176c), lace (158b,179c), luce (58c,117d), Luce (7b,35a), mace (49d,108d,153b,154d,161a,178a), mice, nice (54d,119c,130c), Nice (98c), once (60b,79b), pace (64b,98a,153b, 156a,170b,177d), pice (190), puce (33c,d,52a), race (116a,153b, 154b), Rice (46a), sice (71d,147b), syce (71d), tace (13a,155b), tice (9a,38c,51a,185d), vice (31c,158a), voce (83c,177a)

C - - E   cade (25c,27a,76c,85d,116d), Cade (50c), cafe (36a), cage (36a), cake, cale (72d), came (182b), Came (192), cane (17b,128a,156a,159a, 177d), Cane, cape (75a,96c,124b,161a), care (11b,14c,35d,150a, 184d), case (22c,36c,81c,91a,108c), cate (165c), cave (27d), cede (67b,70c,129d,160a,168b,185d), cene (34c), cepe (48c), cere (19a, 114b,149d,179a), chee (189), cine (104b,152c), cise (147b), cite (15a,98d,126d,159b), cive (110c), clee (19a,129a), Cloe (183c), clue (192), code (21c,31a,40c,161c), coke (32d,64a), cole (25a), Cole, come, cone (66b,150a,157c), cope (12b,26b,36c,65b, 157d,176a), core (28b,51c,75b,81b), cose (29b), cote (19b,143d, 144a,b), cove (17a,73d,107d), coze (29b), Cree (192), cube (66b, 150a), cuke (39b), cure (123b,d), cute (39c), cyke (40c), cyme (58d, 69c)

C - - F   calf, chef, clef (104d,105a), coif (73a), cuff (148a), culf (139a,d, 140c)

C - - G   cang (184a), chug (53a), clog (30c,145b), coag (45d,118a,163b), crag (132c), crig (20d)

CH - -   chaa (162b), chab (184a), Chad (158b), chai (72d), cham (20a,29d), Cham (8c) chan (26c,130c), chap (55b), char (24d,138c,170b), chat (9b,19c,161c), chaw (97c), chay (48a,128d), chee (189), chef, chek (59c), Chen (149b), cher (61b), chew (97c), chez (14b,61a), chia (136d), chib (167a), chic (148d), chid, ch'ih (188), chil, chin, Chin (30b), chip (69d), chir (29b,116d), chit (67b,98c,108b,116c, 177c), chiv (87a), chob (23c), chol (118d), Chol (192), chop (98a), chor (164b), chou (61b), Chou (30b), chow (45a), choy (48a,128d), chub (40c,154c), Chud (191), chug (53a), chum (38d), Chun (30c), chut!

- CH -   ache (79a,112d,185b), acht (66c), achy, echo (130b,d), Echo (105d), icho (67b), ichu (10b,70d), ocha (189), tcha (162c), tche (13d,30b, 105a), tchi, Tchi, tchu

282

- - CH aich (9a), arch (29d,38b,39d,123d,132c), bach, Bach (35c), each, etch, Foch (63b), hoch (52c,66c), Hoch, inch, itch, Koch (66d), lech (102b), loch (88a,139d), much, nach, ouch, rich, Roch (136c), sech (97c), such (146d), Tech, Vach (153b), Zach (96b)

C - - H caph (91c), Caph, cash (101c), ch'ih (188), Cobh (37a), cosh (35a, 97c), cush (101c), Cush (51d,73c)

CI - - cima (83b,c), cine (104b,152c), cinq (61d), cion (42d,70b,145b, 148b,154b,156a), cipo (91d), circ (31a), cirl (24c), cise (147b), cist (22c,29d,156c), cite (15a,98d,126d,159b), cito (89d,126c), cits, city, Civa (56d), cive (110c)

- CI - acid (151a,162a), Acis (64b), Scio

- - CI asci (154a), deci (163b), foci (28b), fuci (132c), loci (66b,118c), Pici (19c,184a), unci (31d)

C - - I cadi (12a,103a,171a), Cadi, caji (180b), cazi (103a), chai (72d), coli, Coni, Cori (138c), cubi (188)

- - CK back (75d,76d,159d), beck (107c), bock (17c,90d,144a), buck, cock (19a,29a,55a,133d,136d,161d,174b), deck (13b,41c, 144d), dick (43a,55b), Dick (96b), dock (40a,117c,144d,179d), duck (26b,53c,179c), hack (40a,77c,184d), heck (100a), hick (185d), hock (91a,115b,182b,c), huck (167d), jack (26c,58a,127c), Jack (96b), jock (96b), Jock (114c), juck (114c), kick, lack (178a), lick lock (54d), luck (28d), mack, mick (82c), mock (131b,162b), muck, neck (83a), nick (30c,108b), nock (13b,108b), pack (24b,140d), peck (24d), pick, puck (44b,68a,77c,100c), Puck (99d,143b), rack (32c,64b), reck (26d,75c), rick (74d,117d), rock (160b), ruck (39a, 185a), sack (43d,118a,119d,182b), seck (173d), sick, sock (157c, 182a), suck (28d,37d,54d), tack (28d,37d,54d), teck (128b), tick (12b,20d,97c), tock (7d,19b), tuck (156b), wick

C - - K calk (78c,109a,141c,178d), cark (26d,184d), cask, cauk (139b), cawk (133c), chek (59c), coak (45d,118a,163b), cock (19a,29a, 55a,133d,136d), conk (41c,108a,156d,157c), cook (137b), cork (119d), cusk (57b)

CL - - clad (46a,82a), clam (20b,101b), clan (169c), clap (58b), claw (29c, 105b,161d,173a), clay, Clay (9d), clee (19a,129a), clef (104d,105a), clem (56b,158b), Cleo (126b), clew (16a,33a,77b,136b,164d), Clim (12b), Clio (104d), clip (54d,143d), clod (22a,45b,157d), Cloe (183c), clog (30c,145b), clop, clot (32d,94d), clou (62b), clow (58c,148c), cloy (61b,137c,159d), club (39c), clue, Clym (12b)

- CL - acle (13d,82c,115d)

C - - L call (145c,159b,176d), carl (115c,135d), Carl (96a), caul (16d,74d), ceil (92c,112a), cell (39b), chil, chol (118d), Chol (192), cirl (24c), coal (49c,64a), coel (39b), coil (39d,171c,185a), cool (25c,107d), cowl (101d), cral (117c), cull (117c), curl (38d,73b,93b,131d)

- CM - acme (39c,115c,186b)

C - - M caam (93d), calm (8d,11d,112b,118d,126c,d,172b), cham (20a,29d), Cham (8c), chum (38d), clam (20b,101b), clem (56b,158b), Clim (12b), Clym (12b), coom (32d,150c,178d), corm (24b,38d,156a), cram (157d), Crom, culm (11a,32d,70d,145a,156a)

CN - - Cnut (40d,50c)

283

- CN - acne (147c)

C - - N Caen, cain (169c), Cain (6a,7a,50d,88a,104c,143a), carn (156c), cern (41c), chan (26c,130c), Chen (149b), chin, Chin (30b), Chun (30c), cion (42d,70b,145b,148b,154c,156a), clan (169c), Coan (37b), coin (19b,37a,100c,101c,179d), conn (43d,156a), coon (121c), corn (39d,95c,123a), coyn (37a), cran (160c), crin (146c), cyan

CO - - coag (45d,118a,163b), coak (45d,118a,163b), coal (49c,64a), Coan (37b), coat (160a), coax (180c), Cobb (9c), Cobh (37a), coca (29d, 33a,105d,113a), cock (19a,29a,55a,133d,136d,161d,174b), coco, (113a), coda (32c,35d,56c), code (21c,31a,40c,161c), codo (188), coed, coel (39b), coho (136d), coif (73a), coil (39d,171c,185a), coin (19b,37a,100c,101c,179d), coir (33a,37a,56a,133d), Coix (70d,85b), coja (103b,166b), coke (32d,64a), coky, cola (25b,108d,149d,168c), cold (65d), cole (25a), Cole, coli, colp (28a,148b), colt (78c,131a, 185d,186b), Colt, coly (104a), coma (91c,157d,170c,172b), comb (38c), come, Como, cond (156a), cone (66b,150a,157c), Coni, conk (41c,108a,156d,157c), conn (43d,156a), cony (127a), cook (137b), cool (25c,107d), coom (32d,150c,178d), coon (121c), coop, Coos, (192), coot (19b,46d,72b,138d,141a,146d,157d), copa (88b,113c), cope (12b,26b,36c,65b,157d,176a), copt (48d), copy, cora (65d), Cora (42b,69c,80c,116b,124d,172b,183c), cord (39b,139a), core (28b,51c,75b,81b), Cori (138c), cork (119d), corm (24b,38d,156a), corn (39d,95c,123a), cose (29b), cosh (35a,97c), coso (152c), coss (98a), cost (29a), cosy (149c), cota (117a), cote (19b,143d,144a,b), coto (16c,90b), Coty (63c), coup (20d,97c,157b,c,162d), cous (38a), cove (17a,73d,107d), cowl (101d), coxa (77b) coyn (37a), coyo (15a,30c), coze (29b), cozy (149c)

- CO - acon (62c,140d), acor (6d), icon (79d,92b,136a), scob (42a), scon (162c), scop (120a), scot (14a,162b), Scot (64b,132c), scow (21a, 58b)

- - CO alco (45b), caco (73b), coco (113a), Duco (169d), fico (169d), loco (38b, 119b,120b), mico (97a), paco (9b,146a), peco (162b), pico (65a, 152c), poco (83b,93a), saco (189), soco (22a), Teco (192), toco (19b,167c), unco (140c), Waco

C - - O caco (73b), calo (72d), cano (152a), caro (83a), Caro (183d), Caso (82d), Cato (132d,133b), cayo (34a), cero (57b,c,d,180c), ceto (34a), cipo (91d), cito (89d,126c), Cleo (126b), Clio (104d), coco, (113a), codo (188), coho (136d), Como, coso (152d), coto (16c,90b), coyo (15a,30c)

C - - P calp (92b), camp (163b), Capp (27a), carp (27d,38d,40c,55a,56c, 57a), caup, chap (55b), chip (69d), chop (98a), clap (58b), clip (54d,143d), clop, colp (28a,148b), coop, coup (20d,97c,157b,c, 162d), crop (38b), cusp (38c,78b,119a,120a,b)

C - - Q cinq (61d)

CR - - crab (39b,144b,181b), crag (132c), cral, cram (157d), cran (160c), craw (38d,72c,156c), Crax (19b,39d), crea (92c,151d), Cree (192), crew (72a,106a), Crex (37a), crib (96b,120d), cric (131c), crig (20d), crin (146c), cris (40b,95d), croc (13a,74a), Crom, crop (38b), crow (19a), crus (91a,143c), crux (39a,151b)

- CR -   **acre** (39b,56a,88b), **Acre, ecru** (17d,23d,172b), **ocra** (72c,175a)

C - - R   **carr** (120d,140a), **caur** (139a), **char** (24d,138c,170b), **cher** (61b), **chir** (29b,116d), **chor** (164b), **coir** (33a,37a,56a,133d), **cuir** (45c,62a), **curr** (104c), **Czar** (42d,49d,60b,135c)

- - CS   **ABC's** (57a), **pacs** (94c)

C - - S   **cass** (140c,177a), **Cass** (147a), **cens** (115b), **cess** (91d,94c,162b), **cits, Coos** (192), **coss** (98a), **cous** (38a), **cris** (40b,95d), **crus** (91a, 143c), **cuss**

- CT -   **acta** (41d,123d,128d,164c), **acth** (13b), **acto** (152b), **Acts, actu** (7a, 89a), **ecto** (34c,122d), **octa** (122c), **octo** (34a,89b,122c)

- - CT   **duct** (170c), **fact** (7a,128b), **lact** (34c), **pact** (8a), **Pict** (23c,47d), **rect** (117b), **sect** (42b,54a,114c), **tact** (43c,d,116a)

C - - T   **cant** (28d,81b,84d,90c,109b,136c,165d,166a), **cart** (171d,175a, 177b), **cast** (165b,167c), **Catt** (9d), **celt** (30c,82c,123a,156c,167b, 179b), **Celt** (10a,180a,b), **cent** (36d), **cest** (18a,67b), **chat** (9b,19c, 161c), **chit** (67b,98c,108b,116c,177c), **chut!, cist** (22c,29d,156c), **clot** (32d,94d), **coat** (160a), **colt** (78c,131a,185d,186b), **Colt** (131a), **coot** (19b,46d,72b,138d,141a,146d,157d), **Copt** (48d), **cost** (29a), **cult** (141d,161c), **curt** (145b,c), **cyst**

CU - -   **cuba** (189), **Cuba** (180b), **cube** (66b,150a), **cubi** (188), **cuca** (33a, 105d), **cuff** (148a), **cuif** (139a,d,140c), **cuir** (45c,62a), **cuke** (39b), **cull** (117c), **culm** (11a,32d,70d,145a,156a), **cult** (141d,161c), **Cuna** (193), **cura** (152c), **curb** (130c,146b), **curd** (99d), **cure** (123b), **curl** (38d,73b,93b,131d), **curr** (104c), **curt** (145b,c), **cush** (101c), **Cush** (51d,73c), **cusk** (57b), **cusp** (38c,78b,119a,120a,b), **cuss, cute** (39c), **cuvy** (141a), **cuya** (39b)

- CU -   **acus** (89d,118a), **scud** (32c,126c,135b,160c), **scum** (129b), **scup** (57a,121b), **scur** (78b), **scut** (145c,161b)

- - CU   **jacu** (19a,151b), **jocu** (45b,57a)

C - - U   **chou** (61b), **Chou** (30b), **clou** (62b)

C - - V   **chiv** (87a)

C - - W   **chaw** (97c), **chew** (97c), **chow** (45a), **claw** (29c,105b,161d,173a), **clew** (16a,33a,77b,136b,164d), **clow** (58c,148c), **craw** (38d,72c, 156c), **crew** (72a,106a), **crow** (19a)

C - - X   **calx** (23c,75c,112c), **Ceyx** (73b), **coax** (180c), **Coix** (70d,85b), **Crax** (19b,39d), **Crex** (37a), **crux** (39a,151b)

CY - -   **cyan, cyke** (40c), **cyma** (101a,b), **cyme** (58d,69c), **cyst**

- CY -   **acyl** (6d)

- - CY   **ancy** (158c), **lacy, Lucy** (183c), **racy** (153b)

C - - Y   **cady** (69d), **cagy** (178b), **caky, cavy** (72b,120d,132c,157b), **cazy** (103a), **chay** (48a,128d), **choy** (48a,128d), **city, clay, Clay** (9d), **cloy** (61b,137c,159d), **coky, coly** (104a), **cony** (127a), **copy, cosy** (149c), **Coty** (63c), **cozy** (149c), **cuvy** (141a)

CZ - -   **czar** (42d,49d,60b,135c)

C - - Z   **chez** (14b,61a)

DA - -   **dace** (57a,b), **Dada** (13b,63a,157d), **dado** (41c,111c,115c, 177d), **daer** (22b), **daez, daff** (125d), **daft** (59c), **dagg** (118c), **dagh**

285

(76d), **Dago**, **Dail** (49a,82b,c), **dain** (188), **dais** (119b), **dale** (43c, 128a,174b), **dali** (168c,169b), **dama** (65d,152b), **dame** (67b,87c, 166b), **damn**, **damp** (101a), **Dana** (28a,96a,171d), **Dane** (85d,107d, 138a), **dang**, **dank** (40b,101a), **dans** (62a), **Danu** (28a), **Dara** (18d), **Dard**, **dare** (28d,41b,42a,74d,175b), **Dare** (57a), **dari** (38a,70b), **dark** (47a,67d,109b,160b), **darn** (130b), **darr** (163c), **dart** (13b,88a, 100c,120b,153a,160c), **dash** (125c,162d), **dasi** (77a), **data** (54a), **date** (64a,153a), **dato** (95c,102c,117a), **datu** (95c,102c,117a), **daub** (148d), **dauk** (95c), **Daur** (139b), **dauw** (24c), **Dave** (96b), **Davy** (96b,136b), **dawk** (95c), **dawm** (190), **dawn** (14d,41b), **Daye** (123d), **days**, **Daza** (191), **daze** (157d), **dazy**

- **DA** -   **adad** (52c,56a), **Adad** (68c,157a,182a), **Adah** (25b,51b), **Adam** (26b,96a,111c), **adan** (102d), **Adar** (85c,102a), **adat** (90b,95d), **Edam** (29c), **Edar** (18d), **Idas** (27b,71c), **odah** (170d), **odal** (48a,88b,112c), **Odax** (132c), **udad** (143d,144a,181c), **udal** (76b, 88b,131c)

- - **DA** **adda** (147d), **Adda** (68c,119d), **Aida** (110d,175c), **alda** (152b), **Alda** (110d,150c), **anda** (23a,168c), **Beda** (101d), **Buda** (83d), **coda** (32c,35d,56c), **Dada** (13b,63a,157d), **Edda** (76b,79b,107d), **Erda** (23d,41a,47d,68d,69a,131d,177b), **Juda**, **kada** (188), **Leda** (27b, 75d,120c,153a,171d,186b), **Lida** (183c), **meda** (110a), **nuda** (39b), **peda** (114d,144b), **rada** (135c,172a), **Roda** (107b), **sida** (37a, 126c,170a), **soda** (19a,149d,181a), **Teda** (191), **Toda** (45d,76d), **Veda** (77a,b), **Vida** (183c)

D - - **A**   **Dada** (13b,63a,157d), **dama** (65d,152b), **Dana** (28a,96a,171d), **Dara** (18d), **data** (54a), **Daza** (191), **deca** (34d,122d), **depa** (188), **dera** (34c), **deva** (23d,42a,b,56d,77a), **dewa**, **dika** (23a), **Disa** (111a), **dita** (117a), **diva** (110d,123c), **dola** (189), **dona** (83d,121c,151d), **dopa** (117d), **dora** (70b), **Dora** (36d,41a,43b), **dosa** (74b), **doxa** (48b), **draa** (188), **Duma** (135c), **dura** (153c), **dyna** (34c)

- - **DB**   **Badb** (82b), **Bodb** (82b), **Medb**

D - - **B**   **daub** (148d), **dieb** (84a), **doab** (157c), **doob** (18b), **doub** (18b), **drab** (23d,29c,33d,46d,53b,d), **drib** (46b), **drub** (17b,39c), **duab** (157c), **dubb** (161c), **dumb** (153b)

D - - **C**   **disc** (31b), **douc** (101d)

DD - -   **DDSC** (42a)

- **DD** -   **adda** (147a), **Adda** (68c,119d,157a,182a), **Addu** (68c,157a,182a), **Addy** (183d), **Edda** (76b,79b), **eddo** (162a), **eddy** (37d, 39d,160d, 180d), **odds** (28d,172d)

- - **DD**   **dodd** (139c,140c), **gedd** (140a), **Ladd** (143c), **ludd** (23c), **mudd** (188), **Nudd** (23c), **Redd** (153a), **Ridd** (94a), **rodd** (38d), **rudd** (26d, 57a,b), **sadd** (33a,40b,58c,107b), **sudd** (40b,58c,107b), **wadd** (109c)

D - - **D**   **dard**, **dead**, **deed** (7a,52d,91a,166c,168b), **diad** (113a), **dord** (42c), **dowd** (143b), **duad** (113a,171d), **dyad** (113a)

DE - -   **dead**, **deaf**, **deal** (11d,16c,36c,44c,81a,168b), **dean** (33c,109d), **dear**, **debt** (91d,109b), **deca** (34d,122d), **deci** (163b), **deck** (13b, 41c,144d), **dedo** (188), **deed** (7a,52d,91a,166c,168b), **deem** (36b, 85c,164c), **deep** (124a), **deer** (28c,135a,154d) **defi** (61b), **deft** (147c), **defy** (28d), **degu** (132c), **deil** (139b), **dein** (66d), **dele** (26a, 49c,51b,53a,110b,123d,124c,130a,145c,161b), **dell** (43c,174b),

deme (71b,c,167d), **demi** (34b,122c), **demo** (122d), **demy** (113d), **dene** (137a), **Dene** (192), **dens** (90a,167b), **dent** (42c,77d), **deny** (36d,43d,129b), **depa** (188), **dera** (34c), **dere** (74a,79c), **derm** (147c,158d), **desi** (85d), **desk**, **deul** (77b), **deus** (68a,89b), **Deva** (23d,42a,b,56d,77a), **Devi** (147b,153b), **dewa, dewy** (101a)

- DE -   **aden** (34b), **Aden, Ader** (18d), **Ades** (73a), **edel** (66c), **Eden** (6b,50d, 107c,113d,123c), **Eder, EDES** (71c), **idea** (54c,108c,124a,164d), **idee** (61d), **idem** (89d,164a), **Iden** (76a), **ideo** (34b,d), **ides** (41a, b,133a), **odea** (105a,164a), **odel** (48a,112c), **Oder** (132a)

- - DE   **aide** (7b,14a,75d), **Ande** (193), **Aude, bade, Bede** (48c,50c,101d, 175b), **bide** (47c,50b,130a,158b,162a), **bode** (14c,60a,110b,121b), **cade** (25c,27a,76c,85d,116d), **Cade** (50c), **cede** (67b,70c,129d, 160a,168b,185d), **code** (21c,31a,40c,161c), **Dode** (96b), **dude** (40d), **eide** (119c), **fade** (181d,183b), **fide, gade, Gide** (63a), **hade** (66a, 148c,173c), **hide** (53a), **hyde** (188), **Hyde** (45a), **inde, jade** (33c, 65d,71d,166a), **Jude** (11c,96a), **kade** (144a), **lade** (24c,26d,43c,93b, 100a,132a,139d,161b,178d), **lode** (42c,99a,111b,175b), **made, Mede** (10a,b,13c), **mide** (110a), **mode** (54d,96b,157d,179a), **nide** (23c,72a,106c,116d), **node** (35c,85b,87c,94d,120a,124d,160c), **nude** (16c), **onde** (63a,178d), **rede** (37c,81d,138d), **ride** (46b,85c), **rode** (46c), **rude** (134b,172b), **sade** (91d), **side** (13d,22a,b,54a,58a,89a, 161b), **tide** (39d,75d,109c,141c,159d), **Tide, tode** (80a,148a), **unde** (179a), **urde** (86b), **vade** (42c,67d,89b), **vide** (89d,126a,142a), **wade, wide** (133d)

D - - E   **dace** (57a,b), **dale** (43c,128a,174b), **dame** (67b,87c,166b), **Dane** (85d,107d,138a), **dare** (28d,41b,42a,74d,175b), **Dare** (57a), **date** (64a,153a), **Dave** (96b), **Daye** (123d), **daze** (157d), **dele** (26a,49c, 51b,53a,110b,123d,124c,130a,145c,161b), **deme** (71b,c,167d), **dene** (137a), **Dene** (192), **dere** (74a,79c), **dice** (65a), **dike** (49c, 91d), **Dike** (78a), **dime, dine, dire** (45d,55a,104a,163c), **dite** (150b), **dive** (42b,74b,119d), **dobe** (159b,c,172b), **Dode** (96b), **doge** (95b), **dole** (44c,118c,121c,129d), **Dole** (74c), **dome** (39c,133c,155d), **done, dope** (46c,105d), **dore** (61d,67b,69d,117d), **Dore** (50d,63a,b), **dose** (123a), **dote** (17a,90b,94b,97a,112a,139d,165d), **dove** (19a, 117d), **doze** (148a), **dree** (139b,140c,158b,172c), **duce** (29d), **dude** (40d), **duff** (125b), **duke** (107c), **dune** (137a), **dupe** (27c,41c, 72c,160c), **duse** (83c), **dyke** (49c,91d), **dyne** (59d)

D - - F   **daff** (125d), **deaf, doff** (130a,161b), **duff** (125b)

- DG -   **edge** (22a,96d,131c,143c,146b), **edgy** (106c)

D - - G   **dagg** (118c), **dang, ding** (130b), **Doeg** (137c), **dong, drag** (74a, 125b), **dreg, drug** (105d)

DH - -   **dhak** (48a,169a), **dhal** (12b), **dhan** (124c), **dhao** (24c), **Dhar, dhaw** (125a), **dhow** (88d,111c,175d)

- - DH   **sadh** (77a), **Sadh, yodh** (91d)

D - - H   **dagh** (76d), **Dagh, dash** (125c,162d), **dish, doth, drah** (188)

DI - -   **diad** (113a), **dial** (25c), **dian** (46c,130d,170b), **Dian** (68d,69a,c, 102b), **Diau** (192), **dibs** (70c), **dice** (65a), **dick** (43a,55b), **Dick** (96b), **dido** (11b,26c,65a,122a), **Dido** (27a,172c), **dieb** (84a), **diem** (89b,116a), **dier, dies** (41b,89b), **diet** (14a,54c,84c,91b,176a), **Dieu** (61d), **dika** (23a), **dike** (49c,91d), **Dike** (78a), **dill** (13a,117c), **dilo**

287

(120d,168c), **dime, dine, ding** (130b), **dino** (34b), **dint** (48c,59d, 122a), **Dion** (96a,152a), **dipt, dire** (45d,55a,104a,163c), **dirk** (40b), **dirt, Disa** (111a), **disc** (31b), **dish, disk** (31b), **diss** (98b), **dita** (117a), **dite** (150b), **diva** (110d,123c), **dive** (42b,74b,119d), **divi, dixi**

- **DI** - **Adib** (155b), **adit** (51a,100a,114d), **edit** (20d,49d,123a,129a,131a), **Idic** (79b), **idio** (34b,c), **odic** (79c,120a), **Odin** (7c,29d,63c,68c,175d, 183b), **odio** (83b), **udic** (108a)

-- **DI** **Andi** (27d), **cadi** (12a,103a), **kadi** (103a,171a), **Lodi** (105d), **ludi** (133b), **Madi** (174a), **medi** (34c), **Midi** (151b), **nidi** (106c), **nodi** (35c,87c), **padi** (131b), **pedi** (34b), **rodi** (98c), **sidi** (103b), **wadi** (46c,106a,109a,128a,132a)

D -- **I** **dali** (168c,169b), **dari** (38a,70b), **dasi** (77a), **deci** (163b), **defi** (61b), **demi** (34b,122c), **desi** (85d), **Devi** (147b,153b), **divi, dixi, doni** (21a,28c,168a), **drei** (66d,165a)

- **DJ** - **Idjo** (191)

-- **DJ** **hadj** (98b,118a)

D -- **K** **dank** (40b,101a), **dark** (47a,67d,109b,160b), **dauk** (95c), **dawk** (95c), **deck** (13b,41c,144d), **desk, dhak** (48a,169a), **dick** (43a,55b), **Dick** (96b), **dirk** (40b), **disk** (31b), **dock** (40a,117c,144d,179d), **dook** (184a), **duck** (26b,53b,179c), **dunk** (43c,79d), **dusk** (171c), **Dyak** (22b)

- **DL** - **idle** (174b,c,178c), **idly**

D -- **L** **Dail** (49a,82b,c), **deal** (11d,16c,36c,44c,81a,168b), **dell** (139b), **dell** (43c,174b), **deul** (77b), **dhal** (12b), **dial** (25c), **dill** (13a,117c), **doll** (125c), **dowl, dual** (45c,171d), **duel, dull** (21a,32c,173a), **Dull** (94b)

- **DM** - **admi** (65d)

D -- **M** **dawm** (190), **deem** (36b,85c,164c), **derm** (147c,158d), **diem** (89b, 116a), **doom** (42d,55a,134d), **dorm, doum** (168c), **dram** (46b,110c, 121d,148c), **drum** (105a), **duim** (188)

- **DN** - **Edna** (183c)

D -- **N** **dain** (188), **darn, damn, dawn** (14d,41b), **dean** (33c,109d), **dein** (66d), **dhan** (124c), **dian** (46c,130d,170b), **Dian** (68d,69a,c,102b), **Dion** (96a,152a), **Domn** (135a), **doon** (140b,168c), **dorn** (164d), **down** (149d), **duan** (64b)

DO -- **doab** (157c), **doat** (17a,94b,112a,165d), **dobe** (159b,c,172b), **doby** (159b,c), **dock** (40a,117c,144d,179d), **dodd** (139c,140c), **Dode** (96b), **dodo** (19b), **Doeg** (137c), **doer** (8a,116b), **does, doff** (130a,161b), **doge** (95b,175b), **dogy** (46d,103c), **doit** (47a,169d,180d), **Doko** (191), **dola** (189), **dole** (44c,118c,121c,129d), **Dole** (74c), **doli, doll** (125c), **dolt** (20c,59c,157d), **dome** (39c,133c,155d), **Domn** (135a), **domy, dona** (83d,121c,151d), **done, dong, doni** (21a,28c, 168a), **don't, doob** (18b), **dook** (184a), **doom** (42d,55a,134d), **doon** (140b,168c), **door** (51a,121b), **dopa** (117d), **dope** (46c,105d), **dopp** (43c), **dora** (70b), **Dora** (36d,41a,43b,183c,d), **dord** (42c), **dore** (61d,67b,69d,117d), **Dore** (50d,63a,b), **dorm, dorn** (164d), **dorp** (73c,176b), **dorr** (32b), **dory** (21b,58b,144c), **dosa** (74b), **dose** (123a), **doss** (17c), **dost, dote** (17a,90b,94b,97a,112a,139d,165d),

288

doth, Doto (141b), **doty** (43d), **doub** (18b), **douc** (101d), **doum** (168c), **dour** (67d,159a), **dove** (19a,117d), **dowd** (143b), **dowl, down** (149d), **doxa** (48b), **doxy** (129d), **doze** (148a), **dozy**

- DO - **ador** (153b), **Edom** (18c,51b,79b,82c,84a), **idol** (48c,54c,55a,75b, 79d,112d,130b,184d), **odor** (138b,156a)

- - DO **Bodo** (88c), **codo** (188), **dado** (41c,111c,115c,177d), **dedo** (188), **dido** (11b,26c,65a,122a), **Dido** (27a,172c), **dodo** (19b), **eddo** (162a), **endo** (34d,122d,183b), **fado** (121c), **Jodo** (113d), **judo** (84b,85c, 142b), **Lido** (83d,175b), **ludo** (65a,112b), **mado** (14d,57a,170b), **ordo** (22a,30d,122a,171a), **pedo** (34b), **redo** (165c), **sado** (26d, 84d), **todo** (22b,24d,35b,64c,156b), **undo** (11a,93d), **Yedo** (166d)

D - - O **dado** (41c,111c,115c,177d), **Dago, dato** (95c,102c,117a), **dedo** (188), **demo** (122d), **dhao** (24c), **dido** (11b,26c,65a,122a), **Dido** (27a,172c), **dilo** (120d,168c), **dino** (34b), **dodo** (19b), **Doko** (191), **Doto** (141b), **Duco, duro** (190)

D - - P **damp** (101a), **deep** (124a), **dopp** (43c), **dorp** (73c,176b), **drap** (61b, c,62a), **drip, drop** (43d,54b,100b,114c,168b), **dump**

DR - - **draa** (188), **drab** (23d,29c,33d,46d,53b,d), **drag** (74a,125b), **drah** (188), **dram** (46b,110c,121d,148c), **drap** (61b,c,62a), **drat** (100a), **Drau, draw** (42c,53a,92b,117c,121c,167d), **dray** (27a,154c,177b), **dree** (139b,140c,158b,172c), **dreg, drei** (66d,165a), **drew, drey** (154c), **drib** (46b), **Drin, drip, drop** (43d,54b,100b,114c,168b), **drub** (17b,39c), **drug** (105d), **drum** (105a), **drun** (132b)

- DR - **adry** (164c)

- - DR **sadr** (94a), **Sadr** (155b)

D - - R **daer** (22b), **darr** (163c), **Daur** (139b), **dear, deer** (28c,135a,154d), **Dhar, dier, doer** (8a,116b), **door** (51a,121b), **dorr** (32b), **dour** (67d, 159a), **duar, Duhr** (155b), **durr** (70b), **dyer**

- DS - **DDSC** (42a)

- - DS **duds** (32c,166d), **Eads** (23b,24b,50b,82a), **odds** (28d,172d), **suds** (59a)

D - - S **dais** (119b), **dans** (62a), **days, dens** (90a,167b), **deus** (68a,89b), **dibs** (70c), **dies** (41b,89b), **diss** (98b), **does, doss** (17c), **duds** (32c,166d), **Duns, Dyas** (66a)

D - - T **daft** (59c), **dart** (13b,88a,100c,120b,153a,160c), **debt** (91d,109b), **deft** (147c), **dent** (42c,77d), **diet** (14a,54c,84c,91b,176a), **dint** (48c,59d,122a), **dipt, dirt, doat** (17a,94b,112a,165d), **doit** (47a, 169d,180d), **dolt** (20c,59c,157d), **don't, dost, drat** (100a), **Duat** (172d), **duct** (170c), **duet** (104d,171d), **duit** (190), **Duit** (192), **dunt, dust**

DU - - **duab** (157c), **duad** (113a,171d), **dual** (45c,171d), **duan** (64b), **duar, Duat** (172d), **dubb** (161c), **duce** (29d), **duck** (26b,53b,179c), **Duco, duct** (170c), **dude** (40d), **duds** (32c,166d), **duel, duet** (104d,171d), **duff** (125b), **Dufy** (63a), **Duhr** (155b), **duim** (188), **duit** (190), **Duit** (192), **duke** (107c), **duku** (95d,168c), **dull** (21a,32c,173a), **Dull** (94b), **Duma** (135c), **dumb** (153b), **dump, dune** (137a), **dunk** (43c, 79d), **Duns, dunt, dupe** (27c,41c,72c,160c), **dura** (153c), **duro** (190), **durr** (70b), **duse** (83c), **dusk** (171c), **dust, duty** (109b,162b)

- DU - **idun** (107d), **odum** (168c,180a)

289

- - DU **Addu** (68c,157a,182a), **jadu** (95a), **Kadu** (191), **kudu** (11a), **ordu** (170d), **pudu** (41d), **Urdu** (77b), **widu** (102d), **wudu** (102d)

D - - U **Danu** (28a), **datu** (95c,102c,117a), **degu** (132c), **Diau** (192), **Dieu** (61d), **Drau**, **duku** (95d,168c)

D - - W **dauw** (24c), **dhaw** (125a), **dhow** (88d,111c,175d), **draw** (42c,53a, 92b,117c,121c,167d), **drew**

DY - - **dyad** (113a), **Dyak** (22b), **Dyas** (66a), **dyer**, **dyke** (49c,91d), **dyna** (34c), **dyne** (59d,173b)

- DY - **idyl** (114a), **Idyo** (191), **odyl** (59d,79c)

- - DY **Addy** (183d), **Andy** (96b), **body** (72a), **cady** (69d), **eddy** (37d,39d, 160d,180d), **fady**, **jady**, **Judy** (125c,183d), **lady**, **sidy** (123b), **tidy** (106a,111b), **tody** (19b,d,59a,166a), **undy** (179a), **urdy** (86b), **wady** (109a,128a,132a)

D - - Y **Davy** (96b,136b), **dazy**, **defy** (28d), **demy** (113d), **deny** (36d,43d, 129b), **dewy** (101a), **doby** (159b,c), **dogy** (46d,103c), **domy**, **dory** (21b,58b,144c), **doty** (43d), **doxy** (129d), **doxy**, **dray** (27a,154c, 177b), **drey** (154c), **Dufy** (63a), **duty** (109b,162b)

- DZ - **adze** (40c,167a), **Idzo** (191)

- - DZ **Lodz**

D - - Z **Daez**

EA - - **each**, **Eads** (23b,24b,50b,82a), **eard** (139d), **earl** (107c,166b), **earn** (42d,64b,99a), **ease** (7c,8d,35a,100d,129d,130b,c,150c), **east**, **East** (111b), **easy** (54a,146d,149d,172b) **eats**, **eaux** (178c), **eave** (133c),

- EA - **bead** (17a,122a,146b), **beak** (19a), **beal** (139d), **beam**, **bean** (91b, 142a,175a), **bear** (27a,50b,113c,155a), **beat** (58c,87b,131a,164d, 165b,180d), **beau**, **dead**, **deaf**, **deal** (11d,16c,36c,44c,81a,168b), **dean** (33c,109d), **dear**, **feak** (39d,171c), **fear** (113c,155a), **feat** (7a, 52d), **geal** (47d,163c), **gean** (29c), **gear** (32c,112a,167b), **geat** (77d, 101a), **Geat** (138a), **head** (29d), **heaf** (144a), **heal**, **heap** (117d), **hear** (75b,c,92d), **heat**, **jean** (37c), **Jean** (183c), **keal** (25a), **lead** (35d,43d,72b,74d,81a), **leaf** (55c,73c,119b), **Leah** (19a,84a,87b, 183c), **leak** (110c), **leal** (54b,94c,139d), **lean** (128a,148b,152d, 164b,166a), **leap** (26c), **lear** (139d), **Lear** (37a,143b), **mead** (46a, 78a,97d,99b), **Mead** (78a), **meal** (72a,130b), **mean** (15a,42b,146c, 156b), **meat** (59b), **neaf** (58a,73c), **Neal**, **neap** (165c,167a,177b), **near** (11d,32c,107b), **neat** (165c,169d), **peag** (144a,178a), **peal** (98b), **peak** (9a,38c,159b,186b), **peal** (131c,d), **pean** (64c,150b), **pear** (64a), **peat** (64a,175a), **read** (116d,157d), **real** (7a), **ream** (18c,37d,50d,113d,171c), **reap** (7a,40a,74a), **rear** (15b,23a,b,24a, 51b,76d,127c), **seah** (188), **seal** (10c,d,54d,64c,96a,118b,128a), **seam** (85b,d,160a,176d,185a), **Sean** (85b,96a), **sear** (23d,27d,72d, 138c), **seat** (98c,156b), **teak** (41a,48a,168c), **teal** (19b,20d,46c,d), **team** (38c,72a,113a), **tean** (140c,167a), **tear** (67c,87b,130a), **veal**, **weak** (55b), **weal** (124d,157c,180c,d), **wean** (8d,42a), **wear** (50b), **yeah**, **Yean** (88a), **year**, **yeas** (177c), **zeal** (12c,55d)

- - EA **Alea** (14b,31c,167d), **area** (37d,38a,44c,53a,93b,110d,127d, 138c,168a,186d), **asea** (39b,177c), **brea** (100b), **crea** (92c,151d), **evea** (82a), **Evea** (95a), **flea** (81b), **Frea**, **Gaea** (47d,69a), **idea** (54c, 108c,124d,164d), **Itea** (145d,160c,181d), **odea** (105a,164a), **olea**

290

(170b), **Olea** (110b), **Otea** (71a,82d), **oxea** (153d), **plea** (51a,52d, 122a,130b), **rhea** (37a,56a,111d,133d), **Rhea** (19b.68d,87c,103c, 186b), **shea** (25a,168c,d), **Thea** (162c), **uvea** (53c,82b)

E - - A **Ecca** (66a), **Edda** (76b,79b,107d,136b), **Edna** (183c), **Egba** (191), **Ekka** (26d), **Elba** (105d), **Elia** (88a,115d), **ella** (152c, 158c), **Ella** (183c), **Elsa** (70a,93c,110d,177b,183c), **Emma** (183c), **Enna** (146a), **epha** (75c), **Erda** (23d,41a,47d,68d,69a,131d,177b), **eria** (13d,146d), **Erma** (183c), **Erua** (103c), **esca** (11c,44a,70c), **esta** (152d,164c), **etna** (75b,153c,157a,175d,177a,c), **Etta** (183c), **evea** (82a,95a), **eyra** (181d), **ezba** (188), **Ezra** (96a)

EB - - **Eben** (96a), **Eber** (51a,75c,99d), **Ebro** (132a), **eboe** (28b,110a,168c, 169b), **Eboe, ebon** (20b), **ebur** (89c)

- EB - **ceba** (169b), **debt** (91d,109b), **Hebe** (39c,69c,186b), **Nebo** (68c, 102d,103d,183a), **peba** (12d), **Peba** (193), **Reba** (18d,86c,144a), **Seba** (18c,39d), **sebi** (34b), **ueba** (188), **zebu** (22d,80d,112c)

- - EB **bleb** (20c,23d,67c), **dieb** (84a), **pleb** (10d,35b,180b), **Sleb** (12a), **sweb** (160d), **theb** (188)

EC - - **ecad** (73a,119b), **Ecca** (66a), **ecce** (17d,89a,c), **echo** (130b,d), **Echo** (105d), **ecru** (17d,23d,172b), **ecto** (34c,122d)

- EC - **beck** (107c), **deca** (34d,122d), **deci** (163b), **deck** (13b,41c,144d), **heck** (100a), **lech** (102b), **neck** (83a), **peca** (190), **peck** (24d), **peco** (162b), **reck** (26d,75c), **rect** (117b), **sech** (97c), **seck** (173d), **sect** (42b,54a,114c), **teca** (192), **Teca** (192), **Tech, teck** (128b), **Teco** (192)

- - EC **alec** (10a,57c,d,76c), **Alec** (137a), **avec** (63a,183a), **haec** (90a, 164c), **spec**

E - - C **epic** (76b,120a), **eric** (115b), **Eric** (71d,96a,107d,138a,164a,176b), **eruc** (37a,56a)

ED - - **Edam** (29c), **Edar** (18d), **Edda** (76b,79b,107d,136b), **eddo** (162a), **eddy** (37d,39d,160d,180d), **edel** (66c), **Eden** (6b,50d,107c,113d, 123c), **Eder, Edes** (71c), **edge** (22a,96d,131c,143c,146b), **edgy** (106c), **edit** (20d,49d,123a,129a,131a), **Edna** (183c), **Edom** (18c, 51b,79b,82c,84a)

- ED - **Beda** (101d), **Bede** (48c,50c,101d,175b), **cede** (67b,70c,129d,160a, 168b,185d), **dedo** (188), **gedd** (140a), **Leda** (27b.75d,120c,153a, 171d,186b), **meda** (110a), **Medb, Mede** (10a,b,13c), **medi** (34c), **peda** (114d,144b), **pedi** (34b), **pedo** (34b), **redd** (153a), **rede** (37c, 81d,138d), **redo** (165c), **Teda** (191), **Veda** (77a,b), **Yedo** (166d)

- - ED **abed** (130c), **aged** (110a), **bled, bred** (23c,48c,127c), **coed, deed** (7a,52d,91a,166c,168b), **feed** (108c), **fled, Fred** (96b), **gled** (19a, 52a,87a), **heed** (14c,75b,109b), **hued, lied** (66d,150b), **meed** (128c, 131a), **Moed** (100c), **need** (42b,52d,87b,122a,178a), **Obed** (135d), **pied** (96c,103c,114b,117c,154a,174d), **reed** (16a,70d,97b,105a, 111b,118b,144b), **Reed** (163a), **roed, seed** (70b,111c,112c,119a, 151b,154a), **shed** (27a,90c,101b,144b), **sled** (40a), **sned** (93d,125a, 140a), **sped, syed** (103b), **tied, toed, used** (6d,73a), **weed**

E - - D **eard** (139d), **ecad** (73a,119b), **egad** (100a,109a), **eild** (138d,140a), **elod** (49b,59d,79c), **emyd** (163c,167c), **Enid** (13b,25d,66b,163a, 183c)

EE - - **eely** (185a), **eery** (172b,180a)

- EE - beef, been (149a), beer (18c), bees (185b), beet (175a), deed (7a, 52d,166c,168b), deem (36b,85c,164c), deep (124a), deer (28c, 135a,154d), feed (108c), feel (72a,142c), fees (128c), Geez (6c, 51d), heed (14c,75b,109b), heel, Heep (41a,43b), heer (47a,184b, 185b), jeel, jeep, jeer (138c,162b), keef (75d), keek (154c), keel (128d,134d,144c,d), keen (15a,88a,177b), keep (123a,130d), keet (72b), leek (58b,76a,110c,177d), leer (9d,58a,67c,93d,112a,148c), lees (46a,142a), leet (26a,38a,139d), meed (128c,131a), meek (93d,99d), meer, meet (11d,13d,36a,50a,81d,142d), need (42b, 52d,87b,122a,178a), neem (96d,168c,169a), neep (140c,171b), neer (14b,86b,108b), peek (93d), peel (53a,114a), peen (73c), peep (93d,115c), peer (51a,107c), peet (64a), reed (16a,70d,97b,105a, 111b,118b,144b), Reed (163a), reef (129a,137a,145a), reek (49d, 53c,64a,148d,149a), reel (21b,40b,d,153c,154a,c,d,180d), reem (18d), seed (70b,111c,112c,119a,151b,154a), seek (141c), seel (20c,32c,143b), seem (11c), seen, seep (110c,116a,154b), seer (60a,124c,150c), teel (142d), teem (6b,121d), teen (139b,c,140b, 158d), teer (25b,69d), Tees (108a), veer (28d,144c,171b), weed week, weel (16d,57d,140d,180d), weep (39b,88a,104a), weet (19d)

- - EE agee (13d,15c,38d), ajee (15c,139a), akee (168c), alee (15c,75d, 144b,157a,182a), bree (139a), byee (189), chee (189), clee (19a, 129a), Cree (192), dree (139b,140c,158b,172c), epee (55c,160d), flee (44a,70d,131b), free (44a,70d,131b), ghee (24d), glee (99a,150b), idee (61d), inee (120b), Klee (113a), knee (85b), ogee (40c,101a,b,120b), pree (139d), Rhee (87c), shee (82b), skee (149c), slee (140b,148c), smee (19b,46c,d,118b,119d,141b,181b), Smee (116d), snee (40a, b,43d,87a), Spee (66d,70b), thee (124b), tree (11d,37a,66a,184b), twee, tyee (29d), usee, whee

E - - E ease (7c,8d,35a,100d,129d,130b,c,150c), eave (133c), eboe (28b, 110a,168c,169b), Eboe, ecce (17d,89a,c), edge (22a,96d,131c, 143c,146b), eide (119c), eine (66c), Eire (82b), Elbe (108a), elle (62b,c), else (18b,79b,111d), ence (158c), enne (34c), ense (139b, 158c), ente (70b,151d), epee (55c,160d), Erie (82c,87d), erne (19c, d,47b,54b,141a), Erse (28a,64b,82b), esce (158d), esne (10c,45b, 142c,148a,164d), esse (7a,18a,52d,89a,90a,159a,166c), este (152b, d,164c), Este (55c,83c,112d), etre (61a,c,62d,166c), ette (158a,c,d), euge (180a), evoe (15b,130d,181c), eyre (23c,31b,85c), Eyre

EF - - Efik (191)

- EF - defi (61b), deft (147c), defy (28d), heft (179d), Heft, jefe (152a), jeff (133d), left (42c), reft (32a,42c,44d,167b), teff (6c), weft (39a,165a,184b)

- - EF alef (91c), atef (39a,48d), beef, chef, clef (104d,105a), elef (91c), fief (55d), keef (75d), kief (75d), lief (181d), reef (129a,137a, 145a), tref (172b)

E - - F elef (91c), Enif (155b)

EG - - egad (100a,109a), Egba (191), Egbo (141d), Eger (49a), eggs (112a), eggy (185d), Egil (107d), egis (14b,d,115a,124d,144b,154a,161a), egol (11b)

- EG - bega (188), degu (132c), hegh, mega (34b,c), pega (57a,130a, 158b), Pegu (24c,102a,127d), sego (24b,25a,92b,174c), tegg (143d,

292

171d), **vega** (110d,152c), **Vega** (155b), **Wega** (155b), **Wegg** (111d), **yegg** (24c)

- - EG **areg** (116a,137a), **Areg, Doeg** (137c), **dreg, Gheg** (8c), **skeg** (7d, 86a,144d,157d,184a), **sneg** (139b), **waeg** (19b,72c,87a)

EH - - **eheu** (52c)

- EH - **behn** (137d), **Hehe** (191), **jehu** (46b), **Jehu** (18c), **lehr** (67c,112a), **peho** (19b,102c,106d), **sehr** (66d), **tehr** (27c,68a)

- - EH **okeh** (8d,37b)

E - - H **each, Elah** (18c,86d), **Esth** (16a,51d), **Etah** (51c,71d), **etch, eyah** (95b,108d,111c)

EI - - **eide** (119c), **eild** (138d,140a), **eine** (66c) **Eire** (82b)

- EI - **Beid** (155b), **ceil** (92c,112a), **deil** (139b), **dein** (66d), **feis** (82b), **gein** (67d), **heii** (74b), **hein** (52c,61c), **heir, keif** (75d), **keir** (20c, 174d), **Leif** (107d), **Leir, mein** (30b), **nein** (66c), **meio** (188), **Neil** (96a), **reim** (112c), **rein** (29b,130c), **reis** (26c,29d,75a,103b), **seid** (103b), **Seid** (42d,101a,171a), **Seik** (77b), **Seim** (120c), **sein** (146c), **seip** (110c), **Seir** (51b,94a,103d), **seis** (147b,152c), **seit** (189), **Teig** (96a), **teil** (92b,c,168c), **veil** (74d,76c), **vein** (20d,157b), **weir** (40b,57d), **zein**

- - EI **drei** (66d,165a), **kuei** (44a), **kwei** (44a), **Omei** (24a), **quei** (189), **vlei** (38c,160a)

E - - I **Ekol** (191), **Enki** (15b), **equi** (122d), **etui** (27a,29b,62c,106b,148d, 166d,174b)

EJ - - **ejoo** (55b,168c)

- EJ - **Beja** (6c,191), **Nejd, reja** (152b), **Sejm** (120c), **teju** (151b)

EK - - **Ekka** (26d), **Ekoi** (191)

- EK - **beka** (189), **feke, Peke** (45a,148d), **Rekl** (16a), **weka** (58c,106d, 107a,127b), **weki** (55c), **Zeke** (96b)

- - EK **chek** (59c), **esek** (18d), **hoek** (39d), **keek** (154c), **leek** (58b,76a, 110c,177d), **meek** (93d,99d), **peek** (93d,115c), **reek** (49d,53c, 64a,148d,149a), **seek** (141c), **trek** (85c,93c,99d,168b)

E - - K **Efik** (191), **esek** (18d)

EL - - **Elah** (18c,86d), **Elam** (18d,37d,82a,116c,144b), **elan** (12c,41a,50d, 62a,153c,177a,186b), **ELAS** (71c), **Elba** (105d), **Elbe** (108a), **elef** (91c), **Elia** (88a,115d), **Elis** (22c,37d,71b,107c), **ella** (152c,158c, 174d), **Ella** (183c), **elle** (62b,c), **elmy, elod** (49b,59d,79c), **Elon** (18c,51b, 108a), **Elsa** (70a,93c,110d,177b,183c), **else** (18b,79b,111d), **Elul** (102b)

- EL - **bela** (12a), **Bela** (18b,48c,78d), **Beli** (23c), **bell** (24c,39d), **Bell** (162d), **belt** (16a,31a), **cela** (62d), **cell** (39b), **celt** (30c,82c,123a, 156c,167b,179b), **Celt** (10a,180a,b), **dele** (26a,49c,51b,53a,110b, 123d,124c,130a,145c,161b), **dell** (43c,174b), **eely** (185a), **fell** (40a, 58b,76c,115d,147d), **felt, geld** (162b), **gelt** (101c), **Hela** (93c), **held, helm** (144d,165d), **help** (14a), **kela** (189), **keld** (154b), **kelp** (82a,141c), **Kelt** (180b), **Lely** (47a), **mele** (74b,150b), **melt, Nell** (110a,183d), **pela** (30c), **Pele** (69c,74c), **pelf** (131b), **pelo** (83b), **pelt** (53a), **pelu** (30a,106d,168c), **rely** (16b,170b), **self** (48d,80d), **sell** (97a,115c,175b), **tela** (22d,98c,121b,166a,179c), **tele** (34b,

293

122c), teli (94b), tell (105d,129c,154b), Tell (160d), vela (98c 136b,149d), Vela (36b,c), veld (151a), velo (175b), weld (47c,85b, 173c), Welf (67a), welk (65c,96d,141b), well, welt (36d,131b, 145a,b,177b,d), yell (145c), yelp (151b)

- - EL Abel (7a,25b), bhel (126d), coel (39b), duel, edel (66c), esel (66b), ezel (47a,85d), feel (72a,142c), fuel (65c), Gael (28a,96c,138d), goel (15a,75c), heel, Jael (147b), jeel, Joel (96a), keel (128d,134d, 144c,d), kiel (128d,134d), Kiel (25d), koel (19a,b,39b), nael (189), noel (26d,150b), Noel (30d,96a), odel (48a,112c), Orel, peel (53a, 114a), reel (21b,40b,d,153c,154a,c,d,180d), Riel (129a), ryel (190), seel (20c,32c,143b), tael (91d,179d), teel (142d), tuel, weel (16d, 57d,140d,180d), wiel (140d,180d)

E - - L earl (107c), edel (66c), Egil (107d), egol (11b), Elul (102b), Emil (96a), enol (29c,158b), eral (51a), esel (66b), etal (89a), evil (79c, 95d,147a,181a,185c), ezel (47a,85d)

EM - - Emer (39b,183c), emeu (111d), Emil (96a), Emim (67a,100d), emir (12a,103a,b,123c,134d,135a,171a), emit (43d,49a,53c,58d,83a, 142c), Emma (183c), emyd (163c,167c), Emys (167c,171b)

- EM - bema (28d,31a,114b,119b,125b,137a), deme (71b,c,167d), demi (34b,122c), demo (122d), demy (113d), feme (181b), hemi (122c), hemo (34a,122b), hemp (26a,37a,56a,133d), kemp (139b), memo (108b), Nema (34d,48c,134b,164d,176c), nemo (34b), Nemo (56a, 85c), Rems, Rems, seme (45c,138b,151b,154b,155c,157b), semi (34b,80b,122c,d), tema (12a,164a), Tema, xema (72c), Xema (12c), zeme (55d,161b,180b), zemi (55d,161b,180b)

- - EM ahem, alem (98b,155a,170d,171a), asem (9a,49a,69c), clem (56b, 158b), deem (36b,85c,164c), diem (89b,116a), haem (122b), idem (89d,164a), item (6d,13b,42d,51a,90d,92d,107a,113d,114c), Khem (113c), neem (96d,168c,169a), poem (51a), reem (18d), riem (76c, 112c,157c,164d), seem (11c), Shem (11c), stem (29b,125a,154d, 155a,156d), teem (6b,121d), them (124b)

E - - M edam (29c), Edom (18c,51b,79b,82c,84a), Elam (18d,37d,82a,116c, 144b), Emim (67a,100d), enam (70c,77a), Enam (85c), etym (133d), exam

EN - - enam (70c,77a,85c), ence (158c), endo (34d,122d,183b), Enid (13b,25d,66b,163a,183c), Enif (155b), enin (20d), Enkl (15b), Enna (146a), enne (34c), enol (29c,158b), Enon (18c,d), Enos (7a,18d,52a, 70c,96a,143a), enow (50d,123a,158b), ense (139b,158c), enso (34d,183b), ente (70b,151d), ento (34b,d,183b), envy (41b), Enyo (12c,69c,178a), Enzu (102b)

- EN - bena (176a), bend (39d,171b), bene (18a,83c,90a,106d,122a, 180a), beng (43a), beni (116a,142b), Beni (191), beno (113b,117a), bent (80b), benu (49a), cena (88d,133a), cene (34c), cens (115b), cent (36d), dene (137a), Dene (192), dens (90a,167b), dent (42c, 77d), deny (36d,43d,129b), fend (114b,178b), gena (29b), gene (54a,76b), Gene (96b), gens (42d,132d), gent, genu (6b,18a,87a, 89c), hens (121d), Jena (105d,165b), keno, Kent (90d), lena (56d), Lena (36b), lend (6d,79d), lene (36b,149a,172b), leno (37c, 53b), lens (67c,95b,111a,129b,162d), lent (54d), Lent (115d,141c), mend (130b), mene (19a,73d,108d,185c), Ment (54b,164a), menu

294

(19a,27a), **Menu, nene** (19b,74c), **pend, pene, pent** (36a), **rena** (25b,132c), **rend** (32a,159c,162c,185a), **Reni** (83d), **Reno, rent** (58a,91b,138b,153d,162c,167c), **send** (42c,44b,95c,121c,130a, 144c,168b), **senn** (76b), **Sens** (63b), **sent, tend** (26d,80b,93d,100a), **tene** (34d,131b), **teng** (188), **tent** (26b,115a), **vena** (90a,175a), **vend** (97a,115c,142b), **Vend** (10b,148a), **vent** (8b,11b,110d,112a), **wend** (67d,123d), **Wend** (10b,148a), **went** (42c), **xeno** (34d), **yeni** (19b,161d), **Zend, Zeno** (71b), **zenu** (143d)

- - EN   **aden** (34b), **Aden, alen** (40d,138a), **amen** (14a,80b,94a,137a,149c, 175c,184b), **Amen** (86d,127d,164a), **aten** (150a,159b), **been** (149a), **bien** (63a,140c,179a,180a), **bren** (72d,95a), **Caen, Chen** (149b), **Eben** (96a), **Eden** (6b,50d,107c,113d,123c), **even** (51a,58b,79d,91d, 149a,173a), **glen** (43c), **hien** (30b), **hoen** (189), **Iden** (76a), **Iren** (127c), **Iten** (192), **keen** (15a,88a,177b), **lien** (65c,91a,124c), **mien** (11c,17b,26d,44c,96b), **omen** (14c,59d,60a,121c,123a,146b), **open** (26a,60d,81a,109b,112c,125b,172b,173c), **oven** (15d,78c,86b), **Owen** (96a,183c), **oxen** (10c), **peen** (73c), **pien** (13b), **rien** (62b), **seen, Shen** (68a), **sken** (164a), **sten** (72c,95a), **teen** (139b,c,140b, 158d), **then, tien** (147d), **T-men** (168b), **when** (180d), **wren** (19b,c), **Wren** (50b)

E - - N   **earn** (42d,64b,99a), **Eben** (96a), **ebon** (20b), **Eden** (6b,50d,107c, 113d,123c), **elan** (12c,41a,50d,62a,153c,177a,186b), **Elon** (18c, 51b), **enin** (20d), **Enon** (18c,d), **Eoan** (41a,85b), **Eoin** (85b), **Erin** (82b), **Eton** (33b,50c,84a), **Evan** (96a), **even** (51a,58b,79d,91d, 149a,173a), **Ewan**

EO - -   **Eoan** (41a,85b), **Eoin** (85b)

- EO -   **feod** (55d), **Leon** (96a), **meou, meow, neon** (65c), **peon** (28c,59c, 99c), **Teos** (82a)

- - EO   **areo** (34c), **Ateo** (120d), **Cleo** (126b), **ideo** (34b,d,164d), **oleo** (34c), **skeo** (57d)

E - - O   **Ebro** (132a), **echo** (130b,d), **Echo** (105d), **ecto** (34c,122d), **eddo** (162a), **Egbo** (141d), **ejoo** (55b,168c), **endo** (34d,122d,183b), **enso** (34d,183b), **ento** (34b,d,183b), **Enyo** (12c,69c,178a), **ergo** (164b)

EP - -   **epee** (55c,160d), **epha** (75c), **epic** (76b,120a), **epos** (51a,76b,120a)

- EP -   **cepa** (110c), **cepe** (48c), **depa** (188), **kepi** (99d), **kept, Nepa** (106b, 178c), **pepo** (39b,64a,70a,98c,125c,154c), **repp** (53b,131a), **seps** (93b,142d), **sept** (31d,82b,143a,149c), **Sept** (45b), **Veps** (191), **wept**

- - EP   **deep** (124a), **Heep** (41a,43b), **jeep, keep** (123a,130d), **neep** (140c, 171b), **peep** (93d,115c), **prep** (138b), **seep** (110c,116a,154b), **skep** (16d,17c,77c), **step** (70b,112b,177b,d), **weep** (39b,88a,104a)

EQ - -   **equi** (122d)

ER - -   **eral** (51a), **erat** (89c), **Erda** (23d,41a,47d,68d,69a,131d,177b), **erer** (17d,150c), **ergo** (164b), **eria** (13d,146d), **eric** (115b), **Eric** (71d, 96a,107d,138a,164a,176b), **Erie** (82c,87d), **Erin** (82b), **Eris** (12c, 68d,109c), **Erma** (183c), **erne** (19c,d,47b,54b,141a), **Eros** (11c, 39c,68b,97c,182d), **Erse** (28a,64b,82b), **erst** (60b), **Erua** (103c), **eruc** (37a,56a), **eryx** (137a)

- ER -   **aera** (8a), **aeri** (34a), **aero** (8b,34a,b,58c,59a), **aery** (47b,51d,106c), **Bera** (86d), **berg** (79b), **berm** (25d,90d,145c), **Bern** (160d), **Bert**

295

(96b), **cera** (152d,161d,179a), **cere** (19a,114b,149d,179a), **cern** (41c), **cero** (57b,c,d, 180b), **dera** (34c), **dere** (74a,79c), **derm** 147c,158d), **eery** (172b,180a), **fern** (142a), **feru** (37a,56a,133d), **gerb** (56d,143d), **Gerd** (63c), **Gere** (183c), **Geri** (183c), **germ** (17d, 99c,134d), **Hera** (69c,85d,110b,126b,186b,d), **herb** (58b,158b), **herd** (39a,46c,72a), **here, herl** (16b,59a), **hero** (42b,124d,137b), **Hero** (90c), **Herr** (66c), **hers** (124c), **jerk** (153a), **kerb** (146b), **kere** (75c,128b), **kerf** (40a,108b), **keri** (75c,128b), **kern** (59c,172a), **Kern** (132b), **Kerr, Lero** (82d), **lerp** (51d,141d), **mere** (16c,22b, 62a,78b,87d,96c,110c,120d,146d,148b), **merl** (20b), **mero** (72a), **Meru** (77a,103d), **Nera** (165b), **Neri, Nero** (8a,126d,133a,172c), **Pera** (60a), **pere** (61c,63b), **peri** (54b,116b,c,122b), **perk** (84d, 93a), **perm** (49b,97d), **pern** (78a), **pero** (152a), **pert** (80a,93a,137c, 154b), **Peru, qere** (75c), **peri** (75c), **sera** (11b,20d,59a,83a,180d), **Serb** (15d,148a,186c), **sere** (24d,46a,46c,138c,183b), **Sere** (158b), **serf** (21d,148a), **seri** (18b), **Seri** (192), **sero** (34d,88d,164b,178d), **Sert** (151d), **tera** (23d,84c), **term** (92b,105b,142b,166b), **tern** (19b, 32d,72c,94a,138c,141a,160a), **terp** (12b,123a), **vera** (140c,151b, 175c), **Vera** (183c), **verb** (7a,114b,184b), **verd** (71d), **veri** (28b), **vert** (71d,166a,171b), **very** (149c), **were** (139b), **werf** (54d), **weri** (15c,27c), **wert, zero** (31a,84c,108c), **Zero** (118d)

- - ER   **Acer** (96c) **Ader** (18d), **afer** (48a,182b), **ager** (47c,56a,89b,c,131d, 133b), **amer** (61b), **aner** (18d,96b), **aper** (32d), **Aser** (84a), **Ater** (18c), **Auer** (79a), **aver** (7c,14a,15c,41c,95c,140d,155c,160b, 184c), **beer** (18c), **bier** (33b,66b), **Boer** (151a), **Brer** (172b), **cher** (61b), **daer** (22b), **deer** (28c,135a,154d), **dier, doer** (8a,116b), **dyer, Eber** (51a,75c,99d), **Eder, Eger** (49a), **Emer** (39b,183c), **erer** (17d, 150c), **eser, euer** (66d), **ever** (9b,14b,80b), **ewer** (84c,85c,118c, 181b), **eyer, gier** (47b), **goer, heer** (47a, 184b, 185b), **hier** (63a, 185d), **Hler** (141a), **hoer, icer, lmer, lser** (49a), **iter** (22d,76c,85c, 89c,114d,132a,b,133a,b), **jeer** (138c,162b), **kier** (20c,174d), **leer** (9d,58a,67c,93d,112a,148c), **meer, neer** (14b,86b,108b), **Oder** (132a), **omer** (51a,75c), **oner** (20d,53a,75c,162d,173a,d), **oser** (61b), **over** (6b,38c,80a,114d,130a), **oxer** (55c), **oyer** (38a,75b,119c), **peer** (51a,93d,107c), **pier** (23a,88b,180c), **rier** (180b), **roer** (72d), **ruer, saer** (163a), **seer** (60a,124c,150c), **sher** (65d,165c), **sier** (57a,118b), **ster** (158c,d), **suer** (124d), **teer** (25b,69d), **tier** (118a,134b), **tyer, uber** (66b), **user** (49d), **veer** (28d,144c,171b), **vier** (66c), **waer** (40b), **Ymer** (67a,131c), **Yser**

E - - R   **Eber** (51a,75c,99d), **ebur** (89c), **Edar** (18d), **Eder, Eger** (49a), **Emer** (39b,183c,), **emir** (12a,103a,b,123c,171a), **erer** (17d,150c), **eser, euer** (66d), **ever** (9b,14b,80b), **ewer** (84d,85c,118c,181b), **eyer**

ES - -   **Esau** (82c,84a,128c), **Esay, esca** (11c,44a,70c), **esce** (158d), **esek** (18d), **esel** (66b), **eser, esne** (10c,45b,142c,148a,164d), **Esop** (53b, 54a), **esox** (57b), **espy** (44a,142a), **esse** (7a,18a,52d,89a,90a,159a, 166c), **esta** (152d,164c), **este** (152b,d,164c), **Este** (55c,83c,d,112d), **Esth** (16a,51d), **Esus**

- ES -   **aesc** (12d,64d), **Besa** (68b,119c), **Bess** (76c,183d), **best** (41d,159c, 160a), **cess** (91d,94c,162b), **cest** (18a,67b), **desi** (85d), **desk, euer** (66d), **fess** (23c,51b), **fest, gest** (7c,41d,52d,133c), **hest** (35a), **jess** (157a), **jest** (169c), **Jesu, less** (100c,108b,141d), **lest** (59d,163d),

296

mesa (49b,76d,119b,161a), mese (71c), mesh (50d,106c), mess (22b,44b,77c,85d,104b,165c,173d), ness (26b,75a,124b), nest (38b, 74b,130d,149c,160b), oese (15d,119c), pesa (190), peso (99c), pest (108c,116b,118d,170a), rese (127b), resh (91d), rest (15d,91b, 104d,105a,115a,b,130a,b,161b), sesi (20b,57a,149b), sess (149c, 162b), Tesa (80c), Tess (73d,164c,183d), test (26a,51c,144a,169c, 170c), vest (32c,177b), West (9c,50b,109b), Yeso (72d), zest (55d, 72d)

- - ES Ades (73a), Ames (9c,82a), anes (110c,140a), Ares (49b,51b,68c, 76a,97a,105c,110b,178a,186d), ates (160c), Aves (19d), bees (185b), Bres, dies (41b,89b), does, EDES (71c), fees (128c), Ghes (193), gres (156d), ides (41a,b,133a), Ives (9c,90b), lees (46a, 142a), ones (116a), oyes (38a,39b,75b), pres (62b), spes, Spes (69a,78a), Tees (108a), tres (19a,52b,63a,152d,165a,175c), uses (18a), wies (185a)

E - - S Eads (23b,24b,50b,82a), eats, EDES (71c), eggs (112a), egis (14b, d,115a,124d,144b,154a,161a), ELAS (71c), Elis (22c,37d,71b, 107c), Emys (167c,171b), Enns, Enos (7a,18d,52a,70c,96a,143a), epos (51a,76b,120a), Eris (12c,68d,109c), Eros (11c,39c,68b,97c, 182d), Esus, etes (177c), eyas (106c,173a)

ET - - Etah (51c,71d), etal (89a), etat (62d), etch, etes (177c), etna (75b, 153c,157a,175d,177a,c), Eton (33b,50c,84a), etre (61a,c,62d,166c), Etta (183c), ette (158a,c,d), etui (27a,29b,62c,106b,148d,166d, 174b), etym (133d)

- ET - Aeta (94d,95d,100a,106b,117a), beta (71a,91c,141d), bete (61a,107c), beth (91c), Beth (8c,183d), cete (180b,c), ceto (34a), fete (55d,129b), geta (84b,145a), gett (44d), Heth (77c), jete (16a), Jeth (102a), keta (45a), Keta, Ketu (48b), lete, Leti (82d), Leto (11c), Lett (16a,90a,93a), meta (132d,133a), Meta, mete (9a, 11d,22b,44c,45b,98a,121c), nete (71c,108b,163d), neti (164a), nett, pete (136b), Pete (96b), peto (57a,177b), Peto (76a), rete (106c,119c), seta (23b,27c,73a,b,123b,153c), seth (98d), Seth (7a, 52b,68a,b,96a,98d), seti (34a), Seti (116d), sett (115a,156d), tete (61d,73b,74d), teth (91d), veta (104a), veto (94a,124a), Veto, weta (93c), yeta (84c), zeta (71b,91c)

- - ET abet (8b,15b,50a,59b,75d,81c,141d,159d), Ahet (49a,102a), anet (43c), Apet (97c), aret (128c), beet (175a), blet (64a), diet (14a, 54c,84c,91b,176a), duet (104d,171d), evet (48d,107a,136c,169d), fret (28c,35b,111c,184d), keet (72b), khet (188), lact (60d), leet (26a,38a), meet (11d,13d,36a,50a,81d,142d), oket (189), peet (64a), piet (29b,95b), plet (135d), poet (49b), pret (188), pyet (95b), spet (16c,57a,142c), stet (91b,123d,124c), suet (54d), tret (9a,178b,179d), voet (188), weet (19d), whet (143c,156b)

E - - T east, East (111b), edit (20d,49d,123a,129a,131a), emit (43d,49a, 53c,58d,83a,142c), erat (89c), erst (60b), etat (62d), evet (48d, 107a,136c,169d), exit (114d), eyot (82d)

EU - - euer (66d), euge (180a)

- EU - deul (77b), deus (68a,89b), feud (55d,126b,175b), Geum (76b), jeux (61d), meum (27a,89c), Meum, neue (66c), peur (61c), Zeus (135a)

- - EU   **bleu** (61b), **Dieu** (61d), **eheu** (52c), **emeu** (111d), **lieu** (118c,155d)

E - -U   **ecru** (17d,23d,172b), **eheu** (52c), **emeu** (111d), **Enzu** (102b), **Esau** (82c,84a,128c)

EV - -   **Evan** (96a), **even** (51a,58b,79d,91d,149a,173a), **evea** (82a,95a), **ever** (9b,14b,80b), **evet** (48d,107a,136c,169d), **evil** (79c,95d,147a, 181a,185c), **evoe** (15b,130d,181c)

- EV -   **bevy** (38a,58c), **Deva** (23d,42a,b,56d,77a), **Devi** (147b,153b), **hevi** (111d), **Leve** (62a), **Levi** (84a,90c), **levo** (91a), **levy** (14a, 162b), **Neva** (91b,132a), **neve** (56d,67c,70c,149b), **peva** (12d), **pevy** (91d,94c), **reve** (61c,104d), **revs** (131a), **seve** (63a,182c)

- - EV   **Kiev**, **Stev** (155b)

EW - -   **Ewan**, **ewer** (84d,85c,118c,181b), **ewry** (133c)

- EW -   **dewa**, **dewy** (101a), **hewn**, **mewl** (180d), **mews** (154c), **news** (165c), **newt** (48d,136c,169d), **sewn**, **Tewa** (193)

- - EW   **anew** (7c), **blew**, **brew** (35d), **chew** (97c), **clew** (16a,33a,77b,136b, 164d), **crew** (72a,106a), **drew**, **flew**, **grew**, **knew**, **Llew** (40c), **phew** (52c), **plew** (17c), **shew** (44c), **skew** (148a,160c,171c), **slew** (160a), **smew** (19b,46d,99a,137d), **spew** (35a,49a), **stew** (21c,44b,184d), **thew** (104c), **view** (93d,138b), **whew**

E - - W   **enow** (50d,123a,158b)

EX - -   **exam**, **exit** (114d)

- EX -   **next** (106a), **sext** (26b,111b,147b), **text** (21c,140d)

- - EX   **Amex** (184d), **apex** (39c,76c,115c,118c,159b,166a,167b), **Crex** (37a), **faex** (46a), **flex** (18a), **ibex** (67d,68a), **ilex** (77d), **obex** (22d), **plex** (60b), **spex**, **Ulex** (153c)

E - - X   **eaux** (178c), **eryx** (137a), **esox** (57b)

EY - -   **eyah** (95b,108d,111c), **eyas** (106c,173a), **eyer**, **eyey** (74b), **eyot** (82d), **eyra** (181d), **eyre** (23c,31b,85c), **Eyre**, **eyry** (47b,106c)

- EY -   **Ceyx** (73b), **teyl** (92b,c,168c)

- - EY   **ahey** (52c), **akey** (189), **brey** (194), **drey** (154c), **eyey** (74b), **fley** (63d), **Frey** (7c,68b,124d), **grey** (33c), **hoey** (114c), **joey** (86a,185d), **Joey** (96b,109c), **obey** (35c,75c), **prey** (119d,176a), **roey** (103d), **skey** (185d), **sley** (179b), **Spey**, **they** (124b), **trey** (26c,165a), **Urey** (14b,107c,138c), **whey** (100a)

E - - Y   **easy** (54a), **eddy** (37d,39d,160d,180d), **edgy** (106c), **eely** (185a), **eery** (172b,180a), **eggy** (185d), **elmy**, **envy** (41b), **esay**, **espy** (44a, 142a), **ewry** (133c), **eyey** (74b), **eyry** (47b,106c)

EZ - -   **exba** (188), **ezel** (47a,85d), **Ezra** (96a)

- - EZ   **chez** (14b,61a), **daez**, **Geez** (6c,51d), **inez** (45c,183c), **juez** (152b), **knez** (123c), **oyez** (38a,39b,75b)

FA - -   **Faam** (111a), **Faba**, **face** (159d,176c), **fact** (7a,128b), **fade** (181d, 183b), **fado** (121c), **fady**, **faex** (46a), **fail**, **fain** (42d,67c,183b), **fair** (17a,55d), **fait** (6d,61b), **fake** (123a,143c), **faky**, **fala** (129b), **fall** (46b,141c), **falx** (133b), **Fama** (130a), **famn** (188), **fana**, **fane** (30d,137a,162d), **fang** (167b), **fano** (51d,96b,113c,d), **faon** (33c,55a), **fard** (112d), **fare** (43c,59b,67d,123b), **farl** (138c, 140b), **farm** (165d), **faro** (65a), **fash** (140c,176a), **fass** (189), **fast** (56d,126c,141d,160c,173a,d), **fate** (42d,52a,87a,94a), **faun** (56a,

68b,137c,161a,184a), **favi** (138a,165d), **fawn** (33c), **faze** (43d)

- **FA** - **afar** (44c), **Afar** (6c)

- - **FA** **Abfa** (76b), **alfa** (70d), **gufa** (21b,99a), **Kafa** (6c), **kufa** (21b,99a), **Offa** (163d), **sofa** (44d), **tufa** (121b,177a), **Urfa** (99a)

F - - **A** **Faba**, **fala** (129b), **Fama** (135a), **fana**, **flea** (81b), **fora** (133a), **Frea**, **Fria**, **fuga**

F - - **B** **flub** (22b), **frab** (138c), **frib** (43d)

F - - **C** **fisc** (52c,134c), **floc** (149a)

- - **FD** **Wafd** (49a)

F - -**D** **fard** (112d), **feed** (108c), **fend** (114b,178b), **feod** (55d), **feud** (55d, 126b,175b), **find** (44a), **fled**, **fold**, **fond** (7c,94b), **food** (109a,176b), **ford** (177b), **foud** (54d,144b), **Fred** (96b), **Fuad** (54d), **fund** (6d, 101c,130c), **fyrd** (110a)

FE - - **feak** (39d,171c), **fear** (113c,155a), **feat** (7a,52d), **feed** (108c), **feel** (72a,142c), **fees** (128c), **feis** (82b), **feke**, **fell** (40a,58b,76c,115d, 147d), **fels** (190), **felt**, **feme** (181b), **fend** (114b,178b), **feod** (55d), **fern** (142a), **feru** (37a,56a,133d), **fess** (23c,51b), **fest**, **fete** (55d, 129b), **feud** (55d,126b,175b)

- **FE** - **afer** (48a,182b)

- - **FE** **cafe**, **fife** (59a,105a), **jefe** (152a), **life** (19a,177a), **nife** (37a), **orfe** (57a,b,185c), **rife** (6b,c,39d,123b), **safe** (141d,157d,174d), **wife** (154a)

F - - **E** **face** (159d,176c), **fade** (181d,183b), **fake** (123a,143c), **fame** (130a), **fane** (30d,137a,162d), **fare** (43c,59b,67d,123b), **fate** (42d,52a,87a, 94a), **faze** (43d), **feke**, **feme** (181b), **fete** (55d,129b), **fide**, **fife** (59a,105a), **fike** (139c), **file** (13a,127d), **fine** (49b,50a,104b,115d, 159a), **fire** (13a,43d,44b), **five flee**, **floe** (79b), **flue** (8b,30a), **fore** (63d,174b), **free** (44a,70d,131b), **froe** (32a,167a,179d), **fume** (129a, 149a,157a), **fuse** (98c), **fute** (51c), **fuze** (98c), **fyke** (15d)

- **FF** - **affy** (18b), **offa**, **Offa** (163d), **offs** (38c)

- - **FF** **baff** (69d), **biff**, **buff** (134c,161d), **cuff** (148a), **daff** (125d), **doff** (130a,161b), **duff** (125d), **gaff** (57c,d,152d,153a), **goff** (32d), **guff**, **huff** (58a), **jeff** (133d), **Jeff**, **jiff** (101c), **kiff** (88c), **koff** (47a), **luff** (136b), **miff** (44c), **moff** (53b,146c), **muff** (24b), **piff** (24b), **puff** (180d), **raff** (75b), **riff** (131d), **Riff** (18b,102c), **ruff** (19b,33b,63d, 137a), **teff** (6c), **tiff** (126b), **toff** (40d), **tuff** (121b,177a)

F - - **F** **fief** (55d)

F - - **G** **fang** (167b), **flag** (16b,50d,82b,88c,115a,155a), **flog** (180d), **Fong** (40b), **frog** (10a,17a,126d), **Fung** (191)

F - - **H** **fash** (140c,176a), **fish**, **Foch** (63b)

FI - - **fiat** (35a,41d,48c,111b,137a), **Fiat** (83c), **fico** (169d), **fide**, **fief** (55d), **fife** (59a,105a), **fike** (139c), **file** (13a,127d), **fili**, **fill** (109b), **film** (164b), **filo**, **fils** (62d,150b), **find** (44a), **fine** (49b,50a,104b, 115d,159a), **fink** (19a,56c,157c), **Finn** (107d), **Fiot** (191), **fire** (13a,43d,44b), **firm** (154c,173d), **firn** (67c,70c,106c,149b), **fisc** (52c,134c), **fish**, **fisk** (24d,52c,134c), **fist** (80c), **five**

- **FI** - **Efik** (191), **ifil** (117a,168c)

- - **FI** **defi** (61b), **Safi** (191), **sufi** (103a,116c)

299

F - - I favi (138a,165d), fili, foci (28b), fuci (132c), fuji (84b), Fuji (84d)

F - - J Funj

F - - K feak (39d,171c), fink (19a,56c,157c), fisk (24d,52c,134c), flak (11a), folk (116a,169c), fork, fulk (173a), funk (63d,113c)

FL - - flag (16b,50d,82b,88c,115a,155a), flak (11a), flam (169c), flan (39d,40a,114d), flap (17b,59a,104a,118d,161a,182d), flat (41b, 124b,173a), flaw, flax, flay (147c,157c), flea (81b), fled, flee, flew, flex (18a), fley (63d), flip (167c), flit (41a), flix, floc (149a), floe (79b), flog (180d), flop (54a), flot (173a), flow (157b), flub (22b), flue (8b,30a), flux (28d,58d)

F - - L fail, fall (46b,141c), farl (138c,140b), feel (72a,142c), fell (40a, 58b,76c,115d,147d), fill (109b), foal (78c), foil (15d,55c,165b), fool (24a,41c,47a,146d), foul (173a), fowl, fuel (65c), full (7b, 130b), furl (132d)

F - - M Faam (111a), farm (165d), film (164b), firm (154c,173d), flam (169c), foam (63d,154b), form (54d,143c), frim (58d), from

F - - N fain (42d,67c,183b), famn (188), faon (33c,55a), faun (56a,68b, 137c,161a,184a), fawn (33c), fern (142a), Finn (107d), firn (67c, 70c,106c,149b), flan (39d,40a,114d), fohn (182b)

FO - - foal (78c), foam (63d,154b), Foch (63b), foci (28b), fogy, fohn (182b), foil (15d,55c,165b), fold, folk (116a,169c), fond (7c,94b), Fong (40b), fono (137a), fons (60c), font (16b,171d,172a), food (109a,176b), fool (24a,41c,47a,146d), foot (115a), fora (133a), ford (177b), fore (63d,174b), fork, form (54d,143c), fort (63d, 157d), foss (44d,100d), foud (54d,144b), foul (173a), four (26c), fowl, foxy (38b,39c,181d)

- - FO Bufo (166c)

F - - O fado (121c), fano (51d,96b,113c,d), faro (65a), fico (169d), filo, fono (137a)

F - - P flap (17b,59a,104a,118d,161a,182d), flip (167c), flop (54a), frap (45d,165c)

FR - - frab (138c), frap (45d,165c), frat, frau (181b), fray (56b,60d), Frea, Fred (96b), free (44a,70d,131b), fret (28c,35b,111c,184d), Frey (7c,68b,124d), Fria, frib (43d), frim (58d), frit (64c,67c), friz (39d), froe (32a,167a,179d), frog (10a,17a,126d), from, frot (28c), frow (47a,167a)

- FR - Afra (183c)

F - - R fair (17a,55d), fear (113c,155a), four (26c)

- - FS offs (38c)

F - - S fass (189), fees (128c), feis (82b), fels (190), fess (23c,51b), fils (62d,150b), fons (60c), foss (44d,100d), fuss (22b,35b)

- - FT baft (14a,53b), daft (59c), deft (147c), gift (123a), haft (76d), heft (179d), Heft, left (42c), lift (49b), loft (14c,69d,104b,178b), raft (27b,33c,58c,75b), reft (32a,42c,44d,167b), rift (30c,32a,58a, 110d), sift (140d,142c,146b), soft (48b,95d,99d,163a), Taft (29d), tuft (24b,32d,38c), waft (20d,58a), weft (39a,165a,184b), yuft (135c)

300

F - - T **fact** (7a,128b), **fait** (6d,61b), **fast** (56d,126c,141d,160c,173a,d), **feat** (7a,52d), **felt, fest, Fiat** (83c), **fiat** (35a,41d,48c,111b,137a), **Fiot** (191), **fist** (80c), **flat** (41b,124b,173a), **flit** (41a), **flot** (173a), **font** (16b,171d,172a), **foot** (115a), **fort** (63d,157d), **frat, fret** (28c, 35b,111c,184d), **frit** (64c,67c), **frot** (28c), **fust** (105c,143b)

FU - - **Fuad** (54d), **fuci** (132c), **fuel** (65c), **fuga, fugu** (84b), **fuji** (84b), **Fuji** (84d), **fulk, full** (173a), **fume** (129a,149a,157a), **fumy, fund** (6d,101c,130c), **Fung** (191), **funk** (63d,113c), **furl** (132d), **fury** (157a), **fuse** (98c), **fuss** (22b,35b), **fust** (105c,143b), **fute** (51c), **fuxe** (98c), **fuzz** (45d)

F - - U **feru** (37a,56a,133d), **frau** (181b), **fugu** (84b)

F - - W **flaw, flew, flow** (157b), **frow** (47a,167a)

F - - X **faex** (46a), **falx** (133b), **flax, flex** (18a), **flix, flux** (28d,58d)

FY - - **fyke** (15d), **fyrd** (110a)

- - FY **affy** (18b), **defy** (28d), **Dufy** (63a)

F - - Y **fady, faky, flay** (147c,157c), **fley** (63d), **fogy, foxy** (38b,39c,181d), **fray** (56b,60d), **Frey** (7c,68b,124d), **fumy, fury** (157a)

F - - Z **friz** (39d), **fuzz** (45d)

GA - - **gaal** (23b,174d), **gabe** (162a), **gabi** (162a), **gaby** (59c,146d), **gade**
Gaea (47d,69a), **Gael** (28a,96c,138d), **gaff** (57c,d,152d,153a),
gage (28d,98a,119c,d), **gagl** (160b), **Gaia** (47d,69a), **gail** (23b,
174d), **Gail** (183d), **gain** (7a,b,124a,181d), **gait** (96b,179a), **gajo**
(107c), **gala** (55d), **Gala** (191), **gale** (181d), **gali** (6c), **gall** (19a,
28c,29b,82c,160c,176a), **galt, Gama** (121c), **game** (64d,154a),
gamp (172a), **gane** (185b), **gang** (38c), **Gano** (132d), **gaol** (123d),
Gaol (164a), **Gaon** (85b), **gape** (185b), **gapo** (60a), **gapy, gara**
(190), **garb** (32c,46a), **gare** (61b,c,62c,127c,184b), **Garm** (178c),
garn (67d,185b), **Garo** (88c), **Gary, gash** (40a), **gasp** (113c), **gata**
(143c), **gate** (51a,121b), **Gath** (117a), **gaub** (116c), **gaud** (169d),
gaue (67a), **Gaul** (10a,60d,63c), **gaup, gaur** (112c,181c), **gaus**
(67a), **gaut** (88b,103d,132a), **gave, gawd** (169c), **gawk** (146d),
gawp, Gaza (117a), **gaze, gazi, gazy**

- GA - **Agag** (18c,86c,137a), **agal** (17c,36b), **Agao** (6c,73c), **agar** (7d,28c,
39c,103c,141c), **Agau** (73c), **Agaz** (193), **egad** (100a,109a), **ngai**
(48a,159c), **ngan, ogam** (82b,c), **Sgau** (88c)

- - GA **alga** (141b,c), **baga** (171b), **bega** (188), **biga** (171d), **boga** (57d,
180b), **fuga, giga** (56a,105a), **goga** (24a), **hoga** (144b), **inga** (145d,
170a), **Jaga** (191), **juga** (27a), **mega** (34b,c), **muga, naga** (13d,
33a,55b,127c), **Naga** (24c,77a,88c,176d), **Olga** (135c,183c), **paga**
(117a), **pega** (57a,130a,158b), **raga** (56d,105a), **riga** (118b), **ruga**
(59b,185a),   **saga**   (79b,91a,138a,157a,161b,c,168a),   **Saga,**
soga (70d,152b), **Soga** (191), **toga** (132d,133a,b), **vega** (152c),
Vega (155b), **Wega** (155b), **yoga** (10b,13c,77a), **Yuga** (76d), **zyga**
(134b)

G - - A **Gaea** (47d,69a), **Gaia** (47d,69a), **gala** (55d), **Gala** (191), **Gama**
(121c), **gara** (190), **gata** (143c), **Gaza** (117a), **gena** (29b), **geta**
(84b, 145a), **giga** (56a, 105a), **gila** (93b), **Gita, Gjoa**
(144d), **glia** (106c), **goga** (24a), **gola** (27b,40c,70c,157c), **Goma**
(191), **Gona** (106d), **gora** (81c), **Goya** (151d), **gufa** (21b,99a),

Guha (191), gula (90a,101a,165b), guna (106a,137b)

- GB - Egba (191), Egbo (141d)

G - - B garb (32c,46a), gaub (116c), gerb (56d,143d), glib (58d,149a,177c), glub, grab (105b,142a,149b), grub (88d), guib (11a)

G - - D gaud (169d), gawd (169c), gedd (140a), geld (162b), Gerd (63c), gild (14a,49c,69c,98b), gird (32c,50a,123a,160a), glad (85c), gled (19a,52a,87a), goad (80b,154b), gold, Gond, good, grad (28b), grid (17a,70d,119b,156d)

GE - - geal (47d,163c), gean (29c), gear (32c,112a,167b), geat (77d,101a), Geat (138a), gedd (140a), Geez (6c,51d), gein (67d), geld (162b), gelt (101c), gena (29b), gene (54a,76b), Gene (96b), gens (42d, 132d), gent, genu (6b,18a,87a,89c), gerb (56d,143d), Gerd (63c), Gere (183c), Geri (183c), germ (17d,99c,134d), gest (7c,41d,52d, 133c), geta (84b,154b), gett (44d), Geum (76b)

- GE - aged (110a), agee (13d,15c,38d), ager (47c,56a,89b,c,131d,133b), Eger (49a), ogee (101a,b,120b)

- - GE ange (61a), auge (123c,132b), cage (36a), doge (95b,175b), edge (22a,96d,131c,143c,146b), euge (180a), gage (28d,98a,119c,d), huge, Inge (24d,67d,117c,119c), kuge (84c), loge (164a), luge (148a), mage (95b), page (51b,59b,142d,159b), rage (10c,30c,157a, 161d), sage (13a,90d,100c,141c,145c,180b,183a), tige (118a), urge (42d,46b,79d,80a,b,81c,124a,150a), wage (27a,115b), yage (23a)

G - - E gabe (162a), gade, gage (28d,98a,119c,d), gale (181d), game (64d, 154a), gane (185b), gape (185b), gare (61b,c,62c,127c, 184b), gate (51a,121b), gaue (67a), gave, gaze, gene (54a,76b), Gene (96b), ghee (24d), gibe (8a,42c,84d,100d,138c,144c,149b), Gide (63a), gime (77d), gite (62a,118d), give (79d,123a), glee (99a, 150b), glue (7b,156a), gone (6b,15c,42c,44c,114d), gore (115d, 117c,154c,169c), guze (128d), gyle (144c), gyle (23b,174d), gyne (34b,55b,183c), gyre (31b,171b), gyve (55d,143b)

G - - F gaff (57c,d,152d,153a), goaf (104b), goff (32d), golf (154a), goof, Graf (37c,66b,67a,107c,186b), guff, gulf (6c)

- GG - eggs (112a), eggy (185b)

- - GG dagg (118c), hagg, hogg (144a), jagg, magg (95b), migg (96c), nogg (48d), tegg (143d,171d), vugg (28a,66a,132b), Wegg (111d), wigg, yegg (24c)

G - - G gang (38c), Gheg (8c), glug, gong, grig (38c,70d,93a), grog (92d, 153d)

GH - - ghat (32d,88b,103d,132a), ghee (24d), Gheg (8c), Ghes (193), ghor (174b), ghos (30b), Ghuz (171a)

- GH - agha (35a,171a)

- - GH dagh (76d), hegh, high, Hugh (96a), Lugh (28b), Magh (102a), nigh (106a), ough, pugh, sigh, vugh (28a,66a,136b), yogh (10c, 185a)

G - - H gash (40a), Gath (117a), gish (102c), gosh, Goth (16c), gush (35a, 154c)

GI - - gibe (8a,42c,84d,100d,138c,144c,149b), Gide (63a), gier (47b),

302

gift (123a), **giga** (56a,105a), **gila** (93b), **gild** (14a,49c,69c,98b), **gill** (22d), **gilo** (48a), **gilt** (69c,77c,151b,185d), **gime** (77d), **gimp** (169d), **gink** (48b), **gird** (32c,50a,123a,160a), **girl**, **giro** (38c,83c, 167c), **girt** (50a), **gish** (102c), **gist** (95c,118c), **Gita**, **gite** (62a, 118d), **give** (79d,123a)

- GI -   **Agib** (12a,42d), **agio** (52c,60a,101c,123a), **Agis** (86d), **Egil** (107d), **egis** (14b,d,115a,124d,144b,154a,161a)

- - GI   **Bugi** (191), **hagi** (84b), **jogi** (76d), **magi** (123c), **Magi** (95b,116c, 183a), **ragi** (28b), **sugi** (84b), **vagi** (38b), **yogi** (76d)

G - - I   **gabi** (162a), **gali** (6c), **gaxi**, **Geri** (183c), **goai** (106d,168c), **gobi**, **Gobi** (42d), **goli** (105c), **Guti**, **gyri** (22d,131b)

GJ - -   **Gjoa** (144d)

G - - J   **gunj** (70c)

G - - K   **gawk** (146d), **gink** (48b), **gowk** (146d)

GL - -   **glad** (85c), **gled** (19a,52a,87a), **glee** (99a,150b), **glen** (43c), **glia** (106c), **glib** (58d,149a,177c), **glim**, **glis** (45c), **glom** (155d,160d, 178c), **glow** (144c), **glub**, **glue** (7b,156a), **glug**, **glum** (102c,159a), **glut** (52c,70a,137c,159d)

- GL -   **agla** (7a), **iglu** (51c,149b), **ogle** (9d,53c,91a,93d,148c)

- - GL   **gagl** (160b)

G - - L   **gaal** (23b,174d), **Gael** (28a,96c,138d), **gagl** (160b), **gall** (23b,174d), **Gail** (183d), **gall** (19a,28c,29b,82c,160a,176a), **gaol** (123d), **Gaol** (164a), **Gaul** (10a,60d,63c), **geal** (47d,163c), **gill** (22d), **girl**, **goal** (8b,109b,120b,125d), **goel** (15a,75c), **Goll**, **goul** (102a), **gowl** (102a, 140d,185b), **gull** (32d,41c,42a,72c,99b,141a)

G - - M   **Garm** (178c), **germ** (99c,134d), **Geum** (76b), **glim**, **glom** (155d, 160d,178c), **glum** (102c,159a), **gram** (29d,99b,148d,160d,180a), **Gram**, **grim** (156a), **grum** (102c), **Guam**

GN - -   **gnar** (72a), **gnat** (59a,81b,99c), **gnaw** (20a,107a,178b)

- GN -   **agni** (88a,89c), **Agni** (56d,68b)

- - GN   **sign** (121c,146c)

G - - N   **gain** (7a,b,124a,181d), **Gaon** (85b), **garn** (67d,185b), **gean** (29c), **gein** (67d), **glen** (43c), **Goan**, **goon** (157c,163c), **gown**, **gran**, **grin**, **guan** (151b), **Gwyn** (40c,50b)

GO - -   **goad** (80b,154b), **goaf** (104b), **goal** (106d,168c), **goal** (8b,109b, 120b,125d), **Goan**, **goat** (135a), **gobi**, **Gobi** (42d), **gobo** (84d), **goby** (57d), **goel** (15a,75c), **goer**, **goff** (32d), **goga** (24a), **gogo** (16b,24a, 149c), **Gogo** (191), **gola** (27b,40c,70c,157a), **gold**, **golf** (154a) **goli** (105c), **Goll**, **Golo** (191), **Goma** (191), **Gona** (106d), **Gond**, **gone** (6b,15c,42c,44c,114d), **gong**, **good**, **goof**, **goon** (157c,163c), **Goop** (107d), **goor**, **gora** (81c), **gore** (115d,117c,154c,169c), **gory**, **gosh**, **Goth** (16c,163d), **goul** (102a), **gour** (112c,181c), **gout**, **gowk** (146d), **gowl** (102a,140d,185b), **gown**, **Goya** (151d)

- GO -   **agog** (47b,52c,86b), **agon** (12c,36c,41b,55d),71b), **egol** (11b), **Igor** (135d), **Ogor** (170d)

- - GO   **ango** (171a), **Argo** (12c,36b,c), **bago** (13d), **bogo** (117a, 168c), **Bogo** (191), **bygo** (114c), **Dago**, **ergo** (164b), **gogo** (16b,24a,

149c), Gogo (191), **Hugo** (63a,96a), **Iago** (54b,111d,143c), **kago** (113a), **Iago** (83b,152b), **mogo** (74b), **Pogo** (121c), **sago** (54c, 59b,113b,125b,155c), **sego** (24b,25a,92b,174c), **upgo** (13c), **zogo** (136a)

G - - O gajo (107c), **Gajo**, **Gano** (132d), **gapo** (60a), **Garo** (88c), **gilo** (48a), giro (38c,83c,167c), **gobo** (84d), **gogo** (16b,24a,149c), **Gogo** (191), Golo (191), **grao** (189), **guao** (168c,169b), **Gulo** (183c), **gyro** (34d)

- GP - Ogpu (135d)

G - - P gamp (172a), **gasp** (113c), **gaup**, **gawp**, **gimp** (169d), **Goop** (107d), gulp (46a,79d,160a), **Gump** (43b), **grip** (159a)

GR - - grab (105b,142a,149b), **grad** (28b), **Graf** (37c,66b,67a,107c,186b), gram (29d,99b,148d,160d,180a), **grao** (189), **gras** (78b), **gray** (33c, 77c), **Gray** (50c), **gres** (156d), **grew**, **grey** (33c), **grid** (17a,70d, 119b,156d), **grig** (38c,70d,93a), **grim** (156a), **grin**, **grip** (159a), **gris** (61d), **grit** (137a,b), **grog** (92d,153d), **gros** (47a,53d,146c), **Gros** (63a), **grot** (27d), **grow** (154b), **grub** (43c,88d), **grum** (102c), **Grus** (36b,c,38b)

- GR - agra (26d,34d), **Agra** (161b), **agri** (89b), **agro** (149d), **ogre** (67a, 102a)

G - - R gaur (112c,181c), **gear** (32c,167b), **Ghor** (174b), **gier** (47b), **gnar** (72a), **goer**, **goor**, **gour** (112c,181c) **guar** (46c,59d), **guhr** (47d)

- - GS eggs (112a), **togs** (32c)

G - - S gaus (67a), **gens** (42d,132d), **Gens**, **Ghes** (193), **ghos** (30b), **glis** (45c), **Glis**, **gras** (78b), **gres** (156d), **gris** (61d), **gros** (47a,53d,146c), **Gros** (63a), **gyps**, **Gyps** (71d)

- - GT togt (77c), **Vogt**

G - - T gait (96b,179a), **galt**, **gaut** (88b,103a,132a), **geat** (77d,101a), **Geat** (138a), **gelt** (101c), **gent**, **gest** (7c,41d,52d,133c), **gett** (44d), **ghat** (32d,88b,103d,132a), **gift** (123a), **gilt** (69c,77c,151b), **girt** (50a), **gist** (95c,118c), **glut** (52c,70a,137c,159d), **gnat** (59a,81b,99c), **goat** (135a), **grit** (137a,b), **grot** (27d), **gust**

GU - - Guam, **guan** (151b), **guao** (168c,169b), **guar** (46c,59d), **gufa** (21b, 99a), **guff**, **gugu**, **Guha** (191), **guhr** (47d), **guib** (11a), **gula** (90a, 101a,165b), **gulf** (6c), **gull** (32d,41c,42a,72c,99b,141a), **Gulo** (183c), **gulp** (46a,79d,160a), **Gump** (43b), **guna** (106a,137b), **gunj** (70c), **guru** (77b), **gush** (35a,154c), **gust**, **Guti**, **guze** (128d)

- GU - agua (152d,166c,178c), **ague** (30a,55d,95c), **ogum** (82b)

- - GU degu (132c), **fugu** (84b), **gugu**, **kagu** (106c), **Pegu** (24c,102a,127d)

G - - U genu (6b,18a,87a,89c), **gugu**, **guru** (77b)

GW - - Gwyn (40c,50b)

G - - W glow (144c), **gnaw** (20a,107a,178b), **grew**, **grow** (154b)

GY - - gybe (144c), **gyle** (23b,174d), **gyne** (34b,55b,183c), **gyps**, **Gyps** (71d), **gyre** (31b,171b), **gyri** (22d,131b), **gyro** (34d), **gyve** (55d, 143b)

- - GY algy, **Algy** (96b), **bogy** (153a), **cagy** (178b), **dogy** (46d,103c), **edgy** (106c), **eggy** (185d), **fogy** (46d), **logy** (46d), **Nagy** (78d), **orgy** (26d,130d, 137c), **pogy** (57a,88a,98d,103c), **sagy**

304

G - - Y   gaby (59c,146d), Gaby, gapy, Gary, gazy, goby (57d), gory, gray (33c,77c), Gray (50c), grey (33c)

G - - Z   Geez (6c,51d), Ghuz (171a)

HA - -   Haab (97d), haaf (57d), haak (57b,178a), haar (139c), haba (151d), Habe (191), hack (40a,77c,184d), hade (66a,148c,173c), hadj (98b,118a), haec (90a,164c), haem (122b), haft (76d), hagg, hagi (84b), haha (55c,159c), haik (57b,65b,108a), hail (6d,15a,71d), hair (56b,164d), haje (33a,48d), hake (57a,b), hakh (46d), hako (115b), haku (86d), hala (112b), hale (125b), Hale (9d,131a), half (101a), hall (37b,114d), halm, halo (14d,31b,92a,107b,131d), Hals (47a), halt (13b,28a,38d,156d), hami (78a), hand (60c,114c,115d,184c), hang (160a), hank (147c), Hano (125b), Hans (66d,96a), hant (67a), Hapi (66a,107b,136a), hapu (106d), Harb (191), hard (109b), hare (91b,132c), hark (92d), harl (16b,56b,59a), harm (40b,81a), harp (105a,129a), hart (41d,154d), hase (74d), hasp (31d, 54d,153c), hast, hate (6a,43a), hath, Hati (48d), haul (27b,45d), have, hawk (19c,115c), hayz, haze (100c,174d), hazy (174b)

- HA -   Ahab (18c,26c,85b,86d,100d,116a,180b), Ahaz (86d), Bhar (191), bhat (80c), chaa (162b), chab (184a), Chad (158b), chai (72d), cham (20a,29d), Cham (8c), chan (26c,130c), chap (55b), char (24d,26c, 170b), chat (9b,19c,161c), chaw (97c), chay (48a,128d), dhak (48a, 169a), dhal (12b), dhan (124c), dhao (24c), Dhar, dhaw (125a), ghat (32d,88b,103d,132a), khan (7c,26c,81b,93d,116c,123c,130c, 166c), khar (189), khas (153a), khat (105d), Phad (155b), shad (27d,57a,b,c), shag (73b,105b,161d,166d), shah (116c), sham (41c, 55b,60d,80a,123a,b,146d), Shan (13c,80d,88c,101d), shap, shat (87d), shaw (164b), Shaw (50c,53b), shay (110c), Thai (146a), than (35b), thar (68a,76d), that (42b,124b,129c), thaw, wham (157c), what (129c), whau (107a,168c)

- - HA   agha (35a,171a), Akha (86a,c), Asha (191), Azha (155b), epha (75c), Guha (191), haha (55c,159c), Isha (174a), kaha (123d), maha (28c,88c,136d), moha (42b,83d), ocha (189), paha (67b), poha (74c), saha (179b), tcha (162c), Usha (16a,150c),

H - - A   haba (151d), Haba, haha (55c,159c), hala (112b), Hela (93c), Hera (69c,85d,110b,126b,186b,d), hila (53c), Hima (191), hoga (144b), hoja (166b), hola (74c,152b), hora (22a,40b), Hova (95a), Hoya (14d), Hsia (30b,47c), huia (19a,106b), hula (74b), Hupa (192), hura (20a,137a), Hura, Hyla (10a,166d,169b)

H - - B   Haab (97d), Harb (191), herb (58b,158b), hobb (124b), hubb (118b)

H - - C   haec (90a,164c)

H - - D   hand (60c,114c,115d,184c), hard (109b), head (29d), heed (14c, 75b,109b), held, herd (39a,46c,72a), Hild, hind (15b,41d,45a), hold (95c,124c,130d), hood (38a,74d), hued

HE - -   head (29d), heaf (144a), heal, heap (117d), hear (75b,c,92d), heat, Hebe (39c,69c,186b), heck (100a), heed (14c,75b,109b), heel, Heep (41a,43b), heer (47a,184b,185b), heft (179d), Heft, hegh, Hehe (191), heii (74b), hein (52c,61c), heir, Hela (93c), held, helm (144d,165d), help (14a), hemi (122c), hemo (34a,122b), hemp (26a, 37a,56a,133d), hens (121d), Hera (69c,85d,110b,126b,186b,d), herb (58b,158b), herd (39a,46c,72a), here, herl (16b,59a), hero

305

(42b,124d,137b), **Hero** (90c), **Herr** (66c), **hers** (124c), **hest** (35-ʹ). **Heth** (77c), **hevi** (111d), **hewn**

- HE -   **ahem, Ahet** (49a,102a), **ahey** (52c), **bhel** (126d), **chee** (189), **chef,** **chek** (59c), **Chen** (149b), **cher** (61b), **chew** (97c), **chez** (14b,61a), **eheu** (52c), **ghee** (24d), **Gheg** (8c), **Ghes** (193), **Hehe** (191), **Khem** (113c), **khet** (188), **phew** (52c), **rhea** (37a,56a,111d), **Rhea** (19b,68d, 87c,103c,186b), **Rhee** (87c), **shea** (25a,168c,d), **shed** (27a,90c,101b, 144b), **shee** (82b), **Shem** (107c), **Shen** (68a), **sher** (65d,165c), **shew** (44c), **Thea** (162c), **theb** (188), **thee** (124b), **them** (124b), **then,** **thew** (104c), **they** (124b), **whee, when** (180d), **whet** (143c,156b), **whew, whey** (100a)

- - HE   **ache** (79a,112d,185b), **Hehe** (191), **Hohe** (192), **tche** (13d,30b,105a)

H - - E   **Habe** (191), **hade** (66a,148c,173c), **haje** (33a,48d), **hake** (57a,b), **hale** (125b), **Hale** (9d,131a), **hare** (91b,132c), **hase** (74d), **hate** (6a, 43a), **have, haze** (100c,174d), **Hebe** (39c,69c,186b), **Hehe** (191), **here, hide** (53a), **hike, hipe** (185a), **hire** (49d,50b,91b,130a), **hive** (17c), **Hohe** (192), **hole** (6c,11b,110d,118c,147a), **home, hone** (110a,143c,180d), **hope** (13d,52d), **hose** (156c), **hove** (92a,157d), **howe** (77d), **Howe** (17a,82a), **huge, hule** (23a,134c), **Hume** (50c), **huse** (180c), **hyde** (188), **Hyde** (45a), **hyke, hyle** (97c), **hype** (185a)

H - - F   **haaf** (57d), **half** (101a), **heaf** (144a), **hoof** (173a), **huff** (58a)

H - - G   **hagg, hang** (160a), **hing** (13c), **hogg** (144a), **hong** (30b), **hung**

- - HH   **sahh** (188)

H - - H   **hakh** (46d), **hash, hath, hegh, Heth** (77c), **high, hish, hoch,** (52c, 66c), **Hoch, hoth, Hoth** (20c), **Hugh** (96a), **hunh?, hush** (17b,146c)

HI - -   **hick** (185d), **hide** (53a), **hien** (30b), **hier** (63a,185d), **high, hike,** **hiku** (57a,106d,138a), **hila** (53c), **Hild, hilo** (74c), **hilt** (73c), **Hima** (191), **hind** (15b,41d,45a), **hing** (13c), **hino** (106d,168c), **hint** (9a,39c,159a), **hipe** (185a), **hire** (49d,50b,91b,130a), **hiro, hish, hiss** (146a), **hist** (25c,93d), **hive** (17c)

- HI -   **Ahir** (27b), **Bhil** (191), **chia** (136d), **chib** (167a), **chic** (148d), **chid,** **ch'ih** (188), **chil, chin, Chin** (30b), **chip** (69d), **chir** (29b,116d), **chit** (67b,98c,108b,116c,177c), **chiv** (87c), **jhil, ohia** (74c,168c), **Ohio,** **Phil** (96b), **phit** (24b), **phiz** (54a), **Rhin, shih** (189), **Shik** (171a), **shim** (91d,144c,162a,179d), **shin** (91a,d,140b,143c), **ship, shir** (36d, 65d,165c), **thin** (43b,c,148b), **this** (42b,124b), **Whig, whim** (26c, 54c,108c), **whin** (64c,70a,132b,181d), **whip** (58c,88d), **whir** (25c, 181a), **whit** (166c), **whiz** (25c)

- - HI   **bahi** (60c), **Bahi, pahi** (21b,26a), **tchi, Tchi, tshi, Tshi** (69c)

H - - I   **hagi** (84b), **hami** (78a), **Hapi** (66a,107b,136a), **Hati** (48d), **heli** (74b), **hemi** (122c), **hevi** (111d), **Holi** (77a), **hopi** (33c), **Hopi** (12c, 102c,125b), **hoti**

H - - J   **hadj** (98b,118a)

H - - K   **haak** (57a,178a), **hack** (40a,77c,184d), **haik** (57b,65b,108a), **hank** (147c), **hark** (92d), **hawk** (19c,115c), **heck** (100a), **hick** (185d), **hock** (91a,115b,182b,c), **hoek** (39d), **honk** (70a), **hook** (27b,39d), **howk** (139b), **huck** (167d), **hulk** (144d,173d), **hunk, husk** (53a,78d, 142a)

HL - -   **Hler** (141a)

- - HL   buhl (81a), kohl (53c), kuhl (53c)

H - - L   hall (6d,15a,71d), hail (37b,114d), harl (16b,56b,59a), haul (27b, 45d), heal, heel, herl (16b,59a), hill, howl (39b), hull (141d,142a, 144c,d), hurl (167c)

H - - M   haem (122b), halm, harm (40b,81a), helm (144d,165d), holm (77d, 82d,109a)

- HN -   ohne (66d,183b)

- - HN   behn (137d), fohn (182b), John (11c,96a,121a,186b)

H - - N   hein (52c,61c), hewn, hien (30b), hoen (189), hoon (190), horn (11a, 105a,170b,182a), hymn (150c)

HO - -   hoar (63d,71a,181a), hoax (41c,122a), hobb (124b), hobo (168a, 174b), hoch (52c,66c), hock (91a,115b,182b,c), hoek (39d), hoen (189), hoer, hoey (114c), hoga (144b), hogg (144a), Hohe (192), hoja (166b), hoju (84b), hola (74c,152b), hold (95c,124c,130d), hole (6c,11b,110d,118c,147a), Holi (77a), holm (77d,82d,109a), holt (36d,119b,184b), holy, home, homo (122d), homy (38b), hone (110a,143c,180d), hong (30b), honk (70a), hood (38a,74d), hoof (173a), hook (27b,39d), hoon (190), hoop (181b), hoot (112c), hope (13d,52d), hopi (33c), Hopi (12c,102c,125b), hops (17c), hora (22a, 40b), horn (11a,105a,170b,182a), hors (62b), hose (156c), host (13a,51d,104c), Hoth (20c), hoti, hour, Hova (95a), hove (92a, 157d), howe (77d), Howe (17a,82a), howk (139b), howl (39b), Hoya (14d)

- HO -   Ahom (88c), ahoy (106a), b'hoy (134b), chob (23c), chol (118d), Chol (192), chop (98a), chor (16b), chou (61b), Chou (30b), chow (45a), choy (48a,128d), dhow (88d,111c,175d), Ghor (174b), ghos (30b), khot, mhor (180b), ohoy (106a), phon (94a), phoo, phos, phot (173b), rhob (64a,85c), Shoa (6c), shod, shoe (166a), shoo (46b,67a,138b), shop, shoq (169a), shor (136d), Shor (162b), shot (9d,43d,90c,174d), shou (41d), show (42b,44c,96b), thob (128a), Thor (7c,68c,99c,100c,109c,165b), Thos (84a,181c), thou (124b), whoa (156d), whom (42b), whoo

- - HO   baho (122a), boho (117a,179d), coho (136d), echo (130b,d), Echo (105d), icho (67b), kiho (82a), moho (19a,78a), otho (133a), paho (122a), peho (19b,102c,106d), Saho (6c), soho!, Soho (93c), toho (79a)

H - - O   hako (115b), halo (14d,31b,92a,107b,131d), Hano (125b), hemo (34a,122b), hero (42b,124d,137b), Hero (90c), hilo (74c), hino (106d,168c), hiro, hobo (168a,174b), homo (168a,174b), Hugo (63a,96a), huso (180c), hypo (117b)

H - - P   harp (105a,129a), hasp (31d,54d,153c), heap (117d), Heep (41a, 43b), help (14a), hemp (26a,37a,56a,133d), hoop (181b), hump (124d)

- HR -   Shri (17c,166c)

- - HR   Bohr (14b,40d,138c), buhr (180d), Duhr (155b), guhr (47d), lehr (67c,112a), mahr (103a), mohr (65d), rohr (72d), Ruhr, sehr (66d), tahr (68a,76d), tehr (27c,68a)

H - - R   haar (139c), hair (56b,164d), hear (75b,c,92d), heer (47a,184b, 185b), heir, Herr (66c), hier (63a,185b), Hier (141a), hoar (63d,

71a,181a), **hoer, hour**

HS - - Hsia (30b,47c)

H - - S Hals (47a), Hans (66d,96a), hens (121d), hers (124c), hiss (146a),
hops (17c), hors (62b), hyps

- - HT acht (66c), baht (146a)

H - - T haft (76d), halt (13b,28a,38d,156d), hant (67a), hart (41d,154d),
hast, heat, heft (179d), Heft (35a), hest (35a), hilt (73c), hint (9a,39c,
159a), hist (25c,93d), holt (36d,119b,184b), hoot (112c), host (13a,
51d,104c), hunt (141c), hurt

HU - - hubb (118b), huck (167d), hued, huff (58a), huge, Hugh (96a),
Hugo (63a,96a), huia (19a,106d), hula (74b), hule (23a,134c), hulk
(144d,173d), hull (141d,142a,144c,d), hulu (55b), Hume (50c),
hump (124d), hung, hunh?, hunk, hunt (141c), Hupa (192), hura
(20a,137a), Hura, hurl (167c), hurt, huse (180c), hush (17b,146c),
husk (53a,78d,142a), huso (180c), huzz

- HU - ahum, bhut (67a), chub (40c,154c), Chud (191), chug (53a), chum,
(38d), Chun (30c), chut!, Ghuz (171a), jhum, Phud (110b), phut
(24b), Phut (110b), rhum (8c), Rhus (159a), shul (161a), shun (15a,
51b,52a), shut, thud, thug (65a), thus (149c), whun (64c,70a)

- - HU ichu (10b,70d), jehu (46b), Jehu (18c), kahu (14d), Oahu, Rahu
(42b,48b), sahu (153d), tchu

H - - U haku (86d), hapu (106d), hiku (57a,106d,138a), hoju (84b), hulu
(55b)

- HV - IHVH (159d), JHVH (159d), YHVH (159d)

- HW - JHWH (159d), YHWH (159d)

H - - X hoax (41c,122c)

HY - - hyde (188), Hyde (45a), hyke, Hyla (10a,166d,169b), hyle (97c),
hymn (150c), hype (185a), hypo (117b), hyps

- HY - whyo (59d,65a)

- - HY achy, ashy (113a,178a)

H - - Y hazy (174b), hoey (114c), holy, homy (38b)

H - - Z Hayz, huzz

IA - - Iago (54b,111d,143c), Ialu (48d), Iamb (59c)

- IA - bias (43b,123a), diad (113a), dial (25c), dian (46c,130d,170b),
Dian (68d,69a,c,102b), Diau (192), fiat (35a,41d,48c,111b,137a),
Fiat (83c), kiak (51c), Liam (181d), liar (98d), Lias (66a), miam
(14d), mian (97c,147b,166b), Miao (30a,b), mias (111a), Mias,
miau (27b,99b), miaw (27b,99b), Nias (82d), Piaf (63c), piat (11a),
piay (98b), rial (190), siak (72d), sial (112a), Siam (163d,181a),
Tiam, tiao, tiar (39a,75a,121a), vial (148c)

- - IA Abia (18d,137a), akia (74c), amia (22c,170a), apia (121b), aria
(8b,98c,150a,c), Asia (48a), chia (136d), Elia (88a,115d), eria (13d,
146d), Fria, Gaia (47d,69a), glia (106c), Hsia (30b,47c), huia (19a,
106d), ilia (21d,77b,115d), inia (9b,109b), Inia (28c,45b), ixia (37a),
Maia (76b,109a,153b,155b,177c), Naia (33a), obia (55d), ohia (74c,
168c), okia (190), raia (107d), Raia (147b), Soia, tsia (162c), Uria
(14c,16d)

308

I - - A   idea (54c,108c,124a,164d), ijma (103b), ikra (27d), Ilia (21d,77b, 115d), Inca (14b,30a), inga (145d), inia (9b,109b), Inia (28c,45b), Inka (193), Iola, Iona (28a,82d), iota (71a,85c,91c,114c,166c,176a, 180d), Iowa (193), Irra (68c,178a), isba (135c), Isha (174a), Itea (145d,160c,181d), Itza (192), ixia (37a)

IB - -   Ibad (191), Iban (47c), ibex (67d,68a), ibid (80a,117a,137a), ibis (48d,49a,177b), ibit (117a)

- IB -   bibb (97c,146b), bibi (87d), dibs (70c), gibe (8a,42c,84d,100d,138c, 144c,149b), jibb, jibe (8a,33b,35d,37b,42c,100d,138c,144c,149b), kibe, kiby (29a), nibs (116c), ribe (139a), Tibu (191)

- - IB   Abib (102a,b), Adib (155b), Agib (12a,42d), chib (167a), crib (96b, 120d), drib (46b), frib (43d), glib (58d,149a,177c), guib (11a), snib (54d,93c), stib (19b,47a,137a)

I - - B   iamb (59c)

IC - -   ical (158c), icer, icho (67b), ichu (10b,70d), icon (79d,92b,136a)

- IC -   aich (9a), bice (20d,117d), Bice (27b), dice (65a), dick (43a,55b), Dick (96b), fico (169d), hick (185d), kick, lick, mica (82c,100b, 146c), mice, mick (82c), mico (97a), Nice (98c), nick (30c,108b), pica (66b,95b,172c), pice (190), Pici (19c, 184a), pick, pico (65a,152c), Pict (23c,47d), rice, Rice (46a), rich, rick (74d,117d,154d), sice (71d,147b), sick, tice (9a,38c,51a,185d), tick (12b,20d,97c), vice (31d,158a), wick

- - IC   amic (9d), chic (148d), cric (131c), epic (76b,120a), eric (115b), Eric (71d,96a,107d,138a,164a,176b), idic (79b), laic (32b,90b,107d, 124a,141d), odic (79c,120a), olic (158b), otic (14c,d,47b), saic (86b, 91d,175d), Udic (108a), Uvic (70c)

I - - C   idic (79b)

ID - -   Idas (27b,71c), idea (54c,108c,124a,164d), idee (61d), idem (89d, 164a), Iden (76a), ideo (34b,d,164d), ides (41a,b,133a), idic (79b), idio (34b,c), Idjo (191), idle (174b,c,178c), idly, idol (48c,54c,55a 75b,79d,112d,130b,184d), Idun (107d), idyl (114d), Idyo (191), Idxo (191)

- ID -   Aida (110d,175c), aide (7b,14a,75d), bide (47c,50b,130a,158b, 162a,177b), dido (11b,26c,65a,122a), Dido (27a,172c), eide (119c), fide, Gide (63a), hide (53a), Lida (183c), Lido (83d,175b), mide (110a), Midi (151b), nide (23c,72a,106c,116d), nidi (106c), Ridd (94a), ride (46b,85c), sida (37a,126c,170a), side (13d,22a,b,54a, 58a,89a,161b), sidi (103b,166b), sidy (123b), tide (39d,75d,109c, 141c,159d), tidy (106a,111b), Vida (183c), vide (89d,126a,142a), wide (133d), widu (102d)

- - ID   acid (151a,162a), amid (9d,50a), arid (46c,85a), avid (47b,71a, 186b), Beid (155b), caid (35a,151d,152b), chid, Enid (13b,25d,66b, 163a,183c), grid (17a,70d,119b,156d), ibid (80a,117a,137a), imid (29c), irid (38d,67c), kaid (29d,66a), laid (45b,142d), naid (63c), olid (55d,60c,148d,157d), ooid (48d), Ovid (132d,133b), oxid (112c), paid (129c), qaid (35a), quid (39b,166d), raid (59d,80c), said (174c), Said (42d,101a,121b), seid (103b), Seid (42d,101a, 171a), skid (148b), slid, uvid (101a), void (11a,49d,108d), zoid

I - - D   Ibad (191), ibid (80a,117a,137a), imid (29c), Irad (18d), irid (38d, 67c)

309

- IE - bien (63a,140c,179a,180a), bier (33b,66b), dieb (84a), diem (89b 116a), dier, dies (41b,89b), diet (14a,54c,84c,91b,176a), Dieu (61d), fief (55d), gier (47b), hien (30b), hier (63a,185d), Kiev, lied (66d,150b) lief (181d), lien (65c,91a,124c), lieu (118c,155d), mien (11c,17b 26d,44c,96b), pied (96c,103c,114b,117c,154a,174d), pien (13b) pier (23a,88b,180c), piet (29b,95b), Riel (129a), riem (76c,112c 157c,164d), rien (62b), rier (180b), sier (57a,118c), tied, tiem (147d), tier (118a,134b), vier (66c), view (93d,138b), wiel (140d 180d), wies (185a)

- - IE Abie (96b,107a), Amie (61d), Brie (29c), Erie (82c,87d), Okie (99d) Opie (50c), plie (32c,59b), soie (62c), unie (173a)

I - - E idee (61d), idle (174b,c,178c), ille (89b,d,163d), imbe (37a,56a 133d), inde, inee (120b), Inge (24d,67d,117c,119c), inre (35d,80a), Iole (52a,76b,123c), Ione (24b,88d,94d), ipse (44d,89c), Irae (43c), isle (8b,53c,81d,82d,86b,88a), ixle (56a)

IF - - ifil (117a,168c)

- IF - biff, fife (59a,105a), gift (123a), jiff (101c), kiff (88c), life (19a,177a), lift (49b), miff (44c), nife (37a), piff (24b), rife (6b,c, 39d,123b), riff (131d), Riff (18b,102c), rift (30c,32a,58a,110d), sift (140d,142c,146b), tiff (126b), wife (154a)

- - IF alif (12b), arif (127d), coif (73a), cuif (139a,d,140c), Enif (155b), kaif (88c), keif (75d), Leif (107d), luif, naif (74b,105a), waif (157b)

IG - - iglu (51c,149b), Igor (135d)

- IG - biga (171d), giga (56a,105a), high, migg (96c), nigh (106a), riga (118b), Riga, sigh, sign (121c,146c), tige (118a), wigg

- - IG brig (72b,106a,144d), crig (20d), grig (38c,70d,93a), prig (112a, 116c), snig (45d), swig (46a,72c), Teig (96a), trig (106a,148d,154b, 169d), twig, Whig

I - - G ilog (132a,161b)

IH - - IHVH (159d)

- IH - kiho (82a)

- - IH ch'ih (188), shih (189)

I - - H IHVH (159d), inch, itch, Ivah (18d)

II - - iiwi (19a,74b)

- II - liin (188), Riis (9d)

- - II alii (74c,134c), apii (74c), Boii (191), heii (74b), Ubii (191)

I - - I liwi (19a,74b), immi (189), impi (86a), Inti (159b), Ioni (192)

IJ - - ijma (103b)

- IJ - bija (168c), lija (57a,90d,173a)

IK - - ikat (53b,159a), ikmo (18b), ikon (79d,136a), ikra (27d)

- IK - bike, bikh (120b), dika (23a), dike (49c,91d), Dike (78a), fike (139c), hike, hiku (57a,106d,138a), kiki (27b), kiku (30d), like (13c,37d,146d), mike, Mike (96b), Nike (69c,100c,182d), pika (93a,128a,132c), pike (57a,b,76c,120b,153a), piki (95c), piky,

- - IT   adit (51a,100a,114d), alit (44b,143a), amit (94a), bait (15d,51a, 94d,167b), brit (76c), chit (67b,98c,108b,116c,177c), doit (47a, 169d,180d), duit (190), Duit (192), edit (20d,49d,123a,129a,131a), emit (43d,49a,53c,58d,83a,142c), exit (114d), fait (6d,61b), flit (41a), frit (64c,67c), gait (96b,179a), grit (137a,b), ibit (117a), knit (173c,179b), lait (62a), nuit (62b), obit (41b,64c), omit (49c, 52c,106b,114c,147d), phit (24b), quit (90d,130c), seit (189), skit (145c), slit (40a), spit (120a,132b,c), suit (38a,58a,91a,112a,119c, 137c), tait (14d), trit (34d,164c), twit (162b,c), unit (101c,110c, 147a), wait (26d,42b,92c,155d,162a), whit (166c), writ (91a), Yuit (51c)

I - - T   ibit (117a), ikat (53b,159a), ilot (82d)

- IU -   biur (35a), Niue (137d), Pius (121a)

I - - U   lalu (48d), ichu (10b,70d), iglu (51c,149b)

IV - -   Ivah (18d), Ivan (40c,85b,96a), Ives (9c,90b)

- IV -   Civa (56d), cive (110c), diva (110d,123c), dive (42b,74b,119d), divi, five, give (79d,123a), hive (17c), jiva (77a), jive (160c), kiva (28c,125b), kive (174d), kivu (170c), live (47c), Livy (132d,133a), rive (32a,153d), siva (67a,120d), Siva (56d,77a), sive (146a), viva (93d), vive (93d), vivo (93a), wive (97a)

- - IV   chiv (87a), skiv (151b)

- IW -   Biwa (93d,168c), iiwi (19a,74b), kiwi (11d,19a,58c)

IX - -   ixia (37a), Ixil (192), ixle (56a)

- IX -   Bixa (145d), dixi, Mixe (192), mixy, pixy (154b)

- - IX   Alix (183c), Coix (70d,85b), flix, noix (67c)

IY - -   Iyar (102b)

- IY -   kiyi (185d)

I - - Y   idly, inky (20b), inly, ismy (45a)

IZ - -   izar (65b,103b), Izar (155b)

- IZ -   bize (182a), bizz, size, sizy (176d), sizz, tiza (172a), zizz (181a)

- - IZ   friz (39d), phiz (54a), swiz (160c), whiz (25c)

I - - Z   Inez (45c,183c)

JA - -   jaca (84a), jack (26c,58a,127c), Jack (96b), jacu (19a,151b), jade (33c,65d,71d,166a), jadu (95a), jady, Jael (147b), Jaga (191), jagg, jail (123d), Jain (77b), jake (40d), Jake (96b), jako (71a), jama (103b), jamb (12d,45c,118a,146b,174a), jami (103b), jane (190), Jane (183c), jann (102d), jaob, jape (85a,b), jarl (40d,107d), jass (160d), jati (27b), jato (173b), jaun (113a), Java (33a), Jave (84d), jawy, jazz

- JA -   ajar (110c), Ajax (71b,162d)

- - JA   Beja (6c,191), bija (168c), caja (152a), coja (103b,166b), hoja (166b), lija (57a,90d,173a), maja (151c), Maja (153b), Naja (33a), puja (77a), raja (77a,123c), reja (152b), soja (151b)

J - - A   jaca (84a), Jaca, Jaga (191), jama (103b), Java (33a), Jena (105d, 165b), jiva (77a), jota (151c), Jova (193), juba (106b), juca (27a), Juda, juga (27a), jula, jura, Juza (155b)

J - - B   jamb (12d,45c,118a,146b,174a), jaob, jibb, Joab (41a)

315

- - JD   **Nejd**

J - - D   **Joad** (50c)

JE - -   **jean** (37c), **Jean** (183c), **jeel**, **jeep**, **jeer** (138c,162b), **jefe** (152a), **jeff** (133d), **Jeff**, **jehu** (46b), **Jehu** (18c), **Jena** (105d,165b), **jerk** (153a), **jess** (157a), **jest** (169c), **Jesu**, **jete** (16a), **Jeth** (102a), **jeux** (61d)

- JE -   **ajee** (15c,139a)

- - JE   **haje** (33a,48d), **yaje** (23a)

J - - E   **jade** (33c,65d,71d,166a), **jake** (40d), **Jake** (96b), **jane** (190), **Jane** (183c), **jape** (85a,b), **Jave** (84d), **jefe** (152a), **jete** (16a), **jibe** (8a, 33b,35d,37b,42c,100d,138c,144c,149b), **jive** (160c), **joke** (183a), **jole** (29b), **Jose** (96a), **Jove** (85d), **jube** (28d), **Jude** (11c,96a), **juke** (114c), **Jule** (183c), **June** (183c), **jupe** (62b,84a), **jure** (90b), **jute** (37a,48a,56a,133d,136a), **Jute**

J - - F   **jeff** (133d), **Jeff**, **jiff** (101c)

J - - G   **jagg**, **joug** (138d), **Jung** (125a)

JH - -   **Jhil**, **jhum**, **JHVH** (159d), **JHWH** (159d)

J - - H   **Jeth** (102a), **josh** (85b), **JHVH** (159d), **JHWH** (159d)

JI - -   **jibb**, **jibe** (8a,33b,35d,37b,42c,100d,138c,144c,149b), **jiff** (101c), **Jill** (183d), **jilt**, **jink**, **jinn** (42b,103b,153c), **jinx** (78a), **jiti**, **jiva** (77a), **jive** (160c)

- - JI   **caji** (180b), **Caji**, **fuji** (84b), **Fuji** (84d), **koji** (185b), **suji** (180c)

J - - I   **jami** (103b), **jati** (27b), **Jati**, **jiti**, **jogi** (76d), **joli** (62b), **joti**

J - - K   **jack** (26c,58a,127c), **Jack** (96b), **jerk** (153a), **jink**, **jock**, **Jock** (96b), **jonk**, **juck** (114c), **junk** (30a,134c)

J - - L   **Jael** (147b), **jail** (123d), **jarl** (40d,107d), **jeel**, **jhil**, **Jill** (183d), **Joel** (96a), **jowl** (29b)

- JM -   **ijma** (103b)

- - JM   **Sejm** (120c)

J - - M   **jhum**, **joom** (39c)

J - - N   **Jain** (77b), **jann**, **Jann** (102d), **jaun** (113a), **jean** (37c), **Jean** (183c), **jinn** (42b,103b,153c), **Joan** (183c), **John** (11c,96a,121a,186b), **join** (36a,173c), **juan** (113a), **Juan** (96a)

JO - -   **Joab** (41a), **Joad** (50c), **Joan** (183c), **joar** (100a), **jobo** (77c), **jock**, **Jock** (96b), **jocu** (45b,57a), **Jodo** (113d), **Joel** (96a), **joey** (86a, 185d), **Joey** (96b,109c), **jogi** (76d), **John** (11c,96a,121a,186b), **join** (36a,173c), **joke** (183a), **joky** (96a), **jole** (29b), **joli** (62b), **jolt** (143b), **jonk**, **joom** (39c), **Jose** (96a), **josh** (85b), **joss** (30b), **Josy** (183d), **jota** (151c), **joti**, **joug** (138d), **Jova** (193), **Jove** (85d), **jowl** 29b), **Jozy**

- JO -   **ajog** (55b,168c), **ejoo** (55b,168c), **Gjoa** (144d)

- - JO   **bojo** (117a), **gajo** (107c), **Idjo** (191), **majo**, **mojo** (177c), **pajo** (122a), **rojo** (129a,152c), **tajo** (152a,d)

J - - O   **jako** (71a), **Jako**, **jato** (173b), **jobo** (77c), **Jodo** (113d), **judo** (84b, 85c,142b), **Juno** (69c,85d,100c,126b)

J - - P   **jeep**, **jump**

316

J - - R   jeer (162b), joar (100a), juar (100a)

J - - S   jass (160d), jess (157a), joss (30b)

J - - T   jest (169c), jilt, jolt (143b), just (51b,54b)

JU - -   juan (113a), Juan (96a), juar (100a), juba (106b), jube (28d), juca (27a), juck (114c), Juda, Jude (11c,96a), judo (84b,85c,142b), Judy (125c,183d), juez (152b), juga (27a), juju (29b,55d), juke (114c), jula, Jule (183d), jump, June (183c), Jung (125a), junk (30a,134c), Juno (69c,85d,100c,126b), jupe (62b,84a), jura, Jura, jure (90b), jury (38a), just (51b,54b), jute (37a,48a,56a,133d, 136a), Jute, Juza (155b)

- - JU   baju (84a), hoju (84b), juju (29b,55d), teju (151b)

J - - U   jacu (19a,151b), jadu (95a), jehu (46b), Jehu (18c), Jesu, jocu (45b,57a), juju (29b,55d)

J - - X   jeux (61d), jinx (78a), jynx (78a), Jynx (184a)

JY - -   jynx (78a), Jynx (184a)

J - - Y   jady, jawy, joey (86a,185d), Joey (96b,109c), joky, Josy (183d), Jozy, Judy (125c,183d), July, jury (38a)

J - - Z   jazz, juez (152b)

KA - -   kaan (93d,116c), kaat (105d), kada (188), kade (144a), kadi (103a, 171a), Kadu (191), Kafa (6c), kago (113a), kagu (106c), kaha (123d), kahu (14d), kaid (29d,66a), kaif (88c) kaik (96c), kail (18c, 22a,25a,79b), Kain, kair, kaka (114b), kaki (84c,106d), kala (19a), kale (22a,25a,119b,175a), kali (26d,67c,136d,167a), Kali (147b), kalo (162a), Kama (56d), kame (67b,139b), Kami (68a,84b,88c, 107c,144c), kana (84d), Kane (74c), k'ang (30a), Kano (84c,177d), kant (28d), Kant (67a), kapa (74b), kaph (91d), Kapp, Kara (132a), Kari (14d), Karl (96a), karn (156c), karo (106d), kasa (48a), kasi (116b), kasm (189), Kate (143c,183d), kath (14a), Katy (183d), kaun (93d), kava (18c,116a), Kavi (84d), kawa (18c,116a), Kawi (84d), kawn (93d), kayo (87c), kazi (103a), kazy (103a)

- KA -   Akal (56d), Akan (191), ikat (53b,159a), okay (8d), skag (7d, 46d), skat (181b), Skat (155b)

- - KA   Akka (125d), Atka (11a), baka (52b), beka (189), dika (23a), Ekka (26d), Inka (193), kaka (114b), loka (173c,184c), pika (93a, 128a,132c), puka (107a,168c), roka (95a,168c,d), Saka (10a), sika (41d,84b), soka (20c), waka (26a), weka (58c,106d,107a,127b), Yaka (191)

K - - A   kada (188), Kafa (6c), kaha (123d), kaka (114b), kala (19a), Kama (56d), kana (84d), kapa (74b), kara (132a), kasa (48a), kava (18c 116a), kawa (18c,116a), kela (189), keta (45a), kina (126d), kiva (28c,125b), koba (11a), kola (25b,84a,108d), Kola (135b,c,d), kona (74c), kora (19a,178c), kota (117a), Kota (45d), kuba (26d,189), kufa (21b,99a), kula (189), kusa

K - - B   kerb (146b), knab (107a), knob (73c,107c,124d), knub (178b)

K - - D   kaid (29d,66a), keid (154b), kind (150d,153a,174d), Kurd (48b, 82a)

KE - -   keal (25a), keef (75d), keek (154c), keel (128d,134d,144c,d), keen (15a,88a,177b), keep (123a,130d), keet (72b), keif (75d), keir

317

(20c,174d), **kela** (189), **keld** (154b), **kelp** (82a,141c), **Kelt** (180b), **kemp** (139b), **keno, Kent** (90d), **kepi** (99d), **kept, kerb** (146b), **kere** (75c,128b), **kerf** (40a,108b), **keri** (75c,128b), **kern** (59c,172a), **Kern** (132b), **Kerr, keta** (45a), **Ketu** (48b)

- KE -   **akee** (168c), **akey** (189), **okeh** (8d,37b), **oket** (189), **skee** (149c), **skeg** (7d,86a,144d,157d,184a), **sken** (164a), **skeo** (57d), **skep** (16d,17c,77c), **skew** (148a,160c,171b,c), **skey** (185d)

- - KE   **bake** (139a), **bike, cake, coke** (32d,64a), **cuke** (39b), **cyke** (40c), **dike** (49c,91d), **Dike** (78a), **duke** (107c), **dyke** (49c,91d), **fake** (123a,143c), **feke, fike** (139c), **fyke** (15d), **hake** (57a,b), **hike, hyke!, jake** (40d), **Jake** (96b), **joke** (183a), **juke** (114c), **lake** (117d), **like** (13c,37d,146d), **Loke** (15d,68b), **luke, Luke** (52a, 96a), **make** (35b,36d,54a,123a), **mike, Mike** (96b), **moke** (45c, 157d), **Nike** (69c,100c,182d), **Peke** (45a,148d), **pike** (57a,b,76c, 120b,153a), **poke** (108c), **rake** (41b,44c,134b,140d), **roke** (174d, 175b), **sake** (84b,125d), **soke** (44c,85d), **syke** (194), **take, tike** (29d), **tuke** (26b,53b), **tyke** (29d), **wake** (134b,168a), **woke, yoke** (85b,92d,173c), **Zeke** (96b)

K - - E   **kade** (144a), **kale** (22a,25a,119b,175a), **kame** (67b,139b), **Kane** (74c), **Kate** (143c,183d), **kere** (75c,128b), **kibe kile** (189), **kine** (38a,112c), **kite** (19c,49a,74c,d), **kive** (174d), **Klee** (113a), **knee** (85b), **koae** (74b), **Kobe** (78a), **Kome** (71d), **kore** (107b) **Kore** (29a, 42b,116b,124d), **kuge** (84c), **Kure** (84c), **kyle** (57a,139c)

- - KF   **wakf** (103a), **wukf** (103a)

K - - F   **kaif** (88c), **keef** (75d), **keif** (75d), **kerf** (40a,108b), **klef** (75d), **kiff** (88c), **koff** (47a)

K - - G   **k'ang** (30a), **king** (26c,29c), **knag** (115d,139c), **krag** (131c), **kung** (125b)

KH - -   **khan** (7c,26c,81b,93d,116c,123c,130c,166c), **khar** (189), **khas** (153a), **khat** (105d), **Khem** (113c), **khet** (188), **khot**

- KH -   **Akha** (86a,c)

- - KH   **ankh** (38d,162b), **bikh** (120b), **bukh** (122a), **hakh** (46d), **lakh** (110c), **rukh** (53b,54a), **Sikh** (77b)

K - - H   **kaph** (91d), **kath** (14a), **kish** (16d,70c), **Kish** (137c), **kith** (63c), **Koch** (66d), **koph** (91d), **Kush, kyah** (19a)

KI - -   **kiak** (51c), **kibe, kiby** (29a), **kick, kief** (75d), **kiel** (128d,134d), **Kiel** (25d), **kier** (20c,174d), **Kiev, kiff** (88c), **kiho** (82a), **kiki** (27b), **kiku** (30d), **kile** (189), **kill** (38c), **kiln** (15d,112a), **kilo** (99b,122d), **kilt, kina** (126d), **kind** (150d,153a,174d), **kine** (38a,112c), **king** (26c,29c), **kink** (38b,171c), **kino** (27c,34c,47c,72c,98b,161d,168c), **kipp, kiri** (86a,87c,115a,168c), **kirk** (31a,139b), **kish** (16d,70c), **Kish** (137c), **kiss** (148c), **kist** (29d,58a,139b), **kite** (19c,49a,74c,d), **kith** (63c), **kiva** (28c,125b), **kive** (174d), **kivu** (170c), **kiwi** (11d, 19a,58c), **kiyi** (185d)

- KI -   **akia** (74c), **Akim** (135d,191), **akin** (8b,92b,129c), **okia** (190), **Okie** (99d), **skid** (148b), **skil** (57a), **skim** (67c), **skin** (53a,76c,115c, d), **skio** (57d), **skip** (110b,114c,147c), **skir, skit** (145c), **skiv** (151b)

- - KI   **Enki** (15b), **kaki** (84c,106d), **kiki** (27b), **Kuki** (191), **Loki** (7c,15d, 68b), **maki** (91b), **moki** (127b), **piki** (95c), **Reki** (16a), **saki** (39c,

318

84b,102a), **Tiki** (120c), **weki** (55c), **yaki** (193)

K - - I   **kadi** (103a,171a), **kaki** (84c,106d), **kali** (26d,67c,136d,167a), **Kall** (147b), **Kami** (68a,84b,88c,107c,144c), **Kari** (14d), **kasi** (116b), **Kavi** (84d), **Kawi** (84d), **kazi** (103a), **kepi** (99d), **keri** (75c,128b), **kiki** (27b), **kiri** (86a,87c,115a,168c), **kiwi** (11d,19a,58c), **kiyi** (185d), **kobi** (84b), **koji** (185b), **Koli** (27b), **Komi** (191), **kopi** (107a, 168c), **Kopi** (172a), **kori** (7d,77a), **kuei** (44a), **Kuki** (191), **Kuli** (27b), **Kuri** (191), **kwei** (44a)

- KK -   **Akka** (125d), **Ekka** (26d)

- - KK   **bukk** (122a), **rikk** (49a)

K - - K   **kaik** (96c), **kiak** (51c), **keek** (154c), **kick**, **kink** (38b,171c), **kirk** (31a,139b), **konk** (41c), **kunk** (188), **kurk** (31a,139b), **kyak** (51c)

KL - -   **klam** (189), **Klee** (113a), **klom** (189), **klop** (150d)

K - - L   **kail** (18c,22a,25a,79b), **Karl** (96a), **keal** (25a), **keel** (128d,134d, 144c,d), **kiel** (128d,134d), **Kiel** (25d), **kill** (38c), **koel** (19a,b,39b), **kohl** (53c), **kral**, **kuhl** (53c)

- KM -   **ikmo** (18b)

K - - M   **kasm** (189), **Khem** (113c), **klam** (189), **klom** (189)

KN - -   **Knab** (107a), **knag** (115d,139c), **knap** (76d,107a,139b,159b,166a, 170c,185b), **knar** (87c,134b), **knee** (85b), **knew**, **knez** (123c), **knip** (115c), **knit** (173c,179b), **knob** (73c,107c,124d), **knop** (124b,170c, 185b), **knor** (87c), **knot** (43c,99d,107c,124d,137b), **knub** (178b), **knur** (67d,87c,107c), **knut**, **Knut** (40d,50c,96a)

K - - N   **kaan** (93d,116c), **Kain**, **karn** (156c), **kaun** (93d), **kawn** (93d), **keen** (15a,88a,177b), **kern** (172a), **Kern** (132b), **khan** (7c,26c,81b,93d, 116c,123c,130c,166c), **kiln** (15d,112a), **kran** (190), **kuan** (30b), **Kuan** (30c), **kwan** (30b)

KO - -   **koae** (74b), **koba** (11a), **Kobe** (78a), **kobi** (84b), **kobu** (84b), **Koch** (66d), **koel** (19a,b,39b), **koff** (47a), **kohl** (53c), **koir** (33a), **koji** (185b), **koko** (106d,114b), **Koko** (93d,186c), **koku** (189), **kola** (25b,84a,108d,168c), **Kola** (135b,c,d), **Koli** (27b), **kolo** (59b,135c), **Kome** (71d), **Komi** (191), **kona** (74c), **konk** (41c), **koop** (16c), **koph** (91d), **kopi** (107a,168c), **Kopi** (172a), **kora** (19a,178c), **Kora**, **kore** (107b), **Kore** (29a,42b,116b,124d), **kori** (7d,77a), **koso** (6c,80d), **Koso** (192,193), **koss** (188), **kota** (117a), **Kota** (45d), **koto** (84b), **kozo** (113d,168c)

- KO -   **akov** (189), **Ekoi** (191), **ikon** (79d,136a)

- - KO   **boko** (52b), **Doko** (191), **hako** (115b), **jako** (71a), **koko** (106d,114b), **Koko** (93d,186c), **mako** (18a,19a,20d,143c,168c,182c), **moko** (96c), **toko** (30c)

K - - O   **kago** (113a), **kalo** (162a), **Kano** (84c,177d), **karo** (106d), **kayo** (87c), **keno** (87c), **kiho** (82a), **kilo** (99b,122d), **kino** (27c,34c,47c,72c, 98b,161d,168c), **koko** (106d,114b), **Koko** (93d,186c), **kolo** (59b, 135c), **koso** (6c,80d), **Koso** (192,193), **koto** (84b), **kozo** (113d,168c), **Kroo** (191)

K - - P   **Kapp** (189), **keep** (123a,130d), **kelp** (82a,141c), **kemp** (139b), **kipp**, **klop** (150d), **knap** (76d,107a,139b,159b,166a,170c,185b), **knip** (115c), **knop** (124b,170c,185b), **koop** (16c)

319

KR - -   krag (131c), kral, kran (190), kras (76d), kris (40b,95d), Kroo (191)

- KR -   akra (176a), Akra (191), ikra (27d), okra (72c,175a), okro (72c, 175a)

- - KR   Askr (107d)

K - - R   kair, keir (20c,174d), Kerr, khar (189), kler (20c,174d), knar (87c,134b), knor (87c), knur (67d,87c,107c), koir (33a), Kuar (102a), kyar (33a)

- - KS   oaks (154d)

K - - S   khas (153a), kiss (148c), koss (188), kras (76d), kris (40b,95d), kvas (135c)

- - KT   takt (105a,163a)

K - - T   kaat (105d), kant (28d), Kant (67a), keet (72b), Kelt (180b), Kent (90d), kept, khat (105d), khet (188), khot, kilt, kist (29d,58a, 139b), knit (173c,179b), knot (43c,99d,107c,124d,137b), knut, Knut (40d,50c,96a), kyat (189)

KU - -   Kuan (30c), kuan (30b), Kuar (102a), kuba (26d,189), kudu (11a), kuei (44a), kufa (21b,99a), kuge (84c), kuhl (53c), Kuki (191), kuku (19a,106d), kula (189), Kuli (27b), kung (125b), kunk (188), Kurd (48b,82a), Kure (84c), Kuri (191), kurk (31a,139b), kusa, Kush

- KU -   akua (120d), skua (19b,72c,84a,141a)

- - KU   baku (26d,157b,168c), duku (95d,168c), haku (86d), hiku (57a, 106d,138a), kiku (30d), koku (189), kuku (19a,106d), Maku (192), poku (11a), puku (11a), Suku (191), Taku (80c)

K - - U   Kadu (191), kagu (106c), kahu (14d), Ketu (48b), kiku (30d), kivu (170c), kobu (84b), koku (189), kudu (11a), kuku (19a,106d)

KV - -   kvas (135c)

- KV -   NKVD (135d)

K - - V   Kiev

KW - -   kwan (30b), kwel (44a)

K - - W   knew, know

KY - -   kyah (19a), kyak (51c), kyar (33a), kyat (189), kyle (57a,139c)

- KY -   Skye (163c), skyr (21d,151a), skyt (138c,140b)

- - KY   alky, caky, coky, faky, inky (20b), joky, laky, oaky, piky, poky (148c), taky, waky

K - - Y   Katy (183d), kazy (103a), kiby (29a)

K - - Z   knez (123c)

LA - -   laap (51d,91b,141d), lace (58b,179c), lack (178a), lact (34c), lacy, Ladd (143c), lade (24c,26d,43c,93b,100a,132a,139d,161b,178d), lady, laet (60d), lago (83b,152b), laic (32b,90b,107d,124a,141d), laid, lain, lair (37c,42b), Lais (17c), lait (62a), lake (117d), lakh (110c), laky, lala (129b), lalo (16b,34d,153a), Lalo (35c), lama (23d,24a,91d,165b), lamb, Lamb (49c), lame (38d,43d,73b), lamp (92a,94c), lana (58a,66a,90a,184b), land (44a,163c), lane (134b, 157b), lank (148b,164b), lant, lanx (133a,b), Laos (80d,129c), Lapp (108a), Lara (25c), lard (54d,61a,71a,110a), lari (78a,101c),

Lari (72c), lark (19a,63d,177b), larp (51d), Lars (51d,121b), lash (58c,87b,165c,180d), Lasi (191), lass (95b), last (36c,50b,145a, 174c), lata (85d,95d), late (128c), lath (157c), latu (190), laud (122a), laun (146b), lava (101c,132b,151a,177a), lave (16d,178b), lawn (20a,37c,53b,92c), laze (79b), Laze (191), Lazi (191), lazo (88d,128b,133d), lazy

- LA - alae (182d), alai (171a), Alai (135c), alan (45a,79a,183c), Alan, alar (15c,145c,182d), alas (52c,136b,183b), alat (136d), alay (96c), blaa, blab (162b), blae (93b), blah, blas (6c,49c), Blas (67b), blat (25b), blay (57d), clad (46a,82a), clam (20b,101b), clan (169c), clap (58b), claw (29c,105b,161d,173a), Clay (9d), Elah (18c,86d), elan (12c,41a,50d,62a,153c,177a,186b), Elam (18d,37d, 82a,116c,144b), ELAS (71c), flag (16b,50d,82b,88c,115a,155a), flak (11a), flam (169c), flan (39d,40a,114d), flap (17b,59a,104a, 118d,161a,182d), flat (41b,124b,173a), flaw, flax, flay (147c,157c), glad (85c), klam (189), Olaf (108a,176b), olam (51a,d,75c,81a), Olan (115c), Olax (52b), olay (113b), plan (99b,124a,138b), plap (54b), plat (22b,96c,114a,119c,133d), play (63d,154a), slab (148b), slag (46c,99a,138c,148d,177a), slam (180d,182d), slap (24a,128c, 148c), slat (58b,89a,117c,184a), Slav (13c,40c,48b,52a,120b,135b), slaw, slay, Ulam (67b), ulan (27d,88a)

- - LA agla (7a), alla (6d), amla (48a,161d,168c,169a), aula (66c,73b), Bala (26c,66a), bela (12a), Bela (18b,48c,78d), bola (16a,179b), cela (62d), cola (25b,108d,149d,168c), dola (189), ella (152c, 158c), Ella (183c), fala (129b), gala (55d), Gala (191), gila (93b), gola (27b,40c,70c,157a), gula (90a,101a,165b), hala (112b), Hela (93c), hila (53c), hola (74c,152b), hula (74b), Hyla (10a,166d, 169b), iola, jula, kala (19a), kela (199), kola (25b,84a,108d,168c), Kola (135b,c,d), kula (189), lala (129b), Lila (183c), Lola (27d,97b), mala (89c,90a,94b,97d,109d,185c), mela (34a,129d), mila (188), Mola (159c), Nala (77a), Nola, olla (36d,44b,84d,113b,121d, 151d,152c,181b), pala (189), Pala (88b), pela (30c), Pola, pyla (22d), sala (50c,152a,b,c), Sala (50c), sola (9a,48a,74b,118c, 154a,167b), Sula (65a), tala (16d,113a,168c,d), tela (22d,98c, 121b,166a,179c), tola (48a,80d,180a), Tola (85b), tula (9a), Tula, upla, vela (98c,136b,149d), Vela (36b,c), vila (54b), vola (89d), Zola (63a)

L - - A lala (129b), lama (23d,24a,91d,165b), lana (58a,66a,90a,184b), Lara (25c), lata (85d,95d), lava (101c,132b,151a,177a), Leda (27b, 75d,120c,153a,171d,186b), lena (56d), Lena (36b), Lida (183c), lija (57a,90d,173a), Lila (183c), lima (17b,152b,174d), Lima (31b), lina (188), Lina (183d), lipa (54d), lira (28b,79a,170d), Lisa (183d), loka (173c,184c), Lola (27d,97b), loma (58b,63d), lora (146b,149b, 151c,169b), Lora (183c), lota (24c,121d,178d), Lota, Iowa (19a), Luba (191), luna (103c), Luna (102b), lura (22d,82a), lyra, Lyra (36b,74a)

- LB - alba (98b,181a), Alba (151d), albe (133a), Albi (58a), albo (34d, 181a), Elba (105d), Elbe (108a)

- - LB bulb (37a,172c)

L - - B lamb, Lamb (49c), limb (12d,22d), lobb (23b,94c,163a)

- LC - Alca (14c,128b), alco (45b)

321

- - LC   talc (28d,63b,99c,100b,122a,149c)

L - - C   laic (32b,90b,107d,124a,141d)

- LD -   Alda (110d,150c), alda (152b)

- - LD   bald (16c), bold (41a), cold (65d), eild (138d,140a), fold, geld (162b), gild (14a,49c,69c,98b), gold, held, Hild, hold (95c,124c, 130d), Keld (154b), meld (26a,41c,99a,118b), mild (32a,66a), mold (54d,143c), sold, suld (188), told (129c), veld (151a), weld (47c, 85b,173c), wild (38b,173d), wold (47c,60a,118d,174a,184a)

L - - D   Ladd (143c), laid (163c), land (44a,163c), lard (54d,61a,71a,110a), laud (122a), lead (35d,43d,72b,74d,81a), lend (6d,79d), lied (66d,150b), load (24c,26d,161b), lood (189) lord (107c), loud (156a), Ludd (23c)

LE - -   lead (35d,43d,72b,74d,81a), leaf (55c,73c,119b), Leah (19a,84a, 87b,183c), leak (110c), leal (54b,94c,139d), lean (128a,148b,152d, 164b,166a), leap (26c), lear (139d), Lear (37a,143b), lech 102b), Leda (27b,75d,120c,153a,171d,186b), leek (58b,76a,110c,177d), leer (9d,58a,67c,93d,112a,148c), lees (46a,142a), leet (26a, 38a,139d), left (42c), lehr (67c,112a) Leif (107d), Leir, Lely (47a), lena (56d), Lena (36b), lend (6d,79d), lene (36b,149a, 172b), leno (37c,53b), lens (67c,95b,111a,129b,162d), lent (54d), Lent (115d,141c), Leon (96a), Lero (82d), lerp (51d,141d), less (100c,108b,141d), lest (59d,163d), lete, Leti (82d), Leto (11c), Lett (16a,90a,93a), leve (62a), Levi (84a,90c), levo (91a), levy (14a, 162b)

- LE -   Alea (14b,31c,167d), alee (10a,57c,d,76c,137c), alee (15c,75d, 144b,157a,182a), alef (91c), alem (98b,155a,170d,171a), alen (40d, 138a), bleb (20c,23d,67c), bled, blet (64a), bleu (61b), blew, clee (19a,129a), clef (104d,105a), clem (56b,158b), clew (16a,33a,77b, 136b,164d), elef (91c), flea (81b), fled, flee, flew, flex (18a), fley (63d), gled (19a,52a,87a), glee (99a,150b), glen (43c), Hler (141a), ilex (77d), Klee (113a), Lleu (40c), Llew (40c), olea (170b), Olea (110b), oleo (34c), plea (51a,52d,122a,130b), pleb (10d,35b,180b), plet (135d), plew (17c), plex (60b), Sleb (12a), sled (40a), slee (140b,148c), slew (160a), sley (179b), Ulex (153c), vlei (38c, 160a), vley (160a)

- - LE   able (26b,35b,126a,147c), acle (13d,82c,115d), aile (62b,63a,182c, d), Alle (14c), atle (136d,161d,169b), axle (153c,180c), bale (24b, 74a), bile (30c), bole (31b,32a,169b), cale (72d), cole (25a), Cole, dale (43c,128a,174b), dele (26a,49c,51b,53a,110b,123d,124c,130a, 145c,161b), dole (44c,118c,121c,129d), Dole (74c), elle (62b,c), file (13a,127d), gale (181d), gyle (23b,174d), hale (125b), Hale (9d,131a), hole (6c,11b,110d,118c,147a), hule (23a,134c), hyle (97c), idle (174b,c,178c), ille (89b,d,163d), Iole (52a,76b,123c), isle (8b,53c,81d,82d,86b,88a), ixle (56a), jole (29b), Jule (183d), kale (22a,25a,119b,175a), kile (189), kyle (57a,139c), male (154d), Male (45d), mele (74b,150b), mile (64c), mole (19d,23a,24d,85a, 117c,155c), Mole (88c), mule (45b,148b,153c,180b), nile (33c, 71d), Nile (106b), ogle (9d,53c,91a,93d,148c), orle (17b,56b,76a, 144b,177a), pale (113a,117c,178a), Pele (69c,74c), pile (45d,75b, 117c), pole (132c,143b,177b,184a), Pole (52a), pule (180d), pyle (34b), Pyle (9c,178a), rale (7c,23a,29d,41b), rile (10c,d,82c,125a,

322

156b,176a), **role** (114b), **rule** (11b,26b,90b), **sale** (14c,61c,62b,c,
168b), **sole** (52c,57a,b,58b,d,110c,115d,150a), **tale** (91a,185b), **tele**
(34b,122c), **tile** (31d,56d,72b,95b,133c,163c), **tole** (9a,51a,99b,
163a), **tule** (24b,27c), **vale** (54c,128a,174b), **Vale** (7c,109c), **vile**
(16c,56c), **vole** (97d,104a), **wale** (70b,131b,157c,163d,179a,180a,
c,d), **wile** (13b,41c,157b,169c), **Yale** (173c), **Yule** (30d)

L - - E   **lace** (58b,179c), **lade** (24c,26d,43c,93b,100a,132a,139d,161b),
178d), **lake** (117d), **lame** (38d,43d,73b), **lane** (134b,157b), **late**
(128c), **lave** (16d,178b), **laze** (79b), **Laze** (191), **lene** (36b,149a,
172b), **lete, leve** (62a), **life** (19a,177a), **like** (13c,37d,146d), **lime**
(25b,27d,31b,33c,102d,168c), **line** (12b,22b,36d,38a,126c,134b,
157b,158b,162d,175c), **lire** (62c), **lite** (158c,d), **live** (47c), **lobe**
(90c,134b), **lode** (42c,99a,111b,175b), **loge** (164a), **Loke** (15d,68b),
Lome, lone (150a), **lope** (48b,64b,d), **lore** (77c,87c,90d,151c,183a),
lose (60a,100c), **lote** (24c,94a), **love** (163a), **lube** (110a), **luce**
(58c,117d), **Luce** (7b,35a), **luge** (148a), **luke, Luke** (52a,96a), **lune**
(38c,73b,74d), **lupe** (19a,64a), **lure** (41c,51a,54b,163a), **lute** (11c,
28b,84d,105a,131d), **luxe** (61c,62d,159c), **lyre** (11c,81c,105a,111c),
lyse

- LF -   **alfa** (70d)

- - LF   **calf, golf** (154a), **gulf** (6c), **half** (101a), **pelf** (22a,56c,131b), **self**
(48d,80d), **Welf** (67a), **wolf**

L - - F   **leaf** (55c,73c,119b), **Leif** (107d), **lief** (181d), **loaf** (49b,94b), **loof**
(144c,153d), **luff** (136b), **luif**

- LG -   **alga** (141b,c), **Algy** (96b), **Olga** (135c,183c)

L - - G   **ling** (24c,57a,b,75b,178c), **long** (38b,185b), **lung, lurg** (96d,141b,
184d)

L - - H   **lakh** (110c), **lash** (58c,87b,165c,180d), **lath** (157c), **Leah** (19a,84a,
87b,183c), **lech** (102b), **lith** (34d,156c), **loch** (88a,139d), **losh**
(178b), **loth** (15a,173d), **Lugh** (28b), **lush** (94d)

LI - -   **Liam** (181d), **liar** (98d), **Lias** (66a), **lick, Lida** (183c), **Lido** (83d,
175b), **lied** (66d,150b), **lief** (181d), **lien** (65c,91a,124c), **lieu** (118c,
155d), **life** (19a,177a), **lift** (49b), **liin** (188), **lija** (57a,90d,173a),
like (13c,37d,146d), **Lila** (183c), **lill** (15d,118a), **lilt** (93a,131a,
147a), **lily, lima** (17b,152b,174d), **Lima** (31b), **limb** (12d,22d),
lime (25b,27d,31b,33c,102d,168c), **limn** (45d,121c), **limp**
(58a,81a,177d), **limu** (141c), **limy** (176d), **Lina** (188), **Lina**
(183d), **line** (12b,22b,36d,38a,126c,134b,157b,158b,162d,175c),
ling (24c,57a,b,75b,178c), **link** (36a,81d,85b), **linn** (120d,140a,c,
168c,178d), **lino, lint** (46a,58d), **liny** (157b), **Linz** (40d), **lion** (55b,
86c), **lipa** (54d), **lira** (28b,79a,170d), **lire** (62c), **Lisa** (183d), **lisp**
153b), **liss** (54b,58b,60c,129d,140a), **list** (26d,27b,75b,83d,134a,
138b,165d), **lite** (158c,d), **lith** (34d,156c), **liti** (60d), **litz** (127b),
live (47c), **Livy** (132d,133a)

- LI -   **alia** (89d), **alif** (12b), **alii** (74c,134c), **alim** (103b,162c) **alin** (188),
alit (44b,143a), **Alix** (183c), **Clim** (12b), **Clio** (104d), **clip** (54d,
143d), **Elia** (88a,115d), **Elis** (22c,37d,71b,107c), **flip** (167c), **flit**
(41a), **flix, glia** (106c), **glib** (58d,149a,177c), **glim, glis** (45c), **ilia**
(21d,77b,115d), **ille** (89b,d), **olic** (158b), **olid** (55d,60c,148d,157d),
olio (44b,77c,98c,100d,121d), **plie** (32c,59b), **slid, slim** (148b,

323

160a), **slip** (67c,119a), **slit** (40a)

- - LI **amli** (48a,161d,168c,169a), **Atli** (14c,72b,79a,107d), **Ball, Beli** (23c), **coli, dali** (168c,169b), **doli, fili, gali** (6c), **goli** (105c), **Holi** (77a), **joli** (62b), **kali** (26d,67c,136d,167a), **Kali** (147b), **Koli** (27b, **Kuli** (27b), **mali** (27b), **pali** (122b), **Pali** (23d,24a,137b,175a), **pill** (34b,108d), **puli** (45a,78d), **soli** (12c,110c), **tali** (189), **teli** (94b), **vali** (171a,176a), **Vali** (7c,109c), **vili** (54b), **Vili** (109c), **wali** (171a), **yali** (171a)

L - - I **Lari** (72c), **lari** (78a,101c), **Lasi** (191), **Lazi** (191), **Leti** (82d), **Levi** (84a,90c), **liti** (60d), **loci** (66b,118c), **Lodi** (105d), **Loki** (7c,15d, 68b), **lori** (91b), **Loti** (63a,176a), **ludi** (133b), **Luri** (191)

- LK - **alky**

- - LK **balk** (118c,146a,156d), **bilk** (29b,41c,42a), **bulk** (97b), **calk** (78c, 109a,141c,178d), **folk** (116a,169c), **fulk** (173a), **hulk** (144d,173d), **milk, mulk** (60d), **polk** (37c), **pulk** (37c,88d), **silk** (53b,179c), **sulk** (159a), **talk, volk** (66c,105d,116a), **Volk, walk, welk** (65c,96d, 141b), **yolk**

L - - K **lack** (178a), **lank** (148b,164b), **lark** (19a,63d,177b), **leak** (110c), **leek** (58b,76a,110c,177d), **lick, link** (36a,81d,85b), **lock** (54d), **lonk** (143d), **look** (11c,53c,142a), **luck** (28d), **lurk** (92a, 147d)

LL - - **llyn** (120d,140a), **Lieu** (40c), **Llew** (40c)

- LL - **alla** (6d), **Alle** (14c), **allo** (34c), **ally** (14a,35c,d,173c), **ella** (152c, 158c), **Ella** (183c), **elle** (62b,c), **ille** (89b,d,163d), **ills** (170a), **olla** (36d,44b,84d,113b,121d,151d,152c,181b), **ullo** (6a,144a), **Ullr** (146b,164d)

- - LL **ball, bell** (24c,39d), **Bell** (162d), **bill** (17b,147a), **Bill** (96b), **boll** (119b,d), **bull** (113c), **call** (145c,159b,176d), **cell** (39b), **cull** (117c), **dell** (43c,174b), **dill** (13a,117c), **doll** (125c), **dull** (21a,32c,173a), **Dull** (94b), **fall** (46b,141c), **fell** (40a,58b,76c,115d,147d), **fill** (109b), **full** (7b,130b), **gall** (19a,28c,29b,82c,160c,176a), **gill** (22d), **Goll, gull** (32d,41c,42a,72c,99b,141a), **hall** (37b,114d), **hill, hull** (141d,142a,144c,d), **Jill** (183d), **kill** (38c), **lill** (15d,118a), **loll** (94b,128c), **lull** (126d,150c), **mall** (95d,124b,143b), **mill** (126c), **moll, Moll** (183d), **mull** (53b,135a,164c), **Nell** (110a,183d), **nill** (173d), **Noll** (96b,110b), **null** (108c,177a), **pall** (32d,81b,112a), **pill, poll** (74d,160a,177c), **pull** (45d,167d), **rill** (23c,102b,132a,148d, 157b), **roll** (134a,160b), **rull** (170b), **sell** (97a,115c,175b), **sill** (45c, 76c,165a,182b), **tall** (118c), **tell** (105d,129c,154b), **Tell** (160d), **till** (39c,101c,173d), **toll** (131c), **vill** (176b), **wall, well, will** (18b,43a, 163c,177c), **yell** (145c)

L - - L **leal** (54b,94c,139d), **lill** (15d,118a), **loll** (94b,128c), **lull** (25c,126d,150c)

- LM - **alma** (40d,53d,146d,147a), **Alma** (38d,183c), **alme** (40d,147a), **alms** (29a), **elmy, ulme** (49c)

- - LM **balm** (110a,172c), **calm** (8d,11d,112b,118d,126c,d,172b,173d), **culm** (11a,32d,70d,145a,156a), **film** (164b), **halm, helm** (144d, 165d), **holm** (77d,82d,109a), **malm** (32a,92b), **palm** (59b,168a,169b)

L - - M **Liam** (181d), **loam** (47d), **loom** (11c,146b,179b), **lyam** (139a)

324

- LN -   **ulna** (21d,39b)

- - LN   **kiln** (15d,112a), **vuln** (184d)

L - - N   **Lain, laun** (146b), **lawn** (20a,37c,53b,92c), **lean** (128a,148b,152d, 164b,166a), **Leon** (96a), **lien** (65c,91a,124c), **lliin** (188), **limn** (45d, 121c), **linn** (120d,140a,c,168c,178d), **lion** (55b,86c), **llyn** (120d, 140a), **loan, loin** (40a,98a), **loon** (19a,b,c,157d,179c), **lorn** (42d, 60b), **loun** (19a,b), **lown** (157d)

LO - -   **load** (24c,26d,161b), **loaf** (79b,94b), **loam** (47d,150a), **loan, lobb** (23b,94c,163a), **lobe** (90c,134b), **lobo** (165d,183c), **loch** (88a,139d), **loci** (66b,118c), **lock** (54d), **loco** (38b,119b,120b), **lode** (42c,99a, 111b,175b), **Lodi** (105d), **Lodz, loft** (14c,69d,104b,178b), **loge** (164a), **logy** (46d), **loin** (40a,98a), **loir** (45c), **Loir, Lois** (165d,183c), **loka** (173c,184c), **Loke** (7c,15d,68b), **Loki** (7c,15d,68b), **Lola** (27d, 97b), **loll** (94b,128c), **Lolo** (27d,30a), **loma** (58b,63d), **Lome, lone** (150a), **long** (38b,185b), **Lonk** (143d), **lood** (189), **loof** (144c,153d) **look** (11c,53c,142a), **loom** (11c,146b,179b), **loon** (19a,b,c,157d, 179c), **loop** (31b,107d), **Loos, loot** (22a,118a,119d,136a,153d), **lope** (48b,64b,d), **lora** (146b,149b,151c,169b), **Lora** (183c), **lord** (107c), **lore** (77c,87c,90d,151c,183a), **lori** (91b), **lorn** (42d,60b), **loro** (19a,114b), **lory** (19a,114a), **lose** (60a,100c), **losh** (178b), **loss** (42c,123d,178b), **lost, lota** (24c,121d,178d), **lote** (24c,94a), **loth** (15a,173d), **Loti** (63a,176a), **loto** (65a,121d,178d), **lots, loud** (156a), **loun** (19a,b), **loup** (61d,62a,90c,139d), **Loup** (193), **lour** (13d,63d), **lout** (15c,22a,24b,45b,109a,157d), **love** (163a), **Iowa** (19a), **lown** (157d), **lowp** (90c,139d)

- LO -   **alod** (51c,55d,88a,124c), **aloe** (7d,20a,76a,b,92b,98b,119b,158b, 167a,183d), **alop** (13d,46b,93d), **alow** (18a,172c), **blob, bloc** (173a), **blot, blow, clod** (22a,45b,157d), **Cloe** (183c), **clog** (30c,145b), **clop, clot** (32d,94d), **clou** (62b), **clow** (58c,148c), **cloy** (61b,137c, 159d), **elod** (49b,59d,79c), **Elon** (18c,51b,108a), **floc** (149a), **floe** (79b), **flog** (180d), **flop** (54a), **flot** (173a), **flow** (157b), **glom** (155d, 160d,178c), **glow** (144c), **ilog** (132a,161b), **ilot** (82d), **klom** (189), **klop** (150d), **Olor** (160a,b), **plod** (170b), **plop** (54b), **plot** (25a,36b, 118d,138b), **plow** (39c,165d), **ploy** (43c), **slob** (173d), **sloe** (14a,20b, 64a,119d,181c), **slog** (157c,170b,177d), **sloo** (160a), **slop, slot** (10d, 11b,41d,110d,167d,168a,181b), **slow** (43c)

- - LO   **allo** (34c), **bilo** (131b), **bolo** (87a), **calo** (72d), **dilo** (120d,168c), **filo, gilo** (48a), **Golo** (191), **Gulo** (183c), **halo** (14d,31b,92a), **hilo** (74c), **kalo** (162a), **kilo** (99b,122d), **kolo** (59b,135c), **lalo** (16b,34d), **Lalo** (35c), **Lolo** (27d,30a), **malo** (23a,74c,152a), **milo** (70b,87c), **Milo, nolo** (42a), **orlo** (56b,119c), **Oslo, palo** (152c), **pelo** (83b), **polo** (154a), **Polo** (175b), **ralo** (188), **silo** (59a), **solo** (12c,89a,110c), **ullo** (6a,144a), **velo** (175b)

L - - O   **lago** (83b,152b), **lalo** (16b,34d), **Lalo** (35c), **lazo** (88d,128b,133d), **leno** (37c,53b), **Lero** (82d), **Leto** (11c), **levo** (91a), **Lido** (83d,175b), **lino, lobo** (165d,183c), **loco** (38b,119b,120b), **Lolo** (27d,30a), **loro** (19a,114b), **loto** (65a,121d), **ludo** (65a,112b)

- LP -   **Alph** (132a), **Alps** (85d), **olpe** (90d,182c)

- - LP   **calp** (92b), **colp** (28a,148b), **gulp** (46a,79d,160a), **help** (14a), **kelp** (82a,141c), **palp** (11a,55b,58b,167c), **pulp, salp** (148d), **yelp**

325

L - - P   laap (51d,91b,141d), lamp (92a,94c), Lapp (108a), larp (51d), leap (26c), lerp (51d,141d), limp (58a,81a,177d), lisp (153b), loop (31b,107d), loup (61d,62a,90c,139d), Loup (193), lowp (90c,139d), lump (45a,160c)

- - LR   Ullr (146b,164d)

L - - R   lair (37c,42b), lear (139d), Lear (37a,143b), leer (9d,58a,67c,93d, 112a,148c), lehr (67c,112a), Leir, liar (98d), loir (45c), Loir, lour (13d,63d)

- LS -   also (10b,18b,80a), Elsa (70a,93c,110d,177b,183c), else (18b,79b, 111d)

- - LS   fels (190), fils (62d,150b), Hals (47a), ills (170a)

L - - S   Lais (17c), Laos (80d,129c), Lars (51d,121b), lass (95b), lees (46a, 142a), lens (95b,111a,129b,162d), less (100c,108b,141d), Lias (66a), liss (54b,58b,60c,129d,140a), Lois (165d,183c), Loos, loss (42c,123d,178b), lots, Lubs (94c), Lyas (66a)

- LT -   alta (89c,152d), alto (152b,176c,177a)

- - LT   Balt (93a), belt (16a,31a), bolt (13b,54d,58b,132d,160a), bult (76d), celt (30c,82c,123a,156c,167b,179b), Celt (10a,180a,b), colt (78c,131a,185d,186b), Colt, cult (141d,161c), dolt (20c,59c,157d), felt, galt, gelt (101c), gilt (69c,77c,151d,185d), halt (13b,28a,38d, 156d), hilt (73c), holt (36d,119b,184b), jilt, jolt (143b), Kelt (180b), kilt, lilt (93a,131a,147a), malt (17c), melt, milt (153d), molt (27a, 143d) pelt (53a), salt (35d,105b,123a,136c,141c,149d), silt (104b, 142a), tilt (26b,d,166a), tolt (49b,78c), volt, Walt (96b), welt (36d,131b,145a,b,177b,d), wilt (46b), yelt (151b)

L - - T   lact (34c), laet (60d), lait (62a), lant, last (36c,50b,145a,174c), leet (26a,38a,139d), left (42c), lent (54d), Lent (115d,141c), lest (59d, 163d), Lett (16a,90a,93a), lift (49b), lilt (93a,131a,147a), lint (46a, 58d), list (26d,27b,75b,83d,134a,138b,165d), loft (14c,69d,104b, 178b), loot (22a,118a,119d,136a,153d), lost, lout (15c,22a,24b,45b, 109a,157d), lust (41b)

LU - -   Luba (191), lube (110a), Lubs (94c), luce (58c,117d), Luce (7b,35a), luck (28d), lucy, Lucy (183c), Ludd (23c), ludi (133b), ludo (65a, 112b), luff (136b), luge (148a), Lugh (28b), luif, luke, Luke (52a, 96a), lull (25c,126d,150c), lulu (19a,57b,112c), Lulu (183d), lump (45a,160c), luna (103c), Luna (102b), lune (38c,73b,74d), lung, luny (38b), lupe (19a,64a), lura (22d,82a), lure (41c,51a,54b,163a), lurg (96d,141b,184d), Luri (191), lurk (92a,147d), lush (94c), lust (41b), lute (11c,28b,84d,105a,131d), luxe (61c,62d,159c)

- LU -   alum (14a,45c), Alur (191), blub, blue (33c,98c,102c,150d,173a), blup, blur, blut (66b), club (39c), clue, Elul (102b), flub (22b), flue (8b,30a), flux (28d,58d), glub, glue (7b,156a), glug, glum (102c, 159a), glut (52c,70a,137c,159d), llus (88d,170b), plug (156d,184d), plum, plup, plus (10b,102c) slub (171c), slue (97b,148b,160a), slug (46b,99b,157c), slum, slur (44b,124c,148b,168a), ulua (57a,74c), Ulua (141b)

- - LU   Aalu (6b,48d), aulu (74c,168c), balu (104b,159a,181d), hulu (55b), lalu (48d), iglu (51c,149b), lulu (19a,57b,112c), Lulu (183d), pelu (30a,106d,168c), pulu (74c), Sulu (102c), tolu (16a), Tulu (45d), zulu (171d,175d), Zulu (86a)

326

L - - U   latu (190), lieu (118c,155d), limu (141c), Lleu (40c), lulu (19a,57b, 112c), Lulu (183d)

- LV -   Alva (151d), Ulva (141b)

LW - -   Lwow

L - - W   Llew (40c), Lwow

- - LX   calx (23c,75c,112c), falx (133b)

L - - X   lanx (133a,b), lynx (26c,181d), Lynx (36b)

LY - -   lyam (139a), Lyas (66a), lynx (26c,181d), Lynx (36b), Lyra (36b, 74a), lyre (11c,81c,105a,111c), lyse

- LY -   Alya (155b,c), Alys (183c), Clym (12b), Ilyn (120d,140a)

- - LY   ably (147c), ally (14a,35c,d,173c), coly (104a), eely (185a), holy, idly, inly, July, Lely (47a), lily, moly (76a,181c), oily (110b, 172c), only (24d,52c,98d,147a,150a), Orly (8b), paly (194), pily, poly (34c,76b), puly, rely (16b,170b), rily (176a), ugly, vily (54b), wily (13b,38b,39c)

L - - Y   Lacy, lady, laky, lazy, Lely (47a), levy (14a,162b), lily, limy (176d), liny (157b), livy (132d,133a), logy (46d), lory (19a,114a), lucy, Lucy (183c), luny (38b)

L - - Z   Linx (40d), litz (127b), Lodz

MA - -   maal (188), ma'am (95a,166b), maar (177a), Maas (132a), Maat (69a,b,85d), Maba (103a,168d), mabi (58d), mace (49d,108d,153b, 154d,161a,178a), mack, made, Madi (174a), mado (14d,57a,170b), mage (95b), magg (95b), Magh (102a), magi (123c), Magi (95b, 116c,183a), maha (28c,88c,136d), mahr (103a), Maia (76b,109a, 153b,155b,177c), maid (45b,142d), mail (12d,99b,121c), maim (43d,81a,105c), main (29d,35d,123d), mais (61b), maja (151c), Maja (153b), majo (85d), make (35b,36d,54a,123a), maki (91b), mako (18a,19a,20d,143c,168c,182c), Maku (192), mala (89b,c,90a,94b, 97d,109d,185c), male (154c), Male (45d), mali (27b), mall (95d, 124b,143b), malm (32a,92b), malo (23a,74c,152a), malt (17c), mama, Mama (116d), mana (19a,74b), mana (30a,120d,122a, 159c), mand (28b), mane, mani (115c), mann (189), Mann (9c, 48c,185c), mano (71d,73d,74b,83b), Mans (30a), Manu (10a,76d, 77a,b), Manx (27b,28a,82d), many (108d), mapo (68a,148d), mara (114d), Mara (24a,d,105b,107b), marc (70c), Marc (96a) mare (78b), Mare (108b), mari (61d), Mari (16a), mark (146b,155a), Mark (52a, 96a), marl (32a,42c,55d), maro (144d), Mars (68c,118d,119a,129a, 178a), mart (49d,97a), Mart (96b,183d), maru (84c,144d), Mary (50c,126b,183c), masa (37a), mash (39b,156c), mask (44a,45c), mass (8a,24b,35b,142d), mast (17c,108d,120b,144d,152d), masu (57a,84c), mate (18c,35b,41d,113a,154a,162c), math (77a), Matt, maty (80c), maud (53d,71a,136d,143c), Maud (181a,183c), Maui (120d), maul (73c,96b), maun (139d), maya (77a,179b), Maya (23d, 186c), Mayo (193), maze (87b,157d)

- MA -   amah (95b,108d,111c), amar (189), imam (25c,102d,103a), Oman (159a), omao (165b), omar (103b), Omar (48c,51b,116c,163b), Xmas

- - MA   alma (40d,53d,146d,147a), Alma (38d,183c), amma (6a), atma (150d), bema (28d,31a,114b,119b,125b,137a), boma (7d),

327

cima (83b,c), coma (91c,157d,170c,172b), cyma (101a,b),
dama (65d,152b), Duma (135c), Emma (183c), Erma (183c),
Fama (135a), Gama (121c), Goma (191), Hima (191), ijma (103b),
Irma (96d), jama (103b), Kama (56d), lama (23d,24a,91d,165b),
lima (17b,152b,174d), Lima (31b), loma (58b,63d), mama, Mama
(116d), mima (185d), Nama (78c), Nema (34d,48c,134b,164d,176c),
Numa (133a), pima (37c), Pima (192), puma (27b,37c,55b,103d),
Rama (77a,80b,176d), rima (23a,30c,32a,58a,110d), Roma (83c,d),
sama (105c,169d), sima (132b), soma (10c,21c,34a,48a,81d,136b),
Tama (192), tema (12a,164a), Toma (191), xema (72c), Xema
(12c), Yama (57a,68a), Yima (84a,116b,c), Yuma, Zama (73d,
141d)

M - - A   Maba (103a,168d), maha (28c,88c,136d), Maia (76b,109a,153b,
155b,177c), maja (151c), Maja (153b), mala (89b,c,90a,94b,97d,
109d,185c), mama, Mama (116d), mana (30a,120d,122a,159c),
mara (114d), Mara (24a,d,105b,107b), masa (37a), maya (77a,
179b), Maya (23d,186c), meda (110a), mega (34b,c), mela (34a,
129d), mesa (49b,76d,119b,161a), meta (132d,133a), Meta, mica
(82c,100b,146c), mila (188), mima (185d), mina (10b,70b,71d,
179d), Mina (23a,183d), mira (174d), Mira (155b), moha (42b,
83d), Mola (159c), mona (72b,101d), mora (42b,65a,72b,83d,99b,
153a,161a), mota (103a), moxa (27d,30c), muga (muga (84d), Mura
(192), Musa (16a), muta (28d,103a), myna (19a,c,70b), Myra (10a,
31b,183c), myxa (168c,169a)

- MB -   amba (161a), ambi (34a,122c), ambo (125b,128b), imbe (37a,56a,
133d), umbo (22b)

- - MB   bomb (144a), comb (38c), dumb (153b), lamb (59c), jamb (12d,
45c,118a,146b,174a), lamb, Lamb (49c), limb (12d,22b), nimb
(31b,73b,92a,107b,131d), numb, rumb (120b), tomb, Zimb (6c)

M - - B   medb, Moab (18d,85a,86d,94a)

M - - C   marc (70c), Marc (96a)

M - - D   maid (45b,142d), mand (28b), maud (53d,71a,136d,143c), Maud
(181a,183c), mead (46a,78a,97d,99b), Mead (78a), meed (128c,
131a), meld (26a,41c,99a,118b), mend (130b), mild (32a,66a),
mind (75c,81d,93d,109b), Moed (100c), mold (54d,143c), mood
(44c), mudd (188), mund (124d)

ME - -   mead (46a,78a,97d,99b), Mead (78a), meal (72a,130b), mean (15a,
42b,146c,156b), meat (59b), meda (110a), Medb, Mede (10a,b,13c),
medi (34c), meed (128c,131a), meek (93d,99d), meer, meet (11d,
13d,36a,50a,81d,142d), mega (34b,c), mein (30b), meio (188),
mela (34a,129d), meld (26a,41c,99a,118b), mele (74b,150b), melt,
memo (108b), mend (130b), mene (19a,73d,108d,185c), Ment
(54b,164a), menu (19a,27a), Menu, meou, meow, mere (16c,22b,
62a,78b,87d,96c,110c,120d,146d,148b), merl (20b), mero (72a),
Meru (77a,103d), mesa (49b,76d,119b,161a), mese (71c), mesh
(50d,106c), mess (22b,44b,77c,85d,104b,165c,173d), meta (132d,
133a), Meta, mete (9a,11d,22b,44c,45b,98a,121c), meum (27a,
89c), Meum, mewl (180d), mews (154c)

- ME -   amen (14a,80b,94a,137a,149c,175c,184b), Amen (86d,127d,159b,
164a), amer (61b), Ames (9c,82a), Amex (184d), Emer (39b,183c),

328

emeu (111d), **Imer, Omei** (24a), **omen** (14c,59d,60a,121c,123a, 146b), **omer** (51a,75c), **smee** (19b,46c,d,118b,119d,141b,181b), **Smee** (116d), **smew** (19b,46d,99a,137d), **T-men** (168b), **Ymer** (67a, 131c)

- - ME **acme** (39c,115c,186b), **alme** (40d), **arme** (63a,179b), **came** (182b), **Came** (192), **come, cyme** (58d,69c), **dame** (67b,87c,166b), **deme** (71b,c,167d), **dime, dome** (39c,133c,155d), **fame** (130a) **feme** (181b), **fume** (129a,149a,157a), **game** (64d,154a), **gime** (77d), **home, Hume** (50c), **kame** (67b,139b), **Kome** (71d), **lame** (38d,43d, 73b), **lime** (25b,27d,31b,102d,168c), **Lome, mime** (24a,71b,85a, 100a), **Mime** (131d,148d), **name** (8a,11b,d,25c,46c,107c,130b,157d, 163b,166b), **nome** (71c,163b), **Nome, oime** (8b), **pome** (11d), **Pume** (137b,175b,185b), **rame** (22d), **rime** (30c,36a,58a,63d,77c), **Rome** (31c,51d), **ryme** (178d), **same** (44d,79b), **seme** (45c,138b,151b, 154b,155c,157b), **sime** (101d), **some** (114b,121c,126a), **tame** (45a, 66a), **Tame, time** (47a,131a), **tome** (21d,177c), **ulme** (49c), **zeme** (55d,161b,180b), **zyme** (55c)

M - - E **mace** (49d,108d,153b,154d,161a,178a), **made, mage** (95b), **make** (35b,36d,54a,123a), **male** (154d), **Male** (45d), **mane, mare** (78b), **Mare** (108b), **mate** (18c,35b,41d,113a,154a,162c), **maze** (87b, 157d), **Mede** (10a,b,13c), **mele** (74b,150b), **mene** (19a,73d,108d, 185c), **mere** (16c,22b,62a,78b,87d,96c,110c,120d,146d,148b), **mese** (71c), **mete** (9a,11d,22b,44c,45b,98a,121c), **mice, mide** (110a), **mike, Mike** (96b), **mile** (64c), **mime** (24a,71b,85a,100a), **Mime** (131d,148d), **mine** (69c,79d,111b,124c), **mire** (21c,104b), **mise** (8a, 10a,70c), **mite** (12b,81b,82a,114a,c,148c,d,181b), **Mixe** (192), **mode** (54d,96b,157d,179a), **moke** (45c,157d), **mole** (19d,23a,24d,85a, 117c,155c), **Mole** (88c), **mope** (92d,159a), **more** (71a), **More** (50b), **Mose** (96b), **mote** (114c,153a), **moue** (61d,62b), **move, mule** (45b, 148b,153c,180b), **mure** (177d), **muse** (65b,93d,120d,164c), **Muse** (68d), **mute** (146c,153b)

M - - F **miff** (44c), **moff** (53b,146c), **muff**

M - - G **magg** (95b), **migg** (96c), **Ming** (30b,c), **morg** (188), **mung** (70d)

MH - - **mhor** (180b)

- - MH **samh** (56b)

M - - H **Magh** (102a), **mash** (39b,156c), **math** (77a), **mesh** (50d,106c), **moth, Moth** (112d), **much, mush** (97d), **muth** (188), **myth** (8b,91a)

MI - - **miam** (14d), **mian** (97c,147b,166b), **Miao** (30a,b), **mias** (111a), **miau** (27b,99b), **miaw** (27b,99b), **mica** (82c,100b,146c), **mice, mick** (82c), **mico** (97a), **mide** (110a), **Midi** (151b), **mien** (11c, 17b,26d,44c,96b), **miff** (44c), **migg** (96c), **mike, Mike** (96b), **mila** (188), **mild** (32a,66a), **mile** (64c), **milk, mill** (126c), **milo** (70b,87c, 150d), **Milo, milt** (153c), **mima** (185d), **mime** (24a,71b,85a,100a), **Mime** (131d,148d), **mimi** (14d), **Mimi** (87b,110d,125b,183d), **mina** (10b,70b,71d,179d), **Mina** (23a,183d), **mind** (75c,81d,93d,109b), **mine** (69c,79d,111b,124c), **ming** (30b,c), **mink** (176d), **mino** (84c), **mint** (13a,33b,58b,76a), **minx** (116c), **miny, Mira** (155b,174b), **mire** (21c,104b), **mirk** (41a,67d), **miro** (19a,106d,184a), **Miro** (113a, 151d), **miry, mise** (8a,10a,70c), **miss, mist** (46b,59b,174d), **mite** (12b,81b,82a,114a,c,148c,d,181b), **mitt** (56c), **mitu** (39d), **mity, Mixe** (192), **mixy**

- MI - amia (22c,170d), amic (9d), amid (9d,50a), amie (61d), amil (45a, 48a,185c), amin (9d), amir (7c,12a,103a,b,123c,170d), amit (94a), Emil (96a), Emim (67a,100d), emir (12a,103a,b,123c,134d,135a, 171a), emit (43d,49a,53c,58d,83a,142c), imid (29c), omit (49c, 52c,106b,114c,147d)

- - MI - admi (65d), ammi (98c), demi (34b,122c), hami (78a), hemi (122c), immi (189), jami (103b), kami (68a,84b), Kami (88c,107c,144c), Komi (191), mimi (14d), Mimi (87b,110d,125b,183d), rami (22d), Remi (10b), romi (72d), semi (34b,80b,122c,d), Simi (82d), zemi (55d,161b,180b)

M - - I Mabi (58d), Madi (174a), magi (123c), Magi (95b,116c,183a), maki (91b), mali (27b), mani (115c), mari (61d), Mari (16a), Maui (120d), medi (34c), Midi (151b), mimi (14d), Mimi (87b,110d,125b,183d), moki (127b), Moki

M - - J munj (70d)

M - - K Mack, mark (146b,155a), Mark (52a,96a), mask (44a,45c), meek (93d,99d), mick (82c), milk, mink (176d), mirk (41a,67d), mock (131b,162b), monk (28b,63c,129d), mosk (97b,103b), muck, mulk (60d), murk (41a,67d), musk (116b)

- ML - amla (48a,161d,168c,169a), amli (48a,161d,168c,169a)

M - - L maal (188), mail (12d,99b,121c), mall (95d,124b,143b), marl (32a, 42c,55d), maul (73c,96b), meal (72a,130b), merl (20b), mewl (180d), mill (126c), moil (46c,184c), moll, Moll (183d), mull (53b, 135a,164c)

- MM - amma (6a), ammi (98c), ammo (9d), ammu (9d), Emma (183c), immi (189)

M - - M ma'am (95a,166b), maim (43d,81a,105c), malm (32a,92b), meum (27a,89c), Meum, miam (14d)

- MN - omni (34a)

- - MN damn, Domn (135a), famn (188), hymn (150c), limn (45d,121c)

M - - N main (29d,35d,123d), mann (189), Mann (9c,48c,185c), maun (139d), mean (15a,42b,146c,156b), mein (30b), mian (97c,147b, 166b), mien (11c,17b,26d,44c,96b), moan, moon (40b,132c,137c), morn, mown

MO - - Moab (18d,85a,86d,94a), moan, moat (44d), mock (131b,162b), mode (54d,96b,157d,179a), Moed (100c), moff (53b,146c), mogo (74b), moha (42b,83d), moho (19a,78a), mohr (65d), moil (46c, 184c), moio (188), mojo (177c), moke (45c,157d), moki (127b), moko (96c), Mola (159c), mold (54d,143c), mole (19d,23a,24d,85a, 117c,155c), Mole (88c), moll, Moll (183d), molt (27a,143d), moly (76a,181c), mona (72b,101d), monk (28b,63c,129d), mono (34c, 78d,122d,147a), Mono (193), mons (89c), Mons (184d), mont (62b), mood (44c), moon (40b,132c,137c), moor (10a,75b,137b,141d, 178b), Moor (102c,d,111d), moot (41b,44c), mope (92d,159a), mora (42b,65a,72b,83d,99b,153a,161a), more (71a), More (50b), morg (188), morn, moro (19a,56c), Moro (100a,103a,117a,159a), Mors (41b), mort (41b,47a,78b,136d), Mose (96b), mosk (97b,103b), moss (91d,104c,114a,170c), most, mosy (67d), mota (103a), mote (114c,153a), moth, Moth (112d), moto (104b), moue (61d,62b), move, mown, moxa (27d,30c), Moxo (192), mozo (152b)

- MO - amoi (62a), amok (18b,63c), Amon (86d,96b,127d,159b,164a),
amor (152b), Amor (39c,68b), Amos (96a,144b), Amoy (88c)

- - MO ammo (9d), atmo (34d,174d), Como, demo (122d), hemo (34a,
122b), homo (122d), ikmo (18b), itmo (18b), mamo (19a,b,74b),
memo (108b), nemo (34b), Nemo (56a,85c), Pomo (192), Sumo

M - O mado (14d,57a,170b), majo (18a,19a,20d,143c,168c,182c),
malo (23a,74c,152a), mamo (19a,74b), mano (71d,73d,74b,83b),
mapo (68a,148d), maro (144d), Mayo (193), meio (188), memo
(108b), mero (72a), Miao (30a,b), mico (97a), milo (70b,87c,
150d), Milo, mino (84c), miro (19a,106d,184a), Miro (113a,151d),
mogo, (74b), moho (19a,78a), moio (188), mojo (177c), moko
(96c), mono (34c,78d,122d,147a), Mono (193), moro (19a,56c),
Moro (100a,103a,117a,159a), moto (104b), Moxo (192), mozo
(152b), Muso (192), Muzo (192), myxo

- MP - impi (86a), umph

- - MP bump, camp (163b), damp (101a), dump, gamp (172a), gimp
(169d), Gump (43b), hemp (26a,37a,56a,133d), hump (124d), jump,
kemp (139b), lamp (92a,94c), limp (58a,81a,177d), lump (45a,
160c), mump (29b,153d), pomp (111d,112d), pump, ramp (65a,
80b,127b,148b), romp (63d), rump, samp (70b,77d,121b), simp
(59c,146d), sump (28c,45d,100b), tamp (46b,112b,121d), tump
(60a,76d,103d), tymp (20c), vamp (80a,145a)

M - - P mump (29b,153d)

- MR - amra (77c), Omri (18c,86d)

M - - R maar (177a), mahr (103a), meer (180b), mhor (65d),
moor (10a,75b,137b,141d,178b), Moor (102c,d,111d), Muir (8b,
142c), murr (72b,128b)

- MS - Omsk

- - MS alms (29a), arms, Rems

M - - S Maas (132a), Mais (61b), Mans (30a), Mars (68c,118a,119a,129a,
178a), mass (8a,24b,35b,142d), mess (22b,44b,77c,85d,104b,165c,
173d), mews (154c), mias (111a), miss, mons (89c), Mons (184d),
Mors (41b), moss (91d,104c,114a,170c), muss (135b,173d)

M - - T Maat (69a,b,85d), malt (17c), mart (49d,97a), Mart (96b,183d),
mast (17c,108d,120b,144d,152d), Matt, meat (59b), meet
(11d,13d,36a,50a,81d,142d), melt, Ment (54b,164a), milt (153d),
mint (13a,33b,58b,76a), mist (46b,59b,174d), mitt (56c), moat
(44d), molt (27a,143d), mont (62b), moot (41b,44c), mort (41b,47a,
78b,136d), most, must (70c,101a,106d,157d,182c), mutt (39c,
101d), myst (71c,123b)

MU - - Muav (66a), much, muck, mudd (188), muff, muga, Muir (8b,
142c), mule (45b,148b,153c,180b), mulk (60d), mull (53b,135a,
164c), mump (29b,153d), mund (124d), mung (70d), munj (70d),
mura (84d), Mura (192), mure (177d), murk (41a,67d), murr (72b,
128b), Musa (16a), muse (65b,93d,120d,164c), Muse (68d), mush
(97d), musk (116b), Muso (192), muss (135b,173d), must (70c,101a,
106d,157d,182c), muta (28d,103a), mute (146c,153b), muth (188),
mutt (39c,101d), Muzo (192)

331

- MU -   **Amun** (86d,127d,159b,164a), **smug, smur** (32c,46b,100c), **smut** (32d,44a,119a,150c)

- - MU   **ammu** (9d), **Atmu** (143a,159b), **limu** (141c), **rimu** (79d, 106d,129a, 168c)

M - - U   **Maku** (192), **Manu** (10a,76d,77a,b), **maru** (84c,144d), **masu** (57a, 84c), **menu** (19a,27a), **Menu, meou, Meru** (77a,103d), **miau** (99b), **mitu** (39d), **Mitu**

M - - V   **Muav** (66a)

M - - W   **meow, miaw** (27b,99b)

M - - X   **Manx** (27b,28a,82d), **minx** (116c)

MY - -   **myna** (19a,c,70b), **Myra** (10a,31b,183c), **myst** (71c,123b), **myth** (8b,91a), **myxa** (168c,169a), **myxo**

- MY -   **amyl** (155c), **emyd** (163c,167c), **Emys** (167c,171b)

- - MY   **army** (78c), **demy** (113d), **domy, elmy, fumy, homy** (38b), **ismy** (45a), **limy** (176d), **rimy** (63d)

M - - Y   **many** (108d), **Mary** (50c,126b,183c), **maty** (80c), **miny, miry, mity, mixy, moly** (76a,181c), **mosy** (67d)

NA - -   **Naab, naam** (44c,150b), **nabk** (30d,164d), **nabo** (117a), **Nabu** (68c, 183a), **nach, nael** (189), **naga** (13d,33a,55b,127c), **Naga** (24c,77a, 88c,176d), **Nagy** (78d), **Naia** (33a), **naid** (63c), **naif** (74b,105d), **naik, nail** (31d,54d,141d,161d,173a), **naio** (107a,168c), **Nair** (45d), **nais** (63c,132a), **Naja** (33a), **Nala** (77a), **Nama** (78c), **name** (8a, 11b,25c,46c,107c,130b,157d,163b,166b), **nana** (118b), **Nana** (15c, 105d,116d,186d), **nane** (139d), **naos** (28a,71c,137a,163a), **Naos** (155b), **napa** (25c,67d,90d), **Napa** (182c), **nape** (15b,108c,d), **napu** (29d,80d), **nard** (13a,97c,102b,110a,153c), **Nare** (93c), **nark** (81a, 156d), **nary** (108b), **nase** (26b,75a,124b), **Nash** (9c), **nasi** (34c,108a, 115a), **Nast** (9c,27a), **nata** (47c), **Nata** (15c), **Nate** (22b), **Nath** (155c), **Nato** (6a,8d), **natr** (189), **Natt** (107b), **naut** (141b), **nave** (30d,31a,78d,114b,180c), **navy** (33c,58b), **naze** (26b,124b), **Nazi**

- NA -   **anai** (163b,181a), **Anak** (67a), **anam** (159a,168c), **Anam, anan** (49a,159a,180c), **Anas** (46c,d), **Anat** (138c,147d), **Anax** (43c, 120c) **anay** (72b,163b,181a), **enam** (70c,77a), **Enam** (85c), **gnar** (72a), **gnat** (59a,81b,99c), **gnaw** (20a,107a,178b), **inar** (65b), **knab** (107a), **knag** (139c), **knap** (76d,107a,139b,159b,166a,170c,185b), **knar** (87c,134b), **Onan** (18c,85c), **snab** (23c,139a), **snag** (11b, 27b,35c,87c,124b,166a), **snap** (23a,36d,38b,48b,54d,56c,58c,149d), **unai** (147a), **unau** (148c,171d)

- - NA   **anna** (190), **Anna** (110c,166d), **arna** (24a,181b), **Bana** (67a), **bena** (176a), **bina** (77a), **bona** (89d), **Bona** (183c), **buna** (161c), **Cana** (57a,64b,100c), **cena** (88d,133a), **Cuna** (193), **Dana** (28a,96a, 171d), **dona** (83d,121c,151d), **dyna** (34c), **Edna** (183c), **Enna** (146a), **etna** (75b,153c,157d,175d,177a,c), **fana, gena** (29b), **Gona** (106d), **guna** (106a,137b), **Iona** (28a,82d), **Jena** (105d,165b), **kana** (84d), **kina** (126d), **kona** (74c), **lana** (58a,66a,90a,184b), **lena** (56d), **Lena** (36b), **lina** (188), **Lina** (183d), **luna** (103c), **Luna** (102b), **mana** (30a,120d,122a,159c), **mina** (10b,70b,71d,179d), **Mina** (23a, 183d), **mona** (72b,101d), **myna** (19a,c,70b), **nana** (118b), **Nana** (15c,105d,116d,186d), **nina** (152a), **Nina** (26c,33d,68d,183d),

332

nona (89b,107b), **Nona** (69a,114a,183c), **orna** (169d,182c), **Pana,
pina** (35d,118b), **puna** (10b,33b,104a,119b,182a), **rana** (77a,123c),
Rana (63d), **rena** (132c), **sana** (56a,166d), **Sana** (185d), **sina** (46c),
Sina (102d,103d), **tana** (159a), **Tana** (87d), **Tina** (183d), **tuna** (57a,
b,123b,170d), **ulna** (21d,39b), **urna** (133a), **vena** (90a,175a), **vina**
(77a,105a), **Xina** (183d), **Yana** (192,193), **zona** (144c,186d)

N - - A   **naga** (13d,33a,55b,127c), **Naga** (24c,77a,88c,176d), **Naia** (33a),
Naja (33a), **Nala** (77a), **Nama** (78c), **nana** (118b), **Nana** (15c,105d,
116d,186d), **napa** (25c,67d,90d), **Napa** (182c), **nata** (47c), **Nata**
(15c), **nema** (34d,48c,134b,164d,176c), **Nepa** (106b,178c), **Nera**
(165c), **Neva** (91b,132a), **Nina** (26c,33d,68d,183d), **nipa** (14b,
46b,48a,164a,168c), **Nola, nona** (89b,107b), **Nona** (69a,114a,183c),
Nora (79b,107a,164c,183c), **nota** (15c,89c), **nova** (20c,106d,155c,
174d), **noxa, Nuba** (108c), **Nuda** (39b), **Numa** (133a)

- NB -   **anba** (36d)

N - - B   **Naab, nimb** (31b,73b,92a,107b,131d), **numb**

- NC -   **ance** (158b,c,d), **ancy** (158c), **ence** (158c), **Inca** (14b,30a), **inch,
onca** (189), **once** (60b,79b), **unca** (49a), **unci** (31d), **unco** (140c),
Ynca (193)

- - NC   **banc** (61a,85c), **zinc** (21a)

- ND -   **anda** (23a,168c), **Ande** (193), **Andi** (27d), **Andy** (96b), **endo** (34d,
122d,183b), **inde, onde** (63a,178d), **unde** (179a), **undo** (11a,93d),
undy (179a)

- - ND   **Arnd** (67a), **band** (72a,157c), **bend** (39d,171b), **bind** (33b,165c),
bond (92a,101c,141d,143b,159b,165c), **bund** (49c,66c,90c), **cond**
(156a), **fend** (114b,178b), **find** (44a), **fond** (7c,94b), **fund** (6d,101c,
130c), **Gond, hand** (60c,114c,115d,184c), **hind** (15b,41d,45a),
kind (150d,153a,174d), **land** (44a,163c), **lend** (6d,79d), **mand** (28b),
mend (130b), **mind** (75c,81d,93d,109b), **mund** (124d), **pend, pond,
pund** (189), **rand** (16d,22a,131b,145a,b), **Rand** (69c), **rend** (32a,
159c,162c,185a), **rind** (53a,115c), **Rind** (109c,174b), **rynd** (100a),
sand (71d,146c), **send** (42c,44b,95c,121c,130a,144c,168b), **Sind,
tend** (26d,80b,93a,100a), **tind** (86b), **tund** (121d), **vend** (97a,115c,
142b), **Vend** (10b,148a), **wand** (120b,132c,156a), **wend** (67d,123d),
Wend (10b,148a), **wind** (33b,39d,171c,185a), **yond** (164d), **Zend**

N - - D   **naid** (63c), **nard** (13a,97c,102b,110a,153c), **need** (42b,52d,87b,
122a,178a), **Nejd, NKVD** (135d), **Nudd** (23c)

NE - -   **neaf** (58a,73c), **Neal, neap** (165c,167a,177b), **near** (11d,32c,107b),
neat (165c,169d), **Nebo** (68c,102d,103d,183a), **neck** (83a), **need**
(42b,52d,87b,122a,178a), **neem** (96d,168c,169a), **neep** (140c,
171b), **neer** (14b,86b,108b), **Neil** (96a), **nein** (66c), **Nejd, Nell**
(110a, 183d), **nema** (34d,48c,134b,164d,176c), **nemo** (34b), **Nemo**
(56a,85c), **nene** (19b,74c), **neon** (65c), **Nepa** (106b,178c), **Nera**
(165b), **Neri, Nero** (8a,126d,133a,150b,172c), **ness** (26b,75a,124b),
nest (38b,74b,130d,149c,160b), **nete** (71c,108b,163d), **neti** (164a),
nett, neue (66c), **Neva** (91b,132a), **neve** (56d,67c,70c,149b), **news**
(165c), **newt** (48d),136c,169d), **next** (106a)

- NE -   **Aner** (18d,96b), **anes** (110c,140a), **anet** (43c), **anew** (7c), **inee**
(120b), **Inez** (45c,183c), **knee** (85b), **knew, knex** (123c), **oner** (20d,
53a,75c,162d,173a,d), **ones** (116a), **sned** (93d,125a,140a), **snee**

333

(40a,43d,87a), **sneg** (139b)

- - NE **acne** (147c), **aine** (49b,62c,142a), **Anne** (50c,84a,143b,183c), **a-one** (52b,167b), **Arne** (35c,50c,134d), **aune** (188), **bane** (74a,106b,120b, 139a), **bene** (18a,83c,90a,106d,122a,180a), **bine** (145b,156a,171c, 176b), **bone**, **cane** (17b,128a,156a,159a,177d), **Cane**, **cene** (34c), **cine** (104b,152c), **cone** (66b,150a,157c), **Dane** (85d,107d,138a), **dene** (137a), **Dene** (192), **dine, done, dune** (137a), **dyne** (59d,173b), **eine** (66c), **enne** (34c), **erne** (19c,d,47b,54b,141a), **esne** (10c, 45b,142c,148a,164d), **fane** (30d,137a,162d), **fine** (49b,50a,104b, 115d,159a), **gane** (185b), **gene** (54a), **Gene** (96b), **gone** (6b,15c,42c, 44c,114d), **gyne** (34b,55b,183c), **hone** (110a,143c,180d), **Ione** (24b,88d,94d), **jane** (190), **Jane** (183c), **June** (183c), **kane** (74c), **kine** (38a,112c), **lane** (134b,157b), **lene** (36b,149a,172b), **line** (12b, 22b,36d,38a,126c,134b,157b,158b,162d,175c), **lone** (150a), **lune** (38c,73b,74d), **mane, mine** (69c,79d,111b,124c), **mene** (19a,73d, 108d,185c), **nene** (19b,74c), **nine** (26c,104d), **none** (108b), **ohne** (66d,183b), **orne** (169d,182c), **Orne** (25b), **pane** (113c,155a,b), **pene, pine** (36a,52a,88c,93c,168c,d,169a), **pone** (37a,85b), **rine** (44d,75d, 135c), **rone** (127c,164b), **rune** (9b,67a,94a,95a,105c,107d,120a, 141d,163d), **sane** (128a), **sine** (64c,66b,90a,97c,126a,163b,169d, 183b), **syne** (140b,147a), **Tane** (120d), **tene** (34d,131b), **tine** (11b, 124b,167b), **tone** (6c,118c,150d), **tune** (8b,12c,98c), **tyne, Tyne** (108a), **vane** (179b,182a), **vine** (32b), **wane** (41c,43c), **wine, zone** (44c,50a,160a)

N - - E **name** (8a,11b,d,25c,46c,107c,130b,157d,163b), **nane** (139d), **nape** (15b,108c,d), **Nare** (93c), **nase** (26b,75a,124b), **Nate** (22b), **nave** (30d,31a,78d,114b,180c), **naze** (26b,124b), **nene** (19b,74c), **nete** (71c,108b,163d), **neue** (66c), **neve** (56d,67c,70c,149b), **nice** (54d, 119c,130c), **Nice** (98c), **nide** (23c,72a,106c,116b), **nife** (37a), **Nike** (69c,100c,182d), **nile** (33c,71d), **Nile** (106b), **nine** (26c,104d), **Niue** (137d), **node** (35c,85b,87c,94d,120a,124d,160c), **nome** (71c,163b), **Nome, none** (108b), **Nore** (163d), **nose** (118c,125a,149b), **note** (98c,109b,124b,128d,130a,177c), **nove** (83b), **noze** (75a), **nude** (16c,172d), **Nupe** (191)

N - - F **naif** (74b,105d), **neaf** (58a,73c)

NG - - **ngai** (48a,159c), **ngan**

- NG - **ange** (61a), **ango** (171a), **inga** (145d,170a), **Inge** (24d,67d,117c 119c)

- - NG **bang** (75d,105d,148a), **beng** (43a), **bing, bong, bung** (119d,156d), **cang** (184a), **dang, ding** (130b), **dong, fang** (167b), **Fong** (40b), **Fung** (191), **gang** (38c), **gong, hang** (160a), **hing** (13c), **hong** (30b), **hung, Jung** (125a), **k'ang** (30a), **king** (26c,29c), **kung** (125b), **ling** (24c,57a,b,75b,178c), **long** (38b), **lung, Ming** (30b,c), **mung** (70d), **pang** (165b), **ping, pong, pung** (22c,148b), **Qung** (191), **rang, ring** (50a), **Rong** (88c), **rung** (28c,39a), **sang, sing** (26d,178a), **song** (12c,170c), **sung, Sung** (30b), **tang** (30b,58b,186b), **teng** (188), **ting** (166a), **Ting** (30c), **tong** (30a,c), **tung** (110a,168c), **uang** (131a), **vang** (72d,134a,140b), **wang** (189), **wing** (10d,58c,59a, 118b,d), **wong** (56a), **yang** (30b,70a), **zing**

N - - G **niog** (33a,168c), **nogg** (48d)

334

- - NH binh (189), hunh?, sinh (97c), tanh (97c)

N - - H Nach, Nash (9c), Nath (155c), nigh (106a), Nish (19d), Noah (88a, 99b)

NI - - Nias (82d), nibs (116c), nice (54d,119c,130c), Nice (98c), nick (30c,108b), nide (23c,72a,106c,116d), nidi (106c), nife (37a), nigh (106a), Nike (69c,100c,182d), nile (33c,71d), Nile (106b), nill (173d), nimb (31b,73b,92a,107b,131d), nina (152a), Nina (26c, 33d,68d,183d), nine (26c,104d), nino (152a), niog (33a,168c), niou (188), nipa (14b,46b,48a,164a,168c), Nish (19d), nisi (90a, 173c), nito (55c), Niue (137d)

- NI - anil (47c,80d,180b), Anim (18d), anis (55c), Enid (13b,25d,66b, 163a,183c), Enif (155b), enin (20d), inia (9b,109b), Inia (28c,45b), knip (115c), knit (173c,179b), snib (54d,93c), snig (45d), snip (32b,40a), unie (173a), Unio (105c), unis (91b), unit (101c,110c, 147a)

- - NI Aani (45a,48d), agni (88a,89c), Agni (56d,68b), arni (24a,181b), bani (190), beni (116a,142d), Beni (191), Bini (191), Boni (63b), Coni, doni (21a,28c,168a), Ioni (192), mani (115c), omni (34a), Pani (120c), rani (72d,77b,123c,127c), Reni (83d), yeni (19b,161d), Zuni (125b)

N - - I nasi (34c,108a,115a), Nazi, Neri, neti (164a), ngai (48a,159c), nidi (106c), nisi (90a,173c), nodi (35c,87c), nori (8c,141c)

- - NJ Funj (70c), gunj (70d), munj (70d)

NK - - NKVD (135d)

- NK - ankh (38d,162b), Enki (15b), Inka (193), inky (20b)

- - NK bank (18a,58c), bonk (190), bunk, conk (41c,108a,156d,157c), dank (40b,101a), dunk (43c,79d), fink (19a,56c,157c), funk (63d, 113c), gink (48b), hank (147c), honk (70a), hunk, jink, jonk, junk (30a,134c), kink (38b,171c), konk (41c), kunk (188), lank (148b, 164b), link (36a,81d,85b), lonk (143d), mink (176d), monk (28b, 63c,129d), pank (189), pink (26d,33c,60c,138a), punk (9b,166a, 167c), rank (31d,55d,70b,92c,94d,157d), rink (147c,154a), sank, sink (41c,43c,46b,158a), sunk (81d), tank (175a,d), tonk (173c), wink (107a), yank, Yank

N - - K nabk (30d,164d), naik (81a,156d), nark (81a,156d), neck (83a), nick (30c, 108b), nock (13b,108b), nook (37a,130d), nubk (30d,164d)

- NL - inly, only (24d,52c,98d,147a,150a)

N - - L nael (189), nail (31d,54d,141d,161d,173a), Neal, Neil (96a), Nell (110a,183d), nill (173d), noel (26d,150b) Noel (30d,96a), noil (87c, 178b), Noll (96b,110b), noyl (87c), null (108c,177a), nurl (33b,87c)

N - - M naam (44c,105b), Naam, neem (96d,168c,169a), norm (15a,115a, 128a,155a)

- NN - Anna (110c,166d,183c), anna (190), Anne (50c,84a,143b,183c), Enna (146a), enne (34c), Enns

- - NN binn (22c), Bonn (17d), bunn (25b), conn (43d,156a), Finn (107d), Jann (102d), jinn (42b,103b,153c), linn (120d,140a,c,168c,178d), mann (189), Mann (9c,48c,185c), rann (175c), senn (76b), sunn (56a), wynn (165d)

335

N - - N nein (66c), neon (65c), ngan, noon, Norn (69a,163d,174b), noun (114b,158a)

NO - - Noah (88a,99b), nobs (38c,87a), nock (13b,108b), node (35c,85b, 87c,94d,120a,124d,160c), nodi (35c,87c), noel (26d,150b), Noel (30d,96a), noes (177c), nogg (48d), noil (87c,178b), noio (107c, 163c), noir (61b,134b), noix (67c), Nola, Noll (96b,110b), nolo (42a), nome (71c,163b), Nome, nona (89b,107b), Nona (69a,114a, 183c), none (108b), nono (83b), nook (37a,130d), noon, Nora (79b, 107a,164c,183c), Nore (163d), nori (8c,141c), norm (15a,115a, 128a,155a), Norn (69a,163d,174b), nose (118d,125a,149b), Nosu (27d), nosy, nota (15c,89c), note (98c,109b,124b,128d,130a,177c), Nott (107b), noun (114b,158a), noup (124b), nous (81d,100a, 128b), nova (20c,106d,155c,174d), nove (83b), nowt (106a,139a), nowy (194), noxa, noyl (87c), noze (75a)

- NO - anoa (28a,60a,112c,181c), anon (7d,14d,79d,80b,123a,145c,150c, 164a), enol (29c,158b), Enon (18c,d), Enos (7a,18d,52a,70c,96a, 143a), enow (50d,123a,158b), knob (73c), knop (124b,170c,185b), knor (87c), knot (43c,99d,107c,124d,137b), know, snob (159c), snod (169d), snow

- - NO Aino (84a,c), Arno (27a), asno (151d), beno (113b,117a), cano (152a), dino (34b), fano (51d,96b,113c,d), fono (137a), Gano (132d), Hano (125b), hino (106d,168c), Juno (69c,85d,100c,126b), Kano (84c,177d), keno (161d,168c), kino (27c,34c,47c,72c,98b), leno (37c,53b), lino (114b), mano (71d,73d,74b,83b), mino (84c), mono (34c,78d,122d,147a), Mono (193), nino (152a), nono (83b), pino (152c), puno (182a), Reno, sano (152b), sino (34a), Tano (192), Tino (136d), tuno (28b,168c), vino (92d,182b), xeno (34d), Zeno (71b)

N - - O nabo (117a), naio (107a,168c), Nato (6a,8d), Nebo (68c,102d,103d, 183a), nemo (34b), Nemo (56a,85c), Nero (8a,126d,133a,150b, 172c), nino (152a), nito (55c), noio (107c,163c), nolo (42a), nono (83b)

N - - P neap (165c,167a,177b), neep (140c,171b), noup (124b)

- - NQ cinq (61d)

- NR - inre (35d,80a), inro (84b,c,106c)

N - - R Nair (45d), natr (189), near (11d,32c,107b), neer (14b,86b,108b), noir (61b,134b), nurr (67d)

- NS - ansa (73c,93d,137c), anse (61d), ansu (11d), ense (139b,158c), enso (34d,183b)

- - NS bans, cens (115b), dans (62a), dens (90a,167b), Duns, Enns, fons (60c), gens (42d,132d), Hans (66d,96a), hens (121d), lens (67c, 95b,111a,129b,162d), Mans (30a), mons (89c), Mons (184d), oons (100a,186d), Pons (13d,63c,110d,150c), sans (63a,183b), Sens (63b), sons (98d,109d), Vans (107d)

N - - S nais (63c,132a), naos (28a,71c,137a,163a), Naos (155b), ness (26b, 75a,124b), news (165c), Nias (82d), nibs (116c), nobs (38c,87a), noes (177c), nous (81d,100a,128b)

- NT - anta (83d,117c,d,121a), Anta (164a), ante (87a,89a,115b,120b, 122b,125d,154d), anti (7d,111a,122b), Anti (193), ente (70b,151d),

336

ento (34b,d,183b), **Inti** (159b), **into** (123a,183b), **onto** (76a,174a), **unto** (166c), **untz** (189)

- - NT   **aint**, **arn't**, **aunt** (129c), **bant** (43c), **bent** (80b), **bunt** (15d,180c), **cant** (28d,81b,84d,90c,109b,136c,165d,166a), **cent** (36d), **dent** (42c,77d), **dint** (48c,59d,122a), **dont**, **dunt**, **font** (16b,171d,172a), **gent**, **hant** (67a), **hint** (9a,39c,159a), **hunt** (141d), **kant** (28d), **Kant** (67a), **Kent** (90d), **lant**, **lent** (54d), **Lent** (115d,141c), **lint** (46a,58d), **Ment** (54b,164a), **mint** (13a,33b,58b,76a), **mont** (62b), **oont** (25d), **pant**, **pent** (36a), **pint** (67b), **pont** (55d,61b), **punt** (21a,58b), **rant** (41c,127d,128a,161d), **rent** (58a,77c,91b,138b, 153d,162c,167c), **runt** (47a,172d), **sent**, **tent** (26b,115a), **tint** (33c, d,114d), **vent** (8b,11b,110d,112a), **vint** (26c,182c), **want** (41b, (38b,74b,106b,122a), **went** (42c), **wont** (6d,40a,73a,174c)

N - - T   **Nast** (9c,27a), **Natt** (107b), **naut** (141b), **neat** (165c,169d), **nest** (38b,74b,130d,149c,160b), **nett**, **newt** (48d,136c,169d), **next** (106a), **Nott** (107b), **nowt** (106a,139a), **nuit** (62b)

NU - -   **Nuba** (108c), **nubk** (30d,164d), **nuda** (39b), **Nudd** (23c), **nude** (16c, 172d), **nuit** (62b), **null** (108c,177a), **Numa** (133a), **numb**, **Nupe** (191), **nurl** (33b,87c), **nurr** (67d)

- NU -   **Cnut** (40d,50c), **knub** (178b), **knur** (67d,87c,107c), **knut**, **Knut** (40d,50c,96a), **onus** (24c,93b,109b), **snub** (128c,148b), **snug** (35a, 38b,165c), **Snug** (99d), **snup** (149b)

- - NU   **Ainu** (84a,c), **benu** (49a), **Danu** (28a), **genu** (6b,18a,87a,89c), **Manu** (10a,76d,77a,b), **menu** (19a,27a), **Menu**, **tunu** (28b), **zenu** (143d)

N - - U   **Nabu** (68c,183a), **napu** (29d,80d), **niou** (188), **Nosu** (27d)

- NV -   **envy** (41b)

- - NX   **jinx** (78a), **jynx** (78a), **Jynx** (184a), **lanx** (133a,b), **lynx** (26c,181d), **Lynx** (36b), **Manx** (27b,28a,82d), **minx** (116c), **Yunx** (184a)

N - - X   **noix** (67c)

- NY -   **Enyo** (12c,69c,178a), **onym** (162c), **onyx** (25d,28d,65d,142b), **Pnyx** (71c)

- - NY   **bony** (147c), **Bony** (96b), **cony** (127a), **deny** (36d,43d,129b), **liny** (157b), **luny** (38b), **many** (108d), **miny**, **piny**, **pony** (55b, 179a), **tiny** (100c,148c), **tony**, **Tony** (96b), **tuny**, **viny**, **wany**, **winy** (176c), **zany** (24a,32d,59c)

N - - Y   **Nagy** (78d), **nary** (108b), **navy** (33c,58b), **nosy**, **nowy** (194)

- NZ -   **anzu** (11d), **Enzu** (102b), **onza** (189), **unze** (189)

- - NZ   **Linz** (40d)

OA - -   **Oahu** (154d), **oaks** (154d), **oaky**, **oary**, **oast** (15d,86b,112a), **oath** (119c, 150a)

- OA -   **boar** (77c,117c,160c,181c), **boat** (27b,106a), **Boaz** (135d), **coag** (45d,118a,163b), **coak** (45d,118a,163b), **coal** (49c,64a), **Coan** (37b), **coat** (160a), **coax** (180c), **doab** (157c), **doat** (17a,94b,112a,165d), **Eoan** (41a,85b), **foal** (78c), **foam** (63d,154b), **goad** (80b,154b), **goaf** (104b), **goai** (106d,168c), **goal** (8b,109b,120b,125d), **Goan**, **goat** (135a), **hoar** (63d,71a,181a), **hoax** (41c,122a), **Joab** (41a), **Joad** (50c), **Joan** (183c), **joar** (100a), **koae** (74b), **load** (24c,26d,161b), **loaf** (79b,94b), **loam** (47d,150a), **loan**, **Moab** (18d,85a,86d,94a),

337

moan, moat (44d), Noah (88a,99b), road (37d,164d), roam (178a)
roan (78b,c,114c,128d,144a,181a), roar (145c), soak (46c,137c),
soap, soar (59a), toad (10a,17a,63d,126d), woad (20d,47c), Zoar,
Zoas (20b)

- - OA   anoa (28a,60a,112c,181c), Aroa (175b), Gjoa (144d), pooa (76a,
125b), proa (21b,26a,95c,d), Shoa (6c) stoa (33c,121a,c), tooa
(17c), whoa (156d)

O - - A   obia (55d), obra (152d,184c), ocha (189), ocra (72c,175a), octa
(122c), odea (105d,164a), Offa (163d), ohia (74c,168c), okla (190),
okra (72c,175a), olea (170b), Olea (110b), Olga (135c,183c), olla
(36d,44b,84d,113b,121d,151d,152c,181b), onca (189), onza (189),
orca (86b), orna (169d,182c), orra (139c,d,140a), ossa (21d), Ossa
(103d,110b,164b), Otea (71a,82d), otra (152c), oxea (153d)

OB - -   oban (190), Obed (135d), obex (22d), obey (35c,75c), obia (55d),
obit (41b,64c), oboe (74b,104d,105a,182a,184a), obol (29b,110a),
obra (152d,184c)

- OB -   boba (29d), bobo (112c,168c), Cobb (9c), Cobh (37a), dobe (159b,
c,172b), doby (159b,c), gobi, Gobi (42d), gobo (84d), goby (57d),
hobb (124b), hobo (168a,174b), jobo (77c), Koba (11a), Kobe
(78a), kobi (84b), kobu (84b), lobb (23b,94c,163a), lobe (90c,
134b), lobo (165d,183c), nobs (38c,87a), robe (65b), Sobk (38d),
Toba (80c), tobe (7d,137b), toby (8c,85c,104b), Toby (96b,125c),
Yobi, zobo (186b)

- - OB   blob (146d), boob (146d), brob (153c), chob (23c), doob (18b), jaob, knob
(73c,107c,124d), rhob (64a,85c), scob (42a), slob (173d), snob
(159c), swob (102b), thob (128a)

OC - -   ocha (189), ocra (72c,175a), octa (122c), octo (34a,89b,122c)

- OC -   boca (152b,c), boce (23b,52a,57b), bock (17c,90d,144a), coca (29d,
33a,105d,113a), cock (19a,29a,55a,133d,136d,161d,174b), coco,
dock (40a,117c,144d,179d), Foch (63b), foci (28b), hoch (52c,
66c), hock (91a,115b,182b,c), jock, Jock (96b), joeu (45b,57a),
Koch (66d), loch (88a,139d), loci (66b,118c), lock (54d), loco (38b,
119b,120b), mock (131b,162b), nock (13b,108b), poco (83b,93a),
Roch (136c), rock (160b), sock (157c,182a), soco (22d), tock (7d,
19b), toco (19b,167c), voce (83c,177a)

- - OC   bloc (173a), croc (13a,74a), floc (149a)

O - - C   odic (79c,120a), olic (158b), otic (14c,d,47b)

OD - -   odah (170d), odal (48a,88b,112c), Odax (132c), odds (28d,172d),
Odea (105a,164a), odel (48a,112c), Oder (132a), odic (79c,120a),
Odin (7c,29d,63c,68c,175d,183b), odio (83b), odor (138b,156a),
odum (168c,180a), odyl (59d,79c)

- OD -   Bodb (82b), bode (14c,60a,110b,121b), Bodo (88c), body (72a),
coda (32c,35d,56c), code (21c,31a,40c,161c), codo (188), dodd
(139c,140c), Dode (96b), dodo (19b), Jodo (113d), lode
(42c,99a,111b,175b), Lodi (105d), Lodz (183c), mode (54d,96b,157d,
179a), node (35c,85b,87c,94d,120a,124d,160c), nodi (35c,87c),
Roda (107b), rodd (38d), rode (46c), rodi (98c), soda (19a,149d,
181a), Toda (45d,76d), tode (80a,148a), todo (22b,24d,35b,64c,
156b), tody (19b,d,59a,166a), yodh (91d)

- - OD   alod (51c,55d,88a,124c), apod (59d), Arod (86c), biod (59d,79c),

338

clod (22a,45b,157d), **elod** (49b,59d,79c), **feod** (55d), **food** (109a, 176b), **good, hood** (38a,74d), **lood** (189), **mood** (44c), **plod** (170b, 177d), **pood** (189), **prod** (67d,80b,106b,120b), **quod** (123d), **rood** (38d,39a,88b), **shod, snod** (169d), **stod** (40d,67d), **trod, wood**

O - - D **obed** (135d), **olid** (55d,60c,148d,157d), **ooid** (48d), **oord** (190), **orad** (104a), **Ovid** (132d,133b), **oxid** (112c)

OE - - **oese** (15d,119c)

- OE - **Boer** (151a), **coed, coel** (39b), **Doeg** (137c), **doer** (8a,116b), **does, goel** (15a,75c), **goer, hoek** (39d), **hoen** (189), **hoer, hoey** (114c), **Joel** (96a), **joey** (86a,185d), **Joey** (96b,109c), **koel** (19a,b,39b), **Moed** (100c), **noel** (26d,150b), **Noel** (30d,96a), **noes** (177c), **poem** (51a), **poet** (49b), **roed, roer** (72d), **roey** (103d), **toed, voet** (188)

- - OE **aloe** (7d,20a,76a,b,92b,98b,119b,158b,167a,183d), **Cloe** (183c), **eboe** (28b,110a,168c,169b), **evoe** (15b,130d,181c), **floe** (79b), **froe** (32a,167a,179d), **oboe** (74b,104d,105a,182a,184a), **Otoe** (147b), **shoe** (166a), **sloe** (14a,20b,64a,119d,181c)

O - - E **oboe** (74b,104d,105a,182a,184a), **oese** (15d,119c), **ogee** (40c,101a, b,120b), **ogle** (9d,53c,91a,93d,148c), **ogre** (67a,102a), **ohne** (66d, 183b), **Oime** (8b), **Oise, Okie** (99d), **olpe** (90d,182c), **once** (60b, 79b), **onde** (63a,178d), **ooze** (53c,104b,116a), **orfe** (57a,b,185c), **orle** (17b,56b,76a,144b,177a), **orne** (169d,182c), **Orne** (25b), **oste** (21d,83b), **Otoe** (147b), **Ouse** (132a,185d), **owse**

OF - - **Offa** (163d), **offs** (38c)

- OF - **doff** (130a,161b), **goff** (32d), **koff** (47a), **loft** (14c,69d,104b, 178b), **moff** (53b,146c), **sofa** (44d), **soft** (48b,95d,99d,163a), **toff** (40d)

- - OF **Azof** (20b,135d), **goof, hoof** (173a), **loof** (144c,153d), **poof, roof** (78d), **stof** (135c), **woof** (39a,163d,165a,179d)

O - - F **Olaf** (108a,176b)

OG - - **ogam** (82b,c), **ogee** (40c,101a,b,120b), **ogle** (9d,53c,91a,93d,148c), **Ogor** (170d), **Ogpu** (135d), **ogre** (67a,102a), **ogum** (82b)

- OG - **boga** (57d,180b), **bogo** (117a,168c), **Bogo** (191), **bogy** (153a), **doge** (95b,175b), **dogy** (46d,103c), **fogy, goga** (24a), **gogo** (16b,24a, 149c), **Gogo** (191), **hoga** (144b), **hogg** (144a), **jogi** (76d), **loge** (164a), **logy** (46d), **mogo** (74b), **nogg** (48d), **Pogo** (121c), **pogy** (57a,88a,98d,103c), **soga** (70d,152b), **Soga** (191), **toga** (132d,133a, b), **togs** (32c), **togt** (77c), **Vogt, yoga** (10b,13c,77a), **yogh** (10c, 185a), **yogi** (76d), **zogo** (136a)

- - OG **agog** (47b,52c,86b), **ajog, clog** (30c,145b), **flog** (180d), **frog** (10a, 17a,126d), **grog** (92d,153d), **ilog** (132a, 161b), **niog** (33a,168c), **slog** (157c,170b,177d), **stog** (155a), **voog** (28a,66a,132b)

OH - - **ohia** (74c,168c), **Ohio, ohne** (66d,183b), **ohoy** (106a)

- OH - **boho** (117a,179d), **Bohr** (14b,40d,138c), **coho** (136d), **fohn** (182b), **Hohe** (192), **John** (11c,96a,121a,186b), **kohl** (53c), **moha** (42b,83d), **moho** (19a,78a), **mohr** (65d), **poha** (74c), **rohr** (72d), **sohol, Soho** (93c), **toho** (79a)

- - OH **booh** (52c), **pooh** (22b,107d)

O - - H **oath** (119c,150a), **odah** (170d), **okeh** (8d,37b), **opah** (23b,57a,b, 86d), **ouch!, ough**

OI - -   **oily** (110b,172c), **oime** (8b), **Oise**

- OI -   **Boii** (191), **boil, bois** (62b,63a,183d), **coif** (73a), **coil** (39d,171c, 185a), **coin** (19b,37a,100c,101c,179d), **coir** (33a,37a,56a,133d), **Coix** (70d,85b), **doit** (47a,169d,180d), **Eoin** (85b), **foil** (15d,55c, 165b), **join** (36a,173c), **koir** (33a), **loin** (40a,98a), **loir** (45c), **Loir, Lois** (165d,183c), **moil** (46c,184c), **moio** (188), **noil** (87c,178b), **noio** (107c,163c), **noir** (61b,134b), **noix** (67c), **ooid** (48d), **roil** (44c, 104b,156b,170d,176a), **Soia, soie** (62c), **soil** (154d,159a,163c), **soir** (61c), **toil** (46c,184c), **void** (11a,49d,108d,174b), **zoid**

- - OI   **amoi** (62a), **Ekoi** (191)

O - - I   **Omei** (24a), **omni** (34a), **Omri** (18c,86d)

- OJ -   **bojo** (117a), **coja** (103b,166b), **hoja** (166b), **hoju** (84b), **koji** (185b), **mojo** (177c), **rojo** (129a,152c), **soja** (151b)

OK - -   **okay** (8d), **okeh** (8d,37b), **oket** (189), **okia** (190), **Okie** (99d), **okra** (72c,175a), **okro** (72c,175a)

- OK -   **boko** (52b), **coke** (32d,64a), **coky, Doko** (191), **joke** (183a), **joky, koko** (106d,114b), **Koko** (93d,186c), **koku** (189), **loka** (173c,184c), **Loke** (15d,68b), **Loki** (7c,15d,68b), **moke** (45c,157d), **moki** (127b), **Moki, moko** (96c), **poke** (108c), **poku** (11a), **poky** (148c), **roka** (95a,168c,d), **roke** (174d,175b), **soka** (20c), **soke** (44c,85d), **toko** (30c), **woke, yoke** (85b,92d,173c)

- - OK   **amok** (18b,63c), **asok** (13d), **book, cook** (137b), **dook** (184a), **hook** (27b,39d), **irok** (55b), **look** (11c,53c,142a), **nook** (37a,130d), **pook** (68a), **rook** (19b,29c,39a), **sook** (22a,25c,97a), **took**

O - - K   **Omsk**

OL - -   **Olaf** (108a,176b), **olam** (51a,d,75c,81a), **Olan** (115c), **Olax** (52b), **olay** (113b), **Olea** (110b,170b), **oleo** (34c), **Olga** (135c,183c), **olic** (158b), **olid** (55d,60c,148d,157d), **olio** (44b,77c,98c,100d,121d), **olla** (36d,44b,84d,113b,121d,151d,152c,181b), **Olor** (160a,b), **olpe** (90d,182c)

- OL -   **bola** (16a), **bold** (41a), **bole** (31d,32a,169b), **boll** (119b,d), **bolo** (87a,179b), **bolt** (13b,54d,58b,132d,160a), **cola** (25b,108d,149d, 168c), **cold** (65d), **cole** (25a), **Cole, coli, colp** (28a,148b), **colt** (78c, 131a,185d,186b), **Colt, coly** (104a), **dola** (189), **dole** (44c,118c, 121c,129d), **Dole** (74c), **doli, doll** (125c), **dolt** (20c,59c,157d), **fold folk** (116a,169c), **gola** (27b,40c,70c,157a), **gold, golf** (154a), **goli** (105c), **Goll, Golo** (191), **hola** (74c,152b), **hold** (95c,124c,130d), **hole** (6c,11b,110d,118c,147a), **Holi** (77a), **holm** (77d,82d,109a), **holt** (36d,119b,184b), **holy, iola, iole** (52a,76b,123c), **jole** (29b), **joli** (62b), **jolt** (143b), **kola** (25b,84a,108d,168c), **Kola** (135b,c,d), **Koli** (27b), **kolo** (59b,135c), **Lola** (27d,97b), **loll** (94b,128c), **Lolo** (27d,30a), **Mola** (159c), **mold** (54d,143c), **mole** (19d,23a,24d,85a, 117c,155c), **Mole** (88c), **moll, Moll** (183d), **molt** (27a,143d), **moly** (76a,181c), **Nola, Noll** (96b,110b), **nolo** (42a), **Pola, pole** (132c,143b,177b,184a), **Pole** (52a), **polk** (37c), **poll** (74d,160a, 177c), **polo** (154a), **Polo** (175b), **poly** (34c,76b), **role** (114b), **roll** (134a,160b), **sola** (9a,48a,74b,118c,154a,167b), **sold, sole** (52c, 57a,b,58b,d,110c,115d,150a), **soli** (12c,110c), **solo** (12c,89a,110c), **tola** (48a,80d), **Tola** (85b,180a), **told** (129c), **tole** (9a,51a,99b,163a), **toll** (131c), **tolt, tolu** (16a), **vola** (89d,150a), **vole** (97d,104a,148a,

340

149b), **volk** (66c,105d,116a,184c), **Volk, volt** (49b,78c,173b), **wold** (47c,60a,118d,174a,184a), **wolf, yolk, Zola** (63a)

- - OL **bool** (39d), **chol** (118d), **Chol** (192), **cool** (25c,107d), **egol** (11b), **enol** (29c,158b), **fool** (24a,41c,47a,146d), **gaol** (123d), **Gaol** (164a), **idol** (48c,54c,55a,75b,79d,112d,130b,184d), **itol** (158b), **obol** (29b, 110a), **pool** (65a,119d,120d), **siol** (82c), **tool** (27c), **viol** (105a), **wool** (58b,179c)

O - - L **obol** (29b,110a), **odal** (48a,88b,112c), **odel** (48a,112c), **odyl** (59d, 79c), **opal** (20a,65d,67b,82b), **oral** (114a,153d,174c,175c), **Orel, oval** (48d,49c), **oxyl** (112c)

OM - - **Oman** (159a), **omao** (165b), **omar** (103b), **Omar** (48c,51b,116c, 163b), **Omei** (24a), **omen** (14c,59d,60a,121c,123a,146b), **omer** (51a,75c), **omit** (49c,52c,106b,114c,147d), **omni** (34a), **Omri** (18c, 86d), **Omsk**

- OM - **boma** (7d), **bomb** (144a), **coma** (91c,157d,170c,172b), **comb** (38c), **come, Como, dome** (39c,133c,155d), **Domn** (135a), **domy, Goma** (191), **home, homo** (122d), **homy** (38b), **Kome** (71d), **Komi** (191), **loma** (58b,63d), **Lome, nome** (71c,163b), **Nome, pome** (11d), **Pomo** (192), **pomp** (111d,112d), **Roma** (83c,d), **Rome** (31c,51d), **romi** (72d), **romp** (63d), **soma** (10c,21c,34a,48a,81d,136b), **some** (114b, 121c,126a), **Toma** (191), **tomb, tome** (21d,177c)

- - OM **Ahom** (88c), **asom** (18d), **atom** (101c,114c,180d), **boom** (152d), **coom** (32d,150c,178d), **Crom, doom** (42d,55a,134d), **Edom** (18c, 51b,79b,82c,84a), **from, glom** (155d,160d,178c), **joom** (39c), **klom** (189), **loom** (11c,146b,179b), **room** (28d), **stom** (34c), **toom** (139b), **whom** (42b), **zoom**

O - - M **odum** (168c,180a), **ogam** (82b,c), **ogum** (82b), **olam** (51a,d,75c, 81a), **onym** (162c), **ovum** (48d)

ON - - **Onan** (18c,85c), **onca** (189), **once** (60b,79b), **onde** (63a,178d), **oner** (20d,53a,75c,162d,173a,d), **ones** (116a), **only** (24d,52c,98d, 147a,150a), **onto** (76a,174a), **onus** (24c,93b,109b), **onym** (162c), **onyx** (25d,28d,65d,142b), **onza** (189)

- ON - **a-one** (52b,167b), **bona** (89d), **Bona** (183c), **bond** (92a,101c,141d, 143b,159d,165c), **bone, bong, Boni** (63b), **bonk** (190), **Bonn** (17d), **bony** (147c), **Bony** (96b), **cond** (156a), **cone** (66b,150a,157c), **Coni, conk** (41c,108a,156d,157c), **conn** (43d,156a), **cony** (127a), **dona** (83d,121c,151d), **done, dong, doni** (21a,28c,168a), **don't, fond** (7c,94b), **Fong** (40b), **fono** (137a), **fons** (60c), **font** (16b,171d,172a), **Gona** (106d), **Gond, gone** (6b,15c,42c,44c,114d), **gong, hone** (110a, 143c,180d), **hong** (30b), **honk** (70a), **Iona** (28a,82d), **Ione** (24b, 88d,94d), **Ioni** (192), **jonk, kona** (74c), **konk** (41c), **lone** (150a), **long** (38b,185b), **lonk** (143d), **mona** (72b,101d), **monk** (28b,63c, 129d), **mono** (34c,78d,122d,147a), **Mono** (193), **mons** (89c), **Mons** (184d), **mont** (62b), **nona** (89b,107b), **Nona** (69a,183c), **none** (108b), **nono** (83b), **oons** (100a,186d), **oont** (25d), **pond, pone** (37a,85b), **pong, Pons** (13d,63c,110d,150c), **pont** (55d,61b), **pony, rone** (127c,164b), **Rong** (88c), **song** (12c,170c), **sons** (98d,109d), **tone** (6c,118c), **tong** (30a,c), **tonk** (173c), **tony, Tony** (96b), **wong** (56a), **wont** (6d,40a,73a), **yond** (164d), **zona** (144c,186d), **zone** (44c,50a,160a)

- - ON   **acon** (62c,140d), **agon** (12c,36c,41b,55d,71b), **Amon** (86d,96b, 127d,159b,164a), **anon** (7d,14d,79d,80b,123a,145c,150c,164a), **aton** (150a,159b), **Avon** (143b), **axon** (106c,153c), **azon** (127b), **bion** (117b), **boon** (18b,20c,55a), **cion** (42d,70b,145b,148b,154b, 156a), **coon** (121c), **Dion** (96a,152a), **doon** (140b,168c),·**ebon** (20b), **Elon** (18c,51b,108a), **Enon** (18c,d), **Eton** (33b,50c,84a), **faon** (33c, 55a), **Gaon** (85b), **goon** (157c,163c), **hoon** (190), **icon** (79d,92b, 136a), **ikon** (79d,136a), **iron** (55c,d,69d,81a,97b,143b,149a,173d, 179c), **Leon** (96a), **lion** (55b,86c), **loon** (19a,b,c,157d,179c), **moon** (40b,132c,137c), **neon** (65c), **paon** (115b), **peon** (28c,59c,99c), **phon** (94a), **pion** (43c,52b), **poon** (97c), **roon** (41a,168b), **scon** (162c), **sion** (125c,158c), **Sion** (75b,c,83a,157d), **soon** (123a), **tion** (158b), **toon** (80c,95b,168c), **tron** (180a), **upon** (6b), **woon** (24c), **Zion** (75b,c,83a,157d) **zoon** (43a)

O - - N   **oban** (190), **Odin** (7c,29d,63c,68c,175d,183b), · **Olan** (115c), **Oman** (159a), **omen** (14c,59d,60a,121c,123a,146b), **onan** (18c), **Onan** (85c), **open** (26a,60d,81a,109b,112c,125b,172b,173c), **Oran** (15d,78c,86b), **Owen** (96a,183c), **oxan** (65c), **oxen** (10c)

OO - -   **ooid** (48d), **oons** (100a,186d), **oont** (25d), **oord** (190), **ooze** (53c, 104b,116a), **oozy** (148b)

- OO -   **boob** (146d), **booh** (52c), **book, bool** (39d), **boom** (152d), **boon** (18b,20c,55a), **boor** (47a,135d,172c), **boot** (128d), **cook** (137b), **cool** (25c,107d), **coom** (32d,150c,178d), **coon** (121c), **coop, Coos** (192), **coot** (19b,46d,72b,138d,141a,146d,157d), **doob** (18b), **dook** (184a), **doom** (42d,55a,134d), **door** (140b,168c), **door** (51a,121b), **food** (109a,176b), **fool** (24a,41c,47a,146d), **foot** (115a), **good, goof, goon** (157c,163c), **Goop** (107d), **goor, hood** (38a,74d), **hoof** (173a), **hook** (27b,39d), **hoon** (190), **hoop** (181b), **hoot** (112c), **joom** (39c), **koop** (16c), **lood** (189), **loof** (144c,153d), **look** (11c,53c,142a), **loom** (11c,146b,179b), **loon** (19a,b,c,157d,179c), **loop** (31b,107d), **Loos, loot** (22a,118a,119d,153d), **mood** (44c), **moon** (40b,132c, 137c), **moor** (10a,75b,137b,141d,178b), **Moor** (102c,d,111d), **moot** (41b,44c), **nook** (37a,130d), **noon, pooa** (76a,125b), **pood** (189), **poof, pooh** (22b,107d), **pook** (68a), **pool** (65a,119d,120d), **poon** (97c), **poop** (41c), **poor** (33a), **poot!, rood** (38d,39a,88b), **roof** (78d), **rook** (19b,29c,39a), **room** (28d), **roon** (41a,168b), **root** (53a), **Roos** (67a), **sook** (22a,25c,97a), **soon** (123a,145c), **soot** (20b, 26c,88a), **tooa** (17c), **took, tool** (27c), **toom** (139b), **toon** (80c, 95b,168c), **toot** (28a,66a,132b), **voog** (28a,66a,132b), **wood, woof** (39a,163d, 165a,179d), **wool** (58b,179c), **woon** (24c), **yoop, zoon** (43a)

- - OO   **aboo** (17a), **aroo** (80c,82b), **broo** (139a), **ejoo** (55b,168c), **Kroo** (191), **phoo, shoo** (46b,67a,138b), **sloo** (160a), **whoo**

O - - O   **octo** (34a,89b,122c), **odio** (83b), **Ohio** (72c,175a), **okro** (34c), **oleo** (34c), **olio** (44b,77c,98c,100d,121c), **omao** (165b), **onto** (76a,174a), **ordo** (22a,30d,122a,171a), **orlo** (56b,119c), **Oslo, otho** (133a), **otro** (151d), **otto** (58d,116b,134a), **Otto** (14c,66d,67a,96a)

OP - -   **opah** (23b,57a,b,86d), **opal** (20a,65d,67b,82b), **open** (26a,60d, 81a,109b,112c,125b,172b,173c), **Opie** (50c), **opus** (35c,105a,184c)

- OP -   **copa** (88b,113c), **cope** (12b,26b,36c,65b,157d,176a), **Copt** (48d),

342

copy, dopa (117d), dope (46c,105d), dopp (43c), hope (13d,52d), hopi (33c), Hopi (12c,102c,125b), hops (17c), koph (91d), kopi (107a,168c), Kopi (172a), lope (48b,64b,d), mope (92d,159a), pope (20a,30d,31c,120d), qoph (91d), rope (36d,88d,128b), ropy (157c, 176d), soph, Sopt (45b), tope (24a,46b,57a,143c,151a), toph (75c), topi (37a,75a,118c), tops (159c)

- - OP   alop (13d,46b,93d), asop (180b), atop (112a,174a), chop (98a), clop, coop, crop (38b), drop (43d,54b,100b,114c,168b), Esop (53b,54a), flop (54a), Goop (107d), hoop (181b), klop (150d), knop (124b,170c,185b), koop (16c), loop (31b,107d), plop (54b), poop (41c), prop (159d), scop (120a), shop, slop, stop (73b,111b), swop (168a), trop (62d,167a), yoop

- - OQ   shoq (169a)

OR - -   orad (104a), oral (114a,153d,174c,175c), Oran, oras (40d), orca (86b), ordo (22a,30d,122a,171a), ordu (170d), Orel, orfe (57a,b, 185c), orgy (26d,130d,137c), orle (17b,56b,76a,144b,177a), orlo (56b,119c), Orly (8b), orna (169d,182c), orne (169d,182c), Orne (25b), orra (139c,d,140a), orts (60d), oryx (11a)

- OR -   bora (181d,182b), bord (100b), bore (14c,25b,46a,116a,165c, 179b), borg (40d), Bori (110d,150c), born, boro (154b), Boro (193), Bors (70b,134b), bort (43b), Bort (134b), cora (65d), Cora (42b, 69c,80c,116b,124d,172b,183c), cord (39b,131a), core (28b,51c, 75b,81b), cork (119d), Cori (138c), corm (24b,38d,156a), corn (39d,95c,123a), dora (70b), Dora (36d,41a,43b,183c,d), dord (42c), dore (61d,67b,69d,117d), Dore (50d,63a,b), dorm, dorn (164d), dorp (73c,176b), dorr (32b), dory (21b,58b,144c), fora (133a), ford (177b), fore (63d,174b), fork, form (54d,143c), fort (63d,157d), gora (81c), gore (115d,117c,154c,169c), gory, hora (22a,40b), horn (11a,105a,170b,182a), hors (62b), kora (178c), Kora, kore (107b), Kore (29a,42b,116b,124d), kori (7d,77a), lora (146b,149b,151c,169b), Lora (183c), lord (107c), lore (77c,87c, 90d,151c,183a), lori (91b), lorn (42d,60b), loro (19a,114b), lory (19a,114a), mora (42b,65a,72b,83d,99b,153a,161a), more (71a), More (50b), morg (188), morn, moro (19a,56c), Moro (100a,103a, 117a,159a), Mors (41b), mort (41b,47a,78b,136d), Nora (79b, 107a,164c,183c), Nore (163d), nori (8c,141c), norm (15a,115a, 128a,155a), Norn (69a,163d,174b), oord (190), pore (59d,110d, 111c,120d,157d), pork, Poro (141d), port (73d,136b,140c,170c,d, 182b,c), Rori (16b), sora (19b,c,127b), sorb (11d,103d,134b,142d), Sorb (148a,180a), sore (23d,142c), sori (55c,64a), sorn (139a,d), sors (44d,89b), sort (31d,39c,70b,86b,153a), sory (176d), tora (11a,44d,74a,75c,85c,90b,102d,115d), tore, tori (101b), torn (130a), toro (38a,107a,152a,168c), torp (54c), tort (31c,91a,185c), Tory (23c,36b,94c,172a), word (124b,165c), wore, work (64c,76b), worm, worn (143b), wort (76a,95d,121d), yore (10b,69d,93c,110b, 165d), york (38c), York (50b,c)

- - OR   acor (6d), ador (153b), amor (152b), Amor (39c,68b), asor (75c, 105a), boor (47a,135d,172c), chor (164b), door (51a,121b), Ghor (174b), goor, Igor (135d), knor (87c), mhor (180b), moor (10a, 75b,137b,141d,178b), Moor (102c,d,111d), odor (138c,156a), Ogor (170b), Olor (160a,b), poor (33a), shor (136d), Shor (162b), Thor

(7c,68c,99c,100c,109c,165b), **utor** (90a,166c)

O - - R Oder (132a), odor (138b,156a), Ogor (170d), Olor (160a,b), omar (103b), Omar (48c,51b,116c), omer (51a,75c), oner (20d,53a,75c, 162d,173a,d), osar (51b,67b,131b), oser (61b), over (6b,38c,80a, 114d), oxer (55c), oyer (38a,75b,119c)

OS - - osar (51b,67b,131b), oser (61b), Oslo, ossa (21d) Ossa (103d,110b, 164b), oste (21d,83b)

- OS - bosa (12a), Bosa, Bosc (115c), bose (163c), bosh, bosk (164b), boss (49d,157d), cosh (35a,97c), cose (29b), coso (152c), coss (98a), cost (29a), cosy (149c), dosa (74b), dose (123a), doss (17c), dost, foss (44d,100d), gosh, hose (156c), host (13a,51d,104c), Jose (96a), josh (85b), joss (30b), Josy (183d), koso (6c,80d), Koso (192,193), koss (188), lose (60a,100c), losh (178b), loss (42c,123d, 178b), lost, Mose (96b), mosk (97b,103b), moss (91d,104c,114a, 170c), most, mosy (67d), nose (118d,125a,149b), Nosu (27d), nosy, pose (14c,15d), posh (49b,148c), post (89a,95c,155d), Rosa (58d, 134a,145d,183c), rose (33c), Rose (6a,50c,183c), ross (16c,161d), Ross (50c), rosy (21a,111a), sosh (81d), soso (99c,114c,166d), tosh (106a), Tosk (8c), toss (24a,132d, Xosa (86a)

- - OS Amos (96a,144b), bios (92a), Coos (192), Enos (7a,18d,52a,70c, 96a,143a), epos (51a,76b,120a), Eros (11c,39c,68b,97c,182d), ghos (30b), gros (47a,53d,146d), Gros (63a), Laos (80d,129c), Loos, naos (28a,71c,137a,163a), Naos (155b), phos, Taos (192), Teos (82a), Thos (84a,181c)

O - - S oaks (154d), odds (28d,172d), offs (38c), ones (116a), onus (24c, 93b,109b), oons (100a,186d), opus (35c,105a,184c), oras (40d), orts (60d), Otis (9c,d,24d,82a,111a), Otus (67a), ours (124c), Ovis (143d), oyes (38a,39b,75b)

OT - - Otea (71a,82d), Otho (133a), otic (14c,d,47b), Otis (9c,d,24d,82a, 111a), Otoe (147b), otra (152c), otro (151d), otto (58d,116b,134a), Otto (14c,66d,67a,96a), Otus (67a)

- OT - bota (189), both, Boto (192), bott (32a,88d), cota (117a), cote (19b,143d,144a,b), coto (16c,90b), Coty (63c), dote (17a,90b,94b, 97a,112a,139d,165d), doth, Doto (141b), doty (43d), Goth (16c, 163d), Hoth (20c), hoti (71a,85c,91c,114c,166c,176a,180d), iota (71a,85c,91c,114c,166c,176a,180d), jota (151c), joti, kota (117a), Kota (45d), koto (84b), Iota (24c, 121d,178d), loth (15a,173d), lote (24c,94a), Loti (63a,176a), loto (65a,121d,178d), lots, mota (103a), mote (114c,153a), moth, Moth (112d), moto (104b), nota (15c,89c), note (98c,109b,124b, 128d,130a,177c), Nott (107b), pott (113d), rota (27c,30d,38a,79a, 92d,133a,134a,b,180c), rote (130b,134b,143a,159d), roti (62c), rotl (103b,111c), roto (30a,122d,127b,152c,171b), sote (150c), tota (71d), tote (27a,73c), toto (8d,15a,34d,89a,181a), toty (87b), vota (133b), vote (60b), Vote (56d), Voth (191), Voto (192), Wote (191)

- - OT Abot (100c), blot, boot (128d), clot (32d,94d), coot (19b,46d,72b, 138d,141a,146d,157d), eyot (82d), Fiot (191), flot (173a), foot (115a), frot (28c), grot (27d), hoot (112c), ilot (82d), khot, knot (43c,99d,107c,124d,137b), loot (22a,118a,119d,136a,153d), moot (41b,44c), phot (173b), piot (95b), plot (25a,36b,118d,138b), pooti, riot (44c,111d,170c,173d), root (53a), ryot (115c), scot (14a,

344

162b), **Scot** (64b,132c), **shot** (9d,43d,90c,174d), **slot** (10d,11b,41d, 110d,167d,168a,181b), **soot** (20b,26c,88a), **spot** (93b,118c,154d, 162a), **stot** (154d,155d,157d,179b,186a), **swot, toot, trot** (85b, 93d,112d)

O - - T oast (15d,86b,112a), obit (41b,64c), oket (189), omit (49c,52c, 106b,114c,147d), oont (25d), oust (44c,49a,52b,125d)

OU - - ouch!, ough!, ours (124c), Ouse (132a,185d), oust (44c,49a,52b, 125d)

- OU - Aoul (191), bout (36c), bouw (188), coup (20d,97c,157b,c,162d), cous (38a), doub (18b), douc (101d), doum (168c), dour (67d, 159a), foud (54d,144b), foul (173a), four (26c), goul (102a), gour (112c,181c), gout, hour, joug (138d), loud (156a), loun (19a,b), loup (61d,62a,90c,139d), Loup (193), lour (13d,63d), lout (15c, 22a,24b,45b,109a,157d), moue (61d,62b), noun (114b,158a), noup (124b), nous (81d,100a,128b), pouf (162d), pour (162d), pous (188), pout (159a), roud (57a,b), roue (41b,44c,127c,134b), roup (44a,121d), rout (41d,44b,46b), souf (146b), souk (22a,97a), soul (10d,125a,153c,176d), soup, sour, sous (62d,172c), toug (171a), toup (95d), tour (31b,85c), tout (61a,127a), youp (185d), your (124c)

- - OU Abou (48b,55a), chou (61b), Chou (30b), clou (67b), meou, niou (188), shou (41d), thou (124b), Tiou (192), Yaou (30c)

O - - U Oahu, Ogpu (135d), ordu (170d)

OV - - oval (48d,49c,127a), oven (15d,78c,86b), over (6b,38c,80a,114d, 130a), Ovid (132a,133b), Ovis (143d), ovum (48d)

- OV - cove (17a,73d,107d), dove (19a,117d), Hova (95a), hove (92a, 157d), Jova (193), Jove (85d), love (163a), move, nova (20c,106d, 155c,174d), nove (83b), rove (127d,132b,178a), wove, Xova (193)

- - OV akov (189), Azov (20b)

OW - - Owen (96a,183c), owse

- OW - bowk (155d), bowl, cowl (101d), dowd (143b), dowl, down (149d), fowl, gowk (146d), gowl (102a,140d,185b), gown, howe (77d), Howe (17a,82a), howl (39b), howk (139b), Iowa (193), iowl (29b), Iowa (19a), lown (157d), lowp (90c,139d), mown (106a,139a), nowy (194), powe, rowy (157b), town (73c), towy (58b), yowl, yowt (139c)

- - OW alow (18a,172c), arow (92c,158b), avow (6d,36a,41c,112c), blow, brow, chow (45a), clow (58c,148c), crow (19a), dhow (88d,111c, 175d), enow (50d,123a,158b), flow (157b), frow (47a,167a), glow (144c), grow (154b), know, Lwow, meow, plow (39c,165d), prow (21b,22c,144d,156a), scow (21a,58b), show (42b,44c,96b), slow (43c), snow, stow (112b), swow (100a), trow (18a,21a,159d,164c, 170b)

OX - - oxan (65c), oxea (153d), oxen (10c), oxer (55c), oxid (112c), oxyl (112c)

- OX - boxy, coxa (77b), doxa (48b), doxy (129d), foxy (38b,39c,181d), moxa (27d,30c), Moxo (192), noxa, Roxy (183d), toxa (153d)

- - OX abox (22d), esox (57b)

O - - X obex (22d), Odax (132c), Olax (52b), onyx (25d,28d,65d,142b), oryx (11a)

OY - - oyer (38a,75b,119c), oyes (38a,39b,75b), oyez (38a,39b,75b)

- OY - coyn (37a), coyo (15a,30c), Goya (151d), Hoya (14d), noyl (87c), soya (151b)

- - OY ahoy (106a), Amoy (88c), b'hoy (134b), buoy (28d,58c), choy (48a,128d), cloy (61b,137c,159d), ohoy (106a), ploy (43c), troy (161c,180a), Troy

O - - Y oaky, oary, obey (35c,75c), ohoy (106a), oily (110b,172c), okay (8d), olay (113b), only (24d,52c,98d,147a,150a), oozy (148b), orgy (26d,130d,137c), Orly (8b)

- OZ - boza (12a), bozo (55b), coze (29b), cozy (149c), doze (148a), dozy, Jozy, kozo (113d,168c), mozo (152b), noze (75a), ooze (53c, 104b,116a), oozy (148b)

O - - Z oyez (38a,39b,75b)

PA - - paal (188), paar (28c), paca (132c,154a), pace (64b,98a,153b,156a, 170b,177d), pack (24b,140d), paco (9b,146d), pacs (94c), pact (8a), padi (131b), paga (117a), page (51b,59b,142d,159b), paha (67b), pahi (21b,26a), paho (122a), paid (129c), pail, pain (7c), pair (22d,37d,85b,171d), pais (37d), pajo (122a), pala (189), Pala (88b), pale (113a,117c,178a), pali (122b), Pali (23d,24a,137b,175a), pall (32d,81b,112a), palm (59b,168c,169b), palo (152c), palp (11a,55b, 58b,167c), paly (194), Pana, pane (113c,155a,b), pang (165b), Pani (120c), pank (189), pant, paon (115b), papa, pape (19b,113a), para (134c,170d), Para (18a,51d), parc (62b,112c), pard (27b, 91b), pare (115c,129a), parf (34a,180a), park, parr (136d,137a, 147c), pars (89d), part (44d,60d,121c,159c), paru (57a), pasa (46a,127c,152c), pasi (94b), pass (110b,155c), past (25c,69d,165d), pata (32c,160d), pate (39a,74d), path (132a,134b), pato (46d), patu (179b), paul, Paul (96a), paun (18b), paut (140a), pave (85a), pavo (115b), Pavo (36b,c), pavy (115b), pawa (189), pawl (43a, 95a), pawn (29c,119c)

- PA - Apap (102a), apar (12d), opah (23b,57a,b,86d), opal (20a,65d,67b, 82b), spad (105b), Spad (118d), spae (139c), span (23b,107b,113a, 128b,162c), spar (22c,24c,64b,97b,100b,144d), spat (112c,126b, 134b), upas (84d,120b,168c,d)

- - PA arpa (83b), capa (152a,166d), cepa (110c), copa (88b,113c), depa (188), dopa (117d), Hupa (192), kapa (74b), lipa (54d), napa (25c, 67d,90d), Napa (182c), Nepa, 106b,178c), nipa (14b,46b,48a,164a, 168c), papa, pipa (159d), pupa (30d,81b,c), ripa (16b,131d), ropa (152a), rupa (60b), sapa (70c), supa (168c), tapa (16c,32c,53b, 56a,74b,104b,112b,113d,120d), yapa (113b), Zipa (29d)

P - - A paca (132c,154a), paga (117a), paha (67b), pala (189), Pala (88b), Pana, papa, para (134c,170d), Para (18a,51d), pasa (46a, 127c,152c), pata (32c,160d), pawa (189), peba (12d), Peba (193), peca (190), peda (114d,144b), pega (57a,130a), pela (30c), Pera (60a), pesa (190), peva (12d), pica (66b,95b,172c), pika (93a,128a, 132c), pima (37c), Pima (192), pina (35d,118b), pipa (159d), Pisa (90c), pita (9c,28b,56a,83a), plea (51a,52d,122a,130b), poha (74c), pola (152a), pooa (76a,125b), proa (21b,26a,95c,d), puca (68a),

puja (77a), **puka** (107a,168c), **puma** (27b,37c,55b,103d), **puna** (10b,33b,104a,119b,182a), **pupa** (30d,81b,c), **Puya** (118b), **pyla** (22d)

P - - B   **pleb** (10d,35b,180b)

P - - C   **parc** (62b,112c)

P - - D   **paid** (129c), **pard** (27b,91b), **pend, Phad** (155b), **Phud** (110b), **pied** (96c,103c,114b,117c,154a,174d), **plod** (170b,177d), **pond, pood** (189), **prod** (67d,80b,106b,120b), **pund** (189), **puud** (189)

PE - -   **peag** (144a,178a), **peai** (98b), **peak** (9a,38c,159b,186b), **peal** (131c,d), **pean** (64c,150b), **pear** (64a), **peat** (64a,175a), **peba** (12d), **Peba** (193), **peca** (190), **peck** (24d), **peco** (162b), **peda** (114d,144b), **pedi** (34b), **pedo** (34b), **peek** (93d,115c), **peel** (53a,114a), **peen** (73c), **peep** (93d,115c), **peer** (51a,93d,107c), **peet** (64a), **pega** (57a,130a,158b), **Pegu** (24c,102a,127d), **peho** (19b,102c,106d), **Peke** (45a,148d), **pela** (30c), **Pele** (69c,74c), **pelf** (22a,56c,131b), **pelo** (83b), **pelt** (53a), **pelu** (30a,106d,168c), **pend, pene, pent** (36a), **peon** (28c,59c,99c), **pepo** (39b,64a,70a,98c,125c,154c), **Pera** (60a), **pere** (61c,63b), **peri** (54b,116b,c,122b), **perk** (84d,93a), **perm** (49b,97d), **pern** (78a), **pero** (152a), **pert** (80a,93a,137c,154b), **Peru, pesa** (190), **peso** (99c), **pest** (108c,116b,118d,170a), **pete** (136b), **Pete** (96b), **peto** (57a,177b), **Peto** (76a), **peur** (61c), **peva** (12d), **pevy** (91d,94c)

- P E -   **aper** (32d), **Apet** (97c), **apex** (39c,76c,115c,118b,159b,166a,167b), **epee** (55c,160d), **open** (26a,60d,81a,109b,112c,125b,172b,173c), **spec, sped, Spee** (66d,70b), **spes, Spes** (69a,78a), **spet** (16c,57a, 142c), **spew** (35a,49a), **spex, Spey**

- - P E   **cape** (75a,96c,124b,161a), **cepe** (48c), **cope** (12b,26b,36c,65b,157d, 176a), **dope** (46c,105d), **dupe** (27c,41c,72c,160c), **gape** (185b), **hipe** (185a), **hope** (13d), **hype** (185a), **jape** (85a,b), **jupe** (62b, 84a), **lope** (48b,64b,d), **lupe** (19a,64a), **mope** (92d), **nape** (15b,108c,d), **Nupe** (191), **olpe** (90d), **pape** (19b,113a), **pipe** (105a,180d,182a), **pope** (20a,30d,31c,120d), **ripe** (58a,97c,98c), **rope** (36d,88d,128b), **rype** (19b,125a), **sipe** (101a,110c,140b), **supe** (53a,154d), **sype** (110c), **tape** (16a,19a,128d), **tipe** (168b), **tope** (24a,46b,57a,143c, 151a), **type** (31d,115a,155a), **wipe, Xipe** (15c)

P - - E   **pace** (64b,98a,153b,156a,170b,177d), **page** (51b,59b,142d,159b), **pale** (113a,117c,178a), **pane** (113c,155a,b), **pape** (19b,113a), **pare** (115c,129a), **pate** (39a,74d), **pave** (85a), **Peke** (45a,148d), **Pele** (69c,74c), **pene, pere** (61c,63b), **pete** (136b), **Pete** (96b), **pice** (190), **pike** (57a,76c,120b,153a), **pile** (45d,75b,117c), **pine** (36a, 52a,88c,93c,168c,d,169a), **pipe** (105a,180d,182a), **pise** (127d), **plie** (32c,59b), **poke** (108c), **pole** (132c,143b,177b,184a), **Pole** (52a), **pome** (11d), **pone** (37a,85b), **pope** (20a,30d,31c, 120d), **pore** (59d,110d,111c,120d,157d), **pose** (14c,15d), **powe, pree** (139d), **puce** (33c,d,52a), **pule** (180d), **pume** (137b), **Pume** (175a,185b), **pure** (29b,172b,173c), **pyle** (34b), **Pyle** (9c,178a), **pyre** (64c)

P - - F   **pelf** (22a,56c,131b), **Piaf** (63c), **piff** (24b), **poor, pouf, puff** (180d)

- P G -   **upgo** (13c)

P - - G   **pang** (165b), **peag** (144a,178a), **ping, plug** (156d,184d), **pong,** prig (112a,116c), **pung** (22c,148b)

PH - -   **Phad** (155b), **phew** (52c), **Phil** (96b), **phit** (24b), **phiz** (54a), **phon** (94a), **phoo**, **phos**, **phot** (173b), **Phud** (110b), **phut** (24b), **Phut** (110b)

- PH -   **epha** (75c)

- - PH   **Alph** (132a), **caph** (91c), **kaph** (91d), **koph** (91d), **qoph** (91d), **soph**, **toph** (75c), **umph**

P - - H   **path** (132a,134b), **pish** (36c,107d), **pith** (37a,51c,67b,95c,97a, 119b,126d), **pooh** (22b,107d), **posh** (49b,148c), **prah** (21b, 26a,95c,d), **Ptah** (48d,98c), **pugh!**, **push** (145c)

PI - -   **Piaf** (63c), **piat** (11a), **piay** (98b), **pica** (66b,95b,172c), **pice** (190), **Pici** (19c,184a), **pick**, **pico** (65a,152c), **Pict** (23c,47d), **pied** (96c, 103c,114b,117c,154a,174d), **pien** (13b), **pier** (23a,88b,180c), **piet** (29b,95b), **piff** (24b), **pika** (93a,128a,132c), **pike** (57a,b,76c,120b, 153a), **piki** (95c), **piky**, **pile** (45d,75b,117c), **pili** (34b,108d), **pill**, **pily**, **pima** (37c), **Pima** (192), **pina** (35d,118b), **pine** (36a,52a,88c, 93c,168c,d,169a), **ping**, **pink** (26d,33c,60c,138a), **pino** (152c), **pint** (67b), **piny**, **pion** (43c,52b), **piot** (95b), **pipa** (159d), **pipe** (105a, 180d,182a), **pipi** (106d,119d), **pipy** (145c), **pirn** (21b,129a,179b), **Piro** (192), **pirr** (181a), **Pisa** (90c), **pise** (127d), **pish** (36c,107d), **pisk** (9c, 19b), **piso** (189), **pist** (25c), **pita** (9c,28b,56a,83a), **pith** (37a, 51c,67b,95c,97a,119b,126d), **pito** (9c,28b,83a), **Pitt** (50d,155d), **pity** (35b), **Pius** (121a), **pixy** (154b)

- PI -   **apia** (121b), **apii** (74c), **apio** (125b), **Apis** (17c,24b,49a,125a,136a), **epic** (76b,120a), **ipil** (117a,168c,169a), **Opie** (50c), **spin** (131a, 180d), **spir** (97c), **spit** (120a,132b,c), **Upis** (13b), ~**ypil** (117a,168c)

- - PI   **aipi** (27a), **Hapi** (66a,107b,136a), **Hopi** (12c,102c,125b), **hopi** (33c), **impi** (86a), **kepi** (99d), **kopi** (107a,168c), **Kopi** (172a), **pipl** (106d,119d), **tipi** (181b), **topi** (37a,75a,118c), **Tupi** (192)

P - - I   **padi** (131b), **pahi** (21b,26a), **pali** (122b), **Pali** (23d,24a,137b,175a), **Pani** (120c), **pari** (34a,180a), **pasi** (94b), **peai** (98b), **pedi** (34b), **peri** (54b,116b,c,122b), **Pici** (19c,184a), **piki** (95c), **pili** (34b, 108d), **pipi** (106d,119d), **puli** (45a,78d), **puri** (80d)

P - - K   **pack** (24b,140d), **pank** (189), **park**, **peak** (9a,38c,159b,186b), **peck** (24d), **peek** (93d,115c), **perk** (84d,93a), **pick**, **pink** (26d,33c,60c, 138a), **pisk** (9c,19b), **polk** (37c), **pook** (68a), **pork**, **puck** (44b,68a, 77c,100c), **Puck** (99d,143b), **pulk** (37c,88d), **punk** (9b,166a,167c)

PL - -   **plan** (99b,124a,138b), **plap** (54b), **plat** (22d,96c,114a,119c,133d), **play** (63d,154a), **plea** (51a,52a,122a,130b), **pleb** (10d,35b,180b), **plet** (135d), **plew** (17c), **plex** (60b), **plie** (32c,59b), **plod** (170b, 177d), **plop** (54b), **plot** (25a,36b,118d,138b), **plow** (39c,165d), **ploy** (43c), **plug** (156d,184d), **plum**, **plup**, **plus** (10b,102c)

- PL -   **upla**

P - - L   **paal** (188), **pail**, **pall** (32d,81b,112a), **paul**, **Paul** (96a), **pawl** (43a, 95a), **peal** (131c,d), **peel** (53a,114a), **Phil** (96b), **pill**, **poll** (74d, 160a,177c), **pool** (65a,119d,120d), **poul** (190), **pull** (45d,167d), **purl** (87c,104c), **pyal** (175c)

P - - M   **palm** (59b,168c,169b), **perm** (49b,97d), **plum**, **poem** (51a), **pram** (15a), **prim** (156b)

348

PN - - Pnyx (71c)

P - - N pain (7c), paon (115b), paun (18b), pawn (29c,119c), pean (64c, 150b), peen (73c), peon (28c,59c,99c), pern (78a), phon (94a), pien (13b), pion (43c,52b), pirn (21b,129a,179b), plan (99b,124a, 138b), poon (97c)

PO - - poco (83b,93a), poem (51a), poet (49b), Pogo (121c), pogy (57a, 88a,98d,103c), poha (74c), poke (108c), poku (11a), poky (148c), pola, pole (132c,143b,177b,184a), Pole (52a), polk (37c), poll (74d,160a,177c), polo (154a), Polo (175b), poly (34c,76b), pome (11d), Pomo (192), pomp (111d,112d), pond, pone (37a,85b), pong, Pons (13d,63c,110d,150c), pont (55d,61b), pony, pooa (76a,125b), pood (189), poof, pooh (22b,107d), pook (68a), pool (65a,119d, 120d), poon (97c), poop (41c), poor (33a), poot!, pope (20a,30d, 31c,120d), pore (59d,110d,111c,120d,157d), pork, Poro (141d), port (73d,136b,140c,170c,d,182b,c), pose (14c,15d), posh (49b, 148c), post (89a,95c,155d), pott (113d), pouf, poul (190), pour (162d), pous (188), pout (159a), powe

- PO - apod (59d), epos (51a,76b,120a), spot (93b,118c,154d,162a), upon (6b)

- - PO cipo (91d), gapo (60a), hypo (117b), mapo (68a,148d), pepo (39b, 64a,70a,98c,125c,154c), sapo (149c,166d), typo (35c,51b)

P - - O paco (9b,146d), paho (122a), pajo (122a), palo (152c), pato (46d), pavo (115a), Pavo (36b,c), peco (162b), pedo (34b), peho (19b, 102c,106d), pelo (83b), pepo (39b,64a,70a,98c,125c,154c), pero (152a), peso (99c), peto (57a,177b), Peto (76a), phoo, pico (65a, 152c), pino (152c), Piro (192), piso (189), pito (9c,28b,83a), poco (83b,93a), Pogo (121c), polo (154a), Polo (175b), Pomo (192), Poro (141d), prao (21b,26a,95c,d), puno (182a), pyro

- - PP Capp (27a), dopp (43c), kapp, kipp, Lapp (108a), repp (53b,131a), typp (185b), wapp (54b,133d,145d), Yapp (22a), zipp

P - - P palp (11a,55b,58b), peep (93d,115c), plap (54b), plop (54b), plup, pomp (111d,112d), poop (41c), prep (138b), prop (159d), pulp, pump

PR - - prah (21b,26a,95c,d), pram (15a), prao (21b,26a,95c,d), prau (21b, 26a,95c,d), pray (18b,51a,159b), pree (139d), prep (138b), pres (62b), pret (188), prey (119d,176a), prig (112a,116c), prim (156b), proa (21b,26a,95c,d), prod (67d,80b,106b,120b), prop (159d), prow (21b,22c,144d,156a), prut!, Prut (41a)

- PR - spry (7a,107b)

P - - R paar (28c), pair (22d,37d,85b,171d), parr (136d,137a,147c), pear (64a), peer (51a,93d,107c), peur (61c), pier (23a,88b,180c), pirr (181a), poor (33a), pour (162d), purr (104c)

- PS - apse (9b,20a,31a,128c,130a,142b,175a), Apsu (29a), ipse (44d, 89c), ipso (89c)

- - PS Alps (85d), gyps, Gyps (71d), hops (17c), hyps, seps (93b,142d), tops (159c), Veps (191), Zips (40c)

P - - S pacs (94c), pais (37d), pars (89d), pass (110b,155c), phos, Pius (121a), plus (10b,102c), Pons (13d,63c,110d,150c), pous (188), pres (62b), puss

PT - -   **Ptah** (48d,98c)

- - PT   **Copt** (48d), **dipt, kept, rapt** (6c,27a,50d), **sept** (31d,82b,143a,149c), **Sept** (45b), **Sopt** (45b), **wept**

P - - T   **pact** (8a), **pant, part** (44d,60d,121c,159c), **past** (25c,69d,165d), **paut** (140a), **peat** (64a,175a), **peet** (64a), **pelt** (53a), **pent** (36a), **pert** (80a,93a,137c,154b), **pest** (108c,116b,118d,170a), **phit** (24b), **phot** (173b), **phut** (24b), **Phut** (110b), **piat** (11a), **Pict** (23c, 47d), **piet** (29b,95b), **pint** (67b), **piot** (95b), **pist** (25c), **Pitt** (50d, 155d), **plat** (22d,96c,114a,119c,133d), **plet** (135d), **plot** (25a,36b, 118d,138b), **poet** (49b), **pont** (55d,61b), **poot!, port** (73d,136b, 140c,170c,d,182b,c), **post** (89a,95c,155d), **pott** (113d), **pout** (159a), **pret** (188), **prut!, Prut** (41a), **punt** (21a,58b), **putt** (69d), **pyat** (95b), **pyet** (95b)

PU - -   **puca** (68a), **puce** (33c,d,52a), **puck** (44b,68a,77c,100c), **Puck** (99d,143b), **pudu** (41d), **puff** (180d), **pugh!, puja** (77a), **puka** (107a,168c), **puku** (11a), **pule** (180d), **puli** (45a,78d), **pulk** (37c, 88d), **pull** (45d,167d), **pulp, pulu** (74c), **puly, puma** (27b,37c,55b, 103d), **pume** (137b), **Pume** (175b,185b), **pump, puna** (10b,33b, 104a,119b,182a), **pund** (189), **pung** (22c,148b), **punk** (9b,166a, 167c), **puno** (182a), **punt** (21a,58b), **puny** (55b,179a), **pupa** (30d, 81b,c), **pure** (29b,172b,173c), **puri** (80d), **purl** (87c,104c), **purr** (104c), **Puru** (192), **push** (145c), **puss, putt** (69d), **puud** (189), **puxy, Puya** (118b)

- PU -   **Apus** (36b,c), **opus** (35c,105a,184c), **spud** (121d,151c), **spun, spur** (10d,67d,167d,168a,181b), **sput** (21c)

- - PU   **hapu** (106d), **napu** (29d,80d), **Ogpu** (135d), **tapu**

P - - U   **paru** (57a), **patu** (179b), **Pegu** (24c,102a,127d), **pelu** (30a,106d, 168c), **Peru, poku** (11a), **prau** (21b,26a,95c,d), **pudu** (41d), **puku** (11a), **pulu** (74c), **Puru** (192)

P - - W   **phew** (52c), **plew** (17c), **plow** (39c,165d), **prow** (21b,22c,144d, 156a)

P - - X   **plex** (60b), **Pnyx** (71c)

PY - -   **pyal** (175c), **pyat** (95b), **pyet** (95b), **pyla** (22d), **pyle** (34b), **Pyle** (9c,178a), **pyre** (64c), **pyro**

- - PY   **copy, espy** (44a,142a), **gapy, pipy** (145d), **ropy** (157c,176d), **typy**

P - - Y   **paly** (194), **pavy** (115b), **pevy** (91d,94c), **piay** (98b), **piky, pily, piny, pipy** (145d), **pity** (35b), **pixy** (154b), **play** (63d,154a), **ploy** (43c), **pogy** (57a,88a,98d,103c), **poky** (148c), **poly** (34c,76b), **pony, pray** (18b,51a,159d), **prey** (119d,176a), **puly, puny** (55b,179a), **puxy**

P - - Z   **phiz** (54a)

QA - -   **Qaid** (35a)

Q - - D   **Qaid** (35a), **quad** (33c,172a), **quid** (39b,166d), **quod** (123d)

QE - -   **qere** (75c), **qeri** (75c)

Q - - E   **qere** (75c), **quae** (176b)

- - QF   **waqf** (103a)

Q - - G   **quag** (21c,102c), **Qung** (191)

Q - - H   **qoph** (91d)

Q - - I   qeri (75c), quai (88b,117c,180c), quei (189)

Q - - N   quan (190)

QO - -   qoph (91d)

Q - - P   quip (183a,b)

Q - - S   quas (135c)

Q - - T   quit (90d,130c)

QU - -   quad (33c,172a), quae (176b), quag (21c,102c), quai (88b,117c,
180c), quan (190), quas (135c), quay (88b,117c,180c), quei (189),
quid (39b,166d), quip (183a,b), quit (90d,130c), quiz, Qung (191),
quod (123d)

- QU -   aqua (90a,178c), equi (122d)

Q - - Y   quay (88b,117c,180c)

Q - - Z   quiz

RA - -   raab (32d), raad (14a,49b,151a,165b), raas (91b), Raba, rabi (38d,
74a), Rabi (14b,117b), raca (19a,59c,130b,184d), race (116a,153b,
154b,169c), rack (32c,64b), racy (153b), rada (135c,172a), rade
(138d), raff (75b), raft (27b,33c,58c,75b), raga (56d,105a), rage
(10c,30c,157a,161d), ragi (28b), Rahu (42b,48b), Raia (107d,147b),
raid (59d,80c), raik (188,189), rail (16b,19b,c,37a,97b,138c,150c,
177b), rain (121d,162d), raip (36d), rais (26c,29d,75a,103b), Rais
(106b), raja (77a,123c), rake (41b,44c,134b,140d), rale (7c,23a,
29d,41b), ralo (188), Rama (77a,80b,176d), rame (22d), rami (22d),
ramp (65a,80b,127b,148b), rana (77a,123c), Rana (63d), rand
(16d,22a,131b,145a,b), Rand (69c), rang, rani (72d,77b,123c,127c),
rank (31d,55d,70b,92c,94d,157d), rann (175c), rant (41c,127b,
128a,161d), rapt (6c,27a,50d), rara (119a), rare (138b,164b,172b,
173d), rasa (51c), rase (42b,91d), rash (75a), rasp (56b,70d,140d),
rata (29d,56b,89d,96c,106d,120c,168c), rate (11d,14a,31d,36b,51d,
52a,70b,85c,112b,123b,127d,128a,138c,143a,174b), rath (29a,
76d,162d), rati (189), rats, rave,(41c,157a,161d), ravi (61b), Ravi
(16b), raya (19b,23c,76d,107d), raze (42b,91d) razz (131b)

- RA -   Arab (30a,78b,c,106a,107c,157b,160c,185d), arad (13a,c,84a),
arah (52c), Aral (135c), Aram (18d,50c,105c,144b,161c), Aran
(18c,48c,64d,82d,174c), arar (137a,168c), Aras, brab (113b), brad
(54d,67c,105b), brae (76d,139a,c,140b,148c), brag (21a,175a),
Bram (96a), bran (23c,39a,70b,72a,79c), Bran (23c,50c), bras
(61a), brat, bray, crab (39b,144b,181b), crag (132c), cral (b),
cram (157d), cran (160c), craw (38d,72c,156c), Crax (19b,39d), draa,
drab (23d,29c,33d,46d,53d), drag (74a,125b), drah (188), dram
(46b,110c,121d,148c), drap (61b,c,62a), drat (100a), Drau,
draw (42c,53a,92b,117c,121c,167d), dray (27a,154c), eral (51a),
erat (89c), frab (138c), frap (45d,165c), frat, frau (181b), fray
(56b,60d), grab (105b,142a,149b), grad (28b), Graf (37c,66b,67a,
107c,186b), gram (29d,99b,148d,160d,180a), grao (189), gras
(78b), gray (33c,77c), Gray (50c), Irad (18d), Irae (43c), Irak
(99a,d), Iran (6a,48c,116b), Iraq (99a,d), Iras (11b,32a), krag
(131c), kral, kran (190), kras (76d), orad (104a), oral (114a,153d,
174c,175c), Oran, oras (40d), prah (21b,26a,95c,d), pram (15a),
prao (21b,26a,95c,d), prau (21b,26a,95c,d), pray (18b,51a,159d),
tram (170a), tran (7a), trap (27b,67b,132b,149b), tray (128c,136d,

351

142d,143c), **ural**, **Ural** (135c), **uran** (101d), **Wraf, wrap** (32b,51a)

- - RA   **abra** (26b), **Abra**, **aera** (8a), **Afra** (183c), **agra** (26d,34d), **Agra** (161b), **Aira** (70d), **akra** (176a), **Akra** (191), **amra** (77c), **arra** (47d, 52c,82b), **aura** (44c,49c,66a,96b,158a,170d,177c), **bara** (188), **Bera** (86d), **bora** (181d,182b), **bura** (182b), **cara** (83a), **Cara** (48b, 183c), **cora** (65d), **Cora** (42b,69c,80c,116b,124d,172b,183c), **cura** (152c), **Dara** (18d), **dera** (34c), **dora** (70b), **Dora** (36d,41a,43b, 183c,d), **dura** (153c), **eyra** (181d), **Ezra** (96a), **fora** (133a), **gara** (190), **gora** (81c), **Hera** (69c,85d,110b,126b,186b,d), **hora** (22a,40b), **hura** (20a,137a), **Hura**, **ikra** (27d), **Irra** (68c, ¹78a), **jura**, **Jura**, **Kara** (132a), **kora** (19a,178c), **Kora**, **Lara** (25c), **liri** (28b,79a,170d), **lora** (146b,149b,151c,169b), **Lora** (183c), **lura** (2²d,82a), **Lyra** (36b,74a), **mara** (114d), **Mara** (24a,d,105b,107b), **mi·a** (174d), **Mira** (155b), **mora** (42b,65a,72b,83d,99b,153a,161a), **¡ra** (84d), **Mura** (192), **Myra** (10a,31b,183c), **Nera** (165b), **Nora** (¯9b,107a,164c,183c), **ocra** (72c,175a), **okra** (72c,175a), **orra** (1³9c,d,140a), **otra** (152c), **para** (134c,170d), **Para** (18a,51d), **Pera** (60a), **Sara** (24d,183c), **sera** (11b,20d,59a,83a,180d), **sora** (19b,c, 127b), **sura** (87c,113b,166d), **Syra**, **tara** (22a,55c,113a,168c), **Tara** (82b,c,138b), **tera** (23d,84c), **tora** (11a,44d,74a,75c,85c,90b,102d, 115d), **vara** (151d), **vera** (140c,151b,175c), **Vera** (183c) **Vira** (191), **zira** (188)

R - - A   **Raba**, **raca** (19a,59c,130b,184d), **rada** (135c,172a), **raga** (56d,105a), **Raia** (107d,147b), **raja** (77a,123c), **Rama** (77a,176d), **rana** (77a,123c), **Rana** (63d), **rara** (119a), **rasa** (51c), **rata** (29d,56b,89d), **96c,106d,120c,168c), **raya** (19b,23c,76d,107d), **reba** (144a), **Reba** (18d,86c), **rede** (37c,81d), **reja** (152b), **rena** (25b,132c), **rhea** (37a, 56a,111d,133d) **Rhea** (19b,68d,87c,103c,186b), **riga** (118b), **Riga**, **rima** (23a,30c,32a,58a,110d), **ripa** (16b,131d), **rita**, **Rita** (37b, 78d,183c,), **Roda** (107b), **roka** (95a,168c,d), **Roma** (83c,d), **ropa** (152a), **Rosa** (58d,134a,145d,183c), **rota** (27c,30d,38a,79a,92d, 133a,134a,b,180c), **ruga** (59b,185a), **rupa** (60b), **rusa**, **Rusa** (41d, 136d), **Ruta** (76b,134d)

- RB -   **arba** (135d,171a)

- - RB   **barb** (20b,57d,78b,117d,120a,b,124b), **curb** (130c,146b), **garb** (32c,46a), **gerb** (56d,143d), **Harb** (191), **herb** (58b,158b), **kerb** (146b), **Serb** (15d,148a,186c), **sorb** (11d,103d,134b,142d), **Sorb** (148a,180a), **verb** (7a,114b,184b)

R - - B   **raab** (32d), **rhob** (64a,85c), **rumb** (120b)

- RC -   **arca** (9a,22c,29d,115a,130a), **Arca** (101b), **arch** (29d,38b,39d,123d, 132c), **orca** (86b)

- - RC   **circ** (31a), **marc** (70c), **Marc** (96a), **parc** (62b,112c)

- RD -   **Erda** (23d,41a,47d,68d,69a,131d,177b), **ordo** (22a,30d,122a,171a), **ordu** (170d), **urde** (86b), **Urdu** (77b), **urdy** (86b)

- - RD   **bard** (12d,120a), **bird**, **bord** (100b), **Byrd** (9c,120b), **card** (33d,114d), **cord** (39b,131a), **curd** (99d), **Dard, dord** (42c), **eard** (139b), **fard** (112d), **ford** (177b), **fyrd** (110a), **Gerd** (63c), **gird** (32c,50a,123a,160a), **hard** (109b), **herd** (39a,46c,72a), **Kurd** (48b, 82a), **lard** (54d,61a,71a,110a), **lord** (107c), **nard** (13a,97c,102b, 110a,153c), **oord** (190), **pard** (27b,91b), **sard** (26d,28d,65d,111a),

352

142b,156d), **Sard, surd** (82c,177a), **verd** (71d), **ward** (31c,55c,86b), **word** (124b,165c), **Wurd, Wyrd** (107d), **yard** (152d)

R - - D   **raad** (14a,49b,151a,165b), **Raad** (151a), **raid** (59d,80c), **rand** (16d, 22a,131b,145a,b), **Rand** (69c), **read** (116d,157d), **redd** (153a), **reed** (16a,70d,97b,105a,111b,118b,144b), **Reed** (163a), **rend** (32a,159c, 162c,185a), **Ridd** (94a), **rind** (53a,115c), **Rind** (109c,174b), **road** (37d,164d), **rodd** (38d), **roed, rood** (38d,39a,88b), **roud** (57a,b), **rudd** (26d,57a,b), **rynd** (100a)

RE - -   **read** (116d,157d), **real** (7a), **ream** (18c,37d,50d,113d,171c), **reap** (7a,40a,74a), **rear** (15b,23a,b,24a,51b,76d,127c), **reba** (144a), **Reba** (18d,86c), **reck** (26d,75c), **rect** (117b), **redd** (153a), **rede** (37c, 81d,138d), **redo** (165c), **reed** (16a,70d,97b,105a,111b,118b,144b), **Reed** (163a), **reef** (129a,137a,145a), **reek** (49d,53c,64a,148d,149a), **reel** (21b,40b,d,153c,154a,c,d,180d), **reem** (18d), **reft** (32a,42c, 44d,167b), **reim** (112c), **rein** (29b,130c), **reis** (26c,29d,75a,103b), **reja** (152b), **Reki** (16a), **rely** (16b,170b), **Remi** (10b), **Rems, rena** (25b,132c), **rend** (32a,159c,162c,185a), **Reni** (83d), **Reno, rent** (58a,77c,91b,138b,153d,162c,167c), **repp** (53b,131a), **rese** (127b), **resh** (91d), **rest** (15d,91b,104d,105a,115a,b,130a,b,161b), **rete** (106c,119c), **reve** (61c,104d), **revs** (131a)

- RE -   **area** (37d,38a,44c,53a,93b,110d,127d,138c,168a,186d), **areg** (116a, 137a), **areo** (34c), **Ares** (49b,51b,68c,76a,97a,105c,110b), **aret** (128c), **brea** (100b), **bred** (23c,48c,127c), **bree** (139a), **bren** (72d, 95a), **Brer** (172b), **Bres, brew** (35d), **brey** (194), **crea** (92c), **Cree** (192), **crew** (72a,106a), **Crex** (37a), **dree** (139b,140c,158b,172c), **drei** (66d,165a), **dreg, drew, drey** (154c), **erer** (17d,150c), **Frea, Fred** (96b), **free** (44a,70d,131b), **fret** (28c,35b,111c,184d), **Frey** (7c, 68b,124d), **gres** (156d), **grew, grey** (33c), **Iren** (127c), **Orel, pree** (139d), **prep** (138b), **pres** (62b), **pret** (188), **prey** (119d), **tree** (11d, 37a,66a,184b), **tref** (172b), **trek** (85c,93c,99d,168b), **tres** (19a,52b, 63a,152d,165a,175c), **tret** (9a,178b,179d), **trey** (26c,165a), **Urey** (107c,138c), **wren** (19b,c), **Wren** (50b)

- - RE   **Aare, acre** (39b,56a,88b), **Acre, aire** (82c), **Aire, bare** (43d,157c), **bore** (14c,25b,46a,116a,165c,179b), **bure** (61b), **byre** (38a), **care** (11b,14c,35d,150a,184d), **cere** (19a,149d,179a), **core** (28b,51c, 75b,81b), **cure** (123b), **dare** (28d,41b,42a,74d,175b), **Dare** (57a), **dere** (74a,79c), **dire** (45d,55a,104a,163c), **dore** (61d,67b,69d, 117d), **Dore** (50d,63a,b), **Eire** (82b), **etre** (61a,c,62d,166c), **eyre** (23c,31b,85c), **Eyre, fare** (43c,59b,67d,123b), **fire** (13a,43d, 44b), **fore** (63d,174b), **gare** (61b,c,62c,127c), **Gere** (183c), **gore** (115d,117c,154c,169c), **gyre** (31b,171b), **hare** (91b,132c), **here, hire** (49d,50b,91b,130a), **inre** (35d,80a), **jure** (90b), **kere** (75c, 128b), **kore** (107b), **Kore** (29a,42b,116b,124d), **Kure** (84c), **lire** (62c), **lore** (77c,87c,90d,151c,183a), **lure** (41c,51a,54b,163a), **lyre** (11c,81c,105a,111c), **mare** (78b), **Mare** (108b), **mere** (16c,22b,62a, 78b,87d,96c,110c,120d,146d,148b), **mire** (21c,104b), **more** (71a), **More** (50b), **mure** (177d), **Nare** (93c), **Nore** (163d), **ogre** (67a,102a), **pare** (115c,129a), **pere** (61c,63b), **pore** (59d,110d,111c,120d,157d), **pure** (29b,172b,173c), **pyre** (64c), **qere** (75c), **rare** (138b,164b, 172b,173d), **rire** (62a), **sere** (24d,46a,c,138c,183b), **Sere** (158b), **sire** (17d,55a,59d,124a,163b,166b), **sore** (23d,142c), **sure** (173d), **tare** (9a,18d,41a,176a,179d), **tire** (15a,22a,52d,55a,179b,180d),

353

tore, tyre (15a), Tyre (31b,90d,117b), vare (179b), vire (11a,13b), ware (27d,35a), were (139b), wire, wore, yare (96b,124b,128b), yore (10b,69d,93c,110b,165d)

R - - E   race (116a,153b,154b,169c), rade (138d), rage (10c,30c,157a, 161d), rake (41b,44c,134b,140d), rale (7c,23a,29d,41b), rame (22d), rare (138b,164b,172b,173d), rase (42b,d,91d), rate 11d,14a,31d,36b,51d,52a,70b,85c,112b,123b,127d,128a,138c,143a, 174b), rave (41c,157a,161d), raze (42b,d,91d), rede (37c,81d,138d), rese (127b), rete (106c,119c), reve (61c,104d), ribe (139a), Rice (46a), ride (46b,85c), rife (6b,c,39d,123b), rile (10c,d,82c,125a, 156b,176a), rime (30c,36a,58a,63d,77c), rine (44d,75d,135c), ripe (58a,97c,98c), rire (62a), rise (49d,80b,155a), Rise (110d,150c), rite (93a,131d), rive (32a,153d), robe (65b), rode (46c), role (114b), Rome (31c,51d), rone (127c,164b), rope (36d,88d,128b), rose (33c), Rose (6a,50c,183c), rote (130b,134b,143a,159d), roue (41b,44c,127c,134b), rove (127d,132b,178a), rube (37d,135d, 185d), Rube (96b), rude (134b,172b), rule (11b,26b,90b), rune (9b,67a,94a,95a,105c,107d,120a,141d,163d), ruse (13b,77c,157b, 169c), rute (188), ryme (178d), rype (19b,125a)

- RF -   orfe (57a,b,185c), Urfa (99a)

- - RF   kerf (40a,108b), serf (21d,148a), surf (23a), turf (115c,149d, 160b), warf, werf (54d), zarf (39c,155a)

R - - F   raff (75b), reef (129a,137a,145a), riff (131d), Riff (18b,102c), roof (78d), ruff (19b,33b,63d,137a)

- RG -   Argo (12c,36b,c), ergo (164b), orgy (26d,130d,137c), urge (42d, 46b,79d,80a,b,81c,124a,150a)

- - RG   berg (79b), borg (40d), burg (22b,73c), lurg (96d,141b,184d), morg (188), Sarg (96d,125c)

R - - G   rang, ring (50a), Rong (88c), rung (28c,39a)

RH - -   rhea (37a,56a,111d,133d), Rhea (19b,68d,87c,103c,186b), Rhee (87c), Rhin, rhob (64a,85c), rhum (8c), Rhus (159a)

R - - H   rash (75a), rath (29a,76d,162d), resh (91d), rich, rick (74d,117d,154d), rukh (53b,54a), rush, ruth (35b,118c), Ruth (105b,183c)

RI - -   rial (190), ribe (139a), rice, Rice (46a), rich, rick (74d,117d,154d), Ridd (94a), ride (46b,85c), Riel (129a), riem (76c,112c,157c,164d), rien (62b), rier (180b), rife (6b,c,39d,123b), riff (131d), Riff (18b, 102c), rift (30c,32a,58a,110d), riga (118b), Riga, Riis (9d), rikk (49a), rile (10c,d,82c,125a,156b,176a), rill (23c102b,132a,148d, 157b), rily (176a), rima (23a,30c,32a,58a,110d), rime (30c,36a,58a, 63d,77c), rimu (79d,106d,129a,168c), rimy (63d), rind (53a,115c), Rind (109c,174b), rine (44d,75d,135c), ring (50a), rink (147c, 154a), riot (44c,111d,170c,173d), ripa (16b,131d), ripe (58a,97c, 98c), rire (62a), rise (49d,80b,155a), Rise (110d,150c), risk (74d), risp (99a), Riss (66a), rita, Rita (37b,78d,183c), rite (93a,131d), rive (32a,153d)

- RI -   aria (8b,98c,150a,c,170c), arid (46c,85a), arif (127d), aril (142a), aris (101b), Brie (29c), brig (72b,106a,144d), brim, brin (32c,54c,146c), brit (76c), crib (96b,120d), cric (131c), crig (20d), crin (146c), cris (40b,95d), drib (46b), Drin, drip, eria (13d,146d), eric (115b), Eric (71d,96a,107d,138a,164d,176b), Erie (82c,87d),

354

Erin (82b), **Eris** (12c,68d,109c), **Fria, frib** (43d), **frim** (58d), **frit** (64c,67c), **friz** (39d), **grid** (17a,70d,119b,156d), **grig** (38c,70d, 93a), **grim** (156a), **grin, grip** (159a), **gris** (61d), **grit** (137a,b), **irid** (38d,67c), **iris** (53c,58a,111c) **Iris** (127c), **kris** (40b,95d), **prig** (112a, 116c), **prim** (156b), **trig** (106a,148d,154b,169d), **trim** (40a,106a, 154b.160a,165c,169d), **trin** (169d), **trio** (104d,165a,169c), **trip** (85c), **tris** (122d), **trit** (34d,164c), **Uria** (14c,16d), **urim** (18d,23a, 110a), **writ** (91a)

- - RI   **abri** (61c,62c,144b), **aeri** (34a), **agri** (89b), **Atri, auri** (34a), **bari** (37c,79c), **Bari** (83d), **Bori** (110d,150c), **buri** (56b), **Cori** (138c), **dari** (38a,70b), **Geri** (183c), **gyri** (22d,131b), **karl** (14d), **keri** (75c,128b), **kiri** (86a,87c,115a,168c), **kori** (7d,77a), **Kuri** (191), **lari** (78a,101c), **Lari** (72c), **lori** (91b), **Luri** (191), **mari** (61d), **Mari** (16a), **Neri, nori** (8c,141c), **Omri** (18c,86d), **pari** (34a, 180a), **peri** (54b,116b,c,122b), **puri** (80d), **qeri** (75c), **Rori** (16b), **sari** (48b,65b,77b), **seri** (18b), **Seri** (192), **Shri** (17c,166c), **siri** (18b), **sori** (55c,64a), **Tari** (47d,69a), **tori** (101b), **Turi** (191), **vari** (34d,91b,134d,174d), **veri** (28b), **weri** (15c,27c)

R - - I   **rabi** (38d,74a), **Rabi** (14b,117b), **ragi** (28b), **rami** (22d), **rani** (72d, 77b,123c,127c), **rati** (189), **ravi** (61b), **Ravi** (16b), **Reki** (16a), **Remi** (10b), **Reni** (83d), **rodi** (98c), **romi** (72d), **Rori** (16b), **roti** (62c)

- - RK   **bark** (115c), **cark** (26d,184d), **cork** (119d), **dark** (47a,67d,109b, 160b), **dirk** (40b), **fork, hark** (92d), **jerk** (153a), **kirk** (31a,139b), **kurk** (31a,139b), **lark** (19a,63d), **lurk** (92a,147d), **mark** (146b, 155a), **Mark** (52a,96a), **mirk** (41a,67d), **murk** (41a,67d), **nark** (81a, 156d), **park, perk** (84d,93a), **pork, Sark** (28d), **Turk** (101d,102d, 106a,111d), **work** (64c,76b), **yark** (22c), **york** (38c), **York** (50b,c)

R - - K   **rack** (32c,64b), **raik** (188,189), **rank** (31d,55d,70b,92c,94d,157c), **reck** (26d,75c), **reek** (49d,53c,64a,148d,149a), **rick** (74d,117d, 154d), **rikk** (49a), **rink** (147c,154a), **risk** (74d), **rock** (160b), **rook** (19b,29c,39a), **ruck** (39a,185a), **rusk** (23a)

- RL -   **orle** (17b,56b,76a,144b,177a), **orlo** (56b,119c), **Orly** (8b)

- - RL   **birl** (93c,131a,153c), **burl** (87c,169a), **carl** (115c,135d), **Carl** (96a), **cirl** (24c), **curl** (38d,73b,93b,131d), **earl** (107c), **farl** (138c,140b), **furl** (132d), **girl, harl** (16b,56b,59a), **herl** (16b,59a), **hurl** (167c), **jarl** (40d,107d), **Karl** (96a), **marl** (32a,42c,55d), **merl** (20b), **nurl** (33b,87c), **purl** (87c,104c), **yarl** (40d,107d)

R - - L   **rail** (16b,19b,c,37a,97b,138c,150c,177b), **real** (7a), **reel** (21b,40b,d, 153c,154a,c,d,180d), **rial** (190), **Riel** (129a), **rill** (23c,102b,132a, 148d,157b), **roil** (44c,104b,156b,170d,176a), **roll** (134a,160b), **rotl** (103b,111c), **rull** (170b), **ryal** (110a,190), **ryel** (190)

- RM -   **arme** (63a,179b), **arms, army** (78c), **Erma** (183c), **Irma** (96d)

- - RM   **barm** (185b), **berm** (25d,90d,145c), **corm** (24b,38d,156a), **derm** (147c,158d), **dorm, farm** (165d), **firm** (154c,173d), **form** (54d, 143c), **Garm** (178c), **germ** (17d,99c,134d), **harm** (40b,81a), **norm** (15a,115a,128a,155a), **perm** (49b,97d), **term** (92b,105b,142b,166b), **turm** (132d), **warm** (7c,75b,163b), **worm, wurm** (67c)

R - -M   **ream** (18c,37d,50d,113d,171c), **reem** (18d), **reim** (112c), **rhum** (8c), **riem** (76c,112c,157c,164d), **roam** (178a), **room** (28d)

- RN -   **arna** (24a,181b), **Arnd** (67a), **Arne** (35c,50d,134d), **arni** (24a,181b),

355

Arno (27a), arn't, erne (19c,d,47b,54b,141a), orna (169d,182c), orne (169d,182c), Orne (25b), urna (133a)

- - RN barn (156d), Bern, 160d), birn (31d), born, burn, carn (156c), cern (41c), corn (39d,95c,123a), darn (130b), dorn (164d), earn (42d, 64b,99a), fern (142a), firn (67c,70c,106c,149b), garn (67d,185b), horn (11a,105a,170b,182a), karn (156c), kern (59c,172a), Kern (132b), lorn (42d,60b), morn, Norn (69a,163d,174b), pern (78a), pirn (21b,129a,179b), sorn (139a,d), tarn (87d,103d,120d), tern (19b,32d,72c,94a,138c,141b,160a), torn (130a), turn (28d,131a, 175a), warn (7b), worn (143b), yarn (154b,161b,184b)

R - - N rain (121d,162d), rann (175c), rein (29b,130c), Rhin, rien (62b), roan (78b,c,114c,128d,144a,181a), roon (41a,168b), ruin (42d)

RO - - road (37d,164d), roam (178a), roan (78b,c,114c,128d,144a, 181a), roar (145c), robe (65b), Roch (136c), rock (160b), Roda (107b), rodd (38d), rode (46c), rodi (98c), roed, roer (72d), roey (103d), rohr (72d), roil (44c,104b,156b,170d,176a), rojo (129a, 152c), roka (95a,168c,d), roke (174d,175b), role (114b), roll (134a, 160b), Roma (83c), Rome (31c,51d), romi (72d), romp (63d), rone (127c, 164b), Rong (88c), rood (38d,39a,88b), roof (78d), rook (19b,29c,39a), room (28d), roon (41a,168b), Roos (67a), root (53a), ropa (152a), rope (36d,88d,128b), ropy (157c,176d), Rori (16b), Rosa (58d,134a,145d,183c), rose (33c), Rose (6a,50c,183c), ross (16c,161d), Ross (50c), rosy (21a,111a), rota (27c,30d,38a,79a,92d, 133a,134a,b,180c), rote (130b,134b,143a,159d), roti (62c), rotl (103b,111c), roto (30a,122d,127b,152c,171b), roud (57a,b), roue (41b,44c,127c,134b), roup (44a,121d), rout (41d,44b,46b), rove (127d,132b,178a), rowy (157b), Roxy (183d)

- RO - Aroa (175b), Arod (86c), aroo (80c,82b), arow (92c,158b), brob (153c), broo (139a), brow, croc (13a,74a), Crom, crop (38b), crow (19a), drop (43d,54b,100b,114c,168b), Eros (11c,39c,68b,97c,182d), froe (32a,167a,179d), frog (10a,17a,126d), from, frot (28c), frow (47a,167a), grog (92d,153d), gros (47a,53d), Gros (63a), grot (27d), grow (154b), irok (55b), iron (55c,d,69d,81a,97b,143b, 149a,173d,179c), Kroo (191), proa (21b,26a,95c,d), prod (67d,80b, 106b,120b), prop (159d), prow (21b,22c,144d,156a), trod, tron (140d,180a), trop (62d,167a), trot (85b,93d,112d), trow (18a,21a, 159d,164c,170b), troy (161c,180a)

- - RO aero (8b,34a,b,58c,59a), agro (149d), arro (52c), baro (71a,122c), boro (154b), Boro (193), caro (83a), Caro (183d), cero (57b,c,d, 180b), duro (190), Ebro (132a), faro (65a), Garo (88c), giro (38c, 167c), gyro (34d), hero (42b,124d,137b), Hero (90c), hiro, inro (84b,c,106c), karo (106d), Lero (82d), loro (19a,114b), maro (144d), mero (72a), miro (19a,106d,184a), Miro (113a,151d), moro (19a,56c), Moro (100a,103a,117a,159a), Nero (8a,126d,133a,150b, 172c), okro (72c,175a), otro (151d), pero (152a), Piro (192), Poro (141d), pyro, sero (34d,88d,164b,178d), taro (13c,48c,49b,64b, 112b,120a,133d,155c,170a,c), tiro (9b,17d,108c), toro (38a,107a, 152a,168c), tyro (9b,17d,108c), xero (31a,84c,108c), Zero (118d)

R - - O ralo (188), redo (165c), Reno, rojo (129a), roto (30a,122d,127b)

- RP - arpa (83b)

- - RP carp (27d,38d,40c,55a,56c,57a), dorp (73c,176b), harp (105a,129a),

356

larp (51d), **lerp** (51d,141d), **tarp** (26b,178d), **terp** (12b,123a), **torp** (54c), **turp**, **warp** (36c,165a,171c), **zarp** (120c)

R - - P **raip** (36d), **ramp** (65a,80b,127b,148b), **rasp** (56b,70d,140d), **reap** (7a,40a,74a), **repp** (53b,131a), **risp** (99a), **romp** (63d), **roup** (44a, 121d), **rump**

- RR - **arra** (47d,52c,82b), **arro** (52c), **Irra** (178a), **orra** (139c,d,140a)

- - RR **barr** (49b), **birr** (180d), **burr** (123b), **carr** (120d,140a), **curr** (104c), **darr** (163c), **dorr** (32b), **durr** (70b), **Herr** (66c), **Kerr**, **murr** (72b,128b), **nurr** (67d), **parr** (136d,137a,147c), **pirr** (181a), **purr** (104c), **turr** (24d,105a), **Tyrr** (68c,109c,163d,178a), **yarr** (72a)

R - - R **rear** (15b,23a,b,24a,51b,76d,127c), **rier** (180b), **roar** (145c), **roer** (72d), **rohr** (72d), **ruer**, **Ruhr**

- RS - **Erse** (28a,64b,82b), **erst** (60b), **Ursa** (17b,36b,43d)

- - RS **airs** (123b), **Bors** (70b,134b), **hers** (124c), **hors** (62b), **Lars** (51d, 121b), **Mars** (68c,118d,119a,129a,178a), **Mors** (41b), **ours** (124c), **pars** (89d), **sors** (44d,89b)

R - - S **raas** (91b), **rais** (26c,29d,75a,103b), **Rais** (106b), **rats**, **reis** (26c, 29d,75a,103b), **Rems**, **revs** (131a), **Rhus** (159a), **Riis** (9d), **Riss** (66a), **Roos** (67a), **ross** (16c,161d), **Ross** (50c), **Russ** (135b)

- RT - **Arta** (72b), **arto** (34a), **arts** (138c), **arty**, **orts** (60d), **Urth** (68d, 107d,163d)

- - RT **Bart** (96b), **Bert** (96b), **bort** (43b), **Bort** (134b), **cart** (171d,175a, 177b), **curt** (145b,c), **dart** (13b,88a,100c,120b,153a,160c), **dirt**, **fort** (63d,157d), **girt** (50a), **hart** (41d,154d), **hurt**, **mart** (49d,97a), **Mart** (96b,183d), **mort** (41b,47a,78b,136d), **part** (44d,60d,121c, 159c), **pert** (80a,93a,137c,154b), **port** (73d,136b,140c,170c,d,182b, c), **Sart** (82b,103b,170d), **Sert** (151d), **sort** (31d,39c,70b,86b,153a), **tart** (114d), **tort** (31c,91a,185c), **vert** (71d,166a,171b), **wart** (124d), **wert**, **wort** (76a,95d,121d), **yurt** (101d)

R - - T **raft** (27b,33c,58c,75b), **rant** (41c,127b,128a,161d), **rapt** (6c,27a, 50d), **rect** (117b), **reft** (32a,42c,44d,167b), **rent** (58a,77c,91b,138b, 153d,162c,167c), **rest** (15d,91b,104d,105a,115a,b,130a,b,161b), **rift** (30c,32a,58a,110d), **riot** (44c,111d,170c,173d), **root** (53a), **rout** (41d,44b,46b), **runt** (47a,172d), **rust** (37b,112c,119a), **ryot** (115c)

RU - - **ruay** (189), **rube** (37d,135d,185d), **Rube** (96b), **ruby** (20a,65d, 179c), **ruck** (39a,185a), **rudd** (26d,57a,b), **rude** (134b,172b), **ruer** **ruff** (19b,33b,63d,137a), **ruga** (59b,185a), **Ruhr**, **ruin** (42d), **rukh** (53b,54a), **rule** (11b,26b,90b), **rull** (170b), **rumb** (120b), **rump**, **rune** (9b,67a,94a,95a,105c,107d,120a,141d,163d), **rung** (28c,39a), **runt** (47a,172d), **rupa** (60b), **ruru** (19b,102c,106d), **rusa**, **Rusa** (41d, 136d), **ruse** (13b,77c,157b,169c), **rush**, **rusk** (23a), **Russ** (135b), **rust** (37b,112c,119a), **Ruta** (76b,134d), **rute** (188), **ruth** (35b,118c), **Ruth** (105b,183c)

- RU - **arui** (11b,143d,144a,181c), **arum** (13a,39b,58d,92b,155c), **Arum** (66a), **bruh** (95a), **brut** (182c), **Brut** (23c), **crus** (91a,143c), **crux** (39a,151b), **drub** (17b,39c) **drug** (105d), **drum** (105a), **drun** (132b), **erua** (103c), **eruc** (37a,56a), **grub** (43c,88d), **grum** (102c), **Grus** (36b,c,38b), **irus** (109d), **prut!**, **Prut** (41a), **true** (7a,8d,37b,54b, 94c,149c), **urus** (14d,53a,112c)

357

- - RU **Aaru** (6b,48d), **baru** (168c), **ecru** (17d,23d,172b), **feru** (37a,56a, 133d), **guru** (77b), **maru** (84c,144d), **Meru** (77a,103d), **paru** (57a), **Peru**, **Puru** (192), **ruru** (19b,102c,106d), **Yaru** (48d)

R - - U **Rahu** (42b,48b), **rimu** (79d,106d,129a,168c), **ruru** (19b,102c,106d)

- RV - **urva** (38b)

RY - - **ryal** (110a,190), **ryel** (190), **ryme** (178d), **rynd** (100a), **ryot** (115c), **rype** (19b,125a)

- RY - **Arya** (80d), **eryx** (137a), **oryx** (11a), **tryp** (114a)

- - RY **adry** (164c), **aery** (47b,51d,106c), **airy** (177a,176d), **atry** (141b), **awry** (13d,38d,171c), **bury** (81d), **dory** (21b,58b,144c), **eery** (172b, 180a), **ewry** (133c), **eyry** (47b,106c), **fury** (157a), **Gary, gory, jury** (38a), **lory** (19a,114a), **Mary** (50c,126b,183c), **miry, nary** (108b), **oary, sory** (176d), **spry** (7a,107b), **Tory** (23c,36b,94c,172a), **vary** (28d,43c), **very** (149c), **wary** (27d,176b), **wiry** (147a,167c)

R - - Y **racy** (153b), **rely** (16b,170b), **rily** (176a), **rimy** (63d), **roey** (103d), **ropy** (157c,176d), **rosy** (21a,111a), **rowy** (157b), **Roxy** (183d), **ruay** (189), **ruby** (20a,65d,179c)

R - - Z **razz** (131b)

SA - - **Saad** (12b), **saah** (188), **saal** (66c,73b), **Saan** (24d), **Saar** (63b,102d, 132a), **saba** (56a,117a), **Saba** (143d), **sabe, sack** (43d,118a,119d, 182b), **saco** (189), **sadd** (33a,40b,58c,107b), **sade** (91d), **sadh** (77a), **sado** (26d,84d), **sadr** (94a), **Sadr** (155b), **saer** (163a), **safe** (141d,157d,174d), **Safi** (191), **saga** (79b,91a,138a,157a,161b,c, 168a), **Saga, sage** (13a,90d,100c,141c,145c,180b,183a), **sago** (54c, 59b,113b,125b,155c), **sagy, saha, sahh** (188), **Saho** (6c), **sahu** (153d), **saic** (86b,91d,175d), **said** (174c), **Said** (42d,101a,121b), **sail** (144c,185a), **sain** (20c,38d,48a), **sair** (140b,150d), **sais** (48d, 71d), **Saka** (10a), **sake** (84b,125d), **saki** (39c,84b,102a), **sala** (152a, b,c), **Sala** (50c), **sale** (14c,61c,62b,c,168b), **salp** (109c,148d), **salt** (35d,105b,123a,136c,141c,149d), **sama** (105c,169d), **same** (44d, 79b), **samh** (56b), **samp** (70b,77d,121b), **sana** (56a,166d), **Sana** (185d), **sand** (71d,146c), **sane** (128a), **sang, sank, sano** (152b), **sans** (63a,183b), **sapa** (70c), **sapo** (149c,166d), **Sara** (24d,183c), **sard** (26d,28d,65d,111a,142b,156d), **Sard, Sarg** (96d,125c), **sari** (48b,65b,77b), **Sark** (28d), **Sart** (82b,103b,170d), **sasa** (55c), **sash** (18a,45c,67b,182b), **sass, sate** (32d,52c,67d,70d,137c,159d), **sati, Sati** (49a,126b,147b), **Sauk** (192), **saul** (48a,168c), **Saul** (18c,86d, 115a), **saum** (189), **save** (52b,110c,123a,173c), **sawk** (188), **sawn saxe** (20d,33c), **saya** (117a)

- SA - **asak** (13d,168c,169a), **asar** (67b), **Esau** (82c,84a,128c), **Esay, Isar** (41a,104c,132a), **osar** (51b,67b,131b), **tsar** (42d,49d,60b,135c), **usar** (8d,16c), **Usas** (68d)

- - SA **ansa** (73c,93d,137c), **Ausa, Besa** (68b,119c), **bisa** (11a), **bosa** (12a), **casa** (152b), **Disa** (111a), **dosa** (74b), **Elsa** (70a,93c,110d, 177b,183c), **kasa** (48a), **kusa, Lisa** (183d), **masa** (37a), **mesa** (49b, 76d,119b,161a), **Musa** (16a), **ossa** (21d), **Ossa** (103d,110b,164b), **pasa** (46a,127c,152c), **pesa** (190), **Pisa** (90c), **rasa** (51c), **Rosa** (58d,134a,145d,183c), **rusa, Rusa** (41d,136d), **sasa** (55c), **Susa** (49a), **Tesa** (80c), **Ursa** (17b,36b,43d), **vasa** (46d,114a,160b,175d), **Vasa, visa** (114d), **Xosa** (86a)

S - - A saba (56a,117a), Saba (143d), saga (79b,91a,138a,157a,161b,c, 168a), saha, Saka (10a), sala (152a,b,c), Sala (50c), sama (105c, 169d), sana (56a,166d), Sana (185d), sapa (70c), Sara (24d,183c), sasa (55c), saya (117a), Seba (18c,39d), sera (11b,20d,59a,83a, 180d), seta (23b,27c,73a,b,123b,153c), shea (25a,168c,d), Shoa (6c), sida (37a,126c,170a), sika (41d,84b), sima (132b), sina (46c), Sina (102d,103d), Sita (127d), siva (67a,120d), Siva (56d,77a), skua (19b,72c,84a,141a), soda (19a,149d,181a), sofa (44d), soga (70d,152b), Soga (191), Soia, soja (151b), soka (20c), sola (9a,48a, 74b,118c,154a,167b), soma (10c,21c,34a,48a,81d,136b), sora (19b, c,127b), soya (151b), stoa (33c,121a,c), Sula (65a), supa (168c), sura (87c,113b,166d), Susa (49a), Syra

- SB - isba (135c)

S - - B scab (80b,107d,157c), scob (42a), Serb (15d,148a,186c), slab (148b), Sleb (12a), slob (173d), slub (171c), snab (23c,139a), snib (54d,93c), snob (159c), snub (128c,148b), sorb (11d,103d,134b, 142d), Sorb (148a,180a), stab (14c,87a,117c), stib (19b,47a,137a), stub (156c), swab (102b), sweb (160d), swob (102b)

SC - - scab (80b,107d,157c), scad (31a,57a,78b,88d,137c), scan (52b,93d, 98a,116d,128b,c,140d), scar (31a,184d), scat (26b,67a,d,126c, 169c), Scio, scob (42a), scon (162c), scop (120a), scot (14a,162b), Scot (64b,132c), scow (21a,58b), scud (32c,126c,135b,160c), scum (129c), scup (57a,121b), scur (78b), scut (145c,161b)

- SC - asci (154a), esca (11c,44a,70c), esce (158d)

- - SC aesc (12d,64d), Bosc (115c), DDSC (42a), disc (31b), fisc (52c,134c)

S - - C saic (86b,91d,175d), spec

S - - D Saad (12b), sadd (33a,40b,58c,107b), said (174c), Said (42d,101a, 121b), sand (71d,146c), sard (26d,28d,65d,111a,142b,156d), Sard, scad (31a,57a,78b,137c), scud (32c,126c,135b,160c), seed (70b, 111c,112c,119a,151b,154a), seid (103b), Seid 42d,101a, 171a), send (42c,44b,95c,121c,130a,144c,168b), shad (27d,57a, b,c), shed (27a,90c,101b,144b), shod, Sind, skid (148b), sled (40a), slid, sned (93d,125a), snod (169d), sold, spad (105b), Spad (118d), sped, spud (121d,151c), stad (151b,167d,176b), stod (40d,67d), stud (22b,25a,42d,54d,111c,143a,174a), sudd (40b,58c,107b), suld (188), surd (82c,177a), swad (94d), syed (103b), syud (103b)

SE - - seah (188), seal (10c,d,54d,64c,96a,118b,128a), seam (85b,d,160a, 176d,185a), Sean (85b,96a), sear (23d,27d,72c,138c), seat (98c, 156b), Seba (18c,39d), sebi (34b), sech (97c), seck (173d), sect (42b,54a,114c), seed (70b,111c,112c,119a,151b,154a), seek (141c), seel (20c,32c,143b), seem (11c), seen, seep (110c,116a, 154b), seer (60a,124c,150c), sego (24b.25a,92b,174c), sehr (66d), seid (103b), Seid (42d,101a,171a), Seik (77b), Seim (120c), sein (146c), seip (110c), Seir (51b,94a,103d), seis (147b,152c), seit (189), Sejm (120c), self (48d,80d), sell (97a,115c,175b), seme (45c, 138b,151b,154b,155c,157b), semi (34b,80b,122c,d), send (42c, 44b,95c,121c,130a,144c,168b), senn (76b), Sens (63b), sent, seps, (93b,142d), sept (31d,82b,143a,149c), Sept (45b), sera (11b,20d, 59a,83a,180d), Serb (15d,148a,186c), sere (24d,46a,c,138c,183b), Sere (158b), serf (21d,148a), seri (18b), Seri (192), sero (34d,88d,

359

164b,178d), **Sert** (151d), **sesi** (20b,57a,149b), **sess** (149c,162b), **seta** (23b,27c,73a,b,123b,153c), **seth** (98d), **Seth** (7a,52b,68a,b,96a, 98d), **seti** (34a), **Seti** (116d), **sett** (115a,156d), **seve** (63a,182c), **sewn, sext** (26b,111b,147b)

- SE -   **asea** (39b,177c), **asem** (9a,49a,69c), **Aser** (84a), **esek** (18d), **esel** (66b), **eser, Iser** (49a), **oser** (61b), **used** (6d,73a), **usee, user** (49d), **uses** (18a), **yser**

- - SE   **anse** (61d), **apse** (9b,20a,31a,128c,130a,142b,175a), **asse** (25a, 60d,74a), **base** (6a,43b,44b,51c,60c,79b,94b,122b), **bise** (182a), **bose** (163c), **case** (22c,36c,81c,91a,108c), **cise** (147b), **cose** (29b), **dose** (123a), **duse** (83c), **ease** (7c,8d,35a,100d,129d,130b,c,150c), **else** (18b,79b,111d), **ense** (139b,158c), **Erse** (28a,64b,82b), **esse** (7a,18a,52d,89a,90a,159a,166c), **fuse** (98c), **hase** (74d), **hose** (156c), **huse** (180c), **ipse** (44d,89c), **Jose** (96a), **lose** (60a,100c), **lyse, mese** (71c), **mise** (8a,10a,70c), **Mose** (96b), **muse** (65b,93d, 120d,164c), **Muse** (68d), **nase** (26b,75a,124b), **nose** (118d,125a, 149b), **oese** (15d,119c), **Oise, Ouse** (132a,185d), **owse** (136b), **pise** (127d), **pose** (14c,15d), **rase** (42b,d,91d), **rese** (127b), **rise** (49d,80b,155a), **Rise** (110d,150c), **rose** (33c), **Rose** (6a,50c,183c), **ruse** (13b,77c, 157b,169c), **sise** (62c,147b), **vase** (6a,50c,183c), **vise** (31d,77d,114d), **wise** (136b)

S - - E   **sabe, sade** (91d), **safe** (141d,157d,174d), **sage** (13a,90d,100c,141c, 145c,180b,183a), **sake** (84b,125d), **sale** (14c,61c,62b,c,168b), **same** (44d,79b), **sane** (128a), **sate** (32d,52c,67d,70d,137c,159d), **save** (52b,110c,123a,173c), **saxe** (20d,33c), **seme** (45c,138b,151b,154b, 155c,157b), **sere** (24d,46a,c,138c,183b), **Sere** (158b), **seve** (63a, 182c), **shee** (82b), **shoe** (166a), **sice** (71d,147b), **side** (13d,22a,b, 54a,58a,89a,161b), **sine** (101d), **sine** (64c,66b,90a,97c,126a,163b, 169d,183b), **sipe** (101a,110c,140b), **sire** (17d,55a,59d,124a,163b, 166b), **sise** (62c,147b), **site** (93b), **sive** (146a), **size, skee** (149c), **Skye** (163c), **slee** (140b,148c), **sloe** (14a,20b,64a,119d,181c), **slue** (97b,148b,160a), **smee** (19b,46c,d,118b,119d,141b,181b), **Smee** (116d), **snee** (40a,b,43d,87a), **soie** (62c), **soke** (44c,85d), **sole** (52c, 57a,b,58b,d,115d,150a), **some** (114b,121c,126a), **sore** (23d, 142c), **sote** (150c), **spae** (139c), **Spee** (66d,70b), **supe** (53a,154d), **sure** (173d), **syce** (71d), **syke** (194), **syne** (140b,147a), **sype** (110c)

S - - F   **self** (48d,80d), **serf** (21d,148a), **souf** (146b), **stof** (135c), **surf** (23a)

SG - -   **Sgau** (88c)

S - - G   **sang, Sarg** (96d,125d), **shag** (73b,105b,161d,166d), **sing** (26d,178a), **skag** (7d,46d), **skeg** (7d,86a,144d,157d,184a), **slag** (46c,99a,138c, 148d,177a), **slog** (157c,170b,177d), **slug** (46b,99b,157c), **smug, snag** (11b,27b,35c,87c,124b,166a), **sneg** (139b), **snig** (45d), **snug** (35a,38b,165c), **Snug** (99d), **song** (12c,170c), **stag** (65a,98d), **stog** (155a), **sung, Sung** (30b), **swag** (22a,156c), **swig** (46a,72c)

SH - -   **shad** (27d,57a,b,c), **shag** (73b,105b,161d,166d), **shah** (116c), **sham** (41c,55b,60d,80a,123a,b,146d), **Shan** (13c,80d,88c,101d), **shap, shat** (87d), **shaw** (164b), **Shaw** (50c,53b), **shay** (110c), **shea** (25a, 168c,d), **shed** (27a,90c,101b,144b), **shee** (82b), **Shem** (107c), **Shen** (68a), **sher** (65d,165c), **shet, shew** (44c), **shih** (189), **Shik** (171a), **shim** (91d,144c,162a,179d), **shin** (91a,d,140b,143c), **ship, shir** (36d, 65d,165c), **Shoa** (6c), **shod, shoe** (166a), **shoo** (46b,67a,138b), **shop, shoq** (169a), **shor** (136d), **Shor** (162b), **shot** (9d,43d,90c,174d), **shou**

(41d), **show** (42b,44c,96b), **Shri** (17c,166c), **shul** (161a), **shun** (15a, 51b,52a), **shut**

- SH - **Asha** (191), **ashy** (113a,178a), **Isha** (174a), **Tshi** (69c), **Usha** (16a, 150c)

- - SH **bash, bish** (120b), **bosh, bush, cash** (101c), **cosh** (35a,97c), **cush** (101c), **Cush** (51d,73c), **dash** (125c,162d), **dish, fash** (140c,176a), **fish, gash** (40a), **gish** (102c), **gosh, gush** (35a,154c), **hash, hish, hush** (17b,146c), **josh** (85b), **kish** (16d,70c), **Kish** (137c), **Kush lash** (58c,87b,165c,180d), **losh** (178b), **lush** (94d), **mash** (39b, 156c), **mesh** (50d,106c), **mush** (97d), **Nash** (9c), **Nish** (19d), **pish** (36c,107d), **posh** (49b,148c), **push** (145c), **rash** (75a), **resh** (91d), **rush, sash** (18a,45c,67b,182b), **sish** (79b), **sosh** (81d), **tash** (154d), **tosh** (106a), **tush** (167b), **wash, wish** (42d)

S - - H **saah** (188), **sadh** (77a), **sahh** (188), **samh** (56b), **sash** (18a,45c,67b, 182b), **seah** (188), **sech** (97c), **seth** (98d), **Seth** (7a,52b,68a,b,96a, 98d), **shah** (116c), **shih** (189), **sigh, Sikh** (77b), **sinh** (97c), **sish** (79b), **soph, sosh** (81d), **such** (146d)

SI - - **siak** (72d), **sial** (112a), **Siam** (163d,181a), **sice** (71d,147b), **sick, sida** (37a,126c,170a), **side** (13d,22a,b,54a,58a,89a,161b), **sidi** (103b, 166b), **sidy** (123b), **sier** (57a,118b), **sift** (140d,142c,146b), **sigh, sign** (121c,146c), **sika** (41d,84b), **Sikh** (77b), **silk** (53b,179c), **sill** (45c,76c,165a,182b), **silo** (59a,156d), **silt** (104b,142a), **sima** (132b), **sime** (101d), **Simi** (82d), **simp** (59c,146d), **sina** (46c), **Sina** (102d, 103d), **Sind, sine** (64c,66b,90a,97a,126a,163b,169d,183b), **sing** (26d,178a), **sinh** (97c), **sink** (41c,43c,46b,158a) **sino** (34a), **siol** (82c), **sion** (125c,158c), **Sion** (75b,c,83a,157d), **sipe** (101a,110c, 140b), **sire** (17d,55a,59d,124a,163b,166b), **siri** (18b), **sise** (62c, 147b), **sish** (79b), **sisi** (121b), **siss, sist** (139d), **Sita** (127d), **site** (93b), **sito** (34b), **siva** (67a,120d), **Siva** (56d,77a), **Sive** (146a), **size, sizy** (176d), **sizz**

- SI - **Asia** (48a), **Asin** (102a), **Hsia** (30b,47c), **Isis** (68d,78c,111d), **tsia** (162c), **Tsin** (30b)

- - SI **Absi** (191), **assi** (77d), **dasi** (77a), **desi** (85d), **kasi** (116b), **Lasi** (191), **nasi** (34c,108a,115a), **nisi** (90a,173c), **pasi** (94b), **sesi** (20b,57a), **sisi** (121b), **susi** (53b,d)

S - - I **Safi** (191), **saki** (39c,84b,102a), **sari** (48b,65b,77b), **sati, Sati** (49a, 126b,147b), **sebi** (34b), **semi** (34b,80b,122c,d), **seri** (18b), **Seri** (192), **sesi** (20b,57a,149b), **seti** (34a), **Seti** (116d), **Shri** (17c,166c), **sidi** (103b,166b), **Simi** (82d), **siri** (18b), **sisi** (121b), **soli** (12c,110c), **sori** (55c,64a), **sufi** (103a,116c), **sugi** (84b), **suji** (180c), **susi** (53b,d)

SK - - **skag** (7d,46d), **skat** (181b), **Skat** (155b), **skee** (149c), **skeg** (7d,86a, 144d,157d,184a), **sken** (164a), **skeo** (57d), **skep** (16d,17c,77c), **skew** (148a,160c,171b,c), **skey** (185d), **skid** (148b), **skil** (57a), **skim** (67c), **skin** (53a,76c,115c,d), **skio** (57d), **skip** (110b,114c,147c), **skir, skit** (145c), **skiv** (151b), **skua** (19b,72c,84a,141a), **Skye** (163c), **skyr** (21d,151a), **skyt** (138c,140b)

- SK - **Askr** (107d)

- - SK **bask** (94d), **bisk** (120b,151a), **bosk** (164b), **busk** (17b,37b,55d, 161b), **cask, cusk** (57b), **desk, disk** (31b), **dusk** (171c), **fisk** (24d,52c,134c), **husk** (53a,78d,142a), **mask** (44a,45c), **mosk** (97b,

361

103b), **musk** (116b), **Omsk, pisk** (9c,19b), **risk** (74d), **rusk** (23a), **task** (156b), **Tosk** (8c), **tusk** (167b)

S - - K   **sack** (43d,118a,119d,182b), **sank, Sark** (28d), **Sauk** (192), **sawk** (188), **seck** (173d), **seek** (141c), **Seik** (77b), **Shik** (171a), **siak** (72d), **sick, silk** (53b,179c), **sink** (41c,43c,46b,158a), **soak** (46c,137c), **Sobk** (38d), **sock** (157c,182a), **sook** (22a,25c,97a), **souk** (22a,97a), **suck, sulk** (159a), **sunk**

SL - -   **slab** (148b), **slag** (46c,99a,138c,148d,177a), **slam** (180d,182d), **slap** (24a,128c,148c), **slat** (58b,89a,117c,184a), **Slav** (13c,40c,48b,52a, 120b,135b), **slaw, slay, Sleb** (12a), **sled** (40a), **slee** (140b,148c), **slew** (160a), **sley** (179b), **slid, slim** (148b,160a), **slip** (67c,119a), **slit** (40a), **slob** (173d), **sloe** (14a,20b,64a,119d,181c), **slog** (157c,170b, 177d), **sloo** (160a), **slop, slot** (10d,11b,41d,110d,167d,168a,181b), **slow** (43c), **slub** (171c), **slue** (97b,148b,160a), **slug** (46b,99b,157c), **slum, slur** (44b,124c,148b,168a)

- SL -   **isle** (8b,53c,81d,82d,86b,88a), **Oslo**

S - - L   **saal** (66c,73b), **sail** (144c,185a), **saul** (48a,168c), **Saul** (18c,86d, 115a), **seal** (10c,d,54d,64c,96a,118a,128a), **seel** (20c,32c,143b), **sell** (97a,115c,175b), **shul** (161a), **sial** (112a), **sill** (45c,76c,165a, 182b) **siol** (82c), **skil** (57a), **soil** (154d,159a,163c), **soul** (10d,125a, 153c,176d)

SM - -   **smee** (19b,46c,d,118b,119b,141b,181b), **Smee** (116d), **smew** (19b, 46d,99a,137d), **smug, smur** (32c,46b,100c), **smut** (32d,44a,119a, 150c)

- SM -   **ismy** (45a)

- - SM   **kasm** (189)

S - - M   **saum** (189), **scum** (129b), **seam** (85b,d,160a,176d,185a), **seem** (11c), **Seim** (120c), **Sejm** (120c), **sham** (41c,55b,60d,80a,123a,b, 146d), **Shem** (107c), **shim** (91d,144c,162a,179d), **Siam** (163d,181a), **skim** (67c), **slam** (180d,182d), **slim** (148b,160a), **slum, stem** (29b, 125a,154d,155a,156d), **stom** (34c), **stum** (70c,105c,131a,173a), **swam, swim** (58c), **swum**

SN - -   **snab** (23c,139a), **snag** (11b,27b,35c,87c,124b,166a), **snap** (23a, 36d,38b,48b,54d,56c,58c,149d), **sned** (93d,125a,140a), **snee** (40a, b,43d,87a), **sneg** (139b), **snib** (54d,93c), **snig** (45d), **snip** (32b, 40a), **snob** (159c), **snod** (169d), **snow, snub** (128c,148b), **snug** (35a,38b,165c), **Snug** (99d), **snup** (149b)

- SN -   **asno** (151d), **esne** (10c,45b,142c,148a,164d)

S - - N   **Saan** (24d), **sain** (20c,38d,48a), **sawn, scan** (52b,93d,98a,116d, 128b,c,140d), **scon** (162c), **Sean** (85b,96a), **seen, sein** (146c), **senn** (76b), **sewn, Shan** (13c,80d,88c,101d), **Shen** (68a), **shin** (91a,d,140b, 143c), **shun** (15a,51b,52a), **sign** (121c,146c), **sion** (125c,158c), **Sion** (75b,c,83a,157d), **sken** (164a), **skin** (53a,76c,115c,d), **soon** (123a, 145c), **sorn** (139a,d), **span** (23b,107b,113a,128b,162c), **spin** (131a, 180d), **spun, sten** (72c,95a), **stun** (145a,157d), **sunn** (56a), **Svan** (27d), **swan** (19b,33a)

SO - -   **soak** (46c,137c), **soap, soar** (59a), **Sobk** (38d), **sock** (157c,182a), **soco** (22d), **soda** (19a,149d,181a), **sofa** (44d), **soft** (48b,95d,99d, 163a), **soga** (70d,152b), **Soga** (191), **soho!, Soho** (93c), **Soia, soie**

362

(62c), **soil** (154d,159a,163c), **soir** (61c), **soja** (151b), **soka** (20c), **soke** (44c,85d), **sola** (9a,48a,74b,118c,154a,167b), **sold**, **sole** (52c,57a,b, 58b,d,110c,115d,150a), **soli** (12c,110c), **solo** (12c,89a,110c), **soma** (10c,21c,34a,48a,81d,136b), **some** (114b,121c,126a), **song** (12c, 170c), **sons** (98d,109d), **sook** (22a,25c,97a), **soon** (123a,145c), **soot** (20b,26c,88a), **soph**, **Sopt** (45b), **sora** (19b,c,127b), **sorb** (11d,103d, 134b,142d), **Sorb** (148a,180a), **sore** (23d,142c), **sori** (55c,64a), **sorn** (139a,d), **sors** (44d,89b), **sort** (31d,39c,70b,86b,153a), **sory** (176d), **sosh** (81d), **soso** (99c,114c,166d), **sote** (150c), **souf** (146b), **souk** (22a,97a), **soul** (10d,125a,153c,176d), **soup, sour, sous** (62d,172c), **soya** (151b)

- SO -   **asok** (13d), **asom** (18d), **asop** (180b), **asor** (75c,105a), **Esop** (53b, 54a), **esox** (57b)

- - SO   **also** (10b,18b,80a), **Caso** (82d), **coso** (152c), **enso** (34d,183b), **huso** (180c), **ipso** (89c), **koso** (6c,80d), **Koso** (192,193), **Muso** (192), **peso** (99c), **piso** (189), **soso** (99c,114c,166d), **yeso** (72d)

S - - O   **saco** (189), **sado** (26d,84d), **sago** (54c,59b,113b,125b,155c), **Saho** (6c), **sano** (152b), **sapo** (149c,166b), **Scio, sego** (24b,25a,92b,174c), **sero** (34d,88d,164b,178d), **shoo** (46b,67a,138b), **silo** (59a,156d), **sino** (34a), **sito** (34b), **skeo** (57d), **skio** (57d), **sloo** (160a), **soco** (22d), **sohol, Soho** (93c), **solo** (12c,89a,110c), **soso** (99c,114c,166d), **Sumo**

SP - -   **spad** (105b), **Spad** (118d), **spae** (139c), **span** (23b,107b,113a,128b, 162c), **spar** (22c,24c,64b,97b,100b,144d), **spat** (112c,126b,134b), **spec, sped, Spee** (66d,70b), **spes, Spes** (69a,78a), **spet** (16c,57a, 142c), **spew** (35a,49a), **spex, spey, spin** (131a,180d), **spit** (97c), **spit** (120a,132b,c), **spot** (93b,118c,154d,162a), **spry** (7a,107b), **spud** (121d,151c), **spun, spur** (10d,67d,167d,168a,181b), **sput** (21c)

- SP -   **espy** (44a,142a)

- - SP   **cusp** (38c,78b,119a,120a,b), **gasp** (113c), **hasp** (31d,54d,153c), **lisp** (153b), **rasp** (56b,70d,140d), **risp** (99a), **wasp, wisp** (24b,148c)

S - - P   **salp** (109c,148d), **samp** (70b,77d,121b), **scop** (120a), **scup** (57a, 121b), **seep** (110c,116a,154b), **seip** (110c), **shap, ship, shop, simp** (59c,146d), **skep** (16d,17c,77c), **skip** (110b,114c,147c), **slap** (24a, 128c,148c), **slip** (67c,119a), **slop, snap** (23a,36d,38b,48b,54d,56c, 58c,149d), **snip** (32b,40a), **snup** (149b), **soap, soup, step** (70b,112b, 177b,d), **stop** (73b,111b), **sump** (28c,45d,100b), **swap** (168a), **swop** (168a)

S - - Q   **shoq** (169a)

S - - R   **Saar** (63b,102d,132a), **sadr** (94a), **Sadr** (155b), **saer** (163a), **sair** (140b,150d), **scar** (31a,184d), **scur** (78b), **sear** (23d,27d,72d,138c), **seer** (60a,124c,150c), **sehr** (66d), **Seir** (51b,94a,103d), **sher** (65d, 165c), **shir** (36d,65d,165c), **shor** (136d), **Shor** (162b), **sier** (57a, 118b), **skir, skyr** (21d,151a), **slur** (44b,124c,148b,168a), **smur** (32c,46b,100c), **soar** (59a), **soir** (61c), **sour, spar** (22c,24c,64b,97b, 100b,144d), **spir** (97c), **spur** (10d,67d,167d,168a,181b), **star** (14a, 21c,94c,100c), **ster** (158c,d), **stir** (8a,13a,35b,78d,100d,104a), **suer** (124d)

- SS -   **asse** (25a,60d,74a), **assi** (77d), **esse** (7a,18a,52d,89a,90a,159a, 166c), **ossa** (21d), **Ossa** (103d,110b,164b)

- - SS   **bass** (57b,c,177a), **Bess** (76c,183d), **boss** (49d,157d), **buss** (87a, 148c), **cass** (140c,177a), **Cass** (147a), **cess** (91d,94c,162b), **coss** (98a), **cuss, diss** (98b), **doss** (17c), **fass** (189), **fess** (23c,51b), **foss** (44d,100d), **fuss** (22b,35b), **hiss** (146a), **jass** (160d), **jess** (157a), **joss** (30b), **kiss** (148c), **koss** (188), **lass** (95b), **less** (100c,108b,141d), **liss** (54b,58b,60c,129d,140a), **loss** (42c,123d,178b), **mass** (8a,24b, 35b,142d), **mess** (22b,44b,77c,85d,104b,165c,173d), **miss, moss** (91d,104c,114a,170c), **muss** (135b,173d), **ness** (26b,75a,124b), **pass** (110b,155c), **puss, Riss** (66a), **ross** (16c,161d), **Ross** (50c), **Russ** (135b), **sass, sess** (149c,162b), **siss, Tass** (107a,135d,151b), **Tess** (73d,164c,183d), **toss** (24a,132d), **viss** (189)

S - - S   **sais** (48d,71d), **sans** (63a,183b), **sass, seis** (147b,152c), **sens** (63b), **seps** (93b,142d), **sess** (149c,162b), **siss, sons** (98d,109d), **sors** (44d, 89b), **sous** (62d,172c), **spes, Spes** (69a,78a), **suds** (59a)

ST - -   **stab** (14c,87a,117c), **stad** (151b,167d,176b), **stag** (65a,98d), **star** (14a,21c,94c,100c), **stat** (72d), **stay** (72d,124c,130a,134a,162a), **stem** (29b,125a,154d,155a,156d), **sten** (72c,95a), **step** (70b,112b, 177b,d), **ster** (158c,d), **stet** (91b,123d,124c), **stev** (155b), **stew** (21c,44b,184d), **stib** (19b,47a,137a), **stir** (8a,13a,35b,78d,100d, 104a), **stoa** (33c,121a,c), **stod** (40d,67d), **stof** (135c), **stog** (155a), **stom** (34c), **stop** (73b,111b), **stot** (154d,155d,157d,179b,186a), **stow** (112b), **stub** (156c), **stud** (22b,25a,42d,54d,111c,143a,174a), **stum** (70c,105c,131a,173a), **stun** (145a,157d), **Styx** (29b,73a,105c)

- ST -   **asta** (188), **Asta** (107a,164c), **Asti** (83d,182b), **esta** (152d,164c), **este** (152b,d,164c), **Este** (55c,83c,d,112d), **Esth** (16a,51d), **oste** (21d,83b)

- - ST   **bast** (16c,56a,117b,184a), **Bast** (27b), **best** (41d,159c,160a), **bust, cast** (165b,167c), **cest** (18a,67b), **dost, dust, east, East** (111b), **erst** (60b), **fast** (56d,126c,141d,160c,173a,d), **fest, fist** (80c), **fust** (105c,143b), **gest** (7c,41d,52d,133c), **gist** (95c,118c), **gust, hast, hest** (35a), **hist** (25c,93d), **host** (13a,51d,104c), **jest** (169c), **just** (51b,54b), **kist** (29d,58a,139b), **last** (36c,50b,145a,174c), **lest** (59d, 163d), **list** (26d,27b,75b,83d,134a,138b,165d), **lost, lust** (41b), **mast** (17c,108d,120b,144d,152d), **mist** (46b,59b,174d), **most, must** (70c,101a,106d,157d,182c), **myst** (71c,123b), **Nast** (9c,27a), **nest** (38b,74b,130d,149c,160b), **oast** (15d,86b,112a), **oust** (44c, 49a,52b,125d), **past** (25c,69d,165d), **pest** (108c,116b,118d,170a), **pist** (25c), **post** (89a,95c,155d), **rest** (15d,91b,104d,105a,115a,b, 130a,b,161b), **rust** (37b,112c,119a), **sist** (139b), **test** (26a,51c,144a, 169c,170c), **vast** (78d,79d), **vest** (32c,177b), **wast, west, West** (9c, 50b,109b), **wist** (87c), **zest** (55d,72d)

S - - T   **salt** (35d,105b,123a,136c,141c,149d), **Sart** (82b,103b,170d), **scat** (26b,67a,d,126c,169c), **scot** (14a,162b), **Scot** (64b,132c), **scut** (145c,161b), **seat** (98c,156b), **sect** (42b,54a,114c), **seit** (189), **sent, sept** (31d,82b,143a,149c), **Sept** (45b), **Sert** (151d), **sett** (115a,156d), **sext** (26b,111b,147b), **shat** (87d), **shot** (9d,43d,90c, 174d), **shut, sift** (140d,142c,146b), **silt** (104b,142a), **skat** (181b), **Skat** (155b), **skit** (145c), **skyt** (138c,140b), **slat** (58b,89a,117c, 184a), **slit** (40a), **slot** (10d,11b,41d,110d,167d,168a,181b), **smut** (32d,44a,119a,150c), **soft** (48b,95d,99d,163a), **soot** (20b,26c,88a), **Sopt** (45b), **sort** (31d,39c,70b,86b,153a), **spat** (112c,126b,134b),

364

spet (16c,57a,142c), **spit** (120a,132b,c), **spot** (93b,118c,154d,162a), **sput** (21c), **stat** (72d), **stet** (91b,123d,124c), **stot** (154d,155d,157d, 179b,186a), **suet** (54d), **suit** (38a,58a,91a,112a,119c,137c), **swat** (15d,20d,32d,157c), **Swat** (103a), **swot**

SU - - **such** (146d), **suck**, **sudd** (40b,58c,107b), **suds** (59a), **suer** (124d), **suet** (54d), **sufi** (103a,116c), **sugi** (84b), **suit** (38a,58a,91a,112a, 119c,137c), **suji** (180c), **Suku** (191), **Sula** (65a), **suld** (188), **sulk** (159a), **Sulu** (102c), **Sumo**, **sump** (28c,45d,100b), **sung**, **Sung** (30b), **sunk**, **sunn** (56a), **supa** (168c), **supe** (53a,154d), **sura** (87c,113b, 166d), **surd** (82c,177a), **sure** (173d), **surf** (23a), **Susa** (49a), **susl** (53b,d), **susu** (20c), **Susu** (191), **Susy** (183d)

- SU - **Asur** (68c), **Esus**, **tsun** (30b), **Usun** (191)

- - SU **ansu** (11d), **Apsu** (29a), **ausu** (168c,180b), **Jesu**, **masu** (57a,84c), **Nosu** (27d), **susu** (20c), **Susu** (191), **vasu** (106c), **Vasu** (176d)

S - - U **sahu** (153d), **Sgau** (88c), **shou** (41d), **Suku** (191), **Sulu** (102c), **susu** (20c), **Susu** (191)

SV - - **Svan** (27d)

S - - V **skiv** (151b), **Slav** (13c,40c,48b,52a,120b,135b), **stev** (155b)

SW - - **swab** (102b), **swad** (94d), **swag** (22a,156c), **swam**, **swan** (19b,33a), **swap** (168a), **swat** (15d,20d,32d,157c), **Swat** (103a), **sway** (104a), **sweb** (160d), **swig** (46a,72c), **swim** (58c), **swiz** (160c), **swob** (102b), **swop** (168a), **swot**, **swow** (100a), **swum**

S - - W **scow** (21a,58b), **shaw** (164b), **Shaw** (50c,53b), **shew** (44c), **show** (42b,44c,96b), **skew** (148a,160c,171b,c), **slaw** (160a), **slew** (160a), **slow** (43c), **smew** (19b,46d,99a,137d), **snow**, **spew** (35a,49a), **stew** (21c, 44b,184d), **stow** (112b), **swow** (100a)

S - - X **spex**, **Styx** (29b,73a,105c)

SY - - **syce** (71d), **syed** (103b), **syke** (194), **syne** (140b,147a), **sype** (110c), **Syra**, **syud** (103b)

- - SY **busy**, **cosy** (149c), **easy** (54a,146d,149d,172b), **Josy** (183d), **mosy** (67d), **nosy**, **rosy** (21a,111a), **Susy** (183d)

S - - Y **sagy** (110c), **shay** (110c), **sidy** (123b), **sizy** (176d), **skey** (185d), **slay**, **sley** (179b), **sory** (176d), **Spey** (7a,107b), **spry** (7a,107b), **stay** (72d,124c,130a, 134a), **Susy** (183d), **sway** (104a)

S - - Z **sizz**, **swiz** (160c)

TA - - **Taal** (7d,88c,151a), **taar** (12b), **tabi** (84c,149d), **tabu** (59d,111d), **tace** (13a,155d), **tack** (28d,37d,54d), **tact** (43c,d,116a), **tael** (91d, 179d), **Taft** (29d), **taha** (179b), **tahr** (68a,76d), **tail** (11d,27d,59b, 143b), **tain** (166a), **tair** (68a,76d), **tait** (14d), **tajo** (152a,d), **take**, **takt** (105a,163a), **Taku** (80c), **taky**, **tala** (16d,113a,168c,d), **talc** (28d,63b,99c,100b,122a,149c), **tale** (91a,185b), **tali** (189), **talk**, **tall** (118d), **Tama** (192), **tame** (45a,b,66a), **Tame**, **tamp** (46b,112b, 121d,127d), **tana** (159a), **Tana** (87d), **Tane** (120d), **tang** (30b,58b, 186b), **tanh** (97c), **tank** (175a,d), **Tano** (192), **Taos** (192), **tapa** (16c, 32c,53b,56a,74b,104b,112b,113d,120d), **tape** (16a,19a,128d), **tapu**, **tara** (22a,55c,113a,168c), **Tara** (82b,c,138b), **tare** (9a,18d,41a, 176a,179d), **Tari** (47d,69a), **tarn** (87d,103d,120d), **taro** (13c,48c, 49b,64b,112b,120a,133d,155c,170a,c), **tarp** (26b,178d), **tart** (114d), **tash** (154d), **task** (156b), **Tass** (107a,135d,151b), **tate** (183a), **tatt**

365

(87c), **tatu** (12d), **Tatu, taun** (188), **taut** (163b,165c), **Tave** (183d), **Tavy** (183d), **tawa** (106d,168c), **taxi** (13a,125b), **taxo** (13a)

- TA - **atap** (113b), **atar** (58d,116b,134a), **Etah** (71d,51c), **etal** (89a), **etat** (62d), **Ptah** (48d,98c), **stab** (14c,87a,117c), **stad** (151b,167d,176b), **stag** (65a,98d), **star** (14a,21c,94c,100c), **stat** (72d), **stay** (72d,124c, 130a,134a,162a), **utac** (22d), **Utah** (180b), **utas** (49a,109c)

- - TA **acta** (41d,123d,128d,164c), **Aeta** (94d,95d,100a,106b,117a), **alta** (89c,152d), **anta** (83d,117c,d,121a), **Anta** (164a), **Arta** (72b), **asta** (188), **Asta** (107a,164c), **atta** (58d,90c,97d,160c,173d), **Atta** (94d,95d,100a,106b,117a), **bata** (30a,142d), **beta** (71a, 91c,141d), **bota** (189), **cata** (122c), **cota** (117a), **data** (54a), **dita** (117a), **esta** (152d,164c), **Etta** (183c), **gata** (143c), **geta** (84b,145a), **Gita, iota** (71a,85c,91c,114c,166c,176a,180d), **jota** (151c), **keta** (45a), **kota** (117a), **Kota** (45d), **lata** (85d, 95d), **lota** (24c,121d,178d), **Lota, meta** (132d,133a), **Meta, mota** (103a), **muta** (28d,103a), **nata** (47c), **Nata** (15c), **nota** (15c, 89c), **octa** (122c), **pata** (32c,160d), **pita** (9c,28b,56a,83a), **rata** (29d,56b,89d,96c,106d,120c,168c), **rita, Rita** (37b,78d,183c), **rota** (27c,30d,38a,79a,92d,133a,134a,b,180c), **Ruta** (76b,134d), **seta** (23b,27c,73a,b,123b,153c), **Sita** (127d), **tota** (71d), **veta** (104a), **vita** (89c,92a), **vota** (133b), **weta** (93c), **yeta** (84c), **zeta** (71b,91c)

T - - A **taha** (179b), **tala** (16d,113a,168c,d), **Tama** (192), **tana** (159a), **Tana** (87d), **tapa** (16c,32c,53b,56a,74b,104b,112b,113d,120d), **tara** (22a, 55c,113a,168c), **Tara** (82b,c,138b), **tawa** (106d,168c), **tcha** (162c), **teca, Teca** (192), **Teda** (191), **tela** (22d,98c,121b,166a,179c), **tema** (12a,164a), **Tema, tera** (23d,84c), **tesa** (80c), **Tewa** (193), **Thea** (162c), **Tina** (183d), **tiza** (172a), **Toba** (80c), **Toda** (45d,76d), **toga** (132d,133a,b), **tola** (48a,80d,180a), **Tola** (85b), **Toma** (191), **tooa** (17c), **tora** (11a,44d,74a,75c,85c,90b,102d,115d), **tota** (71d), **toxa** (153d), **tsia** (162c), **tuba** (105a,137d), **tufa** (121b,177a), **tula** (9a), **Tula, tuna** (57a,b,123b), **tuza** (119d)

T - - B **theb** (188), **thob** (128a), **tomb**

TC - - **tcha** (162c), **tche** (13d,30b,105a), **tchi, Tchi, tchu**

- TC - **etch, itch**

T - - C **talc** (28d,63b,99c,100b,122a,149c)

T - - D **tend** (26d,80b,93d,100a), **thud, tied, tind** (86b), **toad** (10a,17a, 63d,126d), **toed, told** (129c), **trod, tund** (121d)

TE - - **teak** (41a,48a,168c), **teal** (19b,20d,46c,d), **team** (38c,72a,113a), **tean** (140c,167a), **tear** (67c,87b,130a), **teca, Teca** (192), **Tech, teck** (128b), **Teco** (192), **Teda** (191), **teel** (142d), **teem** (6b,121d), **teen** (139b,c,140b,158d), **teer** (25b,69d), **Tees** (108a), **teff** (6c), **tegg** (143d,171d), **tehr** (27c,68a), **Teig** (96a), **teil** (92b,c,168c), **teju** (151b), **tela** (22d,98c,121b,166a,179c), **tele** (34b,122c), **teli** (94b), **tell** (105d,129c,154b), **Tell** (160d), **tema** (12a,164a), **Tema, tend** (26d,80b,93d,100a), **tene** (34d,131b), **teng** (188), **tent** (26b), 115a), **Teos** (82a), **tera** (23d,84c), **term** (92b,105b,142b,166b), **tern** (19b,32d,72c,94a,138c,141a,160a), **terp** (12b,123a), **tesa** (80c), **Tess** (73d,164c,183d), **test** (26a,51c,144a,169c,170c), **tete** (61d,73b,74d), **teth** (91d), **Tewa** (193), **text** (21c,140d), **teyl** (92b, c,168c)

366

- TE - atef (39a,48d), aten (150a,159b), Ateo (120d), Ater (18c), ates (160c), Itea (145d,160c,181d), item (6d,13b,42d,51a,90d,92d,107a, 113d,114c), Iten (192), iter (22d,76c,85c,89c,114d,132a,b,133a,b), Otea (71a,82d), stem (29b,125a,154d,155a,156d), sten (72c,95a), step (70b,112b,177b,d), ster (158c,d), stet (91b,123d,124c), stev (155b), stew (21c,44b,184d)

- - TE - ante (87a,89a,115b,120b,122b,125d,154d), bate (43c,91b,100d), bete (61a,107c), bite (29d,156b), cate (165c), cete (180b,c), cite (15a,98d,126d,159b), cote (19b,143d,144a,b), cute (39c), date (64a,153a), dite (150b), dote (17a,90b,94b,97a,112a,139d,165d), ente (70b,151d), este (152b,d,164c), Este (55c,83c,d,112d), ette (158a,c,d), fate (42d,52a,87a,94a), fete (55d,129b), fute (51c), gate (51a,121b), gite (62a,118d), hate (6a,43a), jete (16a), jute (37a,48a,56a,133d,136a), Jute, Kate (143c,183d), kite (19c,49a, 74c,d), late (128c), lete, lite (158c,d), lote (24c,94a), lute (11c,28b, 84d,105a,131d), mate (18c,35b,41d,113a,154a,162c), mete (9a, 11d,22b,44c,45b,98a,121c), mite (12b,81b,82a,114a,c,148c,d,181b), mote (114c,153a), mute (146c,153b), Nate (22b), nete (71c,108b, 163d), note (98c,109b,124b,128d,130a,177c), oste (21d,83b), pate (39a,74d), pete (136b), Pete, rate (11d,14a,31d,36b,51d,52a,70b, 85c,112b,123b,127d,128a,138c,143a,174b), rete (106c,119c), rite (93a,131d), rote (130b,134b,143a,159d), rute (188), sate (32d,52c, 67d,70d,137c,159d), site (93b), sote (150c), tate (183a), tete (61d, 73b,74d), tote (27a,73c), tute (171b), vite (62b), vote (60b), Vote (56d), Wate (141a), Wote (191), yate (51d,168c)

T - - E tace (13a,155d), take, tale (91a,185b), tame (45a,b,66a), Tame, Tane (120d), tape (16a,19a,128d), tare (9a,18d,41a,176a,179d), tate (183a), Tave (183d), tche (13d,30b,105a), tele (34b,122c), tene (34d,131b), tete (61d,73b,74d), thee (124b), tice (9a,38c,51a, 185d), tide (39d,75d,109c,141c,159d), tige (118a), tike (29d), tile (31d,56d,72b,95b,133c,163c), time (47a,131a), tine (11b,124b, 167b), tipe (168b), tire (15a,22a,52d,55a,179b,180d), tobe (7d, 137b), tode (80a,148a), tole (9a,51a,99b,163a), tome (21d,177c), tone (6c,118c,150d), tope (24a,46b,57a,143c,151a), tore, tote (27a, 73c), tree (11d,37a,66a,184b), true (7a,8d,37b,54b,94c,149c), tube (118b,158a), tuke (26b,53b), tule (24b,27c), tune (8b,12c, 98c), tute (171b), twee (29d), tyee (29d), tyke (29d), tyne, Tyne (108a), type (31d,115a,155a), tyre (15a), Tyre (31b,90d,117b)

T - - F teff (6c), tiff (126b), toff (40d), tref (172b), tuff (121b,177a), turf (115c,149d,160b)

T - - G tang (30b,58b,186b), tegg (143d,171d), Teig (96a), teng (188), thug (65a), ting (166a), Ting (30c), tong (30a,c,), toug (171a), trig (106a,148d,154b,169d), tung (110a,168c), twig

TH - - Thai (146a), than (35b), thar (68a,76d), that (42b,124b,129c), thaw, Thea (162c), theb (188), thee (124b), them (124b), then, thew (104c), they (124b), thin (43b,c,148b), this (42b,124b), thob (128a), Thor (7c,68c,99c,100c,109c,165b), Thos (84a,181c), thou (124b), thud, thug (65a), thus (149c)

- TH - Otho (133a)

- - TH acth (13b), bath, Bath (50d,151c), beth (91c), Beth (8c,183d), both, doth, Esth (16a,51d), Gath (117a), Goth (16c,163d), hath,

367

Heth (77c), **Hoth** (20c), **Jeth** (102a), **kath** (14a), **kith** (63c), **lath** (157c), **lith** (34d,156c), **loth** (15a,173d), **math** (77a), **moth**, **Moth** (112d), **muth** (188), **myth** (8b,91a), **Nath** (155c), **oath** (119c,150a), **path** (132a,134b), **pith** (37a,51c,67b,95c,97a,119b,126d), **rath** (76d,162d), **ruth** (35b,118c), **Ruth** (105b,183c), **seth** (98d), **Seth** (7a,52b,68a,b,96a,98d), **teth** (91d), **Urth** (68d,107d,163d), **Voth** (191), **with** (10b)

T - - H   tanh (97c), **tash** (154d), **Tech**, **teth** (91d), **toph** (75c), **tosh** (106a), **tush** (167b)

TI - -   **Tiam, tiao, tiar** (39a,75a,121a), **Tibu** (191), **tice** (9a,38c,51a,185d), **tick** (12b,20d,97c), **tide** (39d,75d,109c,141c,159d), **tidy** (106a, 111b), **tied, tien** (147d), **tier** (118a,134b), **tiff** (126b), **tige** (118a), **tike** (29d), **Tiki** (120c), **tile** (31d,56d,72b,95b,133c,163c), **till** (39c, 101c,173d), **tilt** (26b,d,166a), **time** (47a,131a), **Tina** (183d), **tind** (86b), **tine** (11b,124b,167b), **ting** (166a), **Ting** (30c), **Tino** (136d), **tint** (33c,d,114d), **tiny** (100c,148c), **tion** (158b), **Tiou** (192), **tipe** (168b), **tipi** (181b), **tire** (15a,22a;52d,55a,179b,180d), **tiro** (9b,17d, 108c), **titi** (20d,102a,145d,168d,181b), **Tito** (186c), **tiza** (172a)

- TI -   **Atik** (155b), **atip** (14b,166a), **atis** (76d,102a), **itis** (158c), **otic** (14c, d,47b), **Otis** (9c,d,24d,82a,111a), **stib** (19b,47a,137a), **stir** (8a, 13a,35b,78d,100d,104a)

- - TI   **anti** (7d,111a,122b), **Anti** (193), **Asti** (83d,182b), **biti** (20b), **Guti**, **Hati** (48d), **hoti**, **Inti** (159b), **jati** (27b), **jiti, joti, Leti** (82d), **liti** (60d), **Loti** (63a,176a), **rati** (189), **roti** (62c), **sati, Sati** (49a,126b,147b), **seti** (34a), **Seti** (116d), **titi** (20d,102a,145d,168d, 181b), **viti** (176b), **yati** (76d), **zati** (21d)

T - - I   **tabi** (84c,149d) **tali** (188), **Tarl** (47d,69a), **taxi** (13a,125b), **tchi, Tchi, teli** (94b), **Thai** (146a), **Tiki** (120c), **tipi** (181b), **titi** (20d,102a, 145d,168d,181b), **topi** (37a,75a,118c), **tori** (101b), **tshi, Tshi** (69c), **Tupi** (192), **Turi** (191), **tuwi** (117a,168c), **Tybi** (102a)

- TK -   **Atka** (11a)

T - - K   **tack** (28d,37d,54d), **talk, tank** (175a,d), **task** (156b), **teak** (41a, 48a,168c), **teck** (128b), **tick** (12b,20d,97c), **tock** (7d,19b),**tonk** (173c), **took, Tosk** (8c), **trek** (85c,93c,99d,168b), **tuck** (156b), **Turk** (101d,102d,106a,111d), **tusk** (167b)

- TL -   **atle** (136d,161d,169b), **Atli** (14c,72b,79a,107d)

- - TL   **roti** (103b,111c)

T - - L   **Taal** (7d,88c,151a), **tael** (91d,179d), **tail** (11d,27d,59b,143b), **tall** (118d), **teal** (19b,20d,46c,d), **teel** (142d), **teil** (92b,c,168c), **tell** (105d,129c,154b), **Tell** (160d), **teyl** (92b,c,168c), **till** (39c,101c, 173d), **toil** (46c,184c), **toll** (131c), **tool** (27c), **tuel**

TM - -   **T-men** (168b)

- TM -   **atma** (150d), **atmo** (34d,174d), **Atmu** (143a,159b), **itmo** (18b)

T - - M   **team** (38c,72a,113a), **teem** (6b), **term** (92b,105b,142b,166b), **them** (124b), **tiam, toom** (139b), **tram** (170a), **trim** (40a,106a,154b, 160a,165c,169d), **turm** (132d)

- TN -   **etna** (75b,153c,157a,175d,177a,c)

T - - N   **tain** (166a), **tarn** (87d,103d,120d), **taun** (188), **tean** (140c,167a), **teen** (139b,c,140b,158d), **tern** (19b,32d,72c,94a,138c,141a,160a),

368

than (35b), **then, thin** (43b.c,148b), **tlen** (147d), **tion** (158b), **T-men** (168b), **toon** (80c,95b,168c), **torn** (130a), **town** (73c), **tran** (7a), **trin** (169d), **tron** (140d,180a), **Tsin** (30b), **tsun** (30b), **tuan** (95d,147b,166c), **turn** (28d,131a,175a), **twin** (45c,171d)

TO - - **toad** (10a,17a,63d,126d), **Toba** (80c), **tobe** (7d,137b), **toby** (8c, 85c,104b), **Toby** (96b,125c), **tock** (7d,19b), **toco** (19b,167c), **Toda** (45d,76d), **tode** (80a,148a), **todo** (22b,24d,35b,64c,156b), **tody** (19b,d,59a,166a), **toed, toff** (40d), **toga** (132d,133a,b), **togs** (32c), **togt** (77c), **toho** (79a), **toil** (46c,184c), **toko** (30c), **tola** (48a,80d,180a), **Tola** (85b), **told** (129c), **tole** (9a,51a,99b,163a), **toll** (131c), **tolt, tolu** (16a), **Toma** (191), **tomb, tome** (21d,177c), **tone** (6c,118c,150d), **tong** (30a,c), **tonk** (173c), **tony, Tony** (96b), **tooa** (17c), **took, tool** (27c), **toom** (139b), **toon** (80c,95b,168c), **toot, tope** (24a,46b,57a,143c,151a), **toph** (75c), **topi** (37a,75a, 118c), **tops** (159c), **tora** (11a,44d,74a,75c,85c,90b,102d,115d), **tore, tori** (101b), **torn** (130a), **toro** (38a,107a,152a,168c), **torp** (54c), **tort** (31c,91a,185c), **Tory** (23c,36b,94c,172a), **tosh** (106a), **Tosk** (8c), **toss** (24a,132d), **tota** (71d), **tote** (27a,73c), **toto** (8d,15a,34d, 89a,181a), **toty** (87b), **toug** (171a), **toup** (95d), **tour** (31b,85c), **tout** (61a,127a), **town** (73c), **towy** (58b), **toxa** (153d)

- TO - **atom** (101c,114c,180d), **aton** (150a,159b), **atop** (112a,174a), **Eton** (33b,50c,84a), **itol** (158b), **Otoe** (147b), **stoa** (33c,121a,c), **stod** (40d,67d), **stof** (135c), **stog** (155a), **stom** (34c), **stop** (73b,111b), **stot** (154d,155d,157d,179b,186a), **stow** (112b), **utor** (90a,166c)

- - TO **acto** (152b), **alto** (152b,176c), **auto** (34d), **bito** (7d,57d,168c), **Boto** (192), **Buto** (142d), **Cato** (132d,133b), **ceto** (34a), **cito** (89d,126c), **coto** (16c,90b), **dato** (95c,102c,117a), **Doto** (141b), **ecto** (34c,122d), **ento** (34b,d), **into** (123a,183b) **jato** (173b), **koto** (84b), **Leto** (11c), **loto** (65a,121d,178d), **moto** (104b), **Nato** (6a,8d), **nito** (55c), **octo** (34a,89b,122c), **onto** (76a,174a), **otto** (58d,116b,134a), **Otto** (14c,66d,67a,96a), **pato** (46d), **peto** (57a,177b), **Peto** (76a), **pito** (9c,28b,83a), **roto** (30a,122d,127b,152c,171b), **sito** (34b), **Tito** (186c), **toto** (8d,15a,34d,89a,181a), **Tyto** (16c), **unto** (166c), **veto** (94a,124a), **Veto, Voto** (192)

T - - O **tajo** (152a,d), **Tano** (192), **taro** (13c,48c,49b,64b,112b,120a,133d, 155c,170a,c), **taxo** (13a), **Teco** (192), **tiao, Tino** (136d), **tiro** (9b, 17d,108c), **Tito** (186c), **toco** (19b,167c), **todo** (22b,24d,35b,64c, 156b), **toho** (79a), **toko** (30c), **toro** (38a,107a,152a,168c), **toto** (8d,15a,34d,89a,181a), **trio** (104d,165a,169c), **tuno** (28b,168c), **typo** (35c,51b,123d), **tyro** (9b,17d,108c), **Tyto** (16c)

T - - P **tamp** (46b,112b,121d,127d), **tarp** (26b,178d), **terp** (12b,123a), **torp** (54c), **toup** (95d), **trap** (27b,67b,132b,149b), **trip** (85c), **trop** (62d,167a), **tryp** (114a), **tump** (60a,76d,103d), **turp, tymp** (20c), **typp** (185b)

TR - - **tram** (170a), **tran** (7a), **trap** (27b,67b,132b149b), **tray** (128c, 136d,142d,143c), **tree** (11d,37a,66a,184b), **tref** (172b), **trek** (85c, 93c,99d,168b), **tres** (19a,52b,63a,152d,165a,175c), **tret** (9a,178b, 179d), **trey** (26c,165a), **trig** (106a,148d,154b,169d), **trim** (40a,106a,154b,160a,165a,169d), **trin** (169d), **trio** (104d,165a, 169c), **trip** (85c), **tris** (122d), **trit** (34d,164c), **trod, tron** (140d, 180a), **trop** (62d,167a), **trot** (85b,93d,112d), **trow** (18a,21a,159d,

369

164c,170b), **troy** (161c,180a), **Troy, true** (7a,8d,37b,54b,94c,149c), **tryp** (114a)

- TR - **Atri, atry** (141b), **etre** (61a,c,62d,166c)

- - TR **natr** (189)

T - - R **taar** (12b), **tahr** (68a,76d), **tair** (68a,76d), **tear** (67c,87b,130a), **teer** (25b,69d), **tehr** (27c,68a), **thar** (68a,76d), **Thor** (7c,68c,99c, 100c,109c,165b), **tiar** (39a,75a,121a), **tier** (118a,134b), **tour** (31b, 85c), **tsar** (42d,49d,60b,135c), **turr** (24d,105a), **tyer, Tyrr** (68c, 109c,163d,178a), **tzar** (42d,49d,60b,135c)

TS - - **tsar** (42d,49d,60b,135c), **tshi, Tshi** (69c), **tsia** (162c), **Tsin** (30b), **tsun** (30b)

- - TS **Acts, arts** (138c), **cits, eats, lots, orts** (60d), **rats**

T - - S **Taos** (192), **Tass** (107a,135d,151b), **Tees** (108a), **Teos** (82a), **Tess** (73d,164c,183d), **this** (42b,124b), **Thos** (84a,181c), **thus** (149c), **tngs** (32c), **tops** (159c), **toss** (24a,132d), **tres** (19a,52b,63a,152d,165a, 175c), **tris** (122d)

- TT - **atta** (58d,90c,97d,160c,173d), **Atta** (94d,95d,100a,106b,117a), **Attu, Etta** (183c), **ette** (158a,c,d), **otto** (58d,116b,134a), **Otto** (14c,66d,67a,96a)

- - TT **batt** (37c), **bitt** (54d,175c), **bott** (32a,88d), **butt** (27a,77b,127d, 162a,182b), **Catt** (9d), **gett** (44d), **Lett** (16a,90a,93a), **Matt, mitt** (56c), **mutt** (39c,101d), **Natt** (107b), **nett, Nott** (107b), **Pitt** (50d,155d), **pott** (113d), **putt** (69d), **sett** (115a,156d), **tatt** (87c), **watt** (173b,177c), **Watt** (82a)

T - - T **tact** (43c,d,116a), **Taft** (29d), **talt** (14d), **takt** (105a,163a), **tart** (114d), **tatt** (87c), **taut** (163b,165c), **tent** (26b,115a), **test** (26a, 51c,144a,169c,170c), **text** (21c,140d), **that** (42b,124b,129c), **tilt** (26b,d,166a), **tint** (33c,d,114d), **todt** (66b), **tolt, toot, toot, tort** (31c,91a,185c), **tout** (61a,127a), **tret** (9a,178b,179d), **trit** (34d,164c), **trot** (85b,93d,112d), **tuft** (24b,32d,38c), **twit** (162b,c)

TU - - **tuan** (95d,147b,166c), **tuba** (105a,137d), **tube** (118b,158a), **tuck** (156b), **tuel, tufa** (121b,177a), **tuff** (121b,177a), **tuft** (24b,32d, 38c), **tuke** (26b,53b), **tula** (9a), **Tula, tule** (24b,27c), **Tulu** (45d), **tump** (60a,76d,103d), **tuna** (57a,b,123b,170d), **tund** (121d), **tune** (8b,12c,98c), **tung** (110a,168c), **tunu** (28b,168c), **tuny** (28b), **tuny, Tupi** (192), **turf** (115c,149d,160b), **Turi** (191), **Turk** (101d,102d, 106a,111d), **turm** (132d), **turn** (28d,131a,175a), **turp, turr** (24d, 105a), **tush** (167b), **tusk** (167b), **tute** (171b), **tutu** (16a,106d,147d), **tuwi** (117a,168c), **tuxa** (119d)

- TU - **atua** (120d), **Atum** (143a,159b), **etui** (27a,29b,62c,106b,148d, 166d,174b), **Otus** (67a), **stub** (156c), **stud** (22b,25a,42d,54d,111c, 143a,174a), **stum** (70c,105c,131a,173d), **stun** (145a,157d), **Utug** (159b), **utum** (19b,112c)

- - TU **actu** (7a,89a), **Attu, datu** (95c,102c,117a), **Ketu** (48b), **latu** (190), **mitu** (39d), **patu** (179b), **tatu** (12d), **Tatu, tutu** (16a,106d,147d), **yutu** (19b,166a)

T - - U **tabu** (59d,111d), **Taku** (80c), **tapu, tatu** (12d), **Tatu, tchu, teju** (151b), **thou** (124b), **Tibu** (191), **Tiou** (192), **tolu** (16a), **Tulu** (45d), **tunu** (28b), **tutu** (16a,106d,147d)

370

TW - - twee, twig, twin (45c,171d), twit (162b,c)

T - - W thaw, thew (104c), trow (18a,21a,159d,164c,170b)

TY - - Tybi (102a), tyee (29d), tyer, tyke (29d), tymp (20c), tyne, Tyne (108a), type (31d,115a,155a), typo (35c,51b,123d), typp (185b), typy, tyre (15a), Tyre (31b,90d,117b), tyro (9b,17d,108c), Tyrr (68c,109c,163d,178a), Tyto (16c)

- TY - etym (133d), Itys (163b), Styx (29b,73a,105c)

- - TY arty, city, Coty (63c), doty (43d), duty (109b,162b), Katy (183d), maty (80c), mity, pity (35b), toty (87b)

T - - Y taky, Tavy (183d), they (124b), tidy (106a,111b), tiny (100c,148c), toby (8c,85c,104b), Toby (96b,125c), tody (19b,d,59a,166a), tony, Tony (96b), tory, Tory (23c,36b,94c,172a), toty (87b), towy (58b), tray (128c,136d,142d,143c), trey (26c,165a), troy (161c,180a), Troy, tuny, typy

TZ - - tzar (42d,49d,60b,135c)

- TZ - Itza (192)

- - TZ batz (190), litz (127b), untz (189)

UA - - uang (131a)

- UA - bual (182c), duab (157c), duad (171d), dual (45c,171d), duan (64b), duar, Duat (172d), Fuad (54d), Guam, guan (151b), guao (168c,169b), guar (46c,59d), juan (113a), Juan (96a), juar (100a), kuan (30b), Kuan (30c), Kuar (102a), Muav (66a), quad (33c,172a), quae (176b), quag (21c,102c), quai (88b,117c,180c), quan (190), quas (135c), quay (88b,117c,180c), ruay (189), tuan (95d,147b, 166c), yuan (190), Yuan (30b,101d)

- - UA agua (152d,166c,178c), akua (120d), aqua (90a,178c), atua (120d), Erua (103c), skua (19b,72c,84a,141a), ulua (57a,74c), Ulua (141b)

U - - A ueba (188), ulna (21d,39b), ulua (57a,74c), Ulua (141b), Ulva (141b), unca (49a), upla, Urfa (99a), Uria (14c,16d), urna (133a), Ursa (17b,36b,43d), urva (38b), Usha (16a,150c), uvea (53c,82b)

UB - - uber (66b), Ubii (191)

- UB - buba (170a), Bube (180b), Bubi (180b), Bubo (112c), cuba (189), Cuba (180b), cube (66b,150a), cubi (188), dubb (161c), hubb (118b), juba (106b), jube (28d), kuba (26d,189), Luba (191), lube (110a), Lubs (94c), Nuba (108c), nubk (30d,164d), rube (37d, 135d,185d), Rube (96b), ruby (20a,65d,179c), tuba (105a,137d), tube (118b,158a)

- - UB blub, chub (40c,154c), club (39c), daub (148d), doub (189), drub (17b,39c), flub (22b), gaub (116c), glub, grub (43c,88d), knub (178b), slub (171c), snub (128c,148b), stub (156c)

- UC - Auca (192), buck, cuca (33a,105d), duce (29d), duck (26b,53b, 179c), Duco, duct (170c), fuci (132c), huck (167d), juca (27a), juck (114c), luce (58c,117d), Luce (7b,35a), luck (28d), lucy, Lucy (183c), much, muck, ouch!, puca (68a), puce (33c,d,52a), puck (44b,68a,77c,100c), Puck (99d,143b), ruck (39a,185a), such (146d), suck, tuck (156b), yuca (27a)

- - UC douc (101d), eruc (37a,56a)

U - - C Udic (108a), Utac (22d)

UD - - udad (143d,144a,181c), udal (76b,88b,131c), Udic (108a)

- UD - Aude, buda (83d), Buda, dude (40d), duds (32c,166d), Juda, Jude (11c,96a), judo (84b,85c,142b), Judy (125c,183d), kudu (11a), Ludd (23c), ludi (133b), ludo (65a,112b), mudd (188), nuda (39b), Nudd (23c), nude (16c,172d), pudu (41d), rudd (26d,57a,b), rude (134b,172b), sudd (40b,58c,107b), suds (59a), wudu (102d)

- - UD baud (162d), Chud (191), feud (55d,126b,175b), foud (54d,144b), gaud (169d), laud (122a), loud (156a), maud (53d,71a,136d,143c), Maud (181a,183c), Phud (110b), puud (189), roud (57a,b), scud (32c,126c,135b,160c), spud (121d,151c), stud (22b,25a,42d,54d, 111c,143a,174a), syud (103b), thud

U - - D udad (143d,144a,181c), used (6d,73a), uvid (101a)

UE - - ueba (188)

- UE - Auer (79a), duel (104d,171d), duet (104d,171d), euer (66d), fuel (65c), hued (188), juez (152b), kuei (44a), quei (189), ruer, suer (124d), suet (54d), tuel

- - UE ague (30a,55d,95c), blue (33c,98c,102c,150d,173a), clue, flue (8b,30a), gaue (67a), glue (7b,156a), moue (61d,62b), neue (66c), Niue (137d), roue (41b,44c,127c,134b), slue (97b,148b,160a), true (7a,8d,37b,54b,94c,149c)

U - - E ulme (49c), unde (179a), unie (173a), unze (189), urde (86b), urge (42d,46b,79d,80a,b,81c,150a), usee

- UF - buff (134c,161d), Bufo (166c), cuff (148a), duff (125b), Dufy (63a), gufa (21b,99a), guff (58a), huff (21b,99a), luff (136b), muff (188), puff (180d), ruff (19b,33b,63d,137a), sufi (103a, 116c), tufa (121b,177a), tuff (121b,177a), tuft (24b,32d,38c), yuft (135c)

- - UF pouf, souf (146b)

UG - - ugly

- UG - auge (123c,132b), Bugi (191), euge (180a), fuga, fugu (84b), gugu, huge, Hugh (96a), Hugo (63a,96a), juga (27a), kuge (84c), luge (148a), Lugh (28b), muga (28b), ough, pugh, ruga (59b,185a), sugi (84b), vugg (28a,66a,132b), vugh (28a,66a,132b), Yuga (76d)

- - UG chug (53a), drug (105d), glug, joug (138d), plug (156d,184d), slug (46b,99b,157c), smug, snug (35a,38b,165c), Snug (99d), thug (65a), toug (171a), Utug (159b)

U - - G uang (131a), Utug (159b)

- UH - buhl (81a), buhr (180d), Duhr (155b), Guha (191), guhr (47d), kuhl (53c), Ruhr

- - UH bruh (95a)

U - - H umph, Urth (68d,107d,163d), Utah (180b)

- UI - cuif (139a,d,140c), cuir (45c,62a), duim (188), duit (190), Duit (192), guib (11a), huia (19a,106d), luif, Muir (8b,142c), nuit (62b), quid (39b,166d), quip (183a,b), quit (90d,130c), quiz (42d), ruin (42d), suit (38a,58a,91a,112a,119c,137c), Yuit (51c)

- - UI arui (11b,143d,144a,181c), equi (122d), etui (27a,29b,62c,106b, 148d,166d,174b), Maui (120d)

U - - I   Ubii (191), unci (31d)

- UJ -   fuji (84b), Fuji (84d), juju (29b,55d), puja (77a), suji (180c)

- UK -   bukh (122a), bukk (122a), cuke (39b), duke (107c), duku (95d, 168c), juke (114c), Kuki (191), kuku (19a,106d), luke, Luke (52a,96a), puka (107a,168c), puku (11a), rukh (53b,54a), Suku (191), tuke (26b,53b), wukf (103a)

- - UK   cauk (139b), dauk (95d), Sauk (192), souk (22a,97a)

UL - -   Ulam (67b̄), ulan (27d,88a), Ulex (153c), ullo (6a,144a), Ullr (146b,164d), ulme (49c), ulna (21d,39b), ulua (57a,74c), Ulua (141b), Ulva (141b)

- UL -   aula (66c,73b), aulu (74c,168c), bulb 37a,172c), bulk (97b), bull (113c), bult (76d), cull (117c), culm (11a,32d,70d,145a,156a), cult (141d,161c), dull (21a,32c,173a), Dull (94b), fulk (173a), full (7b, 130b), gula (90a,101a,165b), gulf (6c), gull (32d,41c,42a,72c,99b, 141a), Gulo (183c), gulp (46a,79d,160a), hula (74b) hule, (23a, 134c), hulk (144d,173d), hull (141d,142a,144c,d), hulu (55b), jula, Jule (183d), July, kula (189), Kuli (27b), lull (25c,126d,150c), lulu (19a,57b,112c), Lulu (183d), mule (45b,148b,153c,180b), mulk (60d), mull (53b,135a,164c), null (108c,177a), pule (180d), pulk (37c,88d), puli (45a,78d), pull (45d,167d), pulp, pulu (74c), puly, rule (11b,26b,90b), rull (170b), Suia (65a), suld (188), sulk (159a), Sulu (102c), tula (9a), Tula, tule (24b,27c), Tulu (45d), vuln (184d), Yule (30d), zulu (171d,175d), Zulu (86a)

- - UL   Aoul (191), azul (151d), baul (18b), caul (16d,74d), deul (77b), Elul (102b), foul (173a), Gaul (10a,60d,63c), goul (102a), haul (27b,45d), maul (73c,96b), paul, Paul (96a), poul (190), saul (48a, 168c), Saul (18c,86d,115a), shul (161a), soul (10d,125a,153c, 176d)

U - - L   udal (76b,88b,131c), unal (147a), Ural (135c), uval (70c)

UM - -   umbo (22b), umph

- UM -   bump, Duma (135c), dumb (153b), dump, fume (129a,149a,157a), fumy, Gump (43b), Hume (50c), hump (124d), jump, lump (45a, 160c), mump (29b,153d), Numa (133a), numb, puma (27b,37c,55b, 103d), Pume (137b,175d,185b), pump, rumb (120b), rump, Sumo, sump (28c,45d), tump (60a,76d,103d), Yuma

- - UM   ahum, alum (14a,45c), arum (13a,39b,58d,92b,155c), Arum (66a), Atum (143a,159b), Baum (9c,112c), chum (38d), doum (168c), drum (105a), Geum (76b), gium (102c,159a), grum (102c), jhum, meum (27a,89c), Meum, odum (168c,180a), ogum (82b), ovuʌ (48d), plum, rhum (8c), saum (189), scum (129b), slum, stum (70c,105c,131a,173a), swum, Ulam (67b), utum (19b,112c)

U - - M   urim (18d,23a,110a), utum (19b,112c)

UN - -   unal (147a), unau (148c,171d), unca (49a), unci (31d), unco (140c), unde (179a), undo (11a,93d), undy (179a), unie (173a), Unio (105c), unis (91b), unit (101c,110c,147a), unto (166c), untz (189), unze (189)

- UN -   aune (188), aunt (129c), buna (161c), bund (49c,66c,90d), bung (119d,156d), bunk, bunn (25b), bunt (15d,180c), Cuna (193), dune (137a), dunk (43c,79d), Duns, dunt, fund (6d,101c,130d), Fung

(191), **Funj, funk** (63d,113c), **guna** (106a,137b), **gunj** (70c), **hung, hunh?, hunk, hunt** (141c), **June** (183c), **Jung** (125a), **junk** (30a, 134c), **Juno** (69c,85d,100c,126b), **kung** (125b), **kunk** (188), **luna** 103c), **Luna** (102b), **lune** (38c,73b,74d), **lung, luny** (38b), **mund** (124d), **mung** (70d), **munj** (70d), **paun** (18b), **puna** (10b,33b,104a, 119b,182a), **pund** (189), **pung** (22c,148b), **punk** (9b,166a,167c), **puno** (182a), **punt** (21a,58b), **puny** (55b,179a), **Qung** (191), **rune** (9b,67a,94a,105c,107d,120a,141d,163d), **rung** (28c,39a), **runt** (47a172d), **sung, Sung** (30b), **sunk, sunn** (56a), **tuna** (57a,b,123b, 170d), **tund** (121d), **tune** (8b,12c,98c), **tung** (110a,168c), **tuno** (28b,168c), **tunu** (28b), **tuny, Yunx** (184a), **Zuni** (125b)

- - **UN** **Amun** (86d,127d,159b,164a), **Chun** (30c), **drun** (132b), **faun** (56a, 68b,137c,161a,184a), **Idun** (107d), **jaun** (113a), **kaun** (93d), **laun** (146b), **loun** (19a,b), **maun** (19d), **noun** (114b,158a), **paun** (18b), **shun** (15a,51b,52a), **spun, stun** (145a,157d), .**taun** (188), **tsun** (30b), **Usun** (191), **whun** (64c,70a)

U - - N **ulan** (27d,88a), **upon** (6b), **uran** (101d), **Usun** (191), **uzan** (189)

- **UO** - **buoy** (28d,58c), **quod** (123d)

U - - O **ullo** (6a,144a), **umbo** (22b), **unco** (140c), **undo** (11a,93d), **Unio** (105c), **unto** (166c), **upgo** (13c)

UP - - **upas** (84d,120b,168c,d), **upgo** (13c), **Upis** (13b), **upla, upon** (6b)

- **UP** - **dupe** (27c,41c,72c,160c), **Hupa** (192), **jupe** (62b,84a), **lupe** (19a, 64a), **Nupe** (191), **pupa** (30d,81b,c), **rupa** (60b), **supa** (168c), **supe** (53a,154d), **Tupi** (192)

- - **UP** **blup, caup, coup** (20d,97c,157b,c,162d), **gaup, loup** (61d,62a,90c, 139d), **Loup** (193), **noup** (124b), **plup, roup** (44a,121d), **scup** (57a, 121b), **snup** (149b), **soup, toup** (95d), **yaup, youp** (185d)

UR - - **Ural** (135c), **uran** (101d), **urde** (86b), **Urdu** (77b), **urdy** (86b), **Urey** (17b,36b,43d), **Urth** (68d,107d,163d), **urus** (14d,53a,112c), **urva** 150a), **Uria** (14c,16d), **urim** (18d,23a,110a), **urna** (133a), **Ursa** (17b,36b,43d), **Urth** (68d,107d,163d), **urus** (14d,53a,112c), **urva** (38b)

- **UR** - **aura** (44c,49c,66a,96b,158a,170d,177c), **auri** (34a), **bura** (182b), **bure** (61b), **burg** (22b,73c), **buri** (56b), **burl** (87c,169a), **burn, burr** (123b), **bury** (81d), **cura** (152c), **curb** (130c,146b), **curd** (99d), **cure** (123b), **curl** (38d,73b,131d), **curr** (104c), **curt** (145b,c), **dura** (153c), **duro** (190), **durr** (70b), **furl** (132d), **fury** (157a), **guru** (77b), **hura** (20a,137a), .**Hura, huri** (167c), **hurt, jura, Jura, jure** (90b), **jury** (38a), **Kurd** (48b,82a), **Kure** (84c), **Kuri** (191), **kurk** (31a,139b), **lura** (22d,82a), **lure** (41c,51a,54b,163a), **lurg** (96d,141b,184d), **Luri** (191), **lurk** (92a,147d), **mura** (84d), **Mura** (192), **mure** (177d), **murk** (41a,67d), **murr** (72b,128b), **nurl** (33b,87c), **nurr** (67d), **ours** (124c), **pure** (29b,172b,173c), **puri** (80d), **purl** (87c,104c), **purr** (104c), **Puru** (192), **ruru** (19b,102c,106d), **sura** (87c,113b,166d), **surd** (82c,177a), **sure** (173d), **surf** (23a), **turf** (115c,149d,160b), **Turi** (191), **Turk** (101d,102d,106a,111d), **turm** (132d), **turn** (28d, 131a,175a), **turp, turr** (24d,105a), **Wurd, wurm** (67c), **yurt** (101d)

- - **UR** **Alur** (191), **Asur** (68c), **biur** (35a), **blur, caur** (139a), **Daur** (139b), **dour** (67d,159a), **ebur** (89c), **four** (26c), **gaur** (112c,181c), **gour** (112c,181c), **hour, knur** (67d,87c,107c), **lour** (13d,63d), **peur** (61c),

374

pour (162d), scur (78b), slur (44b,124c,148b,168a), smur (32c,46b, 100c), sour, spur (10d,67d,167d,168a,181b), tour (31b,85c), your (124c)

U - - R uber (66b), Ullr (146b,164d), usar (8d,16c), user (49d), utor (90a, 166c)

US - - usar (8d,16c), Usas (68d), used (6d,73a), usee, user (49d), uses (18a), Usha (16a,150c), Usun (191)

- US - Ausa, ausu (168c,180b), bush, busk (17b,37b,55d,161b), buss (87a,148c), bust, busy, cush (101c), Cush (51d,73c), cusk (57b), cusp (38c,78b,119a,120a,b), cuss, duse (83c), dusk (171c), dust, fuse (98c), fuss (22b,35b), fust (105c,143b), gush (35a,154c), gust, huse (180c), hush (17b,146c), husk (53a,78d,142a), huso (180c), just (51b,54b), kusa, Kush, lush (94d), lust (41b), Musa (16a), muse (65b,93d,120d,164c), Muse (68d), mush (97d), musk (116b), Muso (192), muss (135b,173d), must (70c,101a,106d,157d,182c), Ouse (132a,185d), oust (44c,49a,52b,125d), push, (145c) puss, rusa, Rusa (41d,136d), ruse (13b,77c,157b,169c), rush, rusk (23a), Russ (135b), rust (37b,112c,119a), Susa (49a), susi (53b,d), susu (20c), Susu (191), Susy (183d), tush (167b), tusk (167b),

- - US acus (89d,118a), Apus (36b,c), avus (89b), cous (38a), crus (91a, 143c), deus (68a,89b), Esus, gaus (67a), Grus (36b,c,38b), Ilus (88d,170b), irus (109d), nous (81d,100a,128b), onus (24c,93b,109b), opus (35c,105a,184c), Otus (67a), Pius (121a), plus (10b, 102c), pous (188), Rhus (159a), sous (62d,172c), thus (149c), urus (14d,53a,112c), Zeus (135a)

U - - S unis (91b), upas (84d,120b,168c,d), Upis (13b), urus (14d,53a, 112c), uses (18a), Usas (68d), utas (49a,109c)

UT - - utac (22d), Utah (180b), utas (49a,109c), utor (90a,166c), Utug (159b), utum (19b,112c)

- UT - auto (34d), Buto (142d), butt (27a,77b,127d,162a,182b), cute (39c), duty (109b,162b), fute (51c), Guti, jute (37a,48a,56a,133d, 136a), Jute, lute (11c,28b,84d,105a,131d), muta (28d,103a), mute (146c,153b), muth (188), mutt (39c,101d), putt (69d), Ruta (76b, 134d), rute (188), ruth (35b,118c), Ruth (105b,183c), tute (171b), tutu (16a,106d,147d), yutu (19b,166a)

- - UT abut (22a,167c), bhut (67a), blut (66b), bout (36c), brut (182c), Brut (23c), chut!, Cnut (40d,50c), gaut (88b,103d,132a), glut (52c,70a,137c,159d), gout, knut, Knut (40d,50c,96a), lout (15c, 22a,24b,45b,109a,157d), naut (141b), paut (140a), phut (24b), Phut (110b), pout (159a), prut!, Prut (41a), rout (41d,44b,46b), scut (145c,161b), shut, smut (32d,44a,119a,150a), sput (21c), taut (163b,165c), tout (61a,127a)

U - - T unit (101c,110c,147a)

- UU - puud (189)

U - - U unau (148c,171d), Urdu (77b)

UV - - uval (70c), uvea (53c,82b), uvic (70c), uvid (101a)

- UV - cuvy (141a)

- UW - tuwi (117a,168c)

- - UW bouw (188), dauw (24c)

375

- UX -   **buxy** (115b), **luxe** (61c,62d,159c), **puxy**

- - UX   **crux** (39a,151b), **eaux** (178c), **flux** (28d,58d), **jeux** (61d), **Vaux** (63b)

U - - X   **Ulex** (153c)

- UY -   **buyo** (18b), **cuya** (39b), **Puya** (118b)

U - - Y   **ugly**, **undy** (179a), **urdy** (86b), **Urey** (14b,107c,138c)

UZ - -   **uzan** (189)

- UZ -   **auzu** (168c,180b), **buzz**, **fuze** (98c), **fuzz** (45d), **guze** (128d), **huzz**, **Juza** (155b), **Muzo** (192), **tuza** (119d), **wuzu** (102d), **zuza** (189)

- - UZ   **Ghuz** (171a)

U - - Z   **untz** (189)

VA - -   **Vach** (153c), **vade** (42c,67d,89b), **vagi** (38b), **vail** (94b,124a,174b), **vain** (81a), **vair** (64c,154c), **vale** (54c,128a,174b), **Vale** (7c,109c), **vali** (171a,176a), **Vali** (7c,109c), **vamp** (80a,145a), **vane** (179b, 182a), **vang** (72d,134a,140b), **Vans** (107d), **vara** (151d), **vare** 179b), **vari** (34d,91b,134d,174d), **vary** (28d,43c), **vasa** (46d,114a, 160b,175d), **Vasa**, **vase**, **vast** (78d,79d), **vasu** (106c), **Vasu** (176d), **Vaux** (63b), **Vayu** (68c,182a), **vaza** (114a)

- VA -   **aval** (70c), **Avar** (27d,108a), **Evan** (96a), **Ivah** (18d), **Ivan** (40c, 85b,96a), **kvas** (135c), **oval** (48d,49c,127a), **Svan** (27d), **uval** (70c)

- - VA   **Alva** (151d), **cava** (116a,175b), **Civa** (56d), **deva** (23d,42a,42b, 56d,77a), **diva** (100d,123c), **Hova** (95a), **Java** (33a), **jiva** (77a), **Jova** (193), **kava** (18c,116a), **kiva** (28c,125b), **lava** (101c,151a, 177a), **Neva** (91b,132a), **nova** (20c,106d,155c,174d), **peva** (12d), **siva** (67a), **Siva** (56d,77a), **Ulva** (141b), **urva** (38b), **viva** (93d), **Xova** (193), **yava**

V - - A   **vara** (151d), **vasa** (46d,114a,160b,175d), **Vasa**, **vaza** (114a), **Veda** (77a,b), **vega** (110d,152c), **Vega** (155b), **vela** (98c,136b,149d), **Vela** (36b,c), **vena** (90a,175a), **vera** (140c,151b,175c), **Vera** (183c), **veta** (104a), **Vida** (183c), **vila** (54b), **vina** (77a,105a), **Vira** (191), **visa** (114d), **vita** (89c,92a), **viva** (93d), **vola** (89d,150a), **yota** (133b)

V - - B   **verb** (7a,114b,184b)

- - VD   **NKVD** (135d)

V - - D   **veld** (151a), **vend** (97a,115c,142b), **Vend** (10b,148a), **verd** (71d), **void** (11a,49d,108d,174b)

VE - -   **veal**, **Veda** (77a,b), **veer** (28d,144c,171b), **vega** (110d,152c), **Vega** (155b), **veil** (74d,76c), **vein** (20d,157b), **vela** (98c,136b,149d), **Vela** (36b,c), **veld** (151a), **velo** (175b), **vena** (90a,175a), **vend** (97a, 115c,142b), **Vend** (10b,148a), **vent** (8b,11b,110d,112a), **Veps** (191), **vera** (140c,151b,175c), **Vera** (183c), **verb** (7a,114b,184b), **verd** (71d), **veri** (28b), **vert** (71d,166a,171b), **very** (149c), **vest** (32c, 177b), **veta** (104a), **veto** (94a,124a), **Veto**

- VE -   **avec** (63a,183a), **aver** (7c,14a,15c,41c,95c,140d,155c,160b,184c), **Aves** (19d), **evea** (82a,95a), **even** (51a,58b,79d,91d,149a,173a), **ever** (9b,14b,80b), **evet** (48d,107a,136c,169d), **Ives** (9c,90b), **oven** (15d,78c,86b), **over** (6b,38c,80a,114d,130a), **uvea** (53c,82b)

- - VE   **bave** (61d,146c), **cave** (27d), **cive** (110c), **cove** (17a,73d,107d),

Dave (96b), **dive** (42b,74b,119d), **dove** (19a,117d), **eave** (133c), **five**, **gave**, **give** (79d,123a), **gyve** (55d,143b), **have** (92a), **hive** (17c), **hove** (92a), **Jave** (84d), **jive** (160c), **jove** (85d), **kive** (174d), **lave** (16d,178b), **leve** (62a), **live** (47c), **love** (163a), **move**, **nave** (30d,31a,78d,114b,180c), **neve** (56d,67c,70c,149b), **nove** (83b), **pave** (85a), **rave** (41c,157a,161d), **reve** (61c,104d), **rive** (32a,153d), **rove** (127d,132b,178a), **save** (52b,110c,123a,173c), **seve** (63a, 182c), **sive** (146a), **Tave** (183d), **vive** (93d), **wave** (19a,59a,111c, 131d,160c,172d), **wive** (97a), **wove**

V - - E **vade** (42c,67d,89b), **vale** (54c,128a,174b), **Vale** (7c,109c), **vane** (179b,182a), **vare** (179b), **vase**, **vice** (31d,158a), **vide** (89d,126a, 142a), **vile** (16c,56c), **vine** (32b), **vire** (11a,13b), **vise** (31d,77d, 114d), **vite** (62b), **vive** (93d), **voce** (83c,177a), **vole** (97d,104a, 148a,149b), **vote** (60b), **Vote** (56d)

V - - G **vang** (72d,134a,140b), **voog** (28a,66a,132b), **vugg** (28a,66a,132b)

- - VH **IHVH** (159d), **JHVH** (159d), **YHVH** (159d)

V - - H **Vach** (153b), **Voth** (191), **vugh** (28a,66a,132b)

VI - - **vial** (148c), **vice** (31d,158a), **Vida** (183d), **vide** (89d,126a,142a), **vier** (66c), **view** (93d,138b), **vila** (54b), **vile** (16c,56c), **vili** (54b), **Vili** (109c), **vill** (176b), **vily** (54b), **vina** (77a,105a), **vine** (32b), **vino** (92d,182b), **vint** (26c,182c), **viny**, **viol** (105a), **Vira** (191), **vire** (11a,13b), **visa** (114d), **vise** (31d,77d,114d), **viss** (189), **vita** (89c, 92a), **vite** (62b), **viti** (176b), **viva** (93d), **vive** (93d), **vivo** (93a)

- VI - **avid** (47b,71a,186b), **avis** (89a), **Avis** (183c), **evil** (79c,95d,147a, 181a,185c), **Ovid** (132d,133b), **Ovis** (143d), **uvic** (70c), **uvid** (101a)

- - VI **Devi** (147b,153b), **divi**, **favi** (138a,165d), **hevi** (111d), **Kavi** (84d), **Levi** (84a,90c), **ravi** (61b), **Ravi** (16b)

V - - I **vagi** (38b), **vali** (171a,176a), **Vali** (7c,109c), **vari** (34d,91b,134d, 174d), **veri** (28b), **vili** (54b), **Vili** (109c), **viti** (176b), **vlei** (38c,160a)

V - - K **volk** (66c,105d,116a,184c)

VL - - **vlei** (38c,160a), **vley** (160a)

V - - L **vail** (94b,124a,174b), **veal**, **veil**, (74d,76b), **vial** (148c), **vill** (176b), **viol** (105a)

V - - N **vain** (81a), **vein** (20d,157b), **vuln** (184d)

VO - - **voce** (83c,177a), **voet** (188), **Vogt**, **void** (11a,49d,108d,174b), **vola** (89d,150a), **vole** (97d,104a,148a,149b), **volk** (66c,105d,116a,184c), **volt** (49b,78c,173b), **voog** (28a,66a,132b), **vota** (133b), **vote** (60b), **Vote** (56d), **Voth** (191), **Voto** (192)

- VO - **Avon** (143b), **Avow** (6d,36a,41c,112c), **evoe** (15b,130d,181c)

- - VO **levo** (91a), **pavo** (115b), **Pavo** (36b,c), **vivo** (93a)

V - - O **velo** (175b), **veto** (94a,124a), **Veto**, **vino** (92d,182b), **vivo** (93a), **Voto** (192)

V - - P **vamp** (80a,145a)

V - - R **vair** (64c,154c), **veer** (28d,144c,171b), **vier** (66c)

- - VS **revs** (131a)

V - - S **Vans** (107d), **Veps** (191), **viss** (189)

V - - T **vast** (78d,79d), **vent** (8b,11b,110d,112a), **vert** (71d,166a,171b), vest (32c,177b), vint (26c,182c), voet (188), Vogt, volt (49b,78c, 173b)

VU – – vugg (28a,66a,132b), vugh (28a,66a,132b), vuln (184d)

– VU – avus (89b), ovum (48d)

– – VU kivu (170c)

V – – U vasu (106c), Vasu (176d), Vayu (68c,182a)

V – – W view (93d,138b)

V – – X Vaux (63b)

– – VY bevy (38a,58c), cavy (72b,120d,132c,157b), cuvy (141a), Davy (96b,136b), envy (41b), levy (14a,162b), Livy (132d,133a), navy (33c,58b), pavy (115b), pevy (91d,94c), Tavy (183d), wavy (147b, 172d)

V – – Y vary (28d,43c), very (149c), vily (54b), viny, vley (160a)

WA – – Waac, waag (71d,101d), Wabi (192), Waco, wadd (109c), wade, wadi (46c,106a,109a,128a,132a), wady (109a,128a,132a), waeg (19b,72c,87a), waer (40b), Wafd (49a), waft (20d,58c), wage (27a, 115b), waif (157b), wail (39b,88a), wain (177b), Wain, wait (26d, 42b,92c,155d,162a), waka (26a), wake (134b,168a), wakf (103a), waky, wale (70b,131b,157c,163d,179a,180a,c,d), wali (171a), walk, wall, Walt (96b), wand (120b,132c,156a), wane (41c,43c), wang (189), want (41b,42d,87b,106b,122a), wany, wapp (54b,133d, 145d), waqf (103a), ward (31c,55c,86b), ware (27d,35a), warf, warm (7c,75b,163b), warn (7b), warp (36c,165a,171c), wart (124d), wary (27d,176b), wash, wasp, wast, Wate (141a), watt (173b, 177c), Watt (82a), wave (19a,59a,111c,131d,160c,172d), wavy (147b,172d), waxy (119c,149d), ways

– WA – Awan (191), away (6b,69d,76a,109d,111d), Ewan, kwan (30b), swab (102b), swad (94d), swag (22a,156c), swam, swan (19b,33a), swap (168a), swat (15d,20d,32d,157c), Swat (103a), sway (104a)

– – WA biwa (93d,168c), dewa, Iowa (193), kawa (18c,116a), Iowa (19a), pawa (189), tawa (160d,168c), Tewa (193)

W – – A waka (26a), Wega (155b), weka (58c,106d,107a,127b), weta (93c), whoa (156d)

W – – C Waac

– – WD dowd (143b), gawd (169c)

W – – D wadd (109c), Wafd (49a), wand (120b,132c,156a), ward (31c,55c, 86b), week, weld (47c,85b,173c), wend (67d,123d), Wend (10b, 148a), wild (38b,173d), wind (33b,39d,171c,185a), woad (20d,47c), wold (47c,60a,118d,174a,184a), wood, word (124b,165c), Wurd, Wyrd (107d)

WE – – weak (55b), weal (124d,157c,180c,d), wean (8d,42d), wear (50b), weed, week, weel (16d,57d,140d,180d), weep (39b,88a,104a), weet (19d), weft (39a,165a,184b), Wega (155b), Wegg (111d), weir (40b,57d), weka (58c,106d,107a,127b), weki (55c), weld (47c,85b, 173c), Welf (67a), welk (65c,96d,141b), well welf (36d,131b,145a, b,177b,d), wend (67d,123d), Wend (10b,148a), went (42c), wept, were (139b), werf (54d), weri (15c,27c), wert, west, West (9c,50b, 109b), weta (93c)

378

- WE -   ewer (84d,85c,118c,181b), kwei (44a), Owen (96a,183c), sweb (160d), twee

- - WE   howe (77d), Howe (17a,82a), powe

W - - E   wade, wage (27a,115b), wake (134b,168a), wale (70b,131b,157c, 163d,179a,180a,c,d), wane (41c,43c), ware (27d,35a), Wate (141a), wave (19a,59a,111c,131d,160c,172d), were (139b), whee, wide (133d), wife (154a), wile (13b,41c,157b,169c), wine, wipe, wire, wise (136b), wive (97a), woke, wore, Wote (191), wove

W - - F   waif (157b), wakf (103a), waqf (103a), warf, Welf (67a), werf (54d), wolf, woof (39a,163d,165a,179d), Wraf, wukf (103a)

W - - G   waag (71d,101d), waeg (19b,72c,87a), wang (189), Wegg (111d), Whig wigg, wing (10d,58c,59a,118b,d), wong (56a)

WH - -   wham (157c), what (129c), whau (107a,168c), wheel, when (180d), whet (143c,156b), whew, whey (100a), Whig, whim (26c, 54c,108c), whin (64c,70a,132b,181d), whip (58c,88d), whir (25c, 181a), whit (166c), whiz (25c), whoa (156d), whom (42b), whoo!, whun (64c,70a), whyo (59d,65a)

- - WH   JHWH (159d), YHWH (159c)

W - - H   wash, wish (42d), with (10b)

WI - -   wick, wide (133d), widu (102d), wiel (140d,180d), wies (185a), wife (154a), wigg, wild (38b,173d), wile (13b,41c,157b,169c), wilk (65c,96d,141b), will (18b,43a,163c,177c), wilt (46b), wily (13b,38b,39c), wind (33b,39d,171c,185a), wine, wing (10d,58c, 59a,118b,d), wink (107a), winy (176c), wipe, wire, wiry (147a, 167c), wise (136b), wish (42d), wisp (24b,148c), wist (87c), with (10b), wive (97a)

- WI -   swig (46a,72c), swim (58c), swiz (160c), twig, twin (45c,171d), twit (162b,c)

- - WI   iiwi (19a,74b), Kawi (84d), kiwi (11d,19a,58c), tuwi (117a,168c)

W - - I   Wabi (192), wadi (46c,106a,109a,128a,132a), wali (171a), weki (55c), weri (15c,27c)

- - WK   bowk (155d), cawk (133c), dawk (95c), gawk (146d), gowk (146d), hawk (19c,115c), sawk (188)

W - - K   walk, weak (55b), week, welk (65c,96d,141b), wick, wilk (65c, 96d,141b), wink (107a), work (64c,76b)

- - WL   bawl, bowl, cowl (101d), dowl, fowl, gowl (102a,140d,185b), howl (39b), jowl (29b), mewl (180d), pawl (43a,95a), yawl (136b,171d, 175d), yowl

W - - L   wail (39b,88a), wall, weal (124d,157c,180c,d), weel (16d,57d,140d, 180d), well, wiel (140d,180d), will (18b,43a,163c,177c), wool (58b, 179c)

- - WM   dawm (190)

W - - M   warm (7c,75d,163b), wham (157c), whim (26c,54c,108c), whom (42b), worm, wurm (67c),

- - WN   bawn (181a), dawn (14d,41b), down (149d), fawn (33c), gown, hewn, kawn (93d), lawn (20a,37c,53b,92c), lown (157d), mown, pawn (29c,119c), sawn, sewn, town (73c), yawn

W - - N   wain (177b), Wain, warn (7b), wean (8d,42d), when (180d), whin

(64c,70a,132b,181d), **whun** (64c,70a), **woon** (24c), **worn** (143b), **wren** (19b,c), **Wren** (50b), **wynn** (165d)

WO - -   **woad** (20d,47c), **woke**, **wold** (47c,60a,118d,174a,184a), **wolf**, **wong** (56a), **wont** (6d,40a,73a,174c), **wood woof** (39a,163d,165a, 179d), **wool** (58b,179c), **woon** (24c), **word** (124b,165c), **wore**, **work** (64c,76b), **worm**, **worn** (143b), **wort** (76a,95d,121d), **Wote** (191), **wove**

- WO -   **Lwow**, **swob** (102b), **swop** (168a), **swot**, **swow** (100a)

W - - O   **Waco**, **whoo**, **whyo** (59d,65a)

- - WP   **gawp**, **lowp** (90c,139d), **yawp**

W - - P   **wapp** (54b,133d,145d), **warp** (36c,165a,171c), **wasp**, **weep** (39b, 88a,104a), **whip** (58c,88d), **wisp** (24b,148c), **wrap** (32b,51a)

WR - -   **Wraf**, **wrap** (32b,51a), **wren** (19b,c), **Wren** (50b), **writ** (91a)

- WR -   **awry** (13d,38d,171c), **ewry** (133c)

W - - R   **waer** (40b), **wear** (50b), **weir** (40b,57d), **whir** (25c,181a)

- WS -   **owse**

- - WS   **mews** (154c), **news** (165c)

W - - S   **ways**, **wies** (185a)

- - WT   **newt** (48d,136c,169d), **nowt** (106a,139a), **yowt** (139c)

W - - T   **waft** (20d,58c), **wait** (26d,42b,92c,155d,162a), **Walt** (96b), **want** (41b,42d,87b,106b,122a), **wart** (124d), **wast**, **watt** (173b,177c), **Watt** (82a), **weet** (19d), **weft** (39a,165a,184b), **welt** (36d,131b, 145a,b,177b,d), **went** (42c), **wept**, **wert**, **west**, **West** (9c,50b,109b), **what** (129c), **whet** (143c,156b), **whit** (166c), **wilt** (46b), **wist** (87c), **wont** (6d,40a,73a,174c), **wort** (76a,95d,121d), **writ** (91a)

WU - -   **wudu** (102d), **wukf** (103a), **Wurd**, **wurm** (67c), **wuzu** (102d)

- WU -   **swum**

W - - U   **whau** (107a,168a), **widu** (102d), **wudu** (102d), **wuzu** (102d)

W - - W   **whew!**

WY - -   **wynn** (165d), **Wyrd** (107d)

- WY -   **Gwyn** (40c,50b)

- - WY   **dewy** (101a), **jawy**, **nowy** (194), **rowy** (157b), **towy** (58b)

W - - Y   **wady** (109a,128a,132a), **waky**, **wany**, **wary** (27d,176b), **wavy** (147b,172d), **waxy** (119c,149d), **whey** (100a), **wily** (13b,38b,39c), **winy** (176c), **wiry** (147a,167c)

W - - Z   **whiz** (25c)

- XA -   **axal** (120b), **exam**, **oxan** (65c)

- - XA   **Bixa** (145d), **coxa** (77b), **doxa** (48b), **moxa** (27d,30c), **myxa** (168c, 169a), **noxa**, **toxa** (153d)

X - - A   **xema** (72c), **Xema** (12c), **Xina** (183d), **Xosa** (86a), **Xova** (193)

XE - -   **xema** (72c), **Xema** (12c), **xeno** (34d)

- XE -   **oxea** (153d), **oxen** (10c), **oxer** (55c)

- - XE   **luxe** (61c,62d,159c), **Mixe** (192), **saxe** (20d,33c)

X - - E   **Xipe** (15c)

XI - -   **Xina** (183d), **Xipe** (15c)

- XI -   axil (10c), axis (28b,41d,77c,153c), exit (114d), ixia (37a), Ixil (192), oxid (112c)
- - XI   dixi, taxi (13a,125b)
- XL -   axle (153c,180c), ixle (56a)
XM - -   Xmas
XO - -   Xosa (86a), Xova (193)
- XO -   axon (106c,153c)
- - XO   Moxo (192), myxo, taxo (13a)
X - - O   xeno (34d), xylo (35a,183d)
X - - S   Xmas
- - XT   next (106a), sext (26b,111b,147b), text (21c,140d)
XY - -   xylo (35a,183d)
- XY -   oxyl (112c)
- - XY   boxy, buxy (115b), doxy (129d), foxy (38b,39c,181d), mixy, pixy (154b), puxy, Roxy (183d), waxy (119c,149d)
YA - -   yage (23a), yaje (23a), Yaka (191), Yaki (193), Yale (173c), yali (171a), Yama (57a,68a), Yana (192,193), yang (30b,70a), yank, Yank, Yaou (30c), yapa (113b), Yapp (22a), yard (152d), yare (96b,124b,128b), yark (22c), yarl (40d,107d), yarn (154b,161b, 184b), yarr (72a), Yaru (48d), yate (51d,168c), yati (76d), yaup, yava, yawl (136b,171d,175d), yawn, yawp, yaya (113c,168c)
- YA -   ayah (108d), cyan, dyad (113a), Dyak (22b), Dyas (66a), eyah (95b, 108d,111c), eyas (106c,173a), Iyar (102b), kyah (19a), kyak (51c), kyar (33a), kyat (189), lyam (139a), Lyas (66a), pyal (175c), pyat (95b), ryal (110a,190)
- - YA   Alya (155b,c), Arya (80d), baya (179b), Baya (191), cuya (39b), Goya (151d), Hoya (14d), maya (77a,179b), Maya (23d,186c), Puya (118b), raya (19b,23c,76d,107d), saya (117a), soya (151b), yaya (113c,168c)
Y - - A   Yaka (191), Yama (57a,68a), Yana (192,193), yapa (113b), yava, yaya (113c,168c), yeta (84c), Yima (84a,116b,c), Ynca (193), yoga (10b,13c,77a), yuca (27a), Yuga (76d), Yuma
- YB -   gybe (144c), Tybi (102a)
- YC -   syce (71d)
- YD -   hyde (188), Hyde (45a)
- - YD   emyd (163c,167c)
Y - - D   yard (152d), yond (164d)
YE - -   yeah, yean (88a), year, yeas (177c), Yedo (166d), yegg (24c), yell (145c), yelp, yelt (151b), yeni (19b,161d), yeso (72d), yeta (84c)
- YE -   ayes (177c), byee (189), dyer, eyer, eyey (74b), oyer (38a,75b, 119c), oyes (38a,39b,75b), oyez (38a,39b,75b), pyet (95b), ryel (190), syed (103b), tyee (29d), tyer
- - YE   Daye (123d), Skye (163c)
Y - - E   yage (23a), yaje (23a), Yale (173c), yare (96b,124b,128b), yate (51d,168c), yoke (85b,92d,173c), yore (10b,69d,93c,110b,165d), Yule (30d)

381

- YG -   **bygo** (114c), **zyga** (134b)

Y - - G   **yang** (30b,70a), **yegg** (24c)

YH - -   **YHVH** (159d), **YHWH** (159d)

Y - - H   **yeah**, **YHVH** (159d), **YHWH** (159d), **yodh** (91d), **yogh** (10c,185a)

YI - -   **Yima** (84a,116b,c)

- YI -   **ayin** (91c)

- - YI   **kiyi** (185d)

Y - - I   **Yaki** (193), **yali** (171a), **yati** (76d), **yeni** (19b,161d), **Yobi**, **yogi** (76d)

- YK -   **cyke** (40c), **dyke** (49c,91d), **fyke** (15d), **hykel**, **syke** (194), **tyke** (29d)

Y - - K   **yank**, **Yank**, **yark** (22c), **yolk**, **york** (38c), **York** (50b,c)

- YL -   **gyle** (23b,174d), **Hyla** (10a,166d,169b), **hyle** (97c), **kyle** (57a, 139c), **pyla** (22d), **pyle** (34b), **Pyle** (9c,178a), **Xylo** (35a,183d)

- - YL   **acyl** (6d), **amyl** (155c), **idyl** (114d), **noyl** (87c), **odyl** (59d,79c), **oxyl** (112c), **teyl** (92b,c,168c)

Y - - L   **yarl** (40d,107d), **yawl** (136b,171d,175d), **yell** (145c), **yowl**, **ypil** (117a,168c)

YM - -   **Ymer** (67a,131c), **Ymir** (67a,131c)

- YM -   **cyma** (101a,b), **cyme** (58d,69c), **hymn** (150c), **ryme** (178d), **tymp** (20c), **zyme** (55c)

- - YM   **clym** (12b), **etym** (133d), **onym** (162c)

YN - -   **Ynca** (193)

- YN -   **dyna** (34c), **dyne** (59d,173b), **gyne** (34b,55b,183c), **jynx** (78a), **Jynx** (184a), **lynx** (26c,181d), **Lynx** (36b), **myna** (19a,c,70b), **rynd** (100a), **syne** (140b,147a), **tyne**, **Tyne** (108a), **wynn** (165d)

- - YN   **coyn** (37a), **Gwyn** (40c,50b), **llyn** (120d,140a)

Y - - N   **yarn** (154b,161b,184b), **yawn**, **yean** (88a), **yuan** (190), **Yuan** (30b, 101d)

YO - -   **Yobi**, **yodh** (91d), **yoga** (10b,13c,77a), **yogh** (10c,185a), **yogi** (76d), **yoke** (85b,92d,173c), **yolk**, **yond** (164d), **yoop**, **yore** (10b,69d,93c, 110b,165d), **york** (38c), **York** (50b,c), **youp** (185d), **your** (124c), **yowl**, **yowt** (139c)

- YO -   **eyot** (82d), **ryot** (115c)

- - YO   **buyo** (18b), **cayo**, **coyo** (15a,30c), **Enyo** (12c,69c,178a), **Idyo** (191), **kayo** (87c), **Mayo** (193), **whyo** (59d,65a)

Y - - O   **Yedo** (166d), **yeso** (72d)

YP - -   **ypil** (117a,168c)

- YP -   **gyps**, **Gyps** (71d), **hype** (185a), **hypo** (117b), **hyps**, **rype** (19b,125a), **sype** (110c), **type** (31d,115a,155a), **typo** (35c,51b), **typp** (185b), **typy**

- - YP   **tryp** (114a)

Y - - P   **Yapp** (22a), **yaup**, **yawp**, **yelp**, **yoop**, **youp** (185d)

- YR -   **Byrd** (9c,120b), **byre** (38a), **eyra** (181d), **eyre** (23c,31b,85c), **Eyre**, **eyry** (47b,106c), **fyrd** (110a), **gyre** (31b,171b), **gyri** (22d,

382

131b), **gyro** (34d), **Lyra** (36b,74a), **lyre** (11c,81c,105a,111c), **Myra** (10a,31b,183c), **pyre** (64c), **pyro**, **Syra**, **tyre** (15a), **Tyre** (31b,90d, 117b), **tyro** (9b,17d,108c), **Tyrr** (68c,109c,163d,178a), **Wyrd** (107d)

- - YR   **skyr** (21d,151a)

Y - - R   **yarr** (72a), **year**, **Ymer** (67a,131c), **Ymir** (67a,131c), **your** (124c), **Yser**

YS - -   **Yser**

- YS -   **cyst, lyse, myst** (71c,123b)

- - YS   **Alys** (183c), **Emys** (167c,171b), **days, Itys** (163b), **ways**

Y - - S   **yeas** (177c)

- YT -   **myth** (8b,91a), **Tyto** (16c)

- - YT   **skyt** (138c,140b)

Y - - T   **yelt** (151b), **yowt** (139c), **yuft** (135c), **Yuit** (51c), **yurt** (101d)

YU - -   **yuan** (190), **Yuan** (30b,101d), **yuca** (27a), **yuft** (135c), **Yuga** (76d), **Yuit** (51c), **Yule** (30d), **Yuma, Yunx** (184a), **yurt** (101d), **yutu** (19b,166a)

- YU -   **syud** (103b)

- - YU   **Vayu** (68c,182a)

Y - - U   **Yaou** (30c), **Yaru** (48d), **yutu** (19b,166a)

- YV -   **gyve** (55d,143b)

- YX -   **myxa** (168c,169a), **myxo**

- - YX   **Ceyx** (73b), **eryx** (137a), **onyx** (25d,28d,65d,142b), **oryx** (11a), **Pnyx** (71c), **Styx** (29b,73a,105c)

Y - - X   **Yunx** (184a)

- - YZ   **hayz**

ZA - -   **Zach** (96b), **zaim** (170d), **zain** (41a), **Zama** (73d,141d), **zany** (24a, 32d,59c), **zarf** (39c,155a), **zarp** (120c), **zati** (21d)

- ZA -   **Azam** (166c), **axan** (102d), **czar** (42d,49d,60b,135c), **izar** (65b, 103b), **Izar** (155b), **tzar** (42d,49d,60b,135c), **Uzan** (189)

- - ZA   **boza** (12a), **caza, Daza** (191), **Gaza** (117a), **Itza** (192), **Juza** (155b), **onza** (189), **tiza** (172a), **tuza** (119d), **vaza** (114a), **zuza** (189)

Z - - A   **Zama** (73d,141d), **zeta** (71b,91c), **Zipa** (29d), **zira** (188), **Zola** (63a), **zona** (144c,186d), **zuza** (189), **zyga** (134b)

- ZB -   **ezba** (188)

Z - - B   **Zimb** (6c)

Z - - C   **zinc** (21a)

Z - - D   **Zend, zoid**

ZE - -   **zeal** (12c,55d), **zebu** (22d,80d,112c), **zein, Zeke** (96b), **zeme** (55d,161b,180b), **zemi** (55d,161b,180b), **Zend, Zeno** (71b), **zenu** (143d), **zero** (31a,84c,108c), **Zero** (118d), **zest** (55d,72d), **zeta** (71b,91c), **Zeus** (135a)

- ZE -   **ezel** (47a,85d)

- - ZE   **adze** (40c,167a), **bize** (182a), **coze** (29b), **daze** (157d), **doze** (148a), **faze** (43d), **fuze** (98c), **gaze, guze** (128d), **haze** (100c,174d), **laze** (79b), **Laze** (191), **maze** (87b,157d), **naze** (26b,124b), **noze** (75a),

383

ooze (53c,104b,116a), raze (42b,d,91d), size, unze (189)

Z - - E   Zeke (96b), zeme (55d,161b,180b), zone (44c,50a,160a), zyme (55c)

Z - - F   zarf (39c,155a)

Z - - G   zing

- ZH -   Azha (155b)

Z - - H   Zach (96b)

ZI - -   Zimb (6c), zinc (21a), zing, Zion (75b,c,83a,157d), Zipa (29d), zipp, Zips (40c), zira (188), zizz (181a)

- - ZI   cazi (103a), gazi, kazi (103a), Lazi (191), Nazi

Z - - I   zati (21d), zemi (55d,161b,180b), Zuni (125b)

Z - - L   zeal (12c,55d)

Z - - M   zaim (170d), zoom

Z - - N   zain (41a), zein, Zion (75b,c,83a,157d), zoon (43a)

ZO - -   Zoar, Zoas (20b), zobo (186b), zodi, zogo (136a), zoid, Zola (63a), zona (144c,186d), zone (44c,50a,160a), zoom, zoon (43a)

- ZO -   Azof (20b,135d), azon (127b), Azov (20b,135d), mozo (152b), Muzo (192)

- - ZO   bozo (55b), Idzo (191), kozo (113d,168c), lazo (88d,128b,133d)

Z - - O   Zeno (71b), zero (31a,84c,108c), Zero (118d), zobo (186b), zogo (136a)

Z - - P   zarp (120c), zipp

- ZR -   Ezra (96a)

Z - - R   Zoar

Z - - S   Zeus (135a), Zips (40c), Zoas (20b)

Z - - T   zest (55d,72d)

ZU - -   zulu (171d,175d), Zulu (86a), Zuni (125b), zuza (189)

- ZU -   azul (151d)

- - ZU   anzu (11d), auzu (168c,180b), Enzu (102b), wuzu (102d)

Z - - U   zebu (22d,80d,112c), zenu (143d), zulu (171d,175d), Zulu (86a)

ZY - -   zyga (134b), zyme (55c)

- - ZY   cazy (103a), cozy (149c), dazy, dozy, gazy, hazy (174b), Jozy, kazy (103a), lazy, oozy (148b), sizy (176d)

Z - - Y   zany (24a,32d,59c)

- - ZZ   bizz, buzz, fuzz (45d), huzz, jazz, razz (131b), sizz, zizz (181a)

Z - - Z   zizz (181a)